COMBINING THE LEGAL AND THE SOCIAL IN SOCIOLOGY OF LAW

This open access book pays homage to Reza Banakar, who passed away in August 2020, exploring the many different areas of socio-legal research that he worked on and influenced. It begins with a summary of his career and explains how he sparked a debate on the identity and aims of legal sociology.

The book is then split into five sections which look at theory, methods and inter-disciplinarity, legal culture, law and sociology of law, and applied sociology of law. As well as honouring Reza Banakar's memory and unique thinking, the book aims to advance the sociology of law by demonstrating the interconnectedness of the legal and the social from a broad range of perspectives.

Oñati International Series in Law and Society

A SERIES PUBLISHED FOR THE OÑATI INSTITUTE
FOR THE SOCIOLOGY OF LAW

General Editors
Rosemary Hunter   David Nelken

Founding Editors
William L F Felstiner   Eve Darian-Smith

Board of General Editors
Carlos Lugo, Hostos Law School, Puerto Rico
Jacek Kurczewski, Warsaw University, Poland
Marie-Claire Foblets, Max Planck Institute for Social Anthropology in Halle, Germany
Ulrike Schultz, Fern Universität, Germany

Recent titles in this series

Fundamental Rights and Legal Consequences of Criminal Conviction
Edited Sonja Meijer, Harry Annison and Ailbhe O'Loughlin

Digital Family Justice: From Alternative Dispute Resolution
to Online Dispute Resolution?
Edited by Mavis Maclean and Bregje Dijksterhuis

The Legacies of Institutionalisation: Disability, Law and Policy in the
'Deinstitutionalised' Community
Edited by Claire Spivakovsky, Linda Steele and Penelope Weller

Gender and Careers in the Legal Academy
Edited by Ulrike Schultz, Gisela Shaw, Margaret Thornton and Rosemary Auchmuty

Contesting Austerity: A Socio-Legal Inquiry
Edited by Anuscheh Farahat and Xabier Arzoz

The Right to the Continuous Improvement of Living Conditions:
Responding to Complex Global Challenges
Edited by Jessie Hohmann and Beth Goldblatt

Supporting Legal Capacity in Socio-Legal Context
Edited by Mary Donnelly, Rosie Harding and Ezgi Tascioglu

What Is a Family Justice System For?
Edited by Mavis Maclean, Rachel Treloar and Bregje Dijksterhuis

Combining the Legal and the Social in Sociology of Law:
An Homage to Reza Banakar
Edited by Håkan Hydén, Roger Cotterrell, David Nelken and Ulrike Schultz

For the complete list of titles in this series
see www.bloomsbury.com/uk/series/oñati-international-series-in-law-and-society/

Combining the Legal and the Social in Sociology of Law

An Homage to Reza Banakar

Edited by
Håkan Hydén
Roger Cotterrell
David Nelken
and
Ulrike Schultz

Oñati International Series in Law and Society

A SERIES PUBLISHED FOR THE OÑATI INSTITUTE
FOR THE SOCIOLOGY OF LAW

·HART·
OXFORD · LONDON · NEW YORK · NEW DELHI · SYDNEY

HART PUBLISHING

Bloomsbury Publishing Plc

Kemp House, Chawley Park, Cumnor Hill, Oxford, OX2 9PH, UK

1385 Broadway, New York, NY 10018, USA

29 Earlsfort Terrace, Dublin 2, Ireland

HART PUBLISHING, the Hart/Stag logo, BLOOMSBURY and the Diana logo are
trademarks of Bloomsbury Publishing Plc

First published in Great Britain 2023

A catalogue record for this book is available from the British Library.

A catalogue record for this book is available from the Library of Congress.

Library of Congress Control Number: 2022950477

ISBN: HB: 978-1-50995-938-9
        ePDF: 978-1-50995-940-2
        ePub: 978-1-50995-939-6

Typeset by Compuscript Ltd, Shannon

To find out more about our authors and books visit www.hartpublishing.co.uk.
Here you will find extracts, author information, details of forthcoming events
and the option to sign up for our newsletters.

Preface

O N 27 AUGUST 2020, the beloved professor Reza Banakar left us mourning his loss. His death resounded far and wide in the academic community and struck a sombre note with all those who knew him. At the time of his death, he held the Chair of Sociology of Law at Lund University, a position he took on returning to Sweden after holding academic posts in Oxford and London. At just 61 years of age, the teacher adored by so many of his students passed away after a long illness.

Reza was born in Shiraz, Iran in 1959, and moved to England in the 1970s, where he both studied and worked. He defended his dissertation at Lund University, Sweden in 1994 and taught socio-legal subjects for a few years thereafter. In 1997, he took up the Paul Dodyk Research Fellowship at the Centre for Socio-Legal Studies at Oxford University. He stayed at Oxford until 2002, where he also served as a Research Fellow at Harris Manchester College. Between 2002 and 2013 he worked at the law faculty at the University of Westminster. In 2013 he returned to Lund University as a Professor in Sociology of Law. Sweden was his last stop before he died.

Reza's intellectual and academic contributions are vast. He tackled many areas of socio-legal interest and paved the way for the development of the field of sociology of law. His remarkable academic contributions are well documented in Chapter 2 of this anthology honouring him. Professor Reza was warm-hearted and will be remembered as an admirable friend, a devoted educator, a kind colleague, and a remarkable scholar in his field.

When Reza Banakar died in August 2020 at much too young an age, our socio-legal community immediately took the decision to honour him with a commemorative publication. He had already left deep traces in our field, particularly in the formation of theory and research methods.

The four editors felt the need to safeguard his scientific legacy. For quite some time there had been plans to update the seminal book by Reza Banakar and Max Travers, *Theory and Method in Socio-Legal Research*, which had become a kind of reference book for all young (and older) socio-legal scholars. While it was no longer possible to realise that ambition, the idea developed somewhat, and it was decided to ask colleagues to write contributions with reflections on the various issues in the book and on other aspects of Reza's work, which are also gathered in the second comprehensive collection he edited with Max Travers, *Law and Social Theory*.

When we sent out a call for contributions, we received an overwhelming response from scholars all around the world. We hope that the various perspectives from a very diverse group of academics may offer new insights and deepen and update our knowledge of important topics of socio-legal research, and can also serve as another guide for our younger generation.

Since Reza earned his doctoral degree at Lund University in 1996 and returned to Lund after having served at different universities in England, being appointed Professor (Chair) in the department of Sociology of Law in 2013, it was natural that the Lund department would take on the practical arrangements for the book in memory of Reza. We thank Tamy Al Saad as coordinator for her comprehensive support with collecting manuscripts and communicating with the authors in order to synchronise style and formats. By publishing within the Onati Series of publications, the book reflects Reza's international profile.

Håkan Hydén, Roger Cotterrell, David Nelken, Ulrike Schultz
October 2022

Contents

Preface .... *v*

Notes on Contributors .... *xi*

PART I
INTRODUCTION AND BIOGRAPHY

1. *Introduction* 3
   Håkan Hydén

2. *Bringing the Social and the Legal Together: An Overview of Reza*
   Banakar's Sociology of Law 23
   Mariana Motta Vivian

3. *Engaging with Reza Banakar* 35
   Max Travers

PART II
SOCIOLOGY OF LAW THEORY,
LEGAL PLURALISM AND LEGAL THEORY

4. *The Place of a Stepchild: Notes on the Establishment of Modern*
   Sociology of Law 47
   Roger Cotterrell

5. *The Stepchild Controversy: Unfortunate Dichotomies in Socio-Legal*
   Theory 59
   Peter Bergwall

6. *Normativity as the Source of Norms* 69
   Håkan Hydén

7. *On the Relationship between Normative Pluralism and Justice*
   after Multiculturalism 83
   Martin Ramstedt

8. *Legal Pluralism and the Army: Legal Sociology as Military Sociology* 93
   Chris Thornhill

9. *Corporate Strategies within a Transnational Regulatory Field* 111
   Isabel Schoultz

10. *Corporate Governance, Soft Law, and Corporate Social Responsibility: Some Legal Theoretical Contributions* 127
Mauro Zamboni

11. *Reflections on Law, Religion, and Technology: Legal Mobilisation in the Area of Egyptian Paternity Law*...145
Monika Lindbekk

PART III
SOCIOLOGY OF LAW METHODS AND INTERDISCIPLINARITY

12. *Knowledge and Opinion about Law – The Importance of Law-related Education*...161
Ulrike Schultz

13. *Rights Consciousness in Hungary. What is Behind the Numbers? Lessons of a Focus Group Study* 173
Balázs Fekete

14. *In Conversation with Reza: Theory and Method in Socio-Legal Research*......189
Linda Mulcahy

15. *'The Light in the Tunnel Can Be a Train': About Kafkaesque Double Thoughts*...199
Karl Dahlstrand and Mikael Furugärde

16. *Socio-Legal Agency in Late Modernity – Reappreciating the Relationship between Normativity and Sociology of Law*...215
Pierre Guibentif

17. *The Quest for Scientific Methods: Sociology of Law, Jurimetrics and Legal Informatics* 227
Peter Wahlgren

18. *Minding the 'Gap' Problem: The Relevance of Combining Top-down and Bottom-up Approaches to the Study of Law's Role in Everyday Life*...239
Stine Piilgaard Porner Nielsen

19. *Doing Fieldwork in Istanbul Courts: Challenges and Strategies*....................249
Seda Kalem

PART IV
COMPARATIVE LEGAL CULTURES

20. *Legal Culture as an Approach to the Study of Law in Russian Society* 263
Marina Kurkchiyan

21. *Flexible Structures: Using the Legal Culture Concept to Study the Law
    of Society* 277
    Carlo Pennisi

22. *Lawyers and Drivers: On Reading Two Works of Reza Banakar* 293
    Lawrence M Friedman

23. *Traffic Justice: Law and Society on the Roads of Iran and
    the Netherlands* 307
    Marc Hertogh

24. *The Cancer of the Law in the Islamic Republic of Iran: Reflections
    on the Iranian Anti-Israel Law of 2020* 319
    Mathieu Deflem

25. *Revolutions and Legal Cultures. Perspectives and Reflections* 331
    Hanne Petersen

PART V
SOCIOLOGY OF LAW AS SCIENCE

26. *Reza Banakar and the Quest for a Sociology of Law* 345
    Ole Hammerslev and Mikael Rask Madsen

27. *Governing through Covid Indicators* 355
    David Nelken

28. *Safe but not Secure? Risk Management, Communication and
    Preparedness for a Pandemic in Aviation* 375
    John Woodlock

29. *The Interlegal Evocation of Peace in Colombia* 391
    Nicolás Serrano C

PART VI
APPLIED SOCIOLOGY OF LAW

30. *Trade Union Solidarity and the Issue of Minimum Wage Regulation
    in the EU* 405
    Ann-Christine Hartzén

31. *Constitutional Imaginaries: A Socio-legal Perspective of Political
    and Societal Constitutions* 417
    Jiří Přibáň

32. *Public Sentiments on Justice, Legal Consciousness, and the Study
    of Marginalised Groups* 429
    Peter Scharf Smith

33. *Challenging Legal Orthodoxy: New Orientations in Space and Time in Discourses Over Land Tenure*..441
Anne Griffiths

34. *Sexual Violence, Standard(s) of Proof, and Arbitrariness in Judicial Decision-Making*..453
Hildur Fjóla Antonsdóttir

Index 465

Notes on Contributors

Håkan Hydén has been a Senior Professor in Sociology of Law at Lund University, Sweden, since 1988. Professor Hydén has also been a Docent in private law. Between 2008 and 2012 he was appointed as a Samuel Pufendorf Professor. In 2009 he was made a fellow of the World Academy of Arts and Sciences. He has also been a member of the Governing board of the IISL in Onati, Spain, as well as the vice President of the governing board of the Research Committee for Sociology of Law. Hydén's main academic ambition is to consolidate the subject Sociology of Law as a Norm Science, and he has recently published his book titled *Sociology of Law as the Science of Norms* (2022). His other research interests concern the ways in which technology affects society and law. Professor Hydén is also interested in how digital technology via AI and algorithms form normativity in society.

Mariana Motta Vivian holds a Master's degree in Sociology of Law from the Oñati International Institute for the Sociology of Law of the University of the Basque Country (IISL/UPV-EHU), Spain, a Master's degree in Sociology from the Graduate Program in Sociology of the Federal University of Rio Grande do Sul (PPGS-UFRGS), Brazil, and a Bachelor's degree in Legal and Social Sciences from the Federal University of Rio Grande do Sul, Brazil. In 2020, she was awarded the André-Jean Arnaud Prize for her IISL Master's thesis titled 'Sociology of Law in between Law's Autonomy and Justice Claims: Theoretical Contributions from Reza Banakar'.

Max Travers is an Associate Professor of Sociology and Criminology in the School of Social Sciences at the University of Tasmania, Australia. He is the author of *The Reality of Law* (1997) and *The Sentencing of Children* (2012), and co-author of *Rethinking Bail* (2020). He co-edited, with Reza Banakar, *Law and Social Theory* (2002 and 2013) and *Theory and Method in Socio-Legal Research* (2005).

Roger Cotterrell is Anniversary Professor of Legal Theory at Queen Mary University of London, UK, and a Fellow of the British Academy and of the UK Academy of Social Sciences. In 2013 he received the Socio-Legal Studies Association award for contributions to the socio-legal community, and in 2022 was awarded the Dennis Leslie Mahoney Prize for Legal Theory. His books include *Sociological Jurisprudence: Juristic Thought and Social Inquiry* (2018); *Living Law: Studies in Legal and Social Theory* (2008); *Law, Culture and Society: Legal Ideas in the Mirror of Social Theory* (2006) and *Law's Community: Legal Theory in Sociological Perspective* (1995).

Peter Bergwall is a Lecturer at the Sociology of Law Department at Lund University, Sweden. In 2021, he defended his doctoral thesis with the title 'Exploring Paths of Justice in the Digital Healthcare: A Socio-Legal Study of Swedish Online Doctors'. In it, the importance of perceptions of justice for the willingness to use a particular online doctor service is studied in light of the increasingly consumer-driven Swedish health system. Peter has a special interest in critical realist perspectives on sociology of law and in the relationship between theory and methodology in social science research.

Martin Ramstedt is currently Research Professor of Ikerbasque/Basque Foundation for Science and Director of the Oñati International Institute for the Sociology of Law in the Basque Autonomous Community in Spain. He obtained a Magister Artium and PhD in Anthropology, European Ethnology and Social Psychology from Ludwig Maximilians University in Munich, and a Dr. phil. habil. in Social and Cultural Anthropology from Martin Luther University Halle-Wittenberg. Ramstedt has done extensive research on normative pluralism at various international research institutions, including the International Institute for Asian Studies in Leiden (Netherlands) and the Max Planck Institute for Social Anthropology in Halle.

Chris Thornhill is Professor in Law at the University of Manchester, UK. He is the author of a number of books on the sociology of law, especially addressing the sociology of constitutions. He is currently working on the relations between legal sociology and military sociology.

Isabel Schoultz is a Senior Lecturer at the Sociology of Law Department, Lund University, Sweden. She has published extensively on corporate crime and corporate defence strategies when accused of crime. She has also written academic papers on a variety of other topics, including state crime in street-level bureaucracy, legal aid in Sweden and access to justice in the European Court and co-authored a book on Edwin Sutherland (2018) (with David Friedrichs and Aleksandra Jordanoska). Schoultz is associate editor of the *Journal of White Collar and Corporate Crime*.

Mauro Zamboni is a Professor in Legal Theory at Faculty of Law, Stockholm University, Sweden. He is also Senior Associate Research Fellow at the Institute of Advanced Legal Studies, University of London (2015–), Co-President of the board for the International Association of Legislation (IAL), member of the Executive Committee of the International Association of Social and Legal Philosophy (IVR), and Korea Legislation Research Institute Global Research Fellow (2012–). His main interests are the relations between law and politics and legislative studies.

Monika Lindbekk is a Research Fellow at the University of Bergen. In 2016, she received her PhD in Sociology of Law at Oslo University. In 2018, she was awarded a Marie Curie Individual Fellowship with the Sociology of Law Department at Lund University as a host academic institution. Before this, she was a Postdoctoral Researcher at Max Planck Institute for Comparative and International Private Law and a Senior Lecturer at the University of Oslo. She is also a co-organiser of an international research collaboration under the Law and Society Association on Gender and Judging (2015–2022).

Ulrike Schultz is a lawyer and retired Senior Academic at the FernUniversität in Hagen, Germany, where she specialised in questions of gender and law, the sociology of the legal professions, ADR, legal education and didactics of law. She has taken part in and organised many national and international socio-legal projects. Together with Gisela Shaw she has edited comprehensive international collections on issues of women/gender in the legal profession. Since 2006 she has been on the IISL board; in 2018 she was elected President of the Research Committee for the Sociology of Law in the International Sociological Association.

Balázs Fekete is Associate Professor in the Department of Law and Society, Faculty of Law, at the Eötvös Loránd University, and Senior Research Fellow at the Centre for Social Sciences, Institute for Legal Studies, both in Budapest. His main areas of research include rights consciousness, legal alienation, and comparative legal studies methodology. His most recent book is *Paradigms in Modern Comparative Law. A History* (Hart Publishing, 2021).

Linda Mulcahy is Professor of Socio-Legal Studies in the Law Faculty, Oxford University, UK where she is also the Director of the Centre for Socio-Legal Studies. Linda has degrees in Law, Sociology and Art History and her work focuses on lay experiences of the justice system. She is currently engaged on an Economic and Social Research Council funded project on digital disadvantage in the age of online trials, and an Arts and Humanities Research Council funded project on an oral history of radical lawyering. Linda teaches Methodology and Law and Society, cultural, and legal change processes.

Karl Dahlstrand, born in 1977 in Gothenburg, received an LLM from Stockholm University in 2003 and a PhD in sociology of law from Lund University in 2012. Since 2014, he has been a lecturer at the Sociology of Law Department at Lund University, Sweden. His research interests concern the disciplinary borders between social science and jurisprudence – how the borders are perceived and the consequences for the application of law. Together with Reza Banakar, Dahlstrand edited the homage volume *Festskrift till Håkan Hydén* and co-supervised doctoral students. He dedicates his leisure time to cultural interests, and through these got to know co-writer Mikael Furugärde in the early 2000s, when the foundation for their current cooperation was laid.

Mikael Furugärde, born in 1968, is a novelist, musician and literary translator. After studying theology, philosophy and aesthetics at Uppsala University, Sweden, he made his debut as a novelist in 1993. In 2001, he co-founded the Grammy-awarded rock band The Plan, with several top chart positions. In 2015, he translated a novel by Nobel Prize laureate Patrick Modiano into Swedish. He is currently studying creative writing at Lund University, Sweden, and is working on a collection of short stories to be published in the near future

Pierre Guibentif, jurist and sociologist, is Full Professor at Iscte University Institute of Lisbon and researcher at DINAMIA'CET_Iscte. He is currently taking part in the management of the Maison des Sciences de l'Homme Paris-Saclay. He has coordination duties in several socio-legal associations and participates in the editorial boards of Droit et Société and Zeitschrift für Rechtssoziologie. From 1998 to 2000 he was scientific director of the International Institute for the Sociology of Law, Oñati, Spain. His recent papers have focused on citizenship in complex societies, based on a reflexive approach to the recent evolution of the scientific domain.

Peter Wahlgren is Professor of Law and Information Technology at The Swedish Law and Informatics Research Institute (IRI), Department of Law, Stockholm University. He is currently Torsten and Ragnar Söderberg Professor of Legal Science and chairman and Director of IRI. He was awarded an LLD degree in 1992, and published *Automation of Legal Reasoning: A Study on Artificial Intelligence and Law* (Kluwer). He was Docent in Jurisprudence (Allmän rättslära), Docent in Law and IT (Rättsinformatik) and appointed Professor in Law and IT in 2001. His research interests cover automated legal methods, IT/AI and law, proactive law, legal risk analysis and legislative techniques.

Stine Piilgaard Porner Nielsen holds a PhD in Sociology of Law from the Department of Law at the University of Southern Denmark and a master's in social science from Roskilde University. Throughout her academic career, Stine has researched legal encounters between welfare professionals and citizens in socially marginalised positions. She combines different qualitative methods and socio-legal theories to bridge methodological gaps related to top-down and bottom-up analyses of law's role in everyday life. In her current position as a postdoctoral researcher, she investigates the role of law in addressing youth homelessness in the context of the Danish welfare state.

Seda Kalem received her PhD in Sociology from The New School for Social Research (NY) in 2010. Currently, she is an Associate Professor of Sociology of Law and the coordinator of the Unit for the Prevention of Sexual Harassment and Assault at Istanbul Bilgi University. Her most recent publications include works on the socio-political history of the legal profession in Turkey and research on gender and judiciary. In Autumn 2018, Kalem was a visiting scholar at Lund University Department of Sociology of Law, where she worked with Reza Banakar.

Marina Kurkchiyan is Emeritus Fellow and former Director of the Centre for Socio-Legal Studies in the University of Oxford, and a Fellow of Wolfson College. She is a sociologist with a variety of publications on comparative legal cultures and the post-communist transition. As a consultant to the World Bank, the EU, the DfID, and the Open Society Institute, she has completed a number of official reports on the interaction between law and society in relation to development. She is a former member of the Executive Committee of the International Sociological Association and the current Chair of the RCSL Comparative Legal Cultures Working Group.

Carlo Pennisi is a Full Professor of Sociology of Law at the University of Catania, Italy. He has carried out, mainly, empirical research on the processes of proceduralisation of the law of administrations, on social policies, on the introduction of evaluation in public administrations and in the Italian University. He has participated in the international debate on the concept of legal culture, supporting its crucial role in defining a specific approach of sociology to legal phenomena. He is currently editing a special issue of the Oñati Socio-Legal Series on the concept of legal culture.

Lawrence M Friedman is Marion Rice Kirkwood Professor of Law at Stanford University, Stanford, California. He is the author of many books on American legal history, and on law and society. His recent works include *Impact: How Law Affects*

Behavior (2016) and *A History of American Law* (4th edn, 2019). He is a member of the American Academy of Arts and Sciences and a former President of the Law & Society Association, the American Society for Legal History, and the Research Committee on the Sociology of Law.

Marc Hertogh is Full Professor of Socio-Legal Studies at the University of Groningen, the Netherlands. His research focuses on law and society, legal consciousness, legal pluralism, and administrative justice. His books include: *The Oxford Handbook of Administrative Justice* (2022) (with Richard Kirkham, Robert Thomas and Joe Tomlinson); *Nobody's Law: Legal Consciousness and Legal Alienation in Everyday Life* (2018); *Research Handbook on the Ombudsman* (2018) (with Richard Kirkham); and *Judicial Review and Bureaucratic Impact* (2004) (with Simon Halliday).

Mathieu Deflem is Professor of Sociology at the University of South Carolina. His research and teaching interests centre on various sociological dimensions of law, social control and policing, popular culture, and social theory. Many of his scholarly efforts are strongly guided by sociological theories in the European and American traditions and situated in an international and global context. He has published widely in journals and anthologies, and has to date authored five books, including *Sociology of Law: Visions of a Scholarly Tradition* (2008).

Hanne Petersen is Emeritus Professor of Legal Cultures, Faculty of Law, University of Copenhagen, Denmark. She has worked on legal pluralism and legal culture in relation to gender, labour, indigenous people (Greenland) and China, and a number of 'law and' areas (eg love, music, environment). She was head of the Nordic critical legal journal *RETFÆRD* for a decade. Her latest coedited publication is *Transnational Solidarity. Concept, Challenges and Opportunities* (2020) (with Helle Krunke and Ian Manners).

Ole Hammerslev is Professor of Sociology of Law at the Department of Law, University of Southern Denmark and guest professor at the Sociology of Law Department, Lund University, Sweden. His main research areas consist of legal professions, state transformations, legal education, legal aid, the pre-dispute phase, legal encounters, the welfare state and socio-legal theory and methodology.

Mikael Rask Madsen is a Professor of European Law and Integration at the Faculty of Law, University of Copenhagen, Denmark, and director of iCourts, Centre of Excellence for International Courts. Trained as both a lawyer and a sociologist, his research focuses on international law and institutions, and the evolution of the legal profession. He is the author of numerous books and articles, including *International Court Authority* (with KJ Alter and LR Helfer) and 'Sovereignty, Substance, and Public Support for European Courts' Human Rights Rulings' *American Political Science Review* (with J Mayoral, E Voeten and A Strezhnev).

David Nelken is Professor of Comparative and Transnational Law and past Vice-Dean for Research, at King's College, London, UK. Widely published in sociology of law and in criminology, he has received awards from the American Sociological Association, the American Society of Criminology, the International Sociological Association, and the (USA) Law and Society Association. He has twice been a Trustee of the LSA and Vice-President of the RSCL. Books include *Comparing Legal Cultures* (1997); *Adapting Legal Cultures* (2001) (with Johannes Feest); *Beyond the Study of 'Law in Context'* (2009); *Comparative Law: A Handbook* (2007) (with Esin Orucu); *European Ways of Law* (2007) (with Volkmar Gessner) and *Comparative Criminal Justice: Making Sense of Difference* (2010).

John Woodlock is a PhD candidate at the Department of Sociology of Law, at Lund University, Sweden. His PhD research focuses on the regulation of civil aviation in the EU and, in particular, from the bottom-up perspectives of licensed aircraft maintenance engineers. By adopting a critical socio-legal approach to explore the professional norms and everyday work practices of these professionals within this heavily regulated socio-technical environment, his research addresses the normative complexity surrounding everyday experiences of law, legality and safety within the European aircraft maintenance sector. He will defend his PhD dissertation in Autumn 2022.

Nicolas Serrano Cardona is a doctoral candidate at the Sociology of Law Department of Lund University, Sweden. His current research interests include legal cultures, legal cartography and interlegality. With a background in Social Anthropology, Habitat and Urban Studies, his work deals with the intersections of culture, cities, and law, particularly the relations between social forces and the state amidst social unrest.

Ann-Christine 'Ankie' Hartzén is a postdoctoral researcher in Labour Law at the Department of Business Law, Lund University, Sweden. Her current research is dedicated to the issue of in-work poverty within the framework of the Horizon 2020 project 'Working, Yet Poor'. Apart from in-work poverty, Ankie's research interests focus on labour law, collective bargaining systems and their impact on labour markets, especially for vulnerable persons. In line with this she also has a deep interest in the European Social Model and international aspects of collective bargaining systems, not least through her previous work on the European Social Dialogue.

Jiří Přibáň is Professor of Law at Cardiff University, UK. He has published extensively in the areas of social theory and sociology of law, legal philosophy, constitutional and European comparative law, and theory of human rights. A loose trilogy of monographs *Constitutional Imaginaries* (2022), *Sovereignty in Post-Sovereign Society* (2015) and *Legal Symbolism* (2007) deals with general themes and problems of constitutional semantics and the book *Dissidents of Law* (2002) addresses the function of dissent in legitimation of positive law. He has also edited numerous books, especially *Research Handbook on The Sociology of Law* (2020), *Self-Constitution of Europe* (2016), *Liquid Society and Its Law* (2007), *Systems of Justice in Transition* (2003), *Law's New Boundaries* (2001) and *The Rule of Law in Central Europe* (1999). He is the founding director of the Centre of Law and Society and an editor of the *Journal of Law and Society*. He regularly contributes to the Czech and international media.

Peter Scharff Smith is Professor in the Sociology of Law at the University in Oslo, Norway. He has studied history and social science, holds a PhD from the University of Copenhagen and has also done research at the University of Cambridge and at the Danish Institute of Human Rights. Peter has published books and articles in Danish,

Norwegian, English and German on prisons, punishment and human rights. He has also published books and articles on the history of the Waffen-SS and the Nazi war of extermination at the Eastern Front. He is the author or co-author of nine monographs and co-editor of several edited collections.

Anne Griffiths is an Emeritus Professor of Anthropology of Law at Edinburgh University, Scotland. Her research focuses on anthropology of law, comparative and family law, African law, gender, culture, and rights. Over the years she has held a number of research grants and affiliations, including a research fellowship on Framing the Global at Indiana University and a senior research fellowship at the International Research Centre on Work and the Human Lifecycle in Global History, Humboldt University, Berlin. She has worked with colleagues at the Max Planck Institute for Social Anthropology in Halle/Saale, Germany and has had visiting appointments at international institution in southern Africa, the United States and Canada.

Hildur Fjóla Antonsdóttir holds a PhD in Sociology of Law from Lund University, Sweden, and is currently a postdoctoral researcher at the EDDA Research Center at the University of Iceland. In her research, she has focused on the meaning of justice for people who have been subjected to sexual violence, with the purpose of exploring how that knowledge can be used to expand and develop strategies that could meet the justice interests of victim-survivors inside and outside the criminal justice system. Currently, her work focuses on the ways in which allegations of sexual violence are framed, procedurally generated, and evaluated outside of the criminal law.

Part I

Introduction and Biography

1

Introduction

HÅKAN HYDÉN

O
UR PURPOSE AS a homage to Reza Banakar is to invite the reader on a journey across the academic field that is the Sociology of Law (SoL), one which he to a large extent himself has shaped. Like his scholarship, the journey covers a vast terrain. To do justice to his significance for the development of the field, the volume is divided into six separate sections, each with its own individual chapters. This Introduction lays out in brief the purpose and content of each section as well as a summary of the various chapters. The presentation is made in a discursive style but for the benefit of the reader each section also lists the authors and the title of their chapters.

PART I: INTRODUCTION AND BIOGRAPHY

Chapter 2   **Mariana Motta Vivian:** Bringing the Social and the Legal Together: An Overview of Reza Banakar's Sociology of Law

Chapter 3   **Max Travers:** Engaging with Reza Banakar

The book starts with a biography of Reza Banakar by Mariana Vivian, who gives an overview of his scientific achievements as a socio-legal scholar, underscoring his multidimensional approach to the sociology of law. She argues that, through multi-faceted insights, Reza Banakar has contributed to the development of the sociology of law as a unique field of study of both the social and the legal. Her chapter shows how Reza's writings engage at different analytical levels of scientific thinking. This is a distinct trait that makes him a unique scholar in the field – one who has much to offer to other socio-legal researchers with diverse academic interests. By making an analytical division between the meta-theoretical, the theoretical-methodological, and the empirical, Reza tried to demonstrate how the scholar may enrich socio-legal research with multifaceted insights.

Chapter 3 by Max Travers provides additional valuable bibliographical information stemming from his close collaboration with Reza in their seminal works regarding theory and method within SoL.[1] Travers has also kept contact with him over the years and is someone who perhaps more than anyone else possesses insights into how he reasoned with respect to central socio-legal problems. Travers's story of his personal interactions with him therefore deepens our understanding of how Reza viewed contemporary sociology of law.

PART II: SOCIOLOGY OF LAW THEORY, LEGAL PLURALISM AND LEGAL THEORY

Chapter 4   **Roger Cotterrell:** The Place of a Stepchild: Notes on the Establishment of Modern Sociology of Law

Chapter 5   **Peter Bergwall:** The Stepchild Controversy: Unfortunate Dichotomies in Socio-Legal Theory

Chapter 6   **Håkan Hydén:** Normativity as the Source of Norms

Chapter 7   **Martin Ramstedt:** On the Relationship between Normative Pluralism and Justice after Multiculturalism

Chapter 8   **Chris Thornhill:** Legal Pluralism and the Army: Legal Sociology as Military Sociology

Chapter 9   **Isabel Schoultz:** Corporate Strategies within a Transnational Regulatory Field

Chapter 10   **Mauro Zamboni:** Corporate Governance, Soft Law, and Corporate Social Responsibility: Some Legal Theoretical Contributions

Chapter 11   **Monika Lindbekk:** Reflections on Law, Religion, and Technology: Legal Mobilisation in the Area of Egyptian Paternity Law

Reza regarded SoL as what he called a stepchild, set uneasily between law and sociology. As Roger Cotterrell discusses in Chapter 4, SoL is most often described as an interdisciplinary field of research between law and sociology. A more specific way of describing the field would be to argue that SoL is the study of law using sociological theories and methods, where the interest is in the role of law in society. Compared to the legal sciences which are about knowledge *in* law, SoL can be said to represent knowledge *about* law. Some scholars elaborate on this difference by identifying an internal and an external perspective of law, SoL being associated with the latter.

In examining the role of SoL Cotterrell points out its strategic function as a specific practice in addressing tensions between the juridical, the political, and the social, which he defines broadly as including civil society. SoL has a strategic mission as a distinctive practice and transdisciplinary science coping with mediating positions between the political, the juridical and the social. This is a parallel to the role played by law as the last resort when conflicts fail to be solved by political or other means.

---

[1] Max Travers was co-editor with Reza Banakar of the following books: *Introduction to Law and Social Theory* (Banakar and Travers 2002); *Theory and Method in Socio-Legal Research* (Banakar and Travers 2005); and *Law and Social Theory* (Banakar and Travers 2013).

As Peter Bergwall argues in Chapter 5, it is necessary to make the distinction between ontology and epistemology when discussing where SoL is situated on the scientific map. Bergwall claims that the key for understanding research in SoL is to regard it as intransitive and ask what is SoL about? It is in this direction that the identity of Sol should be sought. Bergwall briefly discusses the concept of normativity as providing a possible unifying theme. This is also the manner in which Reza uses the concept in one of his last books (Banakar 2016) and the concept is subject to further examination in Chapter 6 by Håkan Hydén and Chapter 16 by Guibentif in this anthology.

In his chapter Hydén shows that there is an extensive discourse on the meaning and use of normativity, but a common definition is lacking. Hydén goes through the different uses of the concept of normativity and finds that the term typically refers to norms or something normative. This is how it is treated especially in philosophical and ethics discourse. For these scholars, normativity seems to be a higher order that defines the good life or the good society. Their preoccupation is focused on selecting which norms should be implemented to realise it.

Reza discusses the relation between norms and normativity from a socio-legal perspective (Banakar 2020: 15–38). He asks if normativity is caused by norms or norms are generated by normativity, concluding that normativity itself can be a source of norms (ibid: 20). More specifically, he points to how normativity may emerge out of system imperatives (purpose or instrumental rationality) as well as lifeworld (value rationality) (ibid: 21). A functional definition of normativity in this perspective would be that normativity is the source within a system from which norms emerge. Bergwall is on similar track in his suggestion that normativity is a possible unifying core for SoL A way of defining the discipline, therefore, would be that it is dealing with normative issues, primarily at the collective level.

In Chapter 7 Martin Ramstedt defines normative order as a broader, more general polythetic category, and law as one of its sub-categories. He distinguishes between normative and legal pluralism and argues for the need to differentiate between the two. Legal pluralism implies the interplay of several normative orders, all of which are recognised by a state or group of states. Normative pluralism, on the other hand, refers to normative orders which exist independently of those sanctioned by the state. These are competing normative orders that sometimes interfere with legal norms in a way which contributes to what Banakar calls the 'gap problem', ie the difference between the normative and the factual dimension of law.

Examples of legal pluralism abound. In Chapter 8, Christopher Thornhill shows how, in a historical perspective, constitutional constructions of the state have moved in a pluralist direction. From having initially been concerned with the mobilisation of military personnel, systematic legal organisation through constitutional law has become increasingly pluralist to cater for the rise of new civil structures. Especially significant is the adoption of international human rights law after the Second World War. This facilitated the integration of national politics into an overarching normative system, which set the parameters for civil-political rights and duties across national boundaries.

This diversification of legal rules makes it harder to claim an unambiguous legal answer to a given legal problem. In a case study of two Swedish companies

(Telia and Lundin Oil) involved in legal battles for suspected misconduct, Isabel Schoultz points out in Chapter 9 how these multinational companies make strategic use of different and competing legal regulations. Multinational corporations are part of a legal pluralistic reality; corporate practices are regulated by domestic law, both where they are registered and where they operate, by international criminal law as well as by non-binding corporate responsibilities such as corporate social responsibility. A transnational legal pluralistic perspective rejects by default the nation-state as the only form of legal order. In this sense, the trans-nationalisation of the legal field, and the notion of transnational legal pluralism, challenges the traditional understanding found in legal and partly in socio-legal research of unified legal systems stemming from the nation-state. Schoultz shows in her chapter how law in its plurality can be utilised by powerful and strategic multinational corporations in their struggle to dominate the interpretation of corporate regulation by appealing to specific laws over others.

Mauro Zamboni uses his chapter (10) to highlight a hybrid form of legal regulation that is usually referred to as 'soft law'. This kind of regulation consists of a variety of voluntary codes, created by private and public actors, which are not formally enacted as legally binding rules. These codes have their origin within other normative orders like technology such as in the case of work environment regulations or security issues as in aircraft safety regulation (Woodlock).[2] This soft law indirectly places obligations, just as positive law does. In practice, large companies, for example, adhere to these regulations as binding because they see it as being in their interest to do so. Soft law concretises the more abstract legal regulation, which indirectly makes soft law equivalent to positive law. Zamboni concludes that the option of hard law regulation is not enough or outright inappropriate when it comes to regulating complex business organisations. Soft law regulation, therefore, is a way of mediating social demands in the operations of these giants.

When different normative orders compete with the law in regulating a specific area, legal arguments many times fall short. It can be conflicts over the letter of the law, different religious arguments, or technological imperatives. This was the situation in a controversial paternity case that took place in Egypt, which Monika Lindbekk uses in Chapter 11 to illustrate the problem with normative pluralism. In such cases, cause lawyering plays a crucial role, not the least by human rights non-governmental organisations. Legal mobilisation outside the courts becomes central and mass media often play an important role.

Most Egyptian family law is codified in the form of modern state legislation applied by civil courts. In expanding the law, the classical scholars relied on a methodology whereby Sharia as Islamic law was derived from specific sources. The fundamental conditions relating to the establishment of paternity are governed by the Hanafi doctrine, which stipulates different ways of establishing paternity, the primary method being through marriage. Customary marriages are not officially registered with the state and fall outside the official legal regime. Thus, the paternity of a child

---

[2] In a Luhmannian perspective soft law can be seen as an instrument for structural coupling between two different autopoeitic systems.

born within the context of a customary marriage is not automatically recognised. With the advent of DNA testing, there is nowadays also a tension between biological and legal conceptions of paternity. Finally, lawyers are now able in specific cases to bring in international conventions signed and ratified by Egypt.

This paternity case illustrates how something which looks rather unambiguous may be swept into the swirl of normative pluralism, making it hard to judge and predict its outcome. From an external perspective, legal pluralism may be a boon but in an internal perspective, it is more often a bane because it complicates the reach of a straightforward verdict.

PART III: SOCIOLOGY OF LAW METHODS AND INTERDISCIPLINARITY

Chapter 12   **Ulrike Schultz:** Knowledge and Opinion about Law – The Importance of Law-related Education

Chapter 13   **Balázs Fekete:** Rights Consciousness in Hungary. What is Behind the Numbers? Lessons of a Focus Group Study

Chapter 14   **Linda Mulcahy:** In Conversation with Reza: Theory and Method in Socio-Legal Research

Chapter 15   **Karl Dahlstrand and Mikael Furugärde:** 'The Light in the Tunnel Can Be a Train': About Kafkaesque Double Thoughts

Chapter 16   **Pierre Guibentif:** Socio-Legal Agency in Late Modernity – Reappreciating the Relationship between Normativity and Sociology of Law

Chapter 17   **Peter Wahlgren:** The Quest for Scientific Methods: Sociology of Law, Jurimetrics and Legal Informatics

Chapter 18   **Stine Piilgaard Porner Nielsen:** Minding the 'Gap' Problem: The Relevance of Combining Top-down and Bottom-up Approaches to the Study of Law's Role in Everyday Life

Chapter 19   **Seda Kalem:** Doing Fieldwork in Istanbul Courts: Challenges and Strategies

This section deals with the question of how SoL researchers have gone about examining the role of law in the broader societal context. It addresses such questions as how widely scholars should cast their net to capture what happens to law and thus examines such issues as what people know about it and how they react. It traces the research that has been carried out under the 'Knowledge of Law' label. It further discusses issues of interdisciplinarity and takes a critical look at the methods that have been used in socio-legal studies. All these issues were prominent in Reza's research, and he addressed them in his writing.

The early research on 'Knowledge and Opinion about Law' (KoL) mainly had the aim of measuring the acceptance of legal rules. The literature also dealt with deviation from norms, penalty and punitive orientation. In the 1960s–1980s questionnaire-based surveys were conducted in several European countries. They formed part of a big international comparative project and followed the same or a similar research design directed towards the acceptance of rules in various social groups with the view to finding out how the knowledge of law (criminal, constitutional, procedural) differs and how the knowledge level varies among social groups based on gender, age, social status, etc. This quantitatively-oriented research was important in establishing levels of legal acceptance, but it has also been criticised for lack of theoretical questioning and being tied to legal policy objectives. Since then, living conditions and democratic values have changed. Updates of this research are timely and make sense. 'When I started to work intensely on women lawyers in Germany in the 1980s', Ulrike Schultz writes in Chapter 12:

> I could state that – at the time – women had a greater cognitive distance to law, ie less knowledge of legal rules than men. Overall, women had a more distanced relation to law. They did not trust in their rights and avoided court cases/legal disputes. Women developed other than legal strategies and problem solutions and they were less likely to ask for legal advice and seek legal help. Men, on the other hand, were more litigious and more often tried to prevail against opponents. In general, terms the law seemed to be alien to many women.

This leads to the question of whether women need more legal education, or rather more legal empowerment.

It is urgent for legal education to focus on questions like: What do students know about law? What should they know? How can they learn what? What is their opinion about law and their attitudes to it? How can these be improved or changed? It is also important and rewarding, according to Schultz, to carry out extended empirical KoL research on young and older citizens (both women and men) as well as members of immigrant communities, to find out where deficits in knowledge exist and empowerment measures are needed. This research ought to be comparative to evaluate the situation across national boundaries.

In Chapter 13, Balacs Fekete argues that while the KoL survey data in Hungary highlighted trends in the country's human rights consciousness, it was not enough to understand the micro dynamics that significantly contribute to the formation of rights consciousness. A new research project was therefore launched in 2017 to specifically dig deeper into the factors determining the state of rights consciousness in Hungary. This project relied on a mixed methods design, combining quantitative and qualitative research tools. The analysis was based on focus group research conducted in late 2020 in order to provide answers to two questions: Why are Hungarian citizens more reluctant to consider any kind of legal procedure in a conflict with an institution than in interpersonal disputes? How and why can previous legal experience have a general positive impact on rights consciousness?

The study showed above all a considerable legal alienation associated with a negative image of 'the law', for example belief that money matters more than trust when it comes to the outcome of legal proceedings. Their stories emphasised two factors that could facilitate change: a positive personal court hearing experience and a personal effort to understand the basics of a given case. The lesson from Fekete's study is that even if people are aware of their rights they may be hesitant to act in order to reach a solution to a legal problem. This finding corroborates Reza's argument that 'a chasm opens up between the rules and principles that mediate moral or legal rights and how they are unfolded in everyday life and legal practice' (Banakar 2010b: 15).

Linda Mulcahy (Chapter 14) raises the fundamental question of whether the researcher needs a theory in advance to frame a project, or whether theory emerges in parallel with the collection and analysis of the data. Reza and Travers suggest (2005) that socio-legal methods can *never* be atheoretical and always reflect a commitment to a particular theoretical perspective or way of understanding the world, even if this is not always explicit. Mulcahy also points out the widespread lack of interest in the question of what constitutes the legal in socio-legal studies (Bradney 1998). There is nowadays an emerging body of work on this topic, encouraging scholars to return to re-engage with doctrine and the technicalities of the legal process (Cowan and Wincott 2005). This ambition, however, raises the issue of how far the boundaries of SoL can be extended without trespassing or losing its prime objective. As argued above, the latter is concerned with knowledge about law, not legal dogmatic.[3]

This observation also raises the issue of whether there is such a thing as a legal methodology or set of methods unique to SoL that can compete with the standards set by other social science disciplines. SoL researchers are generally comfortable with using both quantitative and qualitative methods developed in other social science fields. The crucial question is whether sociology of law requires its own epistemology. The uniqueness of SoL lies in the analysis of normativity with social science methods. Where motives and norms become study objects, certain methods like ethnography become central. In Chapter 15, Karl Dahlstrand and Mikael Furugärde propose the study of law through literature. Seen as a social collective memory of human life, literature consists of different social representations that come to life through narratives.

The humanistic study of law includes imagining the law or ideas of justice through a novel, a piece of art or a cinematic presentation, as well as cultural processes related to interpretation, language use, translation, and narrative and rhetorical aspects of the law. In other words, the empirical material will be constructed and hypothetical in order to discuss different outcomes in the same way that legal dogmatists do when discussing different potential outcomes in interpretation of law. This epistemological strategy can use both existing literature and constructed narratives to illuminate a specific issue or problem area. Dahlstrand and Furugärde use both. Citing Reza's 1994 doctoral thesis *The Dilemma of Law: Conflict Management in a Multi-cultural Society*, the authors discuss ethno-cultural conflicts in Sweden and the dilemmas they pose for the legal system. Their main point is to illustrate the mental pain that is associated with standing 'before the law'. Like Reza, they show how Franz Kafka takes us beyond the instrumental understanding of law and allows us to grasp law as a form of experience.

The relationship between sociology of law and normative debates is highlighted by Pierre Guibentif in Chapter 16 where he takes as his starting point an article by Reza, 'The Identity Crisis of a "Stepchild"' published in 1998, in which he compares SoL with feminist scholarship. The success of feminist scholarship is characterised by a common ideological objective that does not exist to the same extent and with the same intensity in sociology of law. Feminist scholars have 'freed themselves from the

---

[3] This is not the same as the distinction between an internal and an external perspective of law. See Hydén and Wickenberg (2008).

limitations of the traditional and academically established disciplines'. Their starting point is the situation of women, and science is used to illuminate its various aspects. SoL has no corresponding agenda. It does not even have its own praxis field. When SoL engages in normative debates, it relates to something outside its own knowledge field. It can be feminism, environment and sustainable issues, migration, etc. In each case the normative is then subordinated to the specific area under study. Its contribution, therefore, lies in providing a general theoretical perspective without its own agenda.

A considerable portion of academic jurisprudence is still preoccupied with trying to understand the nature of law and law students are taught to solve legal problems in a reactive manner. Countless calls for methodological revision have had little influence, despite being made for well over a century. These calls have been largely motivated by the observation that little is known about the actual impact of law on society. In Chapter 17, Peter Wahlgren discusses how research in SoL and interdisciplinary lines of research has confronted jurisprudence with scientific methods such as jurimetrics and legal informatics. For example, jurimetrics has never became fully integrated with legal sociology or traditional jurisprudence in Scandinavia or elsewhere in the world. With the emergence of computer and system sciences, things have begun to change. With their own technology, power of performance and impact on society these sciences have brought about new solutions and methods. Technology is often a complement or alternative to legal solutions and in this case it has enabled a shift from reactive to proactive problem elimination mechanisms (*cf* Hydén 2022: ch 3). This in turn has led to insights about how technology might be utilised as a legal tool and become a basis for further developments of the legal field. As consequence of digitisation, for example, IT has in a short time become a subject matter for SoL research. In this context it is significant from a methodological point of view that legal informatics now embraces an interest in artificial intelligence.

Stine Piilgaard Porner Nielsen (Chapter 18) emphasises the importance of studying law in social life from both the top and the bottom. Using a group of case workers as empirical illustration she analyses how formal law structures the space of these workers to manoeuvre in handling their cases. This is combined with a bottom-up approach to investigate how caseworkers' and citizens' perception of and experience with law inform their social practice. As an analytical tool she uses the concept of legal consciousness to investigate individual perceptions of law and how these perceptions inform actions. The chapter concludes with reflections on the value of trying to bridge the gap between a top-down and a bottom-up approach in analysing the role of law in everyday life.

Seda Kalem in Chapter 19 discusses the challenges of obtaining access for social science empirical research. In some countries, the researcher needs a permit to conduct interviews and document studies, in many countries for ethical reasons, but in others for murkier reasons. Kalem refers to her own experience in Turkey to show how contingent and problematic such a process might be. For a case file review, she and her fellow researchers filed a petition at the Ministry of Justice asking for permission to examine closed files. The request was initially met with a cold hand but finally approved after six months. The letter issued by the Ministry was written in a technical manner and left the discretion to share files in the hands of the judges and prosecutors. Because most of them were sceptical about the project the research-ers were either dismissed or ignored, sometimes with reference to the independence of the judiciary. Much the same thing happened at lower court levels, where clerks insisted on setting their own terms for access to files. The letter from the Ministry proved to be of little worth. Access became rather a matter of interpersonal dynamics or, as Bourdieu (1987) would call it, a game of (re)determining and (re)negotiating the boundaries of what is possible in the field of law. As such, despite the many hurdles, the research proved to offer valuable information regarding how the convergence of the formal with the informal in a specific judicial setting normalises legal processing.

PART IV: COMPARATIVE LEGAL CULTURES

Chapter 20   **Marina Kurkchiyan:** Legal Culture as an Approach to the Study of Law in Russian Society
Chapter 21   **Carlo Pennisi:** Flexible Structures: Using the Legal Culture Concept to Study the Law of Society
Chapter 22   **Lawrence M Friedman:** Lawyers and Drivers: On Reading Two Works of Reza Banakar
Chapter 23   **Marc Hertogh:** Traffic Justice: Law and Society on the Roads of Iran and the Netherlands
Chapter 24   **Mathieu Deflem:** The Cancer of the Law in the Islamic Republic of Iran: Reflections on the Iranian Anti-Israel Law of 2020
Chapter 25   **Hanne Petersen:** Revolutions and Legal Cultures. Perspectives and Reflections

Few concepts have entered the socio-legal field from within the discipline itself rather than from legal studies or other social science fields. One such exception is the concept of legal culture. It has been criticised as being too vague and hard to apply in empirical studies (Cotterrell 2006: 81–96). Such critique notwithstand-ing, studies of legal culture have flourished (Friedman 1975: 104; Nelken 2004: 1; Merry 2012: 5376). Definitions vary among authors. Marina Kurkchiyan (Chapter 20) uses the concept to refer to socially constructed meanings, images and roles that are attributed to law. Like many other scholars, she treats legal culture as a subset of general culture. It is not independent, however, but embedded in a particular social order and thus encompasses the assumptions about law of people living in that social space. Kurkchiyan understands legal culture as a concept that captures the specificity of the social context, exposing the meanings of law within any particular social unit.

A problem in the study of legal culture is how to locate the legal and how to distinguish law from custom or the multiple norms, rules and practices of everyday life. Kurkchiyan means that what is legal is defined by formal law and its applica-tion. It evolves from the assumption that social facts and their meaning are the result of interactions and learnings that form a localised worldview, a legal culture. This approach depends on being able to locate and interpret law as it is experienced and thought about by the locals. In this perspective, law is what people think it is, and legal culture is what they do in response to it. Her own research in Russia highlights some of the challenges associated with studying legal culture. One is how to build a bridge between contemporary social facts and the past, where the latter is part of the explanation. Another is how to use an analysis of cognition to explain observable behaviour. A third challenge is how to avoid relying on a western-centred perspective but at the same time not just falling back on a form of essentialism. Findings often tend to exaggerate the extent of the uniqueness, and thereby fall into the trap of exceptionalism.

Many of Kurkchiyan's ideas of legal culture are further amplified by Carlo Pennisi in Chapter 21. For him, legal culture goes beyond the mere study of the cultural embeddedness of certain legal practices or how laws are legitimised. Instead, he defines the concept as repeated patterns of legal behaviour that are reproduced in a taken-for-granted manner by officers of the law or by ordinary citizens. Pennisi regards *legal* and *culture* as specifically linked both at the conceptual, theoretical level and empirically by the institutionalisation processes within which the *normative* and *legal* structuring of action mirror each other and differ depending on contexts. This linkage requires a research design about legal phenomena that is expressly sociological because it shifts attention away from institutions to institutionalisation processes, thus focusing on the way in which the legal structures are elaborated and differentiated from other normative structures.

This approach to legal culture is what Reza uses in his research on reckless driving in Iran, *Driving Culture in Iran: Law and Society on the Roads of the Islamic Republic* (Banakar 2016), a subject to which Lawrence Friedman returns in Chapter 22. He is fascinated by the clash of two cultures: one, the culture of the judiciary, the other of Iran's ruling circles – an authoritarian and deeply Islamic version of culture. Drawing on the mentioned study by Iranian researchers (including Reza), Friedman analyses as being the 'most valuable symbolic capital of the juridical field – the authority to determine the law'. While lawyers see law as a rule-based rational construct for decision-making, the judiciary in Iran is imbued with the dominant values of the Islamic Republic and their decision-making is therefore based in part on Sharia but (somewhat paradoxically) also on looser autonomous norms. Friedman emphasises the importance of distinguishing between law and norms and he concludes that drivers in Iran may be more reckless and selfish than those in other countries but even the reckless and selfish obey most of the rules most of the time. Norms that govern driving culture are as much social as they are legal rules which give rise to normative behaviour that is independent of the traffic code. These norms are neither legal nor illegal. They occupy a space in between the two. As Reza stressed in his own study and Friedman shows in his chapter, exploring this space – the domain of social life as people live it – is a key domain in the sociological study of law.

Reza views urban traffic as a social laboratory to pursue the holy grail of law and society research: why people follow or ignore the law. This is a path that Marc Hertogh, in Chapter 23, also treads in his comparison of law and society in Iran and the Netherlands. Using evidence from the two countries, he demonstrates how legal legitimacy shapes legal compliance. People comply with the law if and when they feel that legal authorities are legitimate, and their actions are generally fair. His conclusion is that law can retain its legitimacy only if it is effectively connected to the lifeworld of citizens, an observation that tallies with the one of Kurkchiyan above, but from a slightly different angle.

In Chapter 24, Mathieu Deflem argues that pre-modern conceptions of politics, law, and religion, and their embodiment in a theocracy, are incompatible with the rationalisation that is needed for modern law to guarantee liberty and justice for all. His chapter may be read as a sequitur to Friedman's account above of law in a totalitarian state. Based on sociological theories of the modernisation and rationalisation of law and its relation to culture, Deflem claims that the non-modernity of Iran's legal and political culture only turns into an anti-modernity. In Iran law and politics are so intertwined that they cannot be separated. Authoritarian rule is crystallised in the position of the Supreme Leader as the head of state who has tight control over the government and serves as the last instance over law and the judiciary. An example of the substantive infusion of the Islamic religion is the anti-Israel law, ('Countering Israel's Actions') which the Iranian parliament passed in May 2020, a clear anti-Semitic expression. The Islamic religion provides the anti-Israel law's ultimate justification. Deflem concludes by arguing that for law to be rationalised in a purposive-rational sense, it must be secular or – at least – embody values that are compatible with norms that can function for all, whether the legal subjects are religious or not. These conditions do not exist in Iran today and are not likely to be realised by law and politics. Instead, it has to be brought about by education of modern law and legal empowerment.

Friedman writes that authoritarian societies often begin with a revolution fuelled by ideology. In the case of Iran, the new Islamic regime got rid of the old cadres of lawyers and replaced them with others willing to apply revolutionary justice. His account of Iran sets the tone for Hanne Petersen who, by using a broader set of cases, discusses in Chapter 25 the consequences of revolutions for legal cultures. She suggests that revolutions come in different shapes – social, technological, economic or political. Their common denominator is that they are disruptive as they replace old modes and worldviews with new ones. Referring to Charles Kurzman's book *The Unthinkable Revolution in Iran* (2004), Petersen asserts that the 1979 Islamic Revolution in Iran was possible because of the emergence and existence of a 'viable movement' that could produce an alternative to the corrupt and authoritarian rule of the Shah. This movement consisted primarily of young students at the religious seminaries, particularly the one in Qom, a city considered holy, and the largest centre for Shi'a scholarship in the world. These students were strongly influenced by Ayatollah Khomeini, who after years of exile in Iraq became the leader of the new religious government.

A common feature of revolutions is that they raise people's expectations but rarely produce the expected outcomes. Iran is no exception. The 2021 Iranian elections indicate a widespread disappointment among both young people and women. Despite this, the prospects for change are slim. Revolutions require the concentration of power in the hands of a group of committed few and if they succeed in their pursuit, they become hard to dethrone. At present, there is no 'viable alternative' inside or outside the country capable of bringing about change.

PART V: SOCIOLOGY OF LAW AS SCIENCE

Chapter 26   **Ole Hammerslev and Mikael Rask Madsen:** Reza Banakar and the Quest for a Sociology of Law
Chapter 27   **David Nelken:** Governing through Covid Indicators
Chapter 28   **John Woodlock:** Safe but not Secure? Risk Management, Communication and Preparedness for a Pandemic in Aviation
Chapter 29   **Nicolás Serrano C:** The Interlegal Evocation of Peace in Colombia

Reza's theoretical and methodological work spans the whole field of socio-legal studies, not least, as Mikael Rask Madsen and Ole Hammerslev show in Chapter 26, in his treatment of the dichotomy between law's inside and outside or, put differently, law's internal operations and doctrine, on the one hand and its engagement with society, on the other (Weber 1978; Cotterrell, 1998; Nelken 1993; Habermas 1996; Friedman 1986). This bifurcation reflects a disciplinary tension which in turn has made socio-legal scholars produce a new set of dichotomies, such as 'law on the books' versus 'law in action' or 'formal law' versus 'informal law', all of which are essentially designed to reflect the different research agendas of the two 'parental' disciplines, legal and social sciences. Reza's point is that this tension is innate to SoL and without being able to include both perspectives, the discipline would be empty. Socio-legal studies must grasp the full sociological complexity of the law and its institutions (Banakar 2003). Without basic paradigms, common concepts, theories and methods, however, fragmentation is always a danger. In fact, the very fundamentals for pursuing socio-legal studies as a distinct and valuable scientific discipline might be in jeopardy (ibid). Madsen and Hammerslev suggest that Reza did not claim to provide the solution to this challenge, but he offered a well-argued reflection on how to incorporate the essential insights of the various dichotomies into a more constructive and interpretive, indeed reflexive, socio-legal research methodology and agenda. The field is still somewhat fragmented, but sociology of law clearly relates to international and Nordic sociology while not losing sight of the law.

Social scientists often wish to imitate the scientific methods of the natural sciences but this is a fallacy because accumulating knowledge in the social sciences is different, as the present author has argued elsewhere (Hydén 2022: ch 1). The objects of knowledge in the social sciences and natural sciences are incommensurable. They cannot be studied in the same way. To illustrate, the atom (from the Greek ἄτομος, átomos, meaning 'indivisible') has the same properties no matter where it exists across the globe, while individuals (from the Latin individuum, which in turn means indivisible) differ depending on context. Similar circumstances do not necessarily produce the same results.[4] This problem is further discussed by David Nelken in Chapter 27 with reference to the use of Covid-19 indicators. He shows that differences in the spread of the pandemic and the reasons why some places have suffered more than

---

[4] This does not exclude the possibility that individuals might choose to act the same way. This may especially be the case when people live under similar structural conditions or share a common interest. Yet another example is when a group exerts pressure on individuals to act in the same way.

others are foremost contextual and independent of policy choices (though potentially relevant to them). As a result, he asks himself if it is at all possible to square the circle of establishing global standards that transcend contexts without losing sight of the significance of local variations. Social sciences with international or transnational ambitions tend to become too abstract to be helpful for policymakers. Nelken concludes that concessions to difference are best exercised not at the stage of design but at the time of application (see Desai and Shomerus 2018: 109).

John Woodlock, in Chapter 28, takes as his starting point a statement by Reza in one of his last writings: 'late modern law are forms of legal regulation that increasingly focus on the management of risk and instrumentally seek to control and rationally regulate specific societal domains' (Banakar 2015: 189–90). One such domain that interests Woodlock is aviation. It operates in a labyrinth of norms where successful risk management is critical. The chapter addresses the challenges of cross-sectorial risk management strategies surrounding global public health and aviation in relation to the spread of infectious diseases and the context of the global Covid-19 pandemic. Correct and reliable information is crucial to how the aviation industry is perceived. Airline companies, for example, tend to see safety issues primarily from a perception perspective. They may adopt a proactive form of communication to improve their image in the public arena (Guérard 2018: 136). Woodlock, however, argues that the communication landscape is changing dramatically. Aviation professional experts with knowledge of events provide valid information to reliable mainstream media to inform the public, but in the current information technology world, other information providers have entered the communication scene and relay information of a different nature with different motivations for doing so. This makes understanding the relation between certainty and security important.

Certainty is associated with security and knowledge; uncertainty with insecurity and risk. By discussing increasing uncertainty in relation to the social and cultural consequences of globalisation and the transnational forces reshaping political and legal landscapes, Woodlock argues – like Banakar – that two specific developments have led to a focus on uncertainty. At the micro-level, social actors increasingly reflect on the legal implications associated with the structures and constraints imposed upon them by traditional institutions. At the macro level, uncertainty increases because decision-making and normativity have shifted from the local to the transnational level of society and are therefore harder to control.

'Law conjures peace', Nicolas Serrano Cardona asserts in Chapter 29 on the inter-legal evocation of peace in Colombia. Inspired by Banakar's methodological recommendation of using both a top-down and a bottom-up approach (*cf* Stine Piilgaard Porner Nielsen, Chapter 18 above), Cardona, using municipal Bogota as his case study, explores how different manifestations of the law evoke peace as non-violence in Colombia. The local government interpreted the right to life within its borders as sacrosanct and 'Life is Sacred' became its motto as well as the name of an activist group. The backbone of Bogotá's 'civic culture' strategy, according to its development plan, was to increase voluntary compliance with norms, to foster citizens' ability to enter and comply with agreements and mutual help and help citizens to act according to their conscience and in harmony with the law, as well as to promote communication and solidarity in the community. An intense communication by the authorities within the municipal inter-legal network enabled a flow of relevant legal information aimed at enhancing the sense of peace and safety among city inhabitants.

PART VI: APPLIED SOCIOLOGY OF LAW

Chapter 30   **Ann-Christine Hartzèn:** Trade Union Solidarity and the Issue of Minimum Wage Regulation in the EU

Chapter 31   **Jiří Přibáň:** Constitutional Imaginaries: A Socio-legal Perspective of Political and Societal Constitutions

Chapter 32   **Peter Scharf Smith:** Public Sentiments on Justice, Legal Consciousness, and the Study of Marginalised Groups

Chapter 33   **Anne Griffiths:** Challenging Legal Orthodoxy: New Orientations in Space and Time in Discourses Over Land Tenure

Chapter 34   **Hildur Fjóla Antonsdóttir:** Sexual Violence, Standard(s) of Proof, and Arbitrariness in Judicial Decision-Making

Reza's (2015) meta-methodological framework includes three levels of analysis: (1) How does the law, as a body of rules, interact with society at the macro level? (2) How are legal rules interpreted at the intermediary level of legal institutions? (3) How is law identified, employed, and experienced by ordinary citizens at the level of social action? It is a helpful starting point for analysing SoL in practice. It allows for a closer look at how decision-makers choose when more than one law or norm applies to a given case and when law is independently interpreted or – as it may also be phrased – when law is treated as dependent variable.

Regulators and lawmaking authorities are becoming increasingly aware that interlegality affects their own spheres of action in European countries – despite efforts to harmonise legislation – national and EU regulations may still give room to differences in interpretation (Klabbers and Palombella 2019). Ann-Christine Hartzén (Chapter 30) brings up such a case that illustrates this problem. She is referring to the discussion about minimum wages regulation within the EU and the position of the Nordic countries, more specifically the action by Swedish trade unions on minimum wage regulation. The main issue is how the Nordic labour market model can be accommodated in a proposed Directive on the regulation of minimum wages in the EU. For the Nordic countries which already have high levels of minimum wage (Hartzén 2021; Hällberg and Kjellström 2020; Nelson and Fritzell 2019) the EU proposal is not a step forward. From an EU perspective, the Swedish stand has been interpreted as lack of solidarity. It becomes a hurdle for the broader European trade union movement in establishing a much-needed strategy directed towards the improvement of working conditions for the worst-off workers in the Union.

Hartzén uses a two-step analysis of the communication produced by the system under study, making use of Luhmann's distinction between observation and interpretation. Her analysis demonstrates that the internal solidarity among the Swedish workers overshadows transnational trade union cooperation in the EU. Other arguments than self-interest have been forwarded to justify the position taken by the trade unions. One is that the EU proposal could affect Swedish economic growth negatively by undermining the Swedish system, which is built on negotiations between employers and workers instead of legislation (Arrius 2020). Another is the fear that the whole Swedish model for collective bargaining would come under legal review by the EU Court of Justice.

It should be added here that since Hartzén submitted her chapter there has been some movement regarding the positions discussed above. The European Parliament and the Council of Ministers have proposed changes and additions to the proposed EU directive, which open now new negotiations over the Nordic labour market model. The Directive is no longer presented as regulation but as framework allowing for more flexibility. It now only stipulates procedures for how Member States should achieve adequate minimum wages without determining their level. While the Swedish government has decided to support the new proposal, Denmark has not. Thus, as this case illustrates, it is clear that in an inter-legal perspective, harmonisation within EU has its price and requires compromises and diplomatic skills.

'We imagine the happy state' states Plato in his *Republic* and, to illustrate this constitution of an ideal city, he employs the 'noble lie' as a founding myth of his imaginary polity. The lie is nothing but the fiction behind the imagined community, constituted by different myths. Jiří Přibáň in Chapter 31 examines the constitution as a legal imaginary, Symbols of power structures generate acceptance and unity in the absence of reason and rational consensus. They have greater capacity to guarantee a common consensus than rational discourse, which is the privilege of wise and educated elites and therefore cannot be extended to the whole society. Ideology, as Karl Mannheim would argue, is the set of collective unconscious motives that blurs the true state of society for the purpose of obfuscating and covering its internal conflicts and contradictions. Mannheim (1997) described ideology as the collective unconscious motives blurring the real state of society and thus stabilising its order. Přibáň contrasts the polyvalence and functional differentiation of modern society with the transcendental validity claims generated by specific social systems. The enforcement of these claims through their imaginaries continues, according to Přibáň, to be one of the central themes of both social and legal theory. He analyses social imaginaries as background power communicating the common good in a functionally differentiated system at both national and global level.

Přibáň asserts that symbolic forms of communication constitute social reality. Imaginaries may be analysed in terms of how they expand the potential of the functional rationality of different social systems and thus contribute to their legitimation beyond efficiency and performativity. The specific constitution, function, and operations of imaginaries in legal, political, and other social systems must be examined from both a theoretical and a sociological perspective. Theory may be used to show that social imaginaries are part of the semantics and dramas evolving in modern constitutional politics. The sociology of constitutional imaginaries can reveal their meaning and practice and how they evolve and transform in the systems of positive law and politics. Such an approach becomes especially important for Přibáň, who argues that it is non-political societal constitutions that externally limit power operating in the systems of politics and law.

Peter Scharf Smith in Chapter 32 discusses families and children of prisoners and their marginalised position in the legal system. His study follows in the long Nordic tradition of research on public sentiments toward justice. Taking off from a Danish study by Flemming Balvig, he distinguishes between three different forms of sentiments: the general, the informed, and the concrete sense of justice (Balvig 2015). Together, they constitute what Lotti Ryberg calls people's 'normative opinions on punishment' (Ryberg 2006: 19). Families and children with an incarcerated parent encounter many problems that seriously affect the way that they experience society and state officials like police and prison officers. Encountering the legal system and all the laws governing remand, imprisonment, prison visits, etc can be a stressful and overwhelming experience, especially since families typically know little about their rights regarding visitation and other issues related to detention (Condry and Smith 2019). The criminal justice system is really not designed to balance state power with the rights of prisoners, and third parties such as prisoners' relatives are left out of the equation. The legal consciousness and the sentiments on justice of these families and children have generally been overlooked or simply ignored in the continuous development of the criminal justice system.

Some scholars, like Hertogh (2018: 68 ff), criticise classic legal consciousness research for treating law as an independent variable – ie as a fixed entity that exists regardless of people and their reactions to it. Instead, he urges researchers to make law part of their enquiry and ask how people relate to it and what people 'experience as law' (ibid: 69). Scharff Smith responds to Hertogh's call by focusing on legal alienation, a concept that he believes captures the situation of prisoners' families and children in the legal system. He concludes his chapter by referring to steps that have recently been taken by entities like the UN and the European Council to develop concrete recommendations and standards for how the rights and needs of the children of prisoners should be handled at every stage of the criminal justice system (Donson and Parkes 2021; Smith and Villman 2021).

In Chapter 33, Anne Griffiths explores the role of land in Botswanan discourses on development and livelihoods at both macro and micro levels. In doing so, she engages with concepts of space and time in plural legal settings that are used to challenge the legal orthodoxy centred on a linear approach to the administration and regulation of land. The pressure of access to and control over land transcends nation-states and forms a core component also of macro perspectives on international and transnational engagement with trade and commerce in the global marketplace. At the same time, the issue is also a critical component at the micro level of individual, family and household provision for shelter, livelihoods and processes of capital accumulation.

Debates on land in Botswana are shaped by the country's history of colonialism and its regulatory legacy. Three types of land tenure coexist: (1) tribal land held in customary communal tenure – 70 per cent of the land in the country; (2) state land, previously crown land mostly found in the urban areas; and (3) freehold tenure, with a right to free and undisturbed possession, largely in relation to agricultural land. Griffiths regards them as products of different spatial and temporal logics that reveal how social and property relations are maintained at any given historical moment, providing scope for differing and contested claims to land today. Land administration is not just of importance to Botswana. It also features at the heart of international and transnational approaches to sustainable development and the eradication of poverty. For example, a 2008 report by the United Nations (UN) Development Programme on the 'Legal Empowerment of the Poor' identified property (which includes land) as one of four pillars of legal empowerment. Unlike Ferguson (1992), who argued that globalisation promotes culturally homogenising forces over all others, Griffiths demonstrates the extent to which law is articulated within wider economic, social, and political structures that engage with local, national, international, and transnational domains. Her study raises questions about the relationship between law and power that varies according to the model used.

In Chapter 34, Hildur Fjola Antonsdóttir inspired by Reza's work, conducts a meta-methodological analysis to examine how different standards of proof in evidentiary law apply in cases of sexual violence. A common feature of these cases in the Nordic countries as well as elsewhere in Europe and other parts of the world is that they rarely result in conviction (Lovett and Kelly 2009; Krahé 2016; Antonsdóttir and Gunnlaugsdóttir 2013; Brå 2019). Her starting point is the degree of tension, particularly in civil law countries, that exists between how legal scholars conceptualise standards of proof and the way in which judges apply these standards. As Bourdieu (1987) notes, the process of continuous rationalisation of the law contributes to establishing a social division between ordinary people and legal professionals. Even if ordinary people might share the same concept of the law as legal professionals, this does not mean, according to Banakar (2015), that they experience the relationship between law and morality in the same way. Socio-legal theory must 'transcend the internal/external dichotomy which mainstream jurisprudence employs to place the contradictory outcomes of legal operations outside the juridical gaze' (ibid: 74).

Antonsdóttir concludes based on her interviews with judges and other legal practitioners in Iceland that the application of the standards of proof is not only a question of legal rules but of human sentiments that may change over time. This is detectible not only at the level of individual judges but also at institutional level, which, arguably, reveals the symbolic violence of the law. As she shows, the legal phenomenon of standards of proof is embedded in socio-historical contexts that transcend the self-described internal/external dichotomy of the law.

***

Following this overview of what the journey through the field of Sociology of Law research entails, the time has come to embark on the journey in earnest. Each section that has been identified above may be treated as a major junction, while the chapters are stations that invite the reader to spend time and reflect on the subject matter they raise.

REFERENCES

Antonsdóttir, HF and Gunnlaugsdóttir, ÞS (2013) *Tilkynntar nauðganir til lögreglu á árunum 2008 og 2009: Um afbrotið nauðgun, sakborning, brotaþola og málsmeðferð* (Report) (Reykjavík, EDDA – Center of Excellence at the University of Iceland).

Arrius, G (2020) 'Stå emot EU:s minimilöner, regeringen', debate article published Arbetet 20 October 2020, available at https://www.saco.se/press/aktuellt-fran-saco/debatt/sta-emot-eus-minimiloner-regeringen/ (last accessed 23 September 2022).

Balvig, F (2015) 'Retsfølelse og retsfornuft – i Grønland' 102(1) *Nordisk Tidsskrift for Kriminalvidenskab* 1.

Banakar, R (1994) *Rättens Dilemma: Om konflikthantering i ett mångkulturellt samhälle* (Lund, Bokbox).

—— (1998) 'The Identity Crisis of a "Stepchild": Reflections on the Paradigmatic Deficiencies of Sociology of Law' 81 *Retfærd: Nordisk juridisk tidsskrift* 3.

—— (2003) *Merging Law and Sociology: Beyond the Dichotomies of Socio-Legal Research* (Berlin, Galda and Wilch Publishing).

—— (2010a) 'In Search of Heimat: A Note on Franz Kafka's Concept of Law' 22 *Law and Literature* 463.

—— (2010b) 'Law, Rights and Justice in Late Modern Society: A Tentative Theoretical Framework' in R Banakar (ed), *Rights in Context: Law and Justice in Late Modern Society* (Burlington, Ashgate).

—— (2015) *Normativity in Legal Sociology: Methodological Reflections on Law and Regulation in Late Modernity* (London, Springer).

—— (2016) *Driving Culture in Iran: Law and Society on the Roads of the Islamic Republic* (London, IB Tauris).

—— (2020) 'Iran: A Clash of Two Cultures?' in RL Abel, O Hammerslev, H Sommerlad and U Schultz (eds), *Lawyers in 21st Century Society*, vol 1: National Reports (Oxford, Hart Publishing).

Banakar, R and Travers, M (eds) (2002) *An Introduction to Law and Social Theory* (Oxford, Hart Publishing).

—— (eds) (2005) *Theory and Method in Socio-Legal Research* (Oxford, Hart Publishing).

—— (eds) (2013) *Law and Social Theory*, 2nd edn (Oxford, Hart Publishing).

Bourdieu, P (1987) 'The Force of Law: Towards a Sociology of the Judicial Field' 38 *Hasting Law Journal* 805.

Bradney, A (1998) 'Law as a Parasitic Discipline' 25(1) *Journal of Law and Society* 71.

Brå (2019) *Våldtäkt från anmälan till dom. En studie av rättsväsendets arbete med våldtäktsärenden*. Rapport 2019: 9 (Stockholm, The Swedish National Council for Crime Prevention).

Condry, R and Smith, PS (2019) 'A Holistic Approach to Prisoners' Families – From Arrest to Release' in M Hutton and D Moran (eds), *The Palgrave Handbook of Prison and the Family* (Palgrave).

Cotterrell, R (1998) 'Why Must Legal Ideas Be Interpreted Sociologically' 25 *Journal of Law and Society* 171.

—— (2006) *Law, Culture and Society* (Aldershot, Ashgate).

Cowan, D and Wincott, D (2005) 'Exploring the Legal' in D Cowan and D Wincott (eds), *Exploring the 'Legal' in Socio-Legal Studies* (London, Palgrave Macmillan).

Desai, D and Shomerus, M (2018) '"There Was A Third Man …": Tales from a Global Policy Consultation on Indicators for the Sustainable Development Goals' 49 *Development and Change* 89.

Donson, F and Parkes, A (eds) (2021) *Parental Imprisonment and Children's Rights* (London, Routledge).

Ferguson, M (1992) 'The Mythology about Globalization' (1992) 7 *European Journal of Communication* 69.

Friedman, LM (1975) *The Legal System – A Social Science Perspective* (New York, Russell Sage Foundation).

—— (1986) 'The Law and Society Movement' 38 *Stanford Law Review* 763.

Guérard, M (2018) 'How Safety Communication can Support Safety Management: The Case of Commercial Aviation' in M Bourrier and C Bieder (eds), *Risk Communication for the Future Towards Smart Risk Governance and Safety Management* (Cham, Springer).

Habermas, J (1996) *Between Facts and Norms* (Cambridge, Polity Press).

Hällberg, P and Kjellström, C (2020) *Collective Agreements and Minimum Wages* (Stockholm, Swedish National Mediation Office).

Hartzén, A-C (2021) *Working, Yet Poor: National Report Sweden* (Lund, Lund University).

Hertogh, M (2018) *Nobody's Law. Legal Consciousness and Legal Alienation in Everyday Life* (London, Palgrave).

Hydén, H (2022) *Sociology of Law as the Science of Norms* (London, Routledge).

Hydén, H and Wickenberg, P (eds) (2008) *Contributions in Sociology of Law: Remarks from a Swedish Horizon*, Lund Studies in Sociology of Law; 29 (Lund, Lund University).

Klabbers, J and Palombella, G (eds) (2019) *The Challenge of Inter-legality* (Cambridge, Cambridge University Press).

Krahé, B (2016) 'Societal Responses to Sexual Violence Against Women: Rape Myths and the "Real Rape" Stereotype' in H Kury, R Sławomir and E Shea (eds), *Women and Children as Victims and Offenders: Background, Prevention, Reintegration* (Switzerland, Springer).

Kurzman, C (2004) *The Unthinkable Revolution in Iran* (Harvard, Harvard University Press).

Lovett, J and Kelly, L (2009) *Different Systems, Similar Outcomes? Tracking Attrition in Reported Rape Cases across Europe* (Final report) (London, Child and Woman Abuse Studies Unit, London Metropolitan University).

Luhmann, N (1999) *Ausdifferenzierung des Rechts. Beitrage zur Rechtssoziologie und Rechtstheorie* (Frankfurt, Surhkampf).

Mannheim, K (1997 [1936]) *Ideology and Utopia* (London, Routledge).

Merry, S (2012) 'What is Legal Culture? An Anthropological Perspective' in D Nelken (ed), *Using Legal Culture* (London, Wildy, Simmons and Hill) 53.

Nelken, D (1993) 'The Truth about Law's Truth' *European Yearbook of the Sociology of Law* (Milan, Giuffre).

—— (2004) 'Using the Concept of Legal Culture' 29 *Australian Journal of Legal Philosophy* 1.

Nelson, K and Fritzell, J (2019) *ESPN Thematic Report on In-work Poverty in Sweden* (Brussels, European Commission, Directorate-General for Employment, Social Affairs and Inclusion).

Ryberg, J (2006) *Retsfølelsen. En bog om straf og etik* (København, Roskilde).

Smith, PS and Villman, E (2021) 'Prisons, Families and Human Rights: From Prisoners' Rights to Rights of Prisoners' Children' in F Donson and A Parkes (eds), *Parental Imprisonment and Children's Rights* (London, Routledge).

Teubner, G (2006) 'Rights of Non-Humans? Electronic Agents and Animals as New Actors in Politics and Law' 33 *Journal of Law and Society*.

Weber, M (1978) *Economy and Society* (Berkeley, University of California Press).

2

Bringing the Social and the Legal Together: An Overview of Reza Banakar's Sociology of Law

MARIANA MOTTA VIVIAN

I. INTRODUCTION

REZA BANAKAR'S LEGACY to the sociology of law is beyond measure. For about three decades of contributions to socio-legal studies, he has exhibited a rigorous commitment to the development of the field as well as a rich academic production. Over the years, he proved to be an outstanding scholar within the socio-legal community and became increasingly recognised for the distinguished reflections and questionings that he addressed to social and legal research.

In view of this, the present chapter aims to present an overview of his scholarly work, underscoring his multidimensional approach to the sociology of law. The particular reading here proposed, thus, exhibits Banakar's writings as contributions that engage in different analytical levels of scientific thinking. I would like to argue that this is a distinct trait that makes Reza Banakar a unique scholar in the field – one that has much to offer to socio-legal researchers with the most diverse academic interests.

Beyond this introduction and the concluding remarks, the text is divided into three main sections, which follow the distinct levels of analyses conducted by the scholar throughout his academic path. The first section addresses the meta-theoretical efforts and diagnoses of the sociology of law elaborated by Banakar. The second explores some of the most remarkable theoretical and methodological contributions he made to the field. Finally, the third section presents his empirical studies and the major topics he covered during the course of his career.

Given the brief nature of the overview, the presentation here proposed is not exempt from limitations. As this anthology attests, Reza Banakar's scholarship is fairly extensive, and, as a result, it is likely that certain writings will inevitably be left out or end up under-covered.[1] Hopefully, however, such an attempt to revisit his

---

[1] Apart from the works properly referenced throughout the chapter, I present, at the end of the text, a list containing other publications by Banakar that were not mentioned.

published thoughts will contribute to renewed explorations of his work and spark new interrogations in the sociology of law.

II. META-THEORETICAL EFFORTS AND DIAGNOSES OF THE SOCIOLOGY OF LAW

The sociology of law is an interdisciplinary field of research placed somewhat precariously at the intersection of the disciplines of law and sociology, each of which in turn fosters its own distinct mode of conceptualizing, describing, analysing and experiencing social life.

Reza Banakar (2003: 1)

Reza Banakar made important contributions to the self-reflexivity of the sociology of law as a field of research. On different occasions, he took the sociology of law as his object of analysis and sought to systematise the structuring and contextual elements influencing the development of the field in order to offer an accurate diagnosis of it.

At the end of the 1990s, the scholar initiated a debate concerning the identity of the discipline through the article 'The Identity Crisis of a "Stepchild"' (Banakar 1998a). By seeing the absence of common basic assumptions as a significant issue in the socio-legal field, he argued that the sociology of law faced an identity crisis stemming from a lack of intellectual coherence, which prevented it from producing its own internal paradigms. In his analysis, the sociology of law, as a specific academic specialty, would face a dichotomy engendered by 'inside' and 'outside' perspectives of the legal order, and it could only advance its scientific project by learning how to integrate both standpoints.

Because of its thought-provoking reading and critique, 'The Identity Crisis of a "Stepchild"' produced significant repercussions in the social-legal environment, including a series of replies assessing Banakar's analysis of the field.[2] At the beginning of the 2000s, two relevant articles offering renewed examinations of the sociology of law were published by the scholar. On the one hand, 'A Passage to "India"' (Banakar 2001a) followed the main thesis of the underdeveloped theoretical state of the discipline to propose a socio-legal 'reflexive matrix', which would help the field to constitute itself as more intellectually independent from both sociology and legal practice. On the other hand, 'Reflections on the Methodological Issues of the Sociology of Law' (Banakar 2000) analysed sociology of law from an institutional point of view. Banakar argued that institutional constraints, such as law's mode of domination, communication and legitimacy, would produce particular challenges for the growth of the sociology of law as a scientifically strong and autonomous field of research.

In 2003, Banakar published *Merging Law and Sociology* (Banakar 2003), where he comprehensively dealt with both issues. The first part of the book provided a meta-theoretical reading of the sociology of law in which both the theoretical logic and the institutional arrangements involved in its scientific production were thoroughly

---

[2] See, eg, Mathiesen (1998), Hydén (1999), Dalberg-Larsen (2000), and Sand (2000).

analysed. This analysis was accompanied by a proposal of a general framework for the field founded on the theoretical cores of rationality, system, structure, and agency, which, together with the external-internal dichotomy and the substantive strands specific to legal sociology, Banakar would consistently follow over the course of his research trajectory.

A few years later, he published 'Law Through Sociology's Looking Glass' (Banakar 2009a), a study in which a sociological analysis of the sociology of law was presented. The book chapter explored the conflicts and competitions arising out of the diverse attempts to integrate legal and sociological knowledge on law. Throughout the text, Banakar explained the differences between sociological and legal epistemes, presented various existent approaches in the social scientific study of law, and reflected on the possibilities for law and sociology to learn from one another.

Drawing on all of these insights, 'The Sociology of Law: from Industrialisation to Globalisation' (Banakar 2011a)[3] examined the research field in its historical context, asking to what extent socio-legal scholarship was able to reconsider its premises to grasp those conditions that were specific to global societies of the twenty-first century. In this text, the intellectual origins of the sociology of law were associated with Western industrial societies, and Banakar analysed the challenges that this historical condition posed to socio-legal research conducted in non-Western and contemporary societies, particularly in view of the socio-cultural consequences of globalisation.

III. THEORY AND METHODOLOGY IN SOCIO-LEGAL RESEARCH

> By implication, part of contemporary socio-legal theory, which engages with legal theory and jurisprudence, remains embedded in the paradigm of modernity – which was captured by the debate between Ehrlich and Kelsen – and thus is methodologically constrained by the dichotomy of facts and norms. The question for scholars who work at the cross-section of legal sociology and legal theory is therefore how to break free from the dichotomous tyranny of facticity and normativity and devise a concept of law which reflects the liquidity of late modern society.
>
> Reza Banakar (2012: 31–32)

Alongside many of the field diagnoses he produced, Banakar displayed a keen interest in discussing theoretical and methodological issues in the sociology of law. Together with Max Travers, he edited the books *An Introduction to Law and Social Theory* (Banakar and Travers 2002), *Theory and Method in Socio-Legal Research* (Banakar and Travers 2005a), and *Law and Social Theory* (Banakar and Travers 2013), and he compiled many of his general ideas in the books *Merging Law and Sociology* (Banakar 2003) and *Normativity in Legal Sociology* (Banakar 2015). He was particularly concerned with the theoretical and methodological problems associated with the nature and conceptualisation of law, as well as with the forms of operationalising empirical research within socio-legal studies.

---

[3] A shorter version of this paper appears in Banakar's contribution to the International Sociological Association's sociopedia (Banakar 2011b).

Banakar was both an enthusiast and a critic of classical socio-legal theory. In particular, he paid close attention to the theories produced by Eugen Ehrlich (1862–1922), Leon Petrazycki (1867–1931), and Georges Gurvitch (1894–1965). In 'Integrating Reciprocal Perspectives' (Banakar 2001b), for instance, Banakar defended the importance of certain theoretical ideas from Gurvitch, especially that of 'immediate jural experience'. According to him, the classical thinker provided legal sociology with a theoretical work suitable to be employed in empirical studies attentive to the internal-external realities of law and to integrate the micro and macro levels of analysis. 'Sociological Jurisprudence' (Banakar 2002), on the other hand, highlighted the value of Ehrlich and Petrazycki's conceptual framework for socio-legal studies. For Banakar, their special relevance consisted in the fact that both employed social sciences in order to improve the science of law, refuting natural law theories as well as the claims of legal positivism through the concepts of 'intuitive law' and 'living law'. The importance of classical socio-legal theory was also the central thesis of 'Who Needs the Classics?' (Banakar 2012), a work in which the limits and possibilities of applying the ideas of 'intuitive law' and 'living law' in contemporary empirical research were presented.[4]

In parallel to such efforts of revisiting the classics, Banakar made use of representations of law in literature as part of his theoretical endeavour in the search for a comprehensive understanding of legal phenomena. Noteworthy, in this context, is the paper 'In Search of Heimat' (Banakar 2010a), in which he presented Franz Kafka's concept of law. By making use of the author's writings, Banakar argued that the images of law found in works such as *The Trial* and, most especially, *The Castle* were ambivalent: they presented law as a form of experience marked by the inherent contradictions of the modern world. A similar diagnosis appeared when Banakar discussed Hermann Hesse's novel *Steppenwolf* (Banakar 2008a) and used it to address the multiple and fragmentary nature of the law. Just like the Steppenwolf, law would have several souls, comprising a multitude of rational and non-rational identities.

For Banakar, the methodological implications of such a comprehensive perspective on law would be striking. In writings such as *Merging Law and Sociology* (Banakar 2003) and 'Law, Sociology and Method' (Banakar and Travers 2005b), for instance, he stressed that socio-legal researchers could not ignore the fact that law assumes different forms and that each aspect of it can be seen from contrasting standpoints – ie from inside, outside, experience-near, and experience-distant. Conducting empirical research in legal sociology, in this sense, would mean recognising the dynamic character of legal phenomena and considering the distinctive manifestations and perspectives that are at play in each case studied.

'Power, Culture and Method in Comparative Law' (Banakar 2009b) and 'Having One's Cake and Eating It' (Banakar 2011c), in turn, addressed the contextualisation of law as an indispensable methodological attribute of socio-legal studies. Whereas the former highlighted the importance of combining top-down and bottom-up approaches, especially in comparative research, the latter maintained that such a contextualisation could not be limited to the self-understandings and self-descriptions

---

[4] This text was later published in Banakar (2013a).

of the law itself. Instead, Banakar sustained that contextualisation in socio-legal research would necessarily require questioning positive law's *modus operandi* and, to a certain extent, re-embedding the law.

These ideas concerning the conceptualisation of law were intrinsically attached to the critique of legal positivism found in much of his theoretical and methodological works. 'Can Sociology and Jurisprudence Learn from Each Other?' (Banakar 2006), for instance, exemplifies how the scholar sustained a comprehensive conception of law against traditional, positive legal theory. Likewise, in 'Whose Experience is the Measure of Justice?' (Banakar 2007) Banakar engaged with Robert Alexy's theory of legal argumentation to explore the limits of the separation thesis. He regarded Alexy's thesis as promising in its attempt to link law and justice but problematic in its faithfulness to positive law's institutional framework.

'Law, Rights and Justice in Late Modern Society' (Banakar 2010b) developed and advanced the former claims through a re-examination of the concept of law under the theoretical umbrella of late modernity. Its main argument was that late modernity promoted an increasing marginalisation of moral concerns by making use of a rights discourse that, once employed through law, lost its emancipatory potential. Banakar strongly believed, in this regard, that law and justice could not be set apart, as law without justice could not satisfy the requirement of legitimacy. As a result, a socio-legal theory of law would have to acknowledge the different experiences of justice as an integral part of it, especially in light of the diversity and fragmentation characteristic of late modern conditions.

Along the same lines, Banakar suggested in 'Can Legal Sociology Account for the Normativity of Law?' (Banakar 2013b) that justice would be law's major source of normativity. Because of that, legal sociology could not limit its scope of analysis to the external empirical properties of law. Alternatively, he argued, the sociology of law should overcome the methodological constraints imposed by the positivist separation of facts and values and take part in the study of law's normative dimensions in its own terms.[5]

IV. CASE STUDIES AND EMPIRICAL INTERESTS

As we leave behind the durable social conditions of early modernity, which were shaped by industrial relations, and move towards late modernity, which is characterised by the socio-cultural implications of globalization and the spread of digital technology, the focus of our analysis has to shift from the study of social change (as an event) to the examination of the rate of ongoing change (as an unceasing process) in society. Under late modern conditions, constant change is paradoxically the only empirically consistent property of society.

Reza Banakar (2015: 3)

Banakar's empirical interests were also incredibly rich. Over the course of his career, he was able to produce case studies that touched on topics of major significance to

---

[5] I specifically discuss Banakar's approach to the problem of the relationship between law and justice in Vivian (2020) and Vivian (2021).

the sociology of law and to the social changes of the contemporary world. Notably, the problems associated with globalised, plural societies, and the challenges faced by law in light of such transformations, occupied a significant space in the empirical questions Banakar addressed.

The issue of multiculturalism and of ethno-cultural conflicts, for instance, has been present in his work since his earliest publications in the field. As early as 1994, he published a study that, taking the multicultural environment found in Sweden as its setting, sought to establish the extent to which the law could be used to contain ethnocultural-based conflicts, in particular those involving the Swedish legal system and the various immigrant groups that were part of that multicultural society (Banakar 1994).

This study was part of his doctoral thesis and, years later, it would be revised and updated through the publication of the *Doorkeepers of the Law* (Banakar 1998b), which investigated ethnic discrimination in Sweden through the analysis of several cases processed by the Swedish Ombudsman against Ethnic Discrimination from 1990 to 1995. The problems related to discrimination and legal regulation in Sweden were also the subject of Banakar's analysis in the last part of the book *Merging Law and Sociology* (Banakar 2003) and in the book chapters 'When Do Rights Matter?' (Banakar 2004) and 'Studying Cases Empirically' (Banakar 2005), which involved the study of both ethnic conflicts and gender equality rights.

In addition, Reza Banakar took considerable interest in the particular tension between the Western and Islamic legal cultures of immigrant communities living in the west. This is expressed in works such as 'Poetic Injustice' (Banakar 2008b) and 'The Politics of Legal Cultures' (Banakar 2008a). Through different case studies, the scholar focused on the shift to risk management strategies of late modernity and its impact on such communities, as well as the political processes shaping those interactions and the diversity found within these groups' cultural identities.

The book *Rights in Context* (Banakar 2010c), edited by Banakar in 2010, approached how these and other issues of late modernity were expressed in the context of the rights discourse. As illustrated in his own contribution to the collection (Banakar 2010b), Banakar argued that, under late modernity, the concepts of law, society and state acquire distinct features. On this basis, he examined the ways in which such transformations might influence the debate and employment of rights in practice. In fact, Banakar cultivated a deep concern with late modernity in general and the empirical impact these societal changes had on the workings of law. Many chapters of *Normativity in Legal Sociology* (Banakar 2015) and writings such as 'Law and Regulation in Late Modernity' (Banakar 2013c), 'Law, Policy and Social Control Amidst Flux' (Banakar 2016a) and 'Law, Community and the 2011 London Riots' (Banakar and Phillips 2017) are representative of the increased attention he paid to the topic.

Another related socio-legal subject Banakar has engaged in studying empirically, especially since the second decade of the twenty-first century, is Iranian society and legal culture. 'Driving Dangerously' (Banakar and Fard 2012) and *Driving Culture in Iran* (Banakar 2016b), for instance, approached driving habits in Iran as a way of understanding Iranians' legal culture and the complexities involved in the social order upheld by the contrasts of Iran. 'Double-Thinking and Contradictory Arrangements

in Iranian Law and Society' (Banakar 2018a) explored how Iranians have historically made use of double-thinking to respond to contradictory aspects of their law
and society. Finally, 'The Life of the Law in the Islamic Republic of Iran' (Banakar
and Keyvan 2018) and 'Iran: A Clash of Two Cultures?' (Banakar and Keyvan 2020)
discussed the Iranian legal system through an analysis of its judiciary and legal
profession, outlining the ongoing struggles and clashes that gave the law in Iran a life
of its own.

In parallel to these studies, Banakar conducted research on European Union law in
more recent years. In 'Law, Love and Responsibility' (Banakar 2018b), he focused on
the role of solidarity in EU law and policy and underlined the sources of the problematic form it took in such context. Along the same lines, in 'Brexit: A Note on the EU's
Interlegality' (Banakar 2019), he analysed its integration crisis by focusing on Brexit
and suggested the need for another form of interlegality in the EU.

V. CONCLUDING REMARKS

This chapter has sought to present a general overview of Reza Banakar's body of
work and to highlight the different ways in which such literature has contributed to
the advancement of the sociology of law as a unique field of study of both the social
and the legal. By making an analytical division between the meta-theoretical, the
theoretical-methodological, and the empirical, it tried to demonstrate how Banakar
was able to outline relevant questions at distinct levels of scientific research, providing
socio-legal scholarship with multifaceted insights.

First, it approached Banakar's analyses of the sociology of law as an academic
field. His consistent engagement with the scientific development of legal sociology
over the years allowed him to explore the various challenges it needed to overcome
in order to improve its reflections on legal phenomena. Through several writings,
he was able to point out the theoretical and methodological deficiencies, the socio-
historical conditionings, and the institutional disputes limiting the unfolding of the
field. Beyond providing the field with remarkable intellectual diagnoses, however, he
also employed his theoretical efforts in suggesting innovative responses to such issues.

Second, it addressed the theoretical and methodological thoughts that Banakar
produced in the course of his studies. Apart from co-editing collections on the topic,
he invested a considerable part of his academic inquiries into the development of
diverse proposals of his own in socio-legal theory and methodology. Most of these
insights are synthesised in the books *Merging Law and Sociology* and *Normativity in
Legal Sociology*. Banakar was particularly concerned with devising an encompassing
socio-legal understanding of legal phenomena attentive to the distinct experiences
and standpoints on law. Critical of legal positivism, he believed that law could not be
detached from the demands of justice. Methodologically, he sustained that research
into the sociology of law should consider the societal changes of late modernity,
contextualising and re-embedding the law, as well as overcoming strict divisions
between facts and values.

Finally, the chapter also presented Banakar's empirical research. Bearing in mind
his own notes and critiques, Banakar tried to employ many of his proposals to the

field in concrete case studies. Departing from the tensions emerging out of globalised, plural societies, he conducted empirical studies involving, among others, multiculturalism, the clash of Western and non-Western legal cultures, and late modern forms of domination. Through a combination of analytical rigour, theoretical originality and empirical diversity, Reza Banakar offers indispensable readings for all researchers committed to the refinement of the sociology of law as an autonomous and singular field of knowledge.

REFERENCES

Banakar, R (1994) *Rättens Dilemma: Om konflikthantering i ett mångkulturellt samhälle* (Lund, Bokbox).

—— (1998a) 'The Identity Crisis of a "Stepchild": Reflections on the Paradigmatic Deficiencies of Sociology of Law' 81 *Retfærd: Nordisk juridisk tidsskrift* 3.

—— (1998b) *Doorkeepers of the Law: A Socio-Legal Study of Ethnic Discrimination in Sweden* (Aldershot, Ashgate).

—— (2000) 'Reflections on the Methodological Issues of the Sociology of Law' 27 *Journal of Law and Society* 273.

—— (2001a) 'A Passage to "India": Toward a Transformative Interdisciplinary Discourse on Law and Society' 92 *Retfærd: Nordisk juridisk tidsskrift* 3.

—— (2001b) 'Integrating Reciprocal Perspectives: On Georges Gurvitch's Theory of Immediate Jural Experience' 16 *Canadian Journal of Law and Society* 67.

—— (2002) 'Sociological Jurisprudence' in R Banakar and M Travers (eds), *An Introduction to Law and Social Theory* (Oxford, Hart Publishing).

—— (2003) *Merging Law and Sociology: Beyond the Dichotomies of Socio-Legal Research* (Berlin, Galda and Wilch Publishing).

—— (2004) 'When Do Rights Matter? A Case Study of the Right to Equal Treatment in Sweden' in S Halliday and P Schmidt (eds), *Human Rights Brought Home* (Oxford, Hart Publishing).

—— (2005) 'Studying Cases Empirically: A Sociological Method for Studying Discrimination Cases in Sweden' in R Banakar and M Travers (eds), *Theory and Method in Socio-Legal Research* (Oxford, Hart Publishing).

—— (2006) 'Can Sociology and Jurisprudence Learn from Each Other?: A Reply to Mauro Zamboni' 113 *Retfærd: Nordisk juridisk tidsskrift* 75.

—— (2007) 'Whose Experience is the Measure of Justice?' 10 *Legal Ethics* 209.

—— (2008a) 'The Politics of Legal Cultures' 123 *Retfærd: Nordisk juridisk tidsskrift* 37.

—— (2008b) 'Poetic Injustice: A Case Study of the UK's Anti-Terrorism Legislation' 31 *Retfærd: Nordisk juridisk tidsskrift* 69.

—— (2009a) 'Law Through Sociology's Looking Glass: Conflict and Competition in Sociological Studies of Law' in A Denis and D Kalekin-Fishman (eds), *The ISA Handbook in Contemporary Sociology: Conflict, Competition, and Cooperation* (London, Sage).

—— (2009b) 'Power, Culture and Method in Comparative Law' 5 *International Journal of Law in Context* 69.

—— (2010a) 'In Search of Heimat: A Note on Franz Kafka's Concept of Law' 22 *Law and Literature* 463.

—— (2010b) 'Law, Rights and Justice in Late Modern Society: A Tentative Theoretical Framework' in R Banakar (ed), *Rights in Context: Law and Justice in Late Modern Society* (Burlington, Ashgate Publishing).

—— (ed) (2010c) *Rights in Context: Law and Justice in Late Modern Society* (Burlington, Ashgate Publishing).

—— (2011a) 'The Sociology of Law: From Industrialisation to Globalisation' *University of Westminster –School of Law Research Paper* 11, 1.

—— (2011b) 'Sociology of Law' *Sociopedia.isa*, 2011, 1.

—— (2011c) 'Having One's Cake and Eating It: The Paradox of Contextualisation in Socio-Legal Research' 7 *International Journal of Law in Context* 487.

—— (2012) 'Who Needs the Classics? On the Relevance of Classical Legal Sociology for the Study of Current Social and Legal Problems' *University of Westminster – School of Law Research Paper* 13, 1.

—— (2013a). 'Klassisk retssociologi – og dets relevans for nutidig forskning' in O Hammerslev and MR Madsen (eds), *Retssociologi* (København, Hans Reitzels Forlag).

—— (2013b) 'Can Legal Sociology Account for the Normativity of Law?' in M Baier (ed), *Social and Legal Norms: Towards a Socio-Legal Understanding of Normativity* (Farnham, Ashgate).

—— (2013c) 'Law and Regulation in Late Modernity' in R Banakar and M Travers (eds), *Law and Social Theory*, 2nd edn (Oxford, Hart Publishing).

—— (2015) *Normativity in Legal Sociology: Methodological Reflections on Law and Regulation in Late Modernity* (London, Springer).

—— (2016a) 'Law, Policy and Social Control Amidst Flux' in K Dahlstrand (ed), *Festskrift till Karsten Åström* (Lund, Juristförlaget i Lund).

—— (2016b) *Driving Culture in Iran: Law and Society on the Roads of the Islamic Republic* (London, IB Tauris).

—— (2018a) 'Double-Thinking and Contradictory Arrangements in Iranian Law and Society' 27 *Digest of Middle East Studies* 6.

—— (2018b) 'Law, Love and Responsibility: A Note on Solidarity in EU Law' in R Banakar, K Dahlstrand and LR Welander (eds), *Festskrift till Håkan Hydén* (Lund, Juristförlaget i Lund).

—— (2019) 'Brexit: A Note on the EU's Interlegality' in BL Kristiansen, K Mitkidis, L Munkholm, L Neumann and C Pelaudeix (eds), *Transnationalisation and Legal Actors: Legitimacy in Question* (London, Routledge).

Banakar, R and Fard, SN (2012) 'Driving Dangerously: Law, Culture and Driving Habits in Iran' 39 *British Journal of Middle Eastern Studies* 241.

Banakar, R and Keyvan, Z (2018) 'The Life of the Law in the Islamic Republic of Iran' 51 *Iranian Studies* 717.

—— (2020) 'Iran: A Clash of Two Cultures?' in RL Abel, O Hammerslev, H Sommerlad and U Schultz (eds), *Lawyers in 21st Century Society: vol 1: National Reports* (Oxford, Hart Publishing).

Banakar, R and Phillips, AL (2017) 'Law, Community and the 2011 London Riots' 62 *Scandinavian Studies in Law* 79.

Banakar, R and Travers, M (eds) (2002) *An Introduction to Law and Social Theory* (Oxford, Hart Publishing).

—— (eds) (2005a) *Theory and Method in Socio-Legal Research* (Oxford, Hart Publishing).

—— (2005b) 'Law, Sociology and Method' in R Banakar and M Travers (eds), *Theory and Method in Socio-Legal Research* (Oxford, Hart Publishing).

—— (eds) (2013) *Law and Social Theory*, 2nd edn (Oxford, Hart Publishing).

Dalberg-Larsen, J (2000) 'Sociology of Law from a Legal Point of View' 89 *Retfærd: Nordisk juridisk tidsskrift* 26.

Hydén, H (1999) 'Even a Stepchild Eventually Grows Up: On the Identity of Sociology of Law' 85 *Retfærd: Nordisk juridisk tidsskrift* 71.

Mathiesen, T (1998) 'Is it All That Bad to be a Stepchild? Comments on the State of Sociology of Law' 83 *Retfærd: Nordisk juridisk tidsskrift* 67.

Sand, I-J (2000) 'A Future or a Demise for the Theory of the Sociology of Law: Law as a Normative, Social and Communicative Function of Society' 90 *Retfærd: Nordisk juridisk tidsskrift* 55.

Vivian, M (2020) 'Sociology of Law in Between Law's Autonomy and Justice Claims: Theoretical Contributions from Reza Banakar' (Master's Thesis, UPV/EHU & IISL, Oñati).

—— (2021) 'Law, Justice and Reza Banakar's Legal Sociology' 11 *Oñati Socio-Legal Series* 1.

OTHER NON-REFERENCED PUBLICATIONS

Banakar, R (1989) 'The Dilemma of Law: An Examination of Controvertial Judicial Decisions in Ethno-Culturally Based Legal Disputes' 6 *Tidskrift för rättssociologi* 225.

—— (1990) 'Etnisk diskriminering i arbetslivet' 90 *I & M* 22.

—— (1990) 'Lagen – politikens verktyg' 91 *I & M* 4.

—— (1991) 'Debatt på låtsas' 91 *I & M* 3.

—— (1991) 'Muslimska kvinnor i Norden' (book review) 91 *I & M* 38.

—— (1992) 'Rättslig diskurs i etnokulturella frågor' 57 *Retfærd: Nordisk juridisk tidsskrift* 38.

—— (1992) 'Salman Rushdie och liberalismens heliga ko' 25 *Häften för kritiska studier* 3.

—— (1993) 'Det offentliga samtalet om etnokulturella frågor' 1–2 *Häften för kritiska studier* 81.

—— (1993) 'Svart eller vit i lagens ögon' 60 *Retfærd: Nordisk juridisk tidsskrift* 49.

—— (1995) 'Kvotering skapar inga nya jobb' 95 *I & M* 7.

—— (1995) 'Rättens utveckling i den globala byn' 71 *Retfærd: Nordisk juridisk tidsskrift* 3.

—— (1997) 'Realistic Socio-Legal Theory: Pragmatism and a Social Theory of Law' (book review) 7 *Social and Legal Studies* 580.

—— (1997) 'Samtal som konfliktlösning: En granskning av den svenska lagen mot etnisk diskriminering' *Social forskning – the Journal of the Swedish Council for Social Research* 10.

—— (1998) 'Reflexive Legitimacy in International Arbitration' in V Gessner and AC Budak (eds), *Emerging Legal Certainty: Empirical Studies on the Globalisation of Law* (Farnham, Ashgate).

—— (2001) 'Contrasting Criminal Justice: Getting from Here to There' (book review) 28 *Journal of Law and Society* 451.

—— (2001) 'Review of Organised Cooperation Facing Law: An Anthropological Study' (book review) 24 *Retfærd: Nordisk juridisk tidsskrift* 72.

—— (2005) 'Introduction to Theory and Method in Socio-Legal Research' in R Banakar and M Travers (eds), *Theory and Method in Socio-Legal Research* (Oxford, Hart Publishing).

—— (2005) 'Race, Law, Resistance' (book review) 32 *Journal of Law and Society* 648.

—— (2005) 'Review of Policy of Law: A Legal Theoretical Framework' (book review) 28 *Retfærd: Nordisk juridisk tidsskrift* 82.

—— (2006) 'H.L.A. Hart: A Review of Nicola Lacey's "A Life of HLA Hart"' (book review) 29 *Retfærd: Nordisk juridisk tidsskrift* 96.

—— (2007) 'Gurvitch, Georges (1894–1965)' in DS Clark (ed), *Encyclopedia of Law and Society: American and Global Perspectives – Vol 2* (London, Sage Publications).

—— (2007) 'Race and Ethnicity' in DS Clark (ed), *Encyclopedia of Law and Society: American and Global Perspectives – Vol 3* (London, Sage Publications).

—— (2010) 'Introduction: Snapshots of Rights Discourse' in R Banakar (ed), *Rights in Context: Law and Justice in Late modern Society* (Burlington, Ashgate Publishing).

—— (2010) 'Pre-Empting Terrorism? Two Case Studies of the UK's Anti-Terrorism Legislation' in R Banakar (ed), *Rights in Context: Law and Justice in Late modern Society* (Burlington, Ashgate Publishing).

—— (2010) 'Studying the Rights Discourse: A Tentative Socio-Legal Framework' in BL Kristiansen (ed), *Nordisk Retssociologi* (København, DJØF Forlag).

Banakar, R, Dahlstrand, K and Welander, LR (eds) (2018) *Festskrift till Håkan Hydén* (Lund, Juristförlaget i Lund).

Banakar, R, Flood, J, Webb, J and White, A (2005) *Internal Case Assignment in England* (Utrecht, University of Utrecht).

Banakar, R and Payvar, B (2016) 'Gender and Domination: Interviews with Female Taxi Drivers' in R Banakar (ed), *Driving Culture in Iran: Law and Society on the Roads of the Islamic Republic* (London, IB Tauris).

Banakar, R and Travers, M (2002) 'Law and Sociology' in R Banakar and M Travers (eds), *An Introduction to Law and Social Theory* (Oxford, Hart Publishing).

Flood, J, Whyte, A, Banakar, R and Webb, J (2007) 'Case Assignment English Courts: A Study of Case Assignment and Impartiality in Six European Jurisdictions' in PM Langbroek and M Fabri (eds), *The Right Judge for Each Case* (Antwerp, Intersentia).

3

Engaging with Reza Banakar

MAX TRAVERS

THIS CHAPTER IN honour of Reza Banakar has the following main headings: intellectual contributions; and themes and questions (legal pluralism, black letter law, normativity, and law in late modern societies). Reza was a sociological jurist or legal theorist influenced by sociology, and I will engage critically with his ideas and approach. Law and sociology are each complex disciplines, and it is easy to get things wrong from either side through lack of knowledge or understanding.[1] Reza did more than most in asking interesting questions and crossing intellectual divides.

I. INTELLECTUAL CONTRIBUTIONS

I will discuss Reza's contributions in two sections: sociology of law; and sociological jurisprudence.

A. Sociology of Law

There are only a few people in law schools or social science departments who are interested in how different sociological approaches can be used in researching law. Reza and I identified this as a problem in our doctorates (Travers 1993; Banakar 1998). We later tried to remedy this lack of interest and knowledge by inviting experts, mainly from law schools, to write about different traditions in our collections, *Introduction to Law and Social Theory* (Banakar and Travers 2002) and *Law and Social Theory* (Banakar and Travers 2013).[2] You can learn a lot from these collections about

---

[1] There are some similarities to the ancient parable of blind men meeting an elephant. John Godfey Saxe (2018/1887) wrote a satirical poem about this encounter. The descriptions given by the blind men drew on their limited experiences. Similarly, it is difficult obtaining an understanding of an academic discipline, including an appreciation of internal debates, as an outsider. More positively, we develop an understanding through each encounter with different theorists and traditions.

[2] The title was changed to avoid giving the impression that this was a textbook. This allowed us to submit the second edition as part of university submissions to Research Assessment Exercises without being questioned by auditors.

theorists and theoretical traditions that include Bourdieu, Habermas, Luhmann, Latour, symbolic interactionism and ethnomethodology, postmodernism, feminism, postcolonial theory and critical race theory.[3]

Following a workshop in Onati, we published a collection that invites the reader to think critically about research methods (Banakar and Travers 2005). It starts with a lively debate between an interpretive and structural theorist about how to understand qualitative data. We also planned to co-author accessible textbook introductions. In the end, the only one that resulted was my *Understanding Law and Society* (Travers 2010). This explains the main theoretical traditions in sociology of law to undergraduates in departments of law and sociology. No introductory text on socio-legal research methods has so far been published.[4]

B. Sociological Jurisprudence

Sociological jurisprudence is a sub-field in legal theory. It is distinctive from other sub-fields, such as legal philosophy, because the legal theorist draws on sociological ideas to understand law as a social institution and how this is changing.[5] Another term for a sociological jurist could be a sociologically-oriented legal thinker. In the past, such thinkers have included Frederick Karl von Savigny (1779–1861), William Graham Sumner (1840–1910), Leon Petrazycki (1867–1931), Eugene Ehrlich (1862–1922), Roscoe Pound (1870–1964) and Karl Llewellyn (1893–1962). The only sociological jurists writing today are, to the best of my understanding, Roger Cotterrell (1992; 2018), and – until recently – Reza.

Cotterrell has made the more distinguished contribution over many years. Nevertheless, Reza's work as a younger scholar contains some original ideas and arguments, and has considerable promise. Since the 2000s there has been some cross-fertilisation and even convergence in that they each write about norms, legal pluralism, communities and late modern societies. This might be difficult to see given they have different intellectual styles. Cotterrell has developed a comprehensive legal theory in a similar way to previous sociological jurists, whereas Reza's essays come at the problems from different angles, and raise interesting questions.[6] He was even

---

[3] There were also chapters on globalisation, legal pluralism and comparative research.

[4] Although it has become influential in recognising the relationship between theory and methods, Banakar and Travers (2005) was not a comprehensive introduction to research methods. There was, for example, limited discussion of quantitative methods. This omission has to some extent been remedied by recent handbooks and textbooks on 'empirical legal research' (for example, van den Bos 2020). These have a quantitative bias and are often influenced by psychology or economics.

[5] Cotterrell (2018) distinguishes legal theory from disciplinary sub-fields such as sociology of law and legal philosophy. He sees legal theory as having a distinctive purpose as being concerned with the 'well being' of law.

[6] Isaiah Berlin (1953) made this distinction between two types of thinkers: 'hedgehogs' and 'foxes'. 'Hedgehogs' develop comprehensive theories over the course of their careers, whereas the 'foxes' come at problems from different directions, generating ideas and insights. However, Berlin admitted that classification was only a parlour game. Some people who think like 'hedgehogs' employ the style of 'foxes', making the distinction somewhat problematic.

starting to draw on other disciplines, for example in a thought-provoking discussion of law in Kafka's novels (Banakar 2015a).[7]

In my view, Reza had not yet advanced a compelling theory that speaks to how law is changing or should change in our own times (although he seemed to be moving in this direction). My understanding of the history of sociological jurisprudence is that some nineteenth century jurists, such as Savigny and Ehrlich, were defending local customs and legal institutions against the emergence of the modern unitary state (Trevino 2013). In different historical circumstances, the American realist tradition from the 1890s to 1940s argued for the modernisation of the common law system in response to new social conditions (Hull 1997). Roscoe Pound (1910) argued that a greater willingness of judges to make law was needed to address social change and new social problems.[8] Legal institutions, including law schools, were conservative forces blocking urgently needed reform. Banakar discusses some contemporary issues, including globalisation, at a theoretical level but does not really advance a political agenda about how law should change.[9]

II. THEMES AND QUESTIONS

The second part of this chapter considers some themes or questions from Reza's writings: legal pluralism; black letter law; normativity; and law in late modern societies. I have already characterised Reza as a legal theorist who brought together ideas from sociology and philosophy of law in an interesting way, but without developing or seeking to develop a systematic theory. I am not sure whether I can fill in the gaps in a way that might equally satisfy legal theorists, philosophers and sociologists. My approach will be to summarise Reza's writings about a particular issue, and then make some critical comments.

A. Legal Pluralism

Reza became interested in legal pluralism during his doctorate (Banakar 1998), and he has promoted or canvassed the ideas to a wider readership. The main influence has been the sociological jurist Eugene Ehrlich (1922), who wrote about the relationship between different ethnic groups and attempts by the state to control their affairs in the later years of the Austro-Hungarian empire. Another influence has been

---

[7] A reviewer noted that Kafka was both a novelist and a lawyer.

[8] Pound's paper on law in action was more than a discussion of methodology. It calls for reform in specific areas of law. In some of his writing in the 1930s, this jurist supported Roosevelt's New Deal that took away power and authority from the judiciary. However, matters are more complicated since he opposed the replacement or displacement of the common law by statutes. For details, and how this became part of debates with Llewellyn and others, see Hull (1997).

[9] There seems scope for considering the strains and tensions currently experienced by the legal system, and legal thought, as humanity faces immense challenges. Activists in areas such as animal rights, the environment, sexuality and indigeneity are canvassing alternatives to modern law.

anthropologists writing about multiple systems of law in colonial and post-colonial societies (Griffiths 2002). Some anthropologists have argued that occupational fields and other communities in western societies can be orderly and harmonious without or despite coming into contact with the state legal system (for example, Ellikson 1994). In such communities, law can often feel like an alien force that is irrelevant to how we settle disputes.

How did Reza use these ideas? He argued, quite forcefully, that legal theory in a period of globalisation should recognise and address pluralism. He was, therefore, implicitly critical towards legal theorists who only write about law in western societies. Reza recognised the importance of Sharia law, a system of religious law for migrant communities in western countries that co-exists with state law (Banakar 2015b). In these and other papers, he often discusses pluralism in relation to the systems theorist Jürgen Habermas. During the 1960s and 1970s, Habermas asked questions within systems theory about the effectiveness and legitimacy of the legal and political system ('the system'), and identified tensions or conflicts with 'the lifeworld' (Deflem 2013). Reza also recognised that that there is more to law than the legal system. Legal sociologists should address both the legal system and the lifeworld.

One criticism might be that Reza had not yet completely thought through the implications of legal pluralism. Does pluralism lead to a completely new way to think about law? Or is it only an addition to existing legal theories that focus on state law? He could also have perhaps gone further in advancing the critique that state law is an alien force within everyday life. Here I would recommend looking at a paper by the sociologist Harvey Sacks (1997), published in a collection I co-edited about ethnomethodological and conversation analytic approaches to law (Travers and Manzo 1997). Sacks had taken a course on jurisprudence at university, and was impressed with Ehrlich's ideas. In this short paper, he explains why ordinary people dislike lawyers. It is because the work of a lawyer questions relations of trust. Contract lawyers plan for the worst; and one might add we only take action to enforce rights when relationships have broken down.

B. Black Letter Law

From his first papers and book, Reza recognised the distinction between black letter law and sociology as academic disciplines. Black letter law is the knowledge about law, and skills of interpretation and reasoning, that students learn in law school. Sociologists of law write about law as a social institution from an external perspective. In our collections, we identified three main traditions (Banakar and Travers 2002; 2013). The consensus tradition, which includes theorists such as Durkheim, Parsons, Habermas and Luhmann, offers a positive view of law. It represents a society's shared values, and has the important function of integration and coordination in complex modern societies. By contrast, the conflict tradition, which includes theorists such as Marx, Weber, Bourdieu and Foucault, claims to reveal how law supports dominant groups in society. A third tradition, interpretative sociology, which includes traditions such as symbolic interactionism and ethnomethodology, examines legal processes at the 'micro' level: for example, the interaction between divorce lawyers and their clients (Felstiner and Sarat 1986). The practical considerations in legal practice are not always recognised or seen as important by black letter lawyers.

Reza was most influenced by the consensus tradition. He was an admirer of Talcott Parsons,[10] and often draws on Luhmann's complex ideas. He had little sympathy for conflict theorists such as Marx and Bourdieu who see legal theory reductively as an ideology masking economic and social interests.[11] He would not agree with some interactionists and Weberians (Abel 1988) who have seen lawyers as selfishly advancing their own economic interests. Nevertheless, he accepted that even the sympathetic consensus tradition came nowhere near to addressing the content of black letter law. In a chapter about norms (Banakar 2015d: 230), he presented legal studies as divided into three distinctive fields:

> a three-fold division of labour is largely in force within contemporary legal studies, according to which: 1) legal scholars will study positive law's internal processes; 2) legal sociologists will investigate the empirical foundations of the law, such as its efficacy in regulating behaviour and its impact on social relationships, and vice versa; and 3) legal philosophers will investigate the moral foundations of law, which include justice.

Reza accepted that sociology was incapable of understanding or addressing the content of law as understood by practising lawyers. Here we part company. In my view, it is mistaken to believe that sociologists and anthropologists have never written about case law and legislation; or that they could not conduct more studies if given the opportunity. My own study of bail decision-making with an inter-disciplinary research group describes how magistrates interpret and understand legislation and case law (Travers et al 2020). Bruno Latour (2009) observed the work of a French appeals court over a number of years, and describes decision-making in some detail.

Although law is a demanding, technical discipline, it is possible for the ordinary person to understand legal decisions and legal reasoning, certainly to a greater extent than experimental physics or mathematics.[12] In fact, ethnomethodologists have always recognised that legal decisions are designed to be understood by general audiences. In his study about juries, Harold Garfinkel (1984/1967b) argued that 95 per cent of law consists of shared common-sense knowledge and skills at reasoning. Admittedly, he was not talking about the work of judges interpreting precedents, or technical areas of legal practice. But legal sociologists can address and understand many aspects of black letter law (what Reza calls 'positive law's internal processes'). They can contribute to policy debates, and supply a realistic account of legal practice.

C. Normativity

After moving to Lund, Reza published a difficult but interesting paper in a collection with colleagues titled, 'Can Legal Sociology Account for the Normativity of

---

[10] We tried unsuccessfully to find an expert who could write a critical review of Parsons' approach to law.
[11] See Banakar (2015d: 222): 'Perhaps understandably, from the standpoint of legal philosophers, such sociological explanations miss the target by miles and at best trivialise law's *sui generis* normative property'.
[12] For an ethnomethodological study of mathematics, see Livingston (1986).

Law?' (Banakar 2013a). This was revised and published as a chapter in his collection, *Normativity in Legal Sociology* (Banakar 2015d). The paper is partly a defence of sociology against the criticisms of some legal philosophers that sociology cannot address moral questions. But it is also a subtle and appreciative discussion of the differences, and points of overlap between these disciplines. It is difficult to summarise, since one can ask critical questions about each paragraph. What follows is, therefore, an imaginative construction of some sections that gives a taste of the argument and reflects my own understanding as a sociologist.

By way of ground clearing, one can observe that this discussion of norms and normativity draws heavily on the consensus theorists in sociology, Habermas and Luhmann, who are contrasted favourably in their understanding of law as a moral force holding society together to Bourdieu who sees law in Marxist terms as an ideology supporting power relations. So one way of summarising the paper might be that legal philosophers who criticise sociology have not sufficiently engaged with the consensus tradition. Reza does not explicitly make this argument, but in my view he is suggesting that the consensus tradition in sociology has much to offer legal philosophy.

The paper is also concerned with the criticisms of sociology made by legal philosophers. One is that sociologists are mainly concerned with description, and stay on the surface of social life. They cannot address, or do not address deeply enough, moral questions. This might seem strange to a sociologist given that we often have moral and political objectives. Is it seriously suggested that Marx, Durkheim and Weber did not ask moral questions about industrialisation? What Reza suggests is that, while sociologists often write about *injustice* using empirical methods, they cannot write about *justice* at a deeper philosophical level. This leads to a re-statement of the three-fold division in legal studies:

> Legal sociology neglects the normativity of justice (or is 'blind' to the normative possibilities and constraints of law) and traditional legal philosophy overlooks the empirical dimensions of the legal system and practices (or processes) which reproduce law and its institutions, while doctrinal studies reduce them to rule-based reasoning. (Banakar 2015d: 232)

What is one to make of these fine distinctions and abstract arguments, and what Reza recognises as the competing claims of disciplines for resources and status? One observation is that we can often do our intellectual work, and in the case of the social sciences conduct empirical research, without considering other disciplines or theoretical traditions. For example, as an interpretive sociologist, I have little need to write about theoretical traditions in my own discipline that rarely supply good descriptions of the 'concreteness' of human activities.[13]

---

[13] Unfortunately, Garfinkel often writes at an abstract level in a difficult style. In a theoretical statement, he notes that Parsons and Durkheim were concerned with finding 'objective social facts' as sociology's 'fundamental phenomenon' from the confusing 'concreteness' of everyday activities. This is contrasted with his own programme for addressing or preserving this concreteness:

> 'For ethnomethodology, the objective reality of social facts, in that and just how it is every society's endogenously produced, naturally organized, reflexively accountable, ongoing, practical achievement, being everywhere, always, only, exactly and entirely, members' work with no time out ... is thereby sociology's phenomenon' (Garfinkel 1990: 70).

This leaves unanswered the difficult question of how sociologists understand and study norms. How do different theoretical traditions approach the problem? Consensus theorists, such as Durkheim, Parsons, Luhmann and Habermas, see society as held together by shared norms and values. Conflict theorists, such as Marx and Weber, see norms and values as benefiting dominant economic and social groups. By contrast, ethnomethodology, as an interpretive tradition, looks for how norms are visible, or can be made visible, in everyday life.[14] Garfinkel (1984/1967a) investigated the properties of norms through breaching experiments, for example by asking students to bargain in shops with the aim of generating sanctions and moral disapproval. To complicate matters, sociologists believe that there is more to society than norms, or rather the term cannot encompass the diverse ways in which we understand and produce the meaningful character of our social worlds.[15]

D. Law in Late Modernity

Another theme in Reza's essays, that he canvassed to a sceptical sociologist while we co-edited the second edition of *Law and Social Theory*, was the 'transformation' of law in late modernity (Banakar 2013b). Here are my grounds for scepticism. Some social theorists have argued that we entered a new historical period known as postmodernity (Lyotard 1984) or late modernity (Giddens 1990) during the 1990s, through considering economic and social changes such as post-industrialism or the decline of marriage. But, even if we accept these arguments, it seems harder to show that the legal system has substantially changed.[16] There have always been new areas of law emerging during the modern period. Yet law as an institution has arguably been characterised by remarkable stability and continuity in western countries.

It is certainly possible to identify potentially transformative forces and, in aligning yourself with these trends, to advance a normative argument. In sociology, this research agenda would be concerned with imagining what law could become, as opposed to accepting business as usual at the moment. True disruption and transformation will surely involve pain for practitioners and institutions, and challenge existing ideas. Pound and Llewellyn promoted change of this kind. Today, the prospect of judicial officers being replaced by algorithms to save money and achieve

---

[14] Many norms are taken for granted, and difficult to study (consider the norm that one should not bargain in shops). However, this is not always the case. Professional and political groups debate and challenge norms. There are also cases in which norms that were taken for granted become the subject of debate. Consider, for example, the extensive discussion in the US media, and among the political class, on the norms of transitioning between presidents, and how these have been breached by Donald Trump. I am grateful to Michael Lynch for suggesting this example.

[15] Reza and I differ in how we understand the theoretical argument about norms advanced by Stephen Turner (2010). My reading is that Turner is arguing against those philosophers who see norms as hidden or separate from everyday activities.

[16] Reza suggests, for example, that neoliberalism has weakened the welfare state. Yet one could argue that universal welfare provision has expanded during the pandemic. There have been significant changes, but not a transformation.

justice is an example (Livni 2017).[17] However, the greatest challenge of this century is climate change. Perhaps a new kind of legal theory will emerge that recognises the environment or animal rights as central problems (Convivialist International 2020). In my view, those writing about 'late modern law' have not yet developed a coherent argument or reform agenda. Despite these criticisms, I like the way Reza drew on ideas about late modernity to ask critical questions about law.

III. CONCLUSION

This paper has covered a lot of ground, because Reza wrote about many topics. I have not even mentioned an interesting empirical study about legal culture in Iran (Banakar 2015c). In the last six months of his life, while he was in hospital, he was very interested in Brexit. He could not understand how the public could lose trust in government, and vote for an irrational cause that would harm everyone.

Reza was most distinctive as a sociological jurist, in my view, because he had an informed, scholarly interest in sociology. Although he identified with the consensus tradition, he recognised other approaches, and the debates between them, in this multi-perspectival discipline. Yet he also showed an unusual capacity as a legal theorist for making connections between legal philosophy and sociology of law. Although I am not an expert, his discussions of natural law theory and legal positivism were original and thought provoking. It is often said that positivists accept the world as it is, and can sound highly immoral, whereas natural law theorists make it possible to desire a better world. Yet Reza seems to suggest that positivists could also ask moral questions:

> [natural law philosophers believe that] any society not governed in accordance with the principle of justice is prone to social conflict and political upheaval; in such a case, the society will be no more than a precarious social order maintained over time purely through coercion, oppression and the threat of violence. On this basis, justice becomes the source of law's normativity *par excellence*. This view, however, is not shared by legal positivists who argue that there is no necessarily specific connection between law and morality, and then move on to locate justice (which involves making an ethical judgement) beyond the legal system, in that it becomes not an integral part *of* the law's operations but a moral judgement *about* law). (Banakar 2015d: 224)

A sociologist may find these discussions too general or abstract. However, I can see merit in any approach that asks broader questions than black letter or doctrinal law, the dominant approach or discipline in law schools. I remember my first day at Manchester Polytechnic (now Manchester Metropolitan University) when I started a conversion course in 1986, the Common Professional Examination, after completing a degree in history. The first thing we were told was not to think in broad terms and not to make policy arguments. There was only black letter law to be learnt and applied.

---

[17] See Travers et al (2020). This empirical study explores welfare-oriented changes taking place 'under the radar' in criminal courts.

Like other legal theorists, Reza mainly approaches political and moral issues at a philosophical level. Yet the combination of legal theory and sociology is exciting. He was just getting started and becoming recognised as an interesting and distinctive legal theorist. He had institutional support as a professor in a department at Lund University dedicated to sociology of law. He had the motivation and ability to accomplish a great deal in his sixties. This is an untimely death.

REFERENCES

Abel, R (1988) *The Legal Profession in England and Wales* (Oxford, Blackwell).

Banakar, R (1998) 'The Identity Crisis of a Stepchild' 21 *Retfaerd* 3.

—— (2013a) 'Can Legal Sociology Account for the Normativity of Law?' in M Baier (ed), *Social and Legal Norms* (Farnham, Ashgate).

—— (2013b) 'Law and Regulation in Late Modernity' in R Banakar and M Travers (eds), *Law and Social Theory* (Oxford, Hart Publishing) 305.

—— (2015a) 'A Note on Franz Kafka's Concept of Law' in R Banakar, *Normativity in Legal Sociology: Reflections on Law and Regulation in Late Modernity* (New York, Springer).

—— (2015b) 'The Politics of Legal Cultures' in R Banakar, *Normativity in Legal Sociology: Reflections on Law and Regulation in Late Modernity* (New York, Springer).

—— (2015c) 'A Case Study of Non-Western Legal Systems and Cultures' in R Banakar, *Normativity in Legal Sociology: Reflections on Law and Regulation in Late Modernity* (New York, Springer).

—— (2015d) 'Norms and Normativity in Socio-Legal Research' in R Banakar, *Normativity in Legal Sociology: Reflections on Law and Regulation in Late Modernity* (New York, Springer).

Banakar, R and Travers, M (eds) (2002) *An Introduction to Law and Social Theory* (Oxford, Hart Publishing).

—— (eds) (2005) *Theory and Method in Socio-Legal Research* (Oxford, Hart Publishing).

—— (eds) (2013) *Law and Social Theory* (Oxford, Hart Publishing).

Berlin, I (1953) *The Hedgehog and the Fox: An Essay on Tolstoy's View of History* (London, Weidenfeld & Nicolson).

Convivialist International (2020) 'The Second Convivialist Manifesto: Towards a Post-Neoliberal World' 1 *Civic Sociology* 1 https://online.ucpress.edu/cs/article/1/1/12721/112920/THE-SECOND-CONVIVIALIST-MANIFESTO-Towards-a-Post (last accessed 23 September 2022).

Cotterrell, R (1992) *The Sociology of Law: An Introduction*, 2nd edn (London, Butterworths).

— (2018) *Sociological Jurisprudence: Juristic Thought and Social Inquiry* (London, Routledge).

Deflem, M (2013) 'The Legal Theory of Jurgen Habermas: between the Philosophy and the Sociology of Law' in R Banakar and M Travers (eds), *Law and Social Theory* (Oxford, Hart Publishing).

Ehrlich, E (1922) 'The Sociology of Law' 36 *Harvard Law Review* 130.

Ellikson, R (1994) *Order without Law: How Neighbours Settle Disputes* (Cambridge, MA, Harvard University Press).

Felstiner, B and Sarat, A (1986) 'Law and Strategy in the Divorce Lawyer's Office' 20 *Law and Society Review* 94.

Garfinkel, H (1984/1967a) 'Some Rules of Correct Decisions that Jurors Respect' in H Garfinkel, *Studies in Ethnomethodology* (Cambridge, Polity).

— (1984/1967b) 'Studies of the Routine Grounds of Everyday Activities' in H Garfinkel, *Studies in Ethnomethodology* (Cambridge, Polity).

— (1990) 'The Curious Seriousness of Professional Sociology' 8 *Reseaux* 69.

Giddens, A (1990) *The Consequences of Modernity* (Cambridge, Polity).

— (2002) 'Legal Pluralism' in R Banakar and M Travers (eds), *An Introduction to Law and Social Theory* (Oxford, Hart Publishing).

Griffiths, A (2002) 'Legal Pluralism' in R Banakar and M Travers (eds), *An Introduction to Law and Social Theory* (Oxford, Hart Publishing).

Hull, K (1997) *Roscoe Pound and Karl Llewellyn: Searching for an American Jurisprudence* (Chicago, University of Chicago Press).

Latour, B (2009) *The Making of Law: An Ethnography of the Conseil d'Etat* (Cambridge, Polity).

Livingston, E (1986) *The Ethnomethodological Foundations of Mathematics* (London, Routledge).

Livni, E (2017) 'In the US, Some Criminal Court Judges Now Use Algorithms to Guide Decisions on Bail' *Quartz Media* (28 February), https://qz.com/920196/criminal-court-judges-in-new-jersey-now-use-algorithms-to-guide-decisions-on-bail/ (last accessed 23 September 2022).

Lyotard, J (1984) *The Postmodern Condition: A Report on Knowledge* (Manchester, Manchester University Press).

Pound, R (1910) 'Law in Books and Law in Action' 44 *American Law Review* 12.

Sacks, H (1997) 'The Lawyer's Work' in M Travers and J Manzo (eds), *Law in Action: Ethnomethodological and Conversation Analytic Approaches to Law* (Aldershot, Ashgate).

Saxe, J (2018/1887) *Poems* (London, Forgotten Books).

Travers, M (1993) 'Putting Sociology Back into Sociology of Law' 20 *Journal of Law and Society* 438.

—— (2010) *Understanding Law and Society* (London, Routledge).

Travers, M, Colvin, E, Bartkowiak-Theron, I, Sarre, R, Day, A and Bond, C (2020) *Rethinking Bail: Court Reform or Business as Usual?* (London, Palgrave).

Travers, M and Manzo, J (eds) (1997) *Law in Action: Ethnomethodological and Conversation Analytic Approaches to Law* (Aldershot, Ashgate).

Trevino, J (2013) 'Sociological Jurisprudence' in R Banakar and M Travers (eds), *Law and Social Theory* (Oxford, Hart Publishing).

Turner, S (2010) *Explaining the Normative* (Cambridge, Polity).

van den Bos, K (2020) *Empirical Legal Research: A Primer* (Chichester, Edward Elgar).

Part II

Sociology of Law Theory, Legal Pluralism and Legal Theory

4

The Place of a Stepchild: Notes on the Establishment of Modern Sociology of Law

ROGER COTTERRELL

T HE COMPARATIVE HISTORY of sociology of law is yet to be written, and to write it would certainly be a massive task. There are many studies of the development of the field in particular countries, and some major pioneering efforts have been made in cross-national collaborative surveys (Ferrari 1990; Treves and van Loon 1968). But if a general historical overview could be written it might explain much. In particular, it might show why a self-identifying, institutionalised, collective enterprise of social research on law emerged as a prominent focus of activity in a significant number of highly developed and politically and culturally diverse countries around the same time, generally during the 1950s and 1960s; that is to say, a research enterprise centred on legal phenomena, using modern methods of empirical social research and aiming to be systematic and scientific, linked to the progress of the social sciences.

What needs did modern sociology of law respond to? Were there important common factors in its emergence in different countries? If these questions could be conclusively answered to show distinct historical causes and conditions, other questions about the socio-legal enterprise might receive answers. Within the established array of academic disciplines or fields of practice and inquiry relating to social life, how was it that a *space* became recognised, if sometimes reluctantly, for a distinctive focus on social scientific study of law? What defines that space and its borders? Specifically, what place does sociology of law occupy among the established academic disciplines and research fields that border it?

Prominent among Reza Banakar's[1] many contributions to sociology of law is his careful effort to clarify its methods, the kinds of theory that it could use, and above all its identity as a research field. Influentially, he called it an intellectual 'stepchild'

[1] This chapter is revised and expanded from the text of a lecture in memory of Reza Banakar, organised at the Department of Sociology of Law, Lund University and given on 17 March 2021. I am grateful to David Nelken for many typically insightful comments on a previous draft.

set uneasily between law and sociology (Banakar 1998). As such, sociology of law, largely unclaimed by either juristic studies or academic sociology (both of which have usually showed little interest in it), drifts insecurely in the open sea of social inquiries, lacking theoretical coherence and 'fundamental paradigms' to organise it. Banakar (ibid: 5, 18) denied that sociology of law was a branch of either sociology or of jurisprudence and wished it to 'limit its dependency' on both. Eventually, he defined it as 'an interdisciplinary field of research placed somewhat precariously at the intersection of the disciplines of law and sociology' (Banakar 2003: 1). It had to go its own way intellectually, not seeking 'to reproduce the basic assumptions and academic identities of the parent disciplines' (Banakar 1998: 5).[2]

Figure 1 Sociology of Law as a Stepchild Unclaimed by the Disciplines

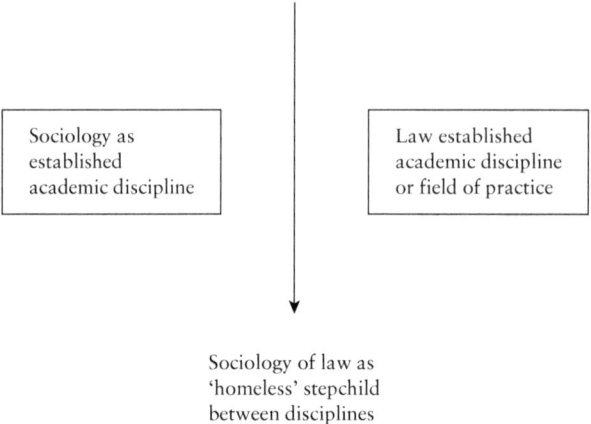

Many would agree with these views, although the severe assessment of sociology of law's intellectual position was questioned in debates provoked by Banakar's stepchild metaphor. However, his major contributions here were surely to insist that the identity of sociology of law is not a matter to be ignored, and to throw down a challenge to look inside the enterprises of socio-legal inquiry for their marks of intellectual pedigree and integrity. Probably most researchers on law as a social phenomenon, whether they call their inquiries sociology of law, socio-legal studies, or 'law and society' scholarship, are mainly concerned to ensure the coherence of their distinct research projects, not that of some much wider intellectual field. But Banakar was right to renew debate on the identity of the socio-legal enterprise, not least because uncertainty about this has sometimes suggested its vulnerability or marginality – perhaps wrongly so when the conditions of its emergence, and of its significance, are understood.

---

[2] Banakar seemed to be concerned both with describing sociology of law as an existing field and advocating directions for its development. But this chapter's focus is mainly conceptual and explanatory – to explore the position of sociology of law as a research enterprise in the light of aspects of its recent history. What this enterprise *should be* becomes a meaningful issue only if the parameters defining its conditions of intellectual and institutional existence can be clarified.

Can the nature of sociology of law be clarified in disciplinary terms? Ultimately, I shall argue, the search for disciplinary pedigree or a clear relationship of sociology of law to its 'parent disciplines' should not be a priority in solving what Banakar called its identity crisis. What constitutes an intellectual discipline can be a controversial matter and the term is often used very loosely. More concretely, if the question of modern sociology of law's identity is considered in relation to its historical emergence – its 'rebirth as an independent science' which Vincenzo Ferrari (1990: xv), in a global survey, dated from the 1960s – it has to be recognised that the prominent pioneers who worked then to establish it were very diverse in their acknowledged disciplinary allegiances.

Some were jurists (eg Jean Carbonnier in France), others were sociologists (eg Adam Podgórecki in Poland, in a direct line of influence from the lawyer-polymath Leon Petrażycki), or were influenced by diverse social science traditions (eg Per Stjernquist in Sweden, trained as a lawyer but strongly drawn to anthropology and socio-economic history).[3] In the United States, 'law and society' studies became a favoured term because of the wide range of disciplinary affiliations (not just sociology or law) contributing to socio-legal research. This is far from saying that disciplinary allegiances were unimportant, but it seems doubtful that they confined the vision that helped form a socio-legal field and facilitated diversity within what was quickly understood as a common transnational enterprise of sociology of law.

Many national studies of the emergence of this enterprise suggest that what is important to the identity of the socio-legal research field (here treated as synonymous with sociology of law) is not a jockeying for position among academic disciplines but the recognition of a new (complex, multifaceted) 'object of study' (Noreau and Arnaud 1998: 270); perhaps a set of problems unseen or neglected in the established disciplines, and perhaps incapable of being fully addressed within them. Sometimes, to confront these problems required much knowledge of law or legal institutions and processes, sometimes of socio-economic conditions. Sometimes, but certainly not always, direct political imperatives from government policy or social control objectives encouraged the institutionalisation of socio-legal research and the teaching of sociology of law (for example in the education of state administrative officials) (Cotterrell 1997).

This is evident in the cases of countries mentioned earlier: in Sweden, teaching in sociology of law, and later a chair in the subject, were established on government initiative (Stjernquist 2000: 65–69); early research initiatives in France were linked to the need for data to inform legislative policy (Andrini and Arnaud 1995: 34–35); in Poland, for a time, research initiatives were promoted by government (Kurczewski 2001: 89), especially focused on popular understandings of and attitudes towards law. Many other instances might be mentioned. Elsewhere, policy interests were sometimes much less direct and obvious in spurring the beginnings of socio-legal research; they provided merely a background, encouraging funding from the state, from within universities, or (especially in the United States) from private foundations

---

[3] See, eg, Andrini and Arnaud 1995 (on Carbonnier); Kojder 1999 and Wicenty 2018 (on Podgórecki); Podgórecki 1980 (on Petrażycki); Cotterrell 1997 and 2006b (on Stjernquist).

aware of the need to adapt law to social change, or to address social issues. But in other cases, implicit policy or political understandings of legal sociologists ultimately ran counter to those of government and were rightly seen as in competition with them (eg Kojder 1999; Wicenty 2018).

The initial engagement of policy interests was often important to fund empirical research, the hallmark of its 1960s 'renaissance' (Ferrari 1990: xlvi) even when those interests made no effort to steer 'pure' research towards specific policy goals. But typically, the 'pull of the policy audience' (Sarat and Silbey 1988) is in the background – in the funding structure of universities, the interests of grant awarding bodies, an atmosphere of national importance informing research. In the foreground is often the researchers' desire to research independently, with scientific credibility and peer respect.

The limits of generalisation are quickly reached but the observations above are intended only to suggest that the identity of sociology of law need not be analysed only as a matter of the positioning of academic disciplines[4] or intellectual fields. It can be considered more empirically in terms of the interrelation of and tensions between *different arenas of action*. Pierre Bourdieu's concept of field (*champ*) is useful here. Banakar (2003: 168–69) uses it in examining the internal organisation and conflicts of sociology of law as a scientific field, but it can be used also to consider tensions and potential conflicts between differentiated fields of action and experience. Sociology of law, as such a field itself, is located at the intersections of other fields: not only the heavily professionalised *juridical* field and what might be called the field of social relations in *civil society* which sociology assumed as a primary research focus. There is also a *political* field – a field of state action, governmental direction and societal steering.[5]

Researchers have often resisted the pull of the policy audience, or not even consciously felt it; they have sought the objectivity and status of science. But my suggestion is that the identity of sociology of law, seen in the light of conditions of its emergence and the kind of tasks that those conditions have created for it, can usefully be understood in terms of the relations between these three fields – the juridical, the political[6] and the social (broadly, civil society).

Sociology of law has the strategic role of addressing tensions between these fields. Its relation to them varies in different contexts depending on the challenges of the time. The political, the juridical and the social can be thought of in this approach as the points of a triangle with sociology of law at its centre. And it is a 'variable

---

[4] For much more wide-ranging debate around the nature and significance of 'disciplinarity' in law and sociology see eg Cotterrell 2006a: ch 3; Nelken 2009: ch 12; Banakar 2003: ch 5.

[5] Bourdieu's idea of field can be very flexibly applied but he seems to see the juridical field (Bourdieu 1987) as conceptually distinct from, but closely interrelated with, state and governmental power. What this chapter calls the social field is not a concept adopted from Bourdieu but a device to characterise, for the purpose of this chapter, the arena of popular societal experience that, in various ways, juridical and political practices address. In sociology various terms such as civil society, the societal community or the civil sphere attempt to characterise it.

[6] 'Political', in this chapter, is taken in what George Orwell (2004:5) called its 'widest possible sense. Desire to push the world in a certain direction, to alter other people's idea of the kind of society they should strive after.'

geometry' triangle. Sometimes one or another of the points is most prominent, encouraging certain emphases in sociology of law. But in all cases, sociology of law is unified by a strategic mission, not by its disciplinary position or by any uniform intellectual sources of its theory or methods. Its mission is to be *a transdisciplinary science* (not beholden to government policy, specific juristic values and commitments, or populist social demands on law) occupying an essential *mediating position between the political, the juridical and the social*, providing forms of knowledge necessary for their continually shifting interrelations as realms of action and experience.

Figure 2 Sociology of Law Located in the Tensions between Different Fields of Action

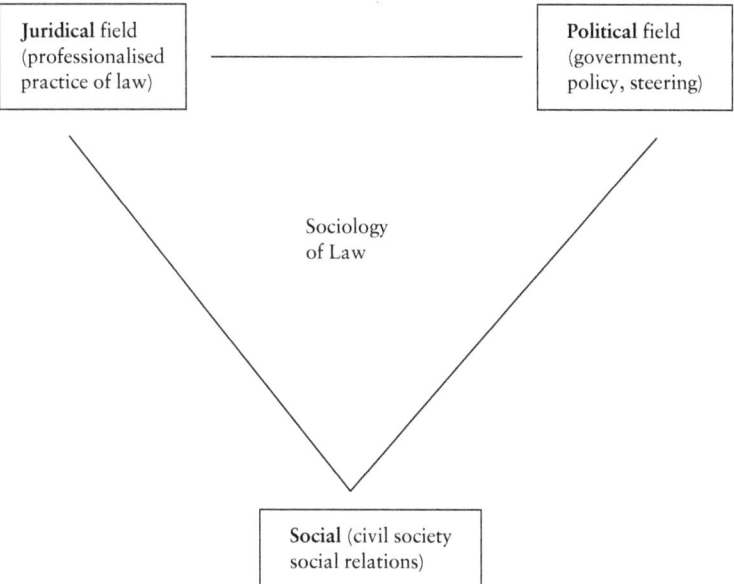

Seen in this perspective, sociology of law could not arise until certain historical conditions, which have been analysed in social theory from many perspectives, were satisfied. A distinct realm of 'the social' had to be recognised, as in the concept of civil society. Government and the state had to evolve to recognise a responsibility for managing or steering society, and so to assume an interest in the social as such, evidenced, for example, by the emergence of the idea of a welfare state (Simon 1999). The juridical, too, had to become a developed professionalised field, somewhat autonomous from the policy imperatives of government and the moral or customary frameworks of everyday social life. The three points of the triangle had to become sufficiently distinct so that sociology of law could begin to find its place inside this structure.

A further question is then: if sociology of law finds its strategic task (and so its identity) in the mediation of tensions inside the triangle of the political, the juridical and the social, what kinds of tensions are these, and when might they arise? I suggest that relevant tensions or conflicts necessarily involve *all three* fields, not just any two. The isolation of the juridical from the social is perennial, long pre-dating the emergence of modern sociology of law. It becomes a catalyst for action usually when the political becomes interested in it – for example when the 'gap' between juristic law and society provokes disquiet registered in government or policy arenas. A similar situation can arise when the juridical and political spheres seem at odds in their responses to social demands and social change.

Again, sociology of law might become relevant when the state seeks to control or steer society through legal instruments and needs to understand their possibilities, effects, and limits; or where the state needs to use law to address perceived problems or demands in the social that have become political or government policy issues (Banakar 2016). In democratic societies such matters increasingly arise; even in societies without effective representative democracy but where government seeks popular acquiescence, sociology of law might (as in communist Poland) be officially supported to some degree as a 'searchlight' shone on the population to inform political powers about the social world they seek to govern (Kurczewski 2001).

Are these generalisations too broad to be useful? As noted earlier, the comparative history of sociology of law remains to be written. It might be said that all hypotheses should be left aside until that distant future date when it is. This chapter's argument is that Banakar was right to argue that the identity of sociology of law needs clarification, not only for intellectual reasons to locate it on the map of social inquiry, but also to assess its ongoing significance as a research enterprise. And he clearly saw the limitations of thinking about that identity in terms of academic disciplinary categories of legal and sociological knowledge which seem to leave no intellectual space between them. Thinking in terms of fields of action provides a way forward. The tensions in a triangle of fields – juridical, political and social – map a space for sociology of law to occupy, and at the same time suggest the strategic necessity of occupying it.

Significantly, socio-legal studies in the United States were established and have developed while avoiding the thickets of disciplinary identity. They grew in conditions where law had, as now, a remarkable centrality in the national culture, especially evidenced in the prominence in both cultural and political life of American courts. So, the juridical field evidenced special prominence in this setting among the components of the triangle of fields. The political, by contrast, was – as probably intended by the framers of the Constitution – weaker specifically in terms of its capacity to respond energetically to developments in the social. But, in the twentieth century, a behavioural case law focus encouraged progressive jurists towards a significant sensitivity to sociological realities of law, especially through the legal realist movement (see eg Schlegel 1995).

Despite the rapid and intense twentieth century professionalisation of sociology in the United States, the strength of the juridical and the relative historical limitations (and frequent distrust) of state governmental direction, perhaps allowed the juridical field to dominate in the triangle of fields. Under the pressures of immense change in the social, and the many challenges faced by post-war American society, a flourishing growth of empirical socio-legal research occurred, as is well-known. But law, rather than sociology, provided its unifying focus. So American sociology of law is explicitly transdisciplinary, and known as 'law and society' studies, even if its practitioners recognise allegiance to particular separate disciplines. The focus of this social research enterprise is some idea of law, even if law is often not seen in juristic terms.

This national case is mentioned here because it has many lessons in considering the identity of sociology of law. In the US (and, to some extent, in other common law countries) the term sociology of law, with its disciplinary connotations, is mainly avoided. Yet much of the work done as socio-legal studies or 'law and society' can hardly be differentiated in scientific character (except perhaps in its balance between empirical research and theory) from that done elsewhere as sociology of law.[7] What unites most inquiries, of whatever national provenance, is the strategic mission that implicitly or explicitly they share through their location at the intersections of the political, the juridical and the social.

Does this approach simply avoid the issues of intellectual coherence and integrity that much concerned Reza Banakar? Does it suggest, at best, some conditions under which socio-legal research emerged in its modern forms, but not address its epistemology as a form of knowledge, or indicate a shared object of study that gives it ontological coherence? The answer, perhaps, is that the nature of the knowledge that characterises sociology of law must be understood outside disciplinary locations. The experience of law and society, socio-legal studies, and transdisciplinary sociology of law in many countries suggests that ultimately what unites all of these varied research enterprises is their focus, in some way, on *law*. However, this cannot simply be law as jurists understand it. The idea of the triangle of fields with sociology of law at its centre, relating to all three of its points, implies that there is no single concept of law that sociology of law can take from any one of the points of the triangle. The nature of law may be understood differently at the different points.

Thus, law typically can appear somewhat differently in each of the three fields – the juridical, the political and the social. Undoubtedly, none of them has any uniform, pervasive understanding of law – an understanding that might be seen, in Bourdieu's terms, as rooted in its habitus (*cf* Bourdieu 1987: 833). The social – an umbrella term here for a vast diversity of social, cultural and economic relations – could hardly be uniform as regards understandings of law. Nevertheless, it is possible to speculate about some contrasting commonplace assumptions in each of the three fields as to law's most obvious nature.

In the political sphere, law is very often seen mainly instrumentally as a tool of government and policy implementation. In the juristic sphere, lawyers like to see it as a (or perhaps the) cohesive, overall normative framework of human life, and the legitimating idea that structures their practice. In the social field, law is sometimes seen, from the 'receiving end', so to speak, as a structure of oppression, and sometimes as a promise (often frustrated) of rights or justice. For this chapter what is important is only the very different emphases in thinking of law indicated by conceptions such as these.

The conclusion should be that (i) law is a necessary unifying idea for sociology of law but (ii) sociology of law has to find its own understanding of the nature of law, reflecting conflicts and convergences in ideas of law at each of the three points of the

---

[7] However, the relation between some kinds of socio-legal history, which have long been prominent in US law and society research, and sociology of law, as understood in many European contexts, might need further discussion. I am grateful to David Nelken for this point.

triangle. It needs understandings of law *for its own purposes* which are not those of the political, the juridical or the social but which exist in the interaction and conflicts between these fields. However, in practice, legal sociologists have tended, when they have expressed or assumed a concept of law for their work, to gravitate in their thinking towards one or other of the points of the triangle.

Often a governmental, primarily instrumental understanding of law has been assumed (especially where the policy relevance of sociology of law has been stressed in research practice). Sometimes, a juristic view centred on law as normative discourse or professional knowledge has been assumed or adopted. In such cases, where a juristic emphasis on legal values conflicts with the research quest for social scientific objectivity, sociology of law risks being seen only through the lens of sociological jurisprudence – the importation of social science perspectives to serve juristic commitments to the well-being of law, understood in the lawyer's sense (Cotterrell 2018). Sociology of law can also adopt concepts of law present in the social field: popular understandings of the nature of law created in experience of law, but such understandings are not necessarily easily identifiable. When legal sociologists have sought to avoid the state's conceptualisations of law (as its governing mechanisms of regulation) or lawyers' concepts, they have sometimes found social concepts of law in classic social theory. Such theory is most useful for this purpose when it offers concepts not confined to state law or 'lawyers' law' but sees law embedded in social experience – eg as in the work of Max Weber, Leon Petrażycki, Eugen Ehrlich or Georges Gurvitch.

Sociology of law cannot do without efforts to conceptualise law because the idea of law has to unify the field intellectually. But there is surely no need for (or possibility of) a single concept agreed on by all researchers. Even jurists do not have such a concept, and legal philosophers argue incessantly around the question 'What is law?', as they have for centuries. Sociology of law needs practical, *provisional models* of what it will treat as law for its own research purposes in mediating between the political, the juridical and the social. Nevertheless, an explicit statement of the model of law with which the researcher is working can help in locating the research on a conceptual map of socio-legal inquiries. That is, it can contribute to an arrangement of understandings of law that makes the comparison and interrelations of law-focused research projects, both theoretical and empirical, potentially more systematic and intellectually integrated.

The consequence of this approach to the nature of law is admittedly paradoxical. In sociology of law, law is an *essentially contested concept*, even though that concept, insofar as it informs action in different ways in different fields, is what intellectually unifies the socio-legal research.[8] Part of the mission of sociology of law is to explore

---

[8] This idea has been resisted by several legal sociologists, because of the difficulty in finding a conclusive definition of law. So, for example, John Griffiths (2006: 63) argues that the focus of sociology of law must be on types of *social control*. But this is to point the research field in a controversial direction (towards the study of authority structures rather than, for example, varieties of social interaction as in Ehrlich's (2002) early sociology of law). A converse approach is found in the attractive argument (in a direct line from Ehrlich) that sociology of law might be re-conceptualised in terms of a wide-ranging sociology of *norms*. But, if research is to avoid the dilemmas that Ehrlich's concept of living law raised a century ago, the question of which norms are to be accepted theoretically as legal needs to be faced by legal sociologists. The best approach, I suggest, is to treat ongoing exploration of the sociological nature of law (at the

the variability of the idea of law – that is, legal understanding and experience – a variability that reflects the very tensions between political, juridical and social fields that justify sociology of law's existence.

Figure 3 Conceptualising Law in Sociology of Law and in its Neighbouring Fields

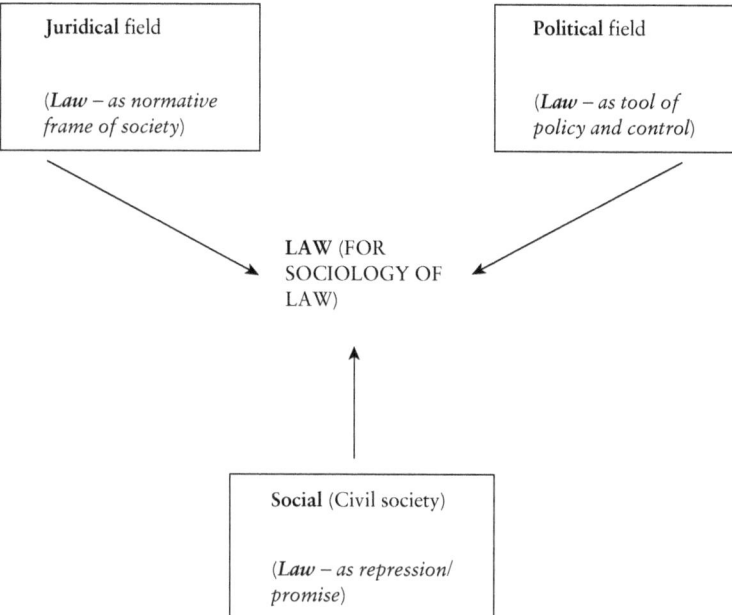

The main focus of sociology of law has rightly been on social action in legal contexts, the forms of consciousness informing such action, and the institutional frameworks in which this action occurs. Sociology of law is centrally concerned with action – social behaviour – but that does not mean it cannot say important things about law as ideas, in whatever fields of social action these ideas are found. Seen in this perspective, sociology of law seeks neither to replace jurisprudence nor to operate without reference to lawyers' concerns.

Part of its destiny is to develop a view of law recognising juristic understandings but relativising them, contrasting them with other understandings of law in other fields of (political and social) experience. In this way sociology of law creates its *own* image of law as its unifying object. It will be an image that reflects the concerns and conclusions of ongoing social research.

Nothing in this chapter is intended to advocate particular directions of socioresearch. The chapter's focus is on the identity of the research enterprise, not its scope or research emphases. But a reader might well be dissatisfied with its apparent

intersection of the juridical, the political and the social) as part of sociology of law's project. This need not be a disabling irresolution since, as suggested in the text, a variety of explicitly developed models of law can be the basis of fruitful empirical research, and comparing them contextually can promote important theoretical development in the field.

dismissal of distinct disciplinary criteria (particular methods, theories or disciplinary traditions). Sociology of law as presented here might seem far too eclectic. However, to maintain its independent position inside the triangle of fields it must have an unshakeable commitment to social science – that is, to the methodologically systematic, empirically informed, theoretical study of social phenomena (Cotterrell 2006a: 54–58) – and, in this, the heritage of academic sociology (as well as other forms of inquiry in the human and social sciences) offers much as a resource of methods, theories and research exemplars.

Sociology of law is probably fated to suffer from permanent instability. It is vulnerable to being co-opted – drawn too firmly towards one point or another in the triangle of fields. One tendency can be called policy-science co-option. Here social research becomes mainly a useful adjunct to *government*, a general aid in governmental tasks and policy formation and implementation. Another tendency is co-option as support for the world of *legal practice*, processes and institutions. Examples are some varieties of 'empirical legal studies' (Eisenberg 2011; Heise 2002), 'legal-empirical research' (Kurczewski 2001: 88) or 'fact research' (eg Rehbinder 1972) organised around legal professionals' agendas. A juristically-oriented outlook might create a space for a sociology of law admittedly 'without rigour' (Carbonnier 2001) as regards social scientific theory but potentially enlightening for lawyers and law students.

Finally, sociology of law might become just a general study of *the social* – general sociology – if its concept of law seems too loose and unclear. So, Ehrlich's (2002) great, pioneering sociology of 'living law' was once criticised juristically as 'megalomaniac jurisprudence' embracing almost everything in social life (Allen 1964: 32). On this view, law just disappears into the social. And theories of legal pluralism, seeing law in many social contexts beyond the state and the lawyer's practice, are sometimes seen as potentially unlimited in scope: 'Where do we stop speaking of law and find ourselves simply describing social life' (Merry 1988: 878).

It is wise just to accept this three-way instability – the risk of co-option or loss of identity within the triangle of fields – as inevitable; something that always needs to be guarded against. But the other face of it is the immense potential variety and scope of sociology of law, its openness, and above all, its natural centrality as a field of inquiry situated between the political, the juridical and the social.

It is important not to be complacent. Sociology of law has usually needed extensive pre-conditions for its firm establishment: (i) a juridical field prepared to co-exist with it, amenable to it or at least not powerful enough to stop its development; (ii) reliable sources of funding (public or private) for empirical research; (iii) some institutional security (usually in a university, and often carrying risks of co-option); (iv) political support or acquiescence; (v) a recognised need (linked to social change or social problems) rooted in civil society; (vi) a sufficiently clear legal focus; and (vii) the availability of existing intellectual resources in social science.

Even where all or most of these conditions have existed, sociology of law has not necessarily been established. Equally, some pioneer socio-legal work was developed largely in the absence of these conditions. Thus, another condition might be added to the list above: intellectual leadership. To adapt Marx, people (not fields of action) make history, but not under conditions of their own choosing. Visionary individual pioneers of the 1950s and 1960s, especially in Europe and North America, created pockets of socio-legal research and teaching, on their own initiative, through their own energy, talent, imagination and personality, and sometimes initially with few of the conditions for success listed above. And socio-legal research began, in isolated, farsighted work by other pioneers, long before what Ferrari saw as the modern 'rebirth' of sociology of law.

The comparative history of all of this deserves to be written and celebrated. To do so would encourage a proper recognition that, despite much variability and contingency in the conditions of its emergence, sociology of law is not a lost step-child among the disciplines. It is an enterprise of great importance set strategically in the midst of governmental imperatives and policies, professionalised legal scholarship and practice, and the ever-shifting challenges and demands thrown up by social change. Surely this is how Reza Banakar hoped it would be seen.

REFERENCES

Allen, CK (1964) *Law in the Making*, 7th edn (Oxford, Oxford University Press).

Andrini, S and Arnaud, A-J (eds) (1995) *Jean Carbonnier, Renato Treves et la sociologie du droit: Archéologie d'un discipline* (Paris, LGDJ).

Banakar, R (1998) 'The Identity Crisis of a 'Stepchild': Reflections on the Paradigmatic Deficiencies of Sociology of Law' 81 *Retfaerd* 3.

—— (2003) *Merging Law and Sociology: Beyond the Dichotomies in Socio-Legal Research* (Glienicke, Berlin, Galda + Wilch Verlag).

—— (2016) 'Law, Policy and Social Control amidst Flux' in K Dahlstrand (ed), *Festskrift till Karsten Åstrom* (Lund, Jurist förlaget i Lund) 47.

Bourdieu, P (1987) 'The Force of Law: Toward a Sociology of the Juridical Field' 38 *Hastings Law Journal* 814.

Carbonnier, J (2001) *Flexible droit: Pour une sociologie du droit sans rigueur*, 10th edn (Paris, LGDJ).

Cotterrell, R (1997) 'Establishing Sociology of Law in Sweden', 23 *Socio-Legal Newsletter* 4.

—— (2006a) *Law, Culture and Society: Legal Ideas in the Mirror of Social Theory* (Abingdon, Routledge).

—— (2006b) 'Per Stjernquist 1912–2005' 48 *Socio-Legal Newsletter* 9.

—— (2018) *Sociological Jurisprudence: Juristic Thought and Social Inquiry* (Abingdon, Routledge).

Ehrlich, E (2002) *Fundamental Principles of the Sociology of Law* (transl WL Moll) (New Brunswick, NJ, Transaction reprint).

Eisenberg, T (2011) 'The Origins, Nature, and Promise of Empirical Legal Studies and a Response to Concerns' *University of Illinois Law Review* 1713.

Ferrari, V (ed) (1990) *Developing Sociology of Law: A World-Wide Documentary Enquiry*. (Milan, Giuffrè).

Griffiths, J (2006) 'The Idea of Sociology of Law and its Relation to Law and to Sociology' in M Freeman (ed), *Law and Sociology* (Oxford, Oxford University Press) 49.

Heise, M (2002) 'The Past, Present, and Future of Empirical Legal Scholarship: Judicial Decision Making and the New Empiricism' *University of Illinois Law Review* 819.

Kojder, A (1999) 'Adam Podgórecki's Vita Activa' 2(126) *Polish Sociological Review* 323.

Kurczewski, J (2001) 'Sociology of Law in Poland' 32(2) *American Sociologist* 85.

Merry, SE (1988) 'Legal Pluralism' 22 *Law & Society Review* 869.

Nelken, D (2009) *Beyond Law in Context: Developing a Sociological Understanding of Law* (Abingdon, Routledge).

Noreau, P and Arnaud, A-J (1998) 'The Sociology of Law in France: Trends and Paradigms' 25 *Journal of Law and Society* 258.

Orwell, G (2004) *Why I Write* (London, Penguin Books reprint of a 1946 essay).

Podgórecki, A (1980) 'Unrecognised Father of Sociology of Law: Leon Petrażycki – Reflections Based on Jan Gorecki's *Sociology and Jurisprudence of Leon Petrażycki*' 15 *Law & Society Review* 183.

Rehbinder, M (1972) 'The Development and Present State of Fact Research in Law in the United States' 24 *Journal of Legal Education* 567.

Sarat, A and Silbey, S (1988) 'The Pull of the Policy Audience' 10 *Law and Policy* 97.

Schlegel, JH (1995) *American Legal Realism and Empirical Social Science* (Chapel Hill, University of North Carolina Press).

Simon, J (1999) 'Law after Society', 24 *Law & Social Inquiry* 143.

Stjernquist, P (2000) *Organized Cooperation Facing Law: An Anthropological Study* (Stockholm, Almqvist & Wiksell).

Treves, R and Glastra van Loon, JF (eds) (1968) *Norms and Actions: National Reports on Sociology of Law* (Hague, Martinus Nijhoff).

Wicenty, D (2018) 'The Experience of Oppression and the Price of Nonconformity: A Brief Biography of Adam Podgórecki' 70 *Studies in East European Thought* 61.

5

The Stepchild Controversy: Unfortunate Dichotomies in Socio-Legal Theory

PETER BERGWALL

R EZA BANAKAR'S INVALUABLE theoretical contribution to Swedish sociology of law is undeniable. This text does not attempt to address Reza's life's work in its entirety. Instead, the text should be seen merely as a comment on a handful of contributions to a classic debate on the state of socio-legal theory,[1] the Stepchild Controversy, as I have chosen to call it. The debate, which was initiated by Banakar (1998) and also concluded by him (2001), represents just a snapshot of Reza's socio-legal thinking at a specific point in time. Then, he moved on and kept on moving.

I. INTRODUCTION

In 1998, *Retfærd* published 'The Identity Crisis of a "Stepchild"', a thought-provoking article written by Reza Banakar on what he at the time considered to be an underdeveloped state of socio-legal theory (Banakar 1998). According to Reza, sociologists of law had not managed to develop a solid theoretical foundation within a scientific paradigm of their own (Niemi-Kiesiläinen 2001). Hence, in the article, Reza set out to investigate the possibility of uniting the fragmented field of sociology of law. In doing so, Reza depicted an academic discipline that was suffering from an identity crisis, being as it were the stepchild of two epistemologically incompatible parent disciplines: law and sociology. Legal science was seen as unequipped to properly tackle social aspects of law, while mainstream sociology failed to grasp the legal system as it is understood by lawyers and policymakers. Reza believed that sociology of law had to break away from predominant paradigms, most notably structural functionalism,

---

[1] Although not stated explicitly, the debate concerned primarily socio-legal theoretical development in Scandinavia. Since I work at a Swedish sociology of law department, my reflections are affected in particular by this 'Swedish experience'. Hence, it is primarily the Swedish tradition in sociology of law that is the main target for my arguments.

and try to integrate the internal perspective on law with 'non-functionalist' sociological perspectives. Reza's initial article prompted replies from Mathiesen (1998), Hydén (1999), Dalberg-Larsen (2000), Hellum (2000), Petersen (2000), and Sand (2000), and caused Reza to return in 2001 with some reflections on the debate, as well as with some clarifications in respect to his initial paper (Banakar 2001). This intellectual discussion, initiated and concluded by Reza, I have chosen to call the Stepchild Controversy.

II. THE CONTROVERSY: RECAPITULATION

In his first article, Banakar (1998: 5) started from three assumptions:

(1) sociology of law lacks theoretical coherence and therefore is unable to produce fundamental paradigms;
(2) this lack of theoretical coherence brings about and sustains the theoretically under-developed state of the field of law and society;
(3) this theoretically underdeveloped state is enhanced by the dominance of a type of structural functional thinking, which is at least in part a product of law's pragmatic properties.

Elaborating on these assumptions, Banakar (ibid) then established that, more than other sociological sub-disciplines, sociology of law is exposed to interdisciplinary and epistemological tensions which cause the fragmentation of the field and impede its theoretical development. As a remedy, the development of several fundamental paradigms, capable of uniting and moulding socio-legal knowledge, is required. However, this development will not be possible 'as long as the scientific goals of the researchers in the field of law and society is to reproduce the basic assumptions and academic identities of their disciplines of origin' (ibid: 5). Reza concluded with a discussion on how the theoretical constructs of legal pluralism and autopoiesis might be developed into the unifying paradigms that he was calling for.

The criticisms of Banakar (1998) were mainly directed – explicitly or implicitly – against Reza's call for paradigmatic unification. For instance, compared to Reza, Mathiesen (1998) displayed a much more relaxed and even embracing attitude towards the 'paradigmatic homelessness' of sociology of law, which Mathiesen (1998) argued had given the discipline a certain degree of academic freedom. Hydén (1999), for his part, pointed out that the goal for sociology of law cannot be to replace scientific paradigms with new, strictly socio-legal paradigms. Instead, Hydén (ibid) called for a common thematic system or object of inquiry, and appointed norms science as his candidate for this purpose. In a very inspiring text, Hellum (2000: 42) identified the typical socio-legal problem as a problem of 'describing and analyzing the normative development situated at the complex interface between law and society – between the established and the emergent'. Hellum (2000), like Petersen (2000), approached the topic from a legal pluralistic perspective, without a sharp disciplinary distinction between law, legal philosophy, legal anthropology and sociology of law. Here, sociology of law's multi- or inter-disciplinarity was seen not as fragmenting but as a something that strengthens the field. In a similar vein, Dalberg-Larsen (2000) viewed sociology of law as a sister discipline of legal science and legal philosophy rather than as the stepchild of law and/or sociology. Finally, Sand (2000), starting from a Habermasian perspective, rejected the idea of a single grand theory, unifying all sociologists of law, and argued instead for a pluralistic theoretical field.

III. PROBLEMATIC DICHOTOMIES IN THE CONTROVERSY

On the surface, the Stepchild Controversy appears to revolve around things like what it is that makes sociology of law unique as an academic discipline, whether it is important to develop research paradigms of your own, and so forth. However, I argue that there is another core problematic that permeates all the contributions in the debate, but without being the expressed subject of discussion. I am talking about what can be referred to in general terms as the *law-society dichotomy*, ie the tendency to conceptualise socio-legal problems as inherently dichotomised problems.[2] Accordingly, it is assumed that 'the legal' and 'the social' are incompatible scientific categories, not only in theory but also in practice, and that the knowledge produced by sociologists is incomprehensible to lawyers, and vice versa. As a direct consequence, mysterious gaps between 'the legal' and 'the social' appear, and sociologists of law rush to the rescue.

Of course, the law-society dichotomy can take on varying forms. Mathiesen (1998), for instance, perceived of two sociologies of law: one approaching law from the inside; and another approaching law from the outside. In Hydén (1999), the sociological understanding of social norms was contrasted with the legal scientific understanding of legal norms. Hellum (2000) referred to an anthropological rule-process dichotomy and, like Reza, she argued for a sociology of law that attempts to simultaneously adopt the inside and outside perspectives of law. For instance, Hellum (2000) argued for what she called 'local law', functioning as a bridge between formal law and customs. In that way, local law transports 'the social' to 'the legal'. Sand (2000), on her part, made a distinction between the normative and social functions of law. In doing so, her arguments echoed the classical fact-value dichotomy that has been incredibly influential in the shaping of the social sciences and arguably of sociology of law as well.[3]

IV. BANAKAR'S INSISTENCE ON THE LAW-SOCIETY DICHOTOMY

However, the insistence on a law-society dichotomy is probably the strongest in Banakar (1998), where differences between 'the legal' and 'the social' are portraited as almost unbridgeable. Reza traced the roots of this dichotomy back to an epistemological tension between law and sociology and argued that 'the dichotomy must be

---

[2] The exception is Dalberg-Larsen (2000), where the law-sociology dichotomy is not prevalent.

[3] The fact-value distinction was first described by Hume (2006). In classical sociology, Max Weber insisted on the necessity to separate facts from values (Gorski 2013), and Weber's influence on sociology of law cannot, of course, be overstated (Přibáň 2017).

systematically addressed by all research conducted within the field' (ibid: 15). I could not disagree more. It is not that I think that sociologists of law should not devote their attention to the tension between conflicting epistemological perspectives. However, a mandatory focus on the law-society dichotomy cannot be a point of departure for a dialectical and critical perspective, one that explicitly denies false dichotomies their status as real objects.

Banakar (1998) claimed that while there is only one legal paradigm, sociology displays multiple scientific paradigms. Still, the version of sociology that Reza extrapolated from the law-society dichotomy seems distinctly macro-oriented, quantitative, and functionalist. Although most of Reza's critics objected to this one-sided view of sociology, they did not seem to object to the dichotomy per se. Indeed, reducing all kinds of law and all kinds of sociology to two opposing categories makes the contours of the law-society dichotomy even sharper.[4] As an illustrative example, Banakar (1998) argues that lawyers do not need sociology to make valid legal decisions. Granted, but neither do most other professions. Also, law is more than 'valid legal decisions'. One does not have to be a sociologist or a lawyer to drive a bus. Still, bus drivers operate in environments that are at once tightly regulated and socially complex. Bus drivers will never be required to make valid legal decisions during drives or master social interactionism in conversations with passengers. Still, 'the social' and 'the legal' are omnipresent in the day of a bus driver. This should basically be all the point of contact needed to attract the interest of a socio-legal scholar.

The disproportionate preoccupation with the actions of lawyers is a peculiarity of sociology of law that has puzzled me ever since I was an undergraduate student. To illustrate: in Banakar (1998), it is argued that interpretative theories, eg phenomenology and symbolic interactionism, have been marginalised in socio-legal research because of their limitations in investigations on how socio-legal issues are perceived by legal scientists and policy-makers. Maybe so, but what about the perceptions of all the rest of us? When the premise of socio-legal inquiry is the law-society dichotomy, socio-legal analyses are often restricted to descriptions of the professional lives of lawyers, perhaps compared to some other group representing 'the social'. Of course, studying lawyers and policymakers is important. But law is for the most part experienced outside of law firms, court rooms, and academic faculties. This circumstance must not go unnoticed by sociology of law.

Socio-legal scholars subscribing to the law-society dichotomy tend to cultivate a strange self-image, sometimes bordering on martyrdom. Hydén (1999: 71) agrees with Banakar (1998) in so far as they both think that sociology of law is 'more than a branch on the tree of sociology'. Moreover, it is implied that the challenges facing sociology of law are far greater than those facing other sociological sub-disciplines, although I suspect that this argument has been put forward by other 'sociological branches' as well.[5] Nevertheless, Banakar's (2001) explanation for the exceptional

---

[4] It also obfuscates an already weak connection between, on the one hand, the real world and, on the other, theories about the real world.

[5] See, for instance, Pescosolido (2010) or Seale (2008) on the atheoretical state of the sociology of health and its ambivalent relationship to medicine and sociology. Also, see Atkinson (2004: 150) on the 'estrangement between mainstream sociology and the sociology of education', Davie (2007) on the sociology of

hardship of the discipline builds on a perception of law as something so mysterious, so unlike any other social phenomenon, that the only way to gain understanding of law seems to be to invent a whole new academic discipline. To me, this is probably the most damaging consequence of a full-blown belief in the law-society dichotomy: sociology not used for the deconstruction of law's mythology but instead used as a vessel, carrying the myth further into the future.[6] At worst, this is anti-sociology.

V. THE META-THEORETICAL PERSPECTIVE OF CRITICAL REALISM

It is as if the law-society dichotomy has traditionally been taken for granted by sociologists of law, or at least by many sociologists of law working in Sweden. This is deeply problematic. However, to be able to fully explain why, I first need to briefly account for critical realism, the meta-theoretical foundation on which I base my arguments, and what this means for my approach to sociology of law.

The label 'critical realism' is a merger of two meta-theoretical positions, *critical naturalism* and *transcendental realism* (Bhaskar 2008a; 2005). Realism refers to the belief in a world that exists independently from our thoughts about it. That reality is transcendental means that reality is perceived as always capable of transcending the limits of human knowledge. We therefore need certain a priori concepts such as time, space and causality to make sense of the world[7] (Norris 2007). Naturalism refers to the epistemological conviction that nature and human life can be explained scientifically in essentially the same way. Critical naturalism acknowledges this but goes on to state that society, unlike nature, can only be reproduced or transformed through the intentional actions of critically reflecting human beings. The study of society therefore requires very different research methods compared to natural science (Bhaskar 2005). Since the world, seen from a realist perspective, proceeds irrespective of our theories about it, it is not possible to proclaim one single theory or paradigm as superior to all others. No theory can perfectly mirror reality, and all knowledge claims about the world are therefore fallible. Critical realists subscribe to this position, which is called epistemic relativism, while they forcefully reject judgmental relativism, the position that all knowledge claims are equally true/untrue. Instead, critical realists advocate judgmental rationality, ie the necessity for social scientists to rationally decide which knowledge claims are the most valid. This requires the researcher to go beneath the empirical surface in search of the most plausible explanation possible.

---

religion and its drift away from mainstream sociology, or Maynard (1990) for an attack on mainstream sociology for its shortcomings in regard to the sociology of gender. These are all sociological perspectives that claim to be uniquely equipped to address very specific problems that mainstream sociology has failed to address.

[6] While legal science, according to Selberg (2020), has moved away from depictions of law and society as a range of binary oppositions, the Swedish socio-legal tradition maintains a distinctive legalistic outlook. Paradoxically, if Selberg (2020) is right, sociology of law has become more legalistic than legal science. And legalism is a myth.

[7] The use of a priori concepts for making sense of the world is referred to as *transcendental deduction*, a concept that Bhaskar brought in from Kant (1996).

VI. LAW, SOCIETY, AND CRITICAL REALISM

To a large extent, critical realists are concerned with causality in society. Under certain conditions, a social mechanism has the tendency or power to cause certain effects in society. From a socio-legal perspective, mechanisms, tendencies, and causal powers are concepts that can be applied in the context of law as a social phenomenon. Importantly, these categories are not static. A crucial point to remember is that causal powers are perceived by critical realists as transfactual, ie they are perceived of as operating in an open world that is differentiated, layered, and multi-dimensional. Consequently, critical realism essentially rejects the possibility of closed social systems.[8] Since law is open and affected by the same causal tendencies as other social phenomena, the alleged closeness of law is merely an ideal.

However, the fact that a social mechanism M tends to cause an event E does not mean that M will always cause E. Whether E takes place ultimately depends on human intentional action, which is never determined but merely conditioned by social structures.[9] Here, the important thing to remember is that even if E does not take place, M's power to influence E under the right structural conditions still exists (Danermark et al 2019). This illustrates how critical realists tackle the structure-agency problem in social science. According to Archer (1995: 198), 'structure necessarily pre-dates the action(s) which transform it, and … structural elaboration necessarily postdates those actions'. While social structure is irreducible to agency, it is through human action that social structures are either reproduced or transformed. This morphogenetic approach, as Archer (1995) calls it, can be applied to sociological studies of law as well.

Accordingly, from the critical realist standpoint, law is seen not as a closed, self-referential system, but as something being in constant engagement with those actors for which law provides structural conditions and whose actions have the potential to reproduce or transform law. Furthermore, I believe that critical realism's strong focus on causal powers, tendencies, and social mechanisms can be extremely useful for sociologists of law with an interest in the causes and effects of normativity in society.[10] Under what conditions does normativity arise? Under what conditions does normativity become law? Under what conditions does it not? These are examples of socio-legal questions that I believe we should ask more often. Answering them will require not only a sociological but also a historical approach, since law is a

---

[8] Since there are obviously social systems (the legal system, the banking system, healthcare, the military) with clear boundaries, critical realists sometimes talk of pseudo-closed systems. (Danermark et al 2019) However, pseudo-closed systems are part of the same open world as other social systems and the human beings acting within them.

[9] Without human interaction social structures would never transform. However, acting intentionally does not always mean acting with the expressed intention to change or uphold social structures.

[10] I deliberately talk of *normativity*, not *norms*. The norm concept has been extensively explored within Swedish sociology of law (Hydén 2011; Hydén and Wickenberg 2008). However, I have always associated norms with the rather static concept of *social facts* (Durkheim 1982), an association that I am uncomfortable with. I prefer 'normativity' because it signals movement, progress, emergence, oppressing or emancipating powers, a causal force always in flux, always interacting with human beings. This captures reality and social change the way I perceive of it in a better way than any kind of 'facts', which appear to be frozen in time.

socio-historical product (Norrie 2017). The causes of law should be looked for in the historical development of society. This requires us to consider other, perhaps unorthodox, dimensions of law. For instance, in my own research on Swedish online doctors, I have made use of what Norrie (2017) refers to as law's architectonic, where the legal is always also the ethico-legal, the juridico-political, and the socio-legal. Within the Swedish health system, these three dimensions are dialectically connected to, but not integrated parts of, Swedish healthcare law. Not least the ethico-legal dimension is essential for understanding how extra-legal but normative causal forces have historically influenced healthcare legislation in Sweden (Bergwall 2021). Of course, other theories or models can be applied; the point is to embrace inter-disciplinary openness and to reject restraining dichotomies and epistemological dogmas.

Another implication following from the assumptions of ontological realism and epistemic relativism is the distinction critical realists make between an intransitive dimension of knowledge and a transitive dimension of knowledge (Bhaskar 2008a):

> Science is about something, and about something that exists independently of science .... The 'results' of scientific inquiry at any time are a set of theories about the nature of the world, which are presumably our best approximation of truth about the world .... [The] work of science at any time takes theories as its raw material, and seeks to transform them into deeper knowledge of the world. These theories are its transitive object .... [Its] aim is knowledge of its intransitive object, the world that exists independently of it. (Collier 1994: 50–51)

The intransitive dimension is synonymous with ontology (being) while the transitive dimension is synonymous with epistemology (the process of inquiry into being) (Hartwig 2007). Intransitivity should not be confused with eternity or immutability. Intransitive knowledge of an object simply entails that the object is what it is at any given point; it does not mean that it stays that way forever. The failure to distinguish between the intransitive and the transitive dimensions of knowledge may lead to a so-called *epistemic fallacy*. An epistemic fallacy is committed when statements about being (ontology) are analysed incorrectly as statements about our knowledge of being (epistemology) (Bhaskar 2008b). For instance, stating that only what can be directly observed exists (empiricism) is to commit an epistemic fallacy (Hartwig 2007). A sociology of law that is occupied predominantly with identity searching takes itself as its study object. This sends the discipline into a transitive loop. The aim of sociology of law should instead be to gain knowledge about its intransitive object. The question is: what is sociology of law's intransitive object? Some sociologists of law will probably and rather unsurprisingly reply: the law. Personally, however, I believe the intransitive object of sociology of law is simply society and the causal forces of normativity dwelling therein. The conventional sources of law are just the tips of icebergs.

VII. LOOKING FORTH: BEYOND DICHOTOMIES

I believe that several of the problems addressed two decades ago by Reza and his critics remain unresolved (see eg Selberg 2020 for a recent critique). In our zeal as sociologists of law to be unique in what we do and who we are, we have neglected normativity as a causal force in society.[11] By neglecting such ontological aspects (or confusing them with epistemological ones), theoretical and methodological socio-legal progress has been hampered in favour of epistemological bickering and, at worst, academic tribalism. In the following, I will try to suggest some possible routes out of this academic dead-end. For the most part, these suggestions will be rooted in a critical realist approach to sociology of law.

As previously mentioned, society provides structural conditions for human beings, but human beings change social structures when they act on them. If we believe (as I do) that this way of seeing things is applicable to sociology of law as well, the law-society dichotomy at once becomes preposterous. Furthermore, as no one can claim to have developed a flawless socio-legal theory or methodology, there is no reason for sociologists of law to submit to and strictly follow any epistemological program or paradigm. As the saying goes, all models are wrong, but some are useful. Also, social structures are real but rarely directly observable. That is why judgmental rationality is so important. Multiple explanations of the unobservable are typically available within social science. It is therefore our obligation as social scientists to make an effort to provide the most rational and plausible explanation possible, even if this entails the combination of what, according to epistemological purists, should not be possible to combine.

The identity crisis that Banakar (1998) referred to, or what is perhaps better described as a lack of academic self-confidence, still plagues Swedish sociology of law. Hence, it is still easy to sympathise with Reza's ambition to defragment socio-legal theory and thereby strengthen the autonomy of sociology of law as an academic discipline. Indeed, theoretical progress is a necessary and ever-ongoing project. The problem with the Stepchild Controversy was not the eagerness to evolve theoretically, but the epistemic fallacy undermining the premises for the discussion. More specifi-cally, the problem addressed by Banakar (1998) – the law-society dichotomy – was, and still is, a strawman. If the law-society dichotomy were real, any kind of sociol-ogy studying law would be an impossibility and law would indeed be sociologically incomprehensible. Banakar (1998: 11) states the problem as follows: '[Sociology] of law is given the difficult (if not impossible) task of uniting two fundamentally differ-ent images of society: a legal image shaped by formal practice and a sociological image formed through intellectual scientific curiosity'. Agreed, this task would prob-ably be impossible to execute. But I do not recognise this as a task given to sociology of law. What would the purpose of that task be? More than once during the Stepchild Controversy, it was held that sociology of law must refrain from reproducing the 'old knowledge' of its parent disciplines (Banakar 1998; Hydén 1999). It is therefore not clear why uniting two pre-existing images, representing two 'old knowledges', would be a priority for sociology of law.

---

[11] I view normativity as something quite unrelated to the norm concept, which has dominated Swedish socio-legal research for decades. I conceive of normativity as a mechanism that needs to be discovered, understood, and explained as a source for social action or suppression. Empirical research on social norms, on the other hand, is often presented as slightly functionalist descriptions of how groups of people tend to behave under certain circumstances, and what effects this might have on law.

VIII. CONCLUSION

The law-society dichotomy is not some monstrous obstacle that sociologists of law have yet to find a way to overcome; it is a fiction. Hence, to base an argument on these premises is to commit an epistemic fallacy. Naturally, getting rid of this mental blockage alone will not save socio-legal theory, but it might help us think and theorise with fresh minds. By thinking of the law-society dichotomy dialectically, it will soon become obvious that the dichotomy is based on false premises. As with any false dichotomy, dialectical thinking will reveal that the descriptions of the two parts making up the law-society dichotomy are distorted and oversimplified. If 'the legal' and 'the social' were described accurately, we would see that the law-society dichotomy is not a dichotomy at all. Of course, the true relationship between 'the legal' and 'the social' is incredibly complex and, unlike dichotomies, such relationships cannot be described in just a couple of sentences. Undoubtedly, no one suggests that the dominance of the law-society dichotomy in Swedish sociology of law is the result of intellectual laziness. The engaged debate during the Stepchild Controversy is proof that the law-society dichotomy still lies deep at the core of Swedish sociology of law. However, although Reza was quite uncompromising in his initial 'stepchild article', in Banakar (2001), he provided a more nuanced depiction of the relationship between law and society, and I think that this shift in perspective continued over time. The Reza that I came to know several years later did not come across as a staunch defender of dichotomic thinking. Unfortunately, I never got the chance to sit down and talk with him about these issues.

REFERENCES

Archer, MS (1995) *Realist Social Theory: The Morphogenetic Approach* (Cambridge, Cambridge University Press).

Atkinson, P (2004) 'Performance, Culture and the Sociology of Education' 14(2) *International Studies in Sociology of Education* 147.

Banakar, R (1998) 'The Identity Crisis of a "Stepchild"' 21(2) *Retfærd* 3.

—— (2001) 'A Passage to "India"' 24(1) *Retfærd* 3.

Bergwall, P (2021) *Exploring Paths of Justice in the Digital Healthcare: A Socio-Legal Study of Swedish Online Doctors* (Lund Studies in Sociology of Law, vol 51; Lund, Lund University).

Bhaskar, R (2005) *The Possibility of Naturalism – A Philosophical Critique of the Contemporary Human Sciences*, 3rd edn (London, Routledge) (orig publ 1979).

—— (2008a) *A Realist Theory of Science* (Abingdon, Routledge) (orig publ 1975).

—— (2008b) *Dialectic – The Pulse of Freedom* (London, Routledge) (orig publ 1993).

Collier, A (1994) *Critical Realism: An Introduction to Roy Bhaskar's Philosophy* (London, Verso).

Dalberg-Larsen, J (2000) 'Sociology of Law from a Legal Point of View' 23(89) *Retfærd* 26.

Danermark, B, Ekström, M, and Karlsson, JC (2019) *Explaining Society – Critical Realism in the Social Sciences*, 2nd edn (Abingdon, Routledge).

Davie, G (2007) *The Sociology of Religion* (Los Angeles, CA, Sage Publications).

Durkheim, É (1982) *The Rules of Sociological Method – And Selected Texts on Sociology and its Method* (ed Anthony Giddens) (London, Macmillan Press) (orig publ 1895).

Gorski, PS (2013) 'Beyond the Fact/Value Distinction: Ethical Naturalism and the Social Sciences', 50(6) *Society* 543.

Hartwig, M (ed) (2007) *Dictionary of Critical Realism* (Abingdon, Routledge).

Hellum, A (2000) 'How to Improve the Doctrinal Analysis of Legal Pluralism: A Comparison of the Legal Doctrine About Custom and Local Law in Zimbabwe and Norway' 23(89) *Retfærd* 40.

Hume, D (2006) *A Treatise of Human Nature* (Project Gutenberg Literary Archive Foundation) (orig publ 1739–40).

Hydén, H (1999) 'Even a Stepchild Eventually Grows Up: On the Identity of Sociology of Law' 22(85) *Retfærd* 71.

—— (2011) *Norms between Law and Society: A Collection of Essays from Doctoral Candidates from Different Academic Subjects and Different Parts of the World*, vol 37 (Lund, Sociology of Law Dept, Lund University).

Hydén, H and Wickenberg, P (eds) (2008) *Contributions in Sociology of Law – Remarks from a Swedish Horizon* (Lund Studies in Sociology of Law, Lund, Sociology of Law Dept, Lund University).

Kant, I (1996) *Critique of Pure Reason* (trans WS Pluhar) (Indianapolis, Hackett Publishing) (orig publ 1781).

Mathiesen, T (1998) 'Is it All That Bad to be a Stepchild? Comments on the State of Sociology of Law' 21(83) *Retfærd* 67.

Maynard, M (1990) 'The Re-Shaping of Sociology? Trends in the Study of Gender' 24(2) *Sociology* 269.

Niemi-Kiesiläinen, J (2001) 'Inledning' 24(92) *Retfærd* 1.

Norrie, A (2017) *Justice and the Slaughter Bench: Essays on Law's Broken Dialectic* (Abingdon, Routledge).

Norris, C (2007) 'Transcendental Realism (TR)' in M Hartwig (ed), *Dictionary of Critical Realism* (Abingdon, Routledge) 474.

Pescosolido, BA (2010) 'Taking "The Promise" Seriously: Medical Sociology's Role in Health, Illness, and Healing in a Time of Social Change' in BA Pescosolido, JK Martin, JD McLeod and A Rogers (eds), *Handbook of the Sociology of Health, Illness, and Healing: A Blueprint for the 21st Century* (New York, Springer) 3.

Petersen, H (2000) 'Forgoing New Identities in the Global Family? Challenges for Prescriptive and Descriptive Normative Knowledge' 23(90) *Retfærd* 46.

Přibáň, J (2017) 'A Sociology of Legal Distinctions: Introducing Contemporary Interpretations of Classic Socio-legal Concepts' 44 (S1) *Journal of Law and Society* S1.

Sand, I-J (2000) 'A Future or Demise for the Theory of the Sociology of Law: Law as a Normative, Social and Communicative Function of Society' 23(90) *Retfærd* 55.

Seale, C (2008) 'Mapping the Field of Medical Sociology: A Comparative Analysis of Journals' 30(5) *Sociology of Health & Illness* 677.

Selberg, N (2020) 'Reflektioner över svensk rättssociologis kunskapsobjekt och teoribildning: Om rättssociologi och Om normer – en recensionsartikel' 133(4) *Tidsskrift for Rettsvitenskap* 481.

6

Normativity as the Source of Norms

HÅKAN HYDÉN

I. INTRODUCTION

INTEREST IN NORMS has been rising in the last 25 years in real life as well as in the sciences (Hydén 2011). One question, which never is raised, is: where do norms come from? One reason for this is that the answer is not straightforward. It is hard to find a common denominator. We generally do not think much about norms because most of the time we take them for granted. One possible answer is that we become aware of the norms that guide our behaviour primarily in times of sudden or radical change. In these situations, we become conscious about our norms because they are challenged and may need to be revised to deal with the new circumstances. I argue that norms arise out of normativity, something which can be seen as the core of various systems: social; economic; bureaucratic; or legal. As actors we participate in these systems and take our leads from what they demand of us. For example, a civil servant becomes a 'bureaucrat' because his behaviour is extensively shaped by being an employee of a hierarchical organisation. A similar socialisation occurs when we participate in the marketplace: its structures encourage us to become optimisers of our own interest.

II. TYPES OF NORMS

I have argued that norms should be regarded as an overarching concept, and social norms as one subcategory of norms (Hydén 2022). The same applies to economic and technical norms. Legal norms are another subcategory of the overarching norm. In the same way, in this chapter I place normativity as a general concept covering different forms of normativity connected to various normative systems. This represent a novelty, being an extension of the norm concept, which assigns to the notion of norm a much broader role in social as well as legal science. It opens up for new approaches and understanding of both law and society. I therefore devote an introductory part of this chapter to a brief description of these norms. Thereafter I turn to the concept of normativity and try to understand what it means. While the meaning of the terms 'norm' and 'normative' is agreed upon, normativity occurs in different contexts without a common understanding or definition.

The ordinary starting point for analysing norms is that they directly or indirectly contain instructions for action (Hydén and Svensson 2008). Built on expectations, norms are present everywhere yet vary in application depending on context. When values in society change, norms are affected. The evolution from collectivism to individualism that has taken place in the West during the past 30 years has involved extensive normative changes, noticeable, for example, in schools and family life. Norms change whether we are aware of it or not. When social life is stable, we do not need to think about what to do because – like our practices – norms are imprinted in the brain through the various experiences stored in every individual. It is when significant changes occur that we become aware of norms, because they are challenged and may need to be re-programmed.

Humans are perpetually involved in creating the world into which they are born. This means that cultural skills are required by the individual to procreate change over time. This applies to both the inner, symbolic world and the outer, material world, in which social norms emerge and change. The culturally created and symbolically constructed world has a longer lifecycle than the physical world, which is renewed at a more rapid rate. The term 'cultural lag' refers to a situation where society's material and technological changes are quicker than its cultural superstructure of values and norms (*Swedish National Encyclopaedia* vol 11: 163; *cf* also Friedman and Ladinsky 1967). This is viewed as a threat to social integration and can result in social unrest.

Social norms contribute to maintaining cultural values, since sanctions and social control articulate what is considered desirable and undesirable behaviour (Ross 2009; Black 1984). Norms, thereby, reinforce the expectation of certain types of behaviour, as Vilhelm Aubert explains in a classic quote: 'Social norms are constituted of expectations' ('Sociala normer er satt samman av forventningar'). He adds that for something to be a norm, the ensuing expectations must have a certain degree of sustainability and stability (Aubert 1976: 34). Based on theories of the Ego (the 'I') and the Alter (the Other), Aubert, in common with many other theorists, emphasises how the individual is generally able to estimate how rules work based on previous experiences of sanctions and statements. This means that norms are not just manifest in the presence of other people; they also have their own motivational force. Requirements that the surrounding social environment demand of the Ego become requirements that the Ego demands of itself. They become a part of their internal norm system, their own morals. This process is described as the norm having become internalised (ibid: 34).

Muzafer Sherif is generally acknowledged as having established the modern understanding of norms in his book, *An Outline of Social Psychology*, which is based on his previous book, *The Psychology of Social Norms*. In the 1936 edition, Sherif describes how norms that arise in uncertain situations result in uniformity due to group pressure. The roots of his concept of norms can be traced back to classical antiquity. It was originally meant to serve as an agreed upon yardstick for measuring goals, validity, and other characteristics of an object (Mortensen 1990: 106). Nils Mortensen argues that the synthesis of moral rules and this ancient concept for evaluating objective characteristics is probably the turning point for how norms are conceptualised within contemporary sociology (ibid). It releases sociology from the conceptual apparatus of moral philosophy and allows it to assume an empirical approach to social rules.

Just as we divide society into different fields such as economics, politics, administration, technology, etc, norms can be similarly differentiated. In this wider normative realm, the legal norms play a special role because they set out the guidelines and principles for collective decision-making in the political-administrative system. **A legal norm** is a binding rule or principle, or norm, that organisations of sovereign power promulgate and enforce in order to regulate social relations. Legal norms determine the rights and duties of individuals within the governing jurisdiction at a given point in time. Competent state authorities issue and publish basic aspects of legal norms through a collection of laws that individuals under that government must abide by, which is further guaranteed by state coercion. Legal norms become validated from the moment they are published as part of legal order and take effect from the moment they bind the subjects of the law.

When a social system has grown sufficiently complex that the legislative and executive processes need to be separated, this is accomplished through norms that describe what actions are expected of each actor. This is how specific bureaucratic norms arise. A bureaucracy typically refers to an organisation that is complex, with multilayered systems and processes. These systems and procedures are designed to maintain uniformity and control within an organisation. To function efficiently, they generate their own **bureaucratic** norms.

Economic norms are based on strategic assessments of what works well in the marketplace. This also means that the economic system is goal-oriented. The various branches of economics can largely be divided into two main sections. Microeconomics studies individual decision-makers in both production and consumption. Macroeconomics studies the economy as a whole, with a focus on aggregate variables such as production, unemployment and inflation. Economic norms are effective because the sanction contained in the norm is activated directly once the norm is violated. For example, a bad investment, ie a deviation from the system's definition of optimal conditions, is visible immediately and therefore signals the need for a change in behaviour.

Expectations are also an outcome of technical endeavours. The ecological system's **technical norms** are at present mainly determinant in actions that relate to the exploitation of nature rather than its preservation. Technical norms built on laws of nature constitute the foundation for calculations about the most rational way for building houses, roads, bridges and more. Breaches are punishable immediately and by themselves. For example, a bridge collapses if the proper norms are ignored. What is regarded as right or wrong is determined by the rationality of the system. Not to construct a bridge according to the necessary principles according to natural science knowledge in the field is regarded as wrongful behaviour and vice versa. There is an important difference between technical norms relating to resource exploitation and those applying to resource conservation. They have different purposes, each with its own rationality being the core of the systems, determining what is right or wrong.

As result of digital technology, technical norms are gaining stronger inherent normativity. This development is mainly manifest in artificial inteligence and the use of algorithms. Digital technology is increasingly becoming a part of our daily lives. It is used in our phones and homes to such an extent that it is hard to imagine a single day passing not in some way or another impacted by artificial inteligence (Alvarez 2017).

III. WHAT IS NORMATIVITY?

There is an extensive discourse on the meaning and use of normativity, but it is hard to find a common definition. It is generally treated as belonging to the normative conceptual world, together with law and morality. Actually, a lot of references to normativity are to norms or something normative. The only explicit example in the literature of an attempt to define normativity is an article by Stephen Finlay (2019), who notes that the concept is arbitrary and not used in a consistent way. Normativity has many faces and, according to Finlay, it is because it is contextually dependent (ibid: 25). With 'context' Finlay refers to a philosopher's metatheoretical claims, such as cognitivism and noncognitivism, naturalism and non-naturalism, or objectivism and subjectivism out of which he constructs his own hybrid view of normative judgment, called perspectivism.

Finlay lists several different definitions, such as the following:

> NORMATIVITY (as an) ontological – judge-relation = the relation that obtains between an agent and an action if a first-personal, robustly normative – judge-ostensive – judgment about that agent and that action would be true. (ibid: 26)

This definition does not say much from a social science point of view. Nor does his footnote example offer additional light:

> This interpretation is consistent, for example, with the way Mark Schroeder introduces his subjectivist theory of reasons, in terms of the psychological difference between Ronnie who has a reason to go to a party, and Bradley who doesn't.

A different definition rests on a quasi-realist concept of normativity formulated as follows:

> NORMATIVITY is from a quasi-ontological point of view to apply the concept to some facts or properties involves having or expressing a favorable attitude towards them.

These definitions belong to the meta-ethic approach to normativity. The philosophical area most distinctively concerned with normativity is ethics, according to the *Routledge Encyclopedia of Philosophy* (Craig 2000). Normativity seems to be a higher order concept that refers to the field of ethics, notably to how we define a good life or society and which norms should be implemented to realise it ('Normativity in Perception' Conference, 2015).

Ethics can also be combined with epistemology such as in a book titled *Normativity: Epistemic and Practical* (McHugh et al 2018: 4). Here normativity 'is a matter of what one should or may do or think, what one has reason or justification to do or not'. Another proposal for an adequate definition, for a particular use of normativity, 'might simply be a description of the facts that fix the reference for that use, such as facts about the causal chain' (Wedgwood 2010: 8). Ethical standards are normative, Judith Thomson explains (Thomson 2008: 8). They do not merely describe a way in which we in fact regulate our conduct. They make claims on us; they command, oblige, recommend, or guide. This position resembles Emile Durkheim's use of the concept 'social facts' (Durkheim 2017: 19). Normativity in the eyes of philosophers tends to entail that a differentiation, attitude or mental state is justified, ie an action one ought to do or a state one ought to be in (Wedgwood 2010: 8).

Another resemblance to Durkheim is the discussion within philosophy about reason (Raz 2011): what motivates the actor to behave in a certain way (Hydén 2022: ch 1). A dominant view takes the concept of reason to be the key to understanding normativity rather than, say, facts about what we ought to do (or the concept of ought) (Star 2018). For example, as Raz argues, reason itself may have normative connotations (Raz 1999: 90–117).

A review of the philosophical, meta-ethical debate confirms that the concept of normativity has no authorised definition. Yet the term is widely used. The reason for the failure to define the concept in a consistent way seems to lie in what it covers – or does not cover. While it is relatively easy to locate 'norms' and 'normative' in the symbolic as well as the material world, the same is not true of the term normativity, the reason being that it lacks denotation, ie references in 'reality' to what the concept is supposed to cover. To rectify this state of affairs, a functionalist definition will help. This is what we turn to in the following analysis.

IV. HOW DO NORMS ORIGINATE?

Christine Horne has developed a general model that explains the emergence of norms (Horne 2001: 3–34). It is based on the premise that social and technological changes lead to cost/benefit allocations which, in combination with group pressure, influence behaviour. Accepting a similar starting point, Robert C Elickson works with the concept of 'change agent' (Elickson 2001: 35–75), thereby highlighting the importance of different actors in the emergence and reproduction of norms. To make his point, Elickson worked on an S-curve that begins with Self-Motivated leaders and Norm Entrepreneurs with Opinion Leaders following behind in an upward curve.[1] Elickson writes that '(w)hen a new norm suddenly becomes manifestly advantageous for a group, many self-motivated individuals with unexceptional leadership abilities may supply it simultaneously', thus making the new norm attributable to particular change agents.

Discussions of normativity are not restricted to ethics only. The concept is also used in different scientific contexts. Reza Banakar claims that '(n)ormativity is used when exploring why, under certain circumstances, we feel obliged to act in specific ways' (Banakar 2015: 218). Normativity also has a presence in psychology. For example, in a study of young children's awareness of the normative structure of games, the

---

[1] *cf* Hydén (2022), Figure 1.6: Different world views in relation to the development of the industrial society.

authors could relate normativity to structural causes, ie the construction of the game (Rakoczy et al 2008: 875–81).

Normativity is especially prominent within legal philosophy. There is a wide-ranging study of the law's normativity, focusing on its conceptual, descriptive and empirical dimensions.[2] Reza Banakar discusses the relation between norms and normativity from a socio-legal perspective (Vivian 2020: 15–38). He asks whether normativity is caused by norms or whether norms are generated by normativity, concluding that normativity per se can be a source of norms (ibid: 20). More specifi-cally, he points to how normativity may emerge out of system imperatives (purpose or instrumental rationality) as well as lifeworld (value rationality) (ibid: 21).

By extending these ideas, normativity can be compared to the inner core of a system or to the source from which the norms emerge. A functional definition of normativity in this perspective would be that normativity is the source within a system from which norms emerge. Furthermore, normativity seems to be the constitutive factor for the system and thereby the definition of the system itself. For example, the economic system is built on economic rationality which – being the normativity – defines the system.

The German legal sociologist Niklas Luhmann (1927–1998) operated with such a systems perspective.[3] He regarded a system as autopoietic, ie capable of reproducing itself from within (Luhmann 1995). Because they reproduce their own elements on the basis of their own elements, they are self-referential. Luhmann built his theory on parallels to the analysis of living systems within biology, developed by the two Chilean biologists Humberto Maturana and Francisco Varela, who showed how a plant reproduces its own cells with its own cells. Luhmann further argues that while systems are open, they have their own internal mechanisms for operational closure and interactional openness. These qualities generate norms and a normative language, which makes learning from the environment as well as communication across systems possible.

A central element within the theory of autopoiesis is the concept of structural coupling which refers to the relation between systems and their environments. For instance, environmental events may trigger internal processes in an autopoietic system, but the concrete processes are determined by the structures of the system,[4] ie by its normativity. A system is said to be structurally linked to its environment (or other systems in its environment) if its structures are in some way or other translated to the normative structures of the environment (or systems in the environment).

Luhmann's autopoietic theory applies to non-living systems. His trans-disciplinary concept of autopoiesis is open to re-specification by the different disciplines, eg law, sociology, economy, biology, and psychology. While living systems reproduce

[2] See, for a collection of essays, Himma 2021.
[3] Niklas Luhmann was a German sociologist, philosopher of social science, and a prominent thinker in systems theory, who is considered one of the most important social theorists of the twentieth century. Luhmann wrote prolifically, with more than 70 books and nearly 400 scholarly articles published on a vari-ety of subjects, including law, economy, politics, art, religion, ecology, mass media, and love. Among the most prominent books, *Theory of Society* vol 1 (2012) and vol 2 (2013a) can be mentioned. In a socio-legal perspective there is reason to point out N Luhmann (2013b), *A Sociological Theory of Law*.
[4] Luhmann (2000: 401) speaks in this sense of a 'trigger-causality'.

themselves on the basis of life, social systems, according to Luhmann, constitute and reproduce themselves on the basis of communication. From a normative perspective, this includes not only communication but also argumentation. Norms develop out of practical motivations to facilitate cooperation and intersubjective communication. That seems also to be the foundation for normativity within social systems, as the next section further illustrates.

V. IN SEARCH OF NORMATIVITY

A. The Social Systems' Normativity

Social action systems are created through interactions between people in line with socio-psychological theories and developed in accordance with the driving forces identified by game theory. This means that the content of a norm, in each single case, is determined by individuals in cooperation with each other, although aspects such as habits, customs and conventions may restrict the set of norms available to the individual (Lloyd 1964: 228).

The function of a social system is to socialise people, ie to encourage individuals to behave socially and to comply with certain socially (collectively) conditioned methods of interaction. For example, individuals socialise into a given society, thereby learning a set of given, normal ways of acting. Normativity stems from the process of socialising individuals into society through interaction and communication with others in both verbal and nonverbal ways. The driving force behind this is the reciprocity principle.[5]

Normativity within the social system boils down to a human need to socialise, stay together and reproduce. From these needs, different social institutions such as the family, schools, and social networks of different kind emerge.

B. The Political/Administrative System

The political system is created to represent society's collective interests, ie the public interest (Rothstein 2010). The establishment of a political system is an expression of the need for a collective order, which is tasked with making decisions on value-based and normative issues that are of importance to the people affected by the system.[6] As such, it is more goal-oriented than the social system.

The political system makes decisions on how to proceed in various situations. Its output largely consists of creating legal norms. From this perspective, law can be seen as a form of standardised politics: it governs and summarises policies in a

---

[5] This so-called golden rule is a fundamental ethical principle and can be found in many religions and philosophical and ethical schools of thought. The oldest known written version comes from Confucius, approximately 500 BC.

[6] This does not prevent the political system, as myriad examples have shown, from being perverted to serve an individual's or group's interests and desire for power.

given sub-section of society (Hydén 2002: ch 8). When society has grown to the extent that the decision-making and executive processes need to be separated, decisions are passed on to those with executive functions. This is accomplished through a division between politics and administration in which the administrative system can be seen as an action system created for a specific purpose.

The normativity in the political system is linked to a need for organisation of decision-making and performance of collective tasks and thereby the exercise of power (Rothstein 2010). The political/administrative systems are based on norms that set out guidelines and principles for collective decision-making, by whom and how the decision-making process should be conducted, ie the principles with which the process should comply, or what kind of issues should be addressed collectively within the political/administrative systems.

C. The Economic System

The economic norm – how we act – depends on our perception of what is most rational, ie the best way to act from an economic perspective. What characterises, then, the economic perspective?

This system is extremely action-oriented. Its very existence is based in inherent normativity. The economic system is constructed to facilitate 'optimal' resource allocation. Not all economic systems are normatively the same. They are constituted differently and operate in variable ways, but they are all highly goal-oriented. The term strategic norm is appropriate when referring to the economic system's norms. Foremost is the notion of self-interest and how it can be secured within a collective framework. **The normativity of the economic system** gives a signal for actors to look for the most rational way to act in a given economic situation.

Thus, to trace the normativity of the economic system it is necessary to know how the economic system is constructed and how it operates in different situations. This is the task of economic science, which is a cognitive science with normative implications for actors in real life. There is an underlying rationality taken for granted that determines what is right or wrong. Economics is empirically oriented and its studies analyse how the economic system behaves and works in different cases, all with the aim of giving as reliable, normative advice as possible on how to act in different situations. The element of cognitive science legitimates economy as a non-normative, neutral and objective, science. Knowledge in these cases works, and has the same function in interpreting economic norms as the preparatory work behind a law has for lawyers when the lawyer seeks to understand the content of a law (Wickenberg 1999: 266–470).

Unlike the social system, where normativity relies on individuals coming together in sharing their values and ambitions, the economic system norms become apparent through the fundamental principle constituting the system itself.[7] The economic system is inherently instrumental. It produces the premises for the actors' actions.

---

[7] *cf* the aforementioned games analogy.

D. The Ecological System

In the industrial era, technology has normative implications related to the use of technology. In the later stage of industrial development, the benefits of technology are increasingly linked to negative external effects. Norms within the framework of the ecological system have a qualitatively different character compared with the norms that belong to the systems emanating from man. While norms in the cases hitherto concerned – the social, political/administrative, and economic systems – are in one way or the other determined by human interaction, norms in the ecological system originate in the regularities exhibited by nature in those respects that man is capable of discovering and formulating. These regularities in nature can be formulated in terms of norms belonging to a system. These norms are in the last instance based on the laws of nature such as the law of gravity, photosynthesis, the first and the second laws of thermodynamics, and so on.

The normativity of ecological systems is a consequence of different laws of nature. The identification of the ecological system's normativity presuppose knowledge about nature in different respects. Science is, according to conventional sources, the study of the physical world, nature. Science uses scientific methods that largely depend on empirical measurements of established hypotheses. Science tries to make theoretical models that can explain as simply as possible what can be observed, measured and tested and thereby made operable for different purposes.

Science is divided into a few main areas, such as physics and chemistry. Physics is about the study of the fundamental forces that govern nature and the building blocks of nature, as well as the phenomena that these together give rise to. This knowledge is fundamental for understanding **the normativity of the technical systems** dealing with production of material goods and constructions for different purposes, such as housing, infrastructure, etc. The normativity is influenced by what science finds out to be possible and most rational in order to fulfil human needs. The same goes for chemistry, the study of the structure and properties of elements and chemical compounds and their reactions with each other. Development of knowledge within this part of nature lays the foundation for certain kinds of normativity.

E. Legal Systems' Normativity

A legal rule as a norm has its source in an authoritative legal source of some kind, usually legislation. There is a well-established technique for identifying and implementing legal norms. These norms belong to openly and explicit normative systems. They point out what has to be done or not be done in different situations of life. Compared to the other systems discussed, the imperative is separate from the sanction stipulated when people do not obey the legal norm.

The legal norm can be understood from a strictly legal point of view and thereby inform us of the correct interpretation and application of the legal rule as an instruction for how to act or how to judge a certain situation. **The normativity of the legal system** is constructed and decided upon by politicians in law or judges in legal decisions, precedents. It is up to legal dogmatic as an authoritative method to analyse how the normativity looks within different fields of the legal system. Legal dogmatic can be illustrated in a vertical perspective since, as an ideal type, it is built on the logic of subsumption and deduction (Hydén and Hydén 2019: ch 1). This process is a matter of the technical application of the normative standpoints in law to factual situations, which may require more or less sophisticated reasoning.

The above-mentioned description of law is valid for private and criminal law, where in both cases the law's normativity is guided by efforts of justice. It is another thing with administrative law and what I call interventional law, ie the type of law with the ambition to partly influence private actors to take external effects into account.

These parts of the legal system require a broader social scientific perspective on law. Legal norms are not neutral but also affect societal functions and have their own consequences for society. It is possible, therefore, to refer to **two different orders of normativity** – the first (the vertical) related to the technical instructions and legal dogmatic, and the second (the horizontal) to the consequences and functions springing from the first order. The horizontal problem area represents something other than legal dogmatic knowledge, although it is of great relevance for understanding the law. It is another perspective on laws paradoxically not regarded as relevant for legal dogmatic.

Legal sociology has not, so far, invented a proper concept which covers these normativities related to the genesis and consequences of law when applied to, and confronted with, societal realities. The concept of law in action is not adequate, nor is the concept of living law. These concepts are directly or indirectly related to the law, while the concept I am looking for is geared towards the social outcome of law and legal regulation. Perhaps the concept of socio-legal norms is the most appropriate one. This normativity is different from the one related to the technical instructions within legal dogmatic. In both cases it is a question of following normative instructions. These are well defined in valid legal sources when it comes to legal dogmatic and represent a kind of inner perspective on law and legal matters. In the case of socio-legal norms, however, normativity presupposes an integration of the internal and external perspectives on the legal norm. The normativity is subordinated to the legally defined purpose and the anticipated factual outcome of the use of the law or legal decision-making. This kind of study belongs to interdisciplinary sub-disciplines, such as implementation studies and evaluation research.

F. The Prediction Strength of Normativity

It might not, for various reasons, always be possible to predict human behaviour. Concepts within (empirically oriented) social science cannot be as precise as in philosophy, which is working with abstract concepts and discourse. Another obvious reason that the norms which follow on normativity might not be obeyed is deviant behaviour. There are always people who ignore or refuse to follow prescriptions. Furthermore, norms stemming from one system might in practice have negative external effects and collide with other norms and values in society. This might give rise to intervention from the state, often using what I refer to as intervening legal rules.

The more a system is based on rational design, the stronger its normativity. In a technical system associated with the laws of nature, such as the laws of gravity, thermodynamics, photosynthesis, etc, the normativity is more decisive for which norms are generated compared to a social system based on interaction between social actors (Hydén 2022: ch 1). While normativity in technical systems gives rise to the same norms independent of context, normativity in social systems varies with each special situation. By understanding how a technical system operates, it is possible to give instructions on how to achieve various goals. However, these norms are both invisible and unknown until they are articulated by science. Technical systems give rise to a kind of conditional or potential normativity that is articulated in professional knowledge systems. The natural sciences lay the foundation for technical applications, where engineers in different fields follow prescriptions for action, which derive from a delimited norm system tied to a knowledge system about a naturally defined phenomenon. The normativity is defined based in the cognitive, where knowledge is a prerequisite.

Less structured systems give rise to less absolute binding normativity (ibid). The political system, which itself seeks to determine normative issues on a collective level, does not create normative expectations in the same way as a scientifically determined physical system. The possible outcomes are simply too many and contingent for normativity to occur. In politics, however, since groups tend to gather around ideologies and commonly shared interests, it is possible to specify normativity in relation to assumed political affiliations. The social system appears to be the least structured and thus least normative,[8] but that does not prevent it from being – and acting as – a norm. There are social contexts in which behavioural expectations appear to be clear to those involved. Primary and secondary socialisation processes contribute. Peer pressure and social control would be other cases in point (Black 1984). In all social systems, a system of reward and punishment encourages members to follow the norms, whether mediated via their family, friends, workmates, or the entire society. The consequence of breaking a norm depends on how important the violation is. For example, murder is punished more severely than a parking offence, because the norm not to kill is more compelling than a parking offence.

Technical norms have an advantage over environmental norms. One could say that technical norms have the same characteristics as the duty norms, while environmental norms correspond better to what might be called normative principles – ie an action that you are obliged or expected to carry out but which is not necessarily as normatively unambiguous as a duty norm. Economic norms, in turn, determine much of how technical norms are applied. Economic norms are based on strategic assessments of what works well in the market. This also means that the economic system is highly goal-oriented. One could say that the normative elements in these cases are mainly determined by their systemic source, ie the normativity. This is not discursively determined by opinions about good or bad, right and wrong; only by the structure of the economic system itself. Economic norms are as effective as technical norms in that the sanction contained in the norm is activated directly if the norm is violated.

---

[8] That is probably the reason for Jurgen Habermas' and other social scientists' interest for what Habermas calls the life-world and discourse on an equal basis.

One might object that the economic system is constantly giving different signals for right and wrong. That is true but my point remains that the rationality/normativity of the economic system decides what will be seen as normatively correct. The normative content of goal-oriented rules is weaker than for duty rules because they[9] require other knowledge in addition to law.[10]

VI. CONCLUSIONS

There is a need for an understanding of what generates norms within different action systems. The answer given in this chapter refers the origin of norms to the concept of normativity. This is a concept widely used within philosophy and meta-ethical theories, however, without bearing on social sciences. The concept of normativity has no authorised definition. The reason for the failure to define the concept in a consistent way is claimed in the chapter to lie in what it covers – or does not cover. The reason seems to be that it lacks denotation, ie references in 'reality' to what the concept is supposed to cover. To rectify this state of affairs, a functionalist definition is introduced based on normativity as the source within a system from which norms are deduced. The concept of normativity fills a gap in the vocabulary related to norms by understanding normativity as the constitutive element in a normative system equivalent to the core from which norms emerge.

REFERENCES

Alvarez-Pereira, C (2017) 'Disruptive Technologies. A Critical Yet Hopeful View' 3(2) *Cadmus*.
Aubert, V (1976) *Rettens sosiale funksjon* (Oslo, Universitetsforlaget).
Banakar, R (2015) *Normativity in Legal Sociology: Methodological Reflections on Law and Regulation in Late Modernity* (Heidelberg, Springer).
—— (2013) 'Can Legal Sociology Account for the Normativity of Law?' in M Baier (ed), *Social and Legal Norms: Towards a Socio-Legal Understanding of Normativity* (Farnham, Ashgate) 15.
Black, DJ (ed) (1984) *Toward a General Theory of Social Control* (New York, Academic Press).
Craig, E (ed) (2000) *Routledge Encyclopedia of Philosophy Online* (electronic resourse) Version 2.0 (New York, Routledge).
Durkheim, É (2017). *The Rules of Sociological Method and Selected Texts on Sociology and its Method* (Johanneshov, MTM).
Elickson, CR (2001) 'The Evolution of Social Norms: Perspectives from the Legal Academy' in M Hechter and KD Opp (eds), *Social Norms* (New York, Russell Sage Foundation).
Finlay, S (2019) 'Defining Normativity', preprint version of article published in D Plunkett et al, *Dimensions of Normativity: New Essays on Metaethics and Jurisprudence* (Oxford, Oxford University Press).
Friedman, LM and Ladinsky, J (1967) 'Social Change and the Law of Industrial Accidents' 67(1) *Columbia Law Review* 50.

---

[9] Aleksander Peczenik distinguishes between action norms and goal-oriented norms and uses the phrase 'regulatory norms' as a common term for these: see Peczenik (1987: 15); *cf* also Graver (1986).
[10] For an example of goal-oriented rules, see Hayek (1993: 138).

Graver, HP (1986) *Den juristskapte virkelighet* (Diss. Oslo, Univ).

Hayek, FA von (1993) *The Law of Legislation and Liberty. A New Statement of the Liberal Principles of Justice and Political Economy* (London, Routledge).

Himma, KE (2021) *Unpacking Normativity: Conceptual, Normative, and Descriptive Issues* (Oxford, Hart Publishing).

Horne, C (2001) 'Sociological Perspective on the Emergence of Social Norms' in M Hechter and KD Opp (eds), *Social Norms* (New York, Russell Sage Foundation).

Hydén, H (2002) *Rättssociologi som rättsvetenskap* (Lund, Studentlitteratur).

—— (2011) 'Looking at the World through the Lenses of Norms. Nine Reasons for Norms: A Plea for Norm Science' in K Papendorf, S Machura and K Andenaes (eds), *Understandig Law in Society. Developments in Socio-legal Studies* (Berlin, LIT Verlag).

—— (2022) *Sociology of Law as the Science of Norms* (New York, Routledge).

Hydén, H and Hydén, T (2019) *Rättsregler* (Legal Rules. An Introduction to the Legal System) (Lund, Studentlitteratur).

Hydén, H and Svensson, M (2008) 'The Concept of Norms in Sociology of Law' in *Scandinavian Studies in Law, Law and Society* vol 53 (Stockholm, Stockholm University Law Faculty).

Lloyd, D (1964) *The Idea of Law* (Harmondsworth, Penguin).

Luhmann, N (1995) *Social Systems* (Stanford, CA, Stanford University Press).

—— (2000) *Art as a Social System* (Stanford, CA, Stanford University Press).

—— (2012) *Theory of Society*, vol 1 (Stanford, CA, Stanford University Press).

—— (2013a) *Theory of Society*, vol 2 (Stanford, CA, Stanford University Press).

—— (2013b) *A Sociological Theory of Law* (Oxford, Routledge).

McHugh, C, Way, J and Whiting, D (eds) (2018) *Normativity: Epistemic and Practical*. (Oxford, Oxford University Press).

Mortensen, N (1990) 'Normer' in P Gundelach, N Mortensen amd JC Tonboe (eds), *Sociologi under forandring* (Köpenhamn, Nordisk förlag Gyldendal).

Peczenik, A (1987) *Rättsnormer* (Stockholm, Norstedt).

Rakoczy, H, Warneken, F and Tomasello, M (2008) 'The Sources of Normativity: Young Children's Awareness of the Normative Structure of Games' 44(3) *Developmental Psychology* 875.

Raz, J (1999) *Engaging Reason: On the Theory of Value and Action* (Oxford, Oxford University Press).

—— (2011) *From Normativity to Responsibility* (Oxford, Oxford University Press).

Ross, EA (2009) *Social Control: A Survey of the Foundations of Order* (New Brunswick, NJ, Transaction Publishers).

Rothstein, B (2010) *Vad bör staten göra?: om välfärdsstatens moraliska och politiska logik*, 3rd edn (Stockholm, SNS förlag).

Sherif, M (1936) *The Psychology of Social Norms* (New York, Harper & Brothers).

—— (1948) *An Outline of Social Psychology* (New York, Harper).

Star, D (ed) (2018) *The Oxford Handbook of Reasons and Normativity* (Oxford, Oxford University Press).

Swedish National Encyclopaedia, vol 11.

Thomson, JJ (2008) *Normativity* (Chicago, IL, Open Court).

Vivian, M (2020) 'Sociology of Law in Between Law's Autonomy and Justice Claims: Theoretical Contributions from Reza Banakar' (Master's Thesis, UPV/EHU & IISL, Oñati).

Wedgwood, R (2010) 'The Nature of Normativity: A Reply to Holton, Railton, and Lenman' 151 *Philosophical Studies* 479.

Wickenberg, P (1999) *Normstödjande strukturer. Miljötematiken börjar slå rot i skolan [Norm Supporting Structures: The Environmental Theme Begins to Take Root in Schools]*, (doctoral thesis) Lund Studies in Sociology of Law 5.

7

On the Relationship between Normative Pluralism and Justice after Multiculturalism

MARTIN RAMSTEDT

I. AN IMAGINARY CONVERSATION WITH REZA BANAKAR

W HEN I WAS invited to contribute a chapter to this volume honouring Reza Banakar, I started to reflect deeply on my relationship with an esteemed colleague I never had – now irrevocably so – the opportunity to meet in person. And yet, for a couple of years, Reza was supervisor for two doctoral candidates at the Department of Sociology of Law, Lund University, who had been my students at the Oñati International Institute for the Sociology of Law (IISL) several years back. Reza's passing brought me into close professional contact with both of them again.

In our recent conversations, I was privileged to learn more about their intellectual relationship with Reza. Their vivid narratives confirmed what Ole Hammerslev had indeed phrased so well in his obituary in the second RCSL Newsletter of 2020, namely that Reza saw sociology of law as a vocation, while having been far from mono-dimensional in his interests and knowledge. I of course knew about the wide spectrum of Reza's published scholarly expertise, ranging from Kafka's concept of law, Iranian driving cultures, ethnic discrimination in Sweden to socio-legal theorisation (Hammerslev 2020). However, through the much more intimate stories of his former mentees I have been able to almost visualise how he revealed to them, time and again, his intellectual vocation, by creatively and engagingly approaching each topic they discussed simultaneously from different theoretical, methodological, and empirical angles.

In the following, I will share some reflections that were as much stimulated by my reading of Reza's work as by my imagination of him as an interlocutor. I will zoom in on what struck me as a central point of Reza's thinking, that is, the increasing social dis-embedding of law under conditions of accelerated globalisation in late modernity, and the role sociology of law can play in attempts to re-embed law in society. This necessitates that we revisit Karl Polanyi's coinage of the term 'double movement' in his seminal book, *The Great Transformation*, which in the first decade of the present millennium was rediscovered primarily in the fields of economic sociology and economic anthropology (see, eg, Block 2008).[1] In relation to that, we will have to inquire into how the social dis-embedding of law impacted on social notions of justice. The question of what 'justice' actually means in the growing plurality of normative orders of today has in point of fact become ever more pressing. Seen from a different angle, we will also have to ask whether the increasing normative and legal pluralism of our time might actually have something to do with both the dis-embedding of law from collective notions of 'justice' and the attempts by social movements to re-embed law in the latter.

In the last three decades, major attempts of to re-embed law into societal notions of justice have consisted of public policies and governance reforms promoting cultural citizenship in connection with liberal multiculturalism and decentralisation. However, many cases, in which religious, ethnic, customary, indigenous, and/or subcultural norms and institutions were accommodated in national law, have roused vocal criticisms by scholars from various disciplines as well all as by stakeholders from all over the political spectrum, to the extent that multiculturalism has been judged a failure, at least in Europe. We are therefore left with the questions, how to conceive of the relation between normative pluralism and 'justice' after multiculturalism?

Before we begin our explorations, let me just state that my reflections are offered in a conversational style, which is appropriate to the nature of this anthology, I believe. They have, moreover, remained somewhat open-ended, which is permissible, I hope, in view of the limited space allotted to me.

II. NORMATIVE PLURALISM, SOCIAL EMBEDDEDNESS, AND THE DOUBLE MOVEMENT OF LAW IN MODERNITY

It makes sense to enter into our conversation by establishing that Reza saw normative pluralism as an integral field of socio-legal research:

> [S]ociology of law studies informal (unofficial) forms of regulation, which can include informal mediation carried out by local communities, the codes of social responsibility which are developed and voluntarily applied by certain international corporations, the Mafia's internal rules, or networks of corruption in some societies. (Banakar 2019: 3)

Consequently, in his reflections on socio-legal methodology, he paid ample attention to a large range of official and unofficial legal forums, encompassing international institutions, such as the European Court of Human Rights or the International Criminal Court, national institutions, like the different levels of national law courts,

---

[1] Karl Polanyi's *The Great Transformation*, first published in 1944, is of course an important reference point for the social embeddedness concept and the social dis-embedding debate (Joerges and Falke 2011: 1). In this work, Polanyi traced 'the great transformation of European civilization from the preindustrial world to the era of industrialization, and the shifts in ideas, ideologies, and social and economic policies accompanying it' (Stiglitz 2001: vii). American economic and political sociologist Fred L. Block incidentally suggested that Polanyi might have encountered the term 'embeddedness' during his research of English economic history in the context of coal mining, subsequently using it as a metaphor in his socioeconomic analysis (Block 2001: xxiv).

religious conflict resolution forums, like Shariah Tribunals or Rabbinical Courts, as well as other communal institutions of conflict management and alternative dispute resolution. Never omitting an actor perspective from his deep analyses, Reza was equally concerned with a whole spectrum of official and unofficial legal specialists. Along with the conventional legal professionals, he included into his consideration ombudsmen, mediators, qadis, and so forth (Banakar and Travers 2005: ix). Reza was of course also well aware of the fact that different normative, or legal orders frequently overlap, which means that one and the same action or case can fall under different official and unofficial jurisdictions, as it were (Banakar 2001: 5–6, 23).

A brief reflection is in order here on what distinguishes official from unofficial law, or normative orders from legal ones. For my article, titled 'Anthropological Perspectives on the Normative and Institutional Recognition of Religion by the Law of the State', published in 2016, I was rereading Brian Z Tamanaha's famous article on 'The Folly of the "Social Scientific" Concept of Legal Pluralism' from 1993. In this article, Tamanaha had rejected the concept of legal pluralism, since its proponents had not been able to agree on a common definition of 'law'. 'Law', Tamanaha had insisted, 'is best seen not as a mechanism for maintaining societal normative order, but as an instrument of power in society, available primarily for the elites' (Tamanaha 1993: 211).

Non-state normative orders are of course also always embedded in concrete power constellations. However, Tamanaha had a point, in that modern elite-driven state bureaucracies have developed increasingly efficient bureaucratic, military, financial, and social psychological technologies (both analogue and digital ones) of control over their subjects that had been unattainable for elites in premodern societies. Modern state law is therefore unique in its being embedded in a completely unprecedented, highly functional system of power. I hence find it useful to conceptually reserve 'law' for those normative orders (including international soft law, like the Declaration of the Principles on Tolerance approved by the member states of UNESCO in 1995, for instance, or the UN Global Compact,[2] supported by 162 states and a host or transnational corporations) which are recognised by a certain modern state or a certain group of modern states. Non-state normative orders, like non-juridified customary, indigenous, Hindu, Jewish, or Islamic law, as well as modern, yet unjuridified forms of alternative dispute resolution, like contemporary neighbourhood mediation, etc, I simply call 'normative orders' (Ramstedt 2016: 53).

I regard the distinction between 'law' and 'normative orders' as methodologically salient for comparative projects. The late Franz von Benda-Beckmann in fact regarded comparison as a major driving force for the deployment of 'law' in a sociological sense. He used the term as a kind of Weberian ideal-type, in order to discover 'similarity and difference in cross-societal and diachronic comparison' (Benda-Beckmann 2002: 40; see also ibid: 42–45). In the absence of a well-developed methodology accompanying von Benda-Beckmann's argument, and in an effort to accommodate both Tamanaha's and von Benda-Beckmann's points, I define 'normative orders' as the broader, more general polythetic class, and 'law' as one of its sub-classes.

---

[2] See, eg, https://www.unglobalcompact.org/.

Moored in Ludwig Wittgenstein's thoughts on 'family resemblance', a polythetic class is characterised by a distinct list of empirically verifiable properties that is actualised to a larger and lesser degree in concrete historical instantiations. Polythetic classes thus provide a valid foundation for comparative analysis (Needham 1975). Of course, one would first have to develop a list of empirically verifiable properties for 'normative orders', or 'law', if space permitted. Suffice it here to underscore von Benda-Beckmann's recommendation to take into account the institutionalisation of norms and procedures as well as the differentiation of expert knowledge from everyday knowledge (Benda-Beckmann 2002: 49–50).

In analogy to my distinction between law and normative orders, I also discriminate between normative and legal pluralism. 'Legal pluralism', in my nomenclature, implies the interplay of a number of normative orders, which are all recognised by a state or group of states, while 'normative pluralism' refers to the interplay of different normative orders, which are not recognised, or not all recognised, by a certain state or group of states (Ramstedt 2016: 53–54).

The frequent overlap of different official as well as unofficial jurisdictions weakens not just legal certainty. The interplay between normative orders of course unfolds with all the implications that Sally Falk Moore unpacked in her classic article on 'Law and Social Change: The Semi-Autonomous Social Field as an Appropriate Subject of Study' from 1972, particularly that rules generated in unofficial jurisdictions could interfere with legal norms issued by the state in such a way that actors might not comply with the latter because of their compliance with the former (Moore 1972: 721).

The multifaceted impact of unofficial normative regimes on people's behaviour and attitudes towards law arguably contributes to what Reza called 'the gap problem', that is, the experiential distinction between the normative and the factual dimension of law (Banakar 2019: 15; 2001: 9–11). The influence of normative pluralism with regard to this problem warrants much more research though. A good window into the range of issues likely to be involved here, to my mind, is Abubakar Samaila's study of informal cross-border trade in Nigeria and the Niger border areas from 2011, which does resonate with Falk Moore's research of the unofficial rules governing the garment industry in the New York of the 1960s. Samaila's study suggests that informal trade in West Africa can be seen 'as a form of indigenous resistance to the imposition of colonial borders and metropolitan economic regulations on traditional African economic social formations' (Samaila 2011: 187).

In other words, colonial and postcolonial metropolitan legal regulations for trade in West Africa have dis-embedded the governance of economic activities from local society, by declaring previous regimes of doing business illegal (see also Banakar 2015: 10; Banakar 2016: 48). Among the wider West African population, resistance against these new regulations 'from above' retained legitimacy over time, because it aligned with socially embedded notions of order and justice. This ties in with yet another 'gap problem', which Reza described as the growing 'separation of positive law, rights, morality and justice' since early modernity (Banakar 2010: 1; 2015: 11–12; see also Banakar 2010: 36; 2009: 87). His description, incidentally, resonates strongly with what Indian-American anthropologist Arjun Appadurai called 'disjunctures between economy, culture, and politics' that have increased under the conditions of accelerating globalisation (Appadurai 2009: 31).

These disjunctures, caused by ever quickening multi-faceted processes of dis-embedding, seem to have fuelled the proliferation of contesting normative positions throughout modernity, by posing constant challenges and overlays of earlier normative regimes with new ones. In this way, the gap between the normative and the factual dimension of law has been enhanced and the separation between law, morality and justice increased. At the same time, normative and even legal certainty has decreased. In fact, the very foundations of society have de-solidified. Whereas premodern social embeddedness of law can be equated, according to Reza, with 'permanence and stability', the dis-embedding and displacement of law in late modernity comes with constant socio-cultural change and an ensuing liquefaction of social structure (Banakar 2015: 15–17, 259–81; 2016: 59–60). Associated with this is a growing 'moral contingency of social action' (Banakar 2015: 272), or, in Émile Durkheim's parlance, a waxing danger of '*anomie*'.

In his famous book, *De la Division du Travail Social*, Durkheim introduced *anomie* as a consequence of 'transitional difficulties' in relation to the rapid modernisation of economic life (Coser 1984: xxii, xxx–xxxii), involving the development of a new, no longer mechanical but intrinsically industrial division of labour, devoid of bonds of solidarity (Durkheim 1984: 304, 309). Anomie here means an unrestricted play of individual and/or collective interests, a kind of normlessness that leaves the interaction between the social classes unregulated, to the extent that no provisions are put in place for any kind of solidarity to ensue (Coser 1984: xx; see also Picciotto 2011: 158–59, 171). Individual and collective states of anomie are furthermore marked by a pervasive suffering for having to live without cohesion and regularity, and hence without any meaningful order and purpose in life (Coser 1984: xxiii, xxxv; Kreide 2011: 44).

That being said, Reza insisted that the dis-embedding or displacement of modern law from society, or from collective notions of justice, has never been absolute, as 'empirically, people's experience of law and legality remains in various ways linked to justice' (Banakar 2015: 6). This, for my part, needs further elucidation, which Reza did not sufficiently provide. However, in my own thinking, the empirical truth of his observation can be attributed to the achievements of different historical social movements in terms of getting their claims to 'justice' accommodated in new legislation and law reforms. And here we encounter what has been portrayed as the so-called 'double movement' of law (see, eg, Kreide 2011).

This brings us back to Karl Polanyi's influential study of *The Great Transformation: The Political and Economic Origins of Our Time*. In this book, he developed the idea of the double movement in relation to the concept of social embeddedness (see also Banakar 2015: 278). According to Polanyi, the great transformation of European societies in the course of industrialisation in the nineteenth and early twentieth centuries was characterised by a double movement of the economy, consisting, on the one hand, of a dis-embedding, 'extension', or 'expansion' of the market, and, on the other, of measures and policies for its re-embedding, that is, its 'restriction', or at least 'checked expansion' (Polanyi 2001: 79, 136; see also ibid: 223). While Polanyi did not expressly mention the role of law in the double movement, he did refer to 'a network of measures and policies' that sought to re-embed the economy into European societies through 'powerful institutions designed to check the action of the market relative to labor, land, and money' (ibid: 79).

In the recent revival of Polanyi's seminal study, economic sociologists outlined in greater detail the legal and regulatory developments contributing to the double movement as described by Polanyi (Joerges and Falke 2011: 5–15; see also Banakar 2015: 278). In her pertinent article on 'Re-embedding the Market through Law? The Ambivalence of Juridification in the International Context' from 2011, Regina Kreide, for example, argued that the transnational law which governs the current global market, consists, on the one hand, of juridification processes commonly experienced as 'unjust' and therefore regarded as lacking legitimacy, and, on the other, of juridification intended to rein in 'unhampered growth of transnational administrative and executive power' (Kreide 2011: 42). The latter, according to Kreide, has the potential to tame dysfunctionalities of the market and to re-embed both the market and the law into legitimate political decision-making (ibid: 63; see also Joerges and Falke 2011: 5).

Apart from juridification geared to the re-embedding of the market and its regulation into fair and just democratic political decision-making, there have been juridifcation efforts also in other fields of governance (marriage, pregnancy, gender and gender relations, religion and religious education, ethnic minorities, communal land ownership, stewardship of natural resources, and so forth) that have sought to socially re-embed the regulation of these fields (see also Banakar 2009: 88–89). These efforts have usually been supported by social movements drawing on various 'rights discourses' (human rights in general, gay rights, indigenous rights, etc). Their increasing success drives home the fact that law production can be, and often is, a consequence of successful bottom-up legal advocacy.

That said, social movements have often brought about new regulations and public policies that have carried their own structural injustice, while at the same time intensifying the legal pluralism of our time. In the next paragraph, I will focus on two related cases revolving around the promotion of cultural citizenship at large: (1) liberal multiculturalism as public policy, striving to reconcile justice and diversity; and (2) increasing juridification of indigenous/customary law, seeking to right colonial and neo-colonial wrongs.

III. DISCONTENTS OF CULTURAL CITIZENSHIP

Instead of providing a detailed discussion of liberal multiculturalism as public policy, permit me to just mention that at the end of 1995 – a few months after the Srebrenica massacre and the rape of thousands of Bosniak Muslim adults and children, in the midst of the genocide in Rwanda, and against the alarming backdrop of a general 'rise in acts of intolerance, violence, terrorism, xenophobia, aggressive nationalism, racism, anti-Semitism, exclusion, marginalisation and discrimination directed against national, ethnic, religious and linguistic minorities, refugees, migrant workers immigrants and vulnerable groups within societies' all around the world (*DoPoT* 1995: 9), the General Conference of UNESCO at its 28th session in Paris proclaimed 'tolerance' as 'the responsibility that upholds human rights, pluralism (including cultural pluralism), democracy and the rule of law' (ibid: 10). Further defined as 'harmony in difference', as 'respect and appreciation of the rich diversity of our world's culture', tolerance was pronounced to be not only a moral duty, but at the same time a political and legal requirement (ibid: 9). Member states of UNESCO were consequentially exhorted to implement impartial legislation and law enforcement, in order to prevent exclusion and marginalisation of vulnerable groups and to enable respect for 'the multicultural character of the human family' (ibid: 10).

Multiculturalism as state policy, however, came under severe attack only a few years later, most of all in Europe, where it had always remained strongly contested even in erstwhile colonising countries, such as Britain, France, or the Netherlands (Chin 2017: 3, 12–18). A major point of criticism was that multiculturalism was not leading to greater social harmony and integration, but to a proliferation of proclaimed primordial identities, and thus to an increase of potentially conflictive identity politics (see also Banakar 2010: 15). Even Canadian philosopher Will Kymlicka, a leading thinker on cultural citizenship, finally conceded that the emancipatory impulse of liberal multiculturalism 'is being subverted by the "essentialist" way that cultures or identities are understood' (Kymlicka 2015: 219; see also Paquet 2005: 223).

Member of the British Socialist Workers Party (SWP) Kenan Malik had already much earlier argued that the multicultural policies of the UK government were not responding to the needs of the Afro-Caribbean, the Bangladeshi, the Pakistani, the Malayan, the Chinese, or the Hindu communities, etc. Instead, these policies would impose state-defined stereotyped collective identities on people (see also Banakar 2015: 133–37). The official assignment of monolithic or blanket ethnic identities would, moreover, ignore the internal conflicts of these supposedly homogeneous communities around gender, class and intra-religious differences, because authority and responsibility were delegated to so-called community leaders who were owning their status mainly to state policies rather than to a well-earned esteem within their own communities (Chin 2017: 265–80).

Moreover, as also Reza rightly argued, liberal multiculturalism had gone awry in its assumption that everything is culturally determined (see also Banakar 2015: 155). While liberal multiculturalism has meanwhile commonly come to be considered a failure in Europe and the UK,[3] if not necessarily in all Anglophone countries, the movement towards juridification of indigenous, or customary law both in classical settler countries and in countries of the Global South, which has been particularly successful since the end of the Cold War, does not seem to have lost momentum.

In the Global South, legal accommodation of ethnic norms and institutions has been facilitated by the fact that the Breton Woods institutions had turned away from centralism and legal unification by the end of the Cold War. This change of policy had been prompted and partly prepared by widespread democratisation movements in the non-Western world since the mid-1980s (Eaton et al 2011: xiii–xvii). Governance reforms, involving decentralisation and an ensuing diversification of power, have in turn encouraged social movements advocating the juridification of indigenous, or customary law (Davidheiser 2007). However, while decentralisation schemes have usually been geared towards democratisation and sustainable local development, the successful emancipation, and occasionally privileging of a range of 'marginalised' ethnic cultures and cosmologies across the Global South has sometimes posed serious challenges to the original objectives of decentralisation (Ribot et al 2008: 3).

---

[3] See, eg, Banakar 2010: 24; Chin 2017: 1, 237–38, 281–92, 304.

The juridification of Hindu-Balinese customary law in the Province of Bali, for instance, which has progressed in stages since the beginning of Indonesia's decentralisation process at the turn of the new millennium, has seriously disadvantaged a range of minority groups on the island, particularly migrant Javanese Muslims, Balinese women, and Balinese adherents of heterodox Hindu sects. Comparable negative effects of the revitalisation and juridification of local customary law on national migrants and/or vulnerable in-group minorities have been reported from other Indonesian provinces, such as West Sumatra, Central and South Sulawesi, West and Central Kalimantan, Lombok and the Moluccas (Ramstedt 2019: 323–25). Human rights infringements have also been observed in indigenous communities throughout the Pacific region, particularly infringements of gender equality and women's rights. It is noteworthy that neither in the Indonesian, nor in the Pacific cases have state courts considered it their duty to end the discriminatory practices, or to provide correctives (see also Zorn 2010: 126–37), which points to a gap between indigenous and state jurisdictions.

IV. IN QUEST OF JUSTICE IN PLURAL NORMATIVE ORDERS

The question that arises is, how can 'justice' be reconceptualised in plural normative orders? One pertinent answer was provided by Ayelet Shachar, former Canada Research Chair in Citizenship and Multiculturalism at Toronto University and current Director of the Ethics, Law, and Politics Department at the Max Planck Institute for the Study of Religious and Ethnic Diversity in Göttingen, in her book on *Multicultural Jurisdictions – Cultural Differences and Women's Rights* from 2001. In this book, she proposed 'transformative accommodation' as a mode of multicultural governance that does not allow any group or community within a given society sole authority over a whole social field (education, family law, urban planning, or environmental protection, etc). Each social field is therefore broken down into sub-fields Shachar called 'sub-matters', which are then allocated under different jurisdictions. In this way, every group has to constantly accommodate 'alien' normative positions at least to a certain degree, which again promises to continuously transform the cultures of all groups involved in the decision-making (Shachar 2001: 117–42). In this model, 'justice' is likely to be a constantly renegotiated and renegotiable benchmark for the heterogeneous people involved in the decision-making process.

In 2005, the late Gilles Paquet, Professor emeritus at the School of Management and Senior Research Fellow at the Centre on Governance at Ottawa University, offered an approach called 'cultural democracy', which he defined as a kind of ecology of governance involving the loose integration of 'uncentralized networks' of people. Since each of these networks would govern a certain issue-domain (Paquet 2005: 227), 'justice' would have to be seen as issue-related, that is, as an understanding shared by those jointly holding authority over a certain issue-domain.

Both Paquet's and Shachar's responses mesh with Reza's observation that there is no monolithic truth of law – or justice – separate from stakeholders' individual and hence divergent experience of it (Banakar 2000: 273–74). 'Justice', therefore, cannot be an absolute category. As an actor-oriented concept, it can only refer to a quality of experience people make in concrete social relations, which themselves are always configured by multiple normative orders.

From this, it follows that we need to pay close attention to the experiences of all stakeholders involved in a situation under investigation. Since experiences always arise in concrete socio-political contexts, we need to thickly describe these contexts, and those beyond, in our research. As teachers of law and society we need to be aware that we require a multi-layered and multifaceted contextualisation of law that transcends the mere understanding of law as a body of rules and doctrine and reveals law's embeddedness in multiple societal relations and structures (Banakar 2009: 69, 73).

REFERENCES

Appadurai, A (2009) 'Disjuncture and Difference in the Global Cultural Economy' in JE Braziel and A Mannur (eds), *Theorizing Diaspora* (Malden, Blackwell) 25.

Banakar, R (2000) 'Reflections on the Methodological Issues of the Sociology of Law' 27(2) *Journal of Law and Society* 273.

—— (2001) 'Integrating Reciprocal Perspectives: On Georges Gurvitch's Theory of Immediate Jural Experience' 16(1) *Canadian Journal of Law and Society/ Revue Canadienne de Droit et Société*.

—— (2009) 'Power, Culture and Method in Comparative Law' 5(1) *International Journal of Law in Context* 69.

—— (2010) 'Introduction: Snapshots of the Rights Discourse' in R Banakar (ed), *Rights in Context: Law and Justice in Late Modern Society* (Farnham, Ashgate).

—— (2015) *Normativity in Legal Sociology: Methodological Reflections on Law and Regulation in Late Modernity* (Cham et al, Springer).

—— (2016) 'Law, Policy and Social Control Amidst Flux' in K Dahlstrand (ed), *Festskrift till Karsten Åström* (Lund, Juristförlaget) 47.

—— (2019) 'On Socio-Legal Design' (Lund, Lund University).

Banakar, R and Travers, M (2005) 'Introduction' in R Banakar and M Travers (eds), *Theory and Method in Socio-Legal Research* (Oxford, Hart Publishing) ix.

Benda-Beckmann, F von (2002) 'Who's Afraid of Legal Pluralism?' 47 *Journal of Legal Pluralism* 37.

Block, FL (2001) 'Introduction'in K Polanyi, *The Great Transformation: The Political and Economic Origins of Our Time* (Boston, Beacon Press) xviii.

—— (2008) 'Polanyi's Double Movement and the Reconstruction of Critical Theory' 38 *Revue Interventions Économique / Papers in Political Economy* 1.

Chin, R (2017) *The Crisis of Multiculturalism in Europe* (Princeton, Princeton University Press).

Coser, L (1984) 'Introduction' in É Durkheim, *The Division of Labour in Society* (Basingstoke, Macmillan) ix.

Davidheiser, M (2007) 'Governance and Legal Reform in Gambia and Beyond: An Anthropological Critique of Current Development Strategies' Halle: Max Planck Institute for Social Anthropology Working Papers (Working Paper No 93).

(*DoPoT*) *Declaration of Principles on Tolerance* (1995) (Paris, UNESCO).

Durkheim, É (1984) *The Division of Labour in Society* (Basingstoke, Macmillan).

Eaton, K, Kaiser, K and Smoke, PJ (2011) *The Political Economy of Decentralization Reforms: Implications for Aid Effectiveness* (Washington, DC, World Bank).

Hammerslev, O (2020) 'In Memoriam: Reza Banakar (1959–2020)' 2 *RCSL Newsletter* 7.

Joerges, C and Falke, J (2011) 'The Social Embeddedness of Transnational Markets: Introducing and Structuring the Project' in C Joerges and J Falke (eds), *Karl Polanyi, Globalization and the Potential of Law in Transnational Markets* (Oxford, Hart Publishing) 1.

Kreide, R (2011) 'Re-embedding the Market through Law? The Ambivalence of Juridification in the International Context' in C Joerges and J Falke (eds), *Karl Polanyi, Globalization and the Potential of Law in Transnational Markets* (Oxford, Hart Publishing) 41.

Kymlicka, W (2015) 'The Essentialist Critique of Multiculturalism: Theories, Policies, Ethos' in V Oberoi and T Modood (eds), *Multiculturalism Rethought: Interpretations, Dilemmas and New Directions* (Edinburgh, Edinburgh University Press) 209.

Moore, SF (1972) 'Law and Social Change: The Semi-Autonomous Social Field as an Appropriate Subject of Study' 7 *Law and Society Review* 719.

Needham, R (1975) 'Polythetic Classification: Convergence and Consequences' 10(3) *Man* 349.

Paquet, G (2005) 'Governance of Culture: Words of Caution' in C Andrew, M Gattinger, MS Jeannotte and W Straw (eds), *Accounting for Culture: Thinking Through Cultural Citzenship* (Ottawa, University of Ottawa Press) 221.

Picciotto, S (2011) 'Dis-embedding and Regulation: The Paradox of International Finance' in C Joerges and J Falke (eds), *Karl Polanyi, Globalization and the Potential of Law in Transnational Markets* (Oxford, Hart Publishing) 157.

Polanyi, K (2001) *The Great Transformation: The Political and Economic Origins of Our Time* (Boston, Beacon Press).

Ramstedt, M (2016) 'Anthropological Perspectives on the Normative and Institutional Recognition of Religion by the Law of the State' in R Bottoni, R Cristoforti and S Ferrari (eds), *Religious Rules, State Law, and Normative Pluralism – A Comparative Overview* (Winterthur, Springer) 45.

—— (2019) 'Prospects of Pluralism in Indonesia Gauged from a Legal Anthropological Perspective' 47(3) *Asian Journal of Social Science* 309.

Ribot, JC, Chhatre, A and Lankina, T (2008) 'Introduction: Institutional Choice and Recognition in the Formation and Consolidation of Local Democracy' 6(1) *Conversation and Society* 1.

Samaila, A (2011) 'Exchange and Marketing Across Borders: A Study of Informal Cross-Border Trade in Nigeria-Niger Border Areas, 1960–1999' 20 *Journal of the Historical Society of Nigeria* 183.

Shachar, A (2001) *Multicultural Jurisdictions: Cultural Differences and Women's Rights.* (Cambridge, Cambridge University Press).

Stiglitz, JE (2001) 'Foreword' in K Polanyi, *The Great Transformation: The Political and Economic Origins of Our Time* (Boston, Beacon Press) vii.

Tamanaha, BZ (1993) 'The Folly of the "Social Scientific" Concept of Legal Pluralism' 20(2) *Journal of Law and Society* 192.

Zorn, JG (2010) 'Issues in Contemporary Law: Women and the Law' in A Jowitt and T Newton Cain (eds), *Passage of Change: Law, Society and Governance in the Pacific* (Canberra, Pandanus Books) 125.

8

Legal Pluralism and the Army: Legal Sociology as Military Sociology

CHRIS THORNHILL

I. INTRODUCTION

T HIS CHAPTER HAS three primary purposes.[1] First, it aims to modify debates about legal pluralism by assessing pluralist legal analyses as broad structural accounts of social formation. It defines such pluralist theory, quite generally, as a body of outlooks, beginning in the nineteenth century but still articulated today, which construct law in society as complex, concurrent sets of rules and expectations, emanating from multiple sources and determining different spheres of action, often possessing deep-lying and informal historical origins, and not reducible to official legal codes or statutes. Today, pluralist theories of law identify pluralism in a wide range of normative arenas – from transnational patterns of norm construction, to global soft law, to professional and associational self-regulatory codes, to the local recesses of national societies.[2] However, pluralist theories originally gained purchase as accounts of legal validity that challenged the monopolistic claims in formal processes of legal codification, ordained by emerging national states. In many respects, from the outset, theories of legal pluralism formed the critical shadow of modern law. They expressed marginal commentaries on the defining trajectories of legal formation from the French revolution through to the period of high positivism, drawing attention to the informal and historical meanings of law not defined by central dictates of legislators. As a result, legal pluralism is understood here, in origin, as a doctrine that claims that the formal organisation of the law may often eradicate vital associational freedoms from the law, law's authority may reside in social contexts wholly separate from institutions vested with legislative power, and modern formal accounts of the law generally attach legal validity to falsely abstracted normative assumptions. This outlook still remains fundamental to theories of pluralism.

---

[1] My thanks are due to Atina Krajewska for discussions before and during the writing of this chapter. She also wishes to register her appreciation of Reza Banakar for his work and influence in the field of legal sociology.
[2] See for key positions Sciulli (1986); Teubner (1997); Galanter (1981); Ellickson (1986).

The underlying claim in the chapter is that theoretical analysis examining the coexistence of plural legal orders in society can be seen, frequently, as a reconstruction of social contexts created by warfare. Accordingly, this chapter outlines an interpretation of theories of legal pluralism that examines such theories as variants on *military sociology*. It explains that, in some respects, the military is a constantly present, although only partly visible, focus of agency in accounts of legal pluralism. It is often argued that the military dimension of society is neglected in sociology.[3] However, it is argued here that, in its origins, legal sociology as a whole was, at one remove, profoundly concerned with legal phenomena related to military aspects of social interaction.

On this basis, second, this chapter argues that, if reconstructed in this way, theories of legal pluralism possess a much broader validity than is usually assumed. Such theories do not merely describe legal conditions in discrete parts of some societies, in particular in societies with experiences of colonial rule. If interpreted in correlation with military sociology, they unearth deep causalities at the core of modern society, and they contain a comprehensive analysis of material social structure. Third, reflecting this thematic focus, this chapter seeks to add a new element to methodological analysis of legal pluralism. It concludes by indicating how analysis of the relation between legal pluralism and war entails a confluence between pluralist theories and social conflict theories, which are usually positioned in distinct theoretical camps.[4]

On each point, this chapter illustrates its claims by returning to the regions in which sociological accounts of legal pluralism were first pioneered – that is, to parts of Central Europe subject to early colonialism, and especially to the Polish-speaking areas of Central Europe. These regions provided decisive original impetus for the formation of sociology as an academic discipline, and the observation of social interaction in these areas shaped both early theories of legal pluralism and early theories of social conflict.[5] In examining these environments, this chapter explores the dialectical linkages between Imperialism, military conflict and the persistence of pluralistic elements within the law.

II. VIOLENCE AND PLURALISM

Theories of legal pluralism are constitutively related to social environments defined by Imperialism. Theories of this kind evolved through observation of law at the boundaries of Empire, and they question the validity of laws imposed through administrative organs enacting Imperial authority. The sense that authentic law is found in the fringes of Empires was first fully articulated by Eugen Ehrlich, whose *Fundamental*

---

[3] For claims to this effect see Joas and Knöbl (2008); Kruse (2009: 198).

[4] See, eg, Max Weber's hostility to pluralist analysis in his positivist account of the state as an *anstaltsmäßiger Herrschaftsverband* (1921/22: 821).

[5] Several vital works in the canon of early sociology reflect on legal-political conditions in these regions. Eugen Ehrlich's work (1913) is the key example. But Max Weber's inaugural lecture of 1895 is focused on this region (1988). Ludwik Gumplowicz's work on racial conflict (1883) is a product of such observation. Analysis of this region in fact gave rise to a distinct sociological tradition – the 'Austrian conflict tradition' (Malešević 2010: 36). On the position of Gumplowicz as part of a hidden 'military tradition in sociology' see Joas (2000: 214).

Principles of the Sociology of Law (1913) addressed legal realities in regions bearing the varied imprints of the Russian, the Ottoman and the Austro-Hungarian Empires. Before Ehrlich, however, the first building blocks of pluralist legal inquiry had been put in place by jurists who were deeply concerned with relations between law and Empire. Close to the beginnings of this tradition, Savigny proposed a historicist account of legal obligation that was born of hostility to the systematised legal codes (based in Roman law) that followed Napoleon across Europe (Savigny 1840). Later, German organic theorists of legal obligation opted for a pluralist construction of law's formation. Their work was shadowed by the consolidation of continental Empires in Europe, a process strongly underpinned by positivist ideals derived from Roman law. Such theorists were deeply hostile to Roman law, which they observed as inimical to the organic legal traditions of Central Europe.[6] Today, the primary focus of pluralistic descriptions of the law falls on legal orders in regions historically subject to colonial administration.[7] In different contexts, diverse analyses of legal pluralism converge around the claim that legal formalisation goes hand in hand with Imperialism and that formal law has a colonising function. Thus, plural legal forms describe obligations between persons in spaces where colonial authority has not penetrated, and legal subjects recognise such forms as familiar descriptions of their personhood.

For related reasons, it is constitutive of pluralistic legal theory that it queries the legitimacy of formal constitutional law. In early pluralistic analysis, description of informal legal variations in society formed part of a critique of constitutional ideals, growing in force after 1848, based in rational or positivist concepts of public law. Such analysis argued that the formation of political institutions reflecting positivist or state-centred constructions of constitutional law, usually rooted in Roman law, created insubstantial systems of government, with flimsy claims to legal validity and personal obligation. Governments premised in formal constitutions, on this account, reflected a sociological misconstruction of the origins of valid law, and they expressed their authority – as a result – in a form that was *inherently subjugating*. Proponents of organic theory were unsparing in their hostility to what they perceived as the reductivism inherent in positivist models of constitutional law.[8] Among others, Otto von Gierke used the vocabulary of Empire to explain that modern constitutions, rooted in the Roman-law ideals of positivism, attach authority to public institutions in simplified fashion, detaching political power from the multiple foundations in society that

---

[6] Most notably, Otto von Gierke argued that Roman law relies on metaphysical 'abstraction', which fatally reduces the complexities of legal status, entitlement and formation (ie citizenship) (1868: 801).

[7] See, eg, Sánchez Botero (2001: 186); Bello (2004: 15).

[8] For instance, this view can be observed in Georg Beseler's argument that the constitutional personality of the state must draw legal substance from the 'associational spirit' of a real political community. Only on this basis can the state acquire true authority, as the living unity of many wills (1847: 353–54). This view was also expressed in Albert Hänel's claim that the legitimate state is founded in 'corporate association', which constantly regenerates its constitution (1892: 106–107). This approach was fleshed out in Otto von Gierke's proto-sociological analysis of constitutional law. For Gierke, legitimate public authority must obtain a legal-constitutional personality by integrating all associations of society and by reflecting the legal agreements between these associations as consolidated elements of its internal structure. In so doing, the state assumes the character of a 'living total personality', constituted by a plurality of consensual wills and consensual laws (1873: 886).

it presupposes for its formation and legitimacy. He argued that modern state constitutions merely cement the legal personality of the state in a form abstracted against society, as a 'will without relations', with little regard for the actual processes of legal interaction in which social agents bring validity to law. Such constitutions, he indicated, could never acquire true legitimacy, and genuine recognition for constitutional law could only flow from a plural opening of law to different associations in society (Gierke 1873: 37). Implicitly, this admonitory position was intended to guide the process of state and nation building in Germany away from mere Imperialism and towards a condition of political order based in full (pluralist) societal integration. This pluralist constitutional tendency culminated in Ehrlich's assertion that the 'state-centred conception of the law is not scientifically tenable. It is based in the fact that [...] we resolutely close our eyes in face of the volume of law which has developed independently of the state and exists in independence of the state' (Ehrlich 1913: 145).

In such outlooks, early theories of pluralism expressly bracketed constitutional law with Imperialism. Central to the early pluralist outlook was the view that constitutional law, observed as a codified legal order framing the power of the state and aiming to define the public-legal form of society in its entirety, was inseparable from practices of colonisation. This critique of constitutional law became fundamental to pluralist legal ideals in the late twentieth and early twenty-first centuries.[9] However, the origins of legal-pluralist thinking were marked by the conviction that positivist constructions of constitutional rule pressed social agents into coercive models of legal subjectivity and stabilised public order as an irreducibly heteronomous form. The basic assumption in classical constitutional law – namely, that constitutional governments are authorised by simple higher laws, and certain laws have primary authority for all parts and members of society – was reflected, implicitly, as an assumption that is essentially Imperialist.

In both respects, classical theories of legal pluralism circled, implicitly, around one primary implication. Expressly, such theories observed the dominant legal forms of modern society as the result of colonial annexation, and they gave voice to the suspicion that formal law and Imperialism were always thickly intertwined. Yet, at a deeper level, such theories implied that, either in Empires or in nations, formal law was structured in analogy to a military system, and formal laws had their origins in military designs. This view was established amongst positivist sociologists, who clearly observed the proximity between formal legal order and military administration (Weber 1921/22: 566). In parallel, however, pluralists described this condition from the other side of the law, measuring legal codification as a trajectory of territorial encroachment. Ehrlich argued that formal law could only presuppose obedience through society because, lastly, it was backed by institutions able to apply military force. He viewed the modern state, in its original and persistently manifest functional nucleus, as a military organisation, not categorically separate from a system of occupation.[10] The expansive administrative and constitutional machinery of

---

[9] For example, the Bolivian constitution of 2009 is explicitly conceived as a post-colonial constitution.

[10] Ehrlich explained that the modern state can be traced directly to modes of military leadership that took form amongst the 'military aristocracy' of medieval Europe, and the 'military interests' that brought the state into being remained present 'at each stage in its development' (1913: 125).

modern government, thus, had grown from military imperatives.[11] In these respects, the original perceptions at the centre of legal pluralism fused legal sociology and military sociology, and they presented paradigms for interpreting the impact of military processes both on legal organisation and on social structure more broadly. In its origins, analysis of legal pluralism always refracted, at least obliquely, a sociology of military force, and the description of law's plurality always contained, in inverse focus, a description of how law refracted integration processes propelled by war. In these respects, theories of legal pluralism mark out vitally important ground, not only in for the sociology of law, but also in military sociology, which is rarely attentive to the ways in which war impacts on law.[12]

III. WAR, LEGAL CODIFICATION AND CONSTITUTIONAL CITIZENSHIP

Reconstructed in this way, theories of legal pluralism intimate a founding association between law and military organisation. As such, these theories contain a deep legal archaeology of modern society, which is just as valuable for what it tells us about the social foundations of formal law as for the material description of law's plurality that it contains.

On one hand, in the positing of a general link between legal formalisation and military order, theories of legal pluralism touch on a genetic element of formal law. In non-European societies, formal legal systems were typically imposed by organisations and institutions forming parts of a military occupation regime (see Harvey 1962: 584). At an earlier historical juncture, however, processes of legal codification in Europe began in the army, and military law formed a template for formal law more widely. At a deep structural level, the first establishment of modern state-like institutions revolved around the codification of military law, in which regents clarified their responsibilities for military administration and exercised control of military organisations. The precondition for the formation of modern states was that procedures relating to military rank, recruitment, payment, and discipline were subject to a formal legal order, and crucial functions of military supply were subject to regal direction and legal control. Such military codification began as early as 1570 in the Holy Roman Empire, when a uniform military code was drafted in peacetime.[13] Codification of military law then became widespread by the early eighteenth century. Such codification was promoted to allow regents to manage recruitment and discipline of soldiers, and, in so doing, to weaken the authority and constitutional leverage of private or familial institutions. This coincided with early patterns of Imperialism; indeed, military codes became common at the precise moment in military history in which long-term overseas deployment of national armed forces became the norm. The period around the Seven Years War (1756–1763) was a period of intense military

---

[11] See discussion of this in Rehbinder (2007: 281); Röhl and Machura (2013: 1119).

[12] Weber is an exception in this regard, as he showed acute awareness of the relation between war and the formation of legal systems. For key positions in recent military sociology that, for all their brilliance, show little regard for law, see Mann (1984); Warburg (2008); Kruse (2009).

[13] This Code, introduced in Speyer by Emperor Maximilian II, was designed to place military regulation on permanent general foundations.

codification. Importantly, those states that did not impose a formal legal order on their armies at this time were often vulnerable to Imperial annexation.[14] Codification in other spheres of law usually occurred at a slightly later stage, after states had established legal norms to control military organisation.

On the other hand, in associating constitutional law with colonialism and military processes more broadly, theories of pluralism bring to light one of the legal mainsprings of modern society. In this respect, theories of pluralism demand a reinterpretation of the basic sources of constitutional law. Constitutional law is typically viewed as a normative order that gives expression to the collective will of a society, and, as such, it is centred on ideas of citizenship that are oriented, at least in principle, towards patterns of social coexistence based in shared integration, personal autonomy and rational purposive agreement.[15] In the pluralist canon, however, constitutional law appears as inherently rooted in Imperialism and military violence, and the basic normative principles that stand at the heart of constitutional order are framed by invasive military pressures.

The correctness of this pluralist intuition can be illustrated through a brief reconstructive discussion of basic principles that define constitutional legitimacy. Central to modern constitutional law is the assumption that norms set out in constitutional texts draw validity and legitimacy from the construct of *the citizen*.[16] In modern constitutional law, the citizen is defined as a *sovereign subject*, and constitutional law produces normative support for legal-political order in society by claiming to derive higher authority for law directly from the will of citizens.[17] At the inception of modern constitutionalism, the construct of the sovereign citizen imprinted within the modern legal system a conception of law's collective origin, which enabled governmental organisations to impute supreme authority to certain laws, and to utilise such laws as premises for subsidiary law making. Through reference to the constitutionally implicated citizen, governments were able to occupy a central legislative position in society. Political leaders then typically acted on this premise to abrogate older, traditional or consuetudinal laws, to eliminate local-informal legal conventions, and generally to present their legal decisions as having primary obligatory force in society as a whole. For this reason, early constitutional government almost invariably entailed processes of legal codification, and states legitimated by constitutions

---

[14] Disorder in the army was rife in eighteenth-century Poland, and many attempts were made to restrict military ill-discipline. New military laws were introduced during the partition era, but this was too late to save the state. For comment see Organiściak (2002: 50); Szczygielski (2009: 65–66). Lack of effective military codification lay at the heart of long-term legal pluralism in Poland.

[15] In the classical formulation of Alexander Hamilton, constitutions appear as texts in which 'societies of men' establish the foundation of 'good government', using rational capacities of 'reflection and choice' (Madison, Hamilton and Jay 1987 [1787–88]: 88).

[16] See the following early declaration in the American Supreme Court: '*Citizenship*, which has arisen from the dissolution of the feudal system [...] is a substitute for allegiance, corresponding with the new order of things. Allegiance and citizenship differ, indeed, in almost every characteristic. Citizenship is the effect of compact; allegiance is the offspring of power and necessity. Citizenship is a political tie; allegiance is a territorial tenure. Citizenship is the charter of equality; allegiance is a badge of inferiority. Citizenship is constitutional; allegiance is personal. Citizenship is freedom': *Talbot v Janson* 3 US 133 (1795).

[17] At the origin of modern European constitutional law, Sieyès claimed that the nation (people) is 'the origin of everything [...] the law itself' (1789: 79).

used their constituted authority to impose heightened legal uniformity on their social environments.[18]

Many sociologists have noted the vital role of the concept of the citizen in the formation of modern society. Many sociologists have observed how primary integration processes, structural for modern society, hinge on constitutional definitions of citizenship (Dahrendorf 1965: 79; Parsons 1965). The significance of the figure of the citizen is also noted in the margins of legal pluralism. The descriptions of constitutional law in pluralist theory are transparent to the figure of the citizen, and, in this refraction, the citizen appears at the core of modern law. To early observers with a pluralist standpoint, however, modern constitutional law defined the citizen in spurious form, and the subjugating force of constitutional law was determined by the image of the citizen with which it was correlated. On this account, modern states explained their legitimacy in reference to a constitutional image of the citizen that was designed to simplify the use of governmental force and to accelerate procedures for legislation. To achieve this, the constitutional image of the citizen was deployed to limit the state's factual recognition of its subjects as objective legal persons.[19] In counterpoint, early pluralist theory in fact proposed a theory of organic citizenship, in which citizens acted in multiple legitimational roles and associations (Gierke 1881: 609).

Importantly, the first projection of the image of the citizen as a figure for distilling higher-order constitutional norms was linked to military pressures. Indeed, the integrational norm of citizenship acquired such broad purchase in emerging nation states because it formed a pivotal instrument for recruiting soldiers for modern national armies. Of course, most previous models of state building had been marked by constitutions designed to extract soldiers from society. Manifestly, citizenship had been linked to military recruitment in classical Empires. In high feudal Europe, privileges of citizenship had been strongly bound to military service and supply, such that the nobility, as the key provider of military force, obtained powerful constitutional leverage in the state. However, except in times of national emergency, the bearing of arms was usually a distinct mark of honour reserved for certain status groups. The military constitutional system created by feudalism depended on the fact that serfs remained tied to the land, and they only exceptionally performed military duties. From the late eighteenth century onwards, however, national polities began to align to a universal model of state building, in which constitutional rights were immediately tied to military participation, and, in principle, such rights were not restricted to defined social groups. In this process, the widening of constitutional rights for social actors (as *citoyens*) was only infrequently separate from the intensification of military burdens placed on these actors (as *soldats*). The constitutional revolutions beginning around 1775 were constitutional revolutions, citizenship revolutions and military revolutions at the same time, in which all groups were drawn close to the governmental apparatus through the allocation of constitutional rights and, simultaneously, the imposition of military duties.

---

[18] The 1790s in France saw the introduction of drafts for a civil code, a criminal code, an agrarian code and even for a code of interstate relations.

[19] See Ehrlich's analysis of the coercive function of constitutions (1913: 168).

By way of example, in revolutionary America, the establishment of a corpus of constitutional law to support emergent political institutions was shaped by the need to recruit citizens as soldiers, in wars of independence against Britain. At the dawn of the American Republic, the creation of constitutions that recognised citizens as actors implicated in government was flanked by laws attempting to enforce involuntary conscription, both in the individual states and, after 1789, in the Republic as a whole. In revolutionary Pennsylvania, in fact, early constitutional experiments were partly led by radical militias (see Rosswurm 1987: 66, 72). In revolutionary France, the advent of constitutional rule was inseparable from military functions. By 1793, the revolutionary government in France had introduced mandatory conscription for male citizens, and citizens acquired constitutional rights and were subject to military obligations as part of one simultaneous process of legal/political integration.[20] Citizens of the revolutionary polity in France became constituent actors within the legal-political system through a constitutional bargain, in which they acquired legal and political rights on terms that, as fair exchange, obliged them to perform military service. In both classical constitutional settings, the form of citizenship was born of war, and military strategies were primary determinants of constitutional norm formation. In both settings, constitutional law took shape through a process of legal codification, in which universal norms were applied across society that focused the obligations of social actors on formally defined state institutions, weakening the force of customary or local legal duties. In both cases, this constitutional construction of the state was promoted to facilitate the maximum mobilisation of military personnel. Systematic legal organisation through constitutional law, in other words, was intended to impose a shared military structure on society.

This classical nexus between citisenship, constitutional law and military recruitment was forged by conditions shaped by Imperialism. It has been noted in broad terms that early constitutional designs were shaped by the transformation of warfare connected to early Imperialism (Colley 2021: 25). This connection can be seen in the causes that gave rise to constitutions. In the British colonies in North America, for example, the rise of constitutionalism was directly stimulated by the intensification of Imperial rule after the end of the Seven Years War (1763). However, this connection can also be seen in the actions of states that had been placed on constitutional foundations. By 1795, revolutionary France was a clearly expansionist state, and, after 1799, it was progressively constituted as an Empire. In the USA, the formation of a constitutional order created the premises on which, after 1789, the national government embarked on a relentless process of territorial expansion, uninhibitedly adding and colonising new states and new regions to the existing geography of the Republic. Yet, the nexus between constitutionalism and Empire is more intricate and more profound than can be ascertained through accounts of military conflict and expansion. The essential principles of citizenship expressed in modern constitutionalism were first consolidated, not in acts of collective self-legislation, but in acts of colonisation, and early constitutionalism translated legal forms underlying Imperial orders into integrational norms of state legitimacy.

---

[20] See extensive analysis in Hippler (2006) and Crépin (2011).

Notably, before the national constitutional revolutions of the 1780s and 1790s, principles of citizenship had already acquired deep importance as norms of social formation. Indeed, the implementation of citizenship laws, reflecting rights and duties connecting social agents and to governmental institutions, had already assumed prominence as a technique for organising military force. This can be seen in the sociological heartlands of legal pluralism, the eastern parts of the Habsburg Empire. Beginning in the 1770s, lands then in the southern regions of Poland were colonised by Habsburg rulers, first by Maria Theresa and then by Joseph II. In this region, Habsburg colonisation was accompanied by the imposition of laws that abolished (or tentatively began to abolish) class-determined variations in legal rights, and which weakened legal obligations attached to land-based tenures.[21] In the 1770s and 1780s, Polish-speaking peasants resident in Austrian Galicia were subject to legislation that transformed their legal status, conferring new personal rights upon them, such that – in principle – they became citizens. In this process, legal rights for (peasant) citizens were strengthened in order to reduce the historical influence of the nobility, to attach persons in society more immediately to the administrative organs of the (colonising) government, and to centralise the coercive powers of government around the (colonising) state. This period of colonial annexation also saw the rapid introduction of modernising legal codes in other fields of law, including currency law, inheritance law, judicial procedure, criminal law and, by the late 1790s, general civil law.[22] This process involved, in 1775, the colonisation of Ehrlich's home town of Czernowitz (Chernovtsy), which, although briefly placed under Russian administration, was transferred from the Ottoman Empire to the Habsburg Empire at this point (Scott 2001: 246). The colonisation of the Polish parts of the Habsburg Empire, in other words, was a process of colonisation *through citizenship*. The formal ordering of legal personhood acted as the centre pin for territorial annexation. Vitally, the introduction of citizenship laws in the Habsburg regions was flanked by provisions for military service, and persons elevated into the system of citizenship rights were required to discharge a debt for such privilege by fighting in Austrian armies. One account describes this process as nothing less than a 'true revolution in the field military law' (Baczkowski 2020: 31). Within a short period of time, the colonised parts of Poland became important recruitment regions within the Habsburg Empire (see Baczkowski 2007: 33).

In key respects, the basic constructs that became vital to early constitutionalism, including norms of citizenship, personal autonomy and legal rights and duties, had been prefigured in processes of Imperial expansion in the Habsburg Empire. These constructs became mainstays of constitutional law in the revolutionary settings of this period and slightly later. In revolutionary France, legal definitions of citizenship performed almost identical functions in propelling institutional centralisation, in promoting the reduction of local authority, and in distilling positive principles to support the law. The basic normative apparatus of constitutionalism, in short, was first devised as an instrument of Imperialism.

---

[21] Abolition of serfdom in Galicia was not completed until after 1848.
[22] See discussion of this question in Grodziski (2007: 14–15).

These deep relations between Imperialism, militarism and national citizenship were clearly visible in social reactions to national citizenship. Although usually seen as the premise for effective social inclusion, early constitutional norms of citizenship were widely experienced by many subjects as norms that imposed upon them a condition of military violation. It is well documented, for example, that revolutionary France experienced mass protests against inclusion in the rights and obligations attached to citizenship. This was first expressed in the counter-revolutionary movement in the Vendée, which was largely induced by hostile reactions to the military duties imposed on populations through their acquisition of citizenship (Tilly 1964: 308). Later, the mobilisation of French citizens for war after 1799 was flanked by waves of mass desertion from the army.[23] Most armies created in Europe in the longer wake of 1789 were recruited through conscription, and most such armies suffered high levels of desertion. Throughout modern history, military desertion has formed a common response to citizenship. Importantly, such reactions to citizenship had been anticipated in pre-revolutionary Poland. Peasants upon whom citizenship was conferred by Maria Theresa and Joseph II often adopted painful measures to avoid the acquisition of the rights and duties accorded to them through citizenship. Frequent amongst such reactions were acts of military desertion, illegal emigration, and – in extreme cases – self-mutilation, all of which helped newly integrated citizens evade the expectations of military service that accompanied the right to be a citizen.[24] Overall, the transformation of the person into the citizen that stands at the beginning of modern constitutional law was not infrequently perceived as an experience of extreme military coercion. Typically, this transformation was driven by military exigencies, in which legal formation and colonisation were very closely connected and the assumption of legal rights was experienced as a state of physical occupation.

Theories of legal pluralism provide a thick description of legal conditions at the margins of formal law. Beneath the lines of this description is a deep insight into the role of military organisations in the creation of modern societies and their legal forms. Theories of legal pluralism appear as texts that trace, in oblique refraction, the residues of military organisation in legal structure, intuiting a deep military nexus connecting the processes of territorial control, legal systematisation and citizenship formation that lie at the centre of modern societies. Unsurprisingly, primary theories of legal pluralism first developed in, and drew substance from, environments in which the connection between these two dimensions was originally consolidated. In the eastward expansion of the Habsburg Empire, Imperialism forged a paradoxical legal template for later processes of national constitution making, which also grew from military impulses.

---

[23] In 1813, the first wave of conscription in Prussia led to almost 25 per cent desertion in some regions. France had a running desertion rate of circa 10 per cent from 1803 to 1814 (Hewitson 2013: 468).

[24] Analysis of these processes can be found in Jewuła et al (2015: 271, 287–88, 293). One account describes how, in face of citizenship laws and the military duties imposed by them, many Polish peasants simply 'escaped to the woods' (Michalski 1964: 21).

IV. MULTIPLE IMPERIALISMS

Such insights provided by pluralist theory are not only valuable in relation to the early legal evolution of modern society. Similar processes can be observed throughout the more recent history of social construction. Indeed, most societies evolved on a pattern in which Imperialism, militarism and constitutionalism fused to create the dominant legal form for modern society. Through the nineteenth century, societies were designed through modes of legal codification and constitutionalisation, in which legal structure was dictated, directly or remotely, by military pressures. The theory of legal pluralism moved around the outer perimeters of this legal structure, mapping the frontiers of society's legal-military form.

The enduring continuity between legal order, citizenship and military organisation became visible in the fact that, in the longer wake of 1789, European polities usually adopted constitutional structures in settings defined by Imperialism and military conflict. As mentioned, the establishment of norms of constitutional citizenship in France in the early 1790s was not easily separable from war. By 1799, French citizenship was strategically devised as the legal premise for external expansion, and citizenship was primarily understood as a relation between citizens and state that gave rise to military duties. The Imperialist construction of citizenship in France resulted in far-reaching patterns of legal codification, especially the Code Civil (1804), which was enforced within France and across many regions occupied by French armies. In other parts of Europe, patterns of citizenship formation after 1789 were also causally linked to territorial expansion. In Prussia, the years following military defeat by Napoleon (1806) saw the widening of some basic citizenship rights to new social groups (peasants). This process was directly propelled by the endeavour amongst Prussian elites to motivate citizens to take up arms against Napoleonic armies, and it culminated in the imposition of conscription laws in 1813–1815. The expansion of Prussian citizenship was not merely a national process. It coincided with the consolidation of Prussian control in Western Poland. The Prussian colonisation of neighbouring parts of Poland, which began in the 1770s and was cemented after 1815, was flanked by the extension of citizenship rights to persons hitherto excluded from citizenship, on whom military duties were also imposed.[25] In this context, laws that promoted general rights of citizenship were used to attach peasant communities more directly to (colonising) state institutions and to extract military loyalty from them.[26] This was also flanked by increasing legal codification, as Prussian administrative norms were imposed on all citizens after 1815.[27]

By the latter part of the nineteenth century, the deep dialectical bond between formal law, constitutional citizenship and militarism was clear. This was spelled out unmistakably in national constitutional law.

---

[25] In former parts of Poland under Prussian rule after 1815, emancipation of Polish peasants began in 1823.

[26] See analysis in Kozłowski (2004: 27).

[27] Western Poland was effectively assimilated in the Prussian administrative order through the Gesetz wegen Anordnung der Provinzial-Stände für das Großherzogthum Posen (27 March 1824). This took place at the same time as the abolition of serfdom.

The unification of Germany in the years 1864–1871 occurred through a process of nation building in which national citizenship was constituted by military means, such that constitutional integration and military annexation were roughly fused. Germany was established as a nation state, primarily, through Prussian military occupation of non-Prussian German territories in 1866–1867, and – ultimately – through the formation of a national army, which was established as Germany (administratively, still Prussia) took temporary military control of France in 1870–1871. In this process of unification, the integration of Germans in the German army and the integration of Germans in the system of German citizenship rights took place together. Unified Germany was formed through a legal sequence in which, first, constitutional rights, including full male enfranchisement from 1867, were extended to all new German citizens, and then, as they received such rights, German citizens were expected to perform military service. By 1900, a generalised and uniform legal system had been imposed on most functional spheres in German society (the vital area of taxation law remained an exception). Importantly, the years after 1871 were also marked by trajectories of *internal colonisation*, in which minorities in Prussia, especially Poles, were coercively aligned to specifically German patterns of citizenship.

In Italy in the 1860s, nation-building processes revolved around three analogous elements: territorial unification through military force; the extension of constitutional law to all citizens; and the imposition of military service on male Italians. This process was flanked by the introduction of formal legal codes in other areas of law, as, before unification was fully complete, Italy saw the general imposition of a codified corpus of civil law.[28] Nation building in the USA during the Civil War of the 1860s can be aligned to this same broad paradigm of violent constitutional inclusion, linked to expanded conscription.[29] In post-1866 Austria, likewise, a new constitution was created (1867) and military conscription was imposed (1868) as two parts of one process of national consolidation. At this time, as in Germany, Austrian citizenship was attached to national military service, and the extension of citizenship rights was expressly viewed as a policy for mobilising military force. From the 1860s, most European polities experienced conjoined legal processes, in which constitutional rights were deepened and military duties were intensified. In most cases, this was linked to crises caused by international military tensions. France introduced a new body of constitutional laws (1875) and new military service laws (1872) after defeat in the Franco-Prussian war. After the Crimean War, the Tsarist regime in Russia implemented revised citizenship laws, abolishing serfdom in 1861 (1864 in Polish-speaking regions), and this was rapidly followed by laws enforcing intensified conscription (1874). This process was supported by policies of legal codification, in the shape of judicial reforms.

On this basis, it is evident that, in broad terms, constitutional law typically evolved as a system of legal coordination whose functions had a primary military emphasis. Constitutions became widespread in Europe – first after 1789, and then, more endur-ingly in the longer aftermath of 1848 – as documents that constructed legitimacy for

---

[28] A *Codice Civile* for all Italy was introduced in 1865.
[29] For recent highly illuminating analysis of similarities between Italy and the USA in this context see Dal Lago (2018: 90–91).

national political systems by positioning the persons acquiring rights of citizenship in military roles. In essence, constitutions were created as military contracts, in which governments transacted political rights, the most important amongst which were electoral rights, in return for the direct provision of military violence. On this premise, the construction of the citizen in constitutional law served as the fulcrum in a trifocal process of colonisation. First, the citizen was constructed, practically, through an institutional process in which states reached into their societies to obtain resources of military force from their populations. Second, the citizen was constructed as a normative premise for the law, in which state organisations were able to enforce legal obligations across the diffuse domains in national society. As mentioned, most states that codified constitutional law also codified other fields of law at the same time, or shortly afterwards. Third, many states that obtained constitutions did so as part of, or perhaps as the prerequisite for, a concerted process of external enlargement.

This dialectic of legal ordering, constitutional citizenship and militarism was clearest in the case of Poland, during the period of partition (1772–1918). As discussed, Poland first served as a testing ground for the colonising functions of national citizenship, and norms of citizenship were imposed on inhabitants of territories historically belonging to Poland as part of a trajectory of Imperialist expansion. This process persisted throughout the nineteenth century, as, by the 1860s, techniques of colonisation through citizenship originally deployed by Austria and Prussia were emulated in Polish regions incorporated by Russia (see Groniowski 1963: 30). Through these developments, Polish regions persisted in a form of linguistic, political and legal pluralism, in which Polish institutions retained a shadowy partial existence, situated beneath the more formal institutions imposed by occupying governments. In this setting, military organisations acquired heightened prominence, as both the institutions supporting occupation and institutions framing resistance to occupation were concentrated around military functions. Indigenous Polish institutions only became fully visible in times of military conflict.

The eventual reemergence of Poland as an independent state after the collapse of the Prussian and Austro-Hungarian Empires and the overthrow of the Tsarist government in the years 1917–1918 was, in many ways, a process that directly mirrored nation-building wars in Germany and Italy over 50 years previously. The formation of the Polish Second Republic occurred through multi-polar warfare, conducted between the newly unified Polish army and armies of Russians, Ukrainians, Czechs, Germans and Lithuanians. Consequently, the Polish army formed the primary nation-building unit (see Wrzosek 1988: 66). Moreover, to an even greater degree than in Germany or Italy in the 1860s, concepts of citizenship used to support and legitimate the new Polish state after 1918 were determined by military conscription. Constitutions implemented in Poland in 1919 and in 1921 were accompanied by laws imposing very far-reaching military duties on new citizens, especially during the Polish-Soviet war. The linkage between citizenship and conscription was used to map out the geographical contours of the Polish state as it emerged through warfare, until the national borders were formally settled in 1922–1923. As the territorial borders of Poland were widened in the course of military conflict, constitutional rights and military duties were imposed on citizens located on the inside of these moving borders. The condition of being a Polish citizen, integrated within Polish national boundaries, immediately involved extremely perilous military duties, as citizens were required to serve in wars with very uncertain outcomes.

Importantly, this dangerous system of rights and duties was used to integrate the many minority groups that fell within the borders of the Polish state after 1918. Military obligations were especially designed to detach pluralistic minority groups from alternative collective affinities, and to connect members of these groups more immediately to the expanding legal and administrative apparatus of the Polish state (Śleszyński 2007: 160). In the last years of Ehrlich's life, this process of integration through Polish citizenship reached almost as far as Czernowitz (by that point Cernăuţi, as part of Romania). In other words, the strategies of colonisation, expressed through citizenship and military formation, which had previously been implemented by occupying powers within Polish territories were rapidly reproduced after 1918, as Poland itself developed a system of independent statehood. During this time, the Polish Republic developed as a highly militarised political entity, which assumed a clearly Imperial role as it expanded to the north and the east, forcibly incorporating regions whose attachment to Polish nationhood was uncertain. As in earlier settings, this induced largescale resistance to citizenship, expressed especially in acts of military desertion (see Kasprzycki 2016: 93). The first years of the Polish Second Republic saw use of extremely repressive techniques to enforce military duties (citizenship). This also triggered military counter-mobilisation of non-Polish ethnic groups, especially in Ukrainian-speaking regions. By the 1930s, this ultimately resulted in the deep militarisation of Polish citizenship, as Polish citizenship was imposed on all groups in an increasingly forceful manner.

Across this spectrum of historical examples, we can observe a deep correlation between unified legal form, constitutional constructions of citizenship and military organisation. In each setting, the unifying aspects of legal order were imposed by military processes, close to colonial occupation. In each context, the specific distinction between Imperialism and national constitutionalism was very blurred, and constitutional law took root both as the result of external conflict and as the functional transposition of such conflict into domestic law.

V. CONCLUSION: CONFLICT THEORY
AND THE DIALECTICAL LIMITS OF PLURALISM

The theory of legal pluralism is interpreted in this chapter as part of military sociology. This reinterpretation reads the theory of legal pluralism as a description of the ways in which modern law is correlated with primary integration processes, drawing attention to the interwovenness between social-legal form and military organisation. However, this reconstruction also implies that the simple pluralist approach to law, describing multiple legal orders in society, has explanatory limits. It suggests that the theory of legal pluralism can never be a simple theory of legal pluralism, and accounts of legal pluralism that merely describe pluralism fall short of capitalising on their intrinsic significance. The theory of legal pluralism realises its full importance when it is subject to a process of meta-reflection, mediated through conflict theory, which attaches it to analysis of the military sources of modern law and modern citizenship.

The full yield of thinking about legal pluralism is only gained if such thinking partly renounces its strict concern with pluralism, if it brings to light the unifying structural figures that determine modern law, and if it promotes analysis of law's residual plurality to interpret the violent forces that impose unity on law.

Ultimately, early theories of legal pluralism proved inaccurate in their claim that increasing legal unity violated authentic legal experience in society. As discussed, beneath the surface of the pluralist theory of law is the suggestion that formal law is created through a construct of legal validity that fuses constitutional citizenship and military force. The effects of this construct became visible in the trajectories of legal formation in Central Europe, where analysis of legal pluralism was born and came of age. Ehrlich's descriptions of plural law, synthesised in his great work of 1913, stand close to (or just before) the apex of European society's structural determination by this construct. The force of this construct was only softened, very gradually, after 1945, when military patterns of citizenship slowly lost influence, and it became possible for citizens to experience integration through multiple legal regimes. As mentioned above, legal pluralism now means many things. However, if it is understood, in its original sense, as a doctrine that argues against the reductive and oppressive weight of formal law and implies that societies allowing liberty in law must recognise multiple patterns of legal inclusion, such pluralism only became consistently visible in the longer wake of 1945. It was only at this time that states began (tentatively) to recognise and permit the coexistence of multiple legal regimes within the frontiers of their territories. However, contrary to the expectations of legal pluralists, the ultimate emergence of legal systems allowing multiple integration processes was not induced by legal forms arising from inner-societal plurality. By this time, new sources of pluralism entered the integrational matrix of national societies, as international norms increasingly penetrated into national jurisdictions, often establishing grounds for recognition of minority populations creating new openings for multi-centric integration. In key respects, recognition of the coexistence of multiple legal orders in many societies was induced, in the longer wake of 1945, by the growth of international human rights law, in which national polities were integrated in overarching normative systems, which alleviated national states of some normative responsibilities. Not less, but greater, legal uniformity proved the key to greater legal pluralism. The explanation of this process also lies, not in the simple analysis of pluralism, but also in a sociology of law which connects legal inquiry with military sociology.

REFERENCES

Baczkowski, M (2007) 'Armia jako czynnik modernizacji Galicji w dobie konstytucyjnej (1867–1914)' in P Franaszek and A Nieczuchrin (eds), *Problemy cywilizacyjnego rozwoju Białorusi, Polski, Rosji i Ukrainy od końca XVIII do XXI wieku* (Krakow, Wydawnictwo Uniwersytetu Jagiellońskiego) 205.

——— (2020) *Wpłw armii austriackiej na miasta Galicji 1772–1815* (Krakow, Towarzystwo Wydawnicze 'Historia Iagellonica').

Bello, Á (2004) *Etnicidad y ciudadanía en América Latina. La Acción colectiva de los pueblos indígenas* (Santiago de Chile, CEPAL).

Beseler, G (1847) *System des gemeinen deutschen Privatrechts*, vol I (Leipzig, Weidmann'sche Buchhandlung).

Colley, L (2021) *The Gun, the Ship and the Pen. Warfare, Constitutions and the Making of the Modern World* (London, Profile).

Crépin, A (2011) *Vers l'armée nationale. Les débuts de la conscription en Seine et-Marne 1795–1815* (Rennes, Presses universitaires de Rennes).

Dahrendorf, R (1965) *Gesellschaft und Demokratie in Deutschland* (Munich, Piper).

Dal Lago, E (2018) *Civil War and Agrarian Unrest. The Confederate South and Southern Italy* (Cambridge, Cambridge University Press).

Ehrlich, E (1989 [1913]) *Grundlegung der Soziologie des Rechts*, 4th edn (Berlin, Duncker und Humblot).

Ellickson, RC (1986) 'Of Coase and Cattle: Dispute Resolution among Neighbors in Shasta County' 38(3) *Stanford Law Review* 623–87.

Galanter, M (1981) 48 'Justice in Many Rooms: Courts, Private Ordering and Indigenous Law' *Journal of Legal Pluralism* 1.

Gierke, O (1868) *Das deutsche Genossenschaftsrecht*, vol I: *Rechtsgeschichte der deutschen Genossenschaft* (Berlin, Weidmann).

—— (1873) *Das deutsche Genossenschaftsrecht*, vol II: *Geschichte des deutschen Körperschaftsbegriffs* (Berlin, Weidmann).

—— (1881) *Das deutsche Genossenschaftsrecht*, vol III: *Die Staats- und Korporationslehre des Althertums und des Mittelalters* (Berlin, Weidmann).

Grodziski, S (2007) *Studia Galicyjskie. Rozprawy i przyczynki do historii ustroju Galicji* (Krakow, Księgarnia Akademicka).

Groniowski, K (1963) *Realizacja reformy uwłaszczeniowej 1864 roku* (Warsaw, Państwowe Wydawnictwo Naukowe).

Gumplowicz, L (1883) *Der Rassenkampf. Sociologische Untersuchungen* (Innsbruck, Wagner).

Hänel, A (1892) *Deutsches Staatsrecht*, vol I: *Die Grundlagen des deutschen Staates und die Reichsgewalt* (Leipzig, Duncker und Humblot).

Harvey, WB (1962) 'The Evolution of Ghana Law since Independence' 27(4) *Law and Contemporary Problems* 581.

Hewitson, M (2013) 'Princes' Wars, Wars of the People, or Total War? Mass Armies and the Question of a Military Revolution in Germany, 1792–1815' 20(4) *War in History* 452.

Hippler, T (2006) *Soldats et citoyens. Naissance du service militaire en France et en Prusse* (Paris, PUF).

Jewuła, Ł, Kargol, T and Ślusarek, K (2015) *Dwór, wieś i plebania. W przestrzeni społecznej zachodniej Małopolski w latach 1772–1815* (Krakow, Towarzystwo Wydawnicze 'Historia Iagellonica').

Joas, H (2000) *Kriege und Werte. Studien zur Gewaltgeschichte des 20 Jahrhunderts* (Weilerswist, Velbrück).

Joas, H and Knöbl, W (2008) *Kriegsverdrängung. Ein Problem in der Geschichte der Sozialtheorie* (Frankfurt am Main, Suhrkamp).

Kasprzycki, R (2016) 'Dezercje i unikanie służby w Wojsku Polskim w latach 1918–1939' 3 *Dzieje Najnowsze* 87.

Kozłowski, J (2004) *Wielkopolska pod zaborem pruskim w latach 1815–1918* (Poznan, Wydawnictwo Poznańskie).

Kruse, V (2009) 'Mobilisierung und kriegsgesellschaftliches Dilemma. Beobachtungen zur kriegsgesellschaftlichen Moderne' 38(3) *Zeitschrift für Soziologie* 198.

Madison, J, Hamilton, A and Jay, J (1987 [1787–1788]) *The Federalist Papers* (London, Penguin).

Malešević, S (2010) *The Sociology of War and Violence*. (Cambridge, Cambridge University Press).

Mann, M (1984) 'The Autonomous Power of the State' 25(2) *Archives européennes de sociologie. European Journal of Sociology* 185.

Michalski, J (1964) *Polska wobec wojny o sukcesje bawarską* (Wrocław, Zakład narodowy imienia ossolińskich wydawnictwo polskiej akademii nauki).

Organiściak, W (2002) 'Polskie "Artykuły wojskowe" z 1775 roku' 109(1) *Kwartalnik Historyczny* 41.

Parsons, T (1965) 'Full Citizenship for the Negro American? A Sociological Problem' 94(4) *Daedalus* 1009.

Rehbinder, M (2007) 'Die politischen Schriften des Rechtssoziologen Eugen Ehrlich auf dem Hintergrund seines bewegten Lebens' 46 *Anuarul Institutului de Istorie »George Barițiu« – Series HISTORICA* 269.

Röhl, KF and Machura, S (2013) '100 Jahre Rechtssoziologie: Eugen Ehrlichs Rechtspluralismus heute' 68 *Juristen-Zeitung* 1117.

Rosswurm, S (1987) *Arms, Country, and Class. The Philadelphia Militia and 'Lower Sort' during the American Revolution, 1775–1783* (New Brunswick, NJ, Rutgers University Press).

Sánchez Botero, E (2001) 'Aproximación desde la antropología jurídica a la justicia de los pueblos indígenas' in BS Santos and M García Vilegas (eds), *El caleidoscopo de las justicias en* Colombia, vol II (Bogota, Siglo de Hombre Ediores) 159.

Savigny, FC von (1840) *Vom Beruf unserer Zeit für Gesetzgebung* (Heidelberg, JCB Mohr).

Sciulli, D (1986) 'Voluntaristic Action as a Distinct Concept: Theoretical Foundations of Societal Constitutionalism' 51(6) *American Sociological Review* 743.

Scott, HM (2001) *The Emergence of the Eastern Powers, 1756–1775* (Cambridge, Cambridge University Press).

Sieyès, E-J (1789) *Qu'est-ce que le Tiers-Etat?*, 2nd edn (Paris).

Śleszyński, W (2007) *Bezpieczeństwo wewnętrzne w polityce państwa polskiego na ziemach połnocno-wschodnich II Rezczypospolitej* (Warsaw, Oficyna Wydawnicza RYTM).

Szczygielski, W (2009) 'Z dyskusji parlamentarnej nad powołaniem Komisji Wojskowej w początkach obrad Sejmu Wielkiego' 8(2) *Przegląd Nauk Humanistycznych* 63.

Teubner, G (1997) 'Global Bukowina: Legal Pluralism in the World Society' in G Teubner (ed), *Global Law without a State* (Dartmouth, Aldershot) 3.

Tilly, C (1964) *The Vendée* (London, Arnold).

Warburg, J (2008) *Das Militär und seine Subjekte. Zur Soziologie des Krieges* (Bielefeld, transcript).

Weber, M (1921/22) *Wirtschaft und Gesellschaft: Grundriß der verstehenden Soziologie* (Tübingen, Mohr).

—— (1988) 'Der Nationalstaat und die Volkswirtschaftspolitik' in M Weber, *Gesammelte politische Schriften* (Tübingen, JCB Mohr) 1.

Wrzosek, M (1988) *Wojsko Polskie i operacje wojenne lat 1918–1920* (Białystok, Dział Wydawnictw Filii UW).

9

Corporate Strategies within a Transnational Regulatory Field

ISABEL SCHOULTZ

I. INTRODUCTION

I N HIS BOOK, *Normativity in Legal Sociology*, Reza Banakar discusses law and regulation in late modernity, including the regulation of global corporations. He describes how globalisation, with intensified economic exchange and trading, has contributed to the emergence of a legal pluralism, 'causing legal fragmentation and normative uncertainty' (Banakar 2015: 3). This chapter will follow in Reza Banakar's footsteps by investigating legal pluralism in a globalised world. I will do this using the empirical examples provided by two multinational corporations and the struggle over the interpretation of different and competing laws. Banakar (ibid: 273) emphasises that there is no single normative system at the global multi-jurisdictional level. In other words, the legal field surrounding transnational corporations is fragmented and plural. Corporate regulations include a plurality of overlapping legal orders: various forms of law (hard law and soft law); different levels of law (global, regional and national legal orders); and different sources of law (public and private). That is to say, the legal regulation of global corporate activities consist of an increasing *legal pluralism* (Cutler 2013) or even a *transnational legal pluralism*, to use Zumbansen's (2011) term. Transnational legal pluralism in the context of corporate governance refers to a 'cross-jurisdictional, transnational regulatory landscape' (ibid: 57). Traditionally, scholars applying a legal pluralism perspective have focused on pluralism within a single geographical area, but an increasing amount of attention is now being focused on pluralism in the global arena, which consists of different sets of overlapping jurisdictional claims (Berman 2009). The rise of multinational corporations in particular has activated a recognition of multiple normative orders that extend across state boundaries in an international and transnational legal terrain (ibid). The legal pluralistic field of corporate governance involves potential conflicts of law when corporations violate any of these norms, and it creates room for corporations to make opportunistic selections between coexisting legal authorities (Tamanaha 2008: 375).

This chapter takes the transnational legal pluralistic reality surrounding corporations as its point of departure and examines how two corporations accused of misconduct manoeuvre around the legal pluralistic terrain to their advantage, and at the same time attempt to define which laws should be applicable within the field of corporate regulation. The examples are taken from two Swedish companies that have been the focus of various legal battles for suspected misconduct: the Telia Company (previously TeliaSonera)[1] and Lundin Energy (previously Lundin Oil and Lundin Petroleum). In the analysis, I utilise Bourdieu's analytical tool of 'field' and of struggles between social agents that possess various forms of capital (Bourdieu 1993), to understand how the two multinational companies make strategic use of different and competing legal regulations. According to Bourdieu (ibid: 133), a field is 'an area, a playing field, a field of objective relations among individuals or institutions competing for the same stakes'. The ability of corporations to invoke various laws, jurisdictions and forums may be understood as a manifestation of how their access to different types of capital (economic, cultural, social and symbolic) mediates the field (Bourdieu 2000). As Reza Banakar and Max Travers point out, Bourdieu directs his focus at 'the *power* relations and how groups and individual agents struggle over the "stakes" in the field' (Banakar and Travers 2005: 200). McBarnet (2006: 1091) also reminds us that law is not simply passively received by corporations but 'actively worked on to alter its consequences'. In other words, corporations can 'invoke, obey, and evade the legal system in order to avoid law's costs and exploit law's benefits' (Edelman and Suchman 1997: 485). In Bourdieu's terms, corporate regulations can be understood as a field of struggle between agents and institutions who are in competition to control the right to determine the law (Bourdieu 1987: 817). To Bourdieu (2000), the unequal distribution of capital (economic, cultural, social and symbolic) constitutes the very structure of a given field, and the distribution of capital shapes the strategies used by the social agents (Bourdieu and Wacquant 1992). Seeing law, and its plurality of forms, as part of an ongoing struggle over the rules of the game is a fruitful way of tackling the complexity of corporate regulation (see Haines and Macdonald 2021). From this perspective, the ability to manoeuvre around a legal pluralistic terrain would then be related to the juridical capital (as well as other forms of capital) possessed by corporations, and their ability to promote which laws have authority within the field of struggle. With this as a point of departure, I ask: How can we understand the social practice of multinational corporations that make strategic use of different and competing legal regulations as part of a struggle for dominance over the field of corporate regulation?

II. THE FIELD OF CORPORATE REGULATION
AND THE LEGAL PLURALISTIC REALITY

Multinational corporations are part of a legal pluralistic reality; corporate practices are regulated by domestic law, both 'at home' and in the countries where the

---

[1] The public monopoly Televerket was transformed into a public sector joint stock company in 1993 and was renamed Telia. In 2002 the company merged with the Finnish company Sonera, and was renamed TeliaSonera. In 2016 TeliaSonera changed name to become the Telia Company AB. At the present time, the Swedish government remains the company's principal shareholder with almost 40 per cent of the company's shares.

businesses operate, by international criminal law and also by non-binding corporate responsibilities, such as corporate social responsibility. Legal pluralism is frequently defined as 'a situation in which two or more legal systems coexist in the same social field' (Merry 1988: 870). However, definitions of legal systems have been the object of intense scholarly debate (see Tamanaha 1993). John Griffiths (1986) introduced the distinction between weak and strong legal pluralism. Within weak (also known as juridical or classic) legal pluralism, the term 'legal system' refers to a state-centred system in which the state validates different bodies of law, for example, for different groups within the population. On the other hand, strong (also known as sociological and new) legal pluralism rejects this state-centred view and legal centralism, and focuses on situations in which 'more than one source of "law", more than one "legal order" is observable' in a social field (J Griffiths 1986: 38). In Griffith's conceptualisation (ibid: 38), legal pluralism is a fact, 'a universal feature of social organization' and is not dependent on state recognition.

A transnational legal pluralistic perspective rejects by default the nation state as the only form of legal ordering (see A Griffiths 2002: 298 ff). In this sense, the transnationalisation of the legal field (Dezalay and Garth 1998), and the notion of transnational legal pluralism (Zumbansen 2011), challenge a traditional understanding found in socio-legal research of unified legal systems stemming from the nation state (Cotterrell 2009: 483). Take for example *lex mercatoria*, the assertedly self-created international law of arbitration, which has been discussed at length by socio-legal scholars (ie Dezalay and Garth 1998; Shaffer and Halliday 2021; Teubner 2002). The regulations of corporations include a range of non-state normative orders. Self-regulation, for example in the form of corporate codes of conduct, the private regulation of financial market activities, such as via International Chambers of Commerce, as well as OECD Guidelines for Multinational Enterprises and regulations governing stock markets, all create standards and norms (Berman 2009; Cutler 2013). However, as Anne Griffiths (2002) has noted, we cannot ignore the role of the nation state. Banakar (2015: 278) has discussed the possibilities for regulating transnational corporations and found that many underestimate the force of nation states. In its attempts to 'protect and promote the global economy', the nation state is also 'expanding its powers of surveillance'. Similarly, Shaffer and Halliday (2021) argue that the state is central to transnational norm-making, rather than bypassed and marginalised (see also Zumbansen 2011).

Even though the regulation of global corporate conduct is multifaceted, the legal field is mainly characterised by deregulation and decriminalisation (Snider 2000; Tombs and Whyte 2015), and a lack of direct legal governance from both a global and domestic perspective (Simons and Macklin 2014: 8). Scholars have also argued that despite existing domestic legal instruments, corporations often escape accountability (Alvesalo-Kuusi et al 2017; Tombs and Whyte 2015). The failure to regulate transnational corporations via internationally binding, hard law, has led to the development of self-regulation and the soft law of voluntary corporate responsibilities (Cutler 2013; Haines and Macdonald 2021). Cutler (2013) recognises that transnational corporations have historically been successful in securing corporate rights through hard law, while at the same time framing corporate responsibilities as soft norms. Further, self-regulatory initiatives do not seem to fill the 'governance gap' when it comes to corporate human rights abuses (Simons and Macklin 2014). At the same time, Baars (2016: 24) has suggested that the issue of whether corporate crime is regulated through self-regulation or legally binding norms is in effect a semantic question, since corporations are rarely prosecuted.

For legal pluralist scholars, the principal interest is not merely which normative system has the formal authority in a certain situation, but which normative systems are treated as binding in practice and by whom (Berman 2009). Thus, an important aim for the legal pluralist is to observe 'how [social actors] invoke and respond to the presence of multiple normative systems' (Tamanaha 2008: 401). In this sense, multinational corporations' activities in a legal pluralist terrain may be understood as their manoeuvring in a field of struggle and competition to determine which laws should be applied. For example, Berman (2009) has noted that while local communities may seek to assert jurisdiction over corporations causing harm, corporations can attempt to avoid local jurisdiction by invoking competing jurisdictions. In situations of legal pluralism, the technique of choosing the most favourable of a number of jurisdictions has been referred to as *forum shopping* (Merry 1988; Tamanaha 2011; von Benda-Beckmann 1981), while the specific practice of selecting between sources of law is referred to as *law shopping* (Lhuilier 2013). In other words, social actors such as corporations may 'actively exploit situations of legal pluralism in the further-ance of group and individual aims' (Tamanaha 2008: 401). In addition, as A Griffiths (2002) has noted, legal pluralism raises important questions about power: 'the power to define law, to apply it and to use it'. In other words, from a Bourdieusian perspec-tive, the struggles within a juridical field are also part of the transformation of the field. Thus, when corporations engage in competition to determine the law, and ulti-mately to dominate the field, they also play a part in forming the field of corporate regulations.

This chapter explores the corporate practice of utilising coexisting legal authori-ties when accused of misconduct. Legal pluralism is here treated as a fact (see J Griffiths 1986: 4) and the empirical question is that of how legal pluralism is utilised by multinational corporations. Stated in Bourdieusian terms, legal pluralism consti-tutes the specific structure of the field of corporate regulation, the context in which the struggle for dominance and recognition takes place. The idea of corporations avoiding or manoeuvring around laws is hardly new. In her pioneering work on tax avoidance, McBarnet (1988: 114) described a game in which: 'legal techniques are brought into play to create strategies for weakening the law by legally avoiding it'. She went on to describe how lawyers are 'creators of legal techniques, definitions, and devices' which corporations use to their benefit (ibid: 118). Corporations that can afford creative lawyers are able to 'buy legal expertise to tailor-make law to fit their own interests' (ibid: 119). In other words, the ability of corporations to escape the law is in effect business as usual. This chapter contributes new empirical exam-ples to this discussion and raises the question of how the social practices used by two multinational corporations' to strategically utilise different and competing legal regulations can be understood in terms of the struggle for dominance over the field of corporate regulation in a Bourdieusian sense. Before moving on to the analy-sis, I will first describe the two corporations that form the basis for the empirical examples.

III. THE COMPANIES

The telecommunications provider Telia's dealings in Central Asia have attracted a substantial amount of media attention. Initially the company was accused of participating in surveillance operations conducted by the secret services linked to several oppressive regimes. Thereafter, corruption accusations led to criminal investigations both in Sweden and abroad. These resulted in a disgorgement (ie the surrender of profits obtained illegally from the Uzbek affair) and a global settlement to resolve charges relating to violations of the Foreign Corrupt Practices Act (FCPA) in the USA and of Dutch law (US Department of Justice 2017). In Sweden, three former Telia executives were brought to trial for bribery offences in September 2018, and later acquitted in both first and second instance courts.

Lundin Energy describes itself as a family business, of which the Lundin family is the principal owner.[2] In November 2021, following an investigation lasting more than ten years into the company's possible complicity in war crimes in Sudan between 1999 and 2003, the Swedish Prosecutor brought criminal charges against two company representatives. One of these is the current company chairman Ian Lundin, a son of the company's founder, while the other is a former CEO of the company.

The analysis is based on material collected during a three-year research project[3] focused on the two companies' responses to the allegations in the public domain, mainly on the basis of press releases, annual reports, letters to shareholders, dominant national newspapers, and radio and TV interviews. The material also includes field notes from observations made during the Telia trial between 5 September and 19 December 2018, at Stockholm District Court.[4] For this chapter, I have only selected material that is relevant to the analysis of different and competing legal regulations, and how the companies have used these competing regulations to navigate the field. Thus, I am interested in how coexisting legal rules create opportunities for corporations (Tamanaha 2008), and how juridical and other forms of capital are used in battles fought to define the field when corporations are accused of misconduct.

Although the field of corporate regulation is understood as a plurality of transnational legal orders (public, private, state and non-state law etc), the examples highlighted here only encompass a narrow range of the broad spectrum of legal pluralism relating to corporate regulation, and they are focused on formal sources of law. The first example provide insights into the struggle over the interpretation of national law in host states, and colliding human rights regulations, when the Telia Company was accused of participating in surveillance activities conducted by the secret services of oppressive regimes. The second example covers the strategies employed by the lawyers of the former executives of the Telia Company during the criminal trial, as they strove to limit the relevance of judicial decisions made in other jurisdictions. The third example illustrates Lundin's legal struggle regarding the relationship between

---

[2] The Lundin family is the largest shareholder in the business, with 30 per cent of the company's shares.

[3] Business as usual: Corporate defence strategies against accusations of crime supported by the Swedish Riksbankens Jubileumsfond (RJ P15-0176:1).

[4] For more information on the data collection, see Schoultz and Flyghed (2020a; 2020b).

national and international law in relation to international crimes. The cases provide examples of the ways in which multinational corporations invoke and respond to a plurality of rules and norms when accused of crime.

IV. INVOKING LOCAL LAWS

In 2006, the telecommunications provider TeliaSonera sought to expand into the Eurasian telecommunication market. As a result of the human rights record of several of these countries, TeliaSonera's presence was criticised from the start by both human rights organisations and the media. However, it was not until 2012, when one of Sweden's leading investigative journalism TV shows presented a number of revelations about TeliaSonera's activities in Central Asia, that the TeliaSonera business in the region became a public scandal. Some of the revelations focused on suspected bribery offences committed in order to establish TeliaSonera as a telecom operator in Uzbekistan, and later also in other Central Asian countries (Uppdrag granskning 2012b). Other significant revelations focused on how the company was participating in surveillance conducted by the secret services of oppressive regimes such as Belarus, Uzbekistan and Azerbaijan (Uppdrag granskning 2012a). The latter revelations resulted in a certain kind of corporate response that will be analysed here in relation to the social practices employed by the corporation to make strategic use of different and competing legal regulations as part of a struggle for recognition and legitimacy, and by extension a struggle for dominance over the interpretation of corporate regulation. The actors at play in these battles with regard to what law is applicable within this field are primarily the corporation and the public (including the media).

In contrast to the corporation's intense denials of the accusations of corruption (see Schoultz and Flyghed 2016; 2020a), the criticism voiced in the Swedish media and elsewhere for allowing repressive governments to use their networks to infringe human rights relating to freedom of expression and privacy have been met with arguments asserting the corporation's compliance with national laws in the countries in which it was operating. Even before the major revelations emerged in 2012 on TeliaSonera co-operating with oppressive dictatorial governments in countries of the former Soviet Union, which involved the company giving national intelligence agencies access to their networks, the company referred to national laws and governments as its guiding principles. Consider the following statement from the company in 2006, published under the headline: 'Human Rights Performance Indicators': 'TeliaSonera does not decide what is legal or illegal in the area of freedom of expression and privacy and leaves this to governments to decide. We must comply with the requests of governments in the countries where we operate' (TeliaSonera 2006: 23). The quote implicitly recognises competing legal orders, with national laws competing with human rights frameworks. Thus, the distinction between hard law (domestic law) and soft law (human rights declarations) is utilised by corporations to define the field, for their own benefit. This form of manoeuvre, with the corporation referring to obedience to governments and national laws in the countries in which the corporation operates, is often an accepted form of corporate response (Huisman 2010: 34). This is hardly surprising, since official legal systems, such as national laws, lend legitimacy and symbolic authority (Tamanaha 2008: 406 ff), but it might also have to do with the ability of corporations, on the basis of the social and economic capital they possess, to dominate the understanding of which legal frameworks should be applied in a particular situation, and as such the definition of the field of corporate regulation. We know from Bourdieu that to gain recognition and legitimacy, agents use various strategies in relation to their position in the field, and that the distribution of capital shapes the strategies used by social agents (Bourdieu and Wacquant 1992). The corporate tactic is then to exploit the pluralistic legal landscape and to define human rights regulations as being less relevant in this field.

However, as Banakar (2015: 276) has noted, the public is capable of exerting regulatory pressure on transnational corporations. Public moral condemnation can constitute a 'normative force' that compels corporations and their representatives, but it is dependent on mass media reporting, and as Banakar (ibid) has argued, is therefore rarely durable and consistent. In the case of Telia, the public criticism of the company's participation in the surveillance conducted by the secret services of oppressive regimes intensified during 2012. As a response to revelations from one of Sweden's leading investigative journalism TV-shows (Uppdrag granskning 2012a), the CEO of Telia wrote a debate article, emphasising that when information from their networks was used to violate human rights, the responsibility rested with the regimes involved and not with the company. He admitted that they were caught in a dilemma but referred to guiding principles from the OECD to support the claim that the primary obligation of companies is to comply with local laws (Dagens Nyheter 2012).

This corporate response was met by stark criticism in media. When analysing the corporate response to the accusations of participation in violations of integrity and freedom of expression, it becomes obvious that the corporate response was adapted to the reactions it elicited. This type of adjustment can be seen in the following statement:

> Once we analysed what we had said and wrote in the spring, it was not so surprising that many of you had interpreted it as though we do not care about human rights, or even actively participate in violating them. We have probably made mistakes along the way, and there are clearly things that we can do better, but I must emphasize that I and TeliaSonera are firmly against violations of human rights .... (TeliaSonera 2012a)

Nonetheless, later in the statement the CEO highlighted the necessity of following the national laws of the host state in order to avoid risking their business:

> If a telecom company does not follow the local regulations, we run the risk that our employees might end up in prison and that our licenses could be revoked – which would mean that we could no longer offer our communication services in the country. Ultimately, this would also mean significant risks to shareholder value. (TeliaSonera 2012a)

Here the CEO also acknowledges the superior legal obligation to provide profit for the company's shareholders. The corporate interest of profit maximisation may be understood as the doxa of the field of corporate regulation, ie the schemes of thought and perception that appear natural and self-evident (Bourdieu 1977). In other words, the legal obligations to the company's shareholders constitute the guiding legal rule, which is often taken for granted.

The corporate strategy in the context of this struggle involves referring to competing normative orders and invoking the legal system that benefits its own claims (see Tamanaha 2011). The social, economic and symbolic power of corporations allows them to shape the interpretation of corporate regulation. In Bourdieusian terms, we can understand corporate power as an ability to dominate the interpretation of which normative system should be treated as binding in practice. However, as this case has shown, the field of corporate regulations is not without struggles, and the corporation continuously had to shift strategy and tactics in relation to other social actors, primarily the public and mass media.

V. CORRUPTION REGULATION – A TRANSNATIONAL FIELD

Following the revelations focused on how the company was participating in surveillance operations linked to oppressive regimes, the investigative TV shows moved on to look at the acquisition by Telia of a 3G licence, frequencies and number series, in order to become established as a telecom operator in Uzbekistan. Information was presented describing extensive financial transactions with a letter-box entity, Takilant. The journalists could show that Takilant was owned by an assistant to the president's daughter, Gulnara Karimova (Uppdrag granskning 2012b). A week later, Telia announced that a Swedish prosecutor had initiated a criminal investigation to examine suspected bribery offences (Telia 2012b).

Five years later, the company officially admitted guilt via a deferred prosecution agreement. This resulted in a disgorgement (ie the surrender of profits obtained illegally from the Uzbek affair) and a global settlement in which Telia agreed to pay $965 million to resolve charges relating to violations of the Foreign Corrupt Practices Act (FCPA) in the USA and of Dutch law (US Department of Justice 2017). The day after Telia announced that a global settlement had been reached, the Swedish Prosecution Authority levelled criminal charges against the former CEO and two other senior company officials for their involvement in the company's bribery scheme in Uzbekistan. In addition to the criminal charges brought against individuals, the Swedish prosecutors also pursued Telia for forfeiture of economic benefits. The trial started at the Stockholm District Court on 5 September and lasted until 19 December 2018, a total of 42 days. The verdict was announced on 15 February 2019; all three defendants were acquitted. The prosecutor appealed to the Court of Appeal and, in February 2021, the defendants were also acquitted in the second instance.

During the trial, arguments around parallel legal rules constituted a recurrent theme. For example, the defence had to argue that a settlement in the US, where the corporation had accepted guilt for bribery offences, had no bearing on the Swedish case in which three individuals were being held to account: 'Telia Sonera's agreement with other countries is meaningless as evidence in this case' (Field notes day 3). The defence was arguing that although the same actions could be prosecuted in several jurisdictions, this did not mean that the jurisdictions overlapped. One of the defence lawyers expressed the following during the closing arguments: 'You get the feeling that the prosecutors are not only working on the basis of a Swedish, but an international concept when pursuing this case. [...] Of course, the Swedish bribery legislation should apply, and it is not identical to that in the USA' (Field notes day 42).

Similarly, when the prosecution argued that the Dutch court had found that Telia had used bribes, that is, the case had been tried and gained legal force in the Netherlands, the defence responded that 'other legal systems are completely irrelevant' (Field notes day 2). Furthermore, the defence argued that in many foreign legal systems, it is sufficient that the object of bribery has in some respect been a 'foreign public official', but this differs from the Swedish legal system, and concluded that 'it is, as is well known, Swedish law that must be tried in this case' (Field notes day 2). The court case against the former Telia employees highlights the transnationalism of the regulation of corruption. While the prosecutor continuously brought up international legal decisions relating to the same case to underscore liability, the defence argued for their irrelevance. The presence of several legal authorities opens up for interpretations, negotiations and different standpoints.

In this case, the company Telia had already reached the global settlement, in which the company had acknowledged guilt. By the time of the trial in Sweden, the company had nothing to lose besides the confiscation of profits if the individuals placed on trial were convicted of criminal offences. And since this amount would be confiscated by the Dutch authorities in the case of the defendants being acquitted, the company was not at risk of having to make any additional payments. In one sense, the global settlement is in itself a form of 'forum shopping' (see Merry 1988; Tamanaha 2011; von Benda-Beckmann 1981), with the company reaching the agreement with authorities from the US, the Netherlands and Sweden in order to defer prosecution and to put the scandal behind it. Regulatory competition or overlaps will facilitate law and forum shopping strategies by multinational corporations. A multinational corporation's ability, through the capital it possesses, to manoeuvre around in this regulatory landscape constitutes an example of the power such corporations possess to play the game on their own terms.

The former executives, on the other hand, who were not part of the settlement, claimed that they had been scapegoated by the company, and in the trial in Sweden they risked being sentenced to six years' imprisonment. Still, part of the defence strategy was to appeal to certain forms of law and to downplay others. This is hardly surprising, since McBarnet (1988: 120) reminds us that: '[l]aw is, in its nature, multifaceted, contradictory, and manipulable, and it is the legal profession's role to take maximum advantage of the contradictions to manipulate the law in the interests of its clients'. In Bourdieu's (1987) terms, we can understand how juridical capital and the competition for control of corporate regulation structure the juridical field. Bourdieu's theoretical framework offers a way of understanding the symbolic struggles of the interpretation of law and the 'unequal ability to marshal the available juridical resources through the exploration and exploitation of "possible rules," and to use them effectively, as symbolic weapons, to win their case' (ibid: 827). Access to this juridical capital may, as discussed above, be a question of economic capital. The former executives of the corporation did not have the capital of a multinational corporation, but they had sufficient economic capital to be able to afford juridical capital. The three teams of defence lawyers comprised what could be described as some of Sweden's top lawyers in the field of white-collar crime. Thus, the defendants had the ability to transform economic capital into juridical capital, and by this means also the ability to participate in the struggle to negotiate the field of transnational corporate regulation.

As in many cases involving multinational corporations, the corporations' employees are not necessarily citizens of the country in which the parent corporation is based, nor do they necessarily work in that country. In the Telia case, two of the defendants were native Finns and had not been based in Sweden. During both the criminal investigation and during the hearings in the both the first and second instance, the defence argued that Swedish law can only be applied if the crime was committed in Sweden, and that the accused had not performed any acts in Sweden. The defence fought for a dismissal of the prosecution on these grounds, but both instances rejected this claim. The power of a court to hear and decide cases and the boundaries of its jurisdiction is particularly challenging when it comes to multinational corporations and the ability of nation states to hold them to account. The legal contest over jurisdiction was also recurrent in the case of Lundin Energy, as discussed below.

VI. VIOLATIONS OF INTERNATIONAL LAW, UNIVERSAL JURISDICTION AND NATIONAL LAW

In 2010, the prosecutor in Stockholm initiated a criminal investigation into suspicions of violations of international law (*folkrättsbrott*) relating to the activities of Lundin Oil in Sudan between 1997 and 2003. Ever since the company was awarded a contract for Block 5A in southern Sudan, the corporation's operations have faced allegations of participating in crimes against humanity. In November 2016, the Swedish Prosecution Authority served Ian Lundin, chairman of the board, and Alexandre Schneiter, the former CEO, with reasonable suspicions concerning complicity in serious crimes against international law. However, it was not until November 2021 that the prosecutor filed an indictment. According to this indictment, both Lundin and Schneiter exerted a decisive influence over Lundin Oil's operations in Sudan during the period in which the military and militia in the country had committed violations of international law against the civilian population, partly in order to enable Lundin Oil's oil exploration in the area. In addition to the criminal charges against the two individuals, the company has been charged to pay a corporate fine of 3 million SEK and to forfeit economic benefits of almost 1.4 billion SEK. The prosecutor has also demanded that the two defendants be banned from business activities for ten years. At the time of writing, the date for the court hearing has not yet been announced, but it is expected to be the longest trial in Swedish history.

The company's legal defence has been massive and has been operating on the basis of several parallel approaches. One of the approaches has involved aspects of legal pluralism, more specifically the relationship between national and international law in relation to international crimes.[5] In other words, the legal battle started long before

---

[5] The defence have also joined forces to argue that the suspects have had their human rights violated, since the investigation has taken an unreasonably long time (see for example Chambers of 9 Bedford Row and RPC Solicitors 2021). The defendants have attempted to have the investigations discontinued on the grounds of violations of the right to a fair trial, an issue which has been examined and rejected in the first and second instances and which will now be examined by the Swedish supreme court.

the case has reached the courts. As in many other cases in which corporations are accused of crime, the aim is to ensure that the case never reaches court.

This case provides an example of the significance of the legal experts employed by the corporations. The ability to shape the field is related to the capital possessed by social agents, and here juridical knowledge is one of the fundamental forms of capital (Bourdieu 1987). The legal capital of legal experts is available to clients who are able to afford it. It is hardly surprising then that a corporation uses its economic capital to acquire the legal capital that provides professional legal advice and legal arguments to shape the interpretation of law in its own interests (see also McBarnet 1988).

As part of the company's legal defence, it has hired legal experts in Sweden and abroad to formulate professional statements that support the defence. One of the issues concerns jurisdiction, and Sweden's ability to prosecute a non-Swedish national, the former CEO who is a Swiss national, who has not resided in Sweden, for acts that did not take place on Swedish territory. One of the legal experts commissioned by the company has argued that the former CEO cannot be prosecuted in Sweden under Swedish law on the basis of universal jurisdiction (Schabas 2018).

There is another issue relating to the legal pluralistic field, however, that is also related to universal jurisdiction and that constitutes a major focus of the professional statement made by the legal experts commissioned by the company. This concerns the application of Swedish legislation to international crimes. In 2014, four years after initiation of the criminal investigation, two Swedish law professors were commissioned by the company to write a statement regarding the application of Swedish law to international crimes. Having conducted a comparison, the law professors concluded that the regulation of complicity in Swedish law is more comprehensive than in the Rome statute. Similarly, they concluded that the regulation of intent under Swedish law is broader than in the Rome statute, particularly with regard to indifference. Furthermore, they argued that the Swedish legislation on complicity and intent cannot be applied, since Sweden has incorporated violations of international law in the Swedish legislation, meaning that international law should be applied in its entirety (Bring and Träskman 2014). Similarly, the legal expert who formed the opinion relating to jurisdiction with regard to the former CEO argued that it is international law on complicity in international crime that must be applied, not Swedish law (Schabas 2018: 7).

The legal pluralistic field opens up for the interpretations of legal experts. In the case of Lundin, this opportunity has been used extensively. A recent 'independent expert report' (Lundin Energy 2021) by two British legal firms led by Steven Kay, mostly known for defending Slobodan Milosevic, which was commissioned by Lundin's board of directors, of which one of the suspects remains the chair, echoes many of the central elements of the company's defence from the last decade. The report claims that the company has contributed to peace in the region (discusssed in depth in Schoultz and Flyghed 2019), that the allegations made by NGOs are false, and that the criminal investigation is seriously flawed and unfair. With regard to this latter issue, the report raises concerns that the prosecutor is not applying the 'the correct principles of law' (Chambers of 9 Bedford Row and RPC Solicitors 2021: 10) and that 'the prosecution's investigation is not in accordance with Sweden's international obligations' (ibid: 103). The report argues that the cases should be dismissed on these grounds.

The legal pluralistic field, in which national law and international law coincide, opens up for interpretations, negotiations and opportunities. Whether or not this may be framed as a form of 'law shopping' (Lhuilier 2013) is open to debate. Perhaps we should understand it merely as a form of appeal to certain laws over others, as part of a legal defence in which the task of the defence is to find 'loopholes' in the prosecutor's interpretation of events. In addition, the list of legal experts commissioned by the company to support their interpretation of the legal pluralistic field is extensive. It is obvious however, that companies, and large transnational corporations in particular, have capital that can be activated in order to strengthen their ability to 'law shop' and 'forum shop', as well as to appeal to selected forms of law when manoeuvring in a legal pluralistic terrain. Multinational corporations have a much greater ability to exploit situations of legal pluralism than many other social actors. From a Bourdieusian perspective, this could be understood as a form of juridical capital (Bourdieu 1987), which corporations can obtain by commissioning legal experts to improve their position within the juridical field. In this sense, economic capital may facilitate juridical capital. The application of Bourdieu's notion of a field can, in this way, assist in developing the analysis of the way in which those with juridical capital (as well as other forms of capital) are able to utilise parallel and competing regulations.

VII. CONCLUDING DISCUSSION

Modern corporations are surrounded by and intertwined with law: 'They were born through the legal act of incorporation, and they die through the legal act of bankruptcy' (Edelman and Suchman 1997: 480). Classical social theorists such as Marx and Durkheim considered the sociology of law and the sociology of organisations to be intimately intertwined (Edelman and Suchman 1997). As has been discussed, corporations are governed on various levels (local to global), by varying forms (soft law and hard law) and sources of law (state and private) (Berman 2009). At the same time, as others have noted, the field is mainly characterised by a lack of direct legal governance from both a global and domestic perspective, particularly with regard to the business operations of transnational corporations in so-called 'weak states' (Simons and Macklin 2014: 8). The legal pluralistic field may impose conflicting demands and norms, generating uncertainty as to which legal regime should apply in a certain situation. Legal pluralism thus creates opportunities for an opportunistic selection between coexisting legal authorities (Tamanaha 2008: 375).

In this chapter, I have discussed how law in its plurality can be utilised as a tool by powerful and strategic multinational corporations as part of their struggle to dominate the interpretation of corporate regulation. I have provided examples of how two corporations, when accused of misconduct, have drawn on and appealed to specific laws over others. First, when accused of contributing to human rights violations, one of the corporations referred to the obligation to follow local laws (instead of international human rights). Second, when former executives from the same company were accused of bribery offences under Swedish law, they rejected the relevance of legal verdicts and settlements from other jurisdictions. The other company appealed to the application of international rather than domestic law when accused of complicity in the commission of war crimes and crimes against humanity. These are just examples, and strategic appeals to specific laws can take many others forms. Strategic actors, such as corporations, may also be inconsistent in their choices, allowing what is estimated to be most successful in a particular case to determine which legal arguments should be used. While official legal systems are often invoked first, since they lend legitimacy, other norms such as soft law may be utilised if there are financial or other reasons to do so (Tamanaha 2008: 406 ff).

The cases I have drawn upon in this chapter provide insights into the dynamics of law that surround corporations, and to cite Reza Banakar (2015: 36) '[r]ecognising the diversity of forms of law has always been the cornerstone of the sociology of law'. Of course, we should not stop at this recognition, but rather attempt to understand what normative systems are treated as binding in practice, by whom and when (see Berman 2009). We can understand the corporate manoeuvres illustrated in this case study as an expression of an exercise of power that determines the outcome of the law when law leaves room for such manoeuvring, as in the case of legal pluralism. We could also ask what the consequence are of the game in which the multinational corporations have engaged. Do the cases provide an insight into the reasons why corporations are seldom held accountable in criminal courts? Cutler (2013: 734) encourages asking the critical question of '"who benefits" from transnational legality – whose interests do these legal regimes, both hard and soft, serve?'

In this chapter, I have used case studies to illustrate how legal pluralism has enabled two multinational corporations, and their former executives, to manipulate law when accused of crime. The Bourdieusian approach contributes with an understanding of how corporations use their economic capital to shape their vision of the law and of its interpretation, and in this way impose a redefinition of the rules regarding how companies should be governed. Thus, it becomes important to study and understand the relationship between the juridical field and the larger field of power (Bourdieu 1987), not at least in situations of legal pluralism. Juridical capital, based on economic capital, provides the power to shape how law(s) are interpreted and which laws are considered valid in the struggle over corporate regulation.

REFERENCES

Alvesalo-Kuusi, A, Bittle, S and Lähteenmäki, L (2017) 'Repositioning the Corporate Criminal: Comparing and Contrasting Corporate Criminal Liability in Canada and Finland' *International Journal of Comparative and Applied Criminal Justice* 1.

Baars, G (2016) '"It's Not Me, It's the Corporation": the Value of Corporate Accountability in the Global Political Economy' 4(1) *London Review of International Law* 127.

Banakar, R (2015) *Normativity in Legal Sociology: Methodological Reflections on Law and Regulation in Late Modernity* (Heidelberg, Springer).

Banakar, R and Travers, M (2005) *Theory and Method in Socio-Legal Research* (Oxford, Bloomsbury Publishing).

Berman, PS (2009) 'The New Legal Pluralism' 5 *Annual Review of Law and Social Science* 225.

Bourdieu, P (1977) *Outline of a Theory of Practice* (Cambridge, Cambridge University Press).

—— (1987) 'Force of Law: Toward a Sociology of the Juridical Field' 38 *Hastings Law Journal* 805.

—— (1993) *Sociology in Question* (London, Sage Publications (CA)).

—— (2000) *Pascalian Meditations* (Cambridge, Polity).

Bourdieu, P and Wacquant, LJD (1992) *An Invitation to Reflexive Sociology* (Cambridge, Polity).

Bring, O and Träskman, PO (2014) *Utlåtande, 19 december 2014.*

Chambers of 9 Bedford Row and RPC Solicitors (2021) *A Report on The Lundin Case.*

Cotterrell, R (2009) 'Spectres of Transnationalism: Changing Terrains of Sociology of Law' 36(4) *Journal of Law and Society* 481.

Cutler, C (2013) 'Legal Pluralism as the "Common Sense" of Transnational Capitalism' 3(4) *Oñati Socio-Legal Series* 719.

Dagens Nyheter (2012) 'Det är inte vi som bryter mot mänskliga rättigheter'.

Dezalay, Y and Garth, BG (1998) *Dealing in Virtue: International Commercial Arbitration and the Construction of a Transnational Legal Order* (Chicago, University of Chicago Press).

Edelman, LB and Suchman, MC (1997) 'The Legal Environments of Organizations' 23 *Annual Review of Sociology* 479.

Griffiths, A (2002) 'Legal Pluralism' in R Banakar and M Travers (eds), *An Introduction to Law and Social Theory* (Oxford, Hart Publishing) 289.

Griffiths, J (1986) 'What is Legal Pluralism?' 18(24) *The Journal of Legal Pluralism and Unofficial Law* 1.

Haines, F and Macdonald, K (2021) 'Grappling with Injustice: Corporate Crime, Multinational Business and Interrogation of Law in Context' 25(2) *Theoretical Criminology* 284.

Huisman, W (2010) *Business as Usual? Corporate Involvement in International Crimes* (Hague, Eleven International).

Lhuilier, G (2013) 'Academic Knowledge. Three Views on Global Law and Global Legal Theory' in *Rethinking the Globalization of Law*, Les cahiers d'Ebisu. Occasional Papers No 3, 51, available at https://www.mfj.gr.jp/publications/_data/e-CahiersEbisu3_pp41-79_GlobalizationLaw_screen.pdf.

Lundin Energy (2021) 'Open Letter from the Board of Directors of Lundin Energy', 10 May 2021 (press release).

McBarnet, D (1988) 'Law, Policy, and Legal Avoidance: Can Law Effectively Implement Egalitarian Policies' 15(1) *Journal of Law and Society* 113.

—— (2006) 'After Enron Will "Whiter than White Collar Crime" Still Wash?' 46(6) *British Journal of Criminology* 1091.

Merry, SE (1988) 'Legal Pluralism' 22(5) *Law & Society Review* 869.

Schabas, WA (2018) *Expert Opinion on Universal Juristiction* (London, 16 August 2018).

Schoultz, I and Flyghed, J (2016) 'Doing Business for a "Higher Loyalty"? How Swedish Transnational Corporations Neutralise Allegations of Crime' 66(2) *Crime, Law and Social Change* 183.

—— (2019) 'From "We Didn't Do It" to "We've Learned Our Lesson": Development of a Typology of Neutralizations of Corporate Crime' 28 *Critical Criminology* 739.

—— (2020a) 'Denials and Confessions. An Analysis of the Temporalization of Neutralizations of Corporate Crime' 61 *International Journal of Law, Crime and Justice* 100389.

—— (2020b) '"We Have Been Thrown Under the Bus": Corporate Versus Individual Defense Mechanisms Against Transnational Corporate Bribery Charges' 2(1) *Journal of White Collar and Corporate Crime* 24.

Shaffer, G and Halliday, T (2021) 'With, Within, and Beyond the State: The Promise and Limits of Transnational Legal Ordering' in P Zumbansen (ed), *The Oxford Handbook of Transnational Law* (Oxford, Oxford University Press) 988.

Simons, P and Macklin, A (2014) *The Governance Gap: Extractive Industries, Human Rights, and the Home State Advantage* (Routledge).

Snider, L (2000) 'The Sociology of Corporate Crime: An Obituary: (Or: Whose Knowledge Claims have Legs?)' 4(2) *Theoretical Criminology* 169.

Tamanaha, BZ (1993) 'The Folly of the "Social Scientific" Concept of Legal Pluralism' 20(2) *Journal of Law and Society* 192.

—— (2008) 'Understanding Legal Pluralism: Past to Present, Local to Global' 30 *Sydney Law Review* 375.

—— (2011) 'The Rule of Law and Legal Pluralism in Development' 3 *Hague Journal on the Rule of Law* 1.

TeliaSonera (2006) *Global Reporting Initiative Indicators (G3) 2006.*

—— (2012a) *Transcript of CEO update on CR priority action plan on August 23 2012.*

—— (2012b) Press release 28 September 2012 *Uppdatering Uzbekistan.*

Teubner, G (2002) 'Breaking Frames: Economic Globalization and the Emergence of Lex Mercatoria' 5(2) *European Journal of Social Theory* 199.

Tombs, S and Whyte, D (2015) *The Corporate Criminal: Why Corporations Must be Abolished* (Abingdon, Routledge).

US Department of Justice (2017) United States v Telia Company AB Deferred Prosecution Agreement.

Uppdrag granskning (2012a) 'Teliasonera i hemligt samarbete med diktaturer', available at https://www.svt.se/nyheter/granskning/ug/teliasonera-i-hemligt-samarbete-med-diktaturer.

—— (2012b) 'Teliasonera i miljardaffär med diktatur', available at https://www.svt.se/nyheter/granskning/ug/teliasonera-gjorde-miljardaffar-med-diktatur-genom-bolag-i-skatteparadis.

von Benda-Beckmann, K (1981) 'Forum Shopping and Shopping Forums: Dispute Processing in a Minangkabau Village in West Sumatra' 13(19) *The Journal of Legal Pluralism and Unofficial Law* 117.

Zumbansen, P (2011) 'Neither "Public" nor "Private", "National" nor "International": Transnational Corporate Governance from a Legal Pluralist Perspective' 38(1) *Journal of Law and Society* 50.

10

Corporate Governance, Soft Law, and Corporate Social Responsibility: Some Legal Theoretical Contributions

MAURO ZAMBONI

I. BACKGROUND

H AVING KNOWN REZA Banakar for many years, at both a professional and personal level, has been a true blessing to me and my intellectual development as legal theoretician. In addition to his humanity and generosity, Banakar's work has been extremely helpful at the professional level, thanks to one particular trait characterising his legal sociology: his deep interest in legal theory. Moving away from the traditional interest of legal sociology in the relations between law and society, Banakar – in many of his writings – underlined the central role that legal theory may play in shaping law-society relations. He described legal theory not just as a 'mirror' of such relations, but also potentially as a guiding light for us to improve our understanding of them and, eventually, to change them for the better. Based on the insightful legacy Banakar has left to legal theoreticians, this chapter explores the possibility of using legal theory to better understand the legal issues of the arena which, at least prima facie, appears most distant from the theoretical dimensions, namely the corporate world.

When reading the title of this chapter, one may question the very idea that legal theory can in some way offer a valuable contribution to practical problems such as corporate governance, the role of soft law in corporate law, and the possibility of having social responsibility legally embedded in the governance of a company. This questioning of the relevance of a theoretical approach in solving some of the concrete issues that corporate legal scholars and corporate lawyers encounter in their everyday work is justified. Part of legal theory deals with rather abstract questions, eg the nature of the law or the elements that constitute valid law (Penner and Melissaris 2012; Dreier and Alexy 1990).

However, there are also legal theoreticians who deal with the more tangible areas of the legal phenomenon, and whose work can directly affect companies' day-to-day operations. This branch of legal theory aims to establish some general, observation-based models of how the law works, how its actors – such as companies or lawyers – operate, the problems company operations may create (eg in relation to certain social conditions or moral requirements); this legal theory also strives to offer strategic solutions that may work within the legal context (Van Hoecke 1999; Hart 1994; Weinberger 1986). This strand of legal theory has traditionally had very strong ties with corporate law, a privileged area of law where new ideas and future development can be found and discussed (Hart 1983; Weber 1978; Cheffins 2004).

Nowadays, this part of legal theory, inspired by developments in the fields of corporate law and corporate governance, deals with issues that are central to the daily work of corporate lawyers, and that have significant influence on this work: how corporate social responsibility (hereinafter CSR), sustainability, and the globalisation of law affect the idea of what is the 'real' law; the normative criteria that should be used to identify the valid (and therefore applicable) law; and whether (and if so, how) it is possible to separate this valid law from the so-called soft law, ie norms that seem to govern action without being binding in the strict sense (Catá Backer 2008; Zumbansen 2012; Horrigan 2010).[1] In particular, soft law has a central place in the contemporary legal theoretical debate, and (as it is also used in this chapter) it indicates a wide variety of voluntary codes, created by private and public actors, which are not formally enacted as legally binding regulations; thus, these codes indirectly place obligations on their addressees as positive law. For various reasons, however, such regulations are accepted (and adhered to) by large companies as binding regulations; they can take very different forms, eg corporate governance codes, codes of conduct, policy documents, restatements, model laws, and guidelines on best practices and standards (Catá Backer 2008; Woodlock and Hydén 2020).

This chapter aims to point out the reasons behind the increasing importance of soft law as one of the most important compliance tools in corporate regulation, especially at a cross-border level, and why soft law should still be retained as the primary regulatory tool, especially when it comes to regulating CSR.[2] To fulfil this goal, section II will start by sketching the difficult situation in which corporate lawyers may find themselves in their daily work, pressured by different forces and value systems; this picture will rely particularly on the Lawrence Lessig's theory of lawyers as 'pathetic dots' among various institutional forces. Section III will then present how this situation has encouraged corporate actors to develop soft law as a tool for regulating behaviour when companies are forced to confront new forces in the form of more 'socially' orientated business. Finally, section IV will discuss from a legal perspective, what might be the best law-making strategy for decision-makers to adopt to regulate this extremely complicated environment where market considerations, socio-ethical considerations, and legal considerations often conflict with each other.

---

[1] In this chapter, the term 'corporate lawyers' means not only in-house lawyers and/or general counsel, but all professional lawyers who operate mostly within or for companies, eg also lawyers working for law firms that work primarily for corporate clients.

[2] As to this chapter, CSR is defined as an effort by the company to balance and satisfy the so-called 'Triple Bottom Line', ie 'profit' (economic demands), 'people' (social demands), and 'planet' (environmental demands) (Kaptein and Wempe 2002; van Marrewijk 2003).

II. CORPORATE LAWYERS AS 'PATHETIC DOTS'

In the late 1990s, Lessig developed the theory of 'pathetic dots' (Lessig 1999a; Lessig 2006). This is a socio-economic theory about regulatory environments, based on the idea that lawyers are 'pathetic dots' in a society (at least in one of the Western types) that is governed by four institutional forces, ie four systems that compel the addressees into certain behaviours, regardless of whether the addressees consider such behaviours to be worth pursuing. These forces are: law (by threatening sanctions); social norms (ie models of behaviours that society considers worthwhile and that are backed by non-legal sanctions); the market (through economic mechanisms of livelihood, demands, and profits); and 'architecture' (Lessig 1999b; Lessig 2006).[3]

This chapter will mainly consider the position of corporate lawyers within the interlaced system of forces produced by the law, social norms, and the market. As to the fourth institutional force, namely 'architecture', Lessig defines it as 'the physical world as we find it, even if "as we find it" is simply how it has already been made' (Lessig 1999b:, 507). This includes facts such as biology (eg one gets old), technology (eg one cannot, yet, colonise the moon), or geography (eg some countries lack certain natural resources, such as oil) (Lessig 2006). In other words, 'architecture' is the structural physical and technical framework within which human beings live and operate (Lessig 1999b). This chapter, therefore, will not deal with architecture to any great extent, because, from a legal perspective, architecture lacks a normative content: it does not tell actors what they should do, but only what they can physically do, and thus becomes a governing force (ie compelling the addressees to adopt certain types of behaviour), but without awareness (ie lacking the normative feature of indicating to the very addressees what 'ought to be done') (Lessig 1999a).

The theory of 'pathetic dots' has been applied by Lessig (and others) mainly to the regulation of the Internet and cyberspace (Lessig 2006; Murray 2016; Lambooy et al 2019). The point of this chapter is that this theory can also be applied to better illustrate the situation in which company actors, and not least corporate lawyers, find themselves. Such lawyers are employed or hired by companies as legal experts: they are expected to contribute to the activity of the company in legal matters, ie helping the company navigate in the complicated labyrinth, created by the dogmas or paradigms, that governs the legal discourse and regulations (Regan 2000; Nelson and Nielsen 2000). However, both the company and the lawyers working within or for it do not live in a 'legal vacuum', that is, in a world where one may solve all problems and make everyone happy by simply following the law and its rules. Companies are primarily economic actors and therefore their primary task is to achieve economic goals, realise profit and preferably increase this profit over time by following economic dogmas, for instance by developing new financial instruments that are favourable for companies' tax planning or risk-taking (Nelson and Nielsen 2000; Dubey and Kripalani 2013). Moreover, companies, while operating on the market, are at the same time part of a larger structure, ie one or more societies. The latter often impose certain

---

[3] It can be noted that the very nature of passive 'pathetic dots' of the actors located among such institutional forces may be questioned (Murray 2008).

tasks upon the companies and their lawyers, undertakings which are often in conflict with their respective economic and legal frameworks; for instance, society can push for the costly improvement of certain working conditions for workers, regardless of whether such improvements are required by the current legislation (Hackett 2002; Regan 2000; Loughrey 2011).

It is worth pointing out that the theory of pathetic dots is not intended to have a negative connotation. On the contrary, it signals that, when examining and evaluating the work of corporate lawyers, one needs to understand the complex regulatory environments in which they operate and the difficulties of balancing different (and often conflicting) types of rationality (Nelson and Nielsen 2000; Paton 2017). In this sense, the situation for corporate lawyers is the quintessence of the role that lawyers generally play in modern society: they attempt to navigate among strong – often conflicting – streams of normative forces, ie forces that tell them the direction in which their work should go. At the same time that they must maintain their role as lawyers and respect the normative force of law to continue to be legitimised as 'lawyers'; they are required to monitor the directions indicated by the form of regulation known as social norms, ie certain basic societal rules, and carry out both tasks while respecting the force of the market in a capitalist society – a force that requires lawyers' activities to produce economically favourable results (Moorhead et al 2019; Loughrey 2011; Kim 2012).

III. SOFT LAW AS THE PREFERRED TYPE OF REGULATORY TOOL

The term soft law can be regarded from a legal perspective as an umbrella definition. Soft law, to a greater extent than for the term hard law, is a terminological ceiling under which different types of regulations are introduced: codes of conduct, corporate governance codes, recommendations or expert standards, to name just a few (Karlsson-Vinkhuyzen 2011; Catá Backer 2008). In particular, soft law as it is used in this chapter covers all types of norms which, due to their legitimacy, the effectiveness of their sanction system, and the acceptance by the major actors in the field, in some way tend to be perceived and applied as binding by these very actors, despite the lack of the immediate and formal binding nature of legislation (van der Sluijs 2016; Cerone 2016).

Defined in this way, one notes immediately how soft law has been an important tool for norm development in many areas, in particular (though not limited to) the regulatory regimes that are now superseding the governance and activities of corporations (Teubner 2009; Hansmann and Kraakman 2001). If one looks at this phenomenon from the perspective of the corporate lawyers, soft law can also be described as a domain for strategic interactions between the institutional actors (and their respective discourses or, in Lessig's terminology, forms of regulation) that populate a particular social, political, or economic context (Woodlock and Hydén 2020). While hard law is dominated by the authoritative imposition of a certain model of behaviour on the actors, soft law resembles instead a (more or less) trade situation where actors (more or less) freely exchange certain behaviours, eg to establish a corporate policy or comply with a code of conduct, against certain behaviours from other actors, eg to avoid blacklisting (Hall and Sosike 2001).

In this respect, it appears prima facie that in the last decades, soft law has generated problems within the corporate legal discourse by pushing corporate lawyers into an uneasy trade position. The emergence of requirements for CSR inevitably means that several companies, not least large and cross-border corporations, are confronted with a new normative reality that lies outside the strictly economic discourse of maximising profits and the previous legal discourse's full support of such dogma (Sjåfjell et al 2015; Calliess and Zumbansen 2010). However, observing the phenomenon from a closer perspective, it can be noted that it is not soft law that has caused the awkward situation for the corporate players. Instead, other regulatory forces surrounding the corporate world have forced such players to find an alternative tool. Soft law has thus not created the problems; on the contrary, it has been an instrument that has enabled some degree of harmony between such forces, which otherwise would have collided more aggressively, creating a more problematic situation for the actors operating in the corporate arena, and not least for the lawyers (Kirton and Trebilcock 2004; Abbott and Snidal 2000).

In any case, regardless of whether soft law can be seen as the cause or an attempt at a solution, it is quite undisputable how corporate lawyers have become more and more like Lessig's pathetic dots in recent decades, particularly due to the increasing demands from the social discourse (or social norms, according to Lessig's theory). On one hand, historical and institutional reasons have firmly anchored the dominance of economic discourse within the regulatory framework of entrepreneurship (or 'market modality,' in Lessig's categorisation of forms of regulation) (Talbot 2012; Eisenberg 1999; Sjåfjell et al 2015). On the other hand, law-makers (in particular the legislative ones) have found it difficult to deal with the increasing conflict between the market modality that pushes for profit maximisation and the demands from the social modality for greater social responsibility – demands that are supported by large sections of the population and thus by large portions of the electorate (McBarnet 2007; Calliess and Zumbansen 2010; Schuck 2018). As a result, many Western legal systems are witnessing an increasing number of hard law solutions, which legalise social discourse, while allowing the market's profit maximisation efforts to continue as before, but now with built-in legal restrictions (Buhmann 2018). For instance, within the European Union, this process of legalisation is illustrated by the introduction of requirements on sustainability reporting for larger corporations and companies in the financial services sector (European Parliament 2020; European Commission 2020).

However, while this process of embedding social demands in the corporate legal discourse through juridification (in particular in the form of legislation enacted by national assemblies) may work within the traditional nation-state system, it is more problematic when transferred to a more global level (Brodie 2012). The transnational arena lacks a traditional legislator and a traditional electorate; the social discourse is not clearly supported by a legal counterpart; and though hard law standards are certainly not lacking and there are initiatives for universal national regulation, the monitoring and sanctions systems are often weak (Scherer and Palazzo 2008; Horrigan 2010).

Therefore, at a global level and in the midst of conflicting regulatory systems and their underlying values (the forces of law, social forces, and the market), the difficult situation for corporate actors and the difficulties encountered by hard law solutions have contributed to the legal actors' increasingly benevolent attitudes towards a 'soft' regulation than would otherwise have been the case (Whelan and Ziv 2013; Voegtlin and Pless 2014). This tolerance towards such an 'unorthodox solution' (at least from the legal actors' perspective) has probably been necessary, given that soft law in some way questions two of the most basic dogmas of Western legal discourse: the idea that the law is either binding or something other than law; and the idea that what is not recognised as law is somehow viewed as a dangerous (or at least foreign) element in regulatory processes, endangering the principles of democracy and rule of law (Teubner 1997; Mörth 2004; Scheuch 2018).[4]

On the one hand, *soft* law is by definition a flexible regulatory tool: it allows law-makers to adapt more quickly and less elaborately (at least in relation to the traditional tools of hard law) to changes taking place in the external world – changes that depend not only on market forces but also on the social perceptions of corporate behaviour (Gabriel 2019; Brownsword and Goodwin 2012). Moreover, as is often the case when it comes to soft law, the creators of the regulation are also the very addressees of the norms; in other words, soft law to a large extent, is a matter of self-regulation, though it may be that actors others than the creators of the norms may also be influenced by the norms (eg NGOs or political parties) (Wawryk 2003; Kirton and Trebilcock 2004). These two qualities of the regulatory tool of soft law – flexibility and self-regulation – allow companies and corporate actors to adapt to changing requirements, without having to hand over the regulation of their economic activities to other actors (eg political legislators) whose logic and value systems may be dominated by non-economic considerations and who could jeopardise the beneficial economic effects of globalisation (Magnier 2017; Gunningham and Rees 1997).

On the other hand, soft *law* is also 'law': it is a set of rules intended to distance itself from non-binding customs or practices by offering a certain degree of stability. Soft law in this sense is expressed in documents (such as codes of conduct) that are a product of a fairly open creation process; they contain fairly clear and concrete rules for implementation, and include a 'sanction-and-control' system aimed at ensuring the addressees' compliance with rules, for instance via naming and shaming (Creutz 2013; Hepple 2002). In addition, soft law usually contains another function that is considered as typical for 'normal law', namely a certain degree of universality. Soft law is not only often available to the public, for example through widely advertised companies' codes of ethics, but it is almost always the soft law creators themselves (eg companies, marketplaces dominated by market participants, or industry associations) who (more or less) aim in well-intentioned efforts to spread knowledge about the existence and content of such regulatory sources (Jackson 2010).

To sum up, the degree of success of soft law as a privileged regulatory system among lawyers, and in particular corporate lawyers operating in a globalised environment, depends largely on the fact that such regulations are structurally flexible,

---

[4] There are, however, several critical voices denying the very term soft law and its legal relevance due to the necessity of law always being fully binding (Shelton 2006) or due to the non-universal binding nature of soft law (Klabbers 1996; Di Robilant 2006).

but also offer (or at least strive to offer) certain features that are typical of hard law – namely a certain degree of stability, an institutional framework for creation and implementation and, more importantly, a high degree of predictability among addressees (Carruthers 2015; Grabosch 2016). All these 'similar-to-hard-law' qualities, as Max Weber pointed out, are fundamental features required for any regulatory system aimed at governing a capitalist economy and its key players – corporations (Weber 1978; Carruthers and Halliday 2007).

IV.   CAN ACTORS OTHER THAN THE SHAREHOLDERS AUTOMATICALLY CLAIM LEGAL RIGHTS AGAINST THE COMPANY?

Though the issue of the corporation and its responsibilities in a broader social context has been the subject of international debate long before now, the debate about the legal nature of corporate governance and whether companies have a social responsibility towards actors other than their shareholders has taken on new life in recent decades (Hill 2005; Catá Backer 2006; Mares 2007).[5] The aim of this section of the chapter is to determine, from a legal theoretical perspective, whether cross-border corporate regulation by default imposes legal obligations on a company towards parties other than the owners. In other words, this section aims to answer a fundamental question for transnational corporate actors: based on the legal definition of what a company is in a cross-border context, do actors other than the shareholders automatically have any legal rights with respect to the company?

The answer to this question is a first, preliminary step in assessing the legitimacy of soft law as a primary tool for addressing the issue of CSR. Due to the self-regulatory nature of soft law, if the legal perception of what a corporation is automatically assigns legal rights to actors other than the owners, this 'by-default-inclusion' will require a more direct law-making intervention from outside the corporate world. Actors other than the very soft law makers, such as states, government agencies, or state-based organisations, should thus be heavily involved in the creation, via hard law, of the corporate regulation to ensure the adherence to and fulfilment of these non-owners' rights in corporate matters (de Jonge 2017; Liu 2017). Traditionally, due to their public character and identification, only state or administrative agencies in general were able to fully guarantee that 'everyone's rights' are respected, ie including rights for actors who do not belong to the business arena (and who thus do not count among soft law creators) (Zerk 2006; Hassan et al 2016). Therefore, the expansion of the scope of existing global corporations for non-owners should be considered as the necessary condition to justify a process for hardening soft law with traditional regulatory tools, namely hard law in both national and international forms (Bijlmakers 2018). However, this hardening of soft law to protect non-owners' rights should take place not in the usual hard law way, ie in the form of a purely

---

[5] The origins of the issue as to the responsibilities of a corporation can be traced back (albeit limited to a national legal and social context) to the famous debate between Adolph Berle and Merrick Dodd in the early 1930s (Berle 1931; Dodd 1932).

top-down regulation, but in some form of collaboration, where corporate actors have considerable influence over the legislative design of the standards of action (Bell and Hindmoor 2009; Scott 2008).

A. Assessment of the Situation

One characteristic feature of modern law globalisation is soft law, ie the fact that there is significant participation of private actors in the phases of law-making and law enforcement. This participation is seldom allowed in advance or subsequently recognised by the state, but it is simply considered a necessary component for using the market as an integral part of society's governance (Salamon 2002; Slaughter 2001). In terms of corporate governance, and especially in recent decades, it is possible to detect how the phenomenon has created a fundamental dilemma.

On the one hand, large parts of the transnational rules regulating multinational corporations are left to private actors; at least from a formal point of view, these private actors tend to create the standards on their own, even if they are informally influenced by other companies' standards and NGOs (Zerk 2006; Danielsen 2005). On the other hand, large corporations have come to play a central role, not only for the global economy but also for other surrounding areas: what companies do and/or should do has become an issue that affects more parties than just the shareholders. Today, a transnational corporation – a private player constructed in accordance with the wishes of the owners – is considered as one of the most important instruments for promoting welfare policy, ie policies that mainly affect actors who are not shareholders (and who often cannot afford to become shareholders) (Artaraz and Hill 2015; Scherer et al 2006). This situation puts transnational corporate regulation in a classic regulatory discrepancy. As in the case of file sharing, lawyers caught between restricted regulatory provisions regarding the use of copyrighted works and tolerance on the part of large sectors of the population lawyers in the regulatory environments of transnational corporations also find themselves to be pathetic dots among different types of norms (Cutler 2008; Ireland and Pillay 2010).

It is true that there are social norms from the surrounding society that point to and emphasise the need for companies to take a larger role when it comes to social issues in the geographical areas in which they operate. However, under the strong influence of the market, the current transnational legal regulation does not allow companies (and, indirectly, their shareholders, managers, and boards of directors) to act in a socially responsible way (Stalley 2009; Hart and Zingales 2017; Knox 2012). This discrepancy is particularly risky because the legal regulation may lose its legitimacy; subsequently, corporations obedient to the letter of the positive law will also lose legitimacy by ignoring signals coming from the surrounding social environments (Lessig 2008; Schiopoiu Burlea and Popa 2013; Fuchs et al 2010). To avoid such risks, the legal actors operating in the area of corporate law (both as law-makers and law-appliers) should thus identify the best legal strategy to enable adjustment in the regulation of transnational corporations to fit the transnational socio-political context and its demands (Melish and Meidinger 2012).

B. Operational Change in Transnational Corporate Governance: Is it Possible?

When it comes to strategies for tackling regulatory discrepancies, one should start by examining the corporate governance discourse to identify two types of possible changes: *operational* (or strategic) *change*, which means that a reform of corporate governance takes place by assigning companies new tasks and obligations while maintaining the same structure of governance; and *structural change*, which instead implies changing the companies' business purpose or structure (Muchlinski 2007; Sims 2002).

Most of the time, the method of change used to reduce discrepancies between legal regulation and socio-political claims in the transnational environment has been *operational change*: the social demand for CSR is forcibly introduced as an essential normative component (ie what 'ought to be done') in the management of corporations, also by assigning a legal or quasi-legal character to this component (Gill 2008; Rühmkorf 2018). This change can take place, for example, through the introduction of a code of ethical business conduct, which most transnational corporations have established; the code is assumed to play a central normative role in the internal decision-making processes of these companies (Draetta 2012).

However introducing the social element of corporate responsibility into the normative discourse of corporations in not without its problems. In particular, the pursuit of economic objectives is still the central legal characteristic of the business institution known as a corporation (ie what a corporation is created for) and therefore, the introduction of additional social responsibility does not guarantee any lasting operational change (Easterbrook and Fischel 1996; Harper Ho 2010; Rose 2007). Using a hypothetical example, a company may decide to fulfil a social responsibility norm when buying coffee beans from small farmers who live in difficult economic conditions, by offering 10 per cent more than the market prices. As consequence, economic growth in the region increases, and it is conceivable that the costs of living will also rise, leaving the farmers without any benefit from the increase in purchase price. In this scenario, cost increases make the entire activity more expensive for both the company and the farmers. In the long run, one of the objectives of the norm of CSR – ie to improve the economic conditions of small-scale farmers – will not be fulfilled; in addition, there is a significant risk that the company will either buy beans from other regions or try to negotiate back to lower purchase prices.

This hypothetical example shows that companies can indeed operate on some occasions so that social responsibility becomes a reality, but in the medium or long term, there is a threshold where profit maximisation becomes decisive (Hanlon 2008; Stephens 2002). The basic idea of an operational change is to maintain the same main structure of a corporation, but making CSR an essential duty of a company would radically change the fundamental nature of a company as a profit-maximisation structure. The legal 'genome' of pursuing economic goals often cannot be maintained in parallel with the obligation to observe social goals, eg to increase the general welfare of the population in the areas in which the company operates, because the two are often incompatible, at least in the medium- or long-term perspective (Monks and Minow 2011; Wearing 2005).

One can also imagine a possible operational change in a company through an external legal regulation (ie new legislation), eg by prescribing that non-profit purposes should be considered part of a corporation's 'natural' legal obligations and, as a consequence, the corporation should by default be considered legally account-able for implementing such non-profit goals. This operational change will also run the concrete risk of transforming the very structure (or 'identity', in organisational theory terminology) of the corporation, namely from being an economic organisa-tion to being a non-economic one (Tricker 2009; Moss Kanter et al 1992). In the Western national regulatory regimes, many such social goals have been imposed upon large corporations by legislation, but very rarely it has been done by incorporating these requirements into the companies' organisational forms (an exception being the Swedish and German models of structural employee influence on company boards). Most legal regimes have opted instead for exogenous forms of CSR, ie to operation-alise CSR outside the company structure itself – an externalisation that enables the company's profit maximisation interest to be maintained as the basic business idea (Ireland 2010; Dine 2000; Lippert et al 2014).

If CSR were to be introduced by law as an endogenous and necessary element within business purposes (ie if CSR should be counted by law as a 'default' part of the corporate goals), revolution would be imminent: it would change the corpo-rate legal structure from a (currently) well-functioning organisation, at least from an economic perspective, to something unrecognised and unpredictable. In simpler terms, by introducing an imaginary operational change in today's companies through hard law, where a corporation's aim ought to include the fulfilment of certain social demands (ie demands coming from outside the circle of the legal owners), a structural change would occur. The legal structure of Coca-Cola as one knows it today would surely disappear, but it would not necessarily be replaced by an equally economically successful and socially responsible company such as Body Shop (Chandler 2020).

It is certainly true that economic considerations can indirectly benefit from social responsibility (Kurucz et al 2008; Salvioni 2018).[6] However, even in these happy cases, the choice in favour of a more socially orientated business operation is based on economic reasons, ie those that form the basis of the legal construction known as a corporation. For example, behind the policy of quota systems in managerial positions favouring members of local populations and/or women, there is usually the basic economic consideration to create a positive image among the clientele or the governing political actors and regulators, or to counteract social instability in the area, and thus to be as economically successful as possible and, in the end, increase profits for the shareholders (Rolland and O'Keefe Bazzoni 2009; Ibrahim 2014).

From a legal perspective, economic considerations are extremely crucial in all so-called *hard cases*, ie in all cases where the legal actors are confronted with two different (and both binding) legal principles that may apply, but with mutually oppos-ing results: one is more favourable for the social aspect, and the other is better for the

---

[6] The results of empirical studies as to whether CSR brings financial benefits to the company remain contradictory (Carroll and Shabana 2010; Millon 2015).

economic aspect. In such cases, the economic function that a transnational corporation has built into its own legal nature will generally lead, and it will almost always push the decision towards a legal solution, both in terms of decision-making and application of law, and thus benefiting the deep economic nature of the organisation known as a company (Hansmann and Kraakman 2001; Catá Backer 2008).

The CSR policy document of Coca-Cola Corporation explicitly states that the company's main task is to strengthen human rights in the countries where the company operates (Coca Cola 2021). Leaving the question unanswered as to whether the authors of this policy document really meant it, or the statement is merely varnish, the reasoning developed up to now in this chapter shows that this humanitarian task can prove to be quite difficult to carry out, at least if the question is analysed in the light of today's legal definition of what constitutes the primary goal of a corporation in a transnational context. Using hard law to coerce law Coca-Cola decision-makers to work in the field of human rights will likely only produce managers who are unable to take care of their business and at the same time will perform poorly as NGO representatives.

It is true that in recent decades, in many national contexts (eg in the USA and the EU), certain operational changes have been made via hard law to reduce the dominance of profit maximisation in favour of a more socially orientated logic, eg protection of consumers and investors. Above all, the regulatory policy pursued to achieve these objectives has been implemented by establishing legal limits on the activities of the company (Beckers 2015; Zhao 2017). The legislative options chosen to implement such policies have been either to restrict corporate activity by transferring some of the legal competences to a public (or quasi-public) body (eg through the Sarbanes-Oxley Act of 2002 or MiFID I and II from 2004 and 2014, respectively) or by expanding the legal competence of actors operating in legal areas bordering on the economic activities of companies (Rahim 2013; Vercelli 2017).[7] For example, freedom in otherwise unregulated areas of companies' activity has been sharply reduced by statutory rules that prevent the award of public contracts to companies that do not meet quotas on gender and ethnicity (Ankersmit 2020; Sarter 2015).

However, so far these types of operational changes in the regulation of corporations have not taken place on a global level (Madeley 2008; Emeseh et al 2010). The global-level regulatory deficit mentioned above is not due to a simple oversight by private and public actors: it has to do with the fundamental fact that such changes in the business operations of the corporation are very difficult to agree on and implement within the transnational context. In contrast to the USA and other national contexts, transnational legal settings are characterised by a lack of a central legal authority, eg an authority such as the US Security and Exchange Commission, which makes it difficult to create and implement an internationally valid CSR regulation with the impact of legislation like the Sarbanes-Oxley Act (Amaeshi et al 2013; Khoury and Whyte 2017; Mares 2012a).

---

[7] MiFID I is Directive 2004/39/EC of the European Parliament and of the Council of 21 April 2004 on markets in financial instruments, while MiFID II is Directive 2014/65/EU of the European Parliament and of the Council of 15 May 2014 on markets in financial instruments.

From these structural constraints on the creation and application of the regulatory provisions that are typical of the transnational legal field in general, it is possible to conclude that it is an extremely difficult and complicated task, using binding hard law norms, to push transnational corporations into adopting a more socially orientated corporate structure – either by reforming corporate power structures (for example, through a hypothetical, international Sarbanes-Oxley Act with a de facto extraterritorial effect) or by reallocating adjacent transnational jurisdictions (for example, by adopting international environmental rules or by introducing internationally certain social norms in public procurement to protect employees' rights) (Mares 2012b; Haines et al 2012).

V. CONCLUSION

In conclusion, one can quite easily affirm that national hard law has no problem in forcing corporate regulations to take social considerations into account; hard law can thereby fill the regulatory deficit that characterises the normative environment in which today's companies operate. It is possible to see such unproblematic solutions in the vast amount of national legislation on occupational safety, employment protection, minimum wages, discrimination protection, environmental protection, etc. Such legislation generally enjoys a high degree of legal legitimacy among corporate actors. However, these hard law regulations are not a 'natural' part of that which defines a company from a legal perspective, and they do not compete internally with the maximisation of profits; they constitute only an external normative environment to which everyone in the corporate world must relate – almost like Lessig's architectural environment.

When one shifts attention to the transnational level, it is possible to note the use of soft law in making corporations more aware of demands coming from the social environment's regulatory system, ie when the actors themselves introduce such social norms; it is clear that this regulatory strategy makes the situation more complicated. On one hand, the use of soft law in making transnational corporations more socially responsible actually means a disruption of the established supremacy of profit maximisation in favour of social considerations. On the other hand, fully aware of this unholy union, the soft law protection of social demands tends to be perceived by the transnational corporate actors as rather weak, and in difficult cases these actors retreat to the promotion of shareholders' economic interests.

This chapter has shown that today, it is not viable to choose the option of hard law regulation to insert socially orientated operational and structural changes into the very legal core of what a corporation is and what it does. Therefore, in the absence of any other available solution, the soft law regulation – as a way to mediate social demands into the operations of the transnational corporations – remains the 'less worst' option, at least by making corporate lawyers less pathetic dots in the corporate world. The soft law regulation allows such lawyers to add social value, albeit in a weak form, to their daily work for profit maximisation-orientated corporate actors. At the same time, the lawyers have regulatory tools that are sufficiently flexible to avoid jeopardising the very idea upon which a corporation is built: to increase the economic profits for its owners. Thus, with these somewhat limited advantages of soft law when it comes to CSR in the transnational arena, it is most likely that in the foreseeable future, corporate lawyers will be forced to continue to operate as pathetic dots, navigating among not only the barriers of the physical environment (architecture), market realities and binding rules, but also the non-binding norms aimed at fulfilling social demands.

REFERENCES

Abbott, KW and Snidal, D (2000) 'Hard and Soft Law in International Governance' 54(3) *International Organization* 421.

Amaeshi, K et al (2013) *Corporate Social Responsibility, Entrepreneurship, and Innovation* (London, Routledge).

Ankersmit, L (2020) 'The Contribution of EU Public Procurement Law to Corporate Social Responsibility' 26(1–2) *European Law Journal* 9.

Artaraz, K and Hill, M (2015) *Global Social Policy* (London, Palgrave Macmillan).

Beckers, A (2015) *Enforcing Corporate Social Responsibility Codes* (Oxford, Hart Publishing).

Bell, S and Hindmoor, A (2009) *Rethinking Governance* (Cambridge, Cambridge University Press).

Berle, AA (1931) 'Corporate Powers as Powers in Trust' 44(7) *Harvard Law Review* 1049.

Bijlmakers, S (2018) *Corporate Social Responsibility, Human Rights and the Law* (London, Routledge).

Brodie, M (2012) 'Pushing the Boundaries: The Role of National Human Rights Institutions in Operationalising the 'Protect, Respect and Remedy' Framework' in R Mares (ed), *The UN Guiding Principles on Business and Human Rights – Foundations and Implementation* (Leiden, Martinus Nijhoff).

Brownsword, R and Goodwin, M (2012) *Law and the Technologies of the Twenty-First Century* (Cambridge, Cambridge University Press).

Buhmann, K (2018) *Power, Procedure, Participation and Legitimacy in Global Sustainability Norms* (London, Routledge).

Calliess, G-P and Zumbansen, P (2010) *Rough Consensus and Running Code* (Oxford, Hart Publishing).

Carroll, AB and Shabana, KM (2010) 'The Business Case for Corporate Social Responsibility' 12(1) *International Journal of Management Reviews* 85.

Carruthers, BG (2015) 'Economy and Law' in P Aspers and N Dodd (eds), *Re-Imagining Economic Sociology* (Oxford, Oxford University Press).

Carruthers, BG and Halliday, TC (2007) 'Law, Economy and Globalization' in V Nee and R Swedberg (eds), *On Capitalism* (Stanford, Stanford University Press).

Catá Backer, L (2006) 'Multinational Corporations, Transnational Law' 37 *Columbia Human Rights Law Review* 287.

—— (2008) 'Multinational Corporations as Objects and Sources of Transnational Regulation' 14(2) *ILSA Journal of International and Comparative Law* 1.

Cerone, J (2016) 'A Taxonomy of Soft Law' in J Cerone (ed), *Tracing the Roles of Soft Law in Human Rights* (Oxford, Oxford University Press).

Chandler, D (2020) *Strategic Corporate Social Responsibility*, 5th edn (Thousand Oaks, Sage Publications).

Cheffins, BR (2004) 'The Trajectory of (Corporate Law) Scholarship' 63(2) *Cambridge Law Journal* 456.

Coca Cola (2021) 'Human Rights Principles', available at https://www.coca-colacompany.com/policies-and-practices/human-rights-principles.

Creutz, K (2013) 'Law Versus Codes of Conduct' in J Klabbers and T Piiparinen (eds), *Normative Pluralism and International Law: Exploring Global Governance* (Cambridge, Cambridge University Press).

Cutler, CA (2008) 'Problematizing Corporate Social Responsibility under Conditions of Late Capitalism and Postmodernity' in V Rittberger et al (eds), *Authority in the Global Political Economy* (London, Palgrave Macmillan).

Danielsen, D (2005) 'How Corporations Govern' 46(2) *Harvard International Law Journal* 411.

de Jonge, A (2017) 'The Evolving Nature of the Transnational Corporation in the 21st Century' in A de Jonge and R Tomasic (eds), *Research Handbook on Transnational Corporations* (Cheltenham, Edward Elgar).

Di Robilant, A (2006) 54(3) 'Genealogies of Soft Law' *American Journal of Comparative Law* 499.

Dine, J (2000) *The Governance of Corporate Groups* (Cambridge, Cambridge University Press).

Dodd, ME (1932) 'For Whom Are Corporate Managers Trustees?' 45(7) *Harvard Law Review* 1145.

Draetta, U (2012) *On the Side of In-House Counsel* (New York, Juris Publishing).

Dreier, R and Alexy, R (1990) 'The Concept of Jurisprudence' 3(1) *Ratio Juris* 1.

Dubey, P and Kripalani, E (2013) *The Generalist Counsel* (Oxford, Oxford University Press).

Easterbrook, FH and Fischel, DR (1996) *The Economic Structure of Corporate Law* (Cambridge, Harvard University Press).

Eisenberg, MA (1999) 'Corporate Law and Social Norms' 99(5) *Columbia Law Review* 1253.

Emeseh, E et al (2010) 'Corporations, CSR and Self Regulation' 11(2) *German Law Journal* 230.

European Commission (2020) *Study on Directors' Duties and Sustainable Corporate Governance* (European Commission, Brussels).

European Parliament (2020) Regulation (EU) 2020/852 of the European Parliament and of the Council of 18 June 2020 on the establishment of a framework to facilitate sustainable investment, and amending Regulation (EU) 2019/2088, *Official Journal of the European Union*, L 198/14.

Fuchs, D et al (2010) 'Democratic Legitimacy of Transnational Corporations in Global Governance' in E Erman, and A Uhlin (eds), *Legitimacy Beyond the State?* (London, Palgrave Macmillan).

Gabriel, HD (2019) 'The Use of Soft Law in the Creation of Legal Norms in International Commercial Law' 40(3) *Michigan Journal of International Law* 413.

Gill, A (2008) 'Corporate Governance as Social Responsibility' 26 *Berkeley Journal of International Law* 452.

Grabosch, R (2016) 'Corporate Social Responsibility im wirtschaftsrechtlichen Mandat' *Anwaltsblatt* 384.

Gunningham, N and Rees, J (1997) 'Industry Self-regulation' 19(4) *Law and Policy* 363.

Hackett, S (2002) 'Inside Out' 44(3–4) *Arizona Law Review* 609.

Haines, F, Macdonald, K and Balaton-Chrimes, S (2012) 'Contextualising the Business Responsibility to Respect: How Much Is Lost in Translation?' in R Mares (ed), *The UN Guiding Principles on Business and Human Rights – Foundations and Implementation* (Leiden, Martinus Nijhoff).

Hall, PA and Sosike, D (2001) 'An Introduction to Varieties of Capitalism' in PA Hall and D Sosike (eds), *Varieties of Capitalism* (Oxford, Oxford University Press).

Hanlon, G (2008) 'Rethinking Corporate Social Responsibility and the Role of the Firm' in A Crane et al (eds), *The Oxford Handbook of Corporate Social Responsibility* (Oxford, Oxford University Press).

Hansmann, H and Kraakman, R (2001) 'The End of History for Corporate Law' 89 *Georgetown Law Journal* 439.

Harper Ho, V (2010) 'Enlightened Shareholder Value' 36 *The Journal of Corporation Law* 59.

Hart, HLA (1983) 'Definition and Theory in Jurisprudence' in HLA Hart, *Essays in Jurisprudence and Philosophy* (Oxford, Clarendon Press).

—— (1994) 'Postscript' in HLA Hart, *The Concept of Law*, 2nd edn (Oxford, Clarendon Press).

Hart, O and Zingales, L (2017) 'Companies Should Maximize Shareholder Welfare Not Market Value' 2 *Journal of Law, Finance, and Accounting* 247.

Hassan, J et al (2016) 'International Business and Human Rights' *International Company and Commercial Law Review* 343.

Hepple, B (2002) 'Enforcement' in B Hepple (ed), *Social and Labour Rights in a Global Context* (Cambridge, Cambridge University Press)

Hill, JG (2005) 'Regulatory Responses to Global Corporate Scandals' 23 *Wisconsin International Law Journal* 367.

Horrigan, B (2010) *Corporate Social Responsibility in the 21st Century* (Cheltenham, Edward Elgar).

Ibrahim, S (2014) 'Creating Social Capital for SMEs' in M Karataş-Özkan et al (eds), *Corporate Social Responsibility and Human Resource Management* (Cheltenham, Edward Elgar)

Ireland, P (2010) 'Limited Liability, Shareholder Rights and Corporate Irresponsibility' 34 *Cambridge Journal of Economics* 837.

Ireland, P and Pillay, RG (2010) 'Corporate Social Responsibility in a Neoliberal Age' in P Utting and J Marquesss (eds), *Corporate Social Responsibility and Regulatory Governance* (Basingstoke, Palgrave Macmillan).

Jackson, K (2010) 'Global Corporate Governance' 35(1) *Brooklyn Journal of International Law* 41.

Kaptein, M and Wempe, J (2002) 'Ethical Criteria for Corporations Ethical Criteria for Corporations' in M Kaptein and J Wempe, *The Balanced Company* (Oxford, Oxford University Press).

Karlsson-Vinkhuyzen, SI (2011) 'Global Regulation through a Diversity of Norms' in D Levi-Faur (ed), *Handbook on the Politics of Regulation* (Cheltenham, Edward Elgar).

Khoury, S and Whyte, D (2017) *Corporate Human Rights Violations* (Abingdon, Routledge).

Kim, SH (2012) 'The Ethics of In-House Practice' in L Mather and L Levin (eds), *Lawyers in Practice: Ethical Decision Making in Context* (Chicago, The Chicago University Press).

Kirton, JJ and Trebilcock, MJ (2004) 'Introduction' in JJ Kirton and MJ Trebilcock (eds), *Hard Choices, Soft Law* (Aldershot, Ashgate).

Klabbers, J (1996) 'The Redundancy of Soft Law' 65 *Nordic Journal of International Law* 167.

Knox, JH (2012) 'The Ruggie Rules: Applying Human Rights Law to Corporations' in R Mares (ed), *The UN Guiding Principles on Business and Human Rights – Foundations and Implementation* (Leiden, Martinus Nijhoff).

Kurucz, EC et al (2008) 'The Business Case for Corporate Social Responsibility' in A Crane et al (eds), *The Oxford Handbook of Corporate Social Responsibility* (Oxford, Oxford University Press).

Lambooy, T et al (2019) *The Regulatory Ecology of Two Severe Sustainability Hot Spots in the Product Life Cycles of a Pair of Jeans and a T-shirt* (Oslo, Sustainable Market Actors for Responsible Trade).

Lessig, L (1999a) *Code and Other Laws of Cyberspace* (New York, Basic Books).

—— (1999b) 'The Law of the Horse' 113(2) *Harvard Law Review* 501.

—— (2006) *Code – Version 2.0* (New York, Basic Book).

—— (2008) *Remix* (London, Penguin Press).

Lippert, I et al (2014) *Corporate Governance, Employee Voice, and Work Organization* (Oxford, Oxford University Press).

Liu, J-h (2017) 'Globalisation of Corporate Governance Depends on Both Soft Law and Hard Law, Corporate Governance Codes for the 21st Century' in JJ du Plessis and C-K Low (eds), *Corporate Governance Codes for the 21st Century* (Cham, Springer).

Loughrey, J (2011) *Corporate Lawyers and Corporate Governance* (Cambridge, Cambridge University Press).

Madeley, J (2008) *Big Business, Poor Peoples*, 2nd edn (London, Zed Books).

Magnier, V (2017) *Comparative Corporate Governance* (Cheltenham, Edward Elgar).

Mares, R (2007) *The Dynamics of Corporate Social Responsibilities* (Leiden, Martinus Nijhoff).

—— (2012a) 'Business and Human Rights After Ruggie: Foundations, the Art of Simplification and the Imperative of Cumulative Progress' in R Mares (ed), *The UN Guiding Principles on Business and Human Rights – Foundations and Implementation* (Leiden, Martinus Nijhoff).

—— (2012b) 'Responsibility to Respect: Why the Core Company Should Act When Affiliates Infringe Human Rights' in R Mares (ed), *The UN Guiding Principles on Business and Human Rights – Foundations and Implementation* (Leiden, Martinus Nijhoff).

McBarnet, D (2007) 'Corporate Social Responsibility Beyond Law, Through Law, for Law' in D McBarnet et al (eds), *The New Corporate Accountability* (Cambridge, Cambridge University Press).

Melish, TJ and Meidinger, E (2012) 'Protect, Respect, Remedy and Participate: 'New Governance' Lessons for the Ruggie Framework' in R Mares (ed), *The UN Guiding Principles on Business and Human Rights – Foundations and Implementation* (Leiden, Martinus Nijhoff).

Millon, D (2015) 'Corporate Social Responsibility and Sustainability' in B Sjåfjell and BJ Richardson (eds), *Company Law and Sustainability* (Cambridge, Cambridge University Press).

Monks, RAG and Minow, N (2011) *Corporate Governance*, 5th edn (Chichester, John Wiley and Sons).

Moorhead, R et al (2019) *In-House Lawyers' Ethics* (Oxford, Hart Publishing).

Mörth, U (2006) 'Soft Regulation and Global Democracy' in M-L Djelic and K Sahlin-Andersson (eds), *Transnational Governance* (Cambridge, Cambridge University Press).

Moss Kanter, R et al (1992) *The Challenge of Organizational Change* (New York, The Free Press).

Muchlinski, PT (2007) *Multinational Enterprises and the Law*, 2nd edn (Oxford, Oxford University Press).

Murray, A (2016) *Information Technology Law*, 3rd edn (Oxford, Oxford University Press).

Murray, AD (2008) 'Conceptualising the Post-regulatory (Cyber)state' in R Brownsword and K Yeung (eds), *Regulating Technologies Legal* (Oxford, Hart Publishing).

Nelson, RL and Nielsen, LB (2000) 'Cops, Counsel, and Entrepreneurs' 34(2) *Law and Society Review* 457.

Paton, PD (2017) 'Lawyers in Organizational Settings' in A Woolley et al (eds), *Lawyers' Ethics and Professional Regulation*, 3rd edn (Toronto, LexisNexis).

Penner, J and Melissaris, E (2012) *McCoubrey and White's Textbook on Jurisprudence*, 5th edn (Oxford, Oxford University Press).

Rahim, MM (2013) *Legal Regulation of Corporate Social Responsibility* (Berlin, Springer).

Regan Jr, MC (2000) 'Professional Responsibility and the Corporate Lawyer' 13(2) *Georgetown Journal of Legal Ethics* 197.

Rolland, D and O'Keefe Bazzoni, J (2009) 'Greening Corporate Identity' 14(3) *Corporate Communications: An International Journal* 249.

Rose, JM (2007) 'Corporate Directors and Social Responsibility: Ethics versus Shareholder Value', 73 *Journal of Business Ethics* 319.

Rühmkorf, A (2018) 'From Transparency to Due Diligence Laws?' in JJ du Plessis et al (eds), *Globalisation of Corporate Social Responsibility and its Impact on Corporate Governance* (Cham, Springer).

Salamon, LM (2002) 'Foreword' in TH Stanton, *Government-sponsored Enterprises* (Washington, AEI Press).

Salvioni, DM (2018) 'Corporate Governance, Ownership and Global Markets' in SM Brondoni (ed), *Competitive Business Management* (Abingdon, Routledge).

Sarter, EK (2015) 'The Legal Framework of Contracting' 14 *WAGADU – A Journal of Transnational Women's and Gender Studies* 55.

Scherer, AG and Palazzo, G (2008) 'Globalisation and Corporate Social Responsibility' in A Crane et al (eds), *The Oxford Handbook of Corporate Social Responsibility* (Oxford, Oxford University Press).

Scherer, AG et al (2006) 'Global Rules and Private Actors' 16(4) *Business Ethics Quarterly* 506.

Scheuch, A (2018) 'Soft Law Requirements with Hard Law Effects?' in JJ du Plessis et al (eds), *Globalisation of Corporate Social Responsibility and its Impact on Corporate Governance* (Cham, Springer).

Schiopoiu Burlea, A and Popa, I (2013) 'Legitimacy Theory' in SO Idowu et al (eds), *Encyclopedia of Corporate Social Responsibility* (Berlin, Springer).

Schuck, PH (2018) *Limits of Law: Essays on Democratic Governance* (London, Routledge).

Scott, C (2008) 'Reflexive Governance, Meta-Regulation and Corporate Social Responsibility' in N Boeger et al (eds), *Perspectives on Corporate Social Responsibility* (Cheltenham, Edward Elgar).

Shelton, D (2006) 'International Law and "Relative Normativity"' in MD Evans (ed), *International Law*, 2nd edn (Oxford, Oxford University Press).

Sims, RR (2002) *Managing Organizational Behavior* (London, Quorum Books).

Sjåfjell, B et al (2015) 'Shareholder Primacy' in B Sjåfjell and BJ Richardson (eds), *Company Law and Sustainability* (Cambridge, Cambridge University Press).

Slaughter, A-M (2001) 'The Accountability of Government Networks' 8(2) *Indiana Journal of Global Legal Studies* 347.

Stalley, P (2009) 'Can Trade Green China?' 18 *Journal of Contemporary China* 567.

Stephens, B (2002) 'The Amorality of Profit' 20 *Berkeley Journal of International Law* 45.

Talbot, L (2012) *Progressive Corporate Governance for the 21st Century* (London, Routledge).

Teubner, G (1997) 'Global Bukowina' in G Teubner (ed), *Global Law Without a State* (Aldershot, Dartmouth).

—— (2009) 'The Corporate Codes of Multinationals' in R Nickel (ed), *Conflict of Laws and Laws of Conflict in Europe and Beyond* (Oxford, Hart Publishing).

Tricker, B (2009) *Corporate Governance Principles, Policies and Practices* (Oxford, Oxford University Press).

van der Sluijs, J (2016) 62 'The Infrastructure of Normative Legitimacy in Domestic Soft Law', *Scandinavian Studies in Law* 245.

Van Hoecke, M (1999) 'Jurisprudence' in CB Gray (ed), *The Philosophy of Law* (New York, Garland Publishing).

van Marrewijk, M (2003) 44 'Concepts and Definitions of CSR and Corporate Sustainability' *Journal of Business Ethics* 95.

Vercelli, A (2017) *Crisis and Sustainability* (London, Palgrave Macmillan).

Voegtlin, C and Pless, N (2014) 'Global Governance' 122(2) *Journal of Business Ethics* 179.

Wawryk, A (2003) 'Regulating Transnational Corporations through Corporate Codes of Conduct' in JG Frynas and S Pegg (eds), *Transnational Corporations and Human Rights* (London, Palgrave Macmillan).

Wearing, RT (2005) *Cases in Corporate Governance* (London, Sage Publications).

Weber, M (1978) *Economy and Society* (Berkeley, University of California Press).

Weinberger, O (1986) 'The Norm as Thought and as Reality' in N MacCormick and O Weinberger, *An Institutional Theory of Law* (Dordrecht, Springer).

Whelan, CJ and Ziv, N (2013) 'Law Firm Ethics in the Shadow of Corporate Social Responsibility' 26 *Georgetown Journal of Legal Ethics* 153.

Woodlock, J and Hydén, H (2020) '(f)Lex Avionica; How Soft Law Serves as an Instrumental Mediator between Professional Norms and the Hard Law Regulation of European Civil Aviation Maintenance' 121 *Safety Science* 54.

Zerk, JA (2006) *Multinationals and Corporate Social Responsibility* (Cambridge, Cambridge University Press).

Zhao, J (2017) 'Promoting More Socially Responsible Corporations through a Corporate Law Regulatory Framework' 37(1) *Legal Studies* 103.

Zumbansen, P (2012) 'Defining the Space of Transnational Law' 21(2) *Transnational Law and Contemporary Problems* 305.

11

Reflections on Law, Religion, and Technology: Legal Mobilisation in the Area of Egyptian Paternity Law

MONIKA LINDBEKK*

I. INTRODUCTION

IN 2005, THE Egyptian interior designer Hind Elhinnawy filed a court case to establish the paternal lineage of her four-month-old daughter Lina who she alleged resulted from a so-called customary marriage contract between her and the actor Ahmed Fishawy. Fishawy repeatedly denied that marriage had occurred between them and that Lina was his daughter. By filing suit, Elhinnawy did more than shatter a social taboo. She attempted to set an Egyptian legal precedent by requesting that the court order Mr Fishawy to submit to a DNA test to establish whether he was the father of Lina. There was no way under Egyptian law to force him to carry it out. In late January 2006, the first-level court turned down Elhinnawys lawsuit because paternity could not be established without evidence of marriage.[1] But the case did not stop there because Elhinnawy appealed. This case raised a public scandal and generated a heated public debate, echoes that continue to reverberate in Egypt and other parts of the Muslim world today.

The chapter aims to contribute to the growing scholarly literature on implementing Sharia-based family law by addressing legal mobilisation by private citizens and human rights lawyers surrounding a contested and conflictive legal matter, namely the use of DNA to prove paternal lineage. As pointed out by Reza Banakar (2015: 169) in his methodological reflections on the Iranian legal system and culture, theories developed based on studying Western legal systems have both limitations and possibilities. This is the case with the theories on legal mobilisation which were developed in North America and have only more recently spread to other regions.

*The research on which this chapter is based was funded by the CanCode Project at the University of Bergen (Project no: TMS 2020STG01).
[1] Family Court of al-Khalifa, case no 547, 26 January 2006.

Legal mobilisation scholarship has developed as an analytic framework that focuses on how individual claimants and collective actors, such as social movements, engage in the process of novel rights formulation through creative framing (Albiston 2010; Burstein 1991; Galanter 1983; McCann 2008; Merry 1990; Scheingold 1974) as well as legal and political structures that enable or counteract it (Epp 1998), but it leaves many unanswered questions. Among other, existing scholarship has to a small extent explored how legal mobilisation operates under conditions of 'state legal pluralism' (Benda-Beckmann and Turner 2018: 265) as found in many postcolonial settings. According to Ahmed Zaki (2017: 7) several legal systems in postcolonial settings are juristically pluralistic in two main ways: (a) normative sources of law such as Islamic Sharia are codified into civil codes; and (b) several different ethnoreligious codes govern the personal status of different ethnic and religious communities; both within the same legal system. An example in point is Egypt, a country that has developed a hybrid legal system over the past two centuries. Evidence of this internal pluralism of state law lies in how the legal system is largely based on the French civil law model. Meanwhile, the constitution of 2014 declares that the principles of Islamic Sharia are the principal source for legislation. Furthermore, there is a tension between a constitutional provision, which on the one hand enshrines the principle of equality before the law for all citizens regardless of religion and gender, while asserting the state's responsibility to protect the family as the nucleus of society, constituted by 'religion, ethics and patriotism' (Article 10) on the other. In this context, according to which different family laws govern Egyptians depending on religious affiliation, the personal status regime is of crucial significance.

Given that Egyptian paternity law is strongly influenced by Sharia, the chapter also analyses the intersection between law, religion, and science in this field. In so doing, it engages with theoretical reflections by Reza Banakar on the application of Islamic law in another legal system structured in accordance with the French civil law system, namely Iran (Banakar and Ziaee 2019). This takes us beyond discussions in terms of modern/traditionalist or secular/religious dichotomies, which is found in much literature on state legal pluralism. Taking the well-publicised case of *Elhinnawy v Fishawy* and its vantage point, the chapter highlights two functions of legal mobilisation in Muslim personal status law. First, I argue that legal mobilisation has taken the form of a collective organisation by non-governmental organisations (NGOs). The goal is to change the law by preparing and trying particularly suitable cases for the court and using the language and symbols of Islam as innovative strategic framing methods. In examining legal mobilisation and its effects, I combine insights from studies on legal mobilisation with recent theory on legal pluralities (Ahmed Zaki 2017; Sieder and McNeish 2013), where previous tendencies to either celebrate or demonise legal pluralities have given way to a more nuanced analysis that strives to understand them as dynamic social formations embedded in society and the state alike with various effects and consequences. Within this perspective, I highlight how cause lawyers underpin their arguments by drawing upon the pluralism of Islamic normativity and look at how it is presented and whether patterns are discernible in its deployment. Second, this perspective also opens up for questioning how legal mobilisation is enabled and counteracted by a legal-political landscape where multiple institutions contend over who has the right to interpret Islamic Sharia authoritatively. To address the question raised by the chapter, I analyse judicial mobilisation in conjunction with legal mobilisation by various actors and institutions, ranging from the Mufti of Egypt to al-Azhar, one of the oldest and most influential seats of learning in Sunni-Islam and situated in Cairo. The chapter draws on an analysis of court documents and fatwas and interviews with litigants, lawyers, and judges.

II. THE ROLE OF RELIGION IN EGYPTIAN PERSONAL STATUS LAW

Today, much of Egyptian family law exists in the form of codes applied by civil courts. In order to understand the significance of this, it is important to have an understanding of how Sharia emerged and developed. Sharia is a highly complex concept, referring to a vast body of historical, social, political, cultural, and religious developments. In scholarly literature, this is frequently referred to as 'Islamic law' or as 'sacred law'. For the purposes of this chapter, it is important to note that Sharia was developed by scholars who, for a long time, were independent of the state and were not government functionaries. A second feature worth highlighting is the fact the law created by the scholars is called *fiqh* ('scholarly understanding') rather than Sharia. Fiqh hence earned the epithet 'jurists' law', marking a distinction from 'God-given law'. In expanding the law, the classical scholars relied on a methodology whereby Sharia was derived from specific sources. The sacred sources were two, namely: the Qur'an, which embodies the revelations of God to humankind; and the Prophet Muhammad's exemplary practice and utterances, called the Sunna as compiled in hadith collections. The two primary sources, the Qur'an and the Sunna, were complemented by two other methods of exerting rules: reasoning characterised by analogical deduction; and scholarly consensus (Banakar and Ziaee 2019: 122). An important aspect of scholarly consensus as a source of law was the defence of the doctrines developed by the four surviving schools of Sunni jurisprudence. The Hanafi school eventually won a special position as the official law school of the Ottoman Empire (Vikør 2005). Despite the consolidation of the aforementioned schools, the resulting corpus of legal doctrines was not recorded in a format that can be considered a code but were dispersed among various manuals and commentaries of a particular school, described as 'atomistic' in style (Kamali 2003). Before the era of nation-states and statutory laws, judges in Sharia courts could decide cases by relying on normative pluralism – that is, by drawing from different schools of law or by reference to local custom.

In the twentieth century, Muslim family law underwent a process of codification whereby it was transformed from jurists' law into statutory law. In Egypt, the process of codification extended to the field of family law with the adoption of a series of legislative enactments, starting in the 1920s. Substantive personal status law reforms were issued again in 1985 and 2000. The process involved doctrines from the Islamic doctrinal schools (*madhhab*, pl *madhahib*) being combined and fused into new legal rules. Reforms in the field of Muslim personal status have proceeded gradually and in a piecemeal manner. As further testimony to the hybrid nature of Muslim family law, Article 3 of Law no 1 of 2000 refers judges to the predominant opinion of the Hanafi school where there are silences in the law (Dupret et al 2019). Hence, old versions of law coexist with modern law codes in a manner which brings into relief the hybrid nature of Muslim family law.

The reforms adopted in Egypt in the domain of paternal filiation have been mainly procedural rather than substantial. Egypt has precluded courts from hearing disputes arising out of marriages where the birth took place six months after the marriage was contracted or one year after the marriage ended through divorce or death. However, the fundamental conditions relating to the establishment of paternity are governed by Hanafi doctrine, which stipulates primary and secondary ways of establishing paternity. The primary method of establishing paternity is through a valid marriage. According to the principle that 'the child is affiliated to the conjugal bed' (*walad li-l-firash*), the husband's paternity of a child born to his wife during their valid marriage (or within the maximum pregnancy period after divorce) is automatically established. In their attempt to ascertain whether a given child was conceived in a marriage ('a conjugal bed'), the period of gestation had to be discussed. Pre-modern Sunni jurists agreed that the minimum period of gestation was six months, but they disagreed over the maximum period, which varied from two years to four years among the different schools.

According to the Ḥanafī school this maximum gestation period was two years (Ibrahim 2019; Shaham 2010; Esposito 2001. In addition to the primary method of establishing paternity through a licit sexual relationship), classical jurists of Islamic law also discussed several other secondary methods. These secondary methods include admission, evidence, and expert examination of the similarity of physical features between a father and a child (*qiyafa*). The latter means tracing the child to their parent by how they look and seeing who they might resemble, which was the same way the Arabs in the past traced a route in the desert, by following the signs (Ibrahim 2019; Shabana 2013). The Hanafis, however, argued against the use of such tracing on the grounds that it amounts to judgment on the basis of conjecture. The tension between biological and legal conceptions of paternity have become particularly urgent in the modern Muslim world with the advent of DNA testing which, in theory, permits the determination of biological paternity with certainty in each case, therefore raising the question of whether Islamic law should simply adopt a biological definition of paternity (Shabana 2013).

The case which will provide the guiding force is *Hind Elhinnawy v Fishawy*. As mentioned, Elhinnawy filed a court case to establish the paternal lineage of her four-month-old daughter Lina who she alleged resulted from a so-called customary marriage contract between her and the actor Ahmed Fishawy. Customary marriages are a form of marriage that is not officially registered with the state. Although there are no exact data on how widespread undocumented marriage is, a considerable amount of scholarship has focused on the diverse motivations and implications of marriages (notably lack of judicial remedy) conducted outside the state system, particularly in Egypt but also in other countries such as Indonesia, Jordan, Morocco, Syria, and UAE (Bedner and Van Huis 2010; Engelcke 2019; Hasso 2010; Sonneveld 2012). It is important to mention that state legislation does not challenge the validity of a marriage contract that has not been registered by a notary. In a sense, this leaves such marriages in a legal limbo, since few rights arise from them – other than paternity – that can be enforced through courts. In public debates, official marriage and customary marriage are often construed as opposites, the first publicly founding a family and conforming to the official and legal norm, the other secretly and flimsily camouflaging the secret affairs of romantic teenagers or film stars. Elhinnawy became pregnant, and Fishawy tried to convince her to have an abortion. They disagreed on this matter. According to Elhinnawy's version of the events, Fishawy then oscillated between accepting the pregnancy and refusing it until its third month, when he agreed that it should continue. Subsequently, he took the marital contract from her to get the signature of another witness on it. The agreement was that he would return the contract (paper) to her the following day so she could go to the notary to document the marriage, to finish all the required paperwork. After visiting a local preacher, Fishawy reportedly changed his mind, and he neither went with her to the notary nor gave her back the contract. He again started to demand that she have an abortion, and by that time, the pregnancy was in its fourth month. When Elhinnawy insisted on keeping the baby, Fishawy abandoned her, denying the marriage and fatherhood after taking the marital contract.[2] These issues are of considerable importance since children born out of wedlock are generally not entitled to carry their (biological) father's name. They have no right to maintenance, nor do they inherit from their father. Besides the legal issues, being born out of wedlock is a cause of considerable social stigma.

A. The Role of Technology

As mentioned earlier, Elhinnawy did more than shatter a social taboo. She attempted to set an Egyptian legal precedent by requesting that the court order Mr Fishawy to submit to a DNA test to establish whether he was Lina's father. The discovery of DNA fingerprinting has been hailed as one of the most important achievements of modern biomedical technology (Shabana 2013: 158; Shaham 2010). The case in question represents an opportunity to observe how lawyers and other legal actors mobilise different normative repertoires by drawing on overlapping legal and normative orders, including statutory law, uncodified Islamic law, custom, and human rights, to challenge hegemonic hermeneutical understandings of Islam.

In a chapter co-authored with Keyvan Ziaee, Reza Banakar asks if the application of classical Islam jurisprudence (*fiqh*) in Iran, which is a civil law system, can be understood as a 'clash between two legal cultures' (Banakar and Ziaee 2019: 122). According to the authors, the training of Iranian judges includes understanding and enforcing the law in terms of fiqh, or Islamic jurisprudence, as developed by Shi'a jurists. Iranian lawyers view this as a form of 'qadi-justice,' a Weberian ideal-type of legal decision-making, which 'knows no rational "rules of decision"'. The other legal culture as embodied by lawyers is based on the jurisprudence of modern law schools, and sees the law as a rule-based rational construct for decision-making. In the context of codified law and due process, Iranian judges' application of Islamic jurisprudence introduces an element of legal uncertainty and arbitrariness that many defence

---

[2] Fatwa no 2821 for 2004 from the Mufti of Egypt.

attorneys find difficult to anticipate and react to. The authors continue to argue that examining the subject in terms of modern/traditionalist or secular/religious dichotomies would overlook two points. First, they point out that the jurisprudence of the Iranian judiciary – however, politicised, illiberal and repressive it may be – contains many innovative ideas challenging a traditional understanding of Sharia. Second, Islamic jurisprudence (*fiqh*) has always contained secular practices and secularisation of the divine since the principle of expediency of the state overrides all religious doctrine (ibid: 122). The same applies in the context of Egypt, where the scholarly literature tends to posit that fiqh, as found in the classical legal manuals, continues to be applied in domains where the statutory codes are silent. This assumption, however, underestimates the fundamental changes brought about by the importation of a civil law model and its influence on the inner dynamics of legal reasoning as well as the social and intellectual diversity in contemporary Muslim societies (Dupret et al 2019). In the following section, I explore the judicial mobilisation of human rights NGOs in the field of personal status law.

B. The Role of Legal Mobilisation

In recent decades there has been a growing body of research on legal mobilisation by private citizens and different social groups lawyers to challenge the Egyptian state's policies (Agrama 2010; El Fegiery 2016; Ezzat 2021; Lindbekk and Bahgat 2021; Lombardi and Cannon 2016). Moustafa and Ginsburg (2008) pointed out that judicial politics in authoritarian states is often far more complex than commonly assumed. Despite decades of authoritarian rule, Egyptian courts 'enjoy a surprising degree of independence and they provide a vital arena of political contention (Moustafa 2008: 151). According to Tamir Moustafa (ibid: 132), the relative independence of the courts, the visibility of the judicial system, and the attention paid by the media to selected cases and decisions encourage individuals and special interest groups to use the courtrooms for strategic purposes. Such legal mobilisation has become an important strategy for human rights lawyers, not only because of the opportunities afforded but due to the myriad obstacles to mobilising broad social movement. In the 1980s and 1990s, a wave of women's rights NGOs was formed, which was intensified with Egypt's participation in the international conferences despite restrictions on civil society organisations and periodic government crackdowns (Abu-Lughod 2010; Pratt 2020). An example in point is the establishment of the Center for Egyptian Women Legal Assistance (CEWLA) in 1995. The goal of CEWLA and other women's NGOs is to offer Egyptian women legal support and assistance regarding their rights under the Egyptian laws, constitution, and international conventions ratified by Egypt. Yet, to date, little scholarly research has been devoted to the use of Islamic law as part of novel rights-based approaches in the domain of Muslim family law. Instead, the academic literature has tended to focus on the constraining role of state legal pluralities. Meanwhile, as pointed out by Ahmed Zaki (2017), this assumption underestimates the pluralism and fluidity in Islamic discourse. In the absence of legislation governing the establishment of paternity, the lawyers in *Elhinnawy v Fishawy* relied on very distinct arguments:

(1) The lawyers framed their defence within the parameters of classical Hanafi doctrine by arguing that Elhinnawy had witnesses to the customary marriage and continued to mention that Sharia is keen to establish paternity. Relying on the predominant Hanafi doctrine, the lawyers argued that it suffices to be established through evidence that the marriage did take place and consummation of it ensued because of contracting it. It is not imperative for witnesses, who testify for the marriage's existence, to have been present at the signing of the contract or to have witnessed it themselves. It suffices that they attest to their knowledge the marriage took place because testimony based on hearsay is permissible in Sharia in this case. Paternity is also established through a corrupt marriage because the rule is that paternity is established whenever possible, even through manipulation, as long as it is done in a manner that defies neither reason nor Sharia, in order to reform a woman's behaviour and protect her and her family's honour and to sustain a child's life and protect their interest.

(2) The lawyers advocated for using DNA evidence for paternity verification by going beyond the bounds of the Ḥanafī school and selecting a variant view found in other law schools, which accepted a type of evidence called *al-qiyafa*; they drew an analogy between this and DNA.

(3) Finally, the lawyers couched the terms of their argument of international conventions signed and ratified by Egypt, in particular the Convention on Rights of the Child, which Egypt ratified in 1993.[3]

Judicial mobilisation constituted one of several parallel processes adopted by Elhinnawy and her lawyers in the campaign to introduce DNA testing in paternity disputes. In addition to the courts, Elhinnawy and her lawyers strategically turned to reform-oriented Islamic legal scholars with interpretations of Islam that worked to their advantage to influence the case. For example, Elhinnawy's father addressed the Mufti of Egypt with an emotional letter after Fishawy had refused to undergo a DNA test while admitting to a sexual relationship with Elhinnawy without the presence of a marriage contract, which made it *zina* (fornication) and a child from zina is not granted paternity. The Mufti of Egypt responded with a fatwa according to which:

> The rule regarding paternal filiation is precaution on the side of proving it. The divine lawmaker desires to prove it by any means possible, such as testimony, admission, tracing (al-qiyafa) and any scientific method available in order to reform a woman's situation and sustain a child.[4]

The Mufti continued by saying that there is no issue with demanding DNA testing when there is a marriage claim, but it is not for unmarried people because zina does not create paternity. While the Mufti of Egypt argued that DNA paternity testing should be used with caution in cases with no proof of marriage, the NGOs also reached out to a minority group of scholars who recognised DNA evidence as a method that can

---

[3] According to Article 7 of the Convention on Rights of the Child, every child shall be registered immediately after birth and shall have the right from birth to a name, the right to acquire a nationality and. as far as possible, the right to know and be cared for by his or her parents.

[4] Fatwa no 2821 for 2004 from the Mufti of Egypt.

establish filiation for children born out of wedlock. Far from signalling the demise of Islamic law, this minority group of Islamic legal scholars from al-Azhar argued that introducing these novel methods of establishing paternity would support Sharia by protecting progeny, one of the five overarching objectives of Islamic law. Among the Islamic legal scholars who endorsed this minority opinion in the *Elhinnawy v Fishawy* case was ʿAbd Allah al-Najjar, an Azhar scholar who also happened to be part of Elhinnawy's team of lawyers. These arguments concerning the admissibility of DNA testing (or lack of such) are increasingly intertwined in international developments in Islamic law (Korbatieh 2020: 15; Shabana 2013). While engaging with transnational discourses, the Egyptian discussions on paternity law are highly localised in that they drew upon indigenous roots. Women's rights NGOs such as CEWLA have published studies (Aboul-Magd 2017) and articles in widely circulated newspapers focusing on the growing problem of illegitimate children in the country, with 14,000 cases of paternal lineage being tried in Egyptian courts. In addition to creative framing, the activists decided to lobby the Egyptian Ministry of Justice and parliamentarians to introduce new legislation to make DNA tests mandatory in cases of paternal filiation (The New Humanitarian 2006) and helped galvanise international pressure on the Egyptian government by participating in shadow reports on the implementation of UN conventions (Marei 2009).

C. The Role of Courts and Mass Media

In May 2006, Cairo Appeal Court ruled in favour of Elhinnawy. Interestingly and despite the line of alternative discourses developed by cause lawyers and individual Islamic scholars, DNA was not the main theme in the court's reasoning. In the judgment, the court cited the predominant opinion of the Hanafi school, according to which paternity can be established through a corrupt marriage 'because the rule is that paternal filiation is established whenever possible, even through manipulation, as long as it is done in a manner that does defies neither reason nor Sharia, to reform a woman's behavior and protect her and her family's honor and to sustain a child's life and protect their interest'.[5] Thus, the Cairo Appeal court ruling reinforced continuity and stability rather than signifying a departure from prevailing legal norms. It is also noteworthy that, although the judges present their reasoning as falling within the parameters of mainstream Hanafi doctrines, the sources and methodology they use differ considerably from it. While some judges are more erudite than others, court records reveal that family court judges rarely seek guidance in the authoritative collections of classical Islamic scholars. Instead, they generally refer to Hanafi fiqh through the medium of the Court of Cassation and a body of contemporary works of jurisprudence. These works, which are clearly embedded in the civil law tradition, are divided into chapters that follow the sequence of articles in the personal status

---

[5] Cairo Appeal Court, case no 1389 and no 1605, judicial year 123, 24 May 2006. See also Bentlage (2020) and Alim (2016).

legislation in chronological order. Thus, while judges deploy a vocabulary connected to classical fiqh, the grammar of their legal reasoning is of that of civil law (see also Dupret et al 2019).

In 2008, the principle that 'the child is affiliated to the conjugal bed' was challenged in law no 126 of 2008, which amended some provisions in the 1996 child law. According to Article 4 of the amended child law, the child shall also have the right to establish his legitimate paternal and maternal lineage, using all lawful scientific means to establish such lineage. This innovation was introduced after the UN Committee on the Rights of the Child and local civil society organisations (including CEWLA) criticised Egypt's implementation of 'the best interests of the child principle' concerning children born outside marriage (Committee on the Rights of the Child 2008: 32). Yet, Article 7 of the same law defers to the provisions set forth under the personal status laws. Despite the 2008 amendment to child law, Egyptian family court judges remain resistant to integrating new technologies in their consideration of paternity claims. The following two cases testify to this trend. In 2014, an actress named 'Zeina' lodged a claim to establish paternal filiation for her twin sons, which resulted in a highly publicised case, as she claimed that her twin boys were the sons of famous actor Ahmed Ezz. The case was thrust into the limelight after the 38-year-old actress returned from the United States to Egypt in January 2014 after giving birth to the children, who she claimed were the sons of the Egyptian actor. Her lawyer said the pair wedded in June 2012 through a customary marriage. Throughout, Ezz consistently denied the marriage and declined to undergo DNA tests required by the court. The actor even went on TV to publicly deny that these were his children, all while making hints about the actress's reputation. However, a verdict from the Nasr City Family Court in June 2015 stated it had been proven that the children were Ezz's. The judgment compelled Ezz to recognise his paternal responsibilities, allowing Zeina to issue birth certificates and other official documents for the children (Mada Masr 2016).

Yet another highly publicised case revolved around Amal Abdel Hameed, a young woman whose daughter was conceived through rape in 2018. Abdel Hameed launched court proceedings on two fronts in July 2020: pursuing a criminal case against her child's biological father for kidnapping, physical assault and rape, and a paternity suit in the family court, seeking the issuance of a birth certificate for her daughter with the father's name listed. However, the case was dismissed since Egypt's personal status laws do not mandate paternity registration for children born out of wedlock. Subsequently, Abdel Hameed published a video testimony online in the summer of 2020. Amal and her lawyers drew momentum from a wave of high-publicity social media campaigns around sexual violence in this connection. As the case became widely publicised, Amal gained a fair amount of public sympathy. Following concerted pressure from NGOs, the public prosecution intervened by ordering a DNA test for Abdel Hameed's daughter, which proved the defendant to be the biological father. Thus, the campaign demonstrates the ways in which NGOs utilise the dual nature of the Egyptian legal system to bring mandatory DNA testing in through the back door, so to speak. According to an interviewed lawyer, this strategy was rooted in a belief that the public prosecutor was more likely than a family court judge to decide in line with 'the spirit of the law'.[6] Yet, the DNA match was not enough for Abdel Hameed to secure a birth certificate for her daughter bearing the biological father's name (Mada Masr 2021). In response to Abdel-Hameed's court battle, women's rights lawyers from CEWLA also organised a workshop in March 2021 where they invoked the notion of *qiyafa* as the modern-day equivalent of DNA, as well Egypt's constitutional commitments to the International Convention on Rights of the Child.[7] Together with a coalition of other women's rights organisations, CEWLA has also produced a legal guide outlining its collective position on the required changes in personal status law. A feature of the law proposal prepared by the NGOs was an article on filiation where female victims of rape were given the right to establish paternity for their children by using modern scientific methods. That said, there seemed to be a general understanding among women's rights lawyers interviewed for this chapter that their influence on policy outcomes is limited by a range of factors, including the degree of distance between women's rights and the ruling political elites.[8] While the institutionalisation of NGOs since the 1980s has been challenging, the relationship between civil society organisations and the state has been further complicated in recent years. Nicola Pratt (2020) has pointed out that human rights NGOs are increasingly the target of criticism and government crackdowns for receiving foreign funding and being critics of the regime's human rights record.

D. The Outcome

While it is difficult to assess the long-term implications of these ongoing struggles, there are at least three dimensions present here that pertain to the central arguments of this chapter. First, we can discern a continuing and dynamic process of creating what counts as Islamic law, some embryonic and novel, and some influenced by past legalities. In the process of legal mobilisation, different notions were invoked, contested, produced, and fused as part of novel rights-based approaches. For example, we see that the human rights lawyers and Islamic legal scholars merged the classical Islamic concept of *qiyafa* with modern scientific evidence, including DNA. Second, it is theoretically interesting that while court proceedings are a laborious process, strategic litigation may have effects that go beyond purely the decision (see Höland 2011), by providing an opportunity to study, promote and support victims of the conservative laws, and develop tactics to confront them by influencing the legal-political agenda. Thanks to the dramatic content of the court cases lodged by Hind Elhinnawy, Zeina, and Amal Abdel-Hameed, the court generated considerable media attention and limited adoption of DNA testing as a method of proving paternity among judges and Islamic legal scholars. According to human rights lawyers interviewed for this research, when a man refuses to submit to a DNA test, the judge sometimes uses this as evidence against men who deny paternity. Similarly, I found

---

[6] Interview by Lindbekk with lawyer, 2 October 2021.
[7] Workshop convened by CEWLA, 31 March 2021.
[8] Interview by author with two human rights lawyers in Cairo, 1 August 2019, and 15 August 2019.

that some judges viewed a husband's unwillingness to undergo a DNA test as a sign of his bad faith and unwillingness 'to acquit himself in front of the child, society, and God' (Lindbekk forthcoming). However, while refusal to undergo a DNA test can be used as supporting evidence together with other evidence such as a marital contract, I have yet to see a case where DNA was used as the only form of proof to establish paternity. Along the same lines, some interviewed family court judges complained of the difficulties posed by lengthy judicial processes and challenges posed by marriages that were entered into without documentation (or documentation inaccessible to the woman) and in the absence of witnesses or other forms of evidence, and which were therefore non-justiciable. In the words of one judge:

> In a case, the husband disputed that the child was his, while the wife alleged that it was his. We had a length debate within the judicial panel about what to do. I was in favour of using DNA and ordered the male defendant do to this. However, because it was expensive for him to do and he lived in a remote area, we could not obligate him. The Ḥanafī technology is 1000 years old – their views were valid 1000 years ago. But today we have different technology which is more suitable. I can't believe we are still doing this.[9]

Thus, whenever there is a potential conflict between existing Sharia principles and the implications of a DNA test, contemporary family court judges continue to opt for continuity with classical Hanafi doctrine at the substantive level. As convincingly argued by Shaham (2010) in his study on the development of expert witnessing in Islamic law, this desire for family stability was to be mobilised by contemporary jurists who strongly oppose DNA testing in paternity disputes which they fear would open a Pandora's box. I would like to add to this the concern with the welfare of the mother and child mentioned above.

Third, in addition to the agency of private citizens and collective actors such as NGOs, the case sheds light on the contours of legal and political structures that support or contain the challenges of individual claimants and social interest groups through legal mobilisation. The state's relationship with organised religion through the personal status regime and the strength and autonomy of civil society organisations each pose different constraints and opportunities. Instead of viewing the state and state law as an internally consistent entity, I considered heterogeneity by looking at multiple state institutions tasked with defining Islam. This was thrown into relief in February 2021 when Egypt's House of Representatives referred a new personal status bill to the Constitutional and Legislative Affairs Committee for review. Interestingly, the cabinet version of the bill in many ways duplicated a previously submitted law draft by al-Azhar. Several women's rights organisations issued statements denouncing the amendment, and complained that they had been completely excluded from the amendment drafting process. Among other provisions, the NGOs were critical of how the personal status law continues to privilege the paternal instinct and their keenness to assign paternity of a child to their father while women face obstacles in establishing the paternity of children born outside of a recognised or provable marital relationship (Ali 2021). Whereas al-Azhar and the Egyptian cabinet have offered

---

[9] Interview with family court judge, 20 August 2019.

institutional support of the status quo with regard to paternity law, the Mufti of Egypt has also issued a fatwa where he reiterated his support for DNA testing as an effective scientific method in paternity disputes by using the same arguments as in the 2004 fatwa.[10] This suggests that the role of DNA testing remains a subject of internal debate within the judiciary and among Islamic legal scholars, and other state institutions tasked with defining Islam. It remains to be seen whether the Egyptian parliament will pursue bold departures from classical Islamic thought and previous political compromises. After more than 100 hundred years of Muslim personal status reform, what continues to single out personal status law reform is that it remains central to the pursuit of Islamic legal identity. Which interpretations of Sharia will be made to apply in Egyptian family law in the future is likely to depend on the dynamics of Egyptian politics, where a variety of actors and institutions claim the interpretive authority as regards Islamic Sharia.

III. SUMMARY AND CONCLUSION

This chapter addressed legal mobilisation in Muslim personal status law by individual women and NGOs. I argued that private citizens and human rights lawyers engaged in several innovative strategic framing methods regarding paternal lineage. Taking the case of *Elhinnawi v Fishawy* as its vantage point, the chapter addressed the contestation surrounding DNA as a method of proving paternal lineage as an area where past legalities intersect with novel rights-based approaches through a process of hybridisation. I argued that private citizens and their lawyers grounded their novel legal claims in the plural nature of Egypt's legal system, where multiple legal orders co-exist and intermingle within the bounds of the nation-state. At no time was DNA considered contrary to the principles of Islamic Sharia, which is the principal source of Egyptian legislation. Instead, DNA intended to complement the sharia in cases in which the predominant Hanafi doctrine made it difficult to establish paternity for children. In parallel, the human rights lawyers approached reform-oriented Islamic legal scholars, such as the Mufti of Egypt and members of al-Azhar. Second, I highlighted how legal mobilisation has had important effects beyond the decisional outcome of courts by building momentum for a legal-political agenda of change and encouraging activists to lobby for more radical change. While the courts were shown to be highly unreliable agents of change, rights-based litigation proved to be an important resource beyond the decisional outcome. Channelled by the media, the court case in question came to the attention of legal scholars and members of the public alike. It also gave impulses to legislative change in terms of an amendment to the child law, an amendment that has not been implemented because of institutional and ideational challenges. Third, in addition to the agency of private citizens and collective actors such as human rights NGOs, the case shed light on the contours of legal and political structures that support or contain citizen challenges through legal mobilisation in a context where there is internal pluralism of state law.

---

[10] Fatwa no 6996 from 2015 by the Mufti of Egypt.

REFERENCES

Aboul-Magd, A (2017) *Waraqa qanuniya min muasasa qadaya al-marra al-misriya hawil ithbat al-nasab* (Cairo, CEWLA).

Abu-Lughod, L (2010) 'The Active Social Life of "Muslim Women's Rights": A Plea for Ethnography, Not Polemic, with Cases from Egypt and Palestine' 6 *Journal of Middle East Women's Studies* 1.

Agrama, H (2010) 'Secularism, Sovereignty, Indeterminacy: Is Egypt a Secular State?' 52 *Comparative Studies in History and Society* 495.

Ahmed Zaki, H (2017) 'Law, Culture, and Mobilization: Legal Pluralism and Women's Access to Divorce in Egypt' 14 *Muslim World Journal of Human Rights* 1.

Albiston, CR (2010) *Institutional Inequality and the Mobilization of the Family and Medical Leave Act: Rights on Leave* (Cambridge, Cambridge University Press).

Ali, S (2021) 'Qawanin al-ahwal al-shakhsiyah, huquq manqusah lil-nisa', *al-Shuruq* 9 March 2021.

Alim, N (2016) 'Tricks, Traps and Grey Zones: A Comparative Analysis of Egypt's Unique Approach to Marriage Registration in Relation to Tunisia and Jordan' (PhD thesis, University of Hamburg).

Banakar, R (2015) *Normativity in Legal Sociology Methodological Reflections on Law and Regulation in Late Modernity* (London, Springer).

Banakar, R and Ziaee, K (2019) 'Iran: Clash of Two Cultures?' in R Abel, O Hammerslev, H Sommerlad and U Schultz (eds), *Lawyers in 21st Century Society: Vol 1* (Oxford, Hart Publishing).

Bentlage, B (2020) *A Tale of Two Stories: Customary Marriage and Paternity. A Discourse Analysis of a Scandal in Egypt* (Berlin, Klaus Schwarz Verlag).

Bedner, A and Van Huis, S (2010) 'Plurality of Marriage Law and Marriage Registration for Muslims in Indonesia: A Plea for Pragmatism' 6 *Utrecht Law Review* 175.

Benda-Beckmann, K and Turner, B (2018) 'Legal Pluralism, Social Theory, and the State' 50 *The Journal of Legal Pluralism and Unofficial Law* 255.

Burstein, P (1991) 'Legal Mobilization as a Social Movement Tactic: The Struggle for Equal Employment Opportunity' 96 *American Journal of Sociology* 1201.

Committee on the Rights of the Child (2008) 'Convention on the Rights of the Child 2008, Consideration of reports submitted by States parties under article 44 of the Convention Third and fourth periodic reports of States parties due in 2007', Committee on the Rights of the Child, 29 December 2008.

Dupret, B, Bouhya, A, Lindbekk, M, Utriza Yakin, A (2019) 'Filling Gaps in Legislation: The Use of Fiqh by Contemporary Courts in Morocco, Egypt, and Indonesia' 4 *Islamic Law and Society* 405.

El Fegiery, M (2016) *Islamic Law and Human Rights: The Muslim Brotherhood in Egypt* (Cambridge, Cambridge Scholars Publishing).

Engelcke, D (2019) 'Establishing Filiation (Nasab) and the Placement of Destitute Children into New Families: What Role Does the State Play?' 34 *Journal of Law and Religion* 408.

Epp, C (1998) *The Rights Revolution: Lawyers, Activists and Supreme Courts in Comparative Perspective* (Chicago, The University of Chicago Press).

Esposito, J (2001) *Women in Muslim Family Law* (Syracuse, NY, Syracuse University Press).

Ezzat, A (2021) 'Challenging the Legal Ideology of the State: Cause Lawyering and Social Movements in Egypt' Arab Reform Initiative, https://www.arab-reform.net/publication/challenging-the-legal-ideology-of-the-state-cause.

Galanter, M (1983) 'The Radiating Effects of Courts' in KD Boyum and L Mather (eds) *In Empirical Theories of Courts* (New York, Longman) 117.

Hasso, F (2010) *Consuming Desires: Family Crisis and the State in the Middle East* (California, Stanford University Press).

Höland, A (2011) 'Which Effects Do Courts Have?' in K Papendorf, S Machura and K Andenæs (eds), *Understanding Law in Society* (Wien/Berlin, Lit Verlag).

Ibrahim, AF (2019) 'Care of Abandoned Children in Sunni Islamic Law: Early Modern Egypt in Theory and Practice' in N Yassari, L-M Möller and M-C Najm (eds), *Filiation and the Protection of Parentless Children* (London, Springer).

Kamali, H (2003) *Islamic Law: An Introduction* (Oxford, Oneworld).

Korbatieh, S (2007) 'Evidence Rules in Sharia and the Impact of Modern Technology and DNA Testing' 5 *Australian Journal of Islamic Studies* 4.

Lindbekk, M (forthcoming) *Adjudicating the Family in Egypt: Continuity and Transformation* (London, Springer).

Lindbekk, M and Bahgat, B (2021) 'Blasphemy and the Cultivation of Religious Sensibilities in Post-2011 Egypt' in A Stensvold (ed), *Blasphemies Compared: Transgressive Speech in a Globalised World* (London, Routledge).

Lombardi, C and Cannon, C (2016) 'Transformations in Muslim Views about "Forbidding Wrong": The Rise and Fall of Islamist Litigation in Egypt' in R Hefner (ed), *Sharia Law and Modern Muslim Ethics* (Bloomington, IN, Indiana University Press).

Mada Masr (2016) 'Actor Ahmed Ezz Sentenced to 3 Years in Prison for Defaming Actress Zeina in Paternity Case' *Mada Masr* (19 June 2016).

—— (2021) 'High-Stakes Rape Trial for Woman Seeking to Record Biological Father on Daughter's Birth Certificate Goes to Final Appeal' *Mada Masr* (28 March 2021).

Marei, A (2009) *Second Shadow Report for the CEDAW Coalition Egypt* (Cairo, The Egyptian Association for Community Participation Enhancement).

McCann, M (2008) 'Litigation and Legal Mobilization' in G Caldeira, RD Kelemen and K Whittington (eds), *The Oxford Handbook of Law and Politics* (Oxford, Oxford University Press).

Merry, S (1990) *Getting Justice and Getting Even: Legal Consciousness Among Working Class Americans* (Chicago, IL, University of Chicago).

Moustafa, T (2008) 'Law and Resistance in Authoritarian States: The Judicialization of Politics in Egypt' in T Ginsburg and T Moustafa (eds), *Rule by Law: the Politics of Courts in Authoritarian Regimes* (Cambridge, Cambridge University Press).

Moustafa, T and Ginsburg, T (2008) 'Introduction: The Functions of Courts in Authoritarian Politics' in T Ginsburg and T Moustafa (eds), *Rule by Law: the Politics of Courts in Authoritarian Regimes* (Cambridge, Cambridge University Press).

Pratt, N (2020) *Embodying Geopolitics: Generations of Women's Activism in Egypt, Jordan, and Lebanon* (California, University of California Press).

Scheingold, S (1974) *The Politics of Rights: Lawyers, Public Policy, and Social Change* (New Haven, CT, Yale University Press).

Shabana, A (2013) 'Negation of Paternity in Islamic Law between *Li'ān* and DNA Fingerprinting' 20 *Islamic Law and Society* 157.

Shaham, R (2010) *The Expert Witness in Islamic Courts: Medicine and Crafts in the Service of Law* (Chicago, University of Chicago Press).

Sieder, R and A McNeish (2013) 'Introduction' in R Sieder and A McNeish (eds), *Gender Justice and Legal Pluralities: Latin American and African Perspectives* (London, Routledge).

Sonneveld, N (2012) *Khul' Divorce in Egypt: Public Debates, Judicial Practices and Everyday Life* (Cairo, The American University in Cairo Press).

The New Humanitarian (2006) 'New Paternity Law Stipulating DNA Testing Proposed' *The New Humanitarian* (13 April 2006).

Vikør, K (2005) *Between God and the Sultan: A History of Islamic Law* (London, Hurst).

Part III

Sociology of Law Methods and Interdisciplinarity

12

Knowledge and Opinion about Law – The Importance of Law-related Education

ULRIKE SCHULTZ

I. KNOWLEDGE AND OPINION ABOUT LAW – THE IMPORTANCE OF LAW-RELATED EDUCATION

I FIRST MET Reza Banakar about 20 years ago. We sat by chance close to each other on a bus from some conference event, started to talk and discovered that we shared an interest in legal culture and legal consciousness, and we discussed issues of identity and individuality. I was impressed by his profound socio-legal knowledge, and we have – thanks also to some other coincidences – remained in contact. In 2018 I asked Reza whether he could help to initiate a comparative project on Knowledge and Opinion about Law (KoL) (or legal consciousness). He was, as I had heard, looking for funding for a project in that context. I have a specific motivation to deal with the issue as I have been teaching law in schools for over four decades, have observed how the attitude to law of pupils has changed, and I am involved in designing courses in law-related education, an area which has gained a new importance with the increased influx of refugees and migrants in Germany.

II. PLANS FOR A PROJECT ON KNOWLEDGE AND OPINION ABOUT LAW/LEGAL CONSCIOUSNESS

I have written about legal consciousness in my work on women lawyers in Germany (Schultz 1990; 1994; 2003) referring to the research on Knowledge and Opinion about Law (KoL) in the second half of the twentieth century,[1] and had always wanted to go

---

[1] A lot of literature has been published (an annotated bibliography by Keßler in 1981); cf also Röhl 2020: 'For 50 years, the sociology of law has been discussing how law is reflected in people's minds and feelings, and from there how it acts and reacts' (translated from German); he gives further references. All this shows the importance which has been attached to KoL and legal consciousness in sociology of law.

deeper into the subject. In 2018 I heard about a Polish project by Grazyna Skapska on 'Legal awareness of Polish society: diagnosis, types, ways of shaping' which aims to compare the knowledge and opinion about law of Ukrainian immigrants in Poland with those of the Polish native population. This inspired me to think more about revisiting the old KoL or similar research on legal consciousness and investigate in what way, in times of migration, legal knowledge differs in different parts of the population. I circulated a call about revisiting KoL, and several colleagues, mainly from Eastern and Northern European countries answered. Obviously, it was timely to again bring legal consciousness to the fore in social legal research. The subject came up at several conferences and meetings in the past decade. At the RCSL Conference in Lisbon in September 2018, in a session on 'Legal Encounters: When People Meets the Law', Marc Hertogh – who had just published his book *Nobody's Law* (2018) – gave a paper titled 'That's Your Law, Not Mine! Legal Consciousness and Legal Alienation in Everyday Life'. Balázs Fekete from Hungary dealt with changes in knowledge about law in Hungary (Fekete and Gajduschek 2015; Fekete and Robert 2018). In October 2018 the Institute for Legal Studies of the Hungarian Academy of Sciences in Budapest hosted a workshop entitled 'Rights Consciousness and Legal Cultures: Empirical Research Experiences', which was part of a government-funded project on 'Lack of Rights Consciousness in the Legal Cultures of Central-Europe and the Balkans. Myth or Reality?'

All this hints towards a gap between, on one side, law and rights and on the other side the perception, use and acceptance of them by the broader population (Hertogh and Kurkchiyan 2016), 'ordinary citizens' as it was phrased in the session description for the Lisbon conference.[2]

At the Conference for the 30th anniversary of the IISL in Onati we organised two sessions titled 'Knowledge and Opinion about Law: Challenges and Opportunities for a New Generation of KOL-Research' where the Hungarian and Danish empirical research were both presented, and methodological questions discussed.

Reza invited those who had shown interest in the new project on revisiting 'Knowledge and Opinion about Law' to a meeting in Lund. He wrote: 'The primary aim of this gathering is to discuss the research potential of legal consciousness generally, to explore possible avenues of enquiry and, above all, collaboration between us.' But when the meeting took place on 10 October 2019 he was not well enough to attend. Due to Reza's illness and sad untimely death less than a year later, in combination with the worldwide Covid-19 restrictions, the project was put on hold. Balázs Fekete had organised a panel for the RCSL conference in Lund which was planned for August 2020 and had to be postponed. He had chosen 'The Study of Legal Consciousness: European Perspectives' as a title, but international work of course goes beyond just Europe (eg Chua and Engel 2019). The question for Europe is whether there is a common European legal culture or shared elements of it.

---

[2] They experience 'legal meaninglessness and powerlessness'. This may explain the growing success of authoritarian regimes.

III. KOL AND LEGAL CONSCIOUSNESS – WHAT ARE WE TALKING ABOUT?

In the abstract for her presentation on 'The Potential and Limitations of the Empirical Study of Legal Consciousness' for the Onati conference in June 2019, Marina Kurkchiyan, who chairs the RCSL Working Group on Legal Culture, had written:

> Legal consciousness[3] is a vibrant research field attracting growing numbers of scholars worldwide. Yet differing assumptions about aims and methods have generated vigorous debates, ... different clusters of scholars are pursuing different goals and deploying the concept of legal consciousness in different ways. ... legal consciousness is actually a flexible paradigm with multiple applications rather than a mono-lithic approach. (*cf* also Röhl 2020; Marschelke 2015)

The picture is further blurred by concepts such as legal sentiments (*Rechtsgefühl*), sense of justice, legal awareness (in German also *Rechtsbewusstsein*) called 'nebulae' in the editorial to the small booklet on Knowledge and Opinion about Law (Campbell et al 1973: 9) which sums up the outcome of the first wave of international comparative work on KoL.

Without going into further detail here, as an empiricist I like the concept of knowledge of law which can be measured on a cognitive level. Opinion about law is more for qualitative research. It is harder to operationalise and harder to break down into categories. But it is important to know about it if it should be acted upon, as it is related to the appreciation of the state and its institutions.

IV. THE 'OLD' KOL RESEARCH

Research on KoL had its heyday in the years of the boom of sociology of law in Europe in the 1960s–1980s. In 1981 an annotated bibliography on KoL was published in the newly founded Zeitschrift für Rechtssoziologie in Germany (Keßler 1981). There was a KoL Center in Copenhagen which collected and circulated information on ongoing research.

The early research on KoL mainly had the aim of measuring the acceptance of legal rules. This gives them a high level of legitimacy which is a demand in democratic societies (Kaupen 1973), and acceptance is the basis for obeying rules. Therefore the literature also dealt with deviations from norms, penalties and punitive orientation. In spite of population movements during and after World War II, in Germany notably by refugees from the East, European societies were in these years culturally rather homogeneous – at least more so than today with migration from all parts of the world.

In the 1960s–1980s questionnaire-based, mainly surveys on KoL, were conducted in several European countries.[4] They formed part of a big international comparative project and followed the same or a similar research design directed towards the

---

[3] In German: *Rechtsbewusstsein*.
[4] But also in Japan (Chiba 1972), for example. And there had been earlier research in the USA (Podgorecki 1973).

acceptance of rules in various social groups to find out how the knowledge of law (criminal, constitutional, procedural) differs; or how the knowledge level of various social groups (based on gender, age, social status etc) varies. The projects were mainly quantitative, aiming for representativeness.

Kálmán Kulcsár, later Hungarian Minister of Justice, carried out a representative survey in Hungary in 1965 to assess the legal knowledge of the Hungarian population. A follow-up was carried out in 2013, focused on measuring how the knowledge of people about some legal rules has changed since (Fekete and Szilágyi 2017).

Adam Podgorecki supervised research in Poland in 1963 with a representative survey of opinion on parental authority which included questions on familiarity with the law (Podgorecki 1973: 71). He was also involved in studies on the prestige of law followed by a general population sample designed to examine the basic moral and level of views of Polish society (ibid: 82).

Joint comparative research on KoL was conducted in the Netherlands and Belgium (van Houtte and Vinke 1973).

Berl Kutchinsky, from Copenhagen, chairman of the international research group on KoL, wrote in the booklet on KoL research: 'I have tried to provide some answers to the question: What is known, at the moment, about the so-called legal consciousness of the common man?' (1973: 132).

KoL research also found immediate practical application: in 1966 in the socialist German Democratic Republic 'it was considered necessary to research the citizens' opinion on the family and family law' to let 'the citizens themselves participate in the shaping of the law and that their opinion is reflected in the law', 'as a basis for the successful implementation of the concern and objectives of the law'[5] (Grandke et al 1966).

However, it should not be concealed that KoL research has also been criticised for being committed to a technocratic ideology, that it lacks theoretical questioning, and that it is therefore diverted to legal policy objectives. It is reprimanded for the fact that the surveys and publications of public opinion on law create legal facts that have a legitimising function for the status quo (Smaus 1981).

V. KOL RESEARCH IN GERMANY

Kol research in Germany by Kaupen et al in 1970 (Kaupen 1973) was geared towards the issue of 'whether the present system of law perhaps ignores the needs and interest of the public'.

The results were also used for a critique of the *Obrigkeitsstaat* (the authoritarian state): 'An analysis of the legal system of the Federal Republic of Germany shows that the dilemma of authoritarian state or democracy has not yet been solved'[6] (Kaupen and Rasehorn 1971).[7]

---

[5] Translated from German.
[6] Translation from German.
[7] This research was also motivated by a desire to overcome the Nazi past. Kaupen and Rasehorn at the same time carried out empirical research on lawyers in Germany, comparing lawyers in the judiciary and

The quantitative representative surveys in the German research included variables: occupation and sex (wm = working male; wf = working female; hw = housewife), age (–35; 36–50; 51 plus), class (low, lower middle, upper middle, upper), religion (catholic, protestant, none) residence (small, middle, big), court experience, and preference of political parties (Social Democrats, Christian Democrats).[8]

Reading the research today shows how time-related it was, and how living conditions and democratic values have changed. Updates to this research are timely and make sense. As Fekete and Gajduschek concluded from their research (2015), one result is that 'the knowledge about law has certainly increased during this period; moreover, the main impetus behind this was the increase of the general educational level in the country'.

In Germany, since 2010, Roland Legal Cost (Protection) Insurance has published annually a 'Rechtsreport' (law report) about public opinion on the German legal system and current legal policy issues (Roland Rechtsreport 2021). The 2021 version was based on 1,286 interviews conducted in November 2020. The quite consistent result over the past decade has been that support for the legal system is high and stable but, despite that, a considerable level of public dissatisfaction was found.

VI. GENDER DIFFERENCES IN KNOWLEDGE AND OPINION ABOUT LAW

When I started to work intensely on women lawyers in Germany in the 1980s, I remembered the representative KoL survey by Kaupen et al and looked at the results for the various categories they had distinguished (wm = working male; wf = working female; hw = housewife). The quantitative survey included answers by 1,100 adults, 612 men and 200 housewives.[9] I was influenced by difference theory, in line with the zeitgeist of the 1980s, and wanted to find out whether there are differences in KoL between men and women – and if so, why. Germany at the time still had very conservative family structures backed up by patriarchal patterns in the relevant legislation (in family, labour, social, pension, tax, as well as criminal law). Women had largely been kept out of legal occupations: the first woman lawyer was admitted in 1922,[10] and until well into the twentieth century women only gradually gained full legal rights and an independent legal status (Schultz 2016b).

---

in legal practice, finding that – as expected – judges and prosecutors are more conservative and alien to society than practitioners (advocates) (1971: 23 ff). They also refer to at the time still unpublished results of Rüschemeyer's work on lawyers and their society (1973/1976). Hoffmann and Volks (1972) conducted KoL research on West German lawyers in private practice, with 787 interviews based on the 1970 edition of the directory of all (22,987) German lawyers.

[8] 'The sample comprises 1,100 adult (at least 18 years old) persons and is a disproportionally stratified random sample. While the male interviewees (612 persons) represent the respective German population, there is an underrepresentation of 200 housewives in the female sample. This underrepresentation has been mathematically corrected for the presentation of the data in the compendium' (Kaupen et al 1970: 1).

[9] *cf* n 8.

[10] In 2022 we celebrate the 100th anniversary of women in the legal profession; Maria Otto was the first to be admitted.

This had led to what we call negative legal consciousness. Consulting other relevant publications in the field (eg Hommerich 1974; Lautmann 1980[11] and Blankenburg 1975; *cf* Schultz 1990: 329 ff and 1994 with further references), I could state that – at the time – women:

— had a greater cognitive distance to law, ie less knowledge of legal rules than men;
— overall, had a more distanced relation to law, they did not trust in their rights, avoided the court cases/legal disputes;
— developed other than legal strategies and problem solutions;
— were less likely to ask for legal advice and seek legal help.

Men, on the other hand, were more litigious and more often tried to prevail against opponents.

I drew the conclusion that, in general terms, the law was alien to many women, as were the legal habitus, the male-dominated patterns of perception, thinking, judgement and action in legal settings.

In recent decades, particularly in the past 20 years, we have seen a rapid modernisation of gender images and roles in Germany: 'pure' housewives have almost disappeared, and most women work – albeit many in part-time work; women participate more in public life – more than 50 per cent of judges and prosecutors are women; and we see a growing number of women in leading positions (though not yet enough); the educational level of women is as high – or even higher– as that of men. It would be very interesting to repeat the research and find out what has changed, how and why. A hint that differences have not altogether disappeared is found in the Roland Rechtsreport (2021), which discovered in the data analysis that 'women and under 30-year-olds … are involved in court proceedings less often than average' (ibid: 19).[12] We also know from practice that more women than men are interested in qualifying in mediation. In a new Austrian multi-methods survey on the knowledge of fundamental rights in Austria for the 100th anniversary of the federal constitutional law in 2020 (Lachmayer and Rothmann 2020) it was mentioned that 'male respondents tended to give more correct answers than female respondents'.

This prompts the question of whether women need more legal education or just more legal empowerment? Between 1985 and 2015 I have given countless presentations and training sessions to women on women's rights, often commissioned by equal opportunities officers. On the other side the question could be: Should men develop in the direction of women, become less assertive and litigious? And what does

---

[11] In his article on 'Negative Legal Consciousness. On gender differentiations in legal agency' Lautmann used 'qualitative data of nondirective interviews and group discussions' to describe gender differences (1980: 165): 'Such differences are demonstrable for cognitive distance to the law, the subjective theories about law, the awareness of claims, the instrumental-vs.-expressive orientation in legal action, the ego vs. alter direction of legal investment, the range of legal interference, the preference of negotiation to legal decision, the perception and acquisition of structural properties of the law, the autonomy in legal acting, the inclination to assert or to resign legal claims, the attribution of legal competence, the access to legal counselling and some inconsistencies in legal consciousness' (from the English version of the abstract).

[12] The question was: 'Have you been involved in a court case once or more in the last 10 years, whether as plaintiff, defendant or witness, or have you not been?' Answer: Yes, once or several times: men 32 per cent; women 19 per cent.

it mean for the application of law in the judiciary and in legal practice when there are gendered differences in KoL? For example, do women judge differently? I have dealt with the question in recent decades based on empirical research (Schultz 2016a; 2017; Schultz and Shaw 2013).

KoL of course also differs according to age, the economic status, and the social situation of citizens. The various variables intersect. Low earners and the unemployed, for example, know more about social law (occupational disability, social assistance etc) than I do as a lawyer. Citizens who have been involved in eg labour disputes, family law and inheritance litigation will gain a special knowledge in these fields.

VII. KOL IN MIGRANT COMMUNITIES

In the recent past Germany has become a country of immigration. After World War II German society was, for decades, very homogeneous – a middle-class society. After recruiting a foreign workforce since the 1960s, massive waves of migrants and refugees have arrived in Germany since the 1990s, with a huge increase in the refugee crisis in 2015 after Chancellor Merkel's 'wir schaffen das' (we make it) speech. In 2020, 26.7 per cent of the population had a migration background, with a very uneven distribution over the federal states; in cities in the Ruhr district where I live the rate can be as high as 50 per cent, or even more. They include 6.7 per cent of Muslims (2021)[13] while the Christian churches are steadily losing membership, which now lies at under 50 per cent.

We know that in Muslim communities there can be deficits in the acceptance of gender equality but differences in the acceptance of norms goes beyond this. In some migrant groups, a general distrust of the law and state institutions has been observed, giving preference to (local) traditions, the family and its value system; conservative Muslims consult dispute mediators rather than seeking access to justice in courts. Over time, this can undermine traditional legal systems and challenge western constitutional values.[14] Also, individuals' knowledge of everyday law differs according to the legal culture and system in which people have been brought up.

The Bavarian Ministry of Justice reacted to the refugee waves immediately in 2015 and produced information leaflets and short introductory films on the German legal system: 'Lessons in law for refugees and asylum seekers' in different languages (German, English, French, Arabic, Urdu, Pashto, Dari and Farsi, Tigrinya and Russian); a film about the basics: 'Unity. Compliance. Freedom. That is how the constitutional state of Germany works', and one on German civil law, including principles of family law, and films on criminal law, juvenile law and about the role of women in German society.[15] For adults, integration courses are offered, which include elements about democracy.

Some federal states like Northrhine-Westfalia also offer integration classes for pupils, which can include some legal instruction as long as volunteering lawyers are

---

[13] In the city where I live, in Hagen, Muslims form 17 per cent of the population.
[14] Interesting reflections are offered by the French author Houellebecq (2018).
[15] See https://www.justiz.bayern.de/service/fluechtlinge-asylbewerber/videos-englisch/.

available. For naturalisation, applicants for German citizenship have to prove knowledge of the basic principles of the state order in a multiple-choice question test. The syllabus for all these measures is based on unstructured experience and assumptions.

Statistics on criminal offences show that 'Ausländer', ie people with a foreign passport,[16] commit (for example) more crimes involving violence.[17] Therefore, systematic research is long overdue on KoL in various groups of the population to define a sound basis for instruction and education on law and institutions with the aim of guiding immigrants to an acceptance and observance of the rules and achieving respect for constitutional principles.[18]

VIII. TEACHING KOL TO YOUNG PEOPLE

After World War I, in the Weimar Republic, there was the first movement towards a regular basic instruction in law for pupils at school. After World War II the Americans carried out a thorough re-education programme with reorientation to democracy and constitutional values in Germany, also with a strong focus on the younger generation. National and state agencies for civic education were founded. The programmes of the Americans left different traces in the federal states.[19] In Northrhine-Westfalia for more than six decades a programme of law-related education, organised by the Ministry of Justice, has been offered by lawyers in schools. It includes 20 hours of instruction and a visit to a court. It is non-obligatory and geared towards 14–16 year olds. Over more than 40 years, I have taught around 60 courses in various types of school: secondary schools, comprehensive schools, and gymnasium, as well as in primary school, and for 30 years I have been in charge of the further training of the lawyers in our justice academy. I have designed curricula, teaching materials, helped to produce audio-visuals and have even composed an interactive self-instructional 'train the trainer' program.[20]

To plan the teaching, it is important to address the following:

—   What do the pupils know about law? What should they know?

—   How can they learn what?

---

[16] The group is much smaller than that of people with a migration background, as the latter includes those who have become naturalised Germans.

[17] See https://polizei.nrw/sites/default/files/2021-06/PKS_Jahrbuch_2020.pdf, 32 ff. In the first years after 2015 there were nasty incidences of young men molesting women, eg in swimming pools, and other kinds of assaults. News spread around the world when on New Year's Eve 2015/16 in Cologne next to the cathedral, groups of young men harassed women and even tried to rape them.

[18] In the Ruhr district groups of so-called south-east Europeans cause a lot of trouble, not following rules and lacking respect for the police and other public authorities.

[19] In Eastern Germany, the former GDR, which was under Russian occupation and influence, particularly in the older generation, democratic values are still less appreciated and there is a divide between East and West in the evaluation of Putin's attack on Ukraine: cf 'A question of origin: Why do East and West Germans view Russia's war so differently?' at https://www1.wdr.de/daserste/hartaberfair/faktencheck/faktencheck-576.html, based on a Civey survey.

[20] See www.rechtskunde.de. For some time my university had offered a degree course for teachers on teaching law at school. As I led a unit for didactics of law, I was tasked with training the teachers in didactics and the methodology of teaching. To do this, I needed teaching practice at school. This is how it started.

— What is their opinion about law and their attitude to it? How can these be improved or changed?

— What are their sources of information? How can they be used? (Private sphere: family, groups; school; church, religion; media: social media, internet, films, TV, radio, newspapers).

I have defined the following as aims of my teaching:

— to raise interest in law, give an overview of the legal system;

— to teach the basics of law that are relevant to daily life (how to conclude a contract, the financial consequence of harmful acts, what minors are allowed to do at which age etc);

— to create legal awareness and consciousness;

— to teach legal values, strengthen legal morale and '*Rechtstreue*' (obedience to law);

— to encourage pupils to understand law as an integral part of society and the social order;

— to relieve or eliminate threshold 'fear' of law courts and other public institutions;

— to exemplify structures of legal thinking and reasoning;

— to work against discriminatory attitudes.

My teaching and training are based on pragmatic knowledge. Over the years, I have gained profound experience stemming from practice, but this does not replace empirical research. A couple of years ago, I had planned a questionnaire survey but then did not get the chance to do it. However, it is still needed, and all the more so with the growing diversity of pupils at school. The sort of problems we face can be illustrated by just a couple of examples: while teaching at a primary school, I was told by a young Arab boy that it is a man's honour to carry a knife. Another announced that graffitiing in public places is allowed, but that it is forbidden at home.

Prior instruction leaves traces, therefore it matters very much which school the pupils attend. When I ask pupils to name a right or a law that they know, in grammar school – as a result of lessons in politics – the answers will include human rights. In secondary schools, criminal offences are mentioned. Of course, the pupils' personal experiences also affect results: in a comprehensive school in a socially deprived area the pupils knew a lot about social law.

Age is also important. Young people tend to have very punitive attitudes: an even greater proportion than in the population at large is in favour of death penalty, and popular legal errors circulate, such as: a life sentence really means only 15 years' imprisonment; offenders always get a sentence on probation; and even that contracts are only valid in writing etc.

IX. NATIONAL DIFFERENCES IN KOL

As well as the individual factors that influence KoL, the overall economic situation in a country and its political system have an impact (Fekete and Szilágyi 2017; Vuković and Cvejić 2019).

In 2010 I helped to introduce basic instruction in law at schools in Georgia as a supporting element in the democratisation process. From 2013 until 2019 I was invited by the Bulgarian Vice-President to teach some basic courses in 'Democracy and law' in 14 Bulgarian schools, each one covering four units in three grades. At the end, 180 judges and prosecutors were brought together for a 'train the trainer' session.

This gave me various insights into the legal and political system in Bulgaria. Using teaching elements from my courses in Germany and vice versa I experienced differences in perception of law and attitude to legal institutions between pupils in a former communist country and Germany as a Western country. The young Bulgarians had an underdeveloped sense of individual rights, an underdeveloped notion of freedom of speech, and strong threshold apprehensions towards public institutions (they thought that attendance at open court sessions was not permitted, as indeed did their teachers).

Parents were seen as responsible for whatever pupils do, even for material damages and criminal offences. And in case of misbehaviour in school, they thought less in formal legal reactions and rather in low threshold conflict solution in the school (cleaning the floors, sweeping the courtyard). They had a more friendly and relaxed relationship with their teachers, as they also spent a lot of time at school for extracurricular activities. Private clubs, societies and instruction (eg for sports and music) are unusual, NGOs were hardly known. Religion and church were held in low esteem. Bulgarian customs were cherished, and folk dance and traditional music practised. When I asked pupils whether there was a law they would like to make, they gave me more examples than pupils in Germany, but had less proposals for what they could do to get the law on track.[21] My overall aim was to activate them and motivate them for civic engagement. When I asked them which institutions they trusted, they ranked the army, the police and churches at the bottom. In Germany, a similar question places the police high on the trust list, after doctors and before courts.[22] Both countries share a disrespect for government and political parties.

The examples given show how important and rewarding it is to do extended empirical research on KoL of young and older citizens, women and men, different migrant communities, to find out where empowerment is needed, where deficits are, and how they could be compensated through teaching on law and democracy. The examples also show how interesting and necessary it is to do comparative research to evaluate the situation in given contexts and countries – in Europe and globally. Connected to opinion about law are questions on why and when people ignore or follow the law, which Reza Banakar has dealt with in his book *Driving Culture in Iran* (2016).

There is a broad spectrum of issues to cover. Reza Banakar has left us a legacy to follow.

REFERENCES

Banakar, R (2016) *Driving Culture in Iran: Law and Society on the Roads of the Islamic Republic* (International Library of Iranian Studies) (London, IB Tauris).

---

[21] I was astonished to learn that letters to the editor, for example, are unknown.
[22] forsa-Institutionen-Vertrauensranking zur Jahreswende 2021/22 (Ranking Trust in Institutions).

Blankenburg, E (1975) 'Review of Knowledge and Opinion about Law by Adam Podgorecki, Wolfgang Kaupen, Jean van Houtte, Peter Vinke, Berl Kutchinsky' 61 *ARSP: Archiv für Rechts- und Sozialphilosophie / Archives for Philosophy of Law and Social Philosophy* 267.

Campbell, CM et al (1973) 'Introductory Note to Knowledge and Opinion about Law' in A Podgorecki et al (eds), *Knowledge and Opinion about Law* (London, Robertson) 7.

Chiba, M (1972) *Results and Problems of KoL Research in Japan. A Preliminary Report* (Tokyo, Tokyo Metropolitan University).

Chua, LJ and Engel, DM (2019) 'Legal Consciousness Reconsidered' 15 *Annual Review of Law and Social Science* 335.

Fekete, B and Gajduschek, G (2015) 'Changes in Knowledge about Law in Hungary in the Past Half Century' 57 *Sociologija* 620.

Fekete, B and Robert, P (2018) 'Understanding Hungarian Attitudes toward Law in an International Context' (9 February 2018), available at https://ssrn.com/abstract=3120933.

Fekete, B and Szilágyi, IH (2017) 'Knowledge and Opinion about Law (KOL) Research in Hungary' 58 *Acta Juridica Hungarica. Hungarian Journal of Legal Studies* 326.

Grandke, A, Kuhrig, H and Weise, W (1966) 'Die öffentliche Meinung in der Deutschen Demokratischen Republik zur Entwicklung der Familie und des Familienrechts und ihr Einfluss auf den Inhalt des Familiengesetzbuches' in R Schulz and H Steiner (eds), *Soziologie und Wirklichkeit, Beiträge zum VI. Weltkongreß für Soziologie in Evian (Frankreich)*, vol 4 Bis 11 (VEB Verlag Deutscher Wissenschaften, Berlin) 173.

Hertogh, M (2018) *Nobody's Law. Legal Consciousness and Legal Alienation in Everyday Life* (London, Palgrave).

Hertogh, M and Kurkchiyan, M (2016) 'When Politics Comes into Play, Law is No Longer Law: Images of Collective Legal Consciousness in the UK, Poland and Bulgaria' 12 *International Journal of Law in Context* 404.

Hoffmann, H and Volks, H (1972) *KoL Survey on West German Lawyers in Private Practice* (Ms Kölner Arbeitskreis für Rechtssoziologie).

Hommerich, C (1974) *Einstellung der Bevölkerung zu Recht und Justiz* (Arbeitskreis für Rechtssoziologie, Hanover).

Houellebecq, M (2018) *Unterwerfung* (Köln, Dumont).

Kaupen, W (1973) 'Public Opinion of the Law in a Democratic Society' in A Podgorecki et al, *Knowledge and Opinion about Law* (London, Robertson) 43.

Kaupen, W and Rasehorn, T (1971) *Die Justiz zwischen Obrigkeitsstaat und Demokratie* (Neuwied, Luchterhand).

Kaupen, W, Volks, H and Werle, R (1970) *Compendium of Results of a Representative Survey among the German Population on Knowledge and Opinion about Law and Legal Institutions (KOL)* (ms, Hannover, Arbeitskreis für Rechtssoziologie).

Keßler, EM (1981) 'Annotierte Bibliographie zu Knowledge and Opinion about Law (KoL)-Untersuchungen' 2 *Zeitschrift für Rechtssoziologie* 278.

Kutchinsky, B (1973) '"The Legal Consciousness": A Survey of Research on Knowledge and Opinion about Law' in A Podgorecki et al (eds), *Knowledge and Opinion about Law* (London, Robertson) 101.

Lachmayer, K and Rothmann, R (2020) 'Grundrechtswissen in Österreich. Eine empirische Untersuchung zum 100-jährigen Bestehen des Bundes-Verfassungsgesetzes 1920' *juridikum* 472.

Lautmann, R (1980) 'Negatives Rechtsbewusstsein. Über Geschlechterdifferenzierungen in der juristischen Handlungsfähigkeit' 1 *Zeitschrift für Rechtssoziologie* 165.

Marschelke, J-C (2015) 'Rechtskultur – Aspekte einer rechtssoziologischen Debatte' 1 *Zeitschrift für Kultur- und Kollektivwissenschaft* 1(2).

Podgorecki, A (1973) 'Public Opinion on Law' in A Podgorecki et al, *Knowledge and Opinion about Law* (London, Robertson) 65.

Podgorecki, A, Kaupen, W, van Houtte, J, Vinke, P and Kutchinsky, B (1973) *Knowledge and Opinion about Law* (London, Robertson).

Röhl, K (2020) 'Schlagwort: Legal Consciousness' (9 March 2020), available at https://www.rsozblog.de/tag/legal-consciousness/.

Roland Rechtsreport (2021), available at https://www.roland-rechtsschutz.de/media/roland-rechtsschutz/pdf-rr/042-presse-pressemitteilungen/roland-rechtsreport/roland_rechtsreport_2021.pdf.

Rüschemeyer, D (1973) *Lawyers and Their Society: A Comparative Study of the Legal Profession in Germany and the United States: A Comparative Study of the Legal Profession* (Boston, Harvard University Press; German edn Stuttgart, Enke 1976).

Schultz, U (1990) 'Wie männlich ist die Juristenschaft?' in U Battis and U Schultz (eds), *Frauen im Recht* (Heidelberg, CF Müller) 319.

—— (1994) 'Women in Law or the Masculinity of the Legal Profession in Germany' in A Febbrajo and D Nelken (eds), *European Yearbook in the Sociology of Law 1993* (Milan, Giuffre) 229.

—— (2003) 'Women in the World's Legal Professions. Overview and Synthesis' in U Schultz and G Shaw (eds), *Women in the World's Legal Professions* (Oxford, Hart Publishing) XXV.

—— (2012) *Rechtskundeunterricht interessant und anspruchsvoll gestalten* (Düsseldorf, Ministerium der Justiz NRW).

—— (2016a) 'Sexism in Law and the Impact of Gender Stereotypes in Legal Proceedings' in Heinrich Boell Stiftung South Caucasus (ed) *Fight for the Public Space: When Personal is Political* (Tiflis, Heinrich Boell Stiftung South Caucasus) 97, https://ge.boell.org/en/2016/12/29/fight-public-space-when-private-political.

—— (2016b) 'Equal Rights for Men and Women in Germany. How a Constitutional Principle was Transformed into Reality' in Heinrich Boell Stiftung South Caucasus (ed) *Fight for the Public Space: When Personal is Political* (Tiflis, Heinrich Boell Stiftung South Caucasus) 85, https://ge.boell.org/en/2016/12/29/fight-public-space-when-private-political.

—— (2017) 'Do Female Judges Judge Better?' in M Lindbekk and N Sonneveld (eds), *Women Judges in the Muslim World* (Leiden, Brill) 23.

Schultz, U and Shaw, G (2013) 'Introduction: Gender and Judging: Overview and Synthesis' in U Schultz and G Shaw (eds), *Gender and Judging* (Oxford, Hart Publishing) 3.

Smaus, G (1981) 'Theorielosigkeit und politische Botmäßigkeit der KOL-Untersuchungen' 2 *Zeitschrift für Rechtssoziologie* 245.

van Houtte, J and Vinke, P (1973) 'Attitudes Governing the Acceptance of Legislation among Various Social Groups' in A Podgorecki et al (eds), *Knowledge and Opinion about Law* (London, Robertson) 13.

Vuković, D and Cvejić, S (2019) 'Attitudes towards the Rule of Law in Contemporary Serbia: A Coherent Legal Culture?' *Internationales Jahrbuch für Medienphilosophie* 203.

13

Rights Consciousness in Hungary. What is Behind the Numbers? Lessons of a Focus Group Study

BALÁZS FEKETE

I. INTRODUCTION

THE ISSUE OF rights consciousness has not attracted wide attention among the Hungarian socio-legal scholarship. Although legal sociology had a certain role in the former Socialist legal academia (Fekete and H. Szilágyi 2017), it mainly subscribed to the so-called 'knowledge and opinion about law' (KOL) tradition of socio-legal research – which was rather popular in the 60s and 70s in Western scholarship (*cf* Podgórecki et al 1973) – thereby turning to quantitative research designs and macro issues. These were, inter alia, knowledge of the law (eg Kulcsár 1967) and the role of law in general social consciousness (eg Sajó 1981), but rights consciousness had only been touched upon marginally by András Sajó (1988–89) in a study addressing legal alienation in Hungarian society during the late 1980s.

A new impetus came to research into rights consciousness from the 2010s, when new research projects to discuss the general features of Hungarian legal culture began. These relied on both quantitative (H. Szilágyi 2018) and qualitative research methodologies (Fleck et al 2017). Thus, in addition to traditional quantitative data analysis and the KOL heritage, the application of qualitative methods and tools, such as life interviews or focus group analyses, also appeared on the Hungarian scene. Additionally, in 2017, a new research project was launched, specifically addressing the state of rights consciousness in Hungary. This project relied on a mixed methodology research design, combining quantitative and qualitative research tools.[1]

This chapter relates to this last project. It was inspired by our slight dissatisfaction with the results of quantitative data analysis. Or, to put it differently, although

---

[1] *Lack of Rights Consciousness in the Legal Cultures of Central-Europe and Balkans. Myth or Reality?* (NKFIH-FK-125520) Project head: Balázs Fekete.

the analysis of survey data was properly able to highlight certain general trends in the recent setting of rights consciousness in Hungary, and also pointed out the role of some socio-demographic variables (for details see Fekete et al 2021), we had only a limited opportunity to understand those micro dynamics that also seriously contribute to the formation of rights consciousness. Therefore – and thanks to some external financial support[2] – it was decided to broaden our room for interpretation by starting a small-scale focus group study within the frame of this general project.[3]

As such, this chapter analyses focus group research conducted in late November and early December in 2020. Its main aim is to provide the reader with an interpretive discussion of some issues of rights consciousness in Hungary. The issues studied here came up in an early empirical survey research project, carried out in the first half of 2019 in Hungary, the Netherlands, and Serbia (ibid: 6–7). It is hoped that the analysis of focus group study data will provide valid and reliable insights that are able to contribute to a more sophisticated view of the complex question of how rights consciousness manifests itself in everyday Hungarian life.

II. STARTING POINTS AND METHODOLOGY

A. Main Findings of the Survey Research

Based on the previous survey research, we were able to formulate some conclusions, with the help of statistical analysis methods, on the recent state of rights consciousness in Hungary. In general, it is argued that legal alienation still widely pervades everyday relations between the citizen and the law, a manifest legacy of the Socialist era, but rights consciousness also has an impact on social behaviour as a normative pattern, albeit fragmented and uncertain. It can be proved statistically that legal awareness, a precondition of rights consciousness, is rather low in Hungarian society. In general, turning to the law is only a second or third best option for the overwhelming majority of society; citizens mostly prefer to rely on interpersonal agreements and expert consultations to solve their ordinary conflicts that may have a legal dimension too. In addition, the language of rights is used only in a very limited way, if at all, to understand the same ordinary disputes. Hence, people are mostly unable to formulate their problems with the help of terms related to rights. Last, legal mobilisation is also rather restricted, as incentives to bring a case to court and disincentives discouraging people to do so are almost equally strong in public attitudes (for details see ibid: 8–19). In addition, the limited extent to which socio-demographic variables have a statistical impact on these dimensions of rights consciousness, if any, is striking

---

[2] The author of this chapter is very grateful for the financial support of the Centre for Social Sciences, Budapest.

[3] On the utility of focus group studies in empirical legal studies see the paper of Bence Ságvári (2020). This excellent paper summarises the latest English methodological discussion in Hungarian and presents some previous examples when focus groups were used for legal research, too. For a good example of the use of focus groups in legal studies see Gunby et al (2013).

(*cf* Gibson and Caldeira 1996: 71–73). All in all, it cannot be argued that legal alienation still exclusively dominates contemporary Hungarian mass thinking about the law but, equally, no one can assert that rights consciousness has replaced the former strongly alienated attitudes. Nonetheless, a delicate transformation definitely began after 1989, parallel to the rule of law-oriented transformation of the entire legal order, and this also implies the strengthening of some attitudes that boost rights-conscious social activities.

The detailed data analysis identified two intriguing features that appeared at various points. First, the analysis of the conflict-solving preferences of citizens revealed that they are rather reluctant to act in a rights-conscious way if a conflict with an institution – either with a private one or a state one, such as an insurance company or the tax authority – is at stake. On the contrary, in interpersonal conflicts, the respondents were more willing to consider initiating a case to secure their rights, especially in child custody issues.[4] Second, although socio-demographic variables had only limited statistical impact on the attitudes related to rights consciousness, there was one obvious exception. It was shown that any kind of personal experience with the law – from reading a bill to participating in a court process – has a clear and positive effect with regard to rights consciousness as such.[5] Both conclusions seem to be relevant in the Hungarian context, and perhaps beyond it too; this chapter will therefore analyse the material of focus group studies with respect to these two problems. In other words, it is hoped that the analysis of the focus group discussions can help to provide a better understanding of these two questions. Why are Hungarian citizens more reluctant to consider any kind of legal procedure in a conflict with an institution than in interpersonal disputes? How and why can previous legal experience have a general positive impact on rights consciousness?

B. Methodology: Design, Recruitment, and Data Analysis

The focus groups – from recruitment to the preparation of transcripts – were managed by a Budapest-based professional market research firm (ResearchCenter Consulting)

---

[4] With regard to legal awareness, we argued this way based on the survey data: 'An important finding is that Hungarian citizens are more willing to start a legal procedure in cases of interpersonal conflicts: for breaching a private verbal agreement (12%) and the hindrance of child custody (19%). At the same time, they are more reluctant to initiate a legal procedure when an official institution, such as an insurance company or a public authority (the tax authority or the police) is the other party in the conflict. The willingness to start a court case is the lowest against the tax authority; it was chosen by only 3% of the respondents as the preferred conflict-solving strategy' (Fekete et al 2022: 229).

[5] As for rights identification, we found that 'in the 50–65 age group, the majority (54%) were able to argue using terms related to rights. This age factor reveals the high relevance of life experience in shaping legal attitudes (...). In addition, there is moderate positive relation between participation in legal procedures and rights identification (Cramer's V=0.15, p<.05)' (Fekete et al 2022: 237). In addition, the same pattern was revealed with respect to legal mobilisation attitudes: 'Those who have ever read any legal text, ever had a consultation with an advocate or other kind of lawyer, or ever participated in a court procedure appear less deterred by the complexity and incomprehensibility of legal procedures. However, when these personal experiences are lacking, Hungarian respondents seem to be estranged from the legal order' (ibid: 241).

with broad experience in the field of qualitative research. It has to be mentioned at the beginning that at that time there was no possibility to carry out conventional focus group discussions, since strict pandemic regulations were in force from November 2020 as the second wave of Covid-19 hit Hungary quite seriously. As such, the focus group discussions occurred in the online space, with the help of an online platform, and the size of the focus groups was also limited to four participants. The qualitative study experts who oversaw moderating and facilitating the focus groups argued that, based on their previous experience, four persons could properly participate in an online focus group. This limited number of participants made it possible to have a lively interactive discussion in which each participant had an equal opportunity to express his or her views.

Three mixed-sex focus groups – two men and two women in each group – were undertaken between late November and early December 2020. Each focus group lasted about 120 minutes. Participants were recruited by the market research firm with respect to two specific points. To test our research questions, one focus group needed to be composed of participants who had been involved in at least one closed legal case. In addition, age was a relevant aspect, as it is strong indicator of life experience, so a focus group with participants in the younger age category and another one with older participants also had to be set up. Applying these criteria, we had a group with younger participants (23–35 years) having no specific legal experience (FG1), another middle-aged group (30–48 years) whose participants had broader legal experience, as they had all initiated and closed a case (FG2), and a group bringing together older participants (48–58 years) with no court experience at all (FG3). The participants had either high school degrees or university degrees, so they represented a relatively well-educated segment of society.

The focus group guide was set up as follows. The discussion started with (1) a brief personal introduction, then the participants mentioned some (2) associations about law and they were also asked to describe (3) how the law appears in their ordinary life. As a closing step in this warm-up phase, they had to answer the question (4) whether they had ever participated in a legal procedure. In FG2, this last component also enabled them to tell their 'legal story' in considerable detail. Thereafter, the moderators briefly described the (5–11) five conflict situations – these were also at the centre of our survey research[6] – in each group in a random order, and asked the participants how they would try to solve them.[7] In essence, they were allowed to express their ideas

---

[6] 1. You have a verbal agreement with someone who agrees to repair your car after a small accident but the other person does not fulfil the commitment (the car bump case); 2. You get a divorce; the court decides that your ex-wife/ex-husband has custody of your child, and you can meet your child only on weekends. Your ex-spouse, however, hinders you from seeing your child (the child custody case); 3. After a serious fire in your house, the insurance company decides to compensate only a small fraction of your damages (the insurance company case); 4. The tax authority prescribes you to pay additional taxes, but you are convinced that you should not have to pay it according to the existing tax regulations (the tax authority case); 5. Your child has been arrested because of any reason and his or her request for a lawyer is denied by the police (the police abuse case).

[7] In order not to influence each other directly at the very beginning, the participants were asked to type a short reply into the chat first, then they had to elaborate on their ideas with the help of the moderator.

freely without any external help regarding the possible conflict-solving alternatives; that is, the law was not mentioned at all by the mediators. Following the first round of these free reflections, the moderators invited the respondents to explain their position in more detail, sometimes by reflecting on the diverging opinions of others. Finally, having discussed each other's positions, the participants were asked specifically what they thought about turning to law in the given case and what kind of rights could be at stake in the given conflict. Most typically, they discussed at this point why they were so reluctant to invoke, or mention at all, legal mechanisms or rights as a potential solution in their initial replies.

The discussion transcripts were analysed by the author. A thematic analysis, based on the two research questions of this chapter, was applied, meaning that broad themes were determined in the first phase and, during the second reading, those passages that related to them were grouped and coded. In some cases, certain specific sub-themes were identified and they were also coded as a lower-level alternative. As a last step, the coding systems were checked from the aspect of consistency and coherence and some refinements were also made.

Some limitations of this research method should also be discussed. First, the online format proved to have a serious limitation, as interpersonal meta-communicative interaction remained almost entirely out of scope. This is an obvious disadvantage as compared with classic focus groups, but this study could not have been undertaken in other ways due to the pandemic situation. Interestingly, a limited part of meta-communication was accessible even using this methodology, as facial expressions – such as happiness, surprise, dissatisfaction or anger – could be noticed surprisingly well due to the online setting. If something like this occurred, the author always recorded it in his notes when following the discussion. Second, the small size of groups and their limited number obviously question the research's capability to formulate generalised claims. However, since focus group research – inter alia – can aim at discovering specific arguments and their relationships with respect to a discussion theme, it can be argued that the findings are relevant for such a study. They are obviously able to establish a detailed collection of ordinary opinions about the motives of why or why not to act in a rights-conscious way and thereby contribute to having a better understanding of such a complex socio-legal issue.[8] We hope that these findings may be able to stimulate further research, using either quantitative or qualitative approaches.

III. KEY FINDINGS

A. Reasons for Reluctance to Act if a Conflict with an Institution is at Stake

In general, our first quantitative finding – a specific reluctance to act in a rights-conscious way if a conflict with either a private or a public institution is at stake, as

---

[8] Qualitative legal research experts argue that the requirement of representativeness can be interpreted another way than its conventional statistical approach focusing on the estimation of the distribution of a given phenomenon. They submit that representativeness can also be approached 'in the sense of capturing

compared to interpersonal conflicts – was not confirmed by the qualitative data at all. The thematic analysis of the focus group transcripts revealed that the participants were reluctant to consider bringing a case to court – or refer to their rights – in any situation in general. That is, it seems that whether an ordinary conflict has an interpersonal nature or an institution or body is involved was irrelevant in the eyes of focus group members.

i. Most Preferred Conflict-solving Strategies: A General Reluctance to Refer to the Law or Rights as a Primary Intent

A major strategy that participants almost always mentioned is personal consultation to reach an agreement. Interestingly, the idea of personal discussion is rather popular in the cases against the tax authority and the insurance company while, as for interpersonal conflicts, this way of conflict management only came up as a major alternative in the child custody case. In the latter case, the willingness to have a personal discussion with the other party, the ex-wife or ex-husband who breaches the child custody agreement, is obviously rooted in the sensitivity of this issue. This is explained by a member of FG2 this way.

> The involvement of an advocate is totally unnecessary as a first step. It is not my aim that each letter of the court decision would be adhered to, but the children should be brought up properly and in an orderly way. If I involved an advocate it would certainly lead to harm to the child. Let's discuss it personally instead. (FG2 M4)[9]

Another rather popular form of conflict management – strongly appearing in the cases of minor car damage, child custody, and police abuse – is turning to an external body. The focus group members explicitly mentioned the National Authority for Consumers, the financial supervisory body, the local family care centres, or the Hungarian Civil Liberties Union. Interestingly, in the car bump case, some of them suggested calling a police officer; however, not as a primary legal authority, but as a helping hand for drivers in trouble. In essence, the main reason for this choice was that participants saw these bodies as being capable of facilitating the successful management of their conflicts. In addition, these bodies' external position may enable them to provide the conflicting parties with unbiased advice. During the discussion of the police abuse case, a member of FG3 suggested that the involvement of the Hungarian Civil Liberties Union (*Társaság a szabadságjogokért*, TASZ in Hungarian) would be a good choice, as this civil body is 'independent from the state'. Another member of this focus group joined him immediately and told a short personal story to the others.

> I would join Tamás (the member who raised this idea) since this is a very good idea. By the way, I've already written to the TASZ and hats off to the fellows at the TASZ! They answered me very quickly and they gave very professional, comprehensive, and clear replies, even for ordinary people. ... My son is a doctor and I wanted to have some answers with

---

the range or variation in a phenomenon' (Webly 2010: 934). In this sense, this focus group study was also devoted to identifying some variations of argumentation with regard to the ordinary role of rights consciousness in everyday conflicts.
    [9] All these focus group transcripts excerpts were translated by the author.

regard to his job conditions during the first wave of Covid19. For instance, to what extent can the hospital oblige him to work within these circumstances, what are the regulations for sending him to another hospital to help, and is he entitled to have various protective equipment? I asked these and fantastic people work there. The replied very quickly and gave professional answers. (FG3 M4)

Having heard this story, the focus group mediator asked this member about his motivation to start an email exchange with this civil body. He explained it by comparing the position of attorneys and that of the TASZ.

I have the impression that the TASZ cannot be intimidated. An attorney can easily be driven to the wall by state power. Unfortunately, I don't have trust in the current state power at all. However, the TASZ is an independent body .... (FG3 M4)

Perhaps surprisingly, the involvement of an advocate, as an expert to help in dealing with legal issues, is not an especially popular option in the first instance. Focus group members sometimes refer to the idea of calling an advocate to represent their interest but, as a major pattern of argumentation, this is only present in the police abuse case. However, in this specific situation, most members seriously considered this option. A member of FG2 pointed out sharply why she would find it necessary to consult with an attorney.

I would definitely look for a criminal lawyer, or I don't know how to call these specialist guys and I would ask him or her what to do. I'm sure that I would read about this too. Although, if I imagine my state of mind in such a case, I would call an advocate. (...) He's professional, he's already had such a case for sure, and I hope I'll never have a similar one. (FG2 M2)

However, in addition, experts also come into play in two special conflict situations, and both are against institutions. When disputes with the insurance company and tax authority were raised, some focus group members argued for asking help from accountancy experts or insurance claim officers. This shows that, when faced by an institution, people may have the feeling that they lack a specific competence otherwise needed for successful conflict management, and consultation with such an expert can enable them to have more chance of reaching a proper solution. That is to say, institutions in general seem to be in a superior position compared to ordinary people due to their specialised professional competences, and people may try to equalise this position with the help of expert consultations.

ii. The Law and Rights as a Last Hope

As the previous section shows, turning to the law because of a supposed violation of a right was almost totally absent from the primary intentions of the focus group members. None of them mentioned that he or she would immediately start a claim before the court, although they were definitely conscious that these cases also imply legal issues. However, this certainly does not mean that they completely disregard the option of turning to the law at a later stage. From this aspect, the discussions in FG2, composed of members with previous legal and court experience, proved to be really intriguing.

In essence, this discussion revealed an interesting pattern on options of conflict management. In numerous cases, some participants gave rather detailed answers in which they ranked the different options – from personal discussion to calling the help of an external body – to manage such a situation. Although these answers were obviously diverse due to their personal preferences and previous experiences, they all shared a common point. These rankings always put the legal route, with special regard to bringing the case to the court, in the last possible place. That is, it seems that some of those who already have legal experience are not ignorant of the possible role that the law, or more specifically rights, may play in conflict management, but for various reasons they regarded it as the option of last resort. For example, an FG2 member explained their position in the context of a conflict with their insurance company these ways:

> If there is a big difference between the two amounts, I would write a complaint to the insurance company about how they come to this point first. Then I would even go to the supervisory authority and the last thing is starting a case. This thing has its own scale. (FG2 M1)

Interestingly, this consideration of various ways to manage the given conflict and ranking them according to the perceived potential was present in some answers of the other two focus groups. Obviously, these respondents did not create such subtle scales as those who had previous experience with the law, but they seemed to recognise that conflict management in these cases may also be a step-by-step process, implying various options for seeking the enforcement of their interests. Unsurprisingly, in these discussions the law could only reach last place, if it was mentioned at all.

iii. In Reality it is not Trust but Money that Counts

The previous discussion leads us to the motivations, or the discouraging factors, influencing the participants in being so reluctant to follow the rights-based legal path of conflict management. Here, the thematic analysis revealed some new insights relevant to some previous findings on the role of institutional trust which argue that institutional trust has a crucial impact on general attitudes toward the law (in general: Boda and Medve-Bálint 2015; Bartha 2013; with regard to the relationship between the institutional trust and the perceived chance of winning a case: Róbert and Fekete 2017: 90). First of all, it has to be mentioned that, in cases of conflict with the tax authority, the focus group members' argumentation showed a surprisingly high level of trust in this institution. Since this was an absolutely unexpected point, the focus group moderators asked the members to elaborate on such statements. For example, a member of FG3, composed of older participants without relevant legal experience,argued that:

> The tax authority[10] used to be an evil office, but since it has prepared the yearly tax declaration it has definitely had a more human face in my eyes. I believe it's good that it prepares

---

[10] Here, the focus group member used the authority's older acronym 'APEH', which was also a rather dirty word besides its conventional meaning – mirroring a lack of public trust and the bad image of this authority – in the slang of the 90s and 2000s.

the yearly tax declaration, which has always been a bugbear for me. I have the impression that if my position is properly grounded by legal provisions then they will tend to be helpful. Their aim is not to torture me. (FG3 M2)

A member of FG2, with some legal experience, set forth similar argumentation.

I believe that there's legal certainty in Hungary and this is based on the law-abiding attitudes of various authorities and administrative bodies. They won't accuse me of owing them without any legal basis. There are, obviously, some misunderstandings but they can be settled with the help of legal provisions. (FG2 M4)

In sum, the lack of institutional trust seemed to have a much less significant role in the focus group members' thinking than was expected. However, the question of what does motivate them to turn or not turn to the law remains valid. Again, the thematic analysis pointed out a partly unusual pattern of argumentation. Basically, in almost all conflicts and in each focus group, when further prospective actions were discussed by the members, the point of 'money' came up regularly. Interestingly, the 'money factor' implied two kinds of considerations. First, it was argued by many members that if the value of the dispute is too low, for instance the car bump case, it is not worth the bother of finding an advocate to consult and then to start a case at the court. Conversely, if bigger amounts are at stake, as for example in a case against the insurance company, some participants were much more willing to consider the legal route. In addition, the cost of a court case, including the costs of legal counsel and representation, was also mentioned as a significant deterring factor. That is, these focus group discussions suggest that the 'money factor,' including both the value of the case and the cost of the legal procedure itself, can have a serious, sometimes overlooked impact on the personal decisions on trying to claim a right. This is well summarised in the opinion of an FG1 member.

It depends on how much money, time and fatigue has to be wasted in the process. In the case of any damage, I would say that, above a few hundred thousand forints[11] it's worth carrying out such a procedure; below this amount I don't think so. (FG1 M4)

B. The Positive Impact of Legal Experience

Another major finding of our earlier survey study was that previous legal experience, ie bringing a case to the court, has a strong positive impact on rights consciousness as such. For instance, those who had such an experience were able to use the language of rights more correctly and/or they had a more positive view on legal mobilisation than the others. To test the role of previous court experiences, there was a focus group (FG2) which consisted entirely of members with a closed court case. Essentially, this finding was confirmed by the focus group discussions as such; the thematic analysis brought up thought-provoking details and refinements.

---

[11] The forint is Hungary's national currency; this amount is less than €1,000.

i. Primary Associations: Law as Restriction and an Institution

As the focus group guide established, following the mutual introduction, the discussion started with giving some ideas and associations that came to the minds of the members when the expression 'the law' was mentioned. The members of each focus group – although they can be differentiated along various factors, such as sex, age, previous legal experience and educational level – submitted surprisingly similar sets of ideas. Prominent among these was the term 'obligation' and once, as a synonym, 'restriction' was also mentioned in this context. The ideas of 'rule' and the synonyms of 'code' – once with the adjective 'thick' – and 'laws' were also mentioned in an almost equal number. Lastly, some members brought 'the law' into association with 'the court' and 'the cost' of the procedure.

Unsurprisingly, as it was suggested by the survey findings, nobody mentioned the term 'right'. Furthermore, it must be noted that all the members associated 'the law' with restrictive or formal ideas. Thus, no positive association came up that is otherwise connected to 'the law' in professional discourse, such as 'rule of law', 'entitlement', 'emancipation' or 'guarantees'. That being said, these surprisingly converging associations show a rather negative image of the law, and, thereby, they may also indicate a relatively high level of legal alienation (*cf* Hertogh 2018: 53–57). This attitude is expressed well in the assertion of a member of FG3:

> This is thick code. I feel that there are more and more restrictions, and I'm slightly concerned, so that's why this came into my mind. We have more obligations than freedom. (FG3 M3)

In sum, the points of focus group members confirmed that legal alienation, associated with a negative image of 'the law,' deeply pervades the Hungarian mass thinking. It had been detected by András Sajó in the 1980s, ie before the start of the political transitions, and this has certainly not changed in qualitative terms according to the latest studies (see Sajó 1988–1989; Fekete and Róbert 2018). So, on this point, the qualitative and quantitative findings converge convincingly.

ii. How Can Personal Experiences Change the General Attitude?

Alienation thus seems to be given as a general attitude towards the law. However, the members of FG2 articulated a much more sophisticated and refined image of law when giving an account of their individual cases.[12] This was especially striking compared to their primary associations. In essence, two of them reported that the trial in which they participated was a very positive experience, while the other two had a less enthusiastic view of their court experiences. One of them criticised the length of the procedure and the inappropriateness of data protection (this case was about the invalidity of a private contract selling a flat to some people who had forced the seller to sign the contract); the other complained that 'the Hungarian legal order is manifestly mother-and child-focused in divorce cases' and, therefore, it disregards the interests of the father. But, even this member accepted that 'the judge was empathic and kind' (FG2 M3).

---

[12] On the formative role of personal court experiences see Ewick and Silbey (1992).

Three out of four focus group members had a positive or a partly positive view of their court hearing. That is, individual involvement in a court process, partly independent of the outcome (as even that member who believed that the court had ignored the interests of the father agreed that the judge was fair) may have a positive impact on the personal assessment of the law. And this may even be capable of changing the general and manifestly alienated attitude. As for a divorce by mutual consent, a focus group member thus described the hearing:

> To be honest, we waited for the hearing, as this was the final point of our case. I expected a huge courtroom, as it is usually in the movies but, instead, they put us into a small office, so it was a disappointment. The building of the court was really beautiful; we admired it. We went there pleasantly; we are still in a good and friendly relationship, and the judge, she was also very kind and very nice, so it can be said that it was a pleasant experience. (FG2 M1)

Another member of this group gave an account of rather similar experiences with respect to a case against the Budapest Transport Corporation:

> By the way, I didn't feel uncomfortable because I had to go to the court; moreover, I found it an exciting thing, so I really enjoyed the hearing. Of course, when I entered the building I felt my mouth drying up, and I was also a bit concerned that I had to speak here and the judge would order me to speak. I was also worried that the law would be perverted here. But when I saw that I was the only one who came to the hearing, I relaxed immediately. (…) It was an absolutely good experience. (FG2 M4)

As such, it can be argued that personal participation in a court hearing – partly independently from the outcome of the case – may have a decisive impact on individual attitudes towards the law. And this impact, in which the personality of the judge has a crucial role through his or her behaviour in the courtroom, can even reverse the generally alienated attitude towards the law. Interestingly, the member who did not find the hearing a positive experience but only a neutral one mostly criticised the length of the procedure and the uncertainty arising from the complexity of the case.

In addition, in relation to this positive hearing experience, there is another factor worth noting. Each focus group member reported that, when preparing for the hearing, he or she had consciously studied those legal provisions – in the Civil Code or other acts – that they thought would be relevant in their cases. That is, they were somewhat prepared for their court hearings, even in legal terms. This preparation should definitely contribute to their positive experiences, as the legal discussion occurring in the courtroom – which can be frightening for all those who are unfamiliar with even the basic legal terms (*cf* Taslitz 1999) – was neither alienated, nor incomprehensible. A member explained well his motivations to read some basic legal texts.

> I also checked the legal provisions related my case. ('But, you had an advocate!' exclaimed the moderator). Even so, one would like to understand it. The advocate frequently thinks that something is natural, about which an ordinary person who has no legal degree has no idea whatsoever, not even whether it can be eaten or drank. (FG2 M2)

In sum, the stories in FG2 showed that the widely-shared alienated attitude towards the law can be tamed or overturned with the help of two points: positive personal court hearing experiences and some personal efforts to understand the basics of a given case. To put it differently, legal alienation may even be a consequence – obviously besides other relevant factors such as cultural or gender issues – of the fact that the most ordinary people not only know almost nothing about the law in practice but also lack personal experience.

iii. No Mercy for Attorneys

However, in contrast, the members of FG2 had a rather negative view of their attorneys. Interestingly, this was also independent of the outcome of the case. None of them thought of their attorneys as a professional and efficient helping hand, but they complained about various points. For example, in one of the divorce cases in which child custody was also at stake, the father claimed that his ex-wife's attorney had abused his professional position and helped to conclude a clearly disadvantageous agreement between him and his ex-wife on child custody. In addition, he was also dissatisfied with his own advocate:

> My attorney did not find my case that interesting. He was there; he helped, but he did not exert himself. I had to make decisions many times by myself; the advocate only gave advice. (FG2 M3)

Another member also heavily criticised her attorney, as 'he only liked writing letters and cost a lot of money' (FG2 M2). Therefore, she decided to look for another attorney and she luckily found one, who represented her interests much more effectively before the court. However, she added, this new attorney was also unable to manage the uncertainties of the case. All in all, these opinions show that a positive experience in legal proceedings does not necessarily mean a positive experience in every respect, as there may be some components in the procedure – in this focus group, the activities of the advocates – that still cause dissatisfaction for most people.

iv. The General Tone of Speaking about the Law if Someone has a Previous Experience

One final general point should be raised. Compared to the two other focus groups in which members had no personal legal experiences, it must be noted that the quality of the narratives in FG2 were rather different. Members had a more refined linguistic and narrative ability when they discussed various legal issues. Their vocabulary was much more complex and much richer in precise legal terms than that of those who lacked these kinds of experiences. In addition, they also set out longer and more coherent argumentations when a given conflict was discussed and they were also more capable of challenging the competing views of other members, partly in legal terms. Moreover, with special regard to rights consciousness, FG2 was the only focus group where the expression 'I have a right to something' was used to any extent during the discussions, and this group even mentioned some specific rights (for example the right to an advocate and fundamental rights). In sum, the discussions in FG2 suggest that any kind of personal experience of a court trial can significantly enhance the 'legal linguistic capacities' of those who participate and this certainly contributes to spreading the language of rights. Needless to say, this seems to be vital from the perspective of rights consciousness.

IV. CONCLUDING REMARKS

In conclusion, I would like to submit three points with some theoretical relevance, too (*cf* Webly 2010: 943–46). First, it should be noted that a conscious differentiation between specific legal terms – broadly speaking, from basic legal concepts such as rights or contract to activities in a court hearing – was extremely rare in the narratives and arguments of the focus group members. When the focus group members talked about a given dispute, they gave an account of all 'legal stuff' that seemed to be relevant or important in the discussion. That is, it seems that most of the ordinary references to legal issues regard the law as a homogenous phenomenon, referring to practically anything that can be somewhat linked to it. So, in ordinary narratives – as suggested by the focus group discussions – law loses its professional complexity and heterogeneity, and becomes similar to any other 'normal' sphere of life. From this perspective, rights consciousness, as a professional capacity to bring cases before the court if a specific right is violated, simply does not exist among the 'laity' (*cf* Engel and Munger 1996: 45). Ordinary people are not conscious of any rights in a dispute, but they are primarily conscious that something wrong happened to them. Rights can only be some components of the broader social and cultural context and they can mostly influence people's behaviour through their indirect effects (*cf* ibid: 44). However, it has to be stressed, this does not mean that people do not know about their rights or about specific rights; this means only that they take them into consideration as secondary or tertiary motivations when they act in a conflict or a dispute.

Second, the extent that moral considerations were lacking from these discussions was striking (*cf* Cotterrell 2015: 7–9). In these three focus groups, only one older member mentioned that the law should be linked to a sense of justice, and she also mentioned that she would be willing to start a case since she has 'a sense of justice' (FG3 M4) that inspires her to fight if she disagrees with something. No other member referred to any moral idea during the discussions. From a moral philosophy angle, it can be argued that these focus group discussions showed the lack of a moral imagination (see Himmelfarb 2012) that could back the law as a set of moral ideas and may be essential for the proper organisation of society. Whether a consequence of the anomie that has pervaded Hungarian society since the 1970s–1980s (Kiss 1999), or linked to the broad influence of legal alienation as an attitude set in Hungary (Sajó 1988–1989; Fekete and Róbert 2018), or whether rooted in other factors, this warning has to be taken seriously in future studies.

Third, it has to be confirmed that Reza Banakar was absolutely right when he pointed out that 'a chasm opens up between the rules and principles that mediate moral or legal rights and how they are unfolded in everyday life and legal practice' (Banakar 2010: 15). These Hungarian focus groups shed light on the fact that in ordinary conflicts – with no political and/or other 'bigger' relevance at stake – rights can only have a very secondary and limited relevance in dispute settlement, although they may fit a given case perfectly. Everyday practice seems to be almost completely disconnected from the legal background to the disputes and the parties are motived to find a solution by other conflict management techniques, such as personal discussion or expert consultation. The otherwise well-developed and logical system of rights has almost no practical relevance in everyday disputes. As such, this chasm between principles and practice seems to be very, very wide, almost unbridgeable – at least according to the experiences of some Hungarian focus group respondents.

REFERENCES

Banakar, R (2010) 'Studying the Rights Discourse: A Tentative Socio-Legal Framework' in B Lemann Kristiansen (ed), *The Nordic Sociology of Law* (Copenhagen, DJØF Forlag), available at https://ssrn.com/abstract=1690531.

Bartha, A (2013) 'Explaining Successes and Failure in Welfare Policy Changes in Europe: Governance, Trust and Legitimacy' 6 *International Journal of Arts and Science* 287.

Boda, Zs and Medve-Bálint, G (2015) 'Procedural Fairness and the Legitimacy of Law in Hungary: an Empirical Analysis' 57 *Sociologija* 662.

Cotterrell, R (2015) 'Leon Petrazycki and Contemporary Socio-Legal Studies' 11 *International Journal of Law in Context* 1.

Engel, DM and Munger, FW (1996) 'Rights, Rememberance, and the Reconiliation of Difference' 30 *Law & Society Review* 7.

Ewick, P and Silbey, SS (1992) 'Conformity, Contestation, and Resistance: An Account of Legal Consciousness' 26 *New England Law Review* 731.

Fekete, B, Bartha, A, Gajduschek, Gy and Gulya, F (2021) 'Rights Consciousness in Hungary and Some Comparative Remarks. Could an Increasing Level of Rights Consciousness Challenge the Autocratic Tradition?' 47(2) *Review of Central and East European Law* 220.

Fekete, B and Róbert, P (2018) 'Understanding Hungarian Attitudes toward Law in an International Context' (9 February 2018), available at https://ssrn.com/abstract=3120933.

Fekete, B and H. Szilágyi, I (2017) 'Knowledge and Opinion about Law (KOL) Research in Socialist Hungary' 58 *Hungarian Journal of Legal Studies* 326.

Fleck, Z, Kiss, V, Tóth F, Neumann L, Kenéz A and Bajnok, D (2017) *A jogtudat narratív értelmezése [A Narrative Interpretation of Legal Consciousness]* (Budapest, ELTE Eötvös).

Gibson, JL and Caldeira, GA (1996) 'The Legal Cultures of Europe' 30 *Law & Society Review* 55.

Gunby, C, Carline, A and Beynon, C (2013) 'Regretting it After? Focus Group Perspectives on Alcohol Consumption, Nonconsensual Sex and False Allegations of Rape' 22 *Social & Legal Studies* 87.

H. Szilágyi, I (ed) (2018) *Jogtudat-kutatások Magyarországon 1967–2017 [Legal Consciousness Studies in Hungary 1967–2017]* (Budapest, Pázmány Press).

Hertogh, M (2018) *Nobody's Law. Legal Consciousness and Legal Alienation in Everyday Life* (London, Palgrave).

Himmelfarb, G (2012) 'Lionel Trilling: The Moral Imagination' in G Himmelfarb, *The Moral Imagination* (Lanham, MD, Rowman and Littlefield) 269.

Kiss, E (1999) 'Where the Hungarian Society is Heading for, or is it a Jungle without Laws?' in V Bialas, HJ Haessler and E Woit (eds), *Die Kultur des Friedens. Weltordnungsstrukturen und Friedensgestaltung* (Würzburg, Königshausen und Neumann).

Kulcsár, K (1967) *A jogismeret vizsgálata [Study of the Peoples' Knowledge about Law]* (Budapest, MTA-JTI).

Podgórecki, A, Van Houtte, J and Kutchinsky, B (1973) *Knowledge and Opinion About Law* (London, Martin Robertson).

Róbert, P and Fekete, B (2017) 'Ki ellen nyerne meg Ön egy pert? Attitűdök jogról, bizalomról rétegződési szempontból' [Winning a Case? Attitudes on Law and Trust from the Aspect of Social Stratification] 13 *Iustum Aequum Salutare* 81.

Sajó, A (1981) 'A jogi nézetek rendszere a gazdasági vezetők jogtudatában' [*Legal Ideas in the Mind of Socialist CEOs*] 24 *Állam- és Jogtudomány* 608.

—— (1988–1989) *A jogosultság-tudat vizsgálata* [*A Study of Rights Consciousness*] (Budapest, ELTE Szociológiai Intézet).

Ságvári, B (2020) 'A fókuszcsoport' ['The Focus Group'] in A Jakab and M Sebők (eds), *Empirikus jogi kutatások* [*Empirical Legal Studies*] (Budapest, Osiris).

Taslitz, A (1999) *Rape and the Culture of Courtroom* (New York, New York University Press).

Webly, L (2010) 'Qualitative Approaches to Empirical Legal Research' in P Cane and HM Kritzer (eds), *The Oxford Handbook of Empirical Legal Research* (Oxford, Oxford University Press).

14

In Conversation with Reza: Theory and Method in Socio-Legal Research

LINDA MULCAHY

I. INTRODUCTION

REZA BANAKAR WAS a much-respected scholar who made a significant contribution to the development of the sub-discipline through his work on the sociology of law and socio-legal methodologies. We have become accustomed to a certain intellectual tension between sociologists of law and socio-legal scholars in the UK, but Reza was committed to both strands of what Campbell and Wiles (1976) once referred to as mutually hostile groups. Reza was both a committed sociologist of law and someone with in-depth interest in empirical research. In this chapter, I reflect on his contributions to debates about this tension between the empirical and the theoretical in the UK. I draw specific attention to the ways in which two particular projects in which he was closely involved mediated the somewhat uncompromising divide between sociologists of law and empiricists through his writings on the theory of socio-legal methods. More particularly, I consider the contributions made to this debate by *An Introduction to Law and Social Theory* (Banakar and Travers 2002) and *Theory and Method in Socio-Legal Research* (Banakar and Travers 2005a).

These two publications were, and continue to be, an important contribution to a field in which debate about methodology – understood here as the theory of method – is often marginalised and sparse. While many in the UK would lay responsibility for this problem at the doorstep of law schools (see for example Bradney 1998; and Genn et al 2006), for Reza Banakar and Max Travers, the causes lay with both law schools *and* sociology departments. In relation to law schools, Reza and Max drew attention to the paucity of methodological training offered and an unwillingness to engage in any significant way with sociological theory. In *Theory and Method*, they outlined what has since become a familiar diagnosis of the problems with the law school curriculum and attitudes of law teachers. In doing so, they pre-empted the arguments that would be made in the Nuffield Foundation's influential report on *Law in the Real World*, published just a year later (Genn et al 2006).

The arguments made about law schools by Reza and Max in their two edited collections had many supporters. Tony Bradney (1996) has argued that the traditional tendency of UK law schools to eschew inter-disciplinary collaborations has been exacerbated by a tradition of weak links to other disciplines which some have traced back to their origins as 'trade schools' with close links to the profession. It has been argued that the dominance and aridity of traditional doctrinal or rule-based approaches in the law school curriculum has a disabling effect on its students (Hepple 1996). Others have drawn attention to the intellectual and physical isolationalism of law schools in the UK academy, the mystique surrounding legal language and discourse or the complicity of legal academics in sustaining myths about the complexity of law (Bradney 1998; Genn et al 2006). For Reza and Max the result has been an inward-looking approach to the study of law and legal phenomena, in which ideas have been adopted from the sociology of law without being entirely understood. Readers of *An Introduction to Law and Social Theory* and *Theory and Method* are left in no doubt about the dangers of lawyers attempting to use sociological method without sufficient training in methodology and sociological theory.

A less familiar aspect of their criticism is the responsibility that Reza and Max lay at the door of sociology departments for the lack of more sophisticated partnerships between lawyers and social scientists (Travers and Banaker 2005c). They argue that while sociology departments do at least expose their students to the concept of law and legal phenomena through the seminal work of scholars such as Weber, Marx, Ehrlich and Petrazycki, the interests of sociologists in law and legal phenomena amongst sociologists has tended to founder in more recent decades. In doing so, they draw attention to the fact that there are very few courses on law in sociology departments despite its importance to an appreciation of how the state wields power. More specifically, they argue that sociological work has failed to address the content of law as a lawyer would understand it, and that sociologists rarely express an interest in the development of legal doctrine with the same intensity as doctrinal scholars. The result is that sociologists have tended to look at the impact of law on society rather than the essence of, and internal understandings of, law itself. Reza's own chapter on ombudsmen in *Theory and Method*, in which he understands legal texts as a form of sociological data, provides an example of the many ways in which legal texts might be interpreted sociologically. Pointing to the way in which this avoidance of law is reflected in methodology textbooks written by social scientists, Reza and Max (2005b) argued:

> ... they do not tell us the first thing about what it means to interview judges or lawyers in different jurisdictions, observe mediation, dispute resolution or other forms of negotiation in the context of different legal cultures or analyse legal documents in a sociological way. (2005b: x)

The ongoing need for debate about the nature of the relationship between law and sociology is reflected in the continuing popularity of the two volumes produced by Reza and Max as well as the absence of significant competition (but see Halliday and Schmidt 2009). As I have re-read these collections in anticipation of writing this chapter, I have been struck by two things: first, the number of challenges that Reza and Max set socio-legal scholars in the UK which have still to be met; and second, the considerable loss to our community in not being able to continue to debate the issues with Reza himself. What follows is a review of some of the most important arguments made in the two volumes, followed by an attempt to prompt debate about the questions this body of work leaves unanswered and the ongoing points of contention.

II. SETTING OUT THE ARGUMENT

Law and Social Theory (2002) and *Theory and Method* (2005) are the fruits of an engagement between 27 scholars drawing on a rich diet of theoretical and methodological debates about Marxism, critical legal studies, race, systems theory, pluralism and globalisation, symbolic interactionism, ethnomethodology, discourse analysis, comparative methods, research ethics, gender, and feminist approaches to fieldwork. These are topics that one might expect to find in any sociology course, but are less commonly discussed in books on legal or socio-legal methods. The table of contents indicates the ambitions of both books, which seek to draw out debates about ontology, epistemology, sociological theory, methodology and method. The best essays in both collections do not reduce the notion of methodology to pragmatic concerns about the 'how' of fieldwork, but elevate it instead to its proper place as the theory or 'why' of fieldwork.

Both books are much more than just collections of discrete essays. Each bears the marks of an enduring debate between a group of scholars and strong editorial engagement. The books emerged as a result of workshops organised by Reza and Max at Wolfson College Oxford in 1999 and 2000, and the Institute for the Sociology of Law in Onati in 2003. There is an overlap in the authors who contribute to the two collections, with six scholars contributing to both.[1] In addition to substantive first chapters in both books, the editors' comments form a series of introductions to each section, allowing them to weave their own reflections and arguments throughout the manuscripts.

Both books contain contributions from very different sorts of scholars, including sociologists of law, empiricists, critical legal scholars and those whose work is policy orientated. The editors do not shy away from controversy in their comments on each contribution, claiming that socio-legal studies in the UK is impoverished by the lack of attention to theory or that scholars in the field are intellectually unambitious and narrow in their focus. Conscious attempts are also made to set debates up within the pages of the collections. Most notably for present purposes, the collections reveal familiar fault lines between sociologists of law based in sociology departments and socio-legal scholars based in law departments. As Reza and Max were to lament in the introduction to *Law and Social Theory*:

> ... despite some attempts to bring the two disciplines closer together, they remain frustratingly apart. Jurists complain that sociologists do not understand or respect the content of

---

[1] In addition to Reza and Max, Klaus A Ziegert, Anne Griffiths, John Flood and David Nelken all contributed to both collections.

law, or seek to understand law as a profession. Sociologists complain that 'law in context' courses, and the research pursued by the Law and Society movement are not sufficiently sociological'. (Banakar and Travers 2002: 1)

In their view, sociological studies of law are inevitably tasked with bringing together two groups of scholars that have fundamentally different approaches. On the one hand it is argued that law focuses on particular rules or cases and preserves particular values and ambitions about how society 'ought' to be, while sociology is more concerned with the generalisable 'is' of society. In their view, this creates a constant tension between these two images of society and ways of seeing it. Seen at their best, these two tribes engage in debate about intermingling themes. At their worse, tribalism manifests itself in hostility and intellectual snobbery which reifies armchair theory and treats socio-legal studies as synonymous with policy orientated work (see further Campbell and Wiles, 1976; Hutter and Lloyd-Bostock 1997; Banakar and Travers 2005c). For Reza and Max this approach promotes the exposition of elaborate theories which are presented as superior to ordinary, common-sense knowledge collected by empiricists in the field (Banakar 2002; Banakar and Travers 2005d).

III. THE THEORY DATA INTERFACE

The two books conceived of a middle ground between these two positions which relies on theory being placed at the core of debate. Unusually, both books place issues around the theory of method at the heart of their discussion. Building on their criticisms of the narrow nature of the law school curriculum, Reza and Max argue that even when taught in the classroom, methods are frequently substituted for discussion of methodologies. In this way, choices in research are presented as a neutral tool kit for social scientists in which all methods have equal status and legitimacy – what Ziegert (2005) has called methods pluralism or even methods indifference. This hiding of the theoretical, and even ideological, underpinnings of methods was something that Reza and Max were keen to open up to critique.

To my mind, one of the most interesting contributions to emerge from the two collections relates to the relationship between knowledge acquired through thinking about the world and knowledge acquired through being in the world. Reducing these ways of understanding the world into 'theory' and 'practice', though frequently done, is neither helpful nor accurate. The armchair theorist inevitably bases descriptions of the world and the invisible forces that motivate behaviour on their own experiences and observations of practice. At the same time the empiricist is bound to understand the behaviour they observe by reference to purely abstract intellectual debate they have engaged with. This action-structure debate was familiar in the nineteenth century in the context of discussions about how sociology should develop as a science. What these collections make clear is that it remains relevant in contemporary discussion, not least because of the rise of postmodernism and interpretative approaches to data collection and analysis. While some have expressed an appetite for moving beyond the paradigm wars of the past, it becomes apparent from *Theory and Method* that this debate is still very much alive when sociologists of law and socio-legal empiricists come together. This is evident, for instance, in discussions of system theory and the dehumanised theory of law and society it proposes (see further Banakar and Travers 2005d). These debates raise critical questions about the extent to which empiricists are capable of developing theories from their data or are mere handmaidens of theorists, sent out to test whether high theory works in the field.

The significance of these issues is made obvious in the positions taken by John Flood and Klaus Ziegert in *Theory and Method*, which expose the opposing assumptions underpinning empirical research. Indeed, these two contributions raise a fundamental question for empiricists: do you need a theory to frame your research before you start or does theory emerge from the data that emerges during fieldwork? Reflecting on the workshop that led to the collection, John Flood recalls the brave decision on the part of the editors to include both authors in the same session:

> I was up in the first session talking about socio-legal ethnography with Klaus Ziegert who was discussing systems theory and qualitative research. We could not have been more diametrically opposed. I came at the topic through the lens of Everett Hughes and Howard Becker, a kind of loose and gangly ethnographic approach – hanging around and seeing what happens. Ziegert talked about the rigour of Luhmannian theory and all that fieldwork would derive from that. Define the systems first then some fieldwork may assist. The arguments became quite heated and fierce. There was no middle or meeting point between us.[2]

In a reminder of the gentle man we are celebrating in this collection, John Flood goes on to make clear that their host went on to take the heat out of the argument that ensued and reconciled both sides. But the issues this particular debate raised remain fundamental to understanding the ongoing chasm between sociologists of law and socio-legal empiricists that Campbell and Wiles (1976) discussed almost 50 years ago.

A close reading of the collections reveals that Reza and Max frequently waver in their assessment of whether theory can emerge solely from data. While both their collections are rich in their promotion of diverse viewpoints, Reza and Max's overall preference for theory-led research is most obvious in *Law and Social Theory*, in which they aim to review a series of theoretical traditions and perspectives that can be used in studying a substantive topic (but see Travers 2002). In the editorial passages that map out the diverse standpoints represented, Reza and Max suggest that socio-legal methods can *never* be atheoretical and always reflect a commitment to a particular theoretical perspective or way of understanding the world, even if this is not always explicit (see for example 2005b). This argument is also apparent in their inclusion of an essay on feminist methodology in *Theory and Method* (Bano 2005) which contends that feminist approaches to research always start from a position which understands women as oppressed (see also Fletcher 2002). In referring to the engaged moral tone of the feminist methodologist, the editors draw attention to what they see as an important link between theory, methodology and ideology. Though the focus on methodology is less immediately obvious in *Law and Social Theory*, the themes developed make clear the relevance of positionality in the field and includes essays on

---

[2] See https://johnflood.blogspot.com/2020/08/requiem-for-reza.html.

Marxist (Fine 2002) feminist, gendered (Fletcher 2002; Pierce 2002; Beger 2002), 'post-modern' (McVeigh 2002) critical race (Pierce 2002) and queer theory (Beger 2002).

IV. CONCLUDING THOUGHTS: THE DEBATE CONTINUES

The debates brought to the fore in *Theory and Method* and *Law and Social Theory* are far from being resolved and in this final substantive section of the essay I consider a variety of ways in which they might be re-invigorated. In doing so, I imagine a second edition of both collections in which additional voices are added to the debate and the arguments refined. It is noticeable, for instance, that despite the prevalence of public discourse that frequently reifies science and statistics there is a complete absence in either of the volumes of a discussion of quantitative methods. While it is argued that lawyers should take sociological debate more seriously, and sociologists are encouraged to '… think critically about the relationship between quantitative and qualitative methods, and … epistemological issues in analysing data' (Banakar and Travers 2002: 350) there is no discussion of particular quantitative methods. This seems a shame given the influence of natural science models in determining what constitutes credible research. A consideration of quantitative methodology would also have proven valuable in discussions about the epistemological foundations of methods.

A future collection could usefully stimulate further debate about the issues by the inclusion of a doctrinal lawyer – all too often held up as a 'straw man' in discussions. There are several contributions to the existing volumes by socio-legal scholars employing sociological lenses on their work, or from sociologists interested in law. But the voices of 'traditional' legal theorists interested in the connection of law with society or social mores are marginalised in these collections, possibly reflecting the inappropriate distain that socio-legal scholars often feel for the doctrinal. This reflects a general lack of interest in the question of what constitutes the legal in socio-legal studies, an issue that Cowan and Wincott (2005) argue has been lost in the eternal search for the social in socio-legal studies. Scholars such as Riles (2005) have also encouraged socio-legal scholars to take more seriously the work that legal technicalities and ways of thinking do (but see for instance, Grabham 2016; 2022). The more fundamental issue of what is legal also raises questions about the extent to which there is any such a thing as a legal methodology or methods which can withstand the rigorous standards set by other social science disciplines. Cowan and Wincott (2005) argue that in common with other disciplines such as political science, law is a borrowing discipline which utilises methods developed in other fields for its own uses. These are arguments that the legal theorist might be well placed to counter or address.

One question which is not considered in depth in either of Reza and Max's collections is whether law is actually a discipline. They propose a reimagining of the field in which a variety of discipline-based studies of law meet in an effort to transcend some of the theoretical and methodological limitations of a single discipline and create a base from which new insights can be offered. This offers a solution to the problem of social science methodologies disciplining disciplines by imposing a methodological canon on them – an issue which Reza and Max express concerns about. However, in positioning the study of legal phenomena as a 'place' where these problems can be attended to, law is reduced to a site rather than a discipline with its own theories and methodologies. This conundrum reflects a tension which is discernible throughout these two collections as to whether law is understood as a discipline, a profession or a body of rules. While jurisprudes and legal theorists may claim disciplinary status for their work, and the sources that lawyers rely on may make their work distinct, it remains the case that law's claim to disciplinary status remains weak when one seeks to find a distinctive methodological perspective underpinning it (Bradney 1998). Reza's work reminds us that, for Marx, law was seen as part of the superstructure of society that reflected the interests of the bourgeosie rather than a discipline in its own right (Banakar 2002).

Another contender for inclusion in a future edition would be a grounded theorist. Flood's essay in *Theory and Method* presents an exemplary case for greater attention being paid to the context and nuance of ethnographic fieldwork. In doing so he draws on a variety of arguments that we now associate with the Chicago school of sociology (see further Travers 2002). This is complemented by Dingwall's (2002) account of ethnomethodology, which draws on the same intellectual tradition. It can be argued, however, that it is grounded theory as first developed by Glaser and Strauss (1967) which provided the most radical and detailed critique of the relationship between data and theory. Whilst most sociologists would argue that it is impossible to conduct empirical work in a theoretical vacuum (Hutter and Lloyd-Bostock 1997), grounded theorists have argued that it is possible to construct hypotheses and theories as they emerge in the collection and analysis of data. Its focus on inductive reasoning and criticisms of structural approaches stand in sharp contrast to the hypothetico-deductive model which is commonly used in scientific research. At its most radical in *The Discovery of Grounded Theory*, Glaser and Strauss argued that researchers should come to the field without any preconceived ideas about relevant concepts and hypotheses. The original theories have since morphed and evolved (see for instance Charmaz 2014; Corbin 2016). Rather than reifying the theorist, which many sociologists of law are wont to do, the bottom up approaches to theory construction position the research subject as expert and the researcher as interpreter.

Subsequent issues of *Theory and Method* might also include a much more robust discussion of what we now mean by socio-legal studies. This is important in an era in which the field appears to be becoming increasingly fragmented, at least in the United States. Many of us have preferred to avoid debate about 'what is socio-legal studies?' which appears to have no clear cut answer or point (see for instance Creutzfeldt et al 2019). However, a clear definition becomes increasingly important as splinter groups emerge. By way of example it is noticeable that despite its efforts to be seen as a development that is respectful of both qualitative and quantitative methods (see for example Kritzer 2021), the recent emergence of the Empirical Legal Studies movement represents a shift towards deductive methods and statistics in the law and society movement.[3] It is also evidenced by the reaction to this new sub-movement by scholars

---

[3] See, for instance, the recently formed Society of Empirical Legal Studies and the *Journal of Empirical Legal Studies* which are predominantly concerned with statistics and statistical method.

calling themselves the New Legal Realists who have been keen to reiterate the significance of qualitative approaches to the study of law. Drawing on the important work undertaken by Reza and Max, these developments force us to bring methodology to the fore as a device that allows sub-disciplines to distinguish themselves from other sub-disciplines, determine the standards which can be used to monitor and sustain the quality of research within the realms of a group, discipline new entrants to a field, and internalise values (Banakar and Travers 2005c).

My second edition of these important collections would also move beyond sociology to consider the interface between law and other disciplines in more depth. Reza and Max (2005c) saw socio-legal studies as an eclectic and tolerant field which provides fertile ground for innovation but the focus of the two books discussed here is predominantly on the relationship between law and sociology. This stands in opposition to other accounts of the field that have viewed the 'socio' of socio-legal studies as reflecting an interest in the social rather than just sociology (see for example Wheeler and Thomas; Harris 1983). This narrow reading of the field by Reza and Max inhibits discussions about the contribution that other disciplines might be able to make to the action-structure debate or the extent to which socio-legal scholars have been influenced by other distinctive disciplinary traditions. It remains the case for instance, that the Centre for Socio-Legal Studies in Oxford, where Reza worked for many years, was set up and continued to welcome economists, social psychologists, anthropologists, historians and social policy specialists alongside lawyers and sociologists in its 50-year history.[4] Moreover, the earliest issues of the *Law and Society Review* bear the clear marks of a new field that has been heavily influenced by anthropology and political science. We might also add geography and visual culture to the mix in the aftermath of spatial and visual turns in socio-legal studies. It is hoped that work of this kind will continue to contribute to the rich vein of scholarship left behind by Reza Banaker.

REFERENCES

Banakar, R (2002) 'Sociological Jurisprudence' in R Banakar and M Travers (eds), *An Introduction to Law and Social Theory* (Oxford, Hart Publishing).
Banakar, R and Travers, M (eds) (2002) *An Introduction to Law and Social Theory* (Oxford, Hart Publishing).
—— (2005a) *Theory and Method in Socio-Legal Research* (Oxford, Hart Publishing).
—— (2005b) 'Introduction' in R Banakar and M Travers (eds), *Theory and Method in Socio-Legal Research* (Oxford, Hart Publishing).
—— (2005c) 'Law, Sociology and Method' in R Banakar and M Travers (eds), *Theory and Method in Socio-Legal Research* (Oxford, Hart Publishing).
—— (2005d) 'Method Versus Methodology' in R Banakar an M Travers (eds), *Theory and Method in Socio-Legal Research* (Oxford, Hart Publishing).
Bano, S (2005) 'Standpoint, Difference and Feminist Research' in R Banaker and M Travers (eds), *Theory and Method in Socio-Legal Research* (Oxford, Hart Publishing).

---

[4] On this point see the range of 'Law and ....' essays included in Creutzfeldt et al 2019.

Beger, N (2002) 'Putting Gender and Sexuality on the Agenda' in R Banakar and M Travers (eds), *An Introduction to Law and Social Theory* (Oxford, Hart Publishing).

Bradney, A (1998) 'Law as a Parasitic Discipline' 25(1) *Journal of Law and Society* 71.

Campbell, CM and Wiles, P (1976) 'The Study of Law in Society in Britain' 10(4) *Law & Society Review* 547.

Charmaz, K (2014) *Constructing Grounded Theory* (London, Sage).

Corbin, J (2016) 'Taking an Analytic Journey' in JM Morse, PN Stern, J Corbin, BJ Bowers, K Charmaz and AE Clarke (eds), *Developing Grounded Theory* (London, Routledge).

Cowan, D and Wincott, D (2005) 'Exploring the Legal' in D Cowan and D Wincott (eds), *Exploring the 'Legal' in Socio-Legal Studies* (London, Palgrave Macmillan).

Creutzfeldt, N, Mason, M and McConnachie, K (eds) (2019) *Routledge Handbook of Socio-Legal Theory and Methods* (London, Routledge).

Dingwall, R (2002) 'Ethnomethodology and Law' in R Banakar and M Travers (eds), *An Introduction to Law and Social Theory* (Oxford, Hart Publishing).

Fine, R (2002) 'Marxism and the Social Theory of Law' in R Banakar and M Travers (eds), *An Introduction to Law and Social Theory* (Oxford, Hart Publishing).

Fletcher, F (2002) 'Feminist Legal Theory' in R Banakar and M Travers (eds), *An Introduction to Law and Social Theory* (Oxford, Hart Publishing).

Flood, J (2002) 'Socio-Legal Ethnography' in R Banakar and M Travers (eds), *Theory and Method in Socio-Legal Research* (Oxford, Hart Publishing).

Genn, HG, Wheeler, S and Partington, M (2006) *Law in the Real World: Improving our Understanding of How Law Works: Final Report and Recommendations* (London, Nuffield Foundation).

Glaser, B and Strauss, A (1967) *The Discovery of Grounded Theory: Strategies for Qualitative Research* (Chicago, Aldine).

Grabham, E (2016) 'Time and Technique: The Legal Lives of the 26-Week Qualifying Period' 45(3–4) *Economy and Society* 379.

—— (2022) 'The Crafty Power of Text: Methods for a Sociology of Legislative Drafting' 49 *Journal of Law and Society* S1.

Halliday, S and Schmidt, P (2009) *Conducting Law and Society Research: Reflections on Methods and Practices* (Cambridge, Cambridge University Press).

Harris, D (1983) 'The Development of Socio-Legal Studies in the United Kingdom' 3(3) *Legal Studies* 315.

Hepple, B (1996) 'The Renewal of the Liberal Law Degree' 55(3) *The Cambridge Law Journal* 470.

Hutter, B and Lloyd-Bostock, S (1997) 'Law's Relationship with Social Science: The Interdependence of Theory, Empirical Work and Social Relevance in Socio-Legal Studies' in K Hawkins (ed), *The Human Face of Law: Essays in Honour of Donald Harris* (Oxford, Clarendon Press).

Kritzer, HM (2021) *Advanced Introduction to Empirical Legal Research* (London, Edward Elgar).

McVeigh, S (2002) 'Law and Postmodernism' in R Banakar and M Travers (eds), *An Introduction to Law and Social Theory* (Oxford, Hart Publishing).

Pierce, J (2002) 'A Raced and Gendered Organisational Logic in Law Firms' in R Banakar and M Travers (eds), *An Introduction to Law and Social Theory* (Oxford, Hart Publishing).

Riles, A (2005) 'A New Agenda for the Cultural Study of Law: Taking on the Technicalities' 53 *Buffalo Law Review* 973.

Travers, M (2002) 'Symbolic Interactionism and Law' in R Banakar and M Travers (eds), *An Introduction to Law and Social Theory* (Oxford, Hart Publishing).

Wheeler, S and Thomas, PA (2000) 'Socio-legal Studies' in D Hayton (ed), *Law(s) Futures* (Oxford, Hart Publishing) 267.

Ziegert, K (2002) 'The Thick Description of Law: An Introduction to Niklas Luhmann's Theory' in R Banakar and M Travers (eds), *An Introduction to Law and Social Theory* (Oxford, Hart Publishing).

—— (2005) 'Systems Theory and Qualitative Socio-legal Research' in R Banakar and M Travers (eds), *Theory and Method in Socio-Legal Research* (Oxford, Hart Publishing) 49.

15

'The Light in the Tunnel Can Be a Train': About Kafkaesque Double Thoughts

KARL DAHLSTRAND AND MIKAEL FURUGÄRDE

I. INTRODUCTION

THIS CHAPTER WILL highlight Banakar's contribution to the Law and Literature Movement as a socio-legal scholar and reader of Franz Kafka, with special focus on his article 'In Search of Heimat: A Note on Franz Kafka's Concept of Law' (2010a) with some references to analytical jurisprudence and philosophy. In the article, Banakar discusses both the novel *The Trial* by Kafka (1999 [1925]) and the parable 'Before the Law', contained in the same novel, in the context of Kafka's legal work as an insurance lawyer. In this essay we also attempt to make a connection between the field of Law as Literature and the Law and Literature Movement. We do so in the short story 'The Light' by using narratives and literary techniques to give a testimony about a fictional character, Lorentz, who finds himself standing before the law. We will at the same time pay attention to the fact that it is now 75 years since the Nuremberg trials took place, 1945–1946. They have been described as the greatest trials in history and have influenced the development of international criminal law as well as the Universal Declaration of Human Rights (1948) and modern anti-discrimination laws, but also the Law as Literature Movement. We want to highlight Banakar's contribution to the Law and Literature Movement as a source for socio-legal studies, and we will also try to present how law and literature in practice can be a method to write about law in literature. Law and literature may be thought to be connected by some essential common features. Our understanding, though, is that law and literature are not only intertwined with language, dramaturgy, storytelling and interpretation but also fantasy and perplexity – or double thoughts – by a series of overlapping similarities, reminiscent of Wittgenstein's 'family resemblance'.

Beyond the dichotomy between internal (juristic) and external (sociological) views of law, in line with a 'legal pluralism theory in sociology of law' (Clark 2007), socio-legal studies can include the relationship between law and culture as well as legal cultures, considering different socio-cultural aspects of social life. Banakar was throughout his career very engaged in grasping the social and cultural forms of different societies dominated by information (technology), legal uncertainty

and legal pluralism (including non-western legal systems and cultures) to understand how legal, social and cultural factors integrate. Law, culture and legal culture
were, for example, of interest to Banakar when he wrote his book about Iranians'
law, culture and driving habits (Banakar 2016a) and 'conflict management in a
multi-cultural society' (Banakar 1994). According to Banakar, law – in contrast
to Western mainstream legal scholarship and various schools of legal positivism –
'consist[s] of countless fragments which are not necessarily related in a formal
rational manner' (Banakar 2015: 123). The limits of rationality, or even 'irrational
elements of modern law, legal thought and legal cultures' (ibid), were a critical
starting point for Banakar. In the intellectual journey of discovering socio-legal
theory and research, a fiction writer such as Franz Kafka (1883–1924) became a
natural travel companion. Hesse's novel *Steppenwolf* also raised Banakar's interest. Harry Haller, a character in the story, experiences himself as consisting of two
parts: part man (a 'normal' middle class man) and part animal (driven by irrational
instincts and displaying wild behaviours). Banakar discusses Hesse's novel in relation to the politics of legal cultures in late modernity by asking two concluding
questions (Banakar 2015: 142):

> Firstly, is it possible that the legal cultural identity of Muslim immigrant communities is
> part of the 'wolf of the Steppes' of Western legal cultures – a wolf which, as mentioned
> above, consists not of one single but of numerous identities? Secondly, is it realistic to
> expect Western legal cultures of the type we find in Britain or Sweden to engage with the
> 'wolf' constructively, whilst they have not as yet discovered and acknowledged their own
> plurality of form?

Banakar, born in 1959 in Iran, moved to England in the 1970s and studied Sociology
of Law at Lund University from the mid-1980s; from the beginning he was constantly
interested in different aspects of multi-cultural society and ethno-cultural conflicts
(Banakar 1994). His background and his lived experience also gave him a critical,
reflective and dialectical intellect with 'double thoughts'. This dual and analytical
mind partly reflects Banakar's own life as an immigrant in Europe and his professional
role within a complex multidisciplinary field like sociology of law. At Banakar's
office you could find not just an extensive library about socio-legal literature but
also books about poets, Islamic culture, gypsy law, religion and biographies about,
for instance, Ingmar Bergman and Kafka. It can be added that Banakar also had an
interest in and knowledge of contemporary art; he used paintings to illustrate socio-
cultural mechanisms and normative imperatives of modernity (Banakar 2016b).

II. LAW AND LITERATURE. A SOCIO-LEGAL PERSPECTIVE

Literature can be seen as a social collective memory of human life. Different social
representations of history transferred to new generations of readers, sometimes
described as a 'literary canon', become a social factor that shapes our notions of right
and wrong or justice. Pillars of the modern Western literary canon are, for example,
novels like *Crime and Punishment* (1866) by Dostoevsky, *The Trial* (1999 [1925]) by

Kafka; and the authorship of Thomas Mann can also be mentioned. Riemen writes, influenced by Mann:

> If humanity, truth, and eternity are big words – bigger, in any event, than what we are accustomed to these days – then let us justify artistic existence as lifelong faithfulness to language. … Language is the essence of being human. We can think, thanks to language, for thought exists only by the grace of words. Our experience and emotions are moulded by language. It is language that allows us to name and know the world. We ourselves are known by language, through prayer, confession, poetry. Language gives us a world that reaches beyond the reality of the moment, to a past (there was …) and the future (there shall be …). It is through language that eternity has a space and that the dead continue to speak. (Riemen 2008: 20)

The humanistic study of law includes imagining the law or ideas of justice through the novel, art or film, and cultural processes in law include interpretation, language, translation and narrative and rhetorical aspects. The constitution of history and memory includes the right to testimony and witnessing. The legal history of humanity can therefore be seen as related to resistance, justice and representation. Legal discourse, as studies in linguistics, rhetoric and legal analysis, is also legal theory, legal practice and legal methods within jurisprudence, even if there is a fine line to socio-legal studies because law and social discourse often overlap when it comes to normativity, justice and rights in context. Ordinary language philosophy developed at Oxford in the 1950s has sharpened our interest in how the legal discipline and legal meaning depend on their concepts of language and how that language is used by both lawyers and others. This is reflected in the late Wittgenstein's use of the concepts language-games and family resemblance (Wittgenstein 1958; Goodrich 1987: 51) as well as Hart's rule of recognition, '… as a complex, but normally concordant, practice of the courts, officials, and private persons in identifying the law by reference to certain criteria. Its existence is a matter of fact' (Hart 1961: 107). Even the anthropologist Malinowski and his early socio-linguistic work can be mentioned when viewing legal text as linguistic practice and law as social discourse or communication. It is important to note that this way of viewing law is not a theoretical nor a critical one but rather a realistic one, even if it invites a dialectic and interdisciplinary perspective. Goodrich (1987: 210 ff) writes:

> Substantive jurisprudence is a matter of legal technique, a question of reading and teaching the law in terms of vague and dubious notions of interpretation and analogy, authority and present. […] There is no guarantee, in other words, that the internal criteria of legality in any sense reflect the actual practices (formal and informal) of the legal institution and legal actors. Nor is there any overriding reason to suppose that the textual discipline of the law is best read in its own terms.

Law and literature, as an interdisciplinary field, often deals with similar perspectives and themes to those in sociology of law and socio-legal studies, for example: history, culture, politics, justice, modernity or traditions, legal ideas and norms. But critical theory, language and cultural studies also share the idea of deconstruction with sociology of law and socio-legal studies; concepts do not have a settled meaning but are affected by social context, culture, politics etc. Or, as summarised by Trevino

(2008: 117), 'Another recent and critical approach in the study of law and society is deconstruction. ... The (legal) text/story is taken apart, deconstructed, and its structure and logic are questioned'. Law and literature can thus be related to postmodernist and critical legal scholarship. Literature as an emotional, creative or non-rational narrative method to understand and reason about values, norms, violence are represented through authors like Ricoeur, Derrida and Lacan, to name just a few (Cornell et al 1992; Sarat et al 2010). Cotterrell writes (2006: 2 ff):

> ... law and social theory need to recognize and address the non-rational or perhaps differently rational aspects of social life. ... Law and social theory both have to find ways to understand the ambiguous, complex meanings of social action, and to recognize that social relations can be of radically different types.

Banakar was influenced by a late modern view of the law, seeing it as something more than state law, and state law having more aspects and dimensions than being a formal legal system. When Banakar writes about legal culture he explains that '"Law" is understood broadly to encompass not only legislation and the rules of the legal system but also certain categories of social norms, which are used to regulate behaviour and social activities' (Banakar 2016a: 10). Banakar describes, in the same book,

> culture as a 'form of life', or a way of going about the world – seeing, making sense of and experiencing social life. We shall initially frame our definition in line with Geertz's understanding of culture as 'socially constructed and historically transmitted patterns of meaning', which are embodied in symbols, values, attitudes, perceptions, worldviews, conventions and customary practices (Geertz 1973: 89). (ibid)

Law in late modern society is, according to Banakar (2010b), related to a (new) sense of disorder. This condition reminds us of the first stage of modernity, about a hundred years ago, when Kafka wrote. Maybe it is the liquid modern life, living in an age of uncertainty, that links law and/as/is/in/ literature together and increases the interest in what has been called 'jurisliterature' (Goodrich 2021). In the next section we will discuss in more detail how Banakar reads Kafka as a socio-legal scholar through the article 'In Search of Heimat: A Note on Franz Kafka's Concept of Law' (Banakar 2010a).

III. BANAKAR READS KAFKA: SOME REMARKS

In his thesis *The Dilemma of Law: Conflict Management in a Multi-cultural Society* (1994) Banakar discusses ethno-cultural conflicts in Sweden and the legal system in terms of a number of dilemmas. His method advocates the integration of the perspective of the legal practitioner and that of an 'informed' outsider; if these perspectives are not integrated, socio-legal problems will not be solved (Banakar 1994: 338). Banakar even problematises different conceptual dichotomies throughout his academic writing, as described above; this is an academic heritage that is important to carry forward in the sociology of law. Kafka takes us beyond the instrumental understanding of law and allows us to grasp law as a form of experience, according to Banakar (2010a). Banakar (ibid) is paying special attention to Kafka's job as an insurance lawyer and bureaucrat and to his legal and clerical writings. By doing so, Banakar indirectly tells us that Kafka's novels have something to contribute to our understanding of law. Even more, Banakar writes in his final words that Kafka is:

> … producing an imaginative understanding of law and legality as integral parts of the human condition under modernity. Without sociological or legal theorising, Kafka's fiction takes us beyond the understanding of law as an instrument of social control and reform and introduces us to law as a form of experience. (ibid: 485)

Banakar thus highlights the fact that Kafka practised as a lawyer in Prague and examines how his day job as an insurance lawyer and his night-time avocation as a fiction writer both involve writing and are in that aspect related. Banakar asks rhetorically:

> Would Kafka have thought the way he did, constantly striving 'to interpret discourse that looks like one thing but might well be another' – often its opposite – had he not been leading a double life, practicing law during the day and producing fiction at night? (ibid: 464)

The external and internal point of view become problematised; the perspective is on the norm-user instead of the norm-giver, the use of language, and people's critical reflective attitude towards rules since the 'language turn' within modern analytical jurisprudence (Bengoetxea 2020). Everyday life or custom, as repetitive praxis and thinking, is woven by many overlapping fibres of culture as literature or art. These 'Kafkaesque double thoughts' become of interest and of relevance to the reader in a context of late modernity, when we get perspective on the time when Kafka writes his best-known works, such as *The Metamorphosis* or *The Trial*. The ending of the 'long nineteenth century' (1789–1914) and beginning of the twentieth century was a special time, characterised by modernity and radical new cultural ideas within modernism.

In his article, Banakar discusses a relativistic, dialectical or even dualistic perception that fits well in late (or liquid) modernity. The popular adjective 'Kafkaesque' usually describes a nightmarish situation, something that is horribly complicated for no reason, usually in reference to bureaucracy and omnipotent power. The fact that the term is relatively often used in everyday 'ordinary' language tells us something about the social 'form of life' or life-world in society. At the same time, the idea of anti-foundationalism or non-essentialism is an integral part of modernity, perhaps most clearly symbolised by the late Wittgenstein (Wittgenstein 1958) and by ordinary language philosophy such as speech acts theory about performative utterances (Austin 1962) and so on. What law is or ought to be is also questioned by critical schools like Scandinavian realism, contemporary with Kafka; showing that essential parts of law such as rights, duties, transfers of rights and so on, are in part composed of superstitious beliefs, 'myths,' 'fictions,' 'magic' or confusion (Hart 1959: 233). As a consequence, the binding force of law becomes a question of suggestion by socio-psychological methods given an 'intersecting model' about the relation between law and political power (Zamboni 2007). The distinction between legal issues and other social dimensions like cultural, fiction or psychological suggestion becomes deliberately unclear – or even Kafkaesque. Another theme is the bureaucratic world, which Kafka described as 'no initiative, no invention, no freedom of action; there are only order and rules: it is the world of obedience' (Kundera 1988: 112); a society Kafka never really knew. He only discovered a human possibility and shed light on the mechanisms he knew from insurance offices (Constable 2005: 130).

So, through a Kafkaesque double thought, Banakar highlights how Kafka as a writer about law and legality is both 'modern' and 'late modern', at the same time. The late modern visibility of the living ruins ('New Life in the Ruins') is a metaphor within the field of law and religion in the post-secular age (Christoffersen et al 2010). Banakar captures this paradox and how he finds it relevant to our understanding of law:

> In *The Trial*, Joseph K. encounters a priest in the Cathedral who tells him, 'The right percep-
> tion of any matter and a misunderstanding of the same matter do not wholly exclude each
> other.' I will argue in the following pages that Kafka's technique of conflating the 'right'
> perception of a matter with the reverse of its everyday logic – a technique that is the hall-
> mark of Kafka's rhetoric – needs to be understood in the discursive context of his work as
> a lawyer. (Banakar 2010a: 464)

Most people 'standing before the law' probably view the law as fixed, magisterial and remote. Through policy-oriented concepts such as 'access to justice' a similar commodification can be discerned. But even within 'modern' or traditional descrip-tions of what law is, there is an awareness of something else. Hart writes, for example, about 'the open texture of law' when he discusses formalism and rule-scepticism' (Hart 1961: 121).

'Before the Law' is a suggestive parable in Kafka's novel *The Trial* that Banakar describes and analyses in his article (2010a). According to Banakar, Kafka underlines how precarious and vulnerable the normality of daily life is; the rational is therefore conflated with the non-rational and the mundane with the extraordinary (ibid: 476). *The Trial* describes how an ordinary man, 'Josef K', gets arrested and prosecuted by a remote, inaccessible court. The nature of his crime is revealed neither to him nor to the reader. Banakar presents the 'Before the Law' part of the novel by concluding with a question about the relevance of Kafka's legal background and with a reference to 'double thought' (ibid: 477):

> In the well-known parable Before the Law, the door of the law is kept open specifically for
> the man from the country, even as the doorkeeper standing in front of the door paradoxi-
> cally denies him entry. The door is both 'dreadful and intoxicating,' and the word 'before'
> lends itself to several interpretations: 'standing outside of something spatially, preceding it
> temporally, awaiting something, or being on display before something or someone.' Would
> Kafka have known how to use this type of formal language, the ostensibly logical construc-
> tion of which vainly attempts to conceal the illogic of the situation it describes, if he had
> not been familiar with legal forms of 'double thought'?

The parable, an allegorical story, often recognised as the centrepiece of Kafka's novel and considered a key to his work (Deinert 1964), ends with a dialogue between the gatekeeper and the man from the country who asks to gain entry to the law (Kafka 1998):

> 'Everyone strives after the law,' says the man, 'so how is that in these many years no one
> except me has requested entry?' The gatekeeper sees that the man is already dying and, in
> order to reach his diminishing sense of hearing, he shouts at him, 'Here no one else can gain
> entry, since this entrance was assigned only to you. I'm going now to close it'.

Banakar discusses several themes in relation to *The Trial* and its parable 'Before the Law' in his article, like different paradoxes. For example, the paradox about the desire for justice: 'This is a paradox that lies at the heart of the relationship between modern law, which strives toward generality and universality, and justice, which requires the recognition of singularity and specificity' (Banakar 2010a: 480). He also discusses Kafka's notion of law as a non-state form of legality and law's reductionism with reference to Luhmann (law is normatively closed, but cognitively open). Banakar also relates to more existential themes, being an exile in life, perceived meaninglessness ('chewing sawdust') and especially 'the modern search for a lost Heimat' (a 'home,' 'native place,' or 'homeland'). Kafka has, according to Banakar, an ambivalent relationship to modern law and legal institutions and *The Trial* can be read as one of 'Kafka's numerous representations of the search for Heimat, the peaceful and harmonious community to which the modern individual would like to belong and with which he or she longs to identify' (ibid: 465). Banakar relates here to how Tönnies has described modernity as the passage from a form of society dominated by *Gemeinschaft* (community) to one dominated by *Gesellschaft* (association) (ibid). He also asks the Hartian-question 'does Kafka have a concept of law?' (Banakar 2015: 117), and answers it by referring to Kafka's work in insurance law as a parallel jurisdiction to state law, an indirect juridification implemented by bureaucrats rather than legal rules enforced by courts of law. Kafka was an insider, aware of the inherently paradoxical nature of modernity and law (ibid: 119). It is important to notice that Banakar, in his reading of Kafka, highlights the fact that he works as a lawyer. This perspective is not self-evident, as Ziolkowski (1997: 224) writes about 'Kafka and the law'; 'For many decades it was widely assumed that "the law", whenever it occurs in Kafka's works, is nothing but an image for concerns that are theological, metaphysical, psychological, or generally sociological in their meaning'. We will elaborate on different interesting legal themes in *The Trial* and about standing 'before the law' more in the next section.

IV. STANDING 'BEFORE THE LAW': SOME SOCIO-LEGAL COMMENTS

The parable 'Before the Law' takes its starting point in the fact that a man from the country seeks 'the law'. In a general sense, every social scientist or lawyer with practical or theoretical interest in law can relate to the protagonist in the parable. Here as well we can relate to Hart:

> Few questions concerning human society have been asked with such persistence and answered by serious thinkers in so many diverse, strange, and even paradoxical ways as the question 'What is law?' … No vast literature is dedicated to answering the question 'What is chemistry?' or 'What is medicine?', as it is to the question 'What is law?' (1961: 1)

So, what is law? From a socio-legal perspective it can be seen as an empirical question. What law is depends on what function law has in society, or with a Wittgensteinian approach; the meaning of law is its use in the language. Regardless of our perspective, access to the field (justice) is of great importance, both for the client and the researcher, and here different forms of gatekeepers often play a key role (from a meta perspective, ethical considerations can also be seen as a gatekeeper). Banakar's thesis on ethnic discrimination in Sweden has the title

The Doorkeepers of the Law in English, and the doorkeepers are here represented by the Swedish Ombudsman against Ethnic Discrimination processing discrimination complaints (Banakar 1998).

One important contribution to the socio-legal field about how people understand and experience law is the book *The Commonplace of Law: Stories from Everyday Life* (Ewick and Silbey 1998). Legal consciousness and legality are the focus of the study. The authors interviewed a random sample of 430 adults of diverse backgrounds in New Jersey to gain insight into their views on law. Ewick and Silbey found that people describe law as something before which they stand, with which they engage, and against which they struggle (ibid: 47). The authors stress participation in the process of constructing legality in everyday life and how life at the same time bears the imprint of law. The idea of the law as magisterial and remote is the narrative of 'Before the Law'; the view of law as a game with rules that can be manipulated to one's advantage is the narrative of 'with the law'; and the third narrative is the narrative of 'against the law', which describes the law as an arbitrary power that is actively resisted. With a critical and empirical method, the authors find that law and legality have different faces and roles depending on the situation and the context. They describe themes similar to Kafka and Banakar's article in their conclusions. 'Mystery and resolution: reconciling the irreconcilable', law and legality have paradoxes, or people have double thoughts about the phenomena, both strange and familiar, imperfect and ordinary (ibid). They also explicitly refer to Kafka's parable: '… a powerful description of a form of legal consciousness we, following Kafka, call "before the law"' (ibid: 75). Banakar writes in line with the empirical finding that '[i]n fact, Kafka is not "inviting" us to think double thoughts, but only holding up a mirror to us' (Banakar 2010a: 476).

If most people find law and legality hardly available and they feel like supplicants in front of the law, as in the narrative 'before the law', like Josef K in *The Trial* and the ordinary man from the country in the parable 'Before the Law', then this is not surprising. If we observe law through Luhmann's systems theory, the legal system closes itself to its environment by establishing a self-referential binary code (Nobles and Schiff 2013). The open texture of rules is obvious and commonsense within legal theory as well as rule-scepticism (Hart 1961; Twining and Miers 1991). People are often disappointed after meeting the court and legal authorities; the perceived informational and interactional justice (Bergwall 2021) or perceived procedural justice and legitimacy may be low and victims can even begin to strive for justice strategies outside the legal system (Antonsdóttir 2020; see also Woodlock 2020; 2022 for similar overviews of the concepts). But, from a socio-legal perspective, the uncertainty can also be seen as something positive: if coincidence plays a significant role in the court, the parties can hardly use the trial strategically. Paradoxically, this is reinforced by the courts' conflict-resolution function (Hydén and Hydén 2019).

Another important contribution to legal consciousness research is Hertogh's book *Nobody's Law: Legal Consciousness and Legal Alienation in Everyday Life* (2018). As the title indicates, people are disappointed, disenchanted, and outraged by the justice system and gradually move away from law. It is hard for people to know – and subsequently identify with –law, because law is irrelevant for most people. Hertogh describes the 'legal alienation' in today's Europe:

> Legal alienation can be defined as a cognitive state of psychological disconnection from official state law and the justice system. When people are listening to the discourse of the law, they are no longer able to identify their voice at all. Instead, they hear a foreign, distant, and incomprehensible voice. (Hertogh 2018: 55)

Thus, Hertogh finds through empirical research that Josef K is in good company about a hundred years later, the Kafkaesque feeling in relation to law has become a social norm in our society. But he does it through different positions on a spectrum of four potential types of legal alienation:

> (1) Legal meaninglessness ('the sensed inability to understand the law and to predict the outcome of legal processes'), (2) Legal powerlessness ('the perceived inability to control the outcome of legal processes'), (3) Legal cynicism ('a state of normlessness in which legal rules are no longer regarded as binding') and finally (4) Legal value isolation ('the values of the law are replaced by one's personal values'). (ibid: 57)

Hertogh also discusses the distinction between internal and external understandings of law in an interesting way. He presents four normative profiles: legalists, loyalists, cynics and outsiders. He argues that the 'homo juridicus model' underlying legal doctrine is not accurate. People are never fully aware of the law and never fully identify with it. On the other hand, people are seldom total outsiders. The normative profiles may, therefore, be read as a sliding scale from 'legal identification' to 'legal alienation' (ibid: 59). If we relate Hertogh's concepts to Josef K and the man from the country in *The Trial* (Kafka 1999 [1925]), we have to use what Banakar discusses as 'double thoughts'; Josef K can be said to exhibit legal meaninglessness, powerlessness and cynicism but at the same time he is loyal in relation to his own trial. In a similar way the man in the parable 'Before the Law' is both an outsider and extremely loyal, waiting his whole life in front of the gatekeeper of the law, in some sense representing legal identification and legal alienation at the same time. These contradictions and paradoxes have captured Kafka's readers for over a hundred years, as well as Banakar, and made the adjective 'Kafkaesque' popular, even among people who have never read Kafka. A common feature of the law in *The Trial* and in Hertogh's study is the impression that the law is hidden, strange, arbitrary and recondite. 'Everything remains hanging in the air', as Brod (1947: 177), editor of Kafka's writing, describes the feeling. Ironically, when the priest tells the mysterious parable in the cathedral and Josef K replies that it sounds like a topic of conversation in the court, the priest explains, admonishing him; 'it talks about this self-deceit in the opening paragraphs to the law'. But there are different interpretations of the parable (*cf* Hegel's master-slave dialectic) at the end '[...] the autonomy of law's authority is shown to have been somewhat illusory, sustained all along by the man's cooperation and defence. Rather than being separate and remote, there is a vital and direct connection between the man and the law' (Ewick and Silbey 1998: 75). There is also a question about which law we are talking about here. Josef K in *The Trial* is aware of his legal rights but he has been caught up in a different jurisdiction; against the court you cannot defend yourself – all you can do is confess (Kafka 1999 [1925]: 106). The different self-proclaimed experts, trying to inform and help Josef K, know the secret law only by hearsay (ibid).

According to some, we are all somehow lost in translation when we interpret *The Trial*, since the German title *Prozeß* refers to the entire proceeding, which may or may not culminate in a formal trial. How readers interpret the novel probably also depends on whether they are living in a legal culture shaped by accusatory or inquisitorial processes (Ziolkowski 1997: 226). In that sense, the parable 'Before the Law' can be applied to the whole trial and every reader of the novel. And Kafkaesque double thoughts can also contain humour and irony. When Kafka read *The Trial* to some friends (including other lawyers) for the first time, he apparently laughed so much that he could not read any further (ibid).

V. THE STORIES OF THE LAW, THE LAW OF THE STORIES

Within victimology it has been acknowledged that victims may perceive the world as meaningless and incomprehensible as a psychological reaction to crimes. Often victims also describe further victim-blaming from the criminal justice authorities, so-called secondary victimisation. As mentioned above, these phenomena can be related to different experiences of law as Kafkaesque. Modern cornerstones of victimology are the Holocaust victims and the Nuremberg trials which established that all of humanity would be guarded from crimes against humanity. What enables restoration and redress for victims is a central question within victimology. One answer is to be listened to and given the opportunity to tell one's story in court. The opposite can be what Antonsdóttir describes as becoming 'a witness in my own case' concerning the victim-survivor's view on the criminal justice process (Antonsdóttir 2020). Many victims of crimes testify about an experience of alienation and surrealism when they perceive and experience the judicial system. Their frequent experience of disappointment is described in empirical studies (Dahlstrand 2012; Bårnås et al 2021). To be able to talk about their experience in a dialogue and hear about the adverse parties' motives can be valuable according to therapeutic jurisprudence and restorative justice. The traditional criminal justice system has been criticised for depriving victims and offenders of resolutions of criminal matters. Within both victimology and the Law as Literature Movement, questions emerge about whose victimhood and whose memories, stories or experiences are interwoven with justice and justification of the subject. Testimony within literature and legal proceedings can be influenced by each other and inspire authors, parties and lawyers as well. There is an extensive literature about real and fictional trials, which portrays law in its social and cultural context. This also applies, of course, to the Nuremberg trials. Rebecca West's coverage and testimony about those trials is both reportage and great literature with percipient judgments, observations and reflections on the trial and the law. Based on her testimony from controversial trials she explores the nature of timeless themes such as guilt, crime, retribution and forgiveness (West 1955).

Below is a newly-written short story by author Mikael Furugärde about a man who seeks contact with the court as a form of existential belonging due to his 'searching for Heimat'. Furthermore we also want to meditate discursively on the way people perceive and experience law, their frequent disappointment with their experience, most people seem to experience a sense of alienation before meeting the court.

VI. THE LIGHT

This is my earliest memory: a Swedish hospital room in the dark of night. I lie newborn at my mother's bosom. She whispers in my ear that I must not ruin her marriage by acting childish, crying and screaming. Deep in my consciousness, I can recall that moment: my envy of the other infants, sharp red-painted nails pressed against my neck, the smell of brandy from her breath.

Many years later, I found out that my mother had received a telegram from my father just a few hours after my birth. It read: Keep him (or whatever it was.) I have often pondered these words. What could he have meant? Was he advising my mother against adoption? Or from giving me away, putting me up for sale or simply killing me? Perhaps it was his generous way of avoiding a custody dispute.

My mother named me Lorentz, after her beloved dwarf poodle. Growing up, I had difficulties connecting with my father. I have no siblings. I never found out if my father ever discovered that I lived with him and his wife in the big villa in Stockholm. His wife was my mother, after all. But she did not really pretend to be when she was alone with me.

Mother belonged to a wealthy old Swedish family which had managed to live in comfortable inactivity since the Thirty Years' War. She had never had a job and she disliked children. I was taken care of by Polish nannies and acquired a Polish accent early on.

Over the years, my mother faded into mental illness. One day in April, she began to hear voices in her head. She claimed that they read backwards from the Swedish Constitution and the Sturlunga Saga. Wearing her private straitjacket, designed at the exclusive department store NK's tailor shop, she was taken to a mental hospital. I was eighteen at the time.

The same year, my father had been indicted in an international court, for war crimes, genocide, slave trade, drug trafficking and crimes against humanity. While awaiting trial, he was held in a detention cell abroad and was not allowed to correspond by neither phone calls nor letters. My mother was blissfully ignorant of all this. I wouldn't have dared to tell her. Anyway, I realised that it was my legal duty, so I went to the mental hospital.

My mother received me in her room. She was standing by the window, dressed in a moss green silk dressing gown and leaning on a silver-crowned cane. Next to her bed was a large well-stocked bar cabinet. Mother often became surprisingly calm and friendly from alcohol.

The nurses had told me that her habit of drinking brandy, just before she fell asleep and just after she woke up, had a good effect on the mental health of the hospital staff.

'Hello, mother', I said. 'How do you do?'

She looked pensively out of the window. The sun had gone into the clouds. A quiet spring rain was falling outside.

'What a beautiful summer night', she said.

I corrected her gently:

'Spring day.'

'It's February', she said firmly and sat down in a large armchair she had had brought from her home; it was made of solid gold with diamond settings in the form of skulls, runes and hourglasses.

She lit a cigarillo and looked at me grimly.

'Who are you, Lorentz? What do you want from me?'

'Dear mother. I'm afraid I have some bad news. My father has been put on trial.'

A gust of wind from the open window made the curtains flutter. A mental patient was screaming anxiously somewhere. Two medicine bottles blew off the bedside table.

My mother calmly drew a puff on her cigarillo.

'So what?' she said. 'I guess we'll just have to change the law.'

'I thought so too', I said. 'But apparently that's no longer possible.'

'Did he accidentally incriminate himself?'

'No', I said. 'Actually, there are some others behind this. For some kind of moral reason, they say.'

My mother looked at me uncomprehendingly.

'What kind of nonsense is that? Should morality be above laws? What is he accused of anyway?'

'A little bit of everything', I said. 'Including crimes against humanity.'

'Maybe I lack imagination', my mother said. 'But I don't see how this is a moral issue.'

'Neither do I', I said sincerely. 'And now my father is in danger of being imprisoned. He who has never done anything illegal in his entire life …'

'Then he'll have to commit suicide', my mother said, without any noticeable sentimentality. 'His reputation is ruined anyway. If he goes to prison, he will not be able to make any valuable contacts with important people. He might as well kill himself.'

'I don't agree', I said. 'I think I like him. For some reason. Possibly.'

My mother ashed the cigarillo on the carpet.

'Then go to court', she said. 'Solve the problem, Lorentz. Get him acquitted. That's the least you can do, isn't it? Afterwards, you two can go sailing.'

'How will that work?' I said.

'You go out in a sailboat.'

'Yes, I understand. But how am I going to get him off?'

'The boat?'

'No. How do you get someone acquitted?'

My mother shrugged.

'No idea. Make something up. Go away now.'

Two days later, I bought a suitcase made of German swine-leather, and left for the foreign capital where the international trial was to take place. I was naturally determined to solve the problem – heeding my mother's orders – but without knowing how to proceed, or what the problem really was. Above all, I didn't know why I had to solve it.

I took a taxi to the courthouse, a three-storey Swiss-style building. Outside the entrance, reporters and press photographers flocked. Staring eyes. Hateful shouts. Camera flashes and screams into microphones. I tried to make my way through the crowds. A uniformed doorkeeper stood in my way.

'The court is closed', he said. 'There is a trial going on.'

'Then I'll just take another entrance', I said kindly. 'There are many others, aren't there?'

'No', said the doorkeeper. 'The accused in here think so too. But this is the only entrance and it's for everyone.'

'Then it's not for me', I said. 'I have nothing in common with anyone. I don't even have anything in common with myself.'

'In that case', said the doorkeeper wearily. 'I refer you to the court's telephone hours, between eleven o'clock and twelve o'clock. Go home. Make a call.'

'But I've never had a real home', I said, confused.

The doorkeeper gave me a curious look.

'I'm sorry to hear that', he said. 'But don't worry. There's always light at the end of the tunnel.'

'It's probably an oncoming train', I said.

The doorkeeper shook his head. He looked at me thoughtfully. Suddenly he leaned over and whispered in my ear:

'You're wrong. There is a light that never goes out.'

He said in a formal tone:

'Anyway, this is a court, not a home.'

The next day, at eleven o'clock sharp, I called the court from my hotel room. Two signals went through before a distant voice answered:

'Hello?'

'Help me', I said. 'Whoever you are.'

There was a silence on the other end. I tried to brace myself for a moment. Then I said:

'No one has ever treated me lovingly. Nothing I've been through has been right. Everything was wrong from the beginning.'

Silence.

'It's as if my life itself is a miscarriage of justice', I said.

No answer. Suddenly I felt a strong longing for human closeness.

'I could love you', I mumbled.

The line was dead.

VII. SEARCHING FOR HEIMAT

This chapter has highlighted Banakar's contribution to the Law and Literature Movement as a socio-legal scholar and dedicated Kafka-reader, with special focus on his article 'In Search of Heimat: A Note on Franz Kafka's Concept of Law' (2010a). The Law and Literature Movement consists of lawyers and literary scholars with different interdisciplinary methods and theories of reading and writing about *law in literature* or *law as literature* (Simonsen and Tamm 2010). In this chapter we wanted to connect the field of the Law as Literature and the Law and Literature Movement. Law as Literature, with different literary theoretical and philosophical angles on law as interpretation and rhetoric, production of aesthetic and ethical values, construction of the reader, the subject of the court or law, the narrative about the citizen, dramatic and theatrical aspects on the trial etc, is of great interest and value when reflecting on law and legality as social and cultural phenomena. Literature can manifest the inherent value of striving for justice as a core element of human existence and a collective commitment, transcendentally contained in communication (Habermas 1990), or the searching for Heimat as a sense of belonging, and possibilities for participation in society. Lorentz in 'The Light' wanted to testify, but the telephone connection with the court was cut off. Heimat can be a '… bounded medium which links the self with something larger through a process of identification signified by a spatial metaphor' (Boa 2002: 61), like the trial for justice. Either the world is unjust, or Lorentz has not understood the laws; or both (Constantine 2002: 22).

With the short story 'The Light' above, we want to give a testimony about a fictional character who finds himself standing before the law, praying to give his testimony during the trial. The court did not reject him and his story: his testimony was never assessed, the interruption was due to technical issues, which offers some hope (or light). By contrast, there has been one historical figure who was rejected by the court during the The Nuremberg trials who has engaged several commentators and whose fate bears also witness to several Kafkaesque themes. Many years later a journalist, biographer and novelist gives the following testimony of this unheard victim:

> [He] … was one of the saddest men I have ever met, and he died a disappointed man at the end of a ruined life; but I hope the aid he gave me in building up a picture of his mother and stepfather will give him (posthumous though it is) the *justification* for his existence for which he was looking. (Mosley 1974: 7) (emphasis added)

We find that by witnessing these fictional and real human destinies which give a testimony about what standing 'Before the Law' can be, and how life can be Kafkaesque, our ability to think *double thoughts* is awakened. While searching for Heimat, the legality of the trial may be questioned or the banality of evil (Arendt 1963) appears, or other Kafkaesque double thoughts may emerge. Literature or other cultural expressions function as a source of knowledge about human existence. How law is described in literature is a testimony of the author, but the meaning of the text, the *storytelling*, appears in the unique meeting with the reader.

REFERENCES

Antonsdóttir, HF (2020) *Decentring Criminal Law* (Lund, Lund University).
Arendt, H (1963) *Eichmann in Jerusalem: A Report on the Banality of Evil* (London, Faber).
Austin, JL (1962) *How to do Things with Words* (London).
Banakar, R (1994) *Rättens dilemma: om konflikthantering i ett mångkulturellt samhälle* (Lund, Lund University).
—— (1998) *The Doorkeepers of the Law: A Socio-legal Study of Ethnic Discrimination in Sweden* (Aldershot, Ashgate).
—— (2010a) 'In Search of Heimat: A Note on Franz Kafka's Concept of Law' 22(3) *Law and Literature* 463.
—— (2010b) *Rights in Context: Law and Justice in Late Modern Society* (Farnham, Ashgate).
—— (2015) *Normativity in Legal Sociology: Methodological Reflections on Law and Regulation in Late Modernity* (Heidelberg, Springer).

—— (2016a) *Driving Culture in Iran: Law and Society on the Roads of the Islamic Republic* (London, IB Tauris).

—— (2016b) 'Law, Policy and Social Control Amidst Flux' in K Dahlstrand (ed), *Festskrift till Karsten Åström* (Lund, Juristförlaget) 47.

Bengoetxea, J (2020) 'Legal theory and sociology of law' in J Přibáň (ed), *Research Handbook on the Sociology of Law* (Cheltenham, Edward Elgar Publishing).

Bergwall, P (2021) *Exploring Paths of Justice in the Digital Healthcare* (Lund, Lund University).

Boa, E (2002) 'The Castle' in J Preece (ed), *The Cambridge Companion to Kafka* (Cambridge, Cambridge University Press) 61.

Brod, M (1947) *The Biography of Franz Kafka* (London, Secker & Warburg).

Bårnås, K, Dahlstrand, K and Knutsen, V (2021) 'Voldsoffererstatningsordningen. Opplevd betydning av voldsoffererstatning blant mottakere' 1 *Tidsskrift for erstatningsrett, forsikringsrett og trygderett* 7.

Christoffersen, L, Modéer, KÅ and Andersen, S (eds) (2010) *Law & Religion in the 21st Century: Nordic Perspectives* (Copenhagen, Djøf).

Clark, DS (ed) (2007) *Encyclopedia of Law and Society: American and Global Perspectives* (London, Sage).

Constable, M (2005) *Just Silences* (Princeton, NJ, Princeton University Press).

Constantine, D (2002) 'Kafka's Writing and Our Reading' in J Preece (ed), *The Cambridge Companion to Kafka* (Cambridge, Cambridge University Press) 9.

Cornell, D, Carlson, D and Rosenfeld, M (eds) (1992) *Deconstruction and the Possibility of Justice* (New York, Routledge).

Cotterrell, R (2006) *Law, Culture and Society: Legal Ideas in the Mirror of Social Theory* (Aldershot, Ashgate).

Dahlstrand, K (2012) *Kränkning och upprättelse: en rättssociologisk studie av kränkningsersättning till brottsoffer* (Lund, Lund University).

Deinert, H (1964) 'Kafka's Parable before the Law' 39(3) *The Germanic Review: Literature, Culture, Theory* 192.

Ewick, P and Silbey, S (1998) *The Common Place of Law: Stories from Everyday Life* (London, University of Chicago Press).

Geertz, C (1973) *The Interpretation of Cultures: Selected Essays* (New York, Basic Books).

Goodrich, P (1987) *Legal Discourse: Studies in Linguistics, Rhetoric and Legal Analysis* (London, Macmillan).

—— (2021) *Advanced Introduction to Law and Literature* (Cheltenham, Edward Elgar).

Habermas, J (1990) *Moral Consciousness and Communicative Action* (Cambridge, Polity).

Hart HLA (1959) 'Scandinavian Realism' 17(2) *The Cambridge Law Journal* 233.

—— (1961) *The Concept of Law* (Oxford, Clarendon).

Hertogh, MLM (2018) *Nobody's Law: Legal Consciousness and Legal Alienation in Everyday Life* (London, Palgrave Macmillan).

Hydén, H and Hydén, T (2019) *Rättsregler: en introduktion till juridiken* (Lund, Studentlitteratur).

Kafka, F (1999 [1925]) *The Trial* (New York, Schocken Books).

Kundera, M (1988) *The Art of the Novel* (New York, Grove Press).

Mosley, L (1974) *The Reich Marshal: A Biography of Hermann Goering* (New York, Doubleday).

Nobles, R and Schiff, D (2013) *Observing Law through Systems Theory* (Oxford, Hart Publishing).

Riemen, R (2008) *Nobility of Spirit: A Forgotten Ideal* (New Haven, Yale University Press).

Sarat, A, Anderson, M and Frank CO (eds) (2010) *Law and the Humanities: An Introduction.* (Cambridge, Cambridge University Press).

Simonsen, K-M and Tamm, D (eds) (2010) *Law and Literature: Interdisciplinary Methods of Reading* (Copenhagen, DJØF).

Treviño, AJ (2008) *The Sociology of Law: Classical and Contemporary Perspectives* (New Brunswick, Transaction Publishers).

Twining, W and Miers, D (1991) *How To Do Things with Rules: A Primer of Interpretation* (London, Weidenfeld and Nicolson).

West, R (1955) *A Train of Powder* (London, Macmillan).

Wittgenstein, L (1958) *Philosophical Investigations* (Oxford, Blackwell).

Woodlock, J (2020) 'Rättsmedvetande' in I Scholultz and I Nafstad (eds) *Om rättssociologisk tillämpning* (Lund, Studentlitteratur).

—— (2022) 'Procedural Justice for All? Legitimacy, Just Culture and Legal Anxiety in European Civil Aviation' 56(3) *Law & Society Review*.

Zamboni, M (2007) *The Policy of Law: A Legal Theoretical Framework* (Oxford, Hart Publishing).

Ziolkowski, T (1997) *The Mirror of Justice: Literary Reflections of Legal Crises* (Princeton, NJ, Princeton University Press).

16

Socio-Legal Agency in Late Modernity – Reappreciating the Relationship between Normativity and Sociology of Law*

PIERRE GUIBENTIF

I. INTRODUCTION

... By studying law's normativity from specific angles – for example by emphasising people's experience of injustice, or alternatively emphasising norms at the expense of social conflicts – (sociological analysis) does, indirectly as it might be, take a stance on the nature of a good society. (Banakar 2015: 236)

THIS IS ONE of the sentences in Reza Banakar's book *Normativity in Legal Sociology* (2015) where the possible role of sociology of law in normative debates is mentioned, and where the concern of Banakar with this issue finds expression. In a time when science finds itself strongly involved in political decision-making processes, as well as in the implementation of public policies, it is important, taking up – actually sharing – this concern, to discuss this role. And it makes sense to put forward a tentative contribution to this discussion in this anthology honouring Reza's memory.

I will take as a starting point a paper of Reza Banakar, published 1998, in which he used more radical formulations than in the 2015 book. In that paper he compared sociology of law with feminist scholarship, arguing, first, that the success of feminist scholarship would be due to the fact that feminist scholars 'share a common ideological objective that does not exist to the same extent and with the same intensity in sociology of law' (Banakar 1998a: 18)[1] and, second, that, just like feminists, who

* A preliminary version of this chapter was presented in July 2021 as a paper at a session organised by the *Comité de Recherche 'Études socio-juridiques – Sociologie du droit'* within the framework of the virtual 2021 conference of the *Association internationale des sociologues de langue française (AISLF)*, and I want to thank the participants in that session for their stimulating comments. That *Comité* welcomed Reza Banakar at the Toulouse RCSL meeting in 2013, where we discussed with him the topic of our sessions: 'Law and the Social Construction of Uncertainty'. I thank Ulrike Schultz for inviting me to present this paper at the opening session of the 2021 Virtual RCSL Conference in September 2021, Håkan Hydén for authorising that presentation, and Roger Cotterrell for his inspiring reviewer's comments.

[1] This 1998 paper gave rise to several critical reactions, after which Banakar reformulated his arguments, without mentioning, however, the one about the 'ideological objectives': Banakar (2001). About the debate triggered by Banakar (1998a), see Motta (2021: 6).

'freed themselves from the limitations of the traditional and academically established disciplines', sociology of law 'must in the same fashion limit its dependency on both law and sociology' (Banakar 1998a: 18).

Tackling these two arguments successively may offer an appropriate structure for a contribution to the discussion about the relationship between sociology of law and normative debates.

II. AN IDEOLOGICAL OBJECTIVE FOR THE SOCIOLOGY OF LAW

Initially, the argument sounds disturbing to a sociologist's ear, as contradicting the seminal distinction defended by Max Weber (1919) between science and politics. In his 1998 paper Banakar did not actually specify any concrete objective of this kind. His 2015 book, however, emphasises a motive which could indicate that, over the years, he found such an objective: it relates to the fact that, in late modernity, 'the individual social actor becomes increasingly independent of social structures which previously exerted a regulating effect on its behaviour' (Banakar 2015: 259). This state of affair, on the one hand, is assessed in critical terms:

> Human agency might be gaining heightened reflexivity vis-à-vis social structures, but individual imagination and transcendental determination remain constrained by the normativity of consumerism and the celebration of hyper-individualism. (Banakar 2015: 284)

But, on the other hand,

> Theoretical constructs such as (…) cosmopolitanism can potentially contribute to the birth of a new 'state of being' by putting ethical conflicts inherent in the global market economy under the spotlight and demanding solution. (ibid)

These statements, in the last pages of *Normativity in Legal Sociology*, suggest a possible function of the law in late modernity: to support individual agency in a sense that makes it more probable for it to contribute to social change towards a 'good society'. This function of the law could be linked to what could be named an 'ideological objective' for the sociology of law: to question the contribution of law and rights nowadays to the shaping of an individual agency likely to contribute to the common good, and the impact of individual agency as stimulated or hampered as a result of law and rights. Through this inquiry, sociology of law could place itself in the condition of contributing to the reinforcement of this type of individual agency.

Such a positioning would converge with several recent references. Manuel Calvo García, who promoted sociology of law in Spain, and who left us a few weeks before Reza Banakar, gave priority in his last works to a sociological analysis of the effectiveness of rights.[2] Christopher Thornhill, in his most recent book, defending a 'global legal sociology', notes that

> A wide sociological reconstruction of the emergence of democracy and the formulation of democratic concepts is required both to clarify the actual nature of democracy, and to avert the tendency of democracy to collapse into populism. (Thornhill 2020)

---

[2] See for example Calvo García (2014).

Jacques Commaille, in a recent review of French socio-legal studies (Commaille 2021), welcomes the shift from a sociology of law focusing on the activities of state agencies, to a sociology of law adopting a bottom-up approach, focusing on, and thereby valuing, the individual practices that actualise the law.

Now the questions are to what extent can it be justified for the sociology of law to contribute to normative debates on individual agency, and how it is advisable to do so.

Let us in a first step tackle a more general issue: the status of norms in scientific discourse in general, considering that sociology of law is linked to science, and that its societal status is conditioned by that of science. The question is whether normative discourses have a place in the discourse of science. A positive answer to this question can be defended, at least in relation to one specific domain: norms governing scientific activity itself.[3] This positive answer requires a justification. As part of society, science as an activity is discussed, in particular in normative terms, not only internally, but also outside the scientific domain.[4] Science is an object of specific legislation, as well as of public policies which relate to political discourses. But according to a certain notion of scientific autonomy, recognised inside and outside the scientific domain, there have to be normative discourses about science produced inside it.[5] Much of the work of Reza Banakar concerns these discourses.

These discourses may be divided in two main categories. Some relate to the intrinsic characteristics of scientific activities; others to the people practising science.

A. Normative Discourses about the Intrinsic Characteristics of Scientific Activities

Science is supposed to produce knowledge; in other words, to offer a cognitive access to the world. This means that scientific discourse has to defend itself as giving a true account of reality. As we know, two set of norms are supposed to enable science to answer this challenge. First there are methodological norms,[6] aimed at organising the process of data collection, processing and interpretation in a way that makes it possible to check the conclusions put forward. Or, as Popper ([1934] 2002) would say, which warrants that the statements defended by scientists can be falsified by empirical observation. Second, and in addition to these methodological norms, there are norms requiring the results of scientific research to be reviewed by peer scientists.

As far as this second type of norm is concerned, we meet institutional arrangements aimed at organising the debates among peers. These arrangements serve two

---

[3] About the relationship between social systems and norms, see Hydén (forthcoming).

[4] The insider/outsider dichotomy, discussed by Banakar (1998a: 8) in the case of law, applies to all functionally differentiated activities developed in modern societies. On functional differentiation in modern society, see Luhmann 1997.

[5] The question of how a normative discourse can be part of the scientific discourse cannot be adequately discussed within the framework of this short contribution. Two important criteria are: the fact that it is connected to scientific arguments, and that it is formulated in a context usually devoted to scientific debates. The two papers of Banakar already quoted may illustrate these criteria: Banakar (1998a) and (2001) defend mainly normative arguments of politics of legal sociology, in a journal which also publishes papers presenting the results of socio-legal research.

[6] Methodology is a concern for Banakar, not only in Banakar (2015: 5), but throughout his career. Remember in particular Banakar (2000) and Banakar and Travers (2005).

opposed purposes. Some are designed to establish arenas where the debate is favoured by a shared background, which means that the access to them is restricted. Here we have, on the one hand, disciplines, ie specialised scientific domains, and, on the other hand, in connection with these disciplines, specialised organisations: university departments, learned societies, and so on. Other arrangements and principles serve, contrarily, to stimulate debates likely to integrate the domain of science as a whole. As a counterpart to locally based organisations, certain norms developed in the scientific milieu directed at internationalising the scientific debate.[7] As a counterpart to disciplinary specialisation, there are, with increasing relevance in recent decades, norms which require interdisciplinary cooperation – and institutions which help with this, such as, in France, the *Maisons des Sciences de l'Homme*.

In a discussion of the norms concerning intrinsic characteristics – modes of operation – of science, two other points have to be mentioned. One concerns the role of individuals. The relationship between science as functionally differentiated activity and individuals is a complex one. Science is the result of communication processes which transcend individual contributions, and which are built by components that are the result of collective action – in the first place, language. But modern science gives special significance to individual contributions by using the category of the author. Modern science in a certain way institutionalises the individual capacity of perception, as likely to originate the stuff to be processed by methodologically sound procedures and discussed in the arenas where peer scientists meet.[8] Moreover, it can be said that science relies on individual creativity to ensure its innovative potential. The relevance of individuality for science, apart from many other mechanisms, is revealed by the practice of honouring, by scientific publications, the memory of the members of the scientific community, as we do here for Reza Banakar.

The other point leads us back to the initial statement, science as an activity specialised in the production of knowledge. Departing from the assumption of a systemic approach to science as a self-referential social system, which to a large extent oriented up to now the reasoning here presented, the accurate perception of this function of knowledge production may be helped by a comparison of, and coupling with, other functionally differentiated activities, in particular those that can be considered as also belonging to the cultural domain, such as art and jurisprudence.[9] This means that

---

[7] Reza Banakar made particular efforts in the internationalisation of sociology of law. Apart from his international career, with moves between Sweden and the United Kingdom, he was secretary of the Research Committee on Sociology of Law of the International Sociological Association, and he carried out research in Iran, his country of origin, in parallel with research carried out in Western Europe. See 'A Case-Study of Non-Western Legal Systems and Cultures' (Banakar 2015: 169).

[8] Up to this point, several references have been made to Luhmann, as an author who proposes an ambitious theory of modern society as comprising differentiated functional systems and organisations. Here it is worth remembering that Luhmann also developed, even if he did it in a more sketchy way, a theory of psychic systems and their relationship to social systems (Guibentif 2013). The present chapter is part of an effort to link these two domains of Luhmann's theoretical work, with a view to the development of tools for a reflexive approach of the scientific domain. The aim is to create the conditions for a productive bridging between the observation of the world of science through the lens of systems theory and concrete experiences gathered in the practice of science.

[9] The emphasis given here to the three domains of law, art and science, is inspired mainly by the work of Habermas, in particular Habermas ([1981] 1984–1987). It is encouraged by Luhmann, who gave priority (indeed after the economy), to science, law and art in the volumes he dedicated to the main functional social systems: Luhmann (1990) ([1993] 2004) ([1995]).

science should take advantage of the differentiation of cognition, expression and volition, without losing sight of the fact that the three have to be recombined in practical activities. I would interpret the interest of Reza Banakar in establishing sociology of law as a domain of its own, independent from law as well as from sociology as a branch of science – an interest less radically expressed in *Normativity in Legal Sociology* (Banakar 2015) than in the paper 'The Identity Crisis' (Banakar 1998a) – as deriving from his perception of the crucial role sociology of law could play as a gatekeeper between these two domains.

B. Normative Discourses about the Addressees and the Functions of Science

Science is practised as a specialised activity, within the framework of a societal division of labour or functional differentiation. This means that it is supposed to produce knowledge to be made available to and used by others. Under these conditions, an issue for scientists is to know to whom the results of their work are made accessible, and to what end they will be used. Even more than in the case of methodological norms, norms concerning the societal uses of science are, by definition, an issue to be tackled outside the scientific domain as well. But, again, if science has to be practised according to a principle of autonomy, this issue also has to be tackled by the scientists themselves. If we admit that modern society comprises many differentiated domains of activities, we could say, inspired by Luhmann, that science, by taking part in the discussion of its uses, takes part in what could be called, in the language in use today, a process of co-construction of society.[10]

A first question to be tackled here is that of the addressees of science. This question has given rise to different responses over the last century. Let us remember Max Weber's statement, formulated at the beginning of the twentieth century, insisting on the need for science to develop autonomously. Arguably a shift took place after World War II. Science at that moment experienced itself as one instrument necessary for the reconstruction of a peaceful international community.[11] As a consequence, science involved itself over the following decades in the implementation of public policies, or in the activities of large firms.[12] A third shift is said to have taken place recently, with an emphasis on the use of scientific results by individuals and grassroots organisations, a shift that is revealed in the socio-legal domain by the growing number of researchers adopting a bottom up approach.[13]

A second question concerns the uses of scientific knowledge. In the case of sociology of law, as viewed by Reza Banakar, the main issue here is the challenge for the discipline to offer useful knowledge. A more specific debate which deserves a mention

---

[10] The notion of a society resulting from the simultaneous processes of operation of differentiated social systems, all of them constructing society as their environment, is to be found in Luhmann (1997: 745).

[11] An example of this self-perception is Talcott Parsons' presidential address at the 1949 annual conference of the American Sociological Society, in which sociology is placed among the 'national resources' that enabled the United States to face its post-war challenges (Parsons 1950: 16).

[12] Reza Banakar discusses the demands of the big players of globalisation, actually in the legal rather than the scientific domain, in Banakar (1998b).

[13] For a reference by Banakar to this trend, see fn 5. Today, this point would deserve to be discussed taking into account the recent development of open science policies.

emerged in relation to the involvement of socio-legal research in the design of policies using 'nudges' (Fluckiger 2018).

Beyond these two classical questions regarding the relationship between science and society (ie whom does it address? And what might be performed with its help?), a third question deserves attention. Scientific activity is a part of society. Society is shaped by the functionally differentiated activities taking place within it. Recent western history suggests the following hypothesis: the establishment of a public sphere, which could later lead to the shaping of democratic political structures, was favoured by the existence of differentiated cultural domains. Within these domains, institutions developed which did recognise individual contributions as providing the substance of cultural outputs likely to be reused by society, and organised the cooperation between the individuals in ways favouring these individual contributions and their combination in a collective cultural output. This could have supplied the organisational skills required for the setting up of the institutional mechanisms of modern democracies, and helped the construction of individualities capable of contributing to the debates in the public sphere. More specifically, three characteristics of such individualities are: (i) the will to defend one's own position; (ii) the capacity to use, for this defence, a sophisticated set of intellectual tools – such as concepts – which gives individuals the possibility of composing contributions that are, at the same time, original and understandable as well as reusable by other people;[14] and (iii) to have acquired the notion that their contribution will be well received if other people can take advantage of it (peer researchers, students, non-scientists), in other words: their self-actualisation as scientists is to a significant extent linked to the self-actualisation of other people.[15]

On the basis of this reasoning, a new question arises, regarding how science has to be practised nowadays: what might be the relevance of the mode of functioning science adopts and defends for itself for the environing society? Having this question in sight, one possible option for scientific policy could be: science has to develop practices and structures likely to have, apart from other characteristics, the potential to value individualities and their contributions to common activities, not only for the sake of scientific productivity, but also because such a functioning of science is likely to favour democratic trends in its societal environment, which, at the end of the day, are likely to improve, from the outside, the conditions of scientific activity.

Let us now come back to the question raised at the beginning of this section. Is it legitimate for sociology of law to have an ideological objective, which would be the defence of a certain place and role of individuals in society, as active contributors?

This question may be answered in two steps. In a first step, we have to recognise that science – the same applies to jurisprudence and art – has reasons to defend that notion of individuality for its own sound functioning, considering the place of this

---

[14] In other words, they experienced, within the cultural domain in which they are specialised, what Axel Honneth ([2011] 2014) calls social freedom.

[15] To duly identify those characteristics, as favoured by the development of the modern cultural domains, does not mean to ignore the fact that these domains also generate inequalities and power strategies, inside and in their societal environment, and deal with inequalities and power strategies which transcend them. The arguments here outlined should be taken as a desirable addition to the critical discussion of these aspects of scientific reality, which is indispensable, but not the object of the present contribution.

notion in the set of norms which characterise science as a differentiated activity, and having in view a possible impact of this notion on its environment, which could serve its own development. This defence, however, takes place in a debate internal to science (where it will have to face, in particular, managerial conceptions of scientific activity, relying on the rationalisation of scientific organisation, and to that end, on an evaluation of individual contributions made by metrics). But this internal debate takes place within the context of a broader societal debate on democracy, and deserves to be taken into account in that broader debate. Not as a privileged debate, but as one among other debates, in particular those which take place in the domains of art, or of jurisprudence.

In a second step, the question of the specific role of sociology of law has to be tackled. Two contributions deserve highlighting. First, as a domain of science, more specifically of social sciences and sociology, it is specialised in the observation of social processes, which provides it with appropriate tools to observe those processes that take place within the scientific domain itself; and it is specialised in particular in the observation of the processes that concern norms (Hydén forthcoming). So it is ideally placed not only to participate in the above-outlined normative debates but also, as a participant observer, to give a particularly dense account of these debates – an account, however, which should not be considered as more than one input among others, to be reworked in discussions gathering scientists of all disciplines. Second, as a discipline observing what happens in the neighbouring cultural domain of jurisprudence, it may help the discussion in the scientific domain to pay attention to that other domain, and to better identify processes which may impact not only on science but more generally on the cultural domain.

This is precisely what Reza Banakar did in his last works, focusing on the evolution of law in late modernity. And his conviction about the relevance of this effort in times of 'emerging legal uncertainties'[16] might be the reason why his appreciation of the role of sociology of law seems somehow less pessimistic in these works than in 'The Identity Crisis'. In this new context, a scholarship such as sociology of law appears as indispensable.

III. BRIDGING BETWEEN LAW AND SOCIOLOGY

As far as the relationship between sociology of law and sociology is concerned I had occasion to defend a position opposed to that of Reza Banakar, arguing for sociology of law to be practised as a sub-discipline of sociology (Guibentif 2003). The foregoing reasoning reinforces my conviction in this sense. The ideological objective which has been reconstructed here is not specific to sociology of law, but to science in general. To consider sociology of law as a discourse likely to enrich the broader

---

[16] This title of the chapter introducing Banakar (2015) has to be related to the title of one of the first international research projects in which Reza Banakar participated, *Emerging Legal Certainties*, a project led by Volkmar Gessner, oriented by the hypothesis that globalisation would generate its own normativity (Banakar 1998b). At that time, this process could be seen as making sociology of law run the risk of being marginalised, an appreciation which may have motivated the publication, in precisely the same period of time, of 'The Identity Crisis' (1998).

scientific debates addressing this objective could strengthen its motivation in better formulating, appreciating, and defending this objective: it puts it in the position to develop a more comprehensive notion of scientific individuality, and to identify a more precise role to play in the defence of that individuality.

Reza Banakar's concern of 'merging law and sociology', however, remains legitimate, in particular if we consider the above highlighted potential of sociology of law to help science to pay attention to what happens in the realm of law.

In line with the above-defended reasoning, which emphasises the relevance of individualities for the functioning of cultural domains, I would like to defend the following, actually obvious, argument. Functionally differentiated activities have to be carried out according to the above-discussed norms that warrant their specificity; sociology of law has to be practised sociologically. Individual specialists of these activities, however, may also carry out other activities. The merging of different activities takes place, among other contexts, in the individual agency.

Arguably, the notion of individuality carried by the notion of author[17] implies this involvement in different social spheres; the recognition of the person, not as an 'official' of the discipline, but as a person who is capable of bringing something new to it, possibly collected in other domains of individual experience. This notion has recently given rise to controversy in cases in which political commitments of certain authors raised doubts about what could be called the legitimacy, or the acceptability, of their contribution to their domain of specialty.[18] Even in the face of such controversies, triggered by particular circumstances, the recognition of the subjectivity of the authors as a driver of scientific or artistic production could be qualified as one of the *Betriebsgeheimnisse* of functional differentiation (Teubner 2012);[19] one of the devices which give functionally differentiated activities their momentum.

To analyse agency as generated by dynamics cutting across differentiated domains of societal activities could lead to the formulation of hypotheses about the generation of social forces. Forces may emerge where correspondences are experienced between what happens at the same time in different domains.[20] These may be individual experiences, but also the experiences of a group. Or better to say, such experience may contribute to the formation of a group. Here a hypothesis could be put forward about the formation, in recent decades, of what has been called the socio-legal field, precisely the field of interest of Banakar. Let us consider his concern – which I share – about 'the lack of common basic assumptions between different orientations constituting the field of sociology of law' (Banakar 1998a: 4). Such a situation could simply have led, without regret, to the development of different separate lines of scientific work. If there is such a concern, it is because there is also a notion of unity, which motivates the appreciation of shortcomings in the effective achievement of that unity. It is an experience of unity – which we made at a global level at occasions such as the foundation of the International Institute for the Sociology of Law in Oñati in

---

[17] For a classical reference on the topic, see Foucault (1969).
[18] For a recent discussion of this issue see Sapiro (2020).
[19] Teubner (2012); terminology of the German version of the book.
[20] For a more developed defence of this argument, see Guibentif (2020: 183).

1989, or the World Law and Society Meeting in Amsterdam in 1991 – that forced us to question what, as a matter of fact, justified that unity. What unites this field, perhaps more than shared scientific paradigms, might be the experience, by individualities, but also by certain communities,[21] of amazing – and productive – correspondences between, to use the cool language of Niklas Luhmann, sociological and legal operations. In other words, this time eschewing the luhmannian terminology, of socio-legal agency.

An intriguing question, to which it is not possible to devote here an expanded analysis, is to know what could be, more precisely, these experiences of correspondences. Two of them may be briefly mentioned. Correspondences – as well as, actually, productive tensions – may be experienced in the realm of concepts. Concepts can be connected to each other in the individual reasoning beyond the schemes that are constructed within particular disciplines, and thereby acquire new meanings. An example could be the concept of legal pluralism, to which Banakar, like many of us, gives centrality (Banakar 1998a: 19).[22] Its meaning, within the socio-legal field, is shaped in particular by the encounter of the notion of unity of the legal system with which jurisprudence struggles, and the many notions converging with plurality which structure sociological theories: inequalities, conflicts, differentiation, and so on. Another level of correspondences are procedures; methodological procedures – reflections on content analysis may enrich reflections on legal interpretation and vice-versa – but also organisational procedures – the experience of the normative debates within the scientific domain analysed in the previous section can be compared with administrative or judicial procedures, or else with political procedures in which researchers may find themselves involved as citizens.

This brings us back to the topic of this chapter, the relationship between sociology of law and normativity. The conclusion of the previous section was that sociology of law has a special role to play within the normative debates internal to the scientific domain. A second conclusion could be that the sociologists of law, as individualities, equipped with their socio-legal habitus, but in their other personal roles – in particular of jurists or of citizens – may be ideally placed to use special intellectual tools in normative debates outside the scientific domain, and to enrich their arguments in these debates by arguments trained within the framework of scientific debates. Among those arguments, let us take, as a conclusive example, the one of pluralism, which can be linked to the defence of a certain modern individuality. Indeed, to recognise individual subjectivities, in functionally differentiated cultural activities as well as in the public sphere, only makes sense if this recognition is connected to the recognition of the plurality of these individualities. This could help to make institutions and procedures sensitive to the variety of human viewpoints, the best warrant for the development of just social arrangements.[23] Perhaps a way of actualising 'the

---

[21] Such research centres as, for example, the Oxford Centre for Socio-Legal Studies, the Sociology of Law Department at the University of Lund, or the CETEL, Centre d'études de technique et d'évaluation législatives, at the University of Geneva.

[22] Legal pluralism is also an issue throughout almost all chapters of Banakar (2015).

[23] To react very tentatively to the interrogation of Douglas-Scott (2013: 16), quoted by André (2019: 258), 'whether pluralism is normatively attractive, and productive of justice'.

theoretical and empirical unoriginality of late modernity (in which) lies latent the promise of a paradigm shift' (Banakar 2015: 284).

REFERENCES

André, P (2019) 'O Direito nas Dinâmicas Paradigmáticas: A Leitura Realista e Pluralista de António Manuel Hespanha' 20(35) *Themis – Revista da Faculdade de Direito UNL* 221.

Banakar, R (1998a) 'The Identity Crisis of a "Stepchild"' *Retfærd: Nordisk juridisk tidsskrift* 3.

—— (1998b) 'Reflexive Legitimacy in International Commercial Arbitration' in V Gessner and A Cem Budak (eds), *Emerging Legal Certainty – Empirical Studies on the Globalization of Law* (Dartmouth, Ashgate) 387.

—— (2000) 'Reflections on the Methodological Issues of the Sociology of Law' 27 *Journal of Law and Society*, 273.

—— (2001) 'A Passage to "India": Toward a Transformative Interdisciplinary Discourse on Law and Society' *Retfærd: Nordisk juridisk tidsskrift* 3.

—— (2015) *Normativity in Legal Sociology. Methodological Reflections on Law and Regulation in Late Modernity* (Cham, Springer)

Banakar, R and Travers, M (eds) (2005) *Theory and Method in Socio-Legal Research* (Oxford, Hart Publishing).

Calvo García, M (2014) 'Crisis económica y efectividad de los derechos sociales' in MJ Bernuz Benéitez and M Calvo García (eds), *La eficacia de los derechos sociales* (Valencia, Tirant lo Blanch) 89.

Commaille, J (2021) 'La *French touch* de la recherche sur le droit' *Droit et Société* Nr 107 203.

Douglas-Scott, S (2013) *Law after Modernity* (Oxford, Hart Publishing).

Fluckiger, A (2018) 'Gouverner par des "coups de pouce" (nudges): instrumentaliser nos biais cognitifs au lieu de légiférer? [Governing by Nudges – Using Cognitive Bias instead of Legislation]' *Les Cahiers de Droit* 199.

Foucault, M (1969) 'What is an author?', available at https://www.open.edu/openlearn/ocw/pluginfile.php/624849/mod_resource/content/1/a840_1_michel_foucault.pdf.

Guibentif, P (2003) 'The Sociology of Law as a Sub-discipline of Sociology' 1(3) *Portuguese Journal of Social Sciences* 175.

—— (2013) 'Rights in Niklas Luhmann's Systems Theory' in A Febbrajo and G Harste (eds), *Law and Intersystemic Communication – Understanding 'Structural Coupling'* (London, Ashgate) 255.

—— (2020) 'The Sociology of Legal Subjectivity' in J Přibáň (ed), *Research Handbook on Sociology of Law* (Cheltenham, Edward Elgar) 177.

Habermas, J ([1981] 1984–1987) *The Theory of Communicative Action* (trans T McCarthy, Boston, MA, Beacon Press).

Honneth, A ([2011] 2014) *Freedom's Right. The Social Foundations of Democratic Life* (New York, Columbia University Press).

Hydén, H (forthcoming) 'Normativity as the Source of Norms' in the present anthology.

Luhmann, N (1990) *Die Wissenschaft der Gesellschaft* (Frankfurt am Main, Suhrkamp).

—— ([1993] 2004) *Law as a Social System* (Oxford, Oxford University Press).

—— ([1995] 2000) *Art as a Social System* (Stanford, Stanford University Press).

—— (1997) *Die Gesellschaft der Gesellschaft* (Frankfurt am Main, Suhrkamp).

Motta, V (2021) 'Law, Justice and Reza Banakar's Legal Sociology' 11(1) *Oñati Socio-Legal Series* 1.

Parsons, T (1950) 'The Prospects of Sociological Theory' 15(1) *American Sociological Review* 3.

Popper, K ([1934] 2002) *The Logic of Scientific Discovery* (London, Routledge).

Sapiro, G (2020) *Peut-on dissocier l'oeuvre de l'auteur ?* (Paris, Seuil).

Teubner, G (2012) *Constitutional Fragments: Societal Constitutionalism and Globalization* (Oxford, Oxford University Press).

Thornhill, C (2020) *Democratic Crisis and Global Constitutional Law* (Cambridge, Cambridge University Press, 2020).

Weber, M (1919) *Wissenschaft als Beruf* (München, Duncker & Humblot), available at https://de.wikisource.org/wiki/Wissenschaft_als_Beruf.

17

The Quest for Scientific Methods: Sociology of Law, Jurimetrics and Legal Informatics

PETER WAHLGREN*

I. INTRODUCTION

A CORE OBJECTIVE of sociology of law is to improve the understanding of how the law operates and is generated by the surrounding society. The research topic thus has a history of pluralism. From a practical point of view the law is a steering instrument and a means to address problems (Hart 1961: 39). Consequently, almost everything has a legal side to it, present or potential, and regarding study objects sociology of law is a wide-ranging subject. Many phenomena and their interdependence with the law have been investigated. In the Scandinavian context this is illustrated by works focusing on different aspects and relationships between a diversity of subject matters and stakeholders (Forslund 1978; Hydén 1997; Saldeen 2004; Wahlgren 2008; Banakar et al 2018).

The broadness of sociology of law is not only reflected in a variety of study objects. Heterogeneity is also apparent in the ways in which studies have been designed and methodological preferences differ. Observations, surveys, statistics, interviews, and many variants thereof abound, and so do theories and discussions on how law, as well as the topic sociology of law as such should be understood and delimited (Kaijus 2008; Ziegert 2018).

An interest in the methodological aspects is present in the writings of Reza Banakar, which make it appropriate to share a few observations concerning research approaches in this context. Consequently, this chapter intends to point out similarities in how research has been motivated and addressed, in sociology of law and interdisciplinary lines of research confronting jurisprudence with scientific methods, viz jurimetrics and legal informatics. The text reflects the development from a Scandinavian perspective.

* This chapter originates from the research project *Legislative Technique*s, financed by Torsten and Ragnar Söderberg's Chair in Legal Science.

II. STARTING POINTS

Sociology of law as we now know it originates from ideas articulated in the late nineteenth century, as a reaction to what were considered to be outdated forms of jurisprudence. The beginning is not homogenous, nor well defined. The efforts made towards a socially oriented jurisprudence reflect a continuation of debates between supporters of legal realism and legal positivists. Forerunners exist (Zabala and Silveira 2019) and early contributions were not coordinated, but the central issue was the same. Should the focus be a deeper understanding of the concept of law, including traditional legal dogma, or should the objective be improved efficiency of law by the introduction of alternative methods?[1]

The calls for reorientation met opposition from traditional jurisprudence with arguments rooted in the established trenches. Supporters of more realistic views were hesitant about a development towards elaborated dogmatism boosted by logic and formal methods. Positivists, on the other hand, were critical of letting jurisprudence be influenced by social science methods, potentially making law unpredictable and unstable. The debates were sometimes hard and the argumentation has been described as antagonistic and hostile (Banakar 2000: 245–46). An insightful comment was articulated by Oliver Wendel Holmes, who added the time aspect to the discussion and suggested that 'for the rational study of the law the black letter man may be the man of the present, but the man of the future is the man of statistics and the master of economics' (Holmes 1897: 457).

Differences between advocates for positivist and realist views are also visible among those criticising traditional jurisprudence from a sociological point of view. Contrasts are reflected in shifting theories on how different social structures affect the legal system and apparent in discussions concerning adequate research approaches (Cotterrell 2020). Variations of this kind prompted several lines of research, sometimes given different names,[2] but not always easy to discern for an outside observer. In this way, sociology of law in its various guises during the first half of the twentieth century stands out as an essentially theoretical activity. Considerable literature was aggregated about how to understand the topic, while presentations of practical and systematic studies were comparatively rare, although a large number of individual exceptions exist, especially in the form of studies focusing on crimes (Foldes 1906) and anthropology (Allwood 1957). In 1960 the Norwegian Torstein Eckhoff summarised the situation from a Scandinavian perspective: 'It is only in the last 10–15 years that these tendencies [to extend the contact between law and social science to other fields than that of crime] have manifested themselves in an amount of research worth mentioning'. (Eckhoff 1960: 32). The preconditions had nevertheless changed and the time was now ripe.

---

[1] Banakar explicitly mentions Leon Petrazycki and Eugen Ehrlich, and that they were both 'specifically interested in employing social scientific methods to *develop* and *improve* the science of law' (Banakar 2006: 248). See also Bengoetxea (2020).

[2] *Inter alia* referred to as Sociological jurisprudence, Law and Society, Empirical Legal Studies, Living Law, Responsive law and Reflexive law.

III. FORMATIVE YEARS

By the mid-twentieth century, while logical positivism and numerous scientific advancements had already had an apparent impact in many sectors of society, it had become obvious that the legal domain lagged behind.[3] Several argumentative works had been published (Stjernquist 1958), and unarguably as part of a growing awareness of the importance of social sciences as such, the first Scandinavian professor in sociology and law was appointed at the Faculty of Law, University of Oslo in 1963. It was followed by the installation of the first Swedish professor at Lund University in 1972.

Internationally, Eckhoff's comment coincided with the setting up of a Working Group on Documentation in sociology of law by The International Sociological Association, which was established as an initiative from the Social Science Department of UNESCO (ISA). A few years later The Law and Society Association was founded in the USA (LSA 2021).

The continued development of sociology of law in Scandinavia is well documented (TfRs 1983–90; Hydén 1996; Hydén 1997; Wahlgren 2008; Banakar et al 2018) and is a description of multifaceted activities, including theoretical analyses of earlier contributions, debates about the proper understanding of the discipline, and empirical studies conducted in various sectors of society. Wide-ranging activities are also a signum on the international scene (Přibáň 2020; Libguides 2021).

Although sociology of law has been vital and rich in expressions, it is difficult to see that the original call for a scientific reorientation has been satisfied and that sociology of law has had a significant impact on jurisprudence. The majority of lawyers appear to move along well-known paths with their heads bowed and jurisprudence can still be characterised as a theoretical discipline in which traditional methods prevail. An ostrich attitude has also hampered interdisciplinary advancements and a fruitful integration of law and sociology. A concerned Reza Banakar in 2000 submitted the fundamental question whether the topics actually were based on incommensurable understandings of the world:

> Could it be that law has its own 'reality' or 'truth', that is, its own way of understanding and describing the world, which cannot be captured by sociological concepts? To put it differently, could it be that sociology can understand the world only in terms of its own concepts, definitions, and assumptions and is, therefore, simply unable to provide insights into legal ideas and clarify questions about legal doctrine, as a result of which the essence of law and legal thinking becomes inaccessible to it? (Banakar 2000: 274)

IV. JURIMETRICS

Although the mid-twentieth century stands out as the formative period, the establishment of sociology of law as a separate discipline was not an isolated occurrence.

---

[3] See eg Strömholm (1996: 119) 'It is not surprising that this situation gave rise to several noteworthy, more or less successful attempts to "save" jurisprudence' (original in Swedish).

As the perspective broadened, the criticism aimed at jurisprudence grew more intense and the search for methodological alternatives became more diversified.

One important contribution from this time is an article by Lee Loevinger, who presented the concept of jurimetrics. The author forcefully argued for a reorientation of jurisprudence and the text was a frontal attack against a permanent status quo '[t]he only important area of human activity which has developed no significant new methods in the last twenty centuries is law' (Loevinger 1949: 473). Although the criticism was devastating, the article was well researched and the conclusions crystal clear. Speculations about the nature of law should be abandoned and the efforts should focus on the development of scientific methods. The purpose should be to improve the efficiency of law as an operative tool:

> The next step forward in the long path of man's progress must be from jurisprudence (which is mere speculation about law) to jurimetrics – which is the scientific investigation of legal problems. In the field of social control (which is law) we must at least begin to use the same approach and the same methods that have enabled us to progress toward greater knowledge and control in every other field. (ibid: 483)

The criticism Loevinger put forward was in no way new, and nor were his ideas, but his argumentation stands out because it included multiple components and suggested concrete ways forward. In addition, he was one of the first to recognise the potential of computers in the legal sector:[4]

> Machines are now in existence which have so far imitated 'thought processes' that they can solve differential equations and other 'logical' operations of equal or greater complexity. The machines can be constructed to solve equations with virtually any number of variables, and with large numbers of variables the operation is much faster than when performed by the human mind. Why should not a machine be constructed to decide lawsuits? The complexity of the problems presented, measured by the number of variables involved, is well within the limits of existing machines. (ibid: 471)

The calls for scientific methods were motivated by the observation that little was known about the actual impact of law in society. Here Loevinger argued for a need of 'macrolegal techniques' of investigation, able to address the most fundamental questions in sociology of law and jurisprudence – 'what indices will most reliably indicate the social results of laws in categories A, B, C, ... N?' and 'how can the data to construct these indices be obtained most efficiently?' (ibid: 488).

The non-existing progress of jurisprudence was obvious for those who had the ability to broaden their perspectives and understood that alternatives as well as new methodological tools were available. Consequently, Loevinger's contribution had an impact and jurimetrics became recognised as an important field of study, especially in the USA. In 1959 the American Bar Association (ABA) set up several committees for the study of related issues, including electronic data retrieval and communications, and started to sponsor the periodic newsletter Modern Uses of Logic in Law (MULL), which later changed its name to Jurimetrics Journal. The work led to the formation of ABA's Standing Committee on Law and Technology, which in 1969 published a second edition of a Handbook on Computers & the Law, in which jurimetrics was used as a headline for articles on symbolic logic, analyses of prediction of judicial decisions

---

[4] Loevinger in this part referred to the work of Norbert Wiener published the year before (Wiener 1948).

and legal education. The support to Jurimetrics Journal continues and the publication is currently in its sixty-second volume (Jurimetrics 2021).

The ABA was not the only organisation ready to give attention to the new concept of jurimetrics. In 1960 The Association of American Law Schools formed a Jurimetrics Committee with the objective to observe the progress in science and technology and its relations to law. Some years later the Working Group on Documentation in sociology of law set up by ISA published an international survey covering activities in sociology of law, including a bibliographical appendix on jurimetrics (Treves 1968). In parallel, starting in the early 1960s, a number of conferences were arranged, focusing on scientific methods, encompassing a number of approaches (for more detailed historical descriptions see Chasalo 1961: 31; Brown 1961; Seipel 1970; Wahlgren 1992: 117–41). In hindsight, however, it is clear that the answer to the call for 'scientific methods' primarily manifested itself in three closely interrelated lines of research: an increased interest in legal logic; potentialities for using computers in the legal sector; and the employment of statistical methods for analysis and prediction – tracks that soon should merge.

In the Scandinavian context pioneering work emerged in the 1970s when a Swedish LLD dissertation was explicitly presented as a study in sociology of law and jurimetrics (Saldeen 1973). The work was based on a statistical analysis of damages in cases of divorce. At the same time a comprehensive article with multiple references to computers and jurimetrics was published in the Swedish leading law journal (Seipel 1970). It is also notable that an interdisciplinary symposium held in 1974 included several references to jurimetrics (Saldeen 1974; Seipel 1974). Additional, but sporadic contributions explicitly referring to jurimetrics followed (Saldeen 1978; 1980), but jurimetrics never became fully integrated with legal sociology or traditional jurisprudence, either in Scandinavia or internationally. A few citations summarise the continued development:

> Jurimetrics, the empirical study of the law, has never really come into existence. Although, given the way in which society has developed during the information age, it could have been expected that jurimetrics would become an important discipline, until now it has not conquered much ground in the universities or outside. (De Mulder et al 2010: 135)

> The world has changed, but law schools and legal professionals seem to be intent to turn a blind eye to science and technology. – Most lawyers are simply not familiar with quantitative, empirical or computer supported approaches. Furthermore, they try to avoid such contact as much as possible. (ibid: 164)

> Among the quantitative methods I have found in legal articles in Sweden, many have only been implicitly applied. The author of the article can, for example, refer to statistics or data, and draw own conclusions or invite the reader to draw conclusions from these without the researcher explaining why the statistics or data really mean what the author thinks it means. In many cases, I have also found it difficult to recreate the models that the author claims to use. (Andersdotter 2018: 54, original in Swedish)

V. A DIFFERENT TURN – LEGAL INFORMATICS

If the legal response to calls for including scientific methods, logic and statistical analyses in the methodological toolbox was hesitant, the opposite is true for the readiness to find uses for computers. The Scandinavian countries were comparatively early to react to potentialities to utilise computers and information technology (IT) in law, and during the 1960s and onwards were able to position themselves at the forefront of the development.

The interest in IT in the Scandinavian setting was in no way a coincidence. With comparatively large public administrative sectors, the Scandinavian countries, especially Sweden, had early on started to invest substantially in computers for the public sector. Consequently, there also existed an interest in finding ways of employing the new technology in the legal domain and in 1966 it was decided that a standing committee for the development of IT for the judiciary should be established. Members included the heads of the authorities in the legal sector and a representative from the parliament. The work was led by the state secretary at the Ministry of Justice. Stakeholders outside the authorities were appointed contact persons and the committee was named *Samarbetsorganet för rättsväsendets informationssystem*, SARI (the cooperation organ for the judiciary's information system) (SARI 1968; Alpsten 2000).

Legal informatics, originally a translation from the Swedish Rättsinformatik, was shortly after recognised as a field of research and one of the world's first academic organisations addressing the topic was the Swedish Working Party for EDP (Electronic Data Processing) and Law, later renamed the Swedish Law and Informatics Research Institute (IRI), established at Stockholm University in 1968 (IRI 2022). IRI was soon followed by The Norwegian Center for Computers and Law (NRCCL), set up at Oslo University 1970. Academic chairs became available in 1982 and 1988 respectively. A Nordic yearbook in legal informatics and a series of Nordic conferences were introduced in 1984. These activities are unbroken and regularly engage researchers and practitioners from Denmark, Finland, Norway and Sweden. The responsibility for the conferences rotates between these countries and the 37th version 2022, held in Copenhagen is given the title Humans, Data and Law: Tectonic Plates in Motion (CIIR 2022). Similar to sociology of law, legal informatics has appeared under several names and the headings have often mirrored the ways in which the technology has been referred to at different points in time.[5]

The development of Legal informatics was prompted by the fact that computers and information systems at an early stage were identified as phenomenon in need of regulation, as it became obvious that established routines on how to manage privacy and security had to be revised. The first IRI seminar in 1968 addressed the issue of to what extent computers posed a threat to privacy and the world's first national Data Act was enacted in Sweden in 1973 (Rudgard 2021: 15), prohibiting data registers comprising personal information without an explicit permit.

For those involved in this process it thus became necessary to develop an understanding of the technique, its subcomponents and underlying methods, including statistics, logic and other formal representations. This in turn led to insights about

---

[5] Apart from Legal informatics, which this chapter uses as a common denominator, *inter alia*, EDP (Electronic Data Processing) and Law, Computing Law, Cybernetics, Electronic Law, Computers and Law, IT Law, ICT Law, AI and Law, Oikeusinformatiikka (Finnish), Droit et informatique (French), Rechtsinformatik (German), informatica giuridica (Italian), Rettsinformatikk (Norwegian), Кибернетика (Russian), Rättsinformatik (Swedish).

how the technology could be utilised as a legal tool and became a basis for further developments. In this way, a number of what frequently had been described as scientific methods became integrated in the legal sector, albeit under different labels and not primarily as a result of theoretical contributions to jurisprudence, but as components incorporated in and adjunct to a technology introduced for practical reasons.

Internationally, legal informatics evolved rapidly, attracting much interest and receiving broad acceptance. The topic was also recommended to be a component in law school curriculums (Council of Europe 1992), and, as a consequence of the digitalisation, IT has in a comparatively short time become a subject matter that everyone has a relationship with. The technology has brought about a number of issues of relevance for the legal sector, inter alia privacy, data quality, security, surveillance, use of digital media for manipulation, intellectual property, transparency, freedom of information, e-governance, e-commerce, regulation of IT systems and new forms of criminal activities.

Although public concern and media discussions have primarily focused on substantive law issues, legal informatics has from the beginning been a science with a practical side (Bing and Harvold 1977; Seipel 1977). The possibility of enhancing the efficiency and quality of legal work has been a focal interest, and the accompanying inclusion of system science has deepened the understanding of the functions of the legal system as such. Concrete illustrations include innumerable projects and applications[6] such as legal databases, document management systems, information services, decision support systems, e-banking, apps for commercial activities and interactive interactions with public agencies via the Internet. The development is reflected in organisational changes at national and international levels, including major reallocations of resources for further advancements.

Significant from a methodological point of view is that legal informatics soon developed an interest for artificial intelligence (AI) and the first conferences on AI and Law were organised during the 1980s (Wahlgren 1992: 133–41). AI is an open, multifaceted discipline with the potential to generate results of relevance for all types of activities that can be described in a sufficiently detailed manner. In this respect AI research is, in principle, a borderless activity in which methods and approaches vary significantly. Digital techniques and computers are essential elements, but in order to develop practical AI, input from a large variety of natural, human and legal sciences must be acknowledged, depending on the type of task that is addressed.

An early illustration of how knowledge and methods of different origin have been integrated as described above is the General Data Protection Regulation (GDPR) adopted by the EU in 2016. In certain circumstances the GDPR stipulates that processing of personal data must be proceeded by an impact assessment and that 'measures which meet … the principles of data protection by design and data protection by default' should be implemented (EU 2016: recital 78). In order to comply with this, it is not only necessary to interpret the meaning and relevance of the relevant legal

---

[6] Among the first SARI projects were computerised analyses of legislative texts, forming KWIC (Key Word In Context) and KWOC (Key Word Out of Context) indexes – necessary components for the design of databases (SARI 1969).

principles for the specific case. It is also necessary to complete a proactive risk analysis, and, based on that, to design and program a solution that is able to technically ensure the upholding of these legal principles.

The GDPR is valid for the processing of personal data, including IT and AI applications, but similar methodological requirements can be related to several regulative issues regarding many types of IT systems. It is foreseeable that there will be a growing need for proactive ELSI (Ethical, Legal, Social Impact) analyses as well as interdisciplinary efforts to develop acceptable technical solutions for various scenarios. The need to merge legal, social and technical methods is obvious.

Looking back, it is clear that the methodological shifts that can be related to practical developments in legal informatics has not happened in the way that might have been predicted, ie as a consequence of internal reconsiderations and methodological developments within jurisprudence. The driving forces have been computer and system sciences, which by their own technology, power of performance and impact on society have brought about new solutions and methods. Legal informatics has in various ways been able to contribute to this development, often with input that has been reflected in methodological developments, but to a large extent this has been a trajectory of its own. Methodological developments originating from jurisprudence are scarce or non-existing, and the effectiveness of IT-related alternatives also makes it relevant to wonder to what extent and in which contexts traditional legal methods and processes will endure.

> While legal problem solving will not be eliminated in tomorrow's legal paradigm, it will nonetheless diminish markedly in significance. The emphasis will shift towards legal risk management supported by proactive facilities which will be available in the form of legal information services and products. As citizens learn to seek legal guidance more regularly and far earlier than in the past, many potential legal difficulties will dissolve before needing to be resolved. Where legal problems of today are often symptomatic of delayed legal input, earlier consultation should result in users understanding and identifying their risk and controlling them before any question of escalation. (Susskind 1998: 290)

For many centuries law has been an important and often unchallenged mechanism for addressing problems and ensuring control. These tasks are now being taken over, and the issue is to see to it that the systems addressing problems and ensuring control can be controlled. This is not primarily a question about formulating legal provisions, but rather a question about developing theoretical models for understanding and sustainable technical methods.

VI. SEPARATION, INTEGRATION OR DOWNFALL?

What has been described here is how an increased awareness of methodological shortcomings, which started as internal discussions within jurisprudence, has come to be expressed in the academic disciplines sociology of law and legal informatics, undertakings which are different but interlinked by common aims – to broaden the jurisprudential perspective and encourage the inclusion of scientific methods. The connection with jurimetrics is also illustrated – an interdisciplinary and bridging approach which initially demonstrated a practical interrelationship between the topics.

Sociology of law and legal informatics have both deepened the understanding of the preconditions for legal solutions and in various ways been able to relate new – as well as previously overlooked – methods to the legal field. It is nevertheless apparent that their practical outcomes are of different kinds and that their influence on traditional jurisprudence has been limited. A considerable portion of academic jurisprudence is still occupied with trying to understand the nature of law, and law students are taught to solve what are considered to be legal problems in reactive manners. Countless calls for methodological revisions have had little influence, despite being articulated for well over a century.

At the same time, it is obvious that the preconditions have changed. Technological progress propelled by digitalisation is affecting all parts of society in a profound way. The legal domain is not immune to this development and technology can in many ways provide complements and alternatives to legal solutions (Wahlgren 2018a). This represent a considerable shift, as reactive problem-solving methods are being replaced by proactive problem-elimination mechanisms. Changes of this kind are already ongoing, often with remarkably good results. The same is true for the impact of digital infrastructures on efficiency and quality in legal management and public administration. It is also undisputable that technical solutions have the potential to verify the effects of various regulative approaches by means of providing mechanisms for collection of control data (Wahlgren 2018b). The latter is a function which until recently has been underdeveloped and frequently non-existent. From this perspective it might therefore appear as if the future is bright. The fact that this development is, to a large extent, driven by technology and non-lawyers nevertheless gives rise to a number of questions.

What if jurisprudence continues to ignore new ways in which human activities are expected to be carried out in order to ensure reasonable demands for efficiency and quality? What if law school curriculums no longer reflect the standardised ways in which transactions and problem solving are managed in society? And, if the answers to these questions give rise to a fear that jurisprudence will continue to be marginalised, is reorientation still an option, or is it already too late? Is Loevinger's more than 70-years-old 'inescapable fact', cited below, still valid, and, if so, are sociology of law and legal informatics able to fill the void? Alternatively, is it unproblematic to recast fundamental legal principles and teleological interpretation methods into technical solutions, and can these tasks therefore be safely entrusted to tech-companies and engineers without legal training? Can ELSI analyses be automated, and, if so, is this the point in time when confused understandings of the function of jurisprudence finally disintegrate? In retrospect, was jurisprudence merely a historical parenthesis; a dubious control and problem-solving mechanism that an immature civilisation all too long clung to?

> In the field of social control (which is law) we must at least begin to use the same approach and the same methods that have enabled us to progress toward greater knowledge and control in every other field. The greatest problem facing mankind … is the inadequacy of socio-legal methods inherited from primitive ancestors to control a society which, in

all other aspects, is based upon the powerful techniques of a sophisticated science. The inescapable fact is that jurisprudence bears the same relation to a modern science ... as astrology does to astronomy, alchemy to chemistry, or phrenology to psychology. (Loevinger 1949: 483)

REFERENCES

Allwood, MS (1957) *Eilert Sundt: A Pioneer in Sociology and Social Anthropology* (Oslo, Nordli).

Alpsten, B (2000) 'Något om utvecklingen av rättsinformation i Sverige' (Universitet i Oslo, Institutt for privatrett, Avdeling for forvaltningsinformatikk, Forvaltningsinformatisk notatserie nr 7/00), https://www.jus.uio.no/ifp/om/organisasjon/afin/forskning/notatserien/2000/7_00.html.

Andersdotter, A (2018) 'Djupare juridisk analys med jurimetri – En fallstudie i upphovsrätten' 2018/19 *Juridisk tidskrift* 54.

Banakar, R (2000) 'Reflections on the Methodological Issues of the Sociology of Law' 27(2) *Journal of Law and Society* 273.

—— (2006) 'Sociological Jurisprudence' in P Wahlgren (ed), *Allmän rättslära* (Juridiska institutionen, Stockholms University) 244.

Banakar, R, Dahlstrand, K, and Ryberg Welander, L (eds) (2018) *Festskrift till Håkan Hydén* (Juristförlaget i Lund).

Bengoetxea, J (2020) 'Legal Theory and Sociology of Law' in J Přibáň (ed), *Research Handbook on the Sociology of Law* (Cheltenham, Edward Elgar) 7.

Bing, J and Harvold, T (1977) *Legal Decisions and Information Systems* (Oslo, Universitetsforlaget).

Brown, JR (1961) 'Electronic Brains and the Legal Mind: Computing the Data Computer's Collision with Law' 71(2) *Yale Law Journal* 239.

Chasalo, I (1961) 'The First National Law and Electronics Conference' 4(7) *The American Behavioral Scientist* 31.

CIIR (2022) Center for Information and Innovation Law, Nordic Conference on Law and Information Technology 2022, https://jura.ku.dk/ciir/english/calendar/2022/nclit2022/.

Cotterrell, R (2020) 'Sociological Jurisprudence: Tradition and Prospects' in J Přibáň (ed), *Research Handbook on the Sociology of Law* (Cheltenham, Edward Elgar) 19.

Council of Europe/Committee of Ministers (1992) 'Recommendation of the Committee of ministers to Member States concerning teaching, research and training in the field of law and information technology', Recommendation No R(92)15, 1992.

De Mulder, R, van Noortwijk, K and Combrink-Kuiters, L (2010) 'Jurimetrics Please!' 1(1) *European Journal of Law and Technology*.

Eckhoff, T (1960) 'Sociology of Law in Scandinavia' in *Scandinavian Studies in Law*, vol 4, 29.

EU (2016) European Union Regulation (EU) 2016/679 of the European Parliament and of the Council of 27 April 2016 on the protection of natural persons with regard to the processing of personal data and on the free movement of such data, and repealing Directive 95/46/EC, recital 78, EUR-Lex – 32016R0679 – EN – EUR-Lex (europa.eu).

Foldes, B (1906) 'The Criminal' 69(3) *Journal of the Royal Statistical Society* 558.

Forslund, A-L (1978) *Vad är rättssociologi?* (Stockholm, Publica).

Hart, HLA (1961) *The Concept of Law*, repr 1986 (Oxford, Clarendon).

Holmes, OW Jr (1897) 'The Path of the Law' 10 *Harvard Law Review* 457.

Hydén, H (1986) 'Sociology of Law in Scandinavia' 13(1) *Journal of Law and Society* 131.

—— (ed) (1997) *Rättssociologi – då och nu: En jubileumsskrift med anledning av rättssociologins 25 år som självständigt ämne i Sverige* (Lund, Lund University).

IRI (2022) *The Swedish Law and Informatics Research Institute*, https://irilaw.org.

ISA (2021) *International Sociological Association International Sociological Association*, isa-sociology.org.

Jurimetrics Journal (2021), https://www.americanbar.org/groups/science_technology/publications/jurimetrics/.

Kaijus, E (2008) 'Sociology of Law as a Multidisciplinary Field of Research' in P Wahlgren and H Hydén (eds), *Law and Society*, Scandinavian Studies in Law vol 5 (Stockholm, Almqvist & Wiksell).

Loevinger, L (1949) 'Jurimetrics: The Next Step Forward' 33(5) *Minnesota Law Review* 455.

Libguides (2021) *Sociology of Law: Scholarly publications* (Lund, Lund University).

LSA (2021) Law & Society Association, Home | Law & Society Association | For Sociolegal Scholars, https://www.lawandsociety.org.

NRCCL (2022) Norwegian Research Center for Computers and Law – Department of Private Law, https://www.jus.uio.no/ifp/english/about/organization/nrccl/.

Přibáň, J (ed) (2020) *Research Handbook on the Sociology of Law* (Cheltenham, Edward Elgar).

Rudgard, S (2021) 'Origins and Historical Context of Data Protection Law' European Privacy Chapter One pdf, https://zdocs.ro/doc/european-privacy-chapter-one-j1jr4m8e8g6e.

Saldeen, Åke (1973) *Skadestånd vid äktenskapsskillnad: En rättssociologisk och jurimetrisk studie* (Uppsala, Uppsala University).

—— (1974) 'Synpunkter på tvärvetenskap och jurimetrik' Original in *Mål och metoder för forskning inom civilrätten, Statens råd för samhällsforskning, 1974, s 55–81* (reprinted and updated in *Några skrifter* (Iustus, Uppsala 2004) (De lege).

—— (1978) *En jurimetrisk metod för en rättssociologisk analys, i Festskrift Per Stjernquist*, (Lund) 55.

—— (1980) *Fastställande av faderskap, Norstedts* (Stockholm).

—— (2004) *Några skrifter, Iustus* (De lege, Uppsala).

SARI (1968) Samarbetsorganet (Ju 1968:59) för rättsväsendets informationssystem (SARI) Kommittéberättelse 1968:Ju59 – Riksdagen.

—— (1969) Samarbetsorganet för ADB inom rättsväsendet ed. Kwoc-register över brottsbalken, Stockholm, Samarbetsorganet för ADB inom rättsväsendet 1969.

Seipel, Pr (1970) Om användning av automatisk databehandlingsteknik inom juridiken, Svensk juristtidning, 1970, Part I p. 267–292, Om användning av automatisk databehandlingsteknik inom juridiken | SvJT & part II p. 722–748.

—— (1974) Tvärvetenskapliga perspektiv på juridiken, in Statens råd för samhällsforskning, ed, Mål och metoder för forskning inom civilrätten. Stockholm 1974 p. 82–118.

—— (1977) *Computing Law, Perspectives on a New Legal Discipline* (Stockholm, Liber Förlag).

Stjernquist, P (1958) 'Gransområden mellan rattsvetenskap och samhallsvetenskap Statsvetenskaplig tidskrift' 61(2–3) *Visar* 141.

Strömholm, S (1996) *Rätt, rättskällor och rättstillämpning*, 5th edn (Stockholm, Norstedts juridik) 119.

Susskind, R (1998) *The Future of Law, Facing the Challenges of Information Technology* (Oxford, Clarendon).

TfRs (1983–90) Tidskrift för rättssociologi, 1983-90 Arkiv | Tidskrift för rättssociologi, https://journals.lub.lu.se/trs/issue/archiv.

Treves, R (ed) (1968) *Nuovi Svi luppi della Sociologia del Diritto* (Milan, Edizione di Comunitá).

Wahlgren, P (1992) *Automation of Legal Reasoning, A Study on Artificial Intelligence and Law* (Boston, Kluwer).

—— (2018a) 'Automatiserade juridiska beslut' in M Nääv and M Zamboni, *Juridisk metod*, 2nd edn (Lund, Studentlitteratur AB) 401.

—— (2018b) 'On Regulatory Impact Assessments' in R Banakar, K Dahlstrand and L Ryberg Welander (eds), *Festskrift Håkan Hydén* (Lund, juristförlaget) 751.

Wahlgren, P (ed) (2008) *Law and Society* (Stockholm, SISL) (Scandinavian Studies in Law, vol 53).

Wiener, N (1948) *Cybernetics: Or Control and Communication in the Animal and the Machine* (Paris, Hermann & Cie).

Zabala, FJ and Silveira, FF (2019) *Decades of Jurimetrics* (School of Technology, Pontifícia Universidade Católica do Rio Grande do Sul).

Ziegert, KA (2018) 'Ernst Rabel's Kaleidoscope: The Quest for Legal Science' in R Banakar, K Dahlstrand and L Ryberg Welander (eds), *Festskrift Håkan Hydén* (Lund, juristförlaget) 793.

18

Minding the 'Gap' Problem: The Relevance of Combining Top-down and Bottom-up Approaches to the Study of Law's Role in Everyday Life

STINE PIILGAARD PORNER NIELSEN

I. INTRODUCTION

THE STUDY AND conceptualisation of law's role in social life and in society have been discussed extensively among sociologists of law, and Reza Banakar's work has contributed widely to these debates on the possibilities, potentials as well as challenges related to socio-legal academic endeavours. He leaves behind ideas and approaches that are, and will continue to be, of great inspiration to socio-legal scholars.

In the late 1990s, Banakar described the discipline of sociology of law as a 'step-child': a discipline which belongs to neither the discipline of law nor to sociology. Banakar argued that the lack of 'intellectual coherence' related to the character of law and the role of law in society results in a fragmented field of research which calls for a systematic development of the discipline of sociology of law (1998). This argument caused quite a debate in which among others Thomas Mathiesen and Jørgen Dalberg-Larsen participated, referring to the fragmented character of the discipline as liberating (Dalberg-Larsen 2000; Mathiesen 1998) and as 'virtues rather than vices' (Mathiesen 1998). Håkan Hydén argued that common themes or fields of research may bridge the differences characterising the discipline of sociology of law, however stressing, as Banakar also did, that the diversity of theoretical perspectives may contribute to insights into the different forms that law may take in social life and in society (Banakar 1998; Hydén 1999). Later, Banakar developed his arguments as a result of the debate caused by his 1998 article. In his book, *Merging Law and Sociology*, Banakar wrote, 'sociology of law has an intrinsic value of its own that lies beyond the disciplinary boundaries of both law and sociology. It can say something about law and society which neither law nor sociology can articulate itself' (Banakar 2003).

The development of sociology of law as a discipline has, among other things, brought along discussion on the so-called gap problem referring to, on the one hand, studies on legislature's intentions, and, on the other hand, studies on law's role in shaping normative practices in ordinary life (Banakar 2015). Studies in the gap problem investigate, for example, law's effectiveness as reflected in discrepancies between legislators' intentions and law's effect in society, and between ordinary people's use of norms to organise social life and formal law's role in organising society (Sarat 1985; Nelken 1981; Pound 1910; Ehrlich 2009). The gap problem thus takes on different forms, including a *methodological* form which refers to the different methodological approaches applied. This methodological gap problem is reflected in a top-down approach that takes a starting point in formal law to analyse its impact on society, and a bottom-up approach that investigates individuals' perception of law (Banakar 2015). This chapter attempts to mind the methodological gap by combining a top-down *and* bottom-up approach to the analysis of law's role in everyday life. To investigate law's role in everyday life, employment case handling in the context of the Danish welfare state is selected as a practice case.

First, the chapter introduces the practice case of employment case handling to provide the reader with an insight into the context of the analysis of law's role in everyday life. Then, a section outlines the methodological approaches applied and the analysis of, first, law's role in everyday life from a top-down approach, drawing on Sheila Jasanoff's co-production theory and empirical data from document analysis of relevant sections of formal law and from observations of caseworkers' practices in the employment case handling process. Then, the section applies a bottom-up approach to investigate how caseworkers' and citizens' perception of and experience with law inform their social practice, drawing on the concept of legal consciousness and empirical data from semi-structured individual interviews with both the citizens and the caseworkers. Subsequently, the chapter is concluded with reflections on the relevance of minding the gap between a top-down and a bottom-up approach in analysing law's role in everyday life and the potential explanatory forces of analyses that mind this methodological gap.

II. EMPLOYMENT CASE HANDLING AS A PRACTICE CASE

From a sociological perspective, cases offer insights into the complexity of social life and allow for analyses that move beyond the specific case in question and relate relevant findings to a societal level (Banakar 2009). In this chapter, employment case handling in the context of the Danish welfare state is included as a practice case to analyse law's role in the social processes pertaining to employment case handling (Flyvbjerg 2001; 2006).

From a socio-legal perspective, employment case handling is relevant as a practice case to understand the role of law in public encounters as these unfold between employment caseworkers and ordinary citizens who experience unemployment. The area of employment is highly legally regulated, subjected to frequent legal changes and complex social law characterised by framework law which regulates competences and procedures that invites professional discretion (Nielsen 2020;

Dalberg-Larsen 1991; Hydén 1985; 1998). The practice case allows for the analysis of law's multiple characters as reflected in, for example, formal law's structuring of employment caseworkers' space for manoeuvre, and of how caseworkers' and citizens' perceptions of law inform their practices (Banakar 2000; Nelken 1998).

Existing research which applies a top-down approach to the study of welfare states' employment policies and law identifies a tendency of so-called workfare and an increased focus on activation as eligibility criteria for income support. In the context of the Danish employment case handling, activation is both a right and an obligation and refers to labour-market related activity initiated for unemployed persons by the jobcentre. This can be, for example, internship at a company or enrolment in an educational programme with the purpose of mapping out and improving unemployed persons' ability to work. This tendency is reflected in, for example, sources of law which outline objectives and procedures for employment case handling, stressing that unemployment is to be addressed through the introduction of incentive structures for unemployed persons, such as reduced social security, stricter work tests and activation obligations (Clasen and Oorschot 2002; Kildal 2001; Handler 2004). Research that applies a bottom-up approach suggests that unemployed citizens as welfare recipients may experience law as 'all over', indicating that law pervades and dominates their ordinary life (Sarat 1990). Additionally, law may be experienced as 'encroaching' on their social as well as private sphere (Zacher 1987), which potentially causes conflicts in the interactions between caseworkers and citizens (Nielsen 2020).

In this chapter, the focus is on the role of formal law in structuring caseworkers' space for manoeuvre in employment case handling *and* on the caseworkers' and citizens' perceptions of and experiences with the law. The empirical data,[1] which consist of document analysis of sources of law, observations of caseworkers' practices in their interactions with the citizens, and semi-structured individual interviews with both caseworkers and citizens, suggest that employment caseworkers perform professional discretion informed by the legal space for manoeuvre, by their perception of law, and by their assessment of the citizens' needs for support. As public officials, the employment caseworkers are powerful actors as they hold authority to exercise professional discretion in the citizens' case handling process (Lipsky 2010; Nielsen 2020; Lemann Kristiansen 2013). The caseworkers enter into employment case handling as part of their everyday job, whereas some of the citizen respondents experience law as, to a large extent, affecting their private sphere, reflecting Sarat's findings of the law as omnipresent in the life of welfare recipients.

III. COMBINING METHODOLOGICAL APPROACHES TO THE STUDY OF LAW'S ROLE IN EVERYDAY LIFE

Some socio-legal researchers argue that sociology of law as a discipline must be empirical to analyse law's constitutive in social relations where 'law may at first glance seem virtually invisible' (Silbey and Sarat 1987). The empirical character of socio-legal

---

[1] The chapter is based on the PhD thesis *Ikke-jurister i et retligt højspændingsfelt – når sagsbehandlere og borgere samproducerer sagsbehandling*. The thesis is available at https://doi.org/10.21996/9c7y-gr54.

studies contributes with analyses of law's role as, for example, an instrument to implement policies, to express societal values, to play a normative role in informing individuals' understandings of their rights and obligations, as well as to have a constitutive effect in guiding actions and shaping social relations, thereby manifesting itself in different forms (Banakar 2003; 2009; 2015; Cotterrell 1992; Hydén 1999; Hammerslev and Nielsen 2020). It may be argued that this fragmented understanding of law's character calls for multiple methodological approaches to understand its role in society. Here, methodology is key, as it strengthens transparency and research quality control through the account of choices of method and theory (Banakar and Travers 2005b).

A. A Top-down Approach: Formal Law Structures Interactions

A top-down approach to the study of law's role in society takes its analytical starting point in formal law and in the attitudes of those responsible for law's implementation, for example public administrators (Banakar 2015), including employment caseworkers. In this chapter, the top-down approach to law's role in society draws on Jasanoff's theory of co-production and on empirical data from document analysis of relevant sources of employment law and on observations of caseworkers' interactions with unemployed citizens. The intention behind applying a top-down approach is to investigate *how formal law structures caseworkers' practices in the case handling process*.

From a co-production perspective, legal texts reflect institutionalised legitimate knowledge on societal (un)accepted behaviour (Jasanoff 1999; 2004; Lee et al 2018), and the texts may be considered a source of sociological data as they contribute to the structuring of social life (Banakar and Travers 2005a). Drawing on Jasanoff's theory of co-production, legal texts are coined as *knowledge actants* which maintain and reproduce knowledge on accepted behaviour and societal ideals. Caseworkers are coined as *knowledge actors* who in their interactions with the citizens exchange and negotiate knowledge which structures the course of the case handling process.

As a knowledge actant, formal law structures the purpose of and the procedures related to the employment case handling, reflecting societal legitimised knowledge of the aim of the process and how to realise this aim. Applying the method of document analysis to relevant sources of law enables analyses of the legislator's intentions and of the space for manoeuvre as structured by law. The objects clause of the Employment Act[2] states that employment case handling is, as quickly and efficiently as possible, to support unemployed citizens' re-entry into the labour market. The objective is to be realised through the legal regulation of procedures pertaining to employment case handling, for example the Act's section 27, part 1, which stresses that adequate support is to be provided in the interactions between employment caseworkers and unemployed persons. These interactions are referred to as job interviews, and the focal point of the job interviews is to discuss and assess the citizens' ability to work and their employment prospect (Nielsen 2020). As part of the

---

[2] The Employment Act, no 548 of 07/05/2019.

assessment process and the mapping of the unemployed citizens' ability to work, the citizens are referred to activation, such as wage subsidy jobs or internships, as regulated in the Act's section 28, part 2. The citizens are obliged to be at the disposable of the labour market, and as stressed in the Act's section 54, part 1, caseworkers may refer citizens to activation if there is doubt related to citizens' willingness to adhere to this obligation or may impose sanctions on citizens if the citizens fail to attend job interviews. The Act's objects clause and sections on caseworkers' options for sanctioning the citizens reflect societal accepted knowledge that the citizens' road to re-entering the labour market is paved with their willingness to contribute actively to the employment-handling process.

To examine caseworkers' practices in the employment case handling process, data was also collected through observations of the job interviews between caseworkers and citizens. The job interviews took place at municipal job centres, and the caseworkers would, as regulated by law, summon citizens to the job interviews; the citizens may, as mentioned, be sanctioned for failing to turn up. Data from the observations of the interactions between caseworkers and citizens reflect a general interaction pattern: the citizens announced their arrival at the job centre's reception desk, and the caseworkers would then come to meet them. Often, the conversations would begin with small-talk related to the citizens' family, pets, or leisure pursuits. As most of the citizen respondents had been unemployed for years, they would have interacted with the employment caseworker several times, and this conversational introduction was a means by which the caseworkers could attune to the citizens before moving on the 'real' focus of the interaction, namely the status and prospect of the citizens' situation. The caseworkers would ask about the citizens' situation, for example their wage subsidy job or internship. This part of the conversation would contribute to uncovering the citizens' experience of their work ability and to assessing the need for support to further the citizens' situation. Often, the conversations would be about the number of hours of the citizens' activation, the number of job applications that the citizens had sent, and the physical and mental state of the citizens. The caseworkers drew on this information to assess the next step in the case handling process, which generally implied an increase in the number of work hours in their wage subsidy job, encouraging the citizens to send out more job applications, and, when relevant, referring the citizens to professional help, for example to physicians, psychologists, and substance abuse centres.

Applying the top-down approach allowed for the analysis of how formal law structured caseworkers' practices in the case handling process, thereby examining the role of law in the practices of caseworkers as public officials. Based on the empirical data, it may from a co-production perspective be argued that the legal texts as knowledge actants reflect knowledge on the accepted focus of the employment case handling related to the increased focus on workfare and activation. Moreover, the legal texts reflect expectations of caseworkers' work performance, namely that of clarifying citizens' ability to work through activation schemes as means to support citizens' re-entry into the labour market. Caseworkers would, as knowledge actors, transform law's focus into practice, as they negotiated knowledge on the further cause of case handling process, drawing on the information exchanged in the interactions with the citizens (Nielsen 2020).

B. A Bottom-up Approach: Perceptions of Law Inform Practices

A bottom-up approach to the study of law focuses on, for example, how people experience law and the meaning that law has to them; the approach contributes by providing insights into individuals' use of law in their organisation of their social life (Banakar 2003; 2015). Drawing on the theoretical concept of legal consciousness and on empirical data from interviews with the unemployed citizens and the employment caseworkers, this section applies a bottom-up approach to investigate how caseworkers' and citizens' legal consciousness affect their social practices in the case handling process.

The concept of legal consciousness contributes to analyses of the construction of meaning in the social world, and it takes on a contingent and subjective character as new experiences, understandings, and perceptions of law shape individuals' legal consciousness (Cowan 2004; Engel 1998; Ewick and Silbey 1998; Hertogh and Kurkchiyan 2016). Thus, legal consciousness may be applied as an analytical tool to investigate individuals' perceptions of law and how the perceptions inform actions (Ewick and Silbey 1999; Hoffmann 2003; Hull 2016; Silbey 2005; Young 2014). Methodologically, semi-structured interviews were in this case conducted with both caseworkers and citizens to allow for the unfolding of respondents' narratives, which enabled the analysis of how their legal consciousness affected their social practices.

In the interviews, the subjective character of legal consciousness was, for example, reflected in the citizens' experience of their agency in the case handling process. One citizen respondent shared his experiences of being neither listened to nor taken seriously in the case handling process. Once, he had been referred to activation, which led to stress, then led to relapse into substance abuse. The experience made him suspicious of plans for future activation, but he considered himself to be 'merely a pawn in the municipality's game' and that he would 'have no say in the process, I just have to do what they tell me to'. His narrative reflected an understanding of being subjected to the municipality's organisation of the case handling process, which caused him to settle into resignation and to display passive behaviour in the process. Another citizen respondent explained that his caseworker had helped him to get clean and to structure his everyday life. 'Just be honest and tell truth. That's how they [the caseworkers] can help you', he said in the interview. His trust in his caseworker's ability to further his situation thus informed his practices and increased his agency and active participation in the encounters. Citizens would also share experiences of conflicts and confrontations in their case handling process. A respondent told me that he was referred to activation, but this was, in his opinion, incompatible with his responsibilities as a parent, as he had 'a child who needs me to be there. And I can't be there when I am off to do some activation'. In this case, his obligations in his private sphere clashed with those in the social sphere of the case handling as formulated in law, resulting in a conflict of interest between him and his caseworker.

From the caseworkers' perspective, law was considered on a general as well as specific level. On a general level, a caseworker explained that 'law is in everything we do. How we assess the citizens and what we plan for the future'. Law's structuring effect thus informed the caseworker's understanding of her work and her practices in the interactions with the citizens. Another caseworker thought of law as potentially obstructive to establishing trust, as 'talking with the citizens about law stresses my authority, and that's no good if I need the citizens to trust me'. The caseworkers are, as public officials, legally obliged to inform the citizens about their rights and obligations, and though aware of law's role in the case handling process, the caseworker would refrain from actively addressing law in the interactions, as law, from the respondent's perspective, spoiled the process of establishing trust. Several caseworkers mentioned trust as a decisive factor for facilitating a positive change in the citizens' situation, and perceiving law as an obstacle to achieving this end indicates that some caseworkers' practices are motivated by social aspects rather than their legal obligations. On a specific level, some caseworkers would instrumentalise law to further the case handling process, as a caseworker explained, 'I sanction the citizens in case of no-show. It's a great way to get them to show up again. Then I can help them again'. In this case, the caseworker's legal consciousness spurred her to translate her powerful position of authority into that of a helper, reflecting a perception of the case handling process as a process of help and support rather than of control and sanctioning where formal law allowed her to actualise mechanisms of help to further the citizens' situation. Another caseworker explained that she would tell the citizens about their rights and obligation 'when it is *needed* for them to know, not [when it is] *nice* to know. They can't cope with the information, anyway'. Her assessment of the individual citizen, based on her interactions with the citizen, would thus determine the legal information she would share, with the potential consequence that the citizens would have only a fragmented legal knowledge. As mentioned, caseworkers are obliged to inform and advise the citizens; however, in this case, the respondent would refrain from carrying out her legal obligation, motivated by a social rather than legal understanding of the citizens' situation.

Applying a bottom-up approach to the study of how caseworkers' and citizens' legal consciousness affect their social practices in the case handling process allowed for the analysis of the complexity of law's role in individuals' organisation of their social life. Based on the empirical data, the subjective character of caseworkers' and citizens' legal consciousness potentially increases the complexity of their encounters as the subjective character informs a variety of social practices which unfold in the case handling process and affects its course.

IV. WHY SHOULD WE MIND THE GAP? REFLECTIONS
ON THE RELEVANCE OF COMBINING METHODOLOGIES

As law may be considered a fragmented phenomenon, taking on a myriad of forms (Aubert 1989), the application of different methodological approaches contributes to a reflexive understanding of the concept of law. When selecting a methodological approach, the researcher also selects a focus for her/his research. This focus allows for an examination of the concept of law within the given focus while excluding other possible foci. Thus, different methodological approaches allow for a broader scope of foci on the character of law (Luhmann 1994). Analysing law's role in everyday life situations, for example as in encounters between public officials and ordinary citizens (Hertogh 2018), through a top-down *and* a bottom-up approach invites insights into law's structuring capacity, and into how individuals' perceptions of and experiences with law guide their social practices. Existing research has, from a top-down approach, shed light upon, among other things, law's role in organising public officials' work, and the relationship between political objectives and the formulation of law (Lemann Kristiansen 2001; Kildal 2001), and, from a bottom-up approach, investigated citizens' experiences with public encounters, and how welfare recipients' perception of access to support in the welfare system affect their practices (Danneris 2018; Høilund and Juul 2015). This chapter attempts to mind the methodological gap by combining the top-down and bottom-up approaches, thereby allowing for the analyses of how formal law as well as subjective experiences and perceptions inform social practices in everyday life situations. Drawing on empirical data, the chapter's analysis investigates law's constitutive effect in the everyday life of employment caseworkers and unemployed citizens. As mentioned, cases may contribute with insights into social life's complexity, and the findings from applying employment case handling as practice case may offer suggestions for the role of law in other encounters involving welfare recipients and public officials.

Minding the methodological gap through the combination of a top-down and a bottom-up approach may strengthen the potential explanatory force related to analyses of law's role in everyday life. The research results presented in the chapter aim to stress the relevance of combining a top-down and bottom-up approach, and when applying a top-down approach, we find that formal law structures the employment caseworkers' work and their approach to the unemployed citizens. This is reflected in law's focus on activation which was also a focal point in the conversations initiated by the caseworkers in the job interviews. Applying a bottom-up approach, we find that perceptions of and experiences with law influence the actors' social practices, and that law from a citizen's perspective may be experienced as dominating, or 'encroaching' on their private sphere; in some situations this causes conflicts that potentially obstruct the case handling process. Also, we find that caseworkers' practices may be motivated by social aspects rather than legal obligations which may conflict with their powerful position and their authority to exercise professional discretion. Minding the methodological gap thus allows for an understanding of law's diverse character which provides analytical insights into law's role in everyday life and in the social complexity of public encounters.

REFERENCES

Aubert, V (1989) *Continuity and Development – in Law and Society* (Oslo, Norwegian University Press/Universitetsforlaget).

Banakar, R (1998) 'The Identity Crisis of a "Stepchild": Reflections on the Paradigmatic Deficiencies of Sociology of Law' 81 *Retfærd: Nordisk juridisk tidsskrift* 3.

—— (2000) 'Reflections on the Methodological Issues of the Sociology of Law' 27 *Journal of Law and Society* 273.

—— (2003) *Merging Law and Sociology: Beyond the Dichotomies of Socio-Legal Research* (Berlin, Galda and Wilch Publishing).

—— (2009) 'Law Through Sociology's Looking Glass: Conflict and Competition in Sociological Studies of Law' in A Denis and D Kalekin-Fishman (eds), *The ISA Handbook in Contemporary Sociology: Conflict, Competition, and Cooperation* (London, Sage).

—— (2015) *Normativity in Legal Sociology: Methodological Reflections on Law and Regulation in Late Modernity* (London, Springer).

Banakar, R and Travers, M (2005a) 'Studying Legal Texts' in R Banakar and M Travers (eds), *Theory and Method in Socio-Legal Research* (Oxford, Hart Publishing).

—— (eds) (2005b) *Theory and Method in Socio-Legal Research* (Oxford, Hart Publishing).

Clasen, J and Oorschot, WV (2002) 'Work, Welfare and Citizenship: Diversity and Variation within European (Un)employment Policy' in J Goul Andersen, J Clasen, WV Oorschot and K Halvorsen (eds), *Europe's New State of Welfare* (Bristol, Policy Press).

Cotterrell, R (1992) *The Sociology of Law: An Introduction* (London, Butterworths).

Cowan, D (2004) 'Legal Consciousness: Some Observations' 67 *The Modern Law Review* 928.

Dalberg-Larsen, J (1991) *Ret, styring og selvforvaltning: retssociologiske artikler og en introduktion til emnet* (Aarhus, Juridisk Bogformidling).

—— (2000) 'Sociology of Law from a Legal Point of View' 89 *Retfærd: Nordisk juridisk tidsskrift* 26.

Danneris, S (2018) 'Ready to Work (Yet)? Unemployment Trajectories among Vulnerable Welfare Recipients' 17 *Qualitative Social Work* 355.

Ehrlich, E (2009) *Fundamental Principles of the Sociology of Law* (New Brunswick, NJ, Transaction).

Engel, DM (1998) 'How Does Law Matter in the Constitution of Legal Consciousness?' in BG Garth and A Sarat (eds), *How Does Law Matter?* (Evanston, IL: Northwestern University Press).

Ewick, P and Silbey, SS (1998) *The Common Place of Law: Stories from Everyday Life* (Chicago, University of Chicago Press).

—— (1999) 'Common Knowledge and Ideological Critique: The Significance of Knowing That the "Haves" Come Out Ahead' 33 *Law & Society Review* 1025.

Flyvbjerg, B (2001) *Making Social Science Matter: Why Social Inquiry Fails and How it Can Succeed Again* (Cambridge, Cambridge University Press).

—— (2006) 'Five Misunderstandings about Case-Study Research' 12 *Qualitative Inquiry* 219.

Hammerslev, O and Nielsen, SPP (2020) 'Retssociologiske metoder' in CR Hamer and S Schaumburg-Müller (eds), *Juraens Verden: metoder, retskilder og discipliner* (Djøf).

Handler, JF (2004) *Social Citizenship and Workfare in the United States and Western Europe: The Paradox of Inclusion* (Cambridge, Cambridge University Press).

Hertogh, M (2018) *Nobody's Law: Legal Consciousness and Legal Alienation in Everyday Life* (UK, Palgrave Macmillan).

Hertogh, M and Kurkchiyan, M (2016) 'When Politics Come into Play, Law is no Longer Law: Images of Collective Legal Consciousness in the UK; Poland and Bulgaria' 12 *International Journal of Law in Context* 404.

Hoffmann, EA (2003) 'Legal Consciousness and Dispute Resolution: Different Disputing Behavior at Two Similar Taxicab Companies' 28 *Law & Social Inquiry* 619.

Hull, KE (2016) 'Legal Consciousness in Marginalized Groups: The Case of LGBT People' 41 *Law & Social Inquiry* 551.

Hydén, H (1985) *Arbetslivets reglering* (Liber Förlag).

—— (1998). *Rättssociologi som rättsvetenskap* (Lund, Lund University).

—— (1999) 'Even a Stepchild Eventually Grows Up: On the Identity of Sociology of Law' 85 *Retfærd: Nordisk juridisk tidsskrift* 71.

Høilund, P and Juul, S (2015) *Anerkendelse og dømmekraft i socialt arbejde* (Copenhagen, Hans Reitzel).

Jasanoff, S (1999) 'The Songlines of Risk' 8 *Environmental Values* 135.

—— (2004) *States of Knowledge: The Co-production of Science and Social Order* (London, Routledge).

Kildal, N (2001) *Workfare Tendencies in Scandinavian Welfare Policies* (Geneva, International Labour Office).

Lee, M, Natarajan, L, Lock, S and Rydin, Y (2018) 'Techniques of Knowing in Administration: Co-production, Models, and Conservation Law' 45 *Journal of Law and Society* 427.

Lemann Kristiansen, B (2001) *Pantefogderne og deres retsanvendelse* (Copenhagen, Jurist- og Økonomforbundet).

—— (2013) 'Udviklingsfaser i forvaltningens regulering' in O Hammerslev and MR Madsen (eds), *Retssociologi: Klassiske og moderne perspektiver* (Hans Reitzels Forlag).

Lipsky, M (2010) *Street-level Bureaucracy: Dilemmas of the Individual in Public Services* (New York, Russell Sage Foundation).

Luhmann, N (1994) '"What is the Case?" and "What Lies behind It?" The Two Sociologies and the Theory of Society' 12 *Sociological Theory* 126.

Mathiesen, T (1998) 'Is it All That Bad to be a Stepchild? Comments on the State of Sociology of Law' 83 *Retfærd: Nordisk juridisk tidsskrift* 67.

Nelken, D (1981) 'The "Gap Problem" in the Sociology of Law: A Theoretical Review (A)' 1 *The Windsor Yearbook of Access to Justice* 35.

—— (1998) 'Blinding Insights? The Limits of a Reflexive Sociology of Law' 25 *Journal of Law and Society* 407.

Nielsen, SPP (2020) *Ikke-jurister i et retligt højspændingsfelt – når sagsbehandlere og borgere samproducerer sagsbehandling* (PhD, University of Southern Denmark).

Pound, R (1910) 'Law in Books and Law in Action' 44 *American Law Review* 12.

Sarat, A (1985) 'Legal Effectiveness and Social Studies of Law: on the Unfortunate Persistence of a Research Tradition' 9 *The Legal Studies Forum* 23.

—— (1990) '"… The Law Is All Over": Power, Resistance and the Legal Consciousness of the Welfare Poor' 2 *Yale Journal of Law and the Humanities* 343.

Silbey, SS (2005) 'After Legal Consciousness' 1 *Annual Review of Law and Social Science* 323.

Silbey, SS and Sarat, A (1987) 'Critical Traditions in Law and Society Research' 21 *Law & Society Review* 165.

Young, KM (2014) 'Everyone Knows the Game: Legal Consciousness in the Hawaiian Cockfight' 48 *Law & Society Review* 499.

Zacher, H (1987) 'Juridification in the Field of Social Law' in G Teubner (ed), *Juridification of Social Spheres: A Comparative Analysis in the Areas of Labor, Corporate, Antitrust and Social Welfare Law* (Berlin, Walter de Gruyter).

19

Doing Fieldwork in Istanbul Courts: Challenges and Strategies

SEDA KALEM

I. INTRODUCTION

IN THE PERIOD from December 2005 to April 2006, we set out to carry out the first project on accessibility and quality of criminal legal aid in Turkey. The main set of data, apart from interviews and observations in trials, was to come from case file reviews, for which we received a permission letter from the Turkish Ministry of Justice, the highest executive organ for judicial affairs. Despite the letter, based on our previous experiences with judges, we believed it would be appropriate to inform them about the project in person. During this 'initial immersion' in the field (Blanck 1987: 343), we were mainly seeking their cooperation. 'Access', however, turned out to be a much more complex issue than we envisioned (Scheffer et al 2010). Our visits soon revealed that not only would we need to convince the judges, but we would also have to play along with the unforeseen yet quite seminal authority of court clerks if we wanted to have access to files. As we proceeded during this permission-seeking phase, we would sometimes be rejected, get caught up in procedural details or be held for hours only to be asked to come back later, all of which required our management so that we could continue our research (Blanck 1987: 345). Therefore, we came up with spontaneous ways to handle these discomforts emerging in the field.

It was only years later, however, when I went back to reading our 'jotted impressions' of these initial encounters with judges and other court staff (ibid: 347), that I came to terms with the situatedness of our knowledge of the field and how that knowledge was bent and twisted on a continuous basis. Our positions at a law faculty, our former encounters with judicial staff and our institutional proximity to the Ministry of Justice all allowed for a certain familiarity with the world of law that we apparently took for granted. In reality, however, our existing knowledge had to be redefined in the context of hierarchies and power relations that we had not previously been aware of. Field access was, after all, not merely a matter of access to data (Scheffer et al 2010: 25): it was a particular challenge that needed to be problematised and managed in an ongoing fashion which ultimately required a more layered understanding of methods in socio-legal research (Banakar and Travers 2005).

This chapter offers a reflexive account of the process of carrying out a socio-legal study in Istanbul courts. It is a methodological exploration of doing field research in judicial settings with a particular focus on the problem of 'access' which seems to be a rather neglected area of study even among court ethnographers. Despite the remarkable collection of ethnographic studies on courts, and of different legal settings like lawyers' offices and police stations, the interest still mostly seems to lie in an exploration of socio-legal issues like dispute management, attitudes and expectations of litigants, decision-making processes or courtroom communication etc. And recent studies in courtroom ethnography take the courtroom as a particular space for observing the intersection of law and everyday practices (Walenta 2019), as a site of embodied exhibits that allows for a feminist ethnographic account (Faria et al 2019), or as an atmosphere with 'feelings' that need to be explored through participant observation (Bens 2018). Reflexive accounts of what it takes to do research in judicial institutions, and more precisely on the issue of 'access' to courts, however, seem to be rather uncommon (Scheffer et al 2010: 33).[1] The openness of courts and trials as public settings seems to have given the impression that they are a 'research-friendly field compared to other "hidden" events in the Justice System'; however, actual engagement with courts has always proved to be more challenging (Scheffer 2002: 5).

In this context, the chapter also aims to contribute to the still limited – albeit growing – socio-legal research field in Turkey.[2] Not only does this contribution set out to offer practical suggestions on how to go about doing research in courts, but, as Hammersley and Atkinson suggest, 'the discovery of obstacles to access, and perhaps of effective means of overcoming them' would in fact themselves 'provide insights into the social organization of the setting' (as cited in Scheffer et al 2010: 25).

II. ACCESS TO THE FIELD

Before case file review, we conducted 75 interviews with judges, prosecutors and lawyers and carried out a non-participant observation at 173 criminal hearings. For interviews, our most important challenge was reaching our sample, which required us to call each name on a randomised list of judges and prosecutors. We would then set a date for an interview with judges we could reach over the phone and would have to knock on the doors of others and most of the prosecutors for an appointment.[3] None of these activities required much bureaucratic involvement. For case file review, however, we filed a petition at the Ministry of Justice asking for permission to examine closed files. Constitutionally, the Ministry has no authority upon courts and judges regarding their work and decisions. Hence, our appeal was not based on any procedural requirement – it was rather a practical decision based on our previous experiences with judicial research. In fact, six months later, when we received

---

[1] One recent exception is the work of Scheffer et al on access to the 'criminal case load' field (2010). There are also notable works on access to lawyers or their offices (Coutin 2002; Flood 1991; Hoy 1995).

[2] Some of the qualitative works on courts and the legal profession in the last decade are Akbaş 2011; Atılgan 2017; Bakıner 2016; Elveriş 2014; Elveriş 2016; Kalem 2020; Kalem Berk 2015.

[3] For more on methodology, see Elveriş et al 2007.

permission, again guided by our existing knowledge of judicial bureaucracy, we also decided to introduce ourselves in person to the presiding judges of the courts.[4]

We were supposed to visit 110 judges from 16 courthouses located in different parts of Istanbul, varying in distance from five kilometres to sixty. We were aware of the possible difficulties of access and of 'gaining trust and cooperation of participants', so we imagined that these visits would enable us to increase our credibility as researchers in the eyes of the judges and prevent possible complications (Blanck 1987: 344). We were not yet aware, however, that these visits would also compel us to question our taken for granted assumptions about the ways in which judicial processes work and force us to reflect upon our own language, conduct and priorities as researchers. From the very beginning, these visits launched a negotiation phase over access to files that required us to convince judges of the relevance of the research to their work and to the criminal justice system (ibid: 344; Scheffer et al 2010: 42). We initially believed in the power of the formal letter in our hands for proving the significance of our project and hoped that it would reinforce our cooperation with judges. As we proceeded with the project, however, throughout our interactions with judges and court clerks, we realised that the issue of permission was much more layered than we had imagined. Access, in fact, was always contingent.

A. Permission à la Judge

The letter from the Ministry was in fact rather technically formulated and basically left the decision to participate in the study to the discretion of the judges and prosecutors as long as 'their participation did not hinder any judicial activity and services'. This wording was, however, also very strategic. It was formulated in a way that would not sound like the Ministry was giving the judiciary any orders which would violate the constitutionally protected principle of separation of powers. During our visits, however, the reference to the letter in fact unravelled complex relations of power between judiciary and executive. In many instances, the submission of the letter intimidated judges because they felt like the Ministry was forcing them. These reactions were not incidental either. In these reactionary moments, *independence* emerged as one of the most significant self-sustaining values of the field which contributed to the making of its relative autonomy from other fields, in this case the political (Bourdieu 1987). At an early stage in our permission-seeking phase, we had a defining encounter with a judge who did not show any interest in our project. Standing at his door, after briefly presenting ourselves as researchers, we said 'we have permission from the Ministry of Justice' to which he immediately responded in an edgy fashion saying 'Tell Master Minister to call me and ask for permission! I do not give permission!'. This incident was above all a moment of consolidation of judicial authority over political one. By denying recognition of any interference from the political field, the judge was not only consolidating his position within the juridical field but was also reaffirming the boundaries of this social space vis-à-vis the political. In fact, his

---

[4] Şentürk talks about a similar permission phase (2016: 90–92).

referring to the Minister of Justice as 'Master Minister' was a sarcastic denial of the implied authority of the executive over the judiciary.

On the other hand, as we were perceived to be outsiders to this field, we were not acknowledged at all in this encounter. We were not only dismissed, but we were also ignored.[5] By denying us any place in this confrontation between himself as the 'judge of the court' and the Minister of Justice, the judge doubly reaffirmed his position in this structurally organised competition. Judges would also often be rather sceptical about the selection of the files, asking us why we chose those cases because they believed we would not be able to find any legal aid lawyer in those files. In one of those instances, the judge explicitly recommended that we make up all data and then claim to have reviewed 900 files. This was not so much an encouragement towards unethical research as it was an exaggerated expression of the 'uselessness' of our efforts, since he was certain we would not be able to find anything in the files, which was yet another moment of consolidating the authority of his situated knowledge over ours. Throughout the process, we also experienced a number of situations where judges made explicit reference to the independence of the judiciary upon our mentioning the official letter. In one case, when we told the judge that we had permission from the Ministry, his immediate response was 'Let me tell you this straight away. I do not give permission. I do not even like it when I give my files to inspectors!'.

After these initial experiences we realised that the letter we had was not so powerful after all. On the contrary, it could even be the reason for why we were denied access. But the real problem in such instances was in fact not so much the letter itself – because judges did not even ask to see it and we were usually kicked out before we could show it. The real problem was with the way in which *we* used the letter. Initially we referred to the permission of the Ministry thinking that it would make it easier for judges to allow us into their courts. As such, we seem to have positioned ourselves as researchers who already got the permission they needed and so were ready to start their work. These encounters, however, made us realise that referring to an *already received* permission in fact jeopardised our access to the field. This led us to reposition ourselves as researchers seeking judges' *permission*, rather than their cooperation. Consequently, rather than telling judges that we had a permission letter, we started to show our recognition of judges' authority explicitly by reformulating our introduction. We started explicitly stating that the Ministry in fact gave the permission to us, *not* to the judges. This was a reintroduction of us as researchers whose work depended on the approval of these judges.[6]

This strategy of acknowledging our dependency would then launch a process of *supplication* which, according to Schopler and Matthews, works best when there is an arbitrary or accidental component in the power differential (as cited in Jones and Pittman 1982: 247). In our case, this strategy seemed to work because it allowed us to readjust our normative schemas and expectations from formal procedures (Banakar 2019). This was particularly important for our lawyer researchers. Throughout our

---

[5] Coşkun refers to such feelings of inconvenience as a natural part of doing research in institutions where 'hierarchy is felt' (2016: 112).

[6] For a similar reintroduction, see Scheffer et al (2010: 44).

encounters, as the sociologist in the group, I often had to remind them not to frame their requests from the judges within a language of rights. Trained in the word of law, they shared similar dispositional tendencies with judges, particularly in terms of legal framing of issues and a common conviction in the 'power of the form' that allowed them to develop expectations regarding how the system should operate (Bourdieu 1987). Technically, closed case files are open to public so there was in fact no legal obstacle to our access to files. However, *legal* did not need to be the defining word in courtroom operations. In fact, in moments of tension when we were denied access, such normative expectations could easily lead to a competitive struggle over the correct interpretation of the written law between different actors in the juridical field – in our case between non-practising lawyers and judges on the bench. And ultimately, lawyers' challenge to the 'legality' of judges' refusal to grant access to files could jeopardise our whole project, so it needed to be negotiated within the field's own protocols. For all of us, however, these were moments of coming to terms with the incompatibility of our knowledge of law with the practical knowledge of the field, so we needed to develop a 'sense of the situation' that would allow us to deem certain lines of action as doable while casting others as undoable. Hence, we *strategised* (Koğacıoğlu 2003: 19).

Appreciation was a strategy that we previously resorted to during our interviews because when we asked judges their opinions about criminal legal aid, often they would go into details about the problems with the system at large. Aside from commenting on the incapacity of legal aid lawyers, for instance, judges also complained about the workload, pending cases, infrastructural difficulties, lack of trained staff and delays. In such narratives, a desire for appreciation usually intertwined with feelings of disappointment and weariness, all of which were expressed by reference to the *sacrifices* made for the profession. Interestingly, even during our relatively brief encounters for permission, judges would often comment on problems with legal aid and express even more vehemently the problems of the judiciary. Two judges, for instance, furiously stated that in a professional environment where they are even denied basic infrastructural utilities like computers or internet access,[7] talking about judicial independence was nothing but demagogy. Another one complained about archives and mentioned how it was almost impossible to keep documents or find anything in such a badly maintained and disorganised space. These narratives would almost always include complaints about workload that were usually framed in reference to personal problems. One judge would tell us how he could not even go to the dentist while another one said that he was so frustrated with not being appreciated for his sacrifices he has made for doing his job in an 'ideal fashion' that he would leave as soon as he qualified for retirement.

In all these encounters, we found ourselves faced with a highly demotivated and exhausted group of professionals who needed not only to be persuaded about the necessity of the project and its relevance for improving their conditions, but who also needed to be understood and even more importantly flattered. Their feelings of exhaustion were usually intertwined with their complaints about 'not being heard'.

---

[7] Given that the research was conducted 15 years ago, one would assume that these particularly technological problems are no longer valid.

One judge asked us to reveal all these problems with the system because otherwise they would only become 'courtroom chats'. Hence, as the field introduced us to the frustration of these people, we felt as though we had to attend to their needs not only because we depended on their approval but also because we genuinely felt they deserved more appreciation for their 'sacrifices'. We no longer just talked about the project and explained to judges what we needed from them; we also became active listeners to their needs and tried to attend to their occasional demands on us, such as helping them out with their applications to graduate schools.[8] Above all, we increasingly developed a feeling of empathy with their problems and praised them for the work they do and the time they spared for our research. Initially, we tried to make our work seem more relevant for these professionals by referring to the planned impact of the research upon decision-making that could lead to more effective measures in improving the judicial system (Blanck 1987: 344). However, as we proceeded, we moved beyond such 'project proposal phrases' to growing a more genuine interest in listening to these complaints and trying to find ways to make these voices heard. As we grew accustomed to listening to problems, we developed a more real sense of being in the field; trying to manage a balance between the *needs of the research* and the *needs of the respondents*.

Strategising about *how* we would approach judges was also accompanied by fellow strategies on *when* to approach them. As we became more familiar with the field, we came to notice the more appropriate or simply the *better* moments to approach judges. We observed that when we approached them just before lunchtime when they were hungry (hence quite edgy), or when they were rushing to the shuttle (hence quite uninterested), or when they had just come out of a hearing (hence extremely tired), we had a high chance of being rejected. Therefore, we started to pay particular attention to this *sui generis* feature of the field and gradually became more intuitive about our practices which allowed us to grow a sense of the field.

B. Permission à la Clerk

However, access was not guaranteed even with permission granted by judges. New negotiations for access were imposed by the field as we were faced with the unanticipated authority of court clerks. In the judicial organisation, court clerks work for judges and prosecutors, which means that every court and prosecution office has its own registry and staff. The chief clerk is responsible for supervising and managing all paperwork, including but not limited to referring documents submitted by the parties to the court, ensuring the protection of relevant documents, preparing documents regarding the calculation and payment of court fees and handling all relevant operations, ensuring the service of summons and court decisions to the parties etc. Clerks, on the other hand, are responsible for carrying out all the secretarial tasks assigned

---

[8] Mutlu talks about how during her field research in Istanbul and Diyarbakır she was sometimes asked for help and had to assume responsibility for those people who have suffered from forced migration (2016: 53–55). Şentürk also talks about how in the neighbourhood she studied, she felt the urge to make herself 'useful' and so helped her respondents' children with their schoolwork (2016: 80).

by the chief clerk, such as registering new files, being present at hearings and during other procedures like field investigation, testimony taking, autopsies etc.[9]

In our research, the relationship between judges and court clerks presented itself as an unpredictably prominent element of the power relations in this field. The permission process always involved informing court clerks about the case file review, since they were in charge of providing us with these documents and, therefore, they would in fact be doing the real job. However, this was not the whole story. Permission would also need to be filtered via these clerks since they were the real gatekeepers in access negotiations. The letter from the Ministry was again challenged this time by the rather practical authority of these clerks who were the real engines behind the scheduling of court cases and general administration of court files. On many occasions, judges would call in their chief clerks, introduce our project and ask them if they could assist us. Or in others, they would send us to the office to tell the chief clerk that we had already spoken to the judge, and ask them for assistance. At one point, one of the judges even told us to 'treat clerks pleasantly and compromise with them'. Not only was the process more complex than we imagined, but it was surprisingly not as direct as the judges foresaw either.

Two of the leading axes of negotiation with the clerks were regarding the date of the review and the number of files to be drawn. These decisions were almost always made by the chief clerk. In one case for instance, the chief clerk told us that they could take out a maximum of ten files from the archive. We asked her if she could not at least provide 15 to which she agreed at the end. At another court, however, we were not so lucky. Although we did negotiate the number of files with the chief clerk, still when our colleagues went to the court on the set date, they saw that only some of the files were in fact ready. The clerks said they could not take out more since they were too busy, so we had to complete that court with missing files, even though the judge had allowed us to review as many files as we requested. In yet another instance, again even though the judge immediately gave us permission, when we went to the court on the assigned day, we noticed that the clerk did not take out the files. Even though we insisted for the files in our list, the clerk said, 'there is no way I will take out these files for you; I already have tons of work to do'. When our colleagues went back to the court another day, the clerk again tried to complicate our access and in fact ultimately took out less files than we requested. Our team had to compensate for the missing files by asking for more files from another court.[10]

The fact that these obstacles emerged during situations where we in fact believed we had the permission we needed from the judge further complicated the process for us. In cases where judges did not introduce us to chief clerks and instruct them to assist us, we were even more dependent upon the mercy of the clerks. In one such instance, the judge told us to treat clerks with respect and negotiate with them, whereas another judge once very explicitly said 'I cannot give you permission; ask the clerk' and delegated full authority to the chief clerk. In yet another instance, we stopped

---

[9] I use court clerks to refer to all clerks and name them specifically as *chief clerk* and *clerk* when needed.
[10] Similarly, Scheffer et al talk about how during their review of files at a German law firm, the lawyer would select the files himself either because he thought they were interesting or because they covered multiple offences (2010: 38).

by the office to request the files, but the chief clerk said in a rather insurgent manner 'We have so much work, why don't you come later?'. When we told her that the judge told us to come in before 10 January, she exclaimed 'As if he does not know our situation! It's the end of the year, we are very busy!'.[11] After our colleague almost begged for the files, she agreed to help. At the end, however, we managed to review the files we intended to only because one of our colleagues went down to the archive at the basement of the courthouse. Hence, not only did we have to negotiate the date of the review and the number of files, but we would also have to expand the terms of our inclusion to such an extent that we would assume duties of clerks. Access, this time, turned out to be very much contingent upon 'local and inter-personal dynamics' (Scheffer et al 2010: 41).

As we proceeded, we realised that court clerks also had many problems regarding their work and that when we introduced ourselves as another group of people who required even more work from them, they would explode. Given that their biggest problem was their workload, asking them to take out cases from the archives was not always welcome. They would also complain about mistreatment from lawyers, which made them feel even more unappreciated: 'They look down on us. They tell us 'you are just a clerk'. It is like they are cursing at us'. Here, once again, we needed to adjust our modes of approaching these people in order to develop working relations for ongoing access. An explicit recognition of the heavy workload of clerks enabled us to reveal our appreciation for their time and energy. The fact that we were dependent on their cooperation dictated the appropriate attitude that we had to adopt when dealing with these clerks. Koğacıoğlu cites a similar case from an Istanbul courthouse where she observed a respected lawyer commonly using 'flattery and mutual remarks of appreciation' during her dialogues with the clerks (2003: 86). In our encounters with clerks, once again we had to adapt to the rules of the game, readjusting our conviction in the power of judicial hierarchy.

III. ACCESS REVISITED

Scheffer et al argue that 'In ethnographic studies, references to access as a problem itself are as rare as they are precious' (2010: 26). They even criticise Max Travers, among others, for failing to elaborate in his 1997 book on how he gained access to the criminal law firm and managed to follow lawyers through their professional practices at or out of the office (as cited in Scheffer et al 2010).[12] Even in cases where the researcher recognises challenges of doing fieldwork in courts, still the question of access to large sets of quantitative data is handled through a simple reference to permission that seems to have been achieved and practised problem free (Biagini 2016: 74). As these documents are publicly accessible, there would usually be no expectation that accessing those data sites would require any special consideration from researchers.

---

[11] All these moments were also occasional opportunities for clerks to overturn the power dynamic between them and the judges. By defying the word of the judge, the clerks were also demonstrating to us their significance in the courtroom operations as the practical authority behind the files.
[12] For other works criticised for failing to elaborate 'access', see Scheffer et al (2010: 25–26).

Problematising access as an ongoing process of continuous negotiation, on the other hand, allows for an observation of the field as a real site with flesh and blood where you are not only concerned with the implications of your data but also with how to reach that data in the first place. This reflexive exploration of what it takes to do fieldwork in Istanbul courts also attests to the impossibility of taking access for granted. In our case, the performances we developed during the initial immersion in the field allowed us to manoeuvre 'in ways that are competent with the field's organisational conditions and cultural conventions' (Alvesson 1994). As we moved in and out of courts, trying to catch judges on their way to hearings, approaching clerks for suggestions on how to reach judges, waiting in their offices for setting a date for case file review, we were constantly made aware of our lack of practical sense of the field. Through the strategies we employed, we in fact developed a 'feel for the game' (Bourdieu 1990: 66). In a way, we gradually learned to show these actors that we were 'willing to take the time to learn about their worlds' (Barrett 2018). Consequently, this entire process of permission-seeking among judges and clerks unfolded as a game of (re)determining and (re)negotiating the boundaries of what was possible in the field of law (Bourdieu 1987). As such, it proved to offer valuable information regarding the normalisation of the convergence of the formal with the informal in a particular judicial setting (Koğacıoğlu 2008: 114). As we observed how informal modes of communication and conduct developed by different actors with different capital in fact challenged our liberal assumptions on a continuous basis, we had to readjust our own positions within this field as actors with certain expectations and skills.

Finally, this problematisation of access 'as a continuous and changeable phenomenon of its own' not only allowed us to see its ongoing nature that extends into each phase of the fieldwork (Scheffer et al 2010: 46), but it also compelled us to continue thinking about its possibilities as a politically and socially contingent issue. I believe that the flexible boundaries of any field which are subject to change with social and political circumstances and developments can perhaps best be observed through a discussion of the contingency of access as a methodological issue. Hostile environments for social research are certainly not limited to conflict zones (Gasser 2006). In fact, issues of access – especially more subtle ones like ensuring the willing cooperation of the actors or convincing them of the academic purposes of the research, guaranteeing confidentiality etc – are significant problems for researchers in particular in all politically unstable settings.

That is why the timing of this piece is not coincidental. It was in fact a decade after the original research that I started to think about the challenges one would face if similar research were to be carried out today. When we were on the field in early 2000s, Turkey was in the midst of accession negotiations with the EU which also instigated a period of sweeping legal changes with an increased cooperation between the Ministry of Justice and legal academia. Today, however, the current political situation in Turkey forces us to question the possibility of such a fieldwork not only in terms of getting the approval of the Ministry but also regarding the possibility of building a partnership with judges and court staff. Especially after the 2016 coup attempt against the government, which resulted in the dismissal and detention of thousands of judges and prosecutors, doing court research today would probably create more diverse and probably more complex barriers for access.

REFERENCES

Akbaş, K (2011) *Avukatlık Mesleğinin Ekonomi Politiği: Avukatların Sınıfsal Konumlarındaki Değişim* (Ankara, NotaBene).

Alvesson, M (1994) 'Talking in Organizations: Managing Identity and Impressions in an Advertising Agency' 15(4) *Organization Studies* 535.

Atılgan, EÜ (2017) *Türkiyede'ki İç Hukuk Kültürü Üzerine Sosyo-Hukuki Bir Araştırma: Haksız Tahrik Kararlarında Eril Tahakküm Kodları* (Ankara, Turhan Kitabevi).

Bakıner, O (2016) 'Judges Discover Politics: Sources of Judges' Off-Bench Mobilization in Turkey' 4(1) *Journal of Law and Courts* 131.

Banakar, R (2019) 'On Socio-Legal Design', available at https://papers.ssrn.com/sol3/papers.cfm?abstract_id=3463028.

Banakar, R and Travers, M (2005) 'Introduction' in R Banakar and M Travers (eds), *Theory and Method in Socio-Legal Research* (Oxford, Hart Publishing).

Barrett, CJ (2018) 'Doing Court Ethnography: How I Learned to Study the Law in Action' in SK Rice and MD Maltz (eds), *Doing Ethnography in Criminology: Discovery Through Fieldwork* (Springer).

Bens, J (2019) 'The Courtroom as an Affective Arrangement: Analysing Atmospheres in Courtroom Ethnography' 50(3) *The Journal of Legal Pluralism and Unofficial Law*.

Biagini, M (2016) 'Revisiting Ethnography for Dialogue Interpreting Research' in C Bendazzoli and C Monacelli (eds), *Addressing Methodological Challenges in Interpreting Studies Research* (Cambridge, Cambridge Scholars Publishing).

Blanck, P (1987) 'The Process of Field Research in the Courtroom: A Descriptive Analysis' 11(4) *Law and Human Behavior* 337.

Bourdieu, P (1987) 'The Force of Law: Toward a Sociology of the Juridical Field' 38(5) *Hastings Law Journal* 814.

—— (1990) *The Logic of Practice* (Cambridge, Polity).

Coşkun, E (2016) 'Bunların Gerçekten Olduğuna İnanmıyor Musunuz?': Araştırma Etiğine Dair 'Yukarıdan' Notlar' in R Harmanşah and Z.N Nahya (eds), *Etnografik Hikayeler: Türkiye'de Alan Araştırması Deneyimleri* (Istanbul, Metis).

Coutin, SB (2002) 'Reconceptualizing Research: Ethnographic Fieldwork and Immigration Politics in Southern California' in J Starr and M Goodale (eds), *Practicing Ethnography in Law: New Dialogues, Enduring Methods* (New York, Palgrave Macmillan).

Elveriş, İ (2014) *Barolar ve Siyaset: Türkiye'de Barolar ve Devlet Kurumları* (Istanbul, İstanbul Bilgi Üniversitesi).

—— (2016) 'Cause Lawyering When It Really Matters: How Istanbul Lawyers Reacted to Events in Gezi' 23(2) *International Journal of the Legal Profession* 131.

Elveriş, İ, Jahic, G and Kalem, S (2007) *Alone in the Courtroom: Accessibility and Impact of Criminal Legal Aid in Istanbul Courts* (Istanbul, İstanbul Bilgi Üniversitesi).

Faria, C, Klosterkamp, S, Torres, RM and Walenta, J (2019) 'Embodied Exhibits: Toward a Feminist Geographic Courtroom Ethnography' 110(4) *Annals of the American Association of Geographers*.

Flood, J (1991) 'Doing Business: The Management of Uncertainty in Lawyer's Work' 25(1) *Law and Society Review* 41.

Gasser, N (2006) *Conducting Field Research in Contexts of Violent Conflict: An Annotated Bibliography. NCCR North–South Dialogue Working Paper No 16* (Bern, NCCR North-South).

Harmanşah, R and Nahya, ZN (eds) (2016) *Etnografik Hikayeler: Türkiye'de Alan Araştırması Deneyimleri* (Istanbul, Metis).

Hoy, JV (1995) 'Selling and Processing Law: Legal Work at Franchise Law Firms' 29(4) *Law and Society Review* 703.

Jones, EE and Pittman, TS (1982) 'Toward a General Theory of Strategic Self-Presentation' in J Suls (ed), *Psychological Perspectives on the Self* (New Jersey, Lawrence Erlbaum).

Kalem, S (2020) 'Being a Woman Judge in Turkish Judicial Culture' 27(2) *International Journal of the Legal Profession* 119.

Kalem Berk, S (2015) 'Arabuluculuk Tartışmaları Üzerinden Türkiye'de Hukuk Mesleğine Bourdieucü Bir Bakış' 132 *Toplum ve Bilim* 191.

Koğacıoğlu, D (2003) 'Law in Context: Citizenship and Reproduction of Inequality in an Istanbul Courthouse' (unpublished doctoral dissertation, Stony Brook University).

—— (2008) 'Conduct, Meaning and Inequality in an Istanbul Courthouse' 39 *New Perspectives on Turkey* 97.

Mutlu, Y (2016) 'Biz ve Onlar Sarkacında: Bir 'Türk' Kadın Araştırmacı Olarak Türkiye'de Zorunlu Kürt Göçü Çalışmanın Şeceresi' in R Harmanşah and ZN Nahya (eds), *Etnografik Hikayeler: Türkiye'de Alan Araştırması Deneyimleri* (Istanbul, Metis).

Scheffer, T (2002) *Exploring Court Hearings – Towards a Research Design for a Comparative Ethnography on 'Witnessing in Court'* (Lancaster, Lancaster University).

Scheffer, T, Kozin, A and Hannken-Illjes, K (2010) *Criminal Defence and Procedure: Comparative Ethnographies in the United Kingdom, Germany, and the United States* (Palgrave Macmillan).

Şentürk, B (2016) 'Mahalle Kahvesinde "abla", Kabul Günlerinde "hanım": Sınıf ve Toplumsal Cinsiyet Bağlamında Gecekonduda Kadın Araştırmacı Olmak' in R Harmanşah and ZN Nahya (eds), *Etnografik Hikayeler: Türkiye'de Alan Araştırması Deneyimleri* (Istanbul, Metis).

Walenta, J (2020) 'Courtroom Ethnography: Researching the Intersection of Law, Space, and Everyday Practices' 72(1) *The Professional Geographer* 131.

Part IV

Comparative Legal Cultures

20

Legal Culture as an Approach to the Study of Law in Russian Society

MARINA KURKCHIYAN

I. INTRODUCTION

R
EZA BANAKAR ONCE pointed out to me that there are only a few concepts that entered the socio-legal field from within the discipline itself rather than from legal studies or other branches of social science. Of these rare offspring, the most notable are 'legal culture', 'legal consciousness' and, to some extent, 'legal pluralism' in its interpretation as a co-existence and interplay of legal cultures within a single political space. Reza had a special interest in using legal culture to link the legal and the social in order to form an empirically grounded and theoretically informed framework that would enable us to study how law is embedded into socio-cultural contexts. In his last publication, on the driving culture in Iran, Reza examined Iranian legal culture as 'a vintage point from which to view how Iranian society is organised' (Banaker 2016: 2).

Having a shared interest with Reza in developing the notion of legal culture, I had many discussions with him on the subject, always thought-provoking, and always containing respectful disagreements scattered among the many views that we shared. Sorting out the disagreements was the part we both valued the most. This paper continues those conversations. It is an attempt to set out my interpretation of the legal culture approach, somewhat divergent from his, but one that reflects the profound benefit I gained from our discussions.

II. LEGAL CULTURE AS AN APPROACH

From a socio-legal perspective, legal culture has been extensively criticised for being too vague and not translatable into an empirical focus of research (Cotterrell 2006: 81–96). For Friedman it is a combination of ideas, attitudes, values, ways of doing and thinking that 'bend social forces toward or away from law (Friedman 1975: 194); for Nelken it is a 'relatively stable pattern of legally-orientated social behaviour and attitudes' (Nelken 2004: 1); for Merry it is a combination of four separate and researchable social facts: the public's attitude towards law, legal consciousness (which she equates to people's awareness of their legal rights), the mobilisation of law (meaning the readiness to use law), and practices within the legal institution (Merry 2012: 53–76). I myself tend to refer to socially constructed meanings, images and roles that are attributed to law. Being such an all-inclusive concept, it is hard to see what exactly the concept covers (see discussion in Nelken 1997: 13–92). Legal culture research very often ends up being a study of just one of those social facts, which is given its own label and arguably does not need to be called 'legal culture'.

The term has received a cool reception from anthropologists as well, who have been having their own in-house battle to get away from the traditional interpretation of culture as a homogenous set of traditions, customs and beliefs that continuously reproduces itself and describes the community (Boellstorff 2003: 225). Arguably, the concept of culture is not equipped to deal sufficiently with the tension between inertia and change. And legal culture being almost universally presented by scholars as a subset of general culture, it has shared the criticism aimed at culture itself.

However, that point is misleading. Undoubtedly there is a big overlap in what the two ideas convey, namely the reproduced patterns of social interaction of a social group and its shared experience of the world around them. But there are also significant differences. In anthropology, 'general culture' carries a meaning of group belonging and identity. For instance, one does not lose easily that sense of identity and cultural capital after moving from one place to another. Legal culture does not have that transportable quality. It describes how law is embedded in one particular social order and identifies the assumptions about law made by people living in that social space. It does not create ties of belonging, so it is much easier to unlearn when people move from one legal environment to another. In making that assertion I take a different view from Nelken, for whom legal culture is about 'who we are' (Nelken 2004: 1). In my understanding, legal culture captures the specificity of the social context, exposing the meanings of law within any particular social unit.

Sociologists, for their part, question the unit of legal culture. There is also an eternal question of how to locate the 'legal' in socio-legal studies, because of the unsolvable dilemmas in how to distinguish law from custom, law from the multiple norms, rules and practices of everyday life. Faced with these ever-decreasing circles of debate, I would rather put my faith in the so-called elephant test: I recognise it when I see it, and importantly, when I see its elephant footprints, even if the elephant is not there. In the socio-legal field we must take care to explain precisely what we mean whenever we use the word 'law' for any particular research purpose. In this paper, I am using the term 'law' straightforwardly, meaning formal law – although in legal culture we often see only the footprints, not the elephant itself.

However, these inconsistencies emerge only if we treat legal culture as a concept, defined by the *Oxford English Dictionary* (*OED*) as 'an abstract idea about social facts used to identify the content or object of specific inquiries. Discussions of concepts in the social sciences tend to be a matter of the choice of terms and, more importantly, of their definitions'. As the debates around legal culture demonstrate, it is difficult to see how legal culture can be reduced to an idea about a particular social fact singled out and defined for the purpose of social enquiry.

Instead, I would argue, legal culture should be treated as an approach. An approach, as the *OED* explains, is a means of access, to take a preliminary step towards consideration, a particular way of dealing with something. It provides a contextual framework for research, a coherent and logical scheme that guides the choices researchers make. To phrase it differently, an approach adjusts the lens that one can use to scrutinise the object of study, in our case laws in societies. It is one of the methodological options in the socio-legal field.

What are the assumptions that tune the lens to bring 'legal culture' into the focus? Epistemologically it is rooted in interpretative approaches in general and constructivism in particular. It evolves from the assumption that social facts are the product of a social context in which their meanings are produced through interactions and learnings to form a localised worldview and, to use Geertz's phrasing, a 'style of social existence' (Geertz 1983: 218). That social existence evolves in the form of 'rules of the game' that are specific to the local context. Law is integrated into that game and plays specific roles that are socially attributed to it within that social fabric.

The legal culture approach takes us to the opposite end of the methodological spectrum from the 'legal family' approach. If the legal family approach is an upward move in the comparative study of legal traditions, and aims to identify similar jurisdictions and assemble them into larger groups (albeit at the expense of marginalising differences), legal culture invites us to make a downward move so that we can spot differences in the nuances of law and describe how they play out in everyday life. The approach requires us to locate and interpret law as it is experienced and thought about by the local people. Looked at from this perspective, law is what people think it is, and legal culture is what they do in response to it.

The approach prompts us to consider a distinct set of questions which point to the convoluted interplay between a way of thinking (legal consciousness) and of acting (observable practice) in the context of legal institutions that evolve through history (Kurkchiyan 2012: 250). But before I demonstrate how the approach guided my years of research in Russia, I would like to discuss some of the challenges that this approach presents.

One of the biggest challenges is to build a bridge between the contemporary social facts and the past, where the past has to be part of the explanation. Any marriage between history and sociology has never been an easy one. It inevitably simplifies whatever version of the past is selected for the explanation and opens up a huge space for speculation. As a result, in many references to legal culture one finds the frequent use of questionable stereotypes about the national character and historically shaped profiles of the psychology of the people. Therefore, looking back into history as an explanation of today's mentality and behaviour must be done with exceptional care. It must be based on accepted historical facts, rather than on assumptions about personalities or superficial cultural descriptions.

The second challenge that the approach presents is how to build a bridge between thinking and acting or how to use an analysis of cognition to explain observable behaviour. In sociology we know very well that there is a big gap between the normative level that people claim to be guided by and their actual behaviour. Behaviour is driven by social expectations and pragmatic calculations, not necessarily by underlying beliefs and attitudes. Therefore, legal culture, an approach that places its questions inside that difficult junction zone, should not be trivialised by simplistic techniques such as measuring attitudes. The legal culture approach invites as to reach much deeper layers of perceptions and meaning, layers that people often do not articulate verbally.

The third challenge is to be consistent in moving away from a western-centred perspective. Taking a western standpoint leads the study of legal culture astray, towards a study focused on legality and the rule of law (Nelken 2020: 136). It usually ends up by questioning what it is that prevents countries outside the western bubble from being able to position law as the key to social order just as it has been positioned across the west. To rephrase the question, this explanatory process is like asking 'why can't they be like us?' As soon as the question is posed in those terms, corruption, politics, national character, tribalism and religion offer themselves as the usual suspects. I would argue that the rule of law model is an ideal type that is relevant only to the western forms of social organisation (Simpson 2000: 53; Kahn 1999). To get away from the western-centred approach is to explore whatever rules may be used to organise life in other communities, like it or not, and possibly emerge from the study with some new ideal types.

And lastly, the legal culture approach poses the challenge of highlighting specific features rather than similarities. Rooted in the ideas that meanings and forms of law emerge from their context, and that each context is marked by distinctiveness, the approach directs us to ask questions and examine the impact of that distinctiveness. As a result, the findings often tend to exaggerate the extent of the uniqueness, and thereby fall into the trap of exceptionalism. It is important not to wriggle out of one mental map only to be caught in another. We need always to bear in mind that a parallel narrative which focused on the similarities would be equally legitimate, even if the two pictures are not placed side by side in a single discourse. Comparative testing of the findings, even if the project itself is not comparative, is essential to highlight the specifics, but also not to overstate them.

III. EXPLORING THE RUSSIAN SOCIO-LEGAL SPACE THROUGH THE LEGAL CULTURE LENS

My instinct to leaning towards the notion of legal culture stemmed from my experience of being an insider as well as a researcher in a variety of settings, including an assortment of western ones as well as Soviet and post-Soviet. When the post-Soviet social order emerged almost overnight out of the ruins of the Soviet era, it catapulted people into a new world that was wholly unfamiliar to them. The transformation of the socio-legal environment was unmissable. The state structures collapsed and institutions ceased to organise the life of the people. Even so, the disrupted social order did not descend into chaos. Instead, a new, bottom-up, self-organised order grew up spontaneously, and developed into a new set of rules of the game. In that new order the former laws remained in play but mutated into insignificant shadows of themselves as the public reconstructed their meanings. Research in the late 1980s and early 1990s in health provision and transport exposed the links between institutional performance, mobilisation of the shared experience of how to make things work, and the formation of social meanings that made sense of the new realities (Kurkchiyan 2000). The very early years of transition openly displayed the socially constructed nature of the law as a social phenomenon with shifting meanings, something that nowadays researchers often take for granted without reflecting on the implications.

The new order achieved a relative stability by the mid-1990s, when the Russian government re-established itself with a policy of embracing a free-market economy. Laws were simply copied from various western jurisdictions and transplanted into the Russian legal soil. It was fascinating to trace out the process by which laws that were highly effective in one context mutated into something quite different when they were inserted into another. Insolvency law is one of many examples. Drafted according to the principles of the 'best practices' learned from western jurisdictions, it was intended to increase debt recovery and to facilitate credit flow. Instead, it became a legitimised means of asset-stripping (Dahan 2003). The problem lay not in the design of the law, which was highly praised by western consultants, nor in any weakness in its implementation and enforcement. The problem lay in the fact that as soon as the law was enacted in Russia, it was adjusted to the local realities by the players on the ground. It was re-interpreted and integrated into the existing game, acquiring a new meaning.

But it is the comparison with the west that brought the notion of legal culture to the centre of my research. I was spurred on by the contrast between the almost-religious faith in the 'the rule of law' that is noticeable in the west, even where the circumstances make it questionable (Ewick and Silbey 1998), and the profound Russian legal nihilism with assumption that law never works, even when there is no reason to doubt that it does work. I call this belief the positive myth versus the negative myth of law. The myths consist of widely shared perceptions of how law works in society, and guides people on what actions to expect from others (Kurkchiyan 2003, 29–34). The question of how to understand this self-reproducing and unfathomable quality of the Russian socio-legal milieu was begging for an answer.

In the attempt to offer that answer, the academic literature almost universally assesses Russia only by its failure to meet western standards. The consensus is that the justice system in Russia is unreliable and corrupt; the judiciary is deemed to be dependent on the state and responds mainly to so-called 'telephone law' (Pastukhov 2002; Ledeneva 2008; Kononenko and Moshes 2011). The question that the commentators usually ask is why law does not work in Russia. The usual answer is because of the Soviet legacy, amplified by the nature of the current political regime. But is it the only answer, or even an accurate one? Can the legal culture approach help to open up a new vision of the role of law in Russian society?

IV. LEGAL FORMALISM AND ITS CONSEQUENCES

The legal culture approach led me to employ a different lens from the mainstream studies of Russian socio-legal space and examine it in its own right. To start my research, I had to demarcate the unit of my analysis. My view is that the notion of legal culture is appropriate to apply to social entities that have sufficient autonomy to generate and modify 'the rules of the game'. Legal culture also requires that experience of the legal environment must have been shared over a sufficiently long period of time to develop relatively stable patterns of legally orientated beliefs, behaviour and institutional tradition. In a few cases such as England, national boundaries contain a relatively homogeneous space with a shared history and experience of law and justice. But in cases such as the Russian Federation, with all its geographical diversity of history, religion, and even contemporary experiences of law in different parts of Russia, it would be misleading to use the national boundaries to discuss a single legal culture. For that reason, I chose to restrict my unit of analysis to the European part of Russia, where law initially evolved from native customs and the people share historical memory over many centuries.

Then, by posing questions at the boundaries of legal consciousness and behaviour, I tried to understand what law means to people and what implications I can link to that state of mind (Kurkchiyan 2009). What became apparent was the extremely formalistic image of law. It is a strong belief that if a law is a good law, it must be applicable to any appropriate circumstance just as it is written. There can be no legitimate requirement for flexibility in implementation. It follows that any discretion in applying the intent of the law to a particular situation must be regarded as manipulation. The tension between the beliefs of how things should be (life regulated by rules that are strict) and how things really are (the perception that law is never accurately applied) generates contradictory feelings. There is a strong drive to bring things under control and at the same time intense disappointment at the repeated failures of all the controlling agencies. This could explain an ongoing attempt in Russian society to impose control systems one above another but without actually trusting anyone to operate them. This interpretation of law has clogged society with petty restrictions. But the people themselves are adaptable, and their experiences have forced them to find ways around restrictions by coming up with a never-ending supply of tricks. That generates the paradox in the Russian approach to law: a powerful demand for formality, legality and better law exists alongside an equally powerful legal nihilism and instinct to solve actual problems informally and whatever means it takes.

The tendency worldwide towards formalism among professionals who work in the civil law tradition is well recorded. It is even more pronounced in Eastern Europe because of the legacy of communist regimes. However, it reaches its extreme in the Russian case, where it has established itself as the only interpretation of the meaning of law. This is not a new phenomenon, or even a Soviet one. Historians of Imperial Russia noted its presence a century earlier as they analysed court archives (Burbank 1997). To explain the origin of this nihilistic mindset we need to briefly trace the trajectory of evolution of law in Russia.

When legal historians describe families of legal traditions, it is routinely assumed that Russian law belongs to the Romano-Germanic tradition, although with some acknowledgment of its peculiarities (Berman 1963: 187). The legal culture approach alerted me that the current closeness of the two systems should not obscure the differences that result from a complicated interplay between native customary law, the western law that was superimposed on it during several phases of modern history, and the disruption caused by the twentieth-century experiment with communism. The result of all this is law as an institution that often exhibits similar forms to the

Western forms, but with diverse meanings, and at other times has identical meanings expressed in different forms.

The Russian legal tradition differs from core civil law in a number of ways. One is the remarkably late – and still only partial – abstraction of law into a distinct social sphere in which lawyers have a demarcated jurisdiction, share a common identity, and hold an established monopoly over legal affairs. Or, to put it differently, law is still only partially professionalised and still retains its 'lay law' meaning, or to use Bourdieu's terminology, a 'vulgar vision' of law (Buordieu 1987: 828)

In Western Europe, the early legal professionals organised themselves way back in the Middle Ages into corporate groups holding a monopoly over studying, interpreting, developing and applying law. Ordinary citizens came to rely on these specialists to find their way through the labyrinths of the law's technical language and distinctive way of reasoning. This shift from amateur to professional lawyers in the twelfth century marks a major turning point in legal history (Brundage 2008).

In contrast 'a lawyer' as a defined social role was not known in pre-modern Russia. This does not mean that law itself did not play an important role – only that it was regarded merely as a 'lay' method of dispute resolution. Early Rus' was a polity with well-established rules of problem solving (Kaiser 1980).

It was not until the early eighteenth century, with the westernisation reforms of Peter the Great, that the Russian legal tradition moved closer to the Western legal system by means of extensive legal borrowings. The reforms set up new legal institutions and were introduced in a manner that was intended to squeeze out 'the old way' of doing things by top-down pressure. The new way succeeded, but only to a limited extent; even as late as the mid-nineteenth century, Russia could still be accurately depicted as a society of 'law without lawyers' (Wortman 1976: 237–40). Legal functions were commonly performed by people with no professional training and drawn from all corners of society: bankrupt nobility, former clerks, retired military personnel, even tavern keepers (Potemkhin 1900: 2217). Any literate person who needed to earn a living could and did get involved in legal affairs. The roles themselves were narrowly bounded. Legal representatives were not expected to appear in court and their job mostly came down to drafting petitions on behalf of claimants.

The move from non-professional to professional law started in earnest only with the judicial reforms of 1864, when a new court structure was introduced as part of a unified system of justice. It is difficult to overstate the importance of the final 50 years of Tsarist Russia with regard to turning law into a professional sphere that could compare with other countries. However, even 50 years was not long enough for the staff of the new institutional structure to monopolise the legal domain, change the public's mentality about law, and construct a new meaning for law in society. It never succeeded in fully squeezing out the non-professional players in legal roles (Huskey 1986). In addition, the ancient customary law remained unchanged and formed a substantial part of the legal landscape. It was practised in village courts where formal written law had little relevance because those courts were outside the general court structure for both civil and criminal cases (Frierson 1997).

The Bolshevik revolution of 1917 changed, once again, the trajectory of the evolution of the Russian legal domain. During the first two decades, the consumption of law shifted back and forth between legal nihilism, declaring that in a communist society there was no need for law or lawyers because justice would be delivered 'by the people and for the people', and extreme legal instrumentalism, based on the assumption that law existed in society to advance political goals (Huskey 1986).

In the later, post-Stalin, period the role of law became more stable. The possession of a legal education became the norm to secure employment in salaried law-related jobs in the state structure. However, Soviet lawyers, as a profession, were more like trained technicians operating the law under the guidance of political authorities without actual jurisdiction over law. Of course, the reality was more complex and there were some highly professional advocates doing their best to represent their clients (Barry and Berman 1968). But that could by no means count as professional institution, gatekeeping its boundaries and monopoly over law. But they were too few to make up a professional institution with recognised autonomy and exert a monopoly over law.

Currently we are observing a post-Soviet phase in which, once again, a Westernised vision of professionalised law is re-emerging in Russia (Kurkchiyan 2018: 25–36). However, it still clashes with the traditional popular mentality that law carries a single meaning that any literate person needs only to read in order to know the correct and only answer. For instance, in a recent focus group lay participants did not hesitate to engage in lengthy debate on the nuances of principles of law, such as the burden of proof. When, on one occasion, such shallow talk was challenged, the reply was 'this is not my opinion; it is the law' (Hendley 2018: 62). Russia is still midway between a 'lay' conception and a professionalised form of law.

This situation has numerous implications. When everyone claims to know for certain what a lawful outcome ought to be, any formal judgment that happens not to correspond to their expectation is perceived as fraudulent and illegitimate. Any discretion exercised by a judge is seen as manipulation or corruption. The 'lay' notion of law is doomed to produce popular distrust of the institutions that delivers justice and to taint all the legal actors involved in the process.

After all, it is acknowledged that the legitimacy of law is not grounded in its quality. Arguably law is legitimate because of the existence of a professional legal group that has successfully created a boundary between laypeople and law itself. When law is abstracted from daily life, laypeople tend to deal with law as it is, rather than to question its substance. (Frier 1985: 272). This pulling of law out of everyone's reach has never been part of the Russian historical memory and experience.

This state of affairs has also important implications for inter-institutional relationships within the Russian polity. I would argue that any major social institution that is not sufficiently professionalised is predestined to have weak internal resistance against external interference. This should not be interpreted as an assertion that political or administrative interference in legal cases is inevitable or common. There is no empirical verification to support such a claim unless attention is fixed on a small number of high-profile, politicised cases. Yet, those egregious cases are of course profoundly important, as the smell coming from just one rotten apple in the barrel can make all the other apples seem to be rotten too, which puts everyone off approaching the barrel.

V. ADMINISTERIAL TRIALS

For a better understanding of the Russian legal space I will now examine the meaning of the trial and the judicial role in Russian courtrooms. The judiciary and what typically happens in court attract the strongest criticism in the literature. The court is a good example of what the legal culture approach allows us to see, which is missed when the mainstream 'law in action' approach is applied in socio-legal studies of Russia.

In western jurisdictions two models of trial are commonly distinguished: the adversarial and the inquisitorial. They differ in the role performance of the actors and the interactions in the courtroom. There are noticeable differences in procedural technique between the two models, but the end goal is the same. The courtroom is the forum where the truth is expected to be revealed and explained before sentence is passed.

With respect to its formal procedures, Russian courtroom practice has been following Western principles, shifting from one model to the other over different historical periods of its modern history. The late Imperial courts began to endorse adversarial procedures; Soviet practices were defined as inquisitorial. Thereafter, post-Soviet reforms brought adversarial procedure back into most courtrooms. However, it is questionable whether the actual practices really conform to either of those models, or even to a combination of them. This is not to deny that elements of models are present in Russian courts, but to argue instead, that the native model, which I labelled the 'administerial' model of a trial, is the dominant form in Russian courtrooms most of the time (Kurkchiyan and Kubal 2018). Its meaning needs to be understood within the entirety of the legal procedure. In the Russian context it is the pre-trial stage that is designed to get to the bottom of the case, to find out the 'truth', leaving the judge with the role of a reviewer and assessor of the work that was done before it is taken to the court.

To start with, in civil cases the legitimate informal pre-trial stage allows for an unlimited number of meetings between the litigant and the judge. In the same manner as one might visit any other government department office, people visit the courthouse to talk to the judge in order to get advice on the merits of their case and establish what documents they need to add to the file. No transcript is made of these conversations. At this preliminary stage, the judge performs multiple roles: that of adviser, of educator, of mediator for reconciliation, and even of the clerk who keeps the file up to date. Meanwhile, the judge gets to know a case and its participants in detail, before it reaches the courtroom. The courtroom hearing itself is rigidly choreographed by the formal rules of due process. However, most cases are not decided in the courtroom. More often than not, the judge comes to the hearing with a draft of the judgment already prepared (Andrianova 2017). In this scenario, the courtroom becomes the forum where the verdict is officially announced. The courtroom, then, is not the place where the truth is unearthed; that will have been determined at the pre-trial stage. The courtroom is used to confer legitimacy upon the judgment that has been reached in the earlier stages of fact collection.

The same pattern is observable in criminal cases. Most cases that reach a criminal court have already passed along an elaborate journey: investigation, prosecutor assessments with the case being sent back and forth for further investigations a number of times, negotiations, plea bargaining, etc. Cases that reach the court are assumed to be already in a shape such that the judge can feel confident in approving the work that has been done in the pre-trial stage. In effect, the role of the judge becomes to evaluate the file that comes in front her (Solomon 2015).

The exception is reserved only for major economic disputes in the commercial courts which are run in an indisputably adversarial format (Bocharov and Titaev 2018). Yet, even in the commercial courts only small number of cases can be described as genuine economic conflicts. For the rest of the time, the courtrooms are used for administrative matters, such as to produce bureaucratic records of a court decision for internal use, to report to the tax authorities, or to legitimise unchallenged administrative penalties. In other words, even economic courts spend a significant proportion of their time on straightforward administrative matters.

It is not surprising, then, that what researchers observe is that the default position of Russian court is to rely on written documents as evidence. Judges are reluctant to question the content of a case file during the trial even when the 'evidence' included in it is doubtful. If the judge finds the file problematic, she would normally request yet another document. During the trial itself the judge does not lead an inquiry to get to the bottom of the case. On the other hand, the lawyers in the courtroom do not have the necessary procedural infrastructure and opportunity to make their case and engage in arguments in earnest that are fundamental if the adversarial rules of the game are to apply.

The public understands very well the need for a written document in order to advance a case, regardless of how absurd the request for any particular document might be. It is not unusual for a party to a case to be in a Catch-22 situation: without a particular written document there can be no court case, and without a court case there can be no pressure on an opponent or third party to produce the document. Because of this awareness of what matters most in court, people tend to take great care to take instruction directly from the judge so as to make quite sure that their case file contains all the paperwork that the court might need as evidence.

This phenomenon is not a contemporary development, nor even a legacy from Soviet times. The use of written papers as the sole basis for a court judgment goes back to the Muscovite period when judges were essentially restricted to writing down all the testimonies and then sending the whole set to a superior governor, who would make a judgment. Imperial courts were also in the habit of treating files as true representations of the facts, without much questioning (Vas'kovskii 1893: 310). One can speculate that this side of the Russian legal tradition is the result of the absence of professional lawyers through history with a say in the process. Without active lawyers in court able to challenge the files, bring in other factual material, cross-examine witnesses in open court, and then argue in defence of the truthfulness of evidence that contradicts the files, the logical and easy solution for a judge is to take whatever is written in the file as solid 'evidence'.

Taken together with observations made in other corners of the Russian institution of justice, I would argue that the meaning of a court hearing, and the purpose that it actually serves, cannot be fully understood from the standpoint of western expectations of law. Instead, it might be more productive to acknowledge that the traditionally developed administerial model for delivering justice is a significant feature of the Russian legal landscape. This acknowledgement would first require a reconceptualisation of the entire delivery of justice in Russia, complete with a better understanding of the place of non-judicial structures in determining the outcome. As to judging the administerial model, the first question to be asked is not whether it is a good model or a bad one, but how it works. Once this question is answered, it is reasonable to consider which aspects of it might realistically be changed to improve it.

VI. CONCLUSION

To conclude, I will highlight the added value of the legal culture approach in my research on Russian law in society. Within this approach, the term 'Russia' neither demarcates the boundaries of the state, nor is it based on the cultural identity of the people. Instead, the inferences have been drawn only from studies of the relatively homogeneous community of European Russia that shares a historical legacy all way from Early Rus' to contemporary Russia.

My projects were concerned with the different aspects of socio-legal realities in Russia. In fact, there was no need to use the term 'legal culture' in any of them. Instead, terms such as 'legal consciousness', 'emerging rules in self-organized social order', 'role performance in the courtrooms', 'evolution of the legal profession', 'legal tradition' and so forth were sufficient to take the projects forward. But the individual projects were all driven by the legal culture approach in terms of the methodological assumption that law was part of a larger game within a particular social order, exploring what law means to people in Russia, how it works in relation to other rules, and why things are as they are. The approach determined the formulation of the questions posed in each of the projects. Through their exploration of the intersection of perceptions, customary practices, and the evolution of the legal institutions through history, the projects aimed to produce a cumulative understanding of the Russian socio-legal space in its own right.

Although in general my projects were not comparative in the way that the data collection was usually designed, comparison was used, nevertheless. It was valuable in highlighting the uniqueness of the Russian consumption of law. Yet, it needs to be borne in mind that quite different narratives could be put together to argue that Roman law exerted a significant influence on Russian legal development as early as the tenth century, followed by further convergence in the modern era. In fact, the uniqueness tends to be overlooked when the similarities are strong, as we observe in Russian studies. The legal culture approach helps to rectify this imbalance.

Finally, despite its strengths, the legal culture approach does not allow me to suggest how legal mentality and associated practices will evolve in the Russian future. There are too many factors that are shaping that future as we watch, such as recently introduced institution of juries for some criminal cases, speeded professionalisation of the legal space, continued western influences, etc. The future will depend on the broader social, political and institutional changes in Russia over the long term.

REFERENCES

Andrianova, V (2017) 'Perceptions of Institutions of Justice: Comparative Study in English and Russian Lower Courts (DPhil thesis, Oxford).

Banakar, R (2016) *Driving Culture in Iran: Law and Society on the Roads of the Islamic Republic* (London, IB Tauris).

Barry, D and Berman HJ (1968) 'The Soviet Legal Profession' 82(1) *Harvard Law Review* 1.

Berman, HJ (1963) *Justice in the USSR: An Interpretation of Russian Law* (Cambridge, MA, Harvard University Press).

Bocharov, T and Titaev K (2018) 'When Business goes to Court: Arbitrazh Courts in Russia' in M Kurkchiyan and A Kubal (eds), *A Sociology of Justice in Russia* (Cambridge, Cambridge University Press) 118.

Boellstorff, T (2003) 'Dubbing Culture: Indonesian Gay and Lesbi Subjectivities and Ethnography in an Already Globalised World' *American Ethnography* 30.

Bourdieu, P (1987) 'The Force of Law: Towards a Sociology of the Judicial Field' 38 *Hasting Law Journal* 805.

Brundage, JA (2008) *The Medieval Origin of the Legal Profession* (Chicago, University of Chicago Press).

Burbank, J (1997) 'Legal Culture, Citizenship, and Peasant Jurisdictions: Perspectives From the Early Twentieth Century' in P Solomon (ed), *Reforming Justice in Russia 1864–1996* (Armonk, NY, ME Sharpe) 82.

Cotterrell, R (2006) *Law, Culture and Society* (Aldershot, Ashgate).

Dahan, F (2003) 'Hope and Bitterness in the Reform of Russian Bankruptcy Law' in D Galligan and M Kurkchiyan (eds), *Law and Informal Practices* (Oxford, Oxford University Press) 135.

Ewick, P and Silbey S (1998) *The Common Place of Law* (Chicago, University of Chicago Press).

Friedman, L (1975) *The Legal System – A Social Science Perspective* (New York, Russell Sage Foundation).

Frier, BW (1985) *The Rise of Roman Jurists* (Princeton, Princeton University Press).

Frierson, CA (1997) 'I Must Always Answer to the Law: Rules and Responses in the Reformed Volost Court' 75(2) *Slavonic and East European Review* 309.

Geertz, C (1983) 'Local Knowledge: Fact and Law in Contemporary Perspective' in C Geertz (ed), *Local Knowledge: Further Essay in Interpretative Anthropology* (New York, Basic Books) 167.

Hendley, K (2018) 'To Go To Court or Not? The Evolution of Disputes in Russia' in M Kurkchiyan and A Kubal (eds), *A Sociology of Justice in Russia* (Cambridge, Cambridge University Press) 40.

Huskey, E (1986) *Russian Lawyers and the Soviet State* (Princeton, Princeton University Press).

Kahn, PW (1999) *The Cultural Study of Law* (Chicago, University of Chicago Press).

Kaiser, DH (1980) *The Growth of Law in Medieval Russia* (Princeton, Princeton University Press) 94.

Kononenko, V and Moshes, A (2011) *Russia as a Network State* (Basingstoke, Palgrave Macmillan).

Kurkchiyan, M (2000) 'The Transformation of the Second Economy into Informal Economy' in M Kurkchiyan and A Ledeneva (eds), *Economic Crime in Russia* (London, Kluwer Law International) 83.

—— (2003) 'The Illegitimacy of Law in Post-Soviet Societies' in D Galligan and M Kurkchiyan (eds), *Law and Informal Practices* (Oxford, Oxford University Press) 25.

—— (2009) 'Russian Legal Culture: An Analysis of Adaptive Response to an Institutional Transplant' 34(2) *Law and Social Inquiry* 337.

—— (2012) 'Comparing Legal Cultures: Three Models of Court for Small Civil Cases' in D Nelken (ed), *Using Legal Culture* (London, Wildy, Simmons and Hill) 218.

—— (2018) 'The Professionalisation of Law in the Context of the Russian Legal Tradition' in M Kurkchiyan and A Kubal (eds), *A Sociology of Justice in Russia* (Cambridge, Cambridge University Press) 12.

Kurkchiyan, M and Kubal, A (2018) 'Administerial Justice: Concluding Remarks on the Russian Legal Tradition' in M Kurkchiyan and A Kubal (eds), *A Sociology of Justice in Russia* (Cambridge, Cambridge University Press) 259.

Ledeneva, A (2008) 'Telephone Justice in Russia' 24(4) *Post-Soviet Affairs* 324.

Merry, S (2012) 'What is Legal Culture? An Anthropological Perspective' in D Nelken (ed), *Using Legal Culture* (London, Wildy, Simmons and Hill) 53.

Nelken, D (ed) (1997) *Comparing Legal Cultures* (Aldershot, Dartmouth).

—— (2004) 'Using the Concept of Legal Culture' 29 *Australian Journal of Legal Philosophy* 1.

—— (2020) 'Sociology of Legal Culture' in J Priban (ed), *Research Handbook on Sociology of Law* (Cheltenham, Edward Elgar) 136.

Pastukhov, V (2002) 'Law under Administrative Pressure in Post-Soviet Russia' 11(3) *East European Constitutional Review* 66.

Potemkhin, PA (1900) 'Fragments from an Advocate's Memo' 47 *Provo* 2217.

Simpson, AWB (2000) *Invitation to Law* (Oxford, Blackwell).

Solomon, P (2015) 'Understanding Russia's Low Rate of Acquittals: Pretrial Screening and the Problem of Accusatorial Bias' 40(1) *Review of Central and East European Law* 1.

Solomon, P and Foglesong, T (2000) *Courts and Transitionin Russia: The Challenge of Judicial Reform* (Oxford, Westview).

Vas'kovskii (1893) *Organizatsiia Advokatury* (St Petersburg, Soikina).

Wortman, R (1976) 'The Development of a Russian Legal Consciousness' (Chicago, Chicago University Press).

21

Flexible Structures:
Using the Legal Culture Concept
to Study the Law of Society

CARLO PENNISI

I. USING BANAKAR IN ORDER TO READ BANAKAR

IN MANY RESPECTS one of Reza Banakar's most significant contributions to the sociology of law is that he has constantly linked his methodological reflections to the concern of identifying and distinguishing the sociology of law from the world of scientific practices that deal with law in reference to society. Research on reckless driving in two large Iranian cities expresses the essential traits of the approach that Banakar will finally specify also through an analysis of research design in the sociology of law (Banakar 2003; 2015; 2019; Banaker et al 2016). This chapter aims to trace the salient features of this approach in the research in Iran to show how the concept of *legal culture* can play an essential and original role. Traffic conditions are considered an interesting area of analysis of the relationship between the legal culture of drivers and pedestrians, the effectiveness of law enforcement, and the psychological implications of the use of technology. The analytical and empirical difficulty of this confluence is common to all countries; nevertheless, the turbulence of Iranian historical events acts on the relationship between law, state, and culture in a particular way due to colonial and post-colonial influences. This raises the question then of the generalisability of the approaches to the sociology of law developed in Europe and the United States. The following section outlines the most relevant research steps from the point of view adopted here that are of use in connecting it to the author's methodological orientations. Of course, much of the book's value will be lost in this way, but it should be possible to enhance its methodological virtue and relevance to the sociology of law (section II). Therefore, the steps identified are attributable to the structure of the research design elucidated by Banakar and to his main methodological concerns (section III). Thereafter, the work specifies how the concept of *legal culture* can play a significant role in that framework (section IV), and will suggest, with reference to some of the proposals in the debate, an analytical perspective through which the concept of *legal culture* can be a criterion for identifying the subject of the sociology of law (section V).

II. THE RESEARCH STEPS ON RECKLESS DRIVING

The essential features of the structure of the research display Banakar's constant attention, expressed in many previous, contemporary and subsequent works, to a methodological system that lends autonomy and originality to the knowledge constructed by the sociology of law (Banakar and Travers 2005). We will summarise the argumentation in five steps to show this.

(1) The abnormal accident rates for Iranian traffic are the subject of two sets of in-depth interviews. The intent is not to look for the 'causes' of the problem through the interviews. Rather, it is to reconstruct the interviewees' experiences of the law and state bureaucracy, through their reasoning regarding their perceptions and opinions, as well as to analyse the link of such experiences with the normative dimensions in which their daily lives take place (Banakar et al 2016: 35). The first set of interviews shows first of all that the traits emerging from the 'unreliability of laws', the 'inconsistency of law enforcement', and 'excessive individualism of Iranians' and the psychological effects of technology, fuel a significant disconnection between perceived regularities in driving behaviour (*descriptive norms*) and the weak prescriptive nature of social norms on traffic (*injunctive norms*) generally referred to as a 'culture of driving'. Banakar then asks himself: 'Why do injunctive norms [...] fail to exert any perceptible regulatory impact on the rampant sense of individualism of Iranian drivers?' (ibid: 50). The distance between *descriptive* and *injunctive norms* appears much more complex than in western countries, where this difference is a common, widespread experience that is normally managed to some extent. Indeed, it consists of a prescriptive, indicative dimension of the opinions of these actors, only generally referred to as a 'culture of driving', but not specified in rules of conduct if not for a general respect for others. Yet, this normative orientation is linked to a descriptive dimension even though it possesses that particular prescriptiveness that instead comes from tradition, and from 'taking something for granted'. The vagueness of the normative reference is fuelled, and in turn fuels, characteristic Iranian individualism, since the latter fosters an interpretation of driving without those legal and formal constraints that instead in western countries, limit the air of freedom, power, status, and identity, to which the use of the particular, normative artifact represented by the car is linked.

(2) The second set of interviews confirms the issues already learned, but accentuates and differentiates the judgment regarding law enforcement and jurisdiction: there is a fundamental mistrust of the reliability of law enforcement and the courts, both seen as hostile and arbitrary. The interviews are more wide-ranging, directed at lawyers, doctors, insurance brokers, teachers, as well as taxi drivers, and are structured in two main parts. The first concerns the interviewees' experience of traffic and understanding of it, their perceptions of the reasons for the disregard of traffic rules, their attitudes towards its regulation and conventions, the way in which they link driving behaviour and social order, and their opinions on the enforcement of traffic regulations. The second part, containing more general questions, instead examines the interviewees' perceptions and attitudes to law and social order. The results from this second set of interviews bring up and examine in depth the issues already raised. Accidents and traffic congestion are blamed on a weak 'culture of driving', ineffective enforcement, and the widespread failure to comply with traffic rules and regulations.

(3) However, this time the judgements regarding law and enforcement are more complex. On the one hand, a predominantly secular conception of law and its sources emerges and a conception of justice as equal treatment that may also be in tune with the religious influences that some attribute to the law. On the other hand, the judgements on the lack of enforcement of traffic regulations reveal a fundamental mistrust of the reliability of law enforcement and the courts, on which negative judgement is more explicitly modulated; this in turn grows in drivers, who feel they have no rights, and a perception of the other traffic actors as *strangers* for whom they are not responsible. Having acquired these descriptions and judgements as *external legal culture* in traffic regulation, Banakar describes the *internal legal culture*, the characteristics of the rules and their application by the courts and law enforcement agencies, as a result of a historical legacy of arbitrariness, and personalistic and despotic regimes (Banakar et al 2016: 54 ff). In this second set of interviews, the lack of a 'culture of driving' and poor enforcement were held to be the main reasons for traffic chaos, despite the importance of aspects not mentioned like the huge growth in traffic, the poor state of the roads and the old age of the vehicles. This leads Banakar to question the links between the *external legal culture* of Iranian drivers that weakens the prescriptive nature of the models underlying social norms for its devaluation of official law and the legal system, and the *internal legal culture* of ineffective enforcement bureaucracy. In order to understand the links between the two aspects, Banakar recalls the events of the construction of the state in Iran. The weak popular legitimacy, which supported the various regimes and dynasties and their relatively short duration, prevented the consolidation of those enduring traditions developed instead in ancient Greece or in Europe under Roman law. The more recent 'Islamisation' of the system, through the Sharia, produced a more permanent basis for the legal system, but its effectiveness was limited by changing state political directions. The rising rejection of the state left a mark on the formation of Iranian society and conditioned the way in which rights and responsibilities are conceived. If one feels one has no rights, it leads to not recognising responsibilities towards others, Banakar affirms, citing the historian Katouzian.

(4) This perspective makes the disconnection between perceived regularities and the normative models of driving conduct clear for Banakar. The personal and arbitrary nature of short-term despotic regimes (*estebdād*) prevented them from developing 'long-term, institutionalised practices' out of social, political, and legal structures. Arbitrary rules create a state and forms of government that are not bound by an autonomous legal framework. In turn, this is reflected in social disorder that becomes political chaos when state bureaucracy loses control of society. The particular Iranian individualism, expressed in clans and families, seems rational in the face of the ephemeral and unstable nature of the way in which social order and collective interests are perceived. The Iranians' traditional cordiality, courtesy, and hospitality are in fact based on the perception of others through personal and individualised interactions, while in the context of technologically mediated relationships, such as driving behaviour, these others become strangers towards whom they feel no responsibilities. Banakar thus connects the role attributed to the community as a source of security, support, and identity, with the mistrust of state law and the courts (Banakar et al 2016: 56 ff, 71 ff, 110 ff, 153 ff). In short, it is a tradition that has prevented the consolidation of institutional practices within which the norms of the *rule of law*

could have taken root by binding the different regimes and bureaucracy to a permanent, autonomous legal framework.

(5) Categorical and defining contrasts, through which the interviewees elaborate both their different diagnoses and different solutions, run through each of these passages. It is through these contrasts that Banakar reconstructs, on a semantic level, the differences in the complex, social structure of Iran (economic, territorial, and political), the different identification structures of the interviewees (family, patriarchy, gender, peer group, neighbours and the clan, wider society and state bureaucracy) and the lines of differentiation through which state power has kept society politically divided, with increasingly variable alliances with social and religious groups. This kaleidoscope-like fragmentation is projected into the diversity of perceptions, judgements, and proposed solutions, giving rise to combinations of modern and traditionalist attitudes that are sometimes surprising. Banakar sharp-wittedly unravels these combinations and reconstructs how references to custom now become acceptance of the regime, now reason for mistrusting the courts and state bureaucracy. In the fabric of these combinations, the normative dimensions of daily life lack consistency (like trust in the effects of educational action on driving that should be carried out precisely by those systems in which they have no confidence), are not unitary (divided between a version of custom metabolised by the legal system and another linked to patriarchy and the traditional, local courts), and never reach degrees of social and cultural generalisation to activate real processes of autonomous institutionalisation from the interactions of the different community levels involved (Banakar et al 2016: 155 ff). In this Banakar finds reason for the distance between *descriptive* and *injunctive norms*:

> Descriptive norms ... often belong to the sociality of immediate community, to the 'private' sphere wherein individuals are related-through kinship, to the 'insiders' ... part of the dichotomies constituting the Iranian culture. ... are based on interpersonal trust and mutual dependency .... Its form of law is that of the customary urf .... By contrast, injunctive norms ... are norms of the larger 'society of strangers' and are the rules dictated by the authorities. These signify the 'public' sphere, people who are 'unrelated', the 'outsiders' (Banakar 2016: 177).

In this tension, the normative dimensions expressed by the research are distinguished by Banakar through the three 'forms of sociality' to which Gurvitch attributed his 'kinds of law' (Banakar 2003: 238–65; 2015: 35). Iran's legal culture thus appears to be the result of three levels of normativity expressed by the peer group, the local community, and the political and administrative system, respectively. However, for each of these levels the reference of normativity to custom is constructed in differentiated ways. The polysemic reference to custom thus makes an *interplay* between them possible, which gives rise to both conflicts and alliances between the different components of Iranian society that affect the political and cultural transition of the country.

Conclusively, Banakar comments on the proposals of Mustashar od-Dawleh, an Iranian intellectual of the late 1800s who inspired the constitutionalist movement. In a country where modernisation was hindered by the traditionalism and arbitrariness of state bureaucracy, he advocated adopting the European model of the *rule of law* and legality, considering it, and the particular conception of Islamic justice, to be alike. Banakar finds this influential work weak in understanding the codification process of law, and above all, 'wanting in respect to the central role of legal institutions and the judiciary, who were to interpret, implement and enforce the codes'. Instead, he agrees with identifying law 'as a mechanism with the social potential to unite an Iran divided along the lines of class, as well as ethnicity and religion'. But the point we are interested in highlighting here is even more incisive:

> We also know that this law is much more than a set of legal codes and principles cohering logically in a larger legal system based on some abstract notion of Western democracy or Perso-Islamic justice. To realise the law that Mustashar od-Dawleh had in mind, we also need a form of institutionalised culture and practice adhering to values and principles enshrined in the Constitution. Such fidelity to the values of law and legality requires rule by law (if not the *rule of law*) and will remain incompatible with the rule of *estebdād*. (ibid: 206)

III. THE FLEXIBILITY OF RESEARCH DESIGN AND THE ROLE OF THE CONCEPT OF LEGAL CULTURE

The structure in which we have simplified the tableau of Iranian society offered by Banakar, expresses the commitment to a sociology of law research design with the characteristic flexibility that it must maintain. The set of interviews highlights a recursive and cumulative learning process designed from the outset (Banakar et al 2016 30). Banakar long sought to overcome the traditional contrasts between the legal and sociological knowledge of the social phenomena in which law matters. And more recently, he entrusted to research design the description of the steps needed to avoid consolidated stereotypes (Banakar 2019). To this end, he took up his own approach to the problem considering, in an *ideal type* way, the legal research normatively oriented by the conception of law as a set of rules, principles and precedents, organised around state sovereignty, aimed at questioning its effectiveness and uniformity, guiding individual behaviour and organised public and private conduct, supported by doctrinal and philosophical contributions, producing internal and systematically self-referring descriptions of law. And still in an *ideal type* way, he considered sociological knowledge aimed at describing how *in actual fact* the law is generated by social practices and how it returns to the social system, or how it is constituted as a social institution such as religion, politics, and economics, or even as a particular manifestation of power. The aim of legal knowledge then is 'doing things' with law, and sociological knowledge is engaged in connecting law to wider social processes. Banakar proposed considering these two approaches, rather than as contrasts, but as valid descriptions of how the law manifests itself at different levels of social reality that are not mutually exclusive and that share the problem of social order and conformity, albeit conceptualised in different ways (Banakar 2003: 25–75; 2015: 21–38, 161–66).

Minimising the (many) internal differences between the two approaches and taking instead their reciprocal differences to extremes (Banakar 2015: 77–96), always in an ideal type key, Banakar had already proposed considering the former as top-down analysis and research, and the sociological ones as bottom-up (ibid: 41–56). He noted how the two orientations tend to have a bearing on research design, methodologies, and privileged techniques. Referring to state law, the top-down perspective favours quantitative and qualitative methods that nevertheless requireit to take for granted the 'project of modernity' (Engel 2010) underlying the descriptions of the rule of law and its attributes: objectivity, universality, generality, and neutrality. The bottom-up perspective instead would move on micro planes where qualitative and ethnographic methods and techniques are privileged, in order to arrive at broader and more pluralistic conceptions of law, legal culture and legal conscience. The empirical 'interplay' of these perspectives, which is in fact realised in law, is detected by research paying attention to the multiplicity of actors involved in its processes and in its decision-making activities, helping to not give exclusivity to either approach. In the analysis and problematisation of Iranian reckless driving, steps (1) and (2) above clearly testify to the indications that that essay analytically exposes. The key to the socio-legal relevance of research design, however, is precisely where a top-down perspective and a bottom-up one cross and account for the specific interplay in which the law is actually realised as a social phenomenon to which steps (3)–(5) are dedicated.

The advantage gained from the two perspectives crossing, in Banakar's reasoning, is twofold. On the one hand, it prevents the *contextualisation* of the legal framework in the context of historical, organisational, and institutional processes, in which it takes shape without closing itself in an exclusively top-down approach and ending up taking for granted the characteristics that legal self-description attributes to the law. On the other hand, the cross inscribes in research design the need to account for how, in our everyday routine, citizens experience and use law in their social relationships (Banakar 2015: 50–52, 161–65). Overall, correct contextualisation and the balanced cross of bottom-up and top-down perspectives, prevent the so-called gap approach, both because it has simply been overtaken by the studies in the 1980s and 1990s (ibid 2015: 52–56) and, above all, because taken uncritically, this approach credits a definition of law that is strictly linked to the self-description of legal positivism. It is precisely the empirical interconnection indicated by Banakar, not in the 'topological' but ideal type sense (the up and the down), that finds a crucial tool in the reference to the concept of legal culture, more than the author showed he believed. For this reason, reference to the distinction between *external legal culture* and *internal legal culture* in the argumentation passages (3) and (5) needs to be investigated specifically. In fact, the interconnection of the perspective that the design constructs for research depends on the reading of the interplay and, with it, the originality of the sociological perspective. Indeed, the two perspectives cannot be understood as two distinct theoretical and empirical 'places', for instance a top and a down of a social and cultural system, the internal and the external of law: the 'sociality' of law and its 'validity' reside in both or are chimeras in both. Thus, the conceptual meeting-point between what Banakar defines as top and down is an extremely useful starting point for further and more specific perspectives on the sociological use of the concept of legal culture, precisely because of the flexibility with which the research design structure is built.

Banakar considers the concept of legal culture to be a subset of the concept of culture. The fundamental traits that he attributes to the former derive from the choices he makes regarding the latter. The main references for the definition of the term culture have been Habermas and his 'lifeworld' approach beginning in 2003 and subsequently, Geertz, Williams, and Wutnow. Culture 'refers to the process of reproducing the beliefs and attitudes people hold about the social world'. Instead, the problems posed by the concept of *legal culture* are dealt with above all in relation to the debate raised in comparative research. Here, according to Banakar, the concept sometimes risks anchoring comparative analysis to western perspectives, confining itself to positive law and implying, in some authors, an unrealistic unity. However, it still remains useful for a conceptualisation aimed at finding the missing link between structure and *agency* or between the micro and macro levels of social analysis, provided that one does not claim to explain everything through the use of culture. For this reason, it can be inscribed in a research design that does not give exclusivity to the content that legal positivism attributes to law (Banakar 2015: 133 ff; 145–66).

In the work on reckless driving, after citing Friedman's studies, Banakar takes on a concise definition of legal culture from Nelken: a concept referring to 'relatively stable patterns of legally-oriented social behaviour and attitudes' which, when referred to law, 'calls for the study of the existence of systematic variations in the models of *law in the book* and *law in action*, especially their relationship' (Nelken 2007: 369–70; 2012). Given the way in which the historical context of enforcement, affecting perceptions, judgements, and evaluations covered by the research, is reconstructed, in addition to Cotterrell's works, the most influential reference nevertheless appears to be that of Marina Kurkchiyan, for whom legal culture:

> is the product of a convoluted interplay between historical legacy, institutional performance and popular attitudes. (S)uch a broad picture does not allow causal analysis, but it does have the potential to explain how law is embedded in the social texture and how it relates to other concepts such as justice, trust and the rule of law. (Kurkchiyan 2012: 250; see also Kurkchiyan 2010)

This is exactly what Banakar's research on reckless driving shows most clearly in point (5) above. Therefore:

> the idea of 'legal culture' goes beyond the mere study of the cultural embeddedness of certain legal practices or how laws are legitimised. Instead, it seeks repeated patterns of legal behaviour, which are reproduced in a taken-for-granted manner by officers of the law or by ordinary citizens. Thus, the concept of legal culture could be used to describe why the majority of people normally follow certain laws or to explain why they collectively ignore them, as in the widespread disregard for traffic rules in Iran. (Banakar 2016: 10)

With these fundamentals, the last three 'steps' in which we have simplified the research describe the normative stratification of Iranian culture, and its variable and differentiated contrast with that expressed by the despotic and confessional systems. The analysis of their 'interplay' constitutes the empirical place and theoretical and methodological fire of Banakar's attempt to address, through research design, the combination of a top-down perspective with a bottom-up type one, to ensure autonomy and originality to the sociology of law. The unified way in which this framework is constructed from the point of view of the definition of the problems of behaviour, and from the point of view of how it is evaluated, but also from the point of view of the differentiations in relation to the levels of sociality that express it, proposes again the classic question that Banakar's methodological concerns precisely make topical:

can we call each of the normative dimensions identified in the levels of 'sociality' by his valuable analysis *legal*?

IV. BEYOND THE DUPLICITY OF LEGAL CULTURE

The inextricability of the normative dimensions involved in any legal action has represented the challenge that has been handed down from Weber and Durkheim, through the generations of Gurvitch and Friedman, to our contemporaries. The role law plays in these normative dimensions is the ground on which Banakar constructed the comparison between the epistemological system of legal doctrines and the sociological one. In this section we will see how the question on the concept of *legal culture* has been at the heart of the debate, but we will merely consider how, especially in the comparative debate, we have tried to make the concept appropriate to that complexity.

Engel (2010) showed how Friedman's intentions, underlying the differentiation between *internal* and *external* culture, and aimed at studying the characteristics of legal change, gave rise to two opposing perspectives. On the one hand, the attention to law was resolved in the role of the cognitive and normative dimensions of social relations in Geertz's system, through the approach that Nelken also identifies as the 'interpretative turn'. On the other, the concept of legal culture served to reveal the distance between the 'project of modernity' underlying the rule of law and the effectiveness of the practices that refer to it, in order to show or refute the specific autonomy it claims. A way of showing the ideological nature often underlying the law's claim of autonomy is the sociocultural embeddedness of its existence. The two approaches are not equivalent to that which they indicate as law. In the latter case, using the concept of legal culture as a means of revealing the ideological nature of the autonomy of law, the law is acquired from the point of view of the process of institutionalisation of the principles that emerged with the secularisation and the birth of nation-states. In the first case, including it in the normative dimensions of society, the law is conceived instead from traditional and everyday contexts, as part of the cosmology and primary relationships from which culture, beliefs and social norms are derived. The apparently paradoxical result is that only in the second case are we left open to the analysis of legal pluralism and to the phenomena of interlegality (De Sousa Santos 2002), that is to say to the types of legal cultures that are under the jurisdiction of sets of rules that coexist with state ones.

The concept has, then, played many different roles in comparative research. Globalisation has raised new issues for lawyers' practices and shown the limits of traditional internationalistic approaches (Örrücü and Nelken 2007). However, as Cotterrell noted, the reference to legal culture has supported the development of a new awareness of the ethical and political dimensions of conflicts between and within laws of different cultural areas. The awareness of cultural dependence also on the same positive law has helped to avoid comparisons between simple textual data, in search of a not always attentive tension towards the harmonisation of specific normative areas, considered, in turn, a condition of economic development. This was the case when we considered the characteristics shared between European legal systems or the issues that best allow them to be compared. While in the first case, however, one is still on levels of abstractness that fall under a reflection on philosophical tradition, in the second the meanings of *legal culture* multiply in relation to each of the terms compared (Cotterrell 2006).

Nelken traced the problems that need to be addressed when referring to legal culture to three areas: (i) the ability of the concept to indicate 'facts'; (ii) its usefulness in determining a specific approach to the study of law of societies; and (iii) the size of the value that it inevitably recalls, not to mention the way each of these aspects relates to other aspects (Nelken 2016). As for the first two problem areas, the gamble is the reliability of the concept, and the judgement as to whether it should be used again. Instead, ambiguities on a value level, if need be, follow on from solutions covered to obtain a specific, empirical referentiality within the framework of the approach made possible precisely by the reference to legal culture. The difficulty of indicating 'facts' still remains linked to the frequent impossibility of separating specifically legal cultural components in operators' attitudes, on the one hand. On the other, it is conditioned by the difficulty to exclude institutional, organisational, and statistical facts, so ending up indicating anything. For our purposes, in this long debate, it is important to point out how constant the proposal has been for *disarticulating*, *unbundling*, and *disaggregating* this concept with reference to sociologically or anthropologically well-founded theoretical perspectives that could define its limits of use in relation to the inextricability of the normative dimension of social life.

It has been proposed that the concept be 'broken down' into elements that are more useful each time, to specify the descriptions and relations to which we refer when studying dimensions, such as cultural ones, of which we can only have 'manifestations' on different levels of the social sphere: individual, collective, and institutional (Von Benda-Beckmann 2012). Simply indicating the values and beliefs incorporated in the procedures and registers of legal practices as legal culture, favours comparative studies and their particular questions. Yet this is of no help when studying just what is being compared. The specific sociological interest is in fact aimed rather at differentiating the contribution of the reference to law, as a social structure, to the reproduction (or transformation) of the conditions of action in a given context (Banakar 2015: 35–37).

Again, from the anthropological tradition on the concept of culture, which Rosen drew from Geertz's works on the cultural dimensions of law (Rosen 2008), Sally Merry had also proposed she would 'unbundle' the concept (Merry 2010: 62–68). The different components could have been treated with specific methods and techniques geared towards different problems: the analysis of the everyday practices and ideologies of the legal system, the study of the public's attitude and expectations that support mobilisation towards the law, as well as the way in which the actors define themselves, through the law, as subjects of legal protection. These analytical plans, sometimes partially overlapping, are identified to analyse the diffusion and generalisation of *hybridisations* between legal systems and the framework of meanings through which the actors experience the law in different contexts. It should be noted that, conversely, they are less useful for questioning how the law differs from other normative structures, as if, precisely attention to the cultural nature of law reduces its distance and heterogeneity compared to other normative dimensions of societies.

Among these attempts, Alberto Febbrajo's proposal should be noted. He advances a 'gradual' conception built on a relationship between social norms and legal norms that takes the variability of the role of law into account. In order to be effectively attributable to the actors, the author feels the internal legal culture, for instance, must be specified in relation to the decision criteria and subjects made by a body whose boundaries are, moreover, more constituted by the variable exercise of particular and variable roles than by their formal pre-definition. The 'legality' of this culture becomes a continuum suitable for showing the variability of the outcomes to which it can give rise, depending on the roles held, the reasoning behind the decisions, and the subjects they concern. He thus proposes a classification of legal cultures based on the relationships established in each type between legal norms and social norms from the point of view of the thematic focus of the research and systemic needs. Within a particular cultural and legal system, four cultural orientations emerge (traditional, reactive, innovative, and applicative) differently directed in relation to the temporal needs of the social system, which respond to the systemic needs common to both legal systems and societies (Febbrajo 2011). On the other hand, when the research focus shifts to comparative intentions, the classification changes on the basis of specific relevance, and the administrative dimension shifts to inter-state planes, focusing on those characteristics of globalisation processes on which the relationship between social norms of specific cultural fields and legal norms is played out in terms of the values and processes of their generalisation (Febbrajo 2019).

Among these authoritative proposals, that of Roger Cotterrell (Cotterrell 2006) stands out. He indicated to some degree a different way of 'unbundling' the concept of legal culture. Indeed, he has long argued the importance not only of observing the differences between legal systems, but of exploiting them – a way of obtaining a broader view of the law than those seeking harmonisation, giving priority only to the economic and instrumental functions of the legal systems. The reference to culture shows that the law is not only a facilitator of the market, but also an instrument for the safeguard of shared beliefs and essential values. It is a way of sharing traditions, the common expression of social expectations and collective emotions, also on the level of the most basic and personal relationships, those of trust, of care, and so on. In this light, the law, in its cultural component, as well as an instrument of economic life, is a guarantee with regard to legislative improvisation, protection of what we now call common goods, and artistic or environmental goods. It is also what, in understanding and using norms or regulatory frameworks, makes them expressions of basic values that, with the same textual data, differentiate the content according to social contexts; an attribution of meanings that guides the content of rules in different ways if they refer, for example, to US freedom or human dignity in the European sense – a role of law that goes beyond its purely economic function, highlighting non-instrumental social relationships. The first step towards unbundling the concept of *legal culture* is thus, for Cotterrell, the distinction between the social relationships involved and the recognition of relevance not only for economic ones but also for traditional, sentimental, and belief-based relationships, rather than levels of 'sociality'.

V. DISCERNING LEGAL CULTURE BY MEANS OF
INSTITUTIONALISATION PROCESSES

The way of unbundling the concept of legal culture proposed by Cotterrell, to refer it to other action areas compared to the market, is particularly useful not only in governing the complexity of the normative dimension to which Banakar referred by dealing with the empirical interplay in which the law is *actually* realised, but also in constituting a criterion of identification of that disciplinary specificity of the sociology of law to which Banakar dedicated himself. Unlike anthropological or interactionist-derived systems, where the law tends to lose specificity among the everyday normative structures, the concept in Cotterrell is used upside down. The reference to legal culture, in fact, highlights how a conception that is not exclusively instrumental or utilitarian, directs the necessary attention to many other important dimensions of social relations. It is a way of saying that the law has a cultural content with which legal texts and decisions connect interests, evaluations, consequences, and distributions of power to history, emotional and sentimental dimensions, and to the framework of belonging within which they only become recognisable as the law. But it is also a way of saying that, if the concept of legal culture is to be unbundled, we should differentiate the role of the law vis-à-vis each of these dimensions of social life and their specific history. Similarities and differences between legal systems or sets of rules can be detected by filtering them through the different role that the law plays between these different action areas in the various cultural contexts.

Legal culture, in short, is more than just an analytical tool and appears, in the contributions to which reference has been made, as a concept to be elaborated gradually in the context of the choices we make in a strategy aimed at controlling, clarifying, and analysing the particular complexity with which the legal dimension emerges, penetrates, and returns to social relations. This is a concept that derives its usefulness precisely from the fact that it forces analytical intent, from which the research moves, to be clarified. Therefore, it is not only a concept aimed at understanding and possibly explaining the autonomy of the law (and possibly criticising its ideological uses) with regard to the normative dimensions of society, but also a concept the use of which is aimed at guaranteeing autonomy to the sociology of law, cognitive this time, from questions that respond to different cognitive, philosophical, political, doctrinal, and legal interests, thus putting it in a position where it can interact in an informative way with the other disciplines that deal with law. Consequently, there is no point questioning which is the best definition outside a theoretical and analytical perspective that provides content and methodological constraints to its use. Apart from these specifications it exposes to polysemic uses, perhaps unproblematic for comparative or culturalist purposes, it lends itself to uses destined to produce specific confusion within a sociological framework. The connection between the use of the concept of legal culture and the approach through which the role of law is to be addressed on a certain sociologically defined phenomenon raises the problem again of the disciplinary identity of the sociology of law, this time at the operational level of the methodological approach and clarification. The functionality of this disciplinary identification, and the judgement that can be given, therefore always remain contingent. They are linked to the maturation of the method, its clarification, the ability to maintain the justification of claims, and the communication with the knowledge that develops around the 'reality' they are dealing with.

For these reasons, Banakar's contributions to research design, and the specificity of the sociology of law approach, are clarifying. Considering in an ideal type way how much he identifies with the top and down, the contributions referred to on the concept of legal culture, on the one hand encourage an unbundling of the cultural component of the law in specific processes of meaning compared to the different social action areas in which they occur, to differentiate the type of reference to the law. On the other hand, however, they call for the need to seek, among these differentiations, a key that holds them together, that makes the differences in the way in which the law may constitute a specific reference for action analytically understandable and empirically compatible. In a traditional way and by making an essential reference to Gurvitch and Durkheim, Banakar finds this unity in the *normativity* and root of the bond generated by the structuring of interaction, according to the well-known models proposed by Giddens and Archer. It reflects on the structure of the legal system through the idea of justice as a source of the specific normativity of the law, highlighted by Luhmann and Bourdieu on opposite fronts, but still little addressed by sociologists (Banakar 2015: 215–36).

In this light, the concept of legal culture may designate both the different role of law in relation to the variation of the contexts of action analysed, and also the invariance of the legal dimension and its very particular social institutionalisation, in relation to the variation of other normative sources. In this sense, it represents the conceptual meeting-point between what Banakar designates as top and down. It is the criterion of orientation between the different levels of analysis the more useful the more specific the reference is to institutionalised practices (both sociologically and legally) of which legal culture ultimately consists. If properly articulated with reference to practices made significant through law, it allows us to grasp the emergence of legal solutions, the evolution of the phenomena to which they are addressed, and the consequences that derive from their use.

For these reasons, it therefore seems useful to distinguish the cultural component of the law from its specific juridical normativity in the use of the concept. The first is readable in reference to specific processes of meaning, areas of social action, where it is not said that legal norms always play the same role, as indicated by Cotterrell and as Banakar showed through the relationship between descriptive and injunctive norms. The second, on the other hand, aims to differentiate the binding nature of the reference to legal norms from obligations and duties that derive from different normative sources: traditional, ethical, political, and religious, and so on. In this way, by culture, the concept of legal culture indicates how jointly legal phenomena participate in the social processes of cognitive and normative meanings of action. However, by only sticking to this path, the law seems to be becoming less interesting to sociologists and disappearing. Instead, by legal, the concept indicates how, how much, and if, the institutionalisation of the legal system has differentiated the law from the other normative structures of social systems. And here, with previous cultural knowledge, the attention of sociologists of law becomes more specific, because the construction of those structures (roles, norms, categories, procedures, decisions, and decision-making programmes), which often remain in the shade in ethnographic studies, comes back into play, in the definition of subjects of analysis, and questions.

Referring normativity to its institutional dimension for sociology means referring to essential social and cultural processes rendering the normative models, within which recognisable social action moves, meaningful and coordinated. These are essential in identifying and evaluating the general orientations of a given set of roles (and in any case of structures: frameworks of meaning, categories, definitions, rules, and so on), in guiding reactions to conduct incompatible with those roles or meanings, in orienting their being reproduced, and the process of their continuous doing and re-proposing with greater or lesser influence on these structures.

Thus, *legal* and *culture* are specifically linked both at the conceptual, theoretical level and empirically by the institutionalisation processes within which the normative and legal structuring of action mirror each other and differ, more or less markedly, depending on contexts, and social and legal systems. This linkage has made research design about legal phenomena expressly sociological because it shifts attention away from institutions to institutionalisation processes, thus focusing on the way in which the legal structures are elaborated and differentiated from the other normative structures, discovering the specific reflexivity that centuries of history have attributed to the law. Besides, it is a sociological perspective because it highlights the mechanisms of reflexivity by which the law represents society, social action represents the law, the transition between the normal reflexivity of basic everyday decisions, even those of legal figures, and the reflexivity of institutions that can reproduce or wear themselves out in representing or not a reference for the reflexivity of action.

Banakar is attentive to the consequences of modernisation on the specific reflexivity of social action, as a component of the relationship between structure and agency. But when we enter into the processes of institutionalisation, where structures and actions are inseparably and distinctly connected, reflexivity takes on a fundamental sociological specificity: a recursiveness that proceeds with the mechanism of progressive, material, social and temporal generalisation of the content that is gradually defined be it categories, ideas, values, or norms. And from Parsons onwards, it has been made clear how these mechanisms have progressively become the subjects of themselves: money as the possibility to exchange possibilities of exchange, ideology as the possibility to evaluate values, or precisely, the law as juridical production of legal normativity (Parsons 1967; Parsons and Shils 2001; Luhmann 1984). This type of reflexivity, then, makes it possible to activate in action that reflexivity on which sociologists, from Giddens onwards, have long been working.

This institutional recursiveness activates *reflexive mechanisms*, which are specific reflexive processes. Everyone decides on decisions. But not everyone can decide what decisions they are deciding on. A reflexive mechanism occurs when you have the tools (categories, concepts, definitions, norms, rules) to decide whether to treat what you are deciding on as a decision, for example, ethical, or political, or legal, or subject to instrumental rationality. This *possibility* of determining the object incorporates decision-making alternatives that remain open, undecided, and make the frame of subsequent choices more complex. The reflexive mechanism is not the repetition of daily reflexivity but the generation of additional possibilities. On these generated possibilities may depend the starting and the direction of their institutionalisation, towards legal, economic, variously cognitive structures, etc (Luhmann 1970; 2008).

The concept of *legal culture* therefore serves to modulate the interconnections between the different theoretical and empirical levels thematised by the sociological attention to law, as well as to bind and specify this attention in a socio-legal sense. To say, as many of Banakar's works invite us to, that interconnections are governed by research design means saying that the *denotata* of the concept of *legal culture* are a direct consequence of the way in which the design is constructed, rather than abstract attributions of meaning or puzzling definitions. Whatever this way or theme is that proves to be privileged, in a sociological framework the historical-cultural content of one's specific subject escapes altogether if one does not go through the tradition of the theory of action. In this sense, 'methodologising' the use of the concept of legal culture means tying the *denotata* to processes by which cultural content becomes such, that is, the processes through which their social institutionalisation takes place. The theory of action and the sociological tradition on social action are those tools that focus on the specificity of institutionalisation processes in the cultural dynamics of social processes, they thematise the reflexivity of legal structure. They trace this reflexivity to the processes of institutionalisation of social action, retrace its common nature (it could be said: *morphogenetic homology*) with every other structuring process. In this way they highlight, in a non-residual way, the *social* nature of the law and the historical-cultural specificity that makes these structures 'legal', with their necessary definitions of society, rather than religious, ethical, aesthetic, or simply 'technical' or 'pragmatic' ones – Weber's 'maxims of conduct' (Weber 1977: 98–115, 156).

REFERENCES

Banakar, R (2003) *Merging Law and Sociology: Beyond the Dichotomies in Socio-Legal Research* (Berlin, Verlag).
—— (2015) *Normativity in Legal Sociology. Methodological Reflections on Law and Regulation in Late Modernity* (Heidelberg, Springer).
—— (2019) 'On Socio-Legal Design' Working paper (Lund, Lund University).
Banakar, R, Fard, SN, Payvar, B and Saeidzadeh, Z (2016) *Driving Culture in Iran. Law and Society on the Roads of the Islamic Republic* (London, IB Tauris).
Banakar, R and Travers, M (2005) 'Law, Sociology and Method' in R Banakar and M Travers (eds), *Theory and Method in Socio-Legal Research* (Oxford, Hart Publishing).
Cotterrell, R (2006) *Law, Culture and Society: Legal Ideas in the Mirror of Social Theory* (Aldershot, Ashgate).
De Sousa Santos, B (2002) *Toward a New Legal Common Sense. Law, Globalization, and Emancipation* (London, Butterworths).
Engel, DM (2010) 'The Uses of Legal Culture in Contemporary Socio-Legal Studies: A Response to Sally Engle Merry' 5 *Journal of Comparative Law* 59.
Febbrajo, A (2011) 'The Failure of Regulatory Institutions. A Conceptual Framework' in PF Kjaer, G Teubner and A Febbrajo, *The Financial Crisis in a Systemic Perspective* (Oxford, Hart Publishing) 269.
—— (2019) 'A Typology of Legal Cultures' in A Febbrajo (ed), *Law, Legal Culture and Society. Mirrored Identities of the Legal Order* (London Routledge) 28.

Kurkchiyan, M (2010) 'Comparing Legal Cultures: Three Models of Court for Small Civil Cases' 5 *Journal of Comparative Law* 169.

—— (2012) 'Perceptions of Law and National Order: A Cross-National Comparison of Collective Legal Consciousness' 29 *Wisconsin International Law Journal* 366.

Luhmann, N (1970) *Soziologische Aufklärung I* (Frankfurt, Suhrkamp, Verlag).

—— (1984) *Soziale Systeme. Grundriß einer allgemeinen Theorie* (Frankfurt, Suhrkamp, Verlag).

—— (2008) *Law as a Social System* (Oxford, Oxford University Press).

Merry, ES (2010) 'What is Legal Culture? An Anthropologial Perspective' 5 *Journal of Comparative Law* 40.

Nelken, D (1997) (ed) *Comparing Legal Cultures* (Routledge).

—— (2007) 'Defining and Using the Concept of Legal Culture' in E Örrücü and D Nelken (eds), *Comparative Law* (Oxford, Hart Publishing) 109.

—— (2012) 'Legal Culture' in DS Clark (ed), *Comparative Law and Society* (Cheltenham, Edward Elgar).

—— (2016) 'Comparative Legal Research and Legal Culture: Facts, Approaches and Values' *Annual Review of Law and Social Science* 12.

Örrücü, E and D Nelken (eds) (2007) *Comparative Law* (Oxford, Hart Publishing).

Parsons, P (1967) *Sociological Theory and Modern Society* (New York, Free Press).

Parsons, P and Shils, EA (2001) *Toward a General Theory of Action* (New Brunswick, NJ, Transaction).

Rosen, L (2008) *Law as Culture* (Princeton, NJ, Princeton University Press).

Von Benda Beckmann, F and K (2012) 'Why not 'Legal Culture'?' in D Nelken (ed), *Using Legal Culture* (London, Wildy) 86.

Weber, M (1977) *Critique of Stammler* (New York, Free Press).

22

Lawyers and Drivers: On Reading Two Works of Reza Banakar

LAWRENCE M FRIEDMAN

I. INTRODUCTION

Reza Banakar was one of the leading law and society scholars of his generation. He was a truly international scholar, a citizen of the world in every sense. He could claim at least three countries as his home: Iran, where he was born; the United Kingdom, where he lived and taught for many years; and Sweden, where he also lived and taught, and where he died. He was active in the international community of law and society scholars. He was deeply read and extremely thoughtful; he was also a warm and friendly human being. This essay is meant to pay him homage; Reza Banakar died far too early. The field lost a great deal when he died, both in human and in scholarly terms.

Reza Banakar's scholarship deals with a number of topics, both empirical and theoretical. In this essay, I want to discuss, briefly, two areas where Reza Banakar made an important recent contribution. The first area is the legal profession; and I will discuss an essay he co-wrote, which deals with the legal profession in Iran. The essay has significant implications for the study of law and the legal profession in authoritarian societies. The second area is a road less travelled: law and the legal order in modern automotive societies. This part of my chapter is a riff on Reza Banakar's important study, *Driving Culture in Iran: Law and Society on the Roads of the Islamic Republic* (2016).

One theme which runs through much of Reza Banakar's work is the need for more attention to sociological theory in studies of the legal system. In an essay written with Max Travers, introducing a collection of essays on socio-legal research, Banakar and Travers distinguish between 'socio-legal' studies, and the 'sociology of law'. 'Socio-legal studies' *use* sociology, but they 'often tend not to address the concerns of sociology', their focus, rather, is on the concerns of 'law and legal studies'. The 'separation' between the sociology of law and 'socio-legal study', they feel, 'hinders the development of the social scientific study of law' (Banakar and Travers 2005: xi–xii). The two works discussed in this chapter do not deal overtly with this distinction; but Reza Banakar's sociological imagination, and his desire to make socio-legal studies more sociological, more in line with mainstream sociology, underpins both of the works I will discuss.

II. LAW IN AUTHORITARIAN SOCIETIES

In 2020, a team of editors, headed by Richard L Abel, published a collection of essays, *Lawyers in 21st Century Society*. This was the first of a two-volume series. Some 40 or so 'National Reports', dealing with aspects of the legal profession in various countries, constitute the bulk of the first volume (Abel et al 2020).[1] Reza Banakar and Keyvan Ziaee wrote the report on Iran. The title is significant: 'Iran: A Clash of Two Legal Cultures?'. The two cultures in question are the professional culture of the trained lawyer, on the one hand, and on the other hand, the culture of the judiciary, and of Iran's ruling circles – an authoritarian and deeply Islamic culture. The two cultures, the authors claim, 'clash' over the 'most valuable symbolic capital of the juridical field – the authority to determine the law'. The legal culture of lawyers 'is based on the jurisprudence of the modern law schools'; lawyers see 'law as a rule-based rational construct for decision-making'. The lawyers also tend to be 'members of the middle class and the intellectual elite'. The judiciary, on the other hand, constitute a 'socially homogeneous group of men', imbued with the dominant values of the Islamic Republic; their decision-making is based in part on Sharia, but also (somewhat paradoxically) on looser and freer norms, so that their rulings almost approximate at times Weberian khadi justice (Banakar and Ziaee 2020: 598). The result is a kind of antagonism between the two cultures. Judges (some lawyers say) treat lawyers as the enemy.

Each society is, of course, unique. Much of what is discussed in this chapter is specific to Iran, a country with a long and singular history. Iran has its own unique mix of languages and ethnic groups. The revolution which overthrew the Shah, and created the Islamic Republic, has put its indelible stamp on Iranian society, including its legal order. That order is unquestionably authoritarian at its core.

The story of the legal profession, since the Islamic Republic was established, has been complex and fraught with difficulties. In the early years the profession had hard times. Many attorneys 'were purged, some were executed, and others fled the country or went into hiding' (ibid: 583). The situation gradually improved. In time, a fairly conventional type of legal profession emerged. Prospective attorneys have to complete four years of 'intensive study' (this includes, to be sure, a fair amount of specifically Islamic courses); they also need to go through a period of pupillage and pass an exam.

The Iranian profession has its problems with official ideology, and with the judiciary. But Iranian lawyers adhere, on the whole, to what we could call the general values of the profession. These values, however, can and do 'clash' with the values of the religious leaders who dominate the government; and with the judges who are allies of the regime. The profession pays respect to the written law, to the actual codes of the Iranian legal system. The profession also values procedural purity. If I read the essay correctly, the authors are saying that the profession finds itself resistant, though rather subtly, to an official ideological code.

---

[1] The second volume (Abel et al 2022) contains comparative and theoretical essays. Richard L Abel and the late Philip Lewis were the guiding spirits behind the three-volume work, *Lawyers in Society*, which appeared in the late 1980s; *Lawyers in 21st Century Society* is modelled on this earlier work, and the research it inspired.

This 'clash' of values can seem somewhat paradoxical, from the standpoint of law and society scholarship. Lawyers in Iran apparently cling to an image of 'law' which is rule-bound, autonomous, independent of politics and policy, and guided by professional values. A mountain of law and society research dismisses this notion of autonomy as unrealistic; and indeed as impossible. And perhaps undesirable. In any event, legal behaviour is not and cannot be autonomous. Norms, values, and (yes) ideologies *always* determine its content. To deny this would be, for a law and society scholar, absolute heresy. And in this regard, Reza Banakar is certainly no heretic.

Still, the lawyers of Iran are not entirely wrong. An independent legal profession, and, indeed, an independent judiciary, is not the same as an *autonomous* profession or judiciary. Judges are independent when the state has no right or power to discipline a judge, or punish a judge, if the judge fails to follow the wishes and dictates of the regime. In most democratic countries, the judiciary is in fact independent; and the judges place a high value on their freedom from official control. But judges also tend to insist that they do not make political or ideological judgments; that they simply follow 'the law'. Yet 'the law' itself, and the decisions of the judges, are not neutral; they follow from the norms, values, and attitudes of society. Or, to be more accurate, the norms, values, and attitudes of the class to which the judges belong. There is a fundamental distinction between decisions which are based on partisan politics (or the will of the regime) and decisions based (perhaps unconsciously) on policy choices which appeal to the judges. The justices of the United States Supreme Court, for example, have life tenure; they can and do disagree with the government whenever they choose to do so. Yet in a deeper sense their decisions are profoundly political. No serious scholar would deny that.

Iranian lawyers, however, do not live in a democracy; and they face a judiciary which is a branch of an authoritarian state. Lawyers in many societies, past and present, have found themselves in a similar situation. The path of the legal profession in Iran, in fact, runs strikingly parallel to the path of legal professions in other authoritarian states: for example, the profession in the GDR (East Germany). At the end of World War II, the Soviet Union installed a communist regime in East Germany. The old legal profession was overthrown. Early on, the government populated the courts with 'people's judges', who typically had no formal legal training. Gradually, however, a more conventional legal profession developed. Over the years, lawyers became more and more 'professional'; lawyers and judges did not, and indeed could not, boldly express opposition to the regime, or to the ideology of the regime. But in their day-to-day work, lawyers and judges often sincerely tried, as best they could, to 'follow the law'.[2] In mainland China, one also finds a divide between 'activist' lawyers and a repressive and ideological state apparatus; a trained and modern legal profession, however, has developed in recent times (Liu 2020). In Vietnam, after the country was unified in 1975, the national government 'dissolved' the bar associations of South Vietnam; many lawyers were 'sent to re-education camps or escaped

---

[2] On East Germany, see in particular the work of Inga Markovits (2010); on the training of lawyers in East Germany, in which a similar class of cultures appears, see Markovits (2020): as the title of this book suggests, the jurists and legal scholars of East Germany have felt they had to serve two masters: legal scholarship and professional habits of thought on the one hand; and the demands of the state on the other.

to foreign countries'; they were replaced by 'people's advocates'. Yet later, the state allowed – or even encouraged – a more traditional profession. Here too, a lawyer who is a dissident, or who is too much of an 'activist' is asking for trouble. But, in general, those lawyers whose practice deals with local and foreign businesses simply carry on their work. They do not face serious difficulties (Nicholson and Ha 2020; see also Carlisle 2020).

A general pattern emerge from these examples. Authoritarian societies often begin with a revolution, a revolution fuelled by ideology. The Russian Revolution was one example; the Iranian revolution another. The new regime gets rid of the old legal cadre of lawyers. It replaces them with some form of revolutionary justice. Ideological loyalists run the legal system. As the revolution matures (if that's the right word), a more traditional legal profession emerges. 'Ordinary' justice – routine, non-political cases – gets handled in ordinary ways; lawyers (and often, judges) follow positive law. Politically charged cases are another matter: they remain under tighter control, perhaps in special courts.

In our times, globalisation has complicated the picture. Even revolutionary societies must deal with economic realities; and in today's world, economic realities usually include international trade. There are no longer any hermit kingdoms (North Korea is perhaps the closest there is). Revolutionary justice does not work with international businesses. Foreign investors have a taste for order and predictability. They want a system which does not tilt too heavily toward local interests – a system that is not totally subservient to the state, or where foreign investments and foreign companies are not constantly at risk. Outsiders want and need a clean, rational code of laws; they want a court system in which their interests will be protected. The small number of political cases are not their concern; or the way the regime deals with dissenters. Business can live with an authoritarian system, so long as it works for them.

III. THE LANGUAGE OF LAW

In country after country, almost without exception, the legal profession has ballooned in size in recent times. The rate of change is different, of course, in different countries. The legal profession may be very large, as in the United States, or much less so, as in Japan. The profession may be differently organised; and training processes can vary, sometimes quite radically. The Iranian experience, and the experience of other autocratic societies, leads us to ask, however, whether there are some common features. Is there something universal, or nearly universal, in the mind-set of lawyers? Is there something in their training that sets them off from the rest of society, and which gives them a distinctive way of thinking? Is there some sort of commitment – to norms of procedure, to ways of thinking and acting – that form the basis of some sort of global kinship among lawyers? Is lawyering, as it were, a kind of common language, spoken from Albania to Zimbabwe, divided no doubt into dialects, but understood more or less by lawyers wherever they are?

This question can be asked about other professions – doctors, for example. But medical science is global in a way that 'legal science' (if there is such a thing) cannot possibly be. A well-trained Albanian doctor could make full use of her medical skills in Zimbabwe, or for that matter in New York City. On the other hand, the well-trained Albanian lawyer would have a hard time functioning in either Zimbabwe or New York. Each legal system is in a real sense unique. Medical licences might be limited to a particular place, but medical science itself has no jurisdictional borders. Law is a network of jurisdictional borders. To be sure, there is such a thing as legal *ethics*, which might be compared to medical ethics. And all professions form guilds, with their own habits, values, norms, and ways of thinking. Whether lawyers from different societies share a common code, a common way of thinking, is of course an empirical question. I suspect the answer is a qualified yes. I do think there exists a kind of common language, as it were, which lawyers in many societies share. This assumption, after all, underlies the project in which the essay by Reza Banakar and Keyvan Ziaee appears. Each essay, each 'national report', is distinct; and yet common threads run through them. The book as a whole presupposes some kind of minimal 'language of law', some minimal commitment to a way of thinking and acting.

This common code or language, if it exists, is probably specific to modern times. It is the product, I think, of cultural and professional convergence. To speak of a 'common language' of lawyers presupposes lawyers, first of all; and many past societies had nothing comparable to a legal profession. Of course, 'lawyer' is a somewhat slippery term. Here I refer essentially to persons who make a living by appearing in court or giving advice about the rules and regulations in their society. In modern societies, they are usually licensed, and form some sort of profession. Just as globalisation has affected the evolutionary arc of Iranian lawyers, it has also affected that arc in other countries. Lawyers who deal with international trade must be able to talk to each other – and to understand each other. These lawyers have to be fluent in the common language. No doubt there are many such lawyers in Iran. But even lawyers who work on local matters, like divorce, or issues arising out of auto accidents, have to be familiar with the common language. All developed countries, and the developed tier of other countries, face a range of common problems. Land-use issues, landlord-tenant questions, custody of children, software patents and copyrights, air and water pollution, wage-earner and business bankruptcy: the precise problem may not go beyond a country's border, and the solutions may not be the same; but the problems themselves are not peculiar to Iran or Mexico or Finland: the problems are global.

IV. LAW IN THE AUTOMOTIVE SOCIETY

I turn now to comments that take off from Reza Banakar's study of driving culture in Iran, one the last major projects he undertook. As Banakar explains at the outset, it is a challenge to do social science research in Iran. The government does not look kindly on such research. Sociology, in the eyes of the regime is essentially 'incompatible with Islamic principles and with religious ethos' (2016: 24). Banakar and his colleagues worked with interview data extensively. But there are gaps in the fabric. The authors were blocked from conducting some interviews they very much wanted to conduct (with traffic police, for example). But despite the problems and the handicaps, *Driving Culture in Iran* is a major sociological achievement.

Iran has had a long and fascinating history; aspects of that history may have become imprinted on Iranian culture. But of course the automobile is not part of the long sweep of Iranian history. Cars were invented at the tail-end of the nineteenth century. Inventors and engineers in Europe then worked on what seemed like the next logical step after the railways: a travel machine that would run on land, without iron rails – in short, a kind of private railway carriage, driven by ordinary people, on ordinary roads. Karl Benz and Gottlieb Daimler, in Germany, independently, produced a successful design; French inventors soon improved on it.[3] The first cars, not surprisingly, were crude, and fairly slow. But technological progress quickly followed. Primitive automobiles were on the road in many countries by 1900.

The first automobiles were not only primitive; they were also expensive. They were essentially toys for rich people. But this situation changed quickly. By about 1920, many middle class families, in developed countries, had become car owners. The industry grew rapidly. In the United States, Henry Ford mass-produced a basic, inexpensive car, the Model T, which appeared on the market in 1908. Ford's company sold more than a quarter of a million cars in 1914; over 450,000 in 1916. By 1921, Ford was selling millions of cars. Ford's production techniques were innovative. But one way or another, the automotive society was bound to happen. Production went international. Ford built a factory in England, for example.[4] British firms date to 1906. One of them, Rolls-Royce, almost became a synonym for luxury cars. The industry boomed in Germany, too. More recently, Japanese and Korean cars have entered the market in a big way. Car manufacturing is an important industry in Iran. Iran produces for the home market, and also for export and assembly in other countries. The largest Iranian company, Iran Khodro, was founded in 1962.

Today, in all developed countries, and in middle-income countries like Iran, the urban middle class considers car ownership as something close to a necessity. Many families, in fact, have two cars, or more. If new cars seem too expensive, families can tap a huge used-car market. Modern societies are very definitely automotive societies. In developed countries, only the very poor lack a car.[5] And cars are not simply urban: indeed, for people in rural areas, suburbs, and small cities, a car may be even more essential than in town. In our 'motorised society', the car is a 'primary' element of 'personal autonomy'. It represents freedom, free choice, the ability to come and go at your own pace, regardless of timetables and schedules. It has worked its way into the life cycle; to get your driver's licence is to 'come of age;' and to lose it because of 'old age or impairment', in old age, is a bitter pill indeed – it represents the loss of freedom and autonomy (Freund and Martin 1993: 3).[6]

---

[3] On these early automobiles, see Goldstone 2016.

[4] So-called Locomotive Acts at first had retarded the use of automobiles in the United Kingdom. The Locomotives on Highways Act (1896) removed the restrictions, and set a speed limit of 14 miles per hour.

[5] In a few great cities, like London and Tokyo, or on Manhattan Island, driving can be a nightmare, and parking even more so. People rely heavily on taxicabs. Venice, a museum city, has no roads and no cars; motorboats cruise up and down its canals.

[6] In the twenty-first century, the automotive age may have crested. Or at least *ownership* of cars. Companies like Uber and its competitors have made a dent in the market for private cars. Car companies and others are experimenting with driverless cars as well. How this will affect the automotive society is hard to predict. The 2020 pandemic radically altered driving habits, at least temporarily. In some ways, it stimulated car ownership: driving your own car was a safe way to get about. The virus might haunt crowded trains, buses, airplanes, and taxis, but alone in your car, you felt protected. Whether this attitude will have any lasting effect on driving habits remains to be seen.

The automobile was invented in the West, but traffic jams in Bangkok or Nairobi or New Delhi – or Tehran – are, alas, as common as in major European or American cities. Nobody thinks of cars as something foreign, or colonial, or imposed. Elites own and drive cars, even in the poorest third-world countries. In Iran, car ownership has mushroomed in recent years; it grew 86.8 per cent between 2006 and 2015. The rate of car ownership in Iran is 158 per thousand population, according to fairly recent figures. This is above the rate in Thailand, and slightly below the rate in Brazil. It is also much greater than the rates in most African and Middle Eastern countries; three times as many Iranians own cars as Egyptians, for example (Economist 2020: 78, 159). Iran also suffers from a fairly high rate of auto accidents. Auto accidents are a leading cause of death. In 2006, according to figures quoted in *Driving Culture in Iran*, nearly 28,000 Iranians died in traffic accidents. Iranians, it seems, are fairly reckless drivers. At least, this is a common belief; drivers interviewed in Banakar's book share this belief; and figures about deaths and injuries in Iran tend to bear out this impression – deaths on the road were seven times as great as in Turkey, and double the rate in the United Kingdom (2016: 6).

In this, and some other respects, Iran differs from its neighbours, and has a distinctive automotive culture (in a negative way). But in Iran, as elsewhere, the automobile has had an incalculable impact on ordinary life. It represented, of course, an enormous liberation. Before cars, people walked, rode on horseback (if they had a horse), or in carriages (if they could afford a carriage). Most people never travelled very far from home. They lived in a circle with a tiny radius. A person might be born in a village, grow up, and die, without ever leaving that circle. Travel was slow and difficult, and relatively rare. In developed societies, the railways and the steamboat led to a radical change in the nineteenth century. Railways carried passengers and freight long distances at high speeds. In big cities, trams and streetcars had routes on main streets. Tramlines were gradually extended into suburban areas. But the automobile was the main engine of suburban growth in the twentieth century. The automobile also made outlying sections of the city livable. For the modern city to function, people had to have ways to get around. Trams were part of the solution; horse-drawn at first. Later came the auto; and, in the cities, buses and taxis and electric trams. In a few cities (London very notably) underground trains – subways, metros – linked different parts of the metropolis; they were fast, and immune to traffic gridlock. In the heart of the cities, cars are not really practical, especially during rush hours. Yet the cars are there – far too many of them. There is probably no large city in the world in which people do not complain about traffic.

There is something of a sociological literature on the automotive society (Redshaw 2008). This is not surprising, considering that cars are supremely important, economically and socially. The law and society branch of that literature, unfortunately, is fairly small. Yet automobile accidents are the bread and butter of tort law, while drunk driving and vehicular homicide are staples of criminal law. H Laurence Ross wrote a classic study of insurance claims, mostly from auto accidents (1970). *Driving Culture in Iran* is an extremely important addition to the literature. The book aimed to explore, through its research on driving culture, the 'social practices of ordinary people', and the way they 'view and experience the law, authority, politics, technology and religion in their daily lives' (Banakar 2016: 207). Its main focus is on Iran, naturally, and on the sociology of driving behaviour in Iran; but the insights are more generally applicable.

Iranians are convinced that their fellow-citizens (if not themselves) drive reck-lessly, as we said; drivers, they report, pay no attention to other people, including pedestrians, or to other drivers. Many of the people interviewed talked about 'the reckless behaviour of Iranian drivers', their utter 'disregard of traffic rules', and 'their inability to respect other people's rights' (ibid: 81). But why should this be the case? Some scholars give a cultural reason. Iranians, it is said, have a particular sense of individualism (or 'personalism') which is 'rooted in the individual's "peer group"' and is 'different from the western idea of individualism' (ibid: 16). The claim is that Iranians, generally speaking, do not care about anyone outside their circle of family and friends, and perhaps their local community. They share a form of individual-ism which is 'disconnected from society at large' (ibid: 57). Banakar expresses some scepticism about this thesis; it seems to him 'too thin, too subtle and too tenuous' to form the 'keystone of Iranian identity' (ibid: 56). Yet in interviews, subjects did seem to blame this feature of Iranian culture for the selfishness and recklessness of drivers. As a doctor said in one interview, 'anything goes' on the road; drive any way you like, so long as you avoid an accident (ibid: 112).

I share Banakar's scepticism about 'personalism'. It does not seem particularly confined to Iran. People naturally tend to favour their own family, clan, group, or circle of friends. In some societies, these ties are stronger than in others. Societies also differ in the sheer *size* of their ingroup. Almost everybody everywhere roots for the home team. Almost everybody prefers relatives and friends to strangers. But societies differ in how they define 'relative' or 'friend'. In some societies, even distant cousins are 'family'; in others, the immediate family is small and circumscribed.

Societies also differ in whether and how much people feel committed to the larger society. East Asian societies are often described in terms of 'personalism' (without using the word).[7] People in these countries, it is said, value close social connections; this is in contrast to the way of life in Europe and North America, which is (suppos-edly) much more individualistic. It is hard to know how much to make of these propositions. What is distinctive about modern societies – *all* modern societies – is that the individual inevitably confronts forces and people outside their immediate circle. Iranians drive cars, they listen to the radio, they have cell phones, they go to schools, they eat in restaurants. Everywhere they are exposed to other people; every day they have contacts with people outside the range of face-to-face experience. The miracles of modern technology have made this possible – the automobile, for one thing. Modern institutions (public education, very notably) have also contributed. Today, most definitely, no man (or woman) is an island.

---

[7] In Edward C Banfield's famous book, *The Moral Basis of a Backward Society* (1958), the author stud-ied 'Montegrano' (not its real name), a town in southern Italy; his description, which is highly negative, used the term 'amoral familism' to describe the mind-set of the people in the village. The villagers lacked any commitment to Italy or to society as a whole – or even to people in their village outside of their own families.

Thus it is no longer possible to live (so to speak) only in your tiny village. You are part of a larger society, whether you choose to be or not. 'Amoral familism', or 'personalism' is not dead. But it has definitely weakened in our times. The larger society, in other words, has shoved its way into the lives of the citizens. Consider, for example, the whole concept of nationalism. The very definition implies some awareness of national identity. In Eugen Weber's classic study, *Peasants into Frenchmen* (1976), he describes how the sense of a distinctively French identity developed in the nineteenth century. Early in the century, millions of people in 'France' did not speak (Parisian) French; and were only loosely connected to the larger society. You could tell a similar story about every modern country; the sense of nationhood developed over time. Almost certainly, one could tell this story about Iran. Among the institutions that (in Weber's book) transformed France were the national army and public education. The development of a road network was another part of the story. Roads (and railways) ended rural isolation. Roads (and railways) bound the country together. In the twentieth century, the explosion of car ownership could be added to the mix. The automobile contributed to the formation of national identity. It stimulated road-building, for one thing. It made internal travel possible; and further diminished the isolation and autonomy of outlying regions.

Also, perhaps paradoxically, the automobile played a role in the rise of internationalism, which is in some ways the opposite of nationalism. In modern times, tourism has become a huge and important industry. Tourist travel was once only for the rich. Now the middle class masses are avid tourists. When people travel, they open themselves up (consciously or not) to other cultures, other societies, other nations. In Europe, people can easily drive across national borders, and experience other societies, other languages, customs, cuisines, and ways of life. In a country like Iran, whose neighbours are not the friendliest, cars probably feature mostly in domestic travel. But even that can be broadening, in a country with many languages and many ethnic groups.

Car-driving, and the automotive experience, illustrates an important trait of modern society: *dependence on strangers*. In traditional societies, people generally interacted with others in their immediate circle: family, friends and members of the local community. The phrase 'disconnected from society at large' fits life in a small, isolated village. Modern society is profoundly different. We eat foods manufactured by strangers; we wear clothes made by strangers; we live in buildings built by strangers. Danger surrounds us – at least potentially. An extreme case is air travel: here we are, passengers, thousands of feet above the earth. If the plane crashed, we would all be killed. Our lives depend on the pilots who fly the planes – not to mention the companies that make the planes, and the mechanics that service them. But all of these people are strangers. We have no control over them, or the institutions they belong to. We rely, instead, on *law*; or, to be more precise, on regulation.

Cars are fast, heavy, and can be dangerous. Unlike airplane passengers, we are their pilots; still, danger is all around us as we drive. We can be careless ourselves, and put ourselves in danger. Other drivers are also a threat. Car-driving is also *anonymous;* the driver may be alone, speeding on a highway full of other cars; or (even worse) crawling or dawdling bumper to bumper on city streets. Traffic is an anonymised flow of 'faceless ghostly machines' (Urry 2004: 25, 30). The automobile represents freedom and choice, as we mentioned; the right to come and go as we please; the right to control many aspects of our lives. Yet, the driver can find himself in a very different situation: trapped in a nerve-wracking and frustrating gridlock, or crawling along at a snail's pace. The stresses of urban driving can lead to 'road rage': aggressive behaviour against other drivers (see, eg, Lupton 2002). Perhaps driving conditions take more of a toll on drivers in Iran than elsewhere. But the frustration is more or less common to all modern societies.

Driving, as we said, is anonymous. Anonymity is a general condition of outdoor urban life. The home is a place of intimacy; a place for family. Walking about on the street, sitting in a café, watching a concert: in these situations, a person is 'in public', and yet almost invisible. Outdoor life is, on the whole, the realm of anonymity. To be seen and yet not seen. Of course, even in public, people can act in such a way as to forfeit their anonymity; can draw attention to themselves – by shouting, brawling, or dressing or undressing in a way that violates accepted norms. To stay anonymous, you have to obey certain rules. For the most part, rules for behaviour in public spaces are simple and easy to follow; most of us know them almost instinctively.

Driving a car is a different form of anonymity. Unlike strolling about, or sitting in a coffee shop, it can be dangerous. And, also unlike other anonymous behaviour, the rules are not simple and easy to follow. Freedom in the automotive society is not unlimited; on the contrary, a tight fabric of rules binds the driver's freedom – rules which act as a kind of counterweight to the driver's autonomy. Iranians might be (comparatively speaking) reckless drivers; they break rules, but like drivers everywhere, they mostly get away with it. But not always. Accidents occur. Lives are lost. Money damages get paid. The law punishes some egregious violators. Moreover, driving is a skill. It has to be learned. Drivers need a licence. Drivers need to exercise control; even 'reckless' driving requires discipline. Discipline is 'part of what is involved in being shaped by automobility'; this implies the 'repression of natural individual desires and impulses' (Redshaw 2008: 142). Discipline, repression, and a measure of *trust*. Drivers are 'mutual strangers', men and women who act for themselves, and yet are able to 'follow … shared rules', to 'communicate through common sets of visual and aural signals, and interact even without eye-contact' (Urry 2004: 29). Some people, and some cultures, are better than others at repression and norm-following. Driving culture, in general, is a complex tangle of rules, laws and norms. Driving and 'automobility', moreover, are vitally important in society. Understanding driving culture is an important key to understanding society generally, what makes it tick, and what makes a particular society like or unlike other societies. These considerations are perhaps what led Reza Banakar to undertake this study in the first place.

V. THE VEILED AND THE UNVEILED

Reza Banakar, in his study of driving culture, refers to earlier studies of Iran, in which a distinction is made between the veiled and the unveiled. A reader will think, immediately, of traditional Islamic societies and their dress codes. Women in these societies may wear head-scarves, or, in even more traditional societies, they may cover themselves up in public from head to toe, their faces invisible except for narrow eye-slits. The 'public sphere' is thus the domain of the 'veiled'. This is because 'it is constituted

by "outsiders"; people who are not "related" or trusted, and thus it is unsafe …
to reveal one's true face or inner self'. Banakar adds, correctly, that the distinction
between inside and outside 'applies to both men and women, albeit in different ways'
(2016: 28). He might have added, too, that the distinction applies to all societies, not
just Islamic societies. And to a whole range of activities and behaviours, in public,
and not merely the dress code. To take an obvious example: people in western societies (as in all societies) can go around at home in their underwear, or even naked if
they choose; but this not permitted (socially at least) on the street. Sexual behaviour,
too, must be kept absolutely private.

There is, in other words, a fundamental distinction between the public and the
private – or, if you will, between the veiled and the unveiled. It varies from society to
society, of course; and from period to period. Women in Europe or North America
or Asia do not need to be 'veiled' in public; they can be mostly unveiled on the beach
(totally so, on nude beaches). But a bathing suit or nudity in a department store would
be considered a breach of decorum if not of law. Rules of modesty in dress are, for
the most part, stricter for women than for men, but a man too would be out of place
wearing a bathing suit in a department store or a classroom. In general, though, the
central distinction between veiled and unveiled domains is important in London or
Buenos Aires though perhaps not as much as in Iran.

Driving culture is a peculiar mixture of the veiled and the unveiled, the public
and the private. Drivers, especially if they have no passengers, can hardly see the
faces or bodies of other drivers. Drivers themselves are basically invisible to other
people, or seen only as a blur. Driving is a public activity; nonetheless, on the road,
the usual norms about behaviour towards other people in public do not apply (at
least not with full force). A driver's 'interactions with other drivers are not mediated face-to-face … or through the use of language'; typically, drivers 'do not, and
cannot orient themselves toward each others' movements through eye contact'
(Banaker 2016: 171–72). This peculiar feature allows drivers to act selfishly and
recklessly – traits which are part of the driving culture of Iran, in the view of many
of the people interviewed in *Driving Culture*. But it would be misleading to buy
this notion wholesale. Selfishness and recklessness are matters of more or less. And
rather less than more.

Driving Culture mentions a distinction between two types of norm: descriptive
and injunctive. Descriptive norms describe how people actually behave. Injunctive
norms are norms about how people *ought* to behave (ibid: 47). In all societies, there
is a gap between the two sets of norms. The gap is probably wider in driving culture
than (say) in the norms about behaviour in offices or restaurants. The gap may also
be particularly wide in Iran; at any rate, subjects interviewed for the book seem to be
think so.

Whether this is true or not is hard to say. But that people think so is a significant
social fact. One reason may be a more general distrust of the regime in power. Iran
is not a dictatorship, but neither is it a democratic state; it is an authoritarian state,
somewhere half way between democracy and dictatorship. We explored the impact of
the system on the structure, behaviour, and culture of the legal profession. Attitudes
toward the system may also impact the driving culture; and what people *think* about
the driving culture. Authoritarian governments tend to be (relatively speaking)
unpopular, and to suffer a deficit in legitimacy. Their very nature offends against the

growing global culture of human rights.[8] This culture percolates into non-democratic countries, and has a negative impact on the legitimacy of their regimes. Democratic countries, of course, have their own pathologies, and their own legitimacy crises. But usually less than autocratic regimes.

An atmosphere of distrust pervades the interviews in *Driving Culture*. As one woman (a taxi driver) put it, the very foundations of the law in Iran are 'flawed'. The police, she said, break the law 'in front of everyone'. She added: 'When I see what they do, I follow the law as long as they see me but break the law behind their back' (Banakar 2016: 143). Another woman flatly stated that 'Iranians are not law-abiding', and that they try to 'circumvent' the laws (ibid: 142).

Probably in every country driving culture is such that selfishness and recklessness are more or less common. Trust and legitimacy matter. But the very nature of driving contributes to the problem. The act of driving a car is hemmed in by many rules. Violating some of the rules is both tempting and easy. Enforcement, on the other hand, is difficult. Or impossible, in fact – because thousands or millions of people are in violation at times – violating rules about speed limits, or U-turns, or parking. One problem is, that in most countries, people see nothing morally wrong in parking for longer than permitted, or making an illegal U-turn; or going a bit faster than the speed limits. The police themselves accept some of these norms. Only gross violators risk trouble with the police. Even for more serious offences, which are not morally neutral, enforcement can be a problem. Drunk driving, for example, is a dangerous practice, and a prime cause of accidents and deaths. Still, the police catch only a tiny proportion of the drivers who are drunk at the wheel.

Could this situation change? Could it become possible to enforce all of the rules, all of the time? This is not science fiction but a practical possibility – or it could be. Surveillance cameras are already in wide use. It would be easy for cameras to capture every driver on the roads who drove too fast; or who made an illegal U-turn. The camera would record the licence plate number; a computer would impose an automatic fine and send out a bill. From one standpoint, this is utopian. It might reduce deaths and injuries on the road. From another standpoint, it would seem like the work of a stifling autocracy. People are used to certain leeways. This is part of modern driving culture, and not only in Iran. But driving culture, like other aspects of culture, is not fixed and changeless. It is constantly in flux.

VI. LAWS AND NORMS

Driving, as we said, is an activity governed (formally at least) by a huge number of rules. The traffic code in modern societies can be truly gargantuan. Before the automobile, there were only a few simple rules of the road. In the automotive age, the rule-book began to grow. And grow and grow: drivers' licences and speed limits; 'rules' which are robotic in nature (traffic lights); rules about car insurance; rules about passing other cars on highways; rules about the protocols to follow in cases of accidents. Drivers in every country have to reckon with all of these rules. Drivers in

---

[8] I considered this issue in Friedman (2011).

Iran may be more reckless and selfish than drivers in other countries. But even reckless and selfish drivers obey most of the rules most of the time.

Moreover, social norms, as we pointed out, govern driving culture as much as legal rules do. This too is surely as true of Iran as it is of other countries. Iranians may think of themselves as drivers who violate rules; but the violations take place within an overarching structure of norms. A careful observer could map out these norms and catalog them. They would probably observe that Iranian drivers, on the whole, observed most of these norms – out of habit, if for no other reason. Norm-following behaviour is an absolute necessity. Otherwise, traffic would turn into total chaos. Traffic at times (rush hour) and in certain places (central cities) may *seem* chaotic, but an underlying order nonetheless pervades it. Perhaps the underlying order is less orderly in Iran than in, say, Finland; but nonetheless it is there.

It is not easy to describe this underlying order precisely. There are clearly informal rules about which car goes first at intersections, how one cuts in ahead of another car (or doesn't), how fast are fast lanes and how slow are slow lanes; much of this is normative behaviour, independent of the traffic code. *Driving Culture* is a study of attitudes, not behaviour; it does not, therefore, explore actual behaviour on the road. But social norms, like the air we breathe, are everywhere. For drivers and car-owners, as for everybody else. Taxicabs waiting at airports, for example, line up in orderly queues. Indeed, the whole notion of a queue is norm-based behaviour. And the norms are for the most part implicit. Implicit norms are in some ways as enforceable as legal norms – perhaps even more so. Jumping the queue can get you a reprimand, and in extreme cases, a punch in the nose. Susan Silbey, in an intriguing essay, described a practice in Boston, and other northern American cities. Heavy snowfalls occur in winter in these cities. Many people park their cars on the street. When they dig their cars out of the snow, to drive to work, they follow the custom of putting a chair or some other object in the parking space. The message is plain: do not park here; this is *my* space. Of course, legally this is just plain wrong. Nobody owns the street or any parking spaces on the street. But people recognise the norm. Your hard work, digging out your car, entitles you to the space. For the most part, people accept the norm. And they enforce it. Violators run real risks. They might, for example, find that their tires have been slashed (Silbey 2010).

The social world, including the world of driving and parking, is full of this kind of implicit norm. The norms are neither legal or illegal. They occupy a space in between. Exploring this space is one of the natural domains of sociology: the domain of social life as people live it. Reza Banakar explores one piece of that domain in his great study of Iranian driving culture. *Driving Culture in Iran* is a major contribution to socio-legal studies and also to the sociology of law. The book reminds us how much was lost to the scholarly world, when Reza Banakar died before his time.

REFERENCES

Abel, RL and Lewis, PSC (eds) (1988–1989) *Lawyers in Society*, vols I–III (Berkeley, University of California Press).

Abel, R, Sommerlad, H, Hammerslev, O and Schultz, U (eds) (2020) *Lawyers in 21st-Century Society*, vol 1: National Reports (Oxford, Hart Publishing).

Abel, R, Sommerlad, H, Hammerslev, O and Schultz, U (eds) (2022) *Lawyers in 21st-Century Society*, vol 2: Comparisons and Theories (Oxford, Hart Publishing)

Banakar, R (2016) *Driving Culture in Iran: Law and Society on the Roads of the Islamic Republic* (London, IB Tauris).

Banakar, R and Travers, M (2005) 'Introduction' in R Banakar and M Travers (eds), *Theory and Method in Socio-Legal Research* (Oxford, Hart Publishing).

Banakar, R and Ziaee, K (2020) 'Iran: A Clash of Two Legal Cultures?' in R Abel et al (eds), *Lawyers in 21st-Century Society*, vol 1: National Reports (Oxford, Hart Publishing) 581.

Banfield, EC (1958) *The Moral Basis of a Backward Society* (Free Press).

Carlisle, J (2020) 'Libya: Lawyers between Ideology and the Market' in R Abel et al (eds), *Lawyers in 21st-Century Society*, vol 1: National Reports (Oxford, Hart Publishing) 619.

Economist (2020) *The Economist: Pocket World in Figures* (Economist Books).

Freund, P and Martin, G (1993) *The Ecology of the Automobile* (Chicago, University of Chicago Press).

Friedman, LM (2011) *The Human Rights Culture: A Study in History and Context* (Quid Pro LLC)

Goldstone, L (2016) *Drive! Henry Ford, George Selden, and the Race to Invent the Auto Age* (New York, Ballantine Books).

Liu, S (2020) 'China: A Tale of Four Decades' in R Abel et al (eds), *Lawyers in 21st-Century Society*, vol 1: National Reports (Oxford, Hart Publishing) 697.

Lupton, D (2002) 'Road Rage: Drivers' Understandings and Experiences' 38(3) *Journal of Sociology* 275.

Markovits, I (2010) *Justice in Lüritz: Experiencing Socialist Law in East Germany* (Princeton University Press).

—— (2020) *Diener zweier Herren: DDR-Juristen zwischen Recht und Macht* (Ch Links Verlag).

Nicholson, P and Ha, DH (2020) 'Vietnam, from Cadres to a "Managed" Profession' in R Abel et al (eds), *Lawyers in 21st-Century Society*, vol 1: National Reports (Oxford, Hart Publishing) 855.

Redshaw, S (2008) *In the Company of Cars: Driving as a Social and Cultural Practice* (CRC Press).

Ross, HL (1970) *Settled Out of Court: The Social Process of Insurance Claims Adjustment* (Routledge).

Silbey, S (2010) 'J Locke, op cit: Invocations of Law on Snowy Streets' 5 *Journal of Comparative Law* 66.

Urry, J (2004) 'The "System" of Automobility' 21(4–5) *Theory, Culture & Society* 25.

Weber, E (1976) *Peasants into Frenchmen: The Modernization of Rural France, 1870–1914* (Stanford University Press).

23

Traffic Justice: Law and Society on the Roads of Iran and the Netherlands

MARC HERTOGH

I. INTRODUCTION

IN *Driving Culture* in Iran: *Law and Society on the Roads of the Islamic Republic*, Reza Banakar (2016) and his collaborators skilfully guide us through everyday life in contemporary Iran. The country has one of the highest rates of road traffic incidents worldwide. The book convincingly argues that 'the driving habits of Iranians, their disregard for traffic laws and their attitude to the rights of other drivers are themselves indicators of how their social identities and relations are forged […] and, ultimately, how Iranian society is organized' (Banakar 2016: 2). In addition, Banakar uses urban traffic as a social laboratory to study the holy grail of law and society research: why do people follow or ignore the law? Previous studies have often claimed that people only comply with legal rules because they fear punishment or because compliance is in their best interest (see, eg, Hyde 1983; Pratt et al 2006). Banakar, by contrast, argues that compliance is also shaped by the perceived legitimacy of law. In his view, Iranian (external) legal culture – in this case understood as Iranians' 'experiences of traffic rules, law and legality' (Banakar 2016: 34) – determines whether people obey the law. Or, in his own words, 'the concept of legal culture could be used to describe why the majority of people normally follow certain laws or to explain why they collectively ignore them, as in the widespread disregard for traffic rules in Iran' (ibid: 10) This chapter will examine this claim by comparing law and society in Iran and in the Netherlands.

First, I will discuss the main findings from international traffic research (section II). These studies focus on two possible explanations for compliance behaviour. The first explanation is based on an 'instrumental' approach and emphasises the importance of deterrence. The second explanation is based on a 'normative' approach and emphasises the importance of legitimacy. I will use this conceptual framework to analyse the main findings from Banakar's study (section III). Next, I will compare these findings from Iran with the outcomes of a study on compliance with traffic rules in the Netherlands (section IV). The cultural and legal context in both countries is, of course, very different. Also, contrary to the situation in Iran, traffic in the Netherlands is characterised by a high level of legal compliance. However, a comparison between two 'extreme cases' is the best approach to achieve a more in-depth understanding of the nature of the phenomenon under study (see Jahnukainen 2010). Based on the comparison between Iran and the Netherlands, I will discuss three general lessons about legal compliance (section V). In the conclusion, I will reflect on the wider significance of Reza Banakar's scholarship (section VI).

II. TRAFFIC RESEARCH

Why do people obey the law? Banakar (2016) discusses two possible answers. First, he shows that both in the literature and in everyday practice there is a 'strong belief in penalties as a deterrent' (ibid: 69). However, sanctions may not always be enough. Building on Habermas' (1975; 1984) distinction between the 'legal system' and the 'lifeworld', Banakar (2016: 187) argues that 'modern liberal law continues to require a degree of legitimacy and moral justification for the way in which it administers society – a form of legitimacy that it can obtain only by maintaining a link with the lifeworld'. Both approaches – deterrence and legitimacy – also play an important role in a growing body of research on compliance with traffic rules among road users.

A. Instrumental and Normative Models of Compliance

Socio-legal traffic research is often based on Tyler's procedural justice model. Tyler (1990) distinguishes between two different perspectives on regulatory compliance: an 'instrumental' and a 'normative' approach. According to the 'instrumental' approach: 'people are viewed as shaping their behavior to respond to changes in the tangible, immediate incentives and penalties associated with following the law' (ibid: 3). This perspective has long dominated the literature on compliance. By contrast, Tyler is more interested in the 'normative' approach. This approach is concerned with 'the influence of what people regard as just and moral as opposed to what is in their self-interest' (ibid: 3). In other words, '[i]f people view compliance with the law as appropriate because of their attitudes about how they should behave, they will voluntarily assume the obligation to follow the rules' (ibid: 3).

An important element of the 'normative' perspective is the idea that people's positive attitudes and opinions about the legitimacy of the authorities will have a positive influence on compliance. To test this idea, Tyler has conducted two surveys of the general population of Chicago. These surveys focused on a range of laws that people deal with in their everyday lives. These laws prohibited six forms of behaviour: making enough noise to disturb the neighbours; littering; driving a car while intoxicated; driving faster than the speed limit; taking inexpensive items from stores without paying; and parking illegally. Tyler examined legitimacy in two ways. First, by measuring the 'perceived obligation to comply with the directives of an authority, irrespective of the personal gains and losses associated with doing so' (ibid: 27). And second, by measuring the extent to which 'authorities enjoy the public's support, allegiance and confidence' (ibid: 28).

Tyler concluded that legitimacy has a significant and independent effect on the level of self-reported compliance (even when other potential causal factors are controlled for). By contrast, deterrence and the risk of punishment have no significant effect on compliance. To quote the jacket of his book, Tyler (1990) argued that 'people comply with the law not so much because they fear punishment as because they feel that legal authorities are legitimate and that their actions are generally fair'. The final part of this citation also emphasises a second important dimension of Tyler's work. He not only found that legitimacy shapes compliance, but also that the level of (perceived) legitimacy is influenced by the perceived procedural fairness of law enforcement authorities.

B. Three Examples: Scotland, Australia, Ghana

Tyler's model has been applied to analyse compliance with traffic rules in a number of countries, including Scotland, Australia and Ghana. Bradford et al (2015) have conducted a survey among 816 motorists in Scotland. Their study was designed to analyse the effects of an experiment in which a group of police officers used a new approach to communicate procedural justice during routine checks. They found that 'experience of procedural justice during encounters with officers appeared to enhance perceptions of police legitimacy' (ibid: 183). Moreover, their findings support 'the idea that there are both instrumental and norms-based "pathways" to compliance with traffic laws' (ibid: 184). In a similar study, Bates et al (2016) have held a survey among 237 young novice drivers in Australia. They focused on how four elements of procedural justice (voice, neutrality, respect and trustworthiness) were perceived in relation to two forms of speed enforcement: average speed and mobile speed cameras. They found 'a significant relationship between perceptions of procedural justice [...] and self-reported speeding behavior' (ibid: 40). Finally, Tankebe et al (2019) have examined traffic violations and cooperative intentions among a sample of 415 commercial vehicle drivers in Ghana. Their study found that personal corruption experiences increased the frequency of self-reported violations of traffic laws. They also found that perceived police fairness significantly increased the likelihood of cooperation with the police (but there was no effect on self-reported compliance).

C. What about Law?

Although Tyler's approach has been very influential, it has also been criticised. As indicated above, Tyler (1990) considered only two elements of legitimacy: the 'perceived obligation to obey the law'; and the level of 'support for legal authorities'. However, several critics have argued that this operationalisation of legitimacy is too limited (Murphy et al 2009; Murphy and Cherney 2010; Murphy and Cherney 2012). According to Murphy et al (2009: 1), 'previous research on procedural justice and legitimacy has examined legitimacy in a limited way by focusing solely on the perceived legitimacy of authorities and ignoring how people may perceive the legitimacy of the laws and rules they enforce'. Although an authority itself may be seen to have legitimate authority, the rules and laws it tries to enforce may be seen to be illegitimate. Following this criticism, this chapter will expand the concept of legitimacy. In addition to *institutional legitimacy* (the 'perceived obligation to obey the law') and *personal legitimacy* ('support for legal authorities'), we will also consider *legal legitimacy* (Crawford and Hucklesby 2013: 2). This third element focuses on the perceived legitimacy of the rules and norms the authorities try to enforce.

To analyse the role of legitimacy, Tyler (1990) also included several other potential motives for compliance, including deterrence, personal morality, peer opinion and procedural justice (as well as several demographic control variables). The next two sections will use this conceptual framework to study compliance with traffic rules among road users in Iran and the Netherlands.

III. LAW AND SOCIETY ON THE ROADS OF IRAN

While most studies that were cited in the previous section are based on surveys, Banakar (2016) has used a qualitative approach. His study is based on over 70 hours of interviews with lawyers, taxi drivers, insurance managers and medical doctors in Shiraz and Teheran. Based on this material, Banakar discusses many different reasons why Iranians follow or (more typically) ignore traffic laws. In this section, these findings will be organised, using the analytical framework (and the variables) from traffic research. I will use fragments from the interviews with Iranians to illustrate 'the words, ideas, images, concepts and terms they use to problematise the traffic situation, reckless driving, the law and law enforcement' (Banakar 2016: 35).

A. Reasons for (Non) Compliance

i. Deterrence

First and foremost, Iranians have a 'strong belief in penalties as a deterrent' (ibid: 69). According to the interviewees the most likely explanation for the lack of compliance with traffic rules in their country is the absence of strict enforcement:

> As long as the rules are not enforced forcefully, very few people will take them seriously and follow them. (ibid: 91)

ii. Personal Morality

Some of the interviewees also suggest that it is important to consider people's own feelings about what is right and wrong. In their view, many Iranians do not feel that it is wrong to break the law:

> Iranians do not experience the rules of traffic as morally binding. (ibid: 101)

> All they [the drivers] care about is driving their cars. They pay no attention to traffic signs. (ibid: 50)

iii. Peer Opinion

The interviewees explain that their friends and family usually do not disapprove of non-compliance with traffic rules:

> In our society lawlessness is tolerated. Breaking the law doesn't cause a person's fall from grace. Far from it, in traffic, if someone breaks the law [...] other drivers will not treat his conduct disapprovingly; instead, they will follow his example. (ibid: 99)

iv. Procedural Justice

Many Iranians also complain about the arbitrary enforcement of traffic rules. The interviewees feel that they are not treated fairly and they experience a lack of procedural justice:

> The law doesn't see or treat everyone in the same way. (ibid: 50)

> The enforcement is entirely selective here, which means that if our traffic officers dislike someone they penalize them. (ibid: 79)

v. Institutional Legitimacy

Signalling a low level of institutional legitimacy, the interviewees indicate that they do not feel obliged to follow the law:

> The arbitrariness of the law turns ordinary people away from the law. (ibid: 51).

> Law doesn't mean a thing. It has no meaning for our people. (ibid: 142)

vi. Personal Legitimacy

During the interviews, many Iranians also indicate that the overall level of respect and support for the police and other state authorities is fairly low:

> Iranians do not trust their rulers ... and therefore they do not submit to the laws imposed on them by their rulers. (ibid: 106)

> The distrust of authorities, coupled with disregard for state law and the rights of others, lay the social foundation upon which Iranian legal culture rests. (ibid: 197)

vii. Legal Legitimacy

The perceived level of legal legitimacy is not very high either. Many of the interviewees do not accept the authority of traffic rules:

> You know, the traffic rules aren't taken seriously by most drivers .... Driving to Iranians means pressing the gas pedal, it isn't about knowing the traffic rules or following the traffic signs. (ibid: 43–44)

> Iranians 'have no respect for the law ...'. (ibid: 98)

viii. Background Variables

Finally, the level of compliance with traffic rules is also influenced by a number of socioeconomic and demographic characteristics of motorists, such as class, gender and age. Some Iranians suggest, for example, that younger drivers are more reckless than older drivers.

B. What Moves Drivers in Iran?

All these reasons for (non)compliance are considered equally important and it is not always clear how they are related. Yet, Banakar focuses on two findings in particular. First, most interviews only point to a limited effect of deterrence. This confirms the experience of some of the male taxi drivers:

> The new increased fines have perhaps had an impact on thirty per cent of drivers, amongst those who have received their driving license more recently. But the drivers haven't changed their ways. (ibid: 69–70)

Second, Banakar's study also shows that legal compliance is shaped by people's own sense of justice and the perceived legitimacy of law:

> Iranians are not law-abiding in so far as they do not readily follow the laws of the State, but they do regard themselves as the source of law and follow a 'personal' set of norms of rules. (ibid: 203)

IV. LAW AND SOCIETY ON THE ROADS OF THE NETHERLANDS[1]

To analyse which factors influence compliance with traffic rules in the Netherlands, survey data were collected from a stratified random sample of 1,182 Dutch traffic offenders.[2] The survey focused on five types of offences: (i) speeding; (ii) ignoring a red traffic light; (iii) illegal parking; (iv) driving a car while intoxicated; and (v) using a mobile phone while driving. The 10-page survey examined a range of issues, including views about Dutch traffic laws, attitudes and beliefs about the Dutch Central Fine Collection Agency (CJIB) and the police, and their personal experiences with legal authorities.

A. Reasons for (Non) Compliance

Because our sample included only traffic offenders, we could not distinguish between those people who did and those who did not break the law. Our scale for self-reported compliance behaviour builds on a scale previously used by Murphy et al (2009) in

---

[1] Parts of his section draw from and build on Hertogh (2015).
[2] For methodological details of this study, see Hertogh (2015).

their study of tax offenders in Australia. Following their example, traffic offenders in our study were asked a series of six questions about how they thought the traffic ticket had affected their behaviour. All responses to the six items were reverse scored to form the traffic rules compliance score. A higher score indicates greater compliance. In general, the self-reported level of compliance among most respondents is quite high, with an average score of 2.41 (on a scale from 0–3). Those offenders who were booked for drunk driving report the highest score (2.56) and those who were caught for the use of a mobile phone report the lowest score (2.32).

i. Deterrence

Deterrence was measured with five items: 'If you did each of the following things, how likely do you think it is that you would be arrested or cited by the police?' (see Tyler 1990: 188). The respondents were asked to answer this question for all five selected offences. The answers were given on a four-point scale (0 = 'very likely' to 3 = 'not at all likely'), with a higher score indicating lower perceptions of deterrence ($\alpha = 0.84$). Nearly three quarter of all respondents think that it is (somewhat or very) likely that they would be cited or get arrested for illegal parking (72.0 per cent) and speeding (70.6 per cent). However, these numbers are lower for driving while intoxicated (61.1 per cent). About one out of every six respondents (17.9 per cent) thinks that it is not likely at all that they will get caught for this offence.

ii. Personal Morality

Personal morality was measured with five items: 'Think about your own feelings about what is right and wrong. How wrong do you think it is to do each of the following things?' (see Tyler 1990: 190). The respondents were asked to answer this question for all five selected offences. The answers were given on a four-point scale (0 = 'very wrong' to 3 = 'not wrong at all'). A higher score on this scale reflects those who perceive these offences as less wrong ($\alpha = 0.69$). All respondents (very) strongly disapprove of drunk driving and ignoring a red traffic light. Of all respondents 90.9 per cent feel that drunk driving is (very) wrong; and 70.2 per cent feel that ignoring a red traffic light is (very) wrong. However, these scores are much lower for illegal parking (16.9 per cent feel this is very wrong) and for speeding (16.1 per cent).

iii. Peer Opinion

Peer opinion was measured with five items: 'Think about the five adults that you know best. If you got a fine or got arrested for doing each of the following things, how much would they disapprove or feel that you had done something wrong?'(see Tyler 1990: 189). The respondents were asked to answer this question for all five selected offences. The answers were given on a four-point scale (0 = 'very much disapprove' to 3 = 'not at all disapprove'). A higher score on this scale reflects lower perceptions of peer disapproval ($\alpha = 0.73$). A majority of our respondents think that their peers would (very) strongly disapprove of drunk driving (73.8 per cent); and ignoring a red light

(52.6 per cent). However, these scores are somewhat lower for speeding (42 per cent) and much lower for illegal parking (19.3 per cent).

iv. Procedural Justice

Procedural justice towards the CJIB was measured with two items: 'I feel that I was treated fairly by the CJIB'; and 'I feel that the procedures used by the CJIB were fair' (see Murphy et al 2009: 25). The answers were given on a four-point scale (0 = 'completely disagree' to 3 = 'completely agree'), with a higher score indicating greater perceptions of procedural justice towards the CJIB ($\alpha = 0.91$). More than half of our respondents (strongly) agree that they were treated fairly by the CJIB (54.6 per cent). Almost half of all our respondents (strongly) agree that the procedure at the CJIB was fair (48.7 per cent).

v. Institutional Legitimacy

Institutional legitimacy was measured with six items (eg 'People should obey the law even if it goes against what they think is right') (see Tyler 1990: 187). The answers were given on a four-point scale (0 = 'completely disagree' to 3 = 'completely agree'). A higher score on this scale reflects those who perceive a larger obligation to obey the law ($\alpha = 0.78$). A large majority of our respondents (85.2 per cent) feel that 'people should obey the law even if it goes against what they think is right'. About two thirds (63.2 per cent) feel that 'disobeying the law is seldom justified'.

vi. Personal Legitimacy

Personal legitimacy was measured with four items (eg 'I have a great deal of respect for the police') (see Tyler 1990: 183). The answers were given on a four-point scale (0 = 'completely disagree' to 3 = 'completely agree'), with a higher score indicating greater support for the police ($\alpha = 0.86$). Most respondents (strongly) agree with the statement 'I feel that one should support the police' (78.2 per cent). However, a smaller number of respondents indicate that they 'trust the police' (52.4 per cent).

vii. Legal Legitimacy

Legal legitimacy was measured with ten items, some of which related to specific traffic laws (eg 'You should always stop for a red traffic light, even if it's on a deserted crossing at midnight') (see Murphy et al 2009: 25) while some related to the law in general (eg 'My own feelings about what is right and wrong usually agree with most laws in our country') (see Murphy and Cherney 2012: 200). The answers were given on a four-point scale (0 = 'completely disagree' to 3 = 'completely agree'). A higher score on this scale reflects those who see laws more legitimate ($\alpha = 0.65$). Two thirds of all respondents (66.4 per cent) feel that, 'if circumstances allow it, it is all right to drive faster than the speed limit'. Also, a majority (55.3 per cent) think that 'good driving is more important than always following traffic rules'. In more general terms, about two thirds (62.8 per cent) agree that 'my own feelings about what is right and wrong usually agree with the laws of our country'.

viii. Background Variables

Finally, our study also included a number of socioeconomic and demographic variables for controlling purposes. Respondents in our sample are mostly male (71 per cent), 'with a Dutch background' (77.7 per cent) and between 14 and 88 years of age (M = 43.1; SD = 15.0). Moreover, 42.2 per cent have received a university or a higher vocational education and 23.6 per cent earn an annual income over €50,000.

B. What Moves Drivers in the Netherlands?

A first statistical analysis of the survey results shows that those with high scores for all three types of legitimacy were also more likely to report a high level of compliance.[3] This holds true for institutional legitimacy, personal legitimacy and legal legitimacy. Similarly, procedural justice was positively correlated with self-reported compliance. A regression analysis further confirmed these findings. A multiple linear regression analysis was performed using instrumental and normative motives as predictors of 'self-reported compliance'.[4] In this analysis, the relation between legitimacy and self-reported compliance was found to be significant. Those offenders who perceive the laws to be highly legitimate were more likely to comply with traffic rules. The same holds true for those offenders who show a high level of support for the police; as well as for those who strongly feel that they have an obligation to obey the law. Moreover, those offenders with a greater perception of procedural justice towards the CJIB were also more likely to comply. Those offenders who do not feel that committing a traffic offence is wrong were less likely to comply with traffic laws. Finally, this analysis also shows that several variables have no significant effect on compliance. Those offenders with a high or low perception of deterrence were not more or less likely to comply with traffic rules. The same holds true for those with high or low perceptions of peer disapproval. Most background variables have no effect on compliance either.

V. DISCUSSION: WHY DO PEOPLE FOLLOW OR IGNORE THE LAW?

Which general conclusions can we draw from these studies in Iran and the Netherlands? Needless to say, that – in cultural, political and legal terms – the two countries could not be more different. This is also reflected in the findings from both studies. While Iran is characterised by a low level of compliance with traffic laws and a corresponding low score on nearly all indicators; the Netherlands has a high level of compliance with traffic laws and a fairly high score on most indicators. However, comparing these two 'extreme cases' is very useful for highlighting 'the most unusual variation in the phenomena under investigation' and to achieve 'a more in-depth understanding of the nature of the phenomenon under study' (Jahnukainen 2010: 378).

---

[3] Table 1 (Hertogh 2015: 221).
[4] Table 2 (Hertogh 2015: 225).

The comparison between Iran and the Netherlands points to three important reasons why people follow or ignore the law.

A. Instrumental and Normative Motives

As Bradford et al (2015: 172) have argued, '[p]erhaps more than other aspects of legal regulation, the enforcement of traffic laws is premised on an instrumental model of human behavior'. However, the empirical evidence from both Iran and the Netherlands shows that the effect of sanctions on compliance with traffic rules is limited. Moreover, both studies demonstrate that people's own views on what is just and moral also play an important role in shaping compliance with traffic rules. In other words, the empirical evidence from both Iran and the Netherlands supports the key finding from previous traffic research that 'while […] instrumental concerns about effective policing and the risk of sanctions play some small role in shaping intentions to comply with the law, normative factors are stronger predictors' (ibid: 174).

B. Legal Legitimacy Shapes Legal Compliance

In addition, the evidence from Iran and the Netherlands shows that people's perceptions of legitimacy are not only related to their views and attitudes about institutions or officials, but also to their views and attitudes about law. Previous research has been criticised for focusing on people's opinions about law and neglecting how their views are reflected in their behaviour. As Abel (2010: 18) has noted in a review of four decades of law-and-society-research: 'Opinions about legal institutions, processes and rules, and events divorced from daily life may be easy to elicit through closed-ended questionnaires, but their meaning is opaque'. In his view, '[w]e need to know whether belief in law's legitimacy makes people more willing to comply against self-interest'. In response to Abel's criticism, the research in Iran and the Netherlands demonstrates how legal legitimacy shapes legal compliance.

C. Congruence Between State Law and Living Law

Finally, the studies in Iran and the Netherlands show that an important dimension of the perceived legitimacy of law is the level of congruence between state law and living law. This is most clearly illustrated in Iran. Banakar (2016: 198) concludes that '[t]he historical rift between state and society, and subsequently between cultural practices of the people and state law, continues to define Iranian society'. In Banakar's (ibid: 184) view, '*urf* [a collection of unwritten local rules and norms] is embodied in the culture of ordinary people and survives as their "living law", distinct from the norms that express the State's political expediency'. This is also clearly reflected in many of the interviews. As one civil servant explains: '*urf* is more powerful than laws and ordinances made in Parliament' (ibid: 43). To some extent, the tension between state law and people's own ideas of law and justice is also present in the Dutch study. For example, one third (30 per cent) of the survey respondents thinks that the laws in the Netherlands do not correspond with their own norms and values.

VI. CONCLUSION

Banakar's brilliant study of driving culture in Iran shows that urban traffic is a good laboratory to study law in everyday life. His book not only explores Iranian legal culture, but it also helps us to answer one of the key questions in law and society research: why do people follow or ignore the law? Although many legal scholars and policymakers still support an instrumental model of compliance, evidence from both Iran and the Netherlands strongly suggests that the effect of sanctions and deterrence is limited. Instead, both studies show that people comply with the law if and when they feel that legal authorities are legitimate and their actions are generally fair. In addition, people's perceptions of legitimacy are not only related to their views and attitudes about institutions or officials, but also to their views and attitudes about law.

A common tread in many of the interviews with Iranians is their mistrust of the legal system. As one medical doctor explains: 'In the same way that [Iranians] hope to avoid ending up in a hospital, they also hope not to come into contact with the law' (Banakar 2016: 108). Although both countries are very different, this is also a valuable lesson for the Netherlands. In times of growing legal alienation in Europe (Hertogh 2018), Iran is the proverbial canary in the coal mine. In this way, Reza Banakar's work not only reminds us of a great scholar who will be dearly missed, but his scholarship also serves as a constant reminder to politicians and lawmakers that law can only retain its legitimacy if it maintains a connection with the lifeworld of its citizens.

REFERENCES

Abel, RL (2010) 'Law and Society: Project and Practice' *Annual Review of Law and Social Science* 1.

Banakar, R (2016) *Driving Culture in Iran. Law and Society on the Roads of the Islamic Republic* (London, IB Tauris).

Bates, L, Allen, S and Watson, B (2016) 'The Influence of the Elements of Procedural Justice and Speed Camera Enforcement on Young Novice Driver Self-Reported Speeding' 92 *Accident Analysis and Prevention* 34.

Bradford, B, Hohls, K, Jackson, J and MacQueen, S (2015) 'Obeying the Rules of the Road: Procedural Justice, Social Identity, and Normative Compliance' 31 *Journal of Contemporary Criminal Justice* 171.

Crawford, A and Hucklesby, A (2013) 'Introduction: Compliance and Legitimacy in Criminal Justice' in A Crawford and A Hucklesby (eds), *Legitimacy and Compliance in Criminal Justice* (New York, Routledge).

Habermas, J (1975) *Legitimation Crisis* (Boston, MA, Heinemann Education).

—— (1984) *The Theory of Communicative Action*, vol I (Boston, MA, Beacon Press).

Hertogh, M (2015) 'What Moves Joe Driver? How Perceptions of Legitimacy Shape Regulatory Compliance among Dutch Traffic Offenders' 43 *International Journal of Law, Crime and Justice* 214.

—— (2018) *Nobody's Law: Legal Consciousness and Legal Alienation in Everyday Life* (London, Palgrave MacMillan).

Hyde, A (1983) 'The Concept of Legitimation in the Sociology of Law' *Wisconsin Law Review* 379.

Jahnukainen, M (2010) 'Extreme Cases' in AJ Mills, G. Durepos and E. Wieber (eds), *Encyclopedia of Case Study Research* (Thousand Oaks, SAGE Publications).

Murphy, K, Tyler, TR and Curtis, A (2009) 'Nurturing Regulatory Compliance: Is Procedural Justice Effective When People Question the Legitimacy of the Law?' 3 *Regulation and Governance*, 1.

Murphy, K and Cherney, A (2010) *Understanding Minority Group Willingness to Cooperate with Police: Taking Another Look at Legitimacy Research*, Working Paper no 15 (Alfred Deakin Research Institute, Deakin University, Australia).

—— (2012) 'Understanding Cooperation with Police in a Diverse Society' 52 *British Journal of Criminology*, 181.

Pratt, TC, Cullen, FT, Blevins, KR, Daigle, LE and Madensen, TD (2006) 'The Empirical Status of Deterrence Theory: A Meta-Analysis' in FT Cullen, JP Wright and KR Blevins (eds), *Taking Stock: The Status of Criminological Theory* (New Brunswick, NJ, Transaction Publishers).

Tankebe, J, Boakye, KE and Amagnya, MA (2019) 'Traffic Violations and Cooperative Intentions among Drivers: The Role of Corruption and Fairness' 30 *Policing and Society* 1081.

Tyler, TR (1990) *Why People Obey the Law* (New Haven, CT, Yale University Press).

24

The Cancer of the Law in the Islamic Republic of Iran: Reflections on the Iranian Anti-Israel Law of 2020

MATHIEU DEFLEM

I. INTRODUCTION

THE STUDY OF culture is essential to the study of law. The study of the culture of law itself must likewise be a central aspect of any serious sociological or socio-legal study of law in society. It is undeniable that the scholar whose life and work we remember in this anthology has devoted arguably better and more efforts than anyone else to the study of legal cultures. It is for this reason not only professionally becoming, but appropriate on scholarly grounds as well, to maintain a conceptual focus on legal cultures and to practise it in our research. Applying a legal cultures perspective to selected cases of law in Iran, further, will also remind us to remember our respective native roots, no matter where we were find ourselves in the present, and foster a mindful comparative dialogue in the global era.

This chapter is indebted to the work of Reza Banakar by analytically considering the role of legal culture in the constellation of the relationship between law and other aspects of society and, additionally, by its thematic focus on a contemporary legal condition in the Islamic Republic of Iran. Banakar's emphasis on the concept of legal culture rhymes well with my own theoretical inclination to focus on the role of culture in relation to law, especially in the context of modern societies (Deflem 2008). The focus on law in Iran, I must approach as an outsider to that particular country, but from an appropriate comparative outlook. I will in this chapter specifically examine and scrutinise the new anti-Israel law that was passed by the Iranian parliament in May 2020 to ban any and all contact between Iran and Israel. Analysing this law in the context of modernisation and counter-modernisation, I will seek to make sense – in strict analytical terms – of the insensible, uncover the reasons for the unreasonable, as Iran's new anti-Israeli law is aimed not only at the destruction of the state of Israel, but the genocide of the Jewish people as well. I shall rely on theoretical advances concerning the rationalisation of law, especially with regard to the independence of the judiciary and its cultural foundations.

II. LAW BETWEEN NORMS AND VALUES

This section is not coincidentally labelled under a heading that invokes the (English-language) title of Jürgen Habermas' (1992) *magnum opus* on law, because my analysis harmonises with long-standing modernist perspectives of law in society (Deflem 2013). It is a mark of modernisation that culture remains related to law, though in markedly different ways than in pre-modern times. I hereby define culture sociologically as the whole of values and their associated practices, while law refers to a system of norms enforced in a given context as well as the institutions and practices associated therewith. Whereas cultural values determine what one ought to do as a member of a group or segment thereof, legal norms prescribe how, within a given jurisdiction, people ought to interact with one another regardless of their potentially varying cultural beliefs and values. As such, culture refers to the substance of a social order (what to do), whereas law and other norms relate to the form of social organisation (how to interact with others). Historically, religion has been a critical element of culture across most if not all known societies, as much as law has been accordingly subject to religious justification or, alternatively, been marked in varying degrees and ways by a process of secularisation.

The development of the changing relationship between law and culture has occupied sociology since the classic era (Deflem 2008: 199–202). Emile Durkheim clarified the relationship between (cultural) values and (legal) norms in terms of a transformation from mechanical to organic societies, whereby the collective conscience changes from a cohesive set of strong beliefs towards an individualist society with a plurality of value systems which modern law needs to integrate (Durkheim 1893). Max Weber described this transformation in terms of a rationalisation of law in the direction of purposive-rational action (Weber 1922). Applying the methodology of '*Wahlverwandtschaft*' (elective affinity), Weber described the conditions of this rationalisation process as resulting from the economic expansion of capitalism, the political development of bureaucracy, a law-internal process of the professionalisation of law, and, culturally, an increasing secularisation of law.

Building on the European classics, Talcott Parsons brought the relationship between values and norms to the centre of sociological theorising. Parsons clearly distinguished values and norms, because, especially after World War II, a variety of ways in which modernity had taken hold (or not) across political and legal communities was revealed. But Parsons could still justifiably conceive of the relation between values and norms in relatively unproblematic terms by arguing that normative integration through law is possible because of freedom-guaranteeing cultural values that form law's sub-constitutional stratum (Parsons 1978). As such, there was an unproblematic relationship between culture and law in the society Parsons described or, at least, thought to describe.

Turning towards contemporary conditions, a perspective must be developed that takes into account increasing societal complexity since the latter half of the twentieth century. At least two avenues are available. One is the post-modern attitude towards wholesale incredulity, a fashionable position that remains alive today. The other route is a modernist theory. Jürgen Habermas's (1992) procedural discourse theory presents a perspective that remains worthy of our attention in the pluralistic societies of today.

Contemporary societies are marked by a high degree of diverse cultural value systems and are, therefore, precisely in need of integration through legal and other normative frameworks. This functional need does not imply that societies must be culturally uniform or cohesive, as a common misconception of Habermas and other modernists would hold. Instead, effective integration efforts through normative regulation are needed when different value systems within societies appear not as mere alternatives, but as consequential conflicts. The integrative function of law is then a necessity for peaceful co-existence and survival of the social order.

Today the most critical challenge to legal systems remains the need to fulfil the primary function of integration in light of a need to preserve cultural differences. The need to have one norm given many cultural values defines the central character of modern society today. But there are limits to tolerance as well. Otherwise, respect for values and cultural self-determination would become self-contradictory when the values to be respected inherently violate the rights of others. When these values are religious in nature, this effort becomes all the more necessary and difficult as religious principles are typically justified in terms of a higher order that is at once considered most fundamental. Minimally, the limits of value-tolerance are presented when certain values and their influence on law and politics become existentially destructive to others. I argue that the autocratic legal system of the Islamist Iranian regime presents such a troubling case.

III. IRAN'S ANTI-ISRAEL LAW

Since the formation of the Islamic Republic of Iran following the 1979 Revolution, the country has generally lacked stability and faced much turmoil, including a nearly eight-year-long war with Iraq, the crippling impact of economic sanctions and political isolation, and the suppression of political protest. Centrally controlled by a Supreme Leader, the regime is a totalitarian Islamic theocracy that violates fundamental rights and liberties, despite the country's otherwise relatively advanced technological and economic conditions.

What is remarkable about present-day Iran is that, unlike many other such autocratic systems today (North Korea, as the most obvious example), the political regime of the country is at once critiqued by many Western nations while still functioning as a player in world affairs. Iran has been facing economic sanctions from many countries and the United Nations, but has also been able to have a Joint Comprehensive Plan of Action (known as the Iran nuclear deal) accepted by the European Union and the five permanent members of the United Nations Security Council (including the United States). Israeli Prime Minister Benjamin Netanyahu had requested the deal to include a basic and more than reasonable 'Iranian commitment of Israel's right to exist', but US President Obama denied the request (Peralta 2015). Whatever its precise terms, the deal has effectively allowed Iran to maintain its role as an active partner in international accords.

In view of longstanding political and cultural traditions in the region, it would almost be redundant to discuss the anti-Israeli aspects of the Iranian Islamic regime. Since the 1979 Revolution, Iran has de facto been engaged in a proxy war with Israel, because such is most typically, if not intrinsically, the nature of an Islamist regime located in the Middle-Eastern region. To the Islamic Republic of Iran, no enemy is worse than Israel, the state and the nation alike. Nonetheless, Iran's recently passed anti-Israel law presents a distinct moment in the development of the country's political and legal system, the dynamics of which reveal, in a concrete and clear way, the nature of the Iranian regime and its legal culture.

Iran's anti-Israel law of 2020 was passed by the Iranian Parliament (the Islamic Consultative Assembly or *Majlis*) on 18 May that year (Joffre 2020; Nadimi 2021; Rose 2020; Seliktar and Rezaei 2020). Voted for unanimously by the 43 members of the Parliament's National Security and Foreign Policy Commission, the law is officially titled 'Countering Israel's Actions' ('*Tarhe Moghabele ba Eghdamat Israel*'). Basically outlawing all contact and agreements between Iran and the 'Zionist enemy' that is Israel (ibid), the law was formally passed to halt alleged 'hostile acts of the Zionist regime against peace and security', including 'spying, terrorism, and martyrdom of Iranian nuclear scientists, cyber and electronic warfare, and cyber-attacks on nuclear and economic centers' (FARS 2020; Joffre 2020). Upon unanimous approval of the bill, Iranian parliamentarians chanted 'down with Israel' (ibid).

The passing of Iran's anti-Israel law came shortly before planned Quds Day rallies had to be drastically scaled back in view of the impact of the coronavirus pandemic (Vahdat and Gambrell 2020). Sanctioned by the Iranian government, Quds Day or Jerusalem Day (Al-Quds, literally 'The Holy', is the Arabic name for Jerusalem) is held annually on the last Friday of Ramadan to protest against Israel and, its major ally, the United States. The day is infamous for its participants gleefully chanting 'Death to Israel!', 'Death to the United States!'.

Iran's anti-Israel law consists of 14 articles. Among the specific provisions, the law criminalises the use of Israeli flags and symbols that favour Israel, bans any and all financial assistance from Iranian citizens to Israel, and advocates the boycotting of all Israeli institutions and companies registered in Israel. Also banned are any forms of cooperation between Iranian universities and medical institutions, public as well as private organisations, and conferences with Israeli members or affiliation. The law further criminalises contact with all organisations that are sanctioned by Israel to advance the 'goals of the Zionist regime' (Joffre 2020), and it bans the use of products and technology manufactured in Israel or by companies that have branches in the country. Any kind of political agreements between Iran and the state of Israel are explicitly outlawed as well.

Iranian citizens violating the anti-Israel law can be fined, dismissed from public office, or imprisoned. All contacts and communications with Israeli nationals are punishable unless they can be proven to have taken place accidentally. The law also applies to Israeli citizens by prohibiting them from entering Iran and from travelling to what is referred to as the 'occupied Palestinian territories' (Rose 2020). Upon Iran's government officials, the law imposes obligations not only to abide by the various bans, but also to actively promote and engage in the prosecution of Israeli politicians and officials for 'crimes against humanity, war crimes, genocide, aggression and terrorist acts inside and outside the occupied territories' (Joffre 2020). The law further seeks to bring awareness to alleged 'Zionist apartheid' among international organisations (ibid). Finally, the law calls for a referendum among the people residing in 'Palestine' to determine the future of the region and recommends the establishment of a virtual Iranian embassy for this country in Jerusalem (ibid).

IV. CONDITIONS AND CONSEQUENCES

Looking at the context in which Iran's anti-Israel law has come about, several internal and external factors must be considered. At the time of the law's passage, the Iranian regime was facing internal difficulties in terms of formulating an effective response against the Covid-19 pandemic (Times of Israel 2020). Failures in terms of health-care provision also motivated efforts to clamp down on popular opposition against the Islamist regime (Avraham 2020). Two of the sponsors of the law may have had more immediate ambitions of self-survival, as they were facing charges of corruption and economic fraud (Seliktar and Rezaei 2020). Considering external factors, the law passed at a time when Israel had been stepping up efforts to take up more land in the administered territories. Israeli authorities had also accused Iran of engaging in cyberattacks against Israeli water and sewage installations, while, in turn, airstrikes targeting Iran-backed militias and the Lebanese Hezbollah had been attributed to Israeli forces.

The passage of the anti-Israel law may at first appear paradoxical because of its explicit listing of all kinds of contact and communications with Israel when the Islamic Republic does not even acknowledge the legitimate existence of the Jewish state and, worse yet, is unambiguously engaged in efforts to bring about its destruction. But there are many reasons to pass a law, not all of which are instrumental. From a practical viewpoint, it is unclear if the law can even be enforced, especially because its scope is so broad that it would inevitably affect many Iranians in their routine daily lives. As the law prohibits even indirect forms of contact with Israel, including electronic equipment with components manufactured by companies with branches in Israel, Iranian iPhone users were reportedly alarmed about what the law could mean for the use of their favourite communication device (Seliktar and Rezaei 2020). The only exception that has been granted to an all-out ban on contacts with Israel was an initially planned prohibition on international sports activities involving Israeli athletes. Iran's Ministry of Sport successfully lobbied against this provision, not for any love of Israel, but because it might have meant that Iran would be excluded from all international sports (ibid).

The new Iranian law is not merely opposed to certain Israeli policies, but decidedly framed as being against Israel as such. It puts into law the goal to abolish the state of Israel by arguing that the 'historical and integrated land of Palestine belongs to the original Palestinian peoples, including Muslims, Christians and Jews' (Joffre 2020). Jerusalem is consequently referred to as 'the permanent capital of Palestine' (ibid). Plainly, the law aims to destroy Israel, while Jews are acknowledged only as Palestinians, thereby effectively denying their true cultural identity.

The law bans any and all engagements with 'Zionist' causes, not just in or from within Israel, but also in connection with 'international Zionism all over the world' (Joffre 2020). The trope of international Jewry is an all too familiar one. But the anti-Semitism of the Iranian regime is no secret. Shortly after the anti-Israel law had passed, Iran's Supreme Leader Sayyid Ali Khamenei, who has been in office since he took over from Ruhollah Khomeini in 1989, referred to the very establishment of Israel as a 'crime against humanity' (Harpin 2020). The statement came just a few days after the Iranian head of state had published a poster on his website that read 'Palestine Will Be Free. The final solution: Resistance until referendum' (Lipin and Aryan 2020).

Although the poster displayed by Khamenei, directly referencing the Nazi policy to exterminate the Jews of Europe, was eventually removed, Iran's Supreme Leader has not backed down from continuing to voice anti-Semitism at every chance. On his Twitter account, which remains active until today, Khamenei has regularly turned to naming and blaming the Jews. At the time of the anti-Israel law's passage in May 2020, the Iranian leader argued that his country's policy of 'Eliminating the Zionist regime doesn't mean eliminating Jews', only to continue that the only acceptable Jews are 'Jewish Palestinians' (Khamenei 2020a). In no uncertain terms, he added, 'This is 'Eliminating Israel' & it will happen' (ibid). Similarly, following the decision by the United Arab Emirates in the fall of 2020 to normalise diplomatic relations with Israel, Khamenei took to Twitter to condemn the Arab country's actions for being 'in agreement with the Israelis & filthy Zionist agents of the U.S. – such as the Jewish member of Trump's family' (Khamenei 2020b). It is this explicit culture of anti-Semitism, which is historically embedded in Iran's political and legal system (Litvak 2006), that finds concrete expression in the 'Countering Israel's Actions' law.

Turning to its impact, it is striking to observe that Iran's anti-Israel law has received little coverage in the international news media, except in selected sources specialised in the Middle East and, for obvious reasons and good cause, the Israeli press. Anti-Semitism and anti-Israeli actions from the Iranian government, it appears, are too routine to warrant special attention. Among the few countries to respond has been the United States, but even the reaction from Israel's most trusted ally has been relatively mild. Upon passage of the law, US State Department officials simply stated that they believe that the people of Iran will reject their leaders' anti-Semitic rhetoric (Lipin and Aryan 2020). While it would have been more accurate had US officials stated that Iranians should, rather than will, reject the anti-Israel law, the implied realisation is that the will of the people matters as a source of legitimacy of law. Even in a theocracy as authoritarian as the Islamic Republic, this cultural dimension is indeed important to take into account, especially in view of any possibilities towards modernisation.

V. THE CHALLENGES OF CULTURE AND LEGAL CULTURE

If the study of culture (values) matters for the study of law (norms), it is evidently because culture matters to law. From the classics to contemporary sociology, the relation between cultural values, on the one hand, and legal norms, on the other, has remained a central concern in the development of modernity. Among the hallmarks of modern law is the independence of the judiciary as one dimension of a broader differentiation process. In autocratic regimes lacking this aspect of modernisation, by contrast, law and politics are so closely intertwined that politicisation cannot even appear as a problem. In Iran, this characteristic of authoritarian rule is crystalised in the position of the Supreme Leader as the head of state who also has tight control over the government as well as the judiciary. In the case of Iran's anti-Israel law, specifically, the close connection between politics and law is shown from the fact that the administration of the law was by order of the Iranian President assigned to the Ministries of the Interior, Intelligence, Foreign, and Defense, the judiciary, and the Supreme National Security Council (FARS 2020). Moreover, the Supreme Leader is an Islamic religious figure who reigns over all important functions of government, military, and law, in which sense the Iranian legal system is deeply and unavoidably entrenched by Islamic precepts. The constitution of the Islamic Republic of Iran not only does not accept religious freedom, but proscribes Sharia Islam as its foundational principle.

Modernity not only applies to politics and law, but also to culture, including religion, and the role thereof in shaping law. In the West, the modernisation of culture in relation to law especially pertains to secularisation in the form of a relegation of religion to the private sphere. In theocratic regimes, by contrast, law not only exists in close relation to religion, but is essentially justified in religious terms as well. As legal cultures are situated in a broader cultural context, the non-modern nature of Iran's legal system is indeed primarily demonstrated from its substantive infusion of the Islamic religion. In the case of the anti-Israel law, Iran's Guardian Council, which is responsible for ensuring that all laws passed by the parliament abide by the country's constitution as well as the principles of Islam, reviewed the law and 'did not find it against the religion and Constitution' (FARS 2020). The Islamic religion therefore provides the anti-Israel law's ultimate justification in that any cooperation with the 'Zionist regime' would be 'an act against God', considered 'equal to enmity towards God and corruption on earth' (Times of Israel 2020).

Especially in the aftermath of the terrorist attacks of 9/11, Reza Banakar (2008) had good reasons to remind us that it is incorrect as well as wrong to make any references to the Muslim community and to Islam in monolithic term. Yet Banakar also acknowledged 'that the practices of Sharia have taken inhumane and oppressive forms in some Islamic states' (ibid: 47). It therefore remains imperative to analyse the dynamics and implications of those expressions of Islam that are violent and destructive towards the state and people of Israel and other nations and cultures. Not all interpretations of Islam imply virulent anti-Semitism, but some of them clearly and openly do. Besides, while different interpretations of Islam may exist even in Iran, unless they are effectively voiced in the public arena, the non-secular nature of Iranian society will inevitably inhibit the modernisation of Iranian politics and law. The victims of Iran's autocratic rule are the Iranian citizens as well.

Looking at its religious cultural underpinnings, the Iranian regime today is not only characterised by, but deeply committed to, an anti-Semitism of the most extreme kind. Speaking on TV on Quds Day in May 2020 shortly after the anti-Israel law was passed, Supreme Leader Khamenei remarked that the 'struggle for the liberation of Palestine is a jihad for the sake of God and a desirable Islamic duty' (Fazeli 2020). Making it clear that this idea of Palestine was to replace the state of Israel, Khamenei went on to say that the 'Zionist regime is a deadly, cancerous growth' and that 'It will undoubtedly be uprooted and destroyed' (Vahdat and Gambrell 2020).

Such pronouncements make it clear, in no uncertain terms, that the non-modernity of Iran's legal and political culture turns into an anti-modernity that expresses an anti-Semitism which poses an existential threat to Israel and its people. It is in this respect incomprehensible to observe that former US President Obama realised that an Iran nuclear deal that included an Iranian recognition of Israel would be 'really akin to saying that we won't sign a deal unless the nature of the Iranian regime completely transforms' (Peralta 2015). Requesting a partner in negotiations to recognise the mere existence of another state might have been becoming for the United States and its moral authority on the world stage.

I agree with Banakar that it would be unwise to impose the standards of Western (secularised Christian) values on Islamic legal cultures because and when these are 'neither based on Western democratic principles nor are sensitive to Western standards of human rights' (Banakar 2008: 37). Regarding the prospects of the development of secularised legal systems in traditionally Muslim countries, it is therefore opportune to look at other Islamic cultures, rather than impose any ideas derived from traditionally Christian nations. Among the obvious cases is the secular state of the Republic of Turkey, at least up until the Constitutional Reform of 2017 since when not only Turkey's President functions as both head of state and head of the government, but a gradual Islamisation of Turkish politics and law has begun to manifest itself as well (Akyol 2019). But in other historically Muslim nations, the situation is more troubling. In May 2021, five parliamentarians in Kuwait introduced a new law that would ban any contact with Israel, imposing jail sentences for Kuwaiti citizens and officials dealing with or travelling to the Jewish state (Nasrallah 2021). Yet, showing that Islamic cultures need not be anti-Semitic nor anti-Israel, the chief executive body of the Cabinet of Sudan in April 2021 approved a bill to repeal a 63-year-old law that banned Arab nations from doing business with Israel (VOA News 2021). Seeking to restore diplomatic and economic ties with Israel, Sudan's efforts do not stand alone as the country became one of four member-countries of the Arab League, along with Bahrain, the United Arab Emirates, and Morocco, to formally recognise the state of Israel.

Even in the context of the Islamic Republic, Banakar has argued, 'Iranian law lives a life of its own' (Banakar and Ziaee 2018: 717). The dynamics of this 'life of routine practices of judges, court clerks, lawyers and clients' (ibid) principally take place in a battle between the Iranian judiciary's notion of law as Islamic jurisprudence, on the one hand, and the legal professionals' purposive-rational understanding thereof, on the other. I agree that there is no need to deny the relevance of professional autonomy even in a state as autocratic as Iran, but, I argue, it is an altogether different matter to estimate what the consequences of this battle between substantive and formal rationalisation are. Whereas a separation of powers is fully institutionalised in highly differentiated societies, in states like Iran, the substantive rationality that is at once both culturally entrenched and enforced from the top down by theocratic principles will always trump whatever formal-rational choices can be made among legal professionals and in the judiciary.

It is not possible for law to be divorced from culture. Societies that have undergone a secularisation of their legal systems, by example, are not necessarily less religious in their culture, but underwent a change in when and where religion matters or not. Legal and political reforms in Iran and other autocratic regimes, therefore, cannot be brought about only through changes in law and politics but will also have to rely on cultural changes. Only when culture is modernised as well, is it possible for a society to be duly differentiated and rationalised. For law to be rationalised in a purposive-rational sense, it must be secular or, at least, embody values that are compatible with norms that can function for all, whether the legal subjects are religious or not. In the Islamic Republic of Iran these conditions are not met. Under Iran's current conditions of religious might, there can be no disputes over the direction of Iran's modernity as there is as yet no modernity to speak of. To reverse the path of the Iranian regime and offer a cure against the cancer that is its legal system, the people of Iran will have to modernise their culture as well as their political and legal institutions in order to reverse the course of their history, lest the genocidal anti-Semitism of their government de facto turn them into the Supreme Leader's executioners, willingly or not.

Whether political isolation and imposed economic sanctions can help bring about the changes needed for a modernisation and rationalisation of Iran's politics, law, and wider society is not nearly as important as the undeniable reality that any necessary cultural changes, especially in terms of secularisation, must be adopted by the Iranian people themselves. Some observers have argued that Iran's anti-Israel law should not be considered nor feared as an achievement in the autocratic path of Iranian Islamist rule, but instead reflects ongoing chaos within the regime (Seliktar and Rezaei 2020). In view of the increasing voices of dissent Iran has been witnessing, the regime is in any case shown to be lacking in legitimacy, leaving only coercion and highly symbolic laws to sustain its might. Regardless of whether this chaos will result in a collapse of the regime or not, anti-Semitism and anti-Israel attitudes cannot possibly be condoned nor can they be useful. It is, of course, up to the people of Iran to decide what they want for themselves, but they cannot expect to impose without consequence beyond their national bounds a culture that does not even recognise others and, worse yet, wishes them to die. In its politically sanctioned and legalised form, the anti-Semitism of Iran's religious culture will have to be reversed if a path of Iranian modernisation is to become possible. Until that time has come, the people of Israel may well argue – and not without justification – that they have no other choice but to defend themselves against the existential threats they face.

REFERENCES

Akyol, M (2019) 'Turkey's Troubled Experiment with Secularism' *The Century Foundation*, 25 April 2019, available at https://tcf.org/content/report/turkeys-troubled-experiment-secularism/.

Avraham, R (2020) 'Iran Exploits Pandemic to Increase Misconduct' *Israel Hayom*, 27 May 2020, available at https://www.israelhayom.com/opinions/iran-exploits-pandemic-to-increase-human-rights-violations/.

Banakar, R (2008) 'The Politics of Legal Cultures' 31(4) *Retfærd: The Nordic Journal of Law and Justice* 37–60.

Banakar, R and Ziaee, K (2018) 'The Life of the Law in the Islamic Republic of Iran' 51 *Iranian Studies* 717.

Deflem, M (2008) *Sociology of Law: Visions of a Scholarly Tradition* (Cambridge, Cambridge University Press).

—— (2013) 'The Legal Theory of Jürgen Habermas' in R Banakar and M Travers (eds), *Law and Social Theory, Second Edition* (Oxford, Hart Publishing) 75.

Durkheim, E ([1893] 1984) *The Division of Labor in Society* (New York, The Free Press).

FARS (2020) 'Iranian President Communicates Law to Confront Hostile Acts of Zionists Against Peace, Security' *FARS News Agency*, 26 May 2020, www.farsnews.ir/en/news/13990306000578/Iranian-Presiden-Cmmnicaes-Law-Cnfrn-Hsile-Acs-f-Ziniss-agains-Peace-.

Fazeli, Y (2020) 'Iran's Khamenei on Quds Day: Israel Will Be Eradicated' *Al Arabiya News*, 22 May 2020, available at https://english.alarabiya.net/News/middle-east/2020/05/22/Iran-s-Khamenei-on-Quds-Day-Israel-will-be-eradicated.

Habermas, J ([1992] 1996) *Between Facts and Norms: Contributions to a Discourse Theory of Law and Democracy* (Cambridge, MIT Press).

Harpin, L (2020) 'Iran's Ayatollah calls Zionism a "virus"' *The Jewish Chronicle*, 27 May 2020, available at https://www.thejc.com/news/israel/iran-s-ayatollah-calls-zionism-a-virus-1.500113.

Joffre, T (2020) 'Iran Progresses Anti-Israel Bill, Plans to Establish Embassy in Jerusalem' *Jerusalem Post*, 20 May 2020, available at https://www.jpost.com/middle-east/iran-passes-anti-israel-law-plans-to-establish-embassy-to-jerusalem-627744.

Khamenei, SA (2020a) Twitter post, 20 May 2020, at 1:51 PM, twitter.com/khamenei_ir/status/1263165539167371267.

—— (2020b) Twitter post, 1 September 2020, at 8:21 AM, twitter.com/khamenei_ir/status/1300770840175407111.

Lipin, M and Aryan G (2020) 'US: Iran's People Will Reject Islamist Rulers' Anti-Semitic Threats against Israel' VOA, 22 May 2020, available at https://www.voanews.com/middle-east/voa-news-iran/us-irans-people-will-reject-islamist-rulers-anti-semitic-threats-against.

Litvak, M (2006) 'The Islamic Republic of Iran and the Holocaust: Anti-Semitism and Anti-Zionism' 25 *Journal of Israeli History* 267.

Nadimi, F (2021) 'New Iranian Bill Aims to Officialize a Policy of Avenging Soleimani and Destroying Israel' *The Washington Institute for Near East Policy* (PolicyWatch 3415), 12 January 2021, available at https://www.washingtoninstitute.org/policy-analysis/new-iranian-bill-aims-officialize-policy-avenging-soleimani-and-destroying-israel.

Nasrallah, T (2021) 'Kuwaiti MPs Submit Bill Banning Any Dealings with Israel' *Gulf News*, 22 May 2021, available at gulfnews.com/world/gulf/kuwait/kuwaiti-mps-submit-bill-banning-any-dealings-with-israel-1.79384064.

Parsons, T (1978) 'Law as an Intellectual Stepchild' in HM Johnson (ed), *Social System and Legal Process* (San Francisco, Jossey-Bass) 11.

Peralta, E (2015) 'Obama: "Misjudgment" to Make Iran Deal Contingent on Recognizing Israel' *NPR*, 6 April 2015, available at https://www.npr.org/sections/thetwo-way/2015/04/06/397892256/obama-conditioning-iran-nuclear-deal-on-recognition-of-israel-is-misjudgment.

Rose, M (2020) 'Iranian Parliament Passes Sweeping Anti-Israel Legislation' *Our Politics*, 20 May 2020, available at http://ourpolitics.net/iranian-parliament-passes-sweeping-anti-israel-legislation/.

Seliktar, O, Rezaei, F (2020) 'Iran's Anti-Israel Bill: Desperation Masquerading as Legislation' *BESA Center Perspectives Paper No. 1,603*, 11 June, available at http://besacenter.org/iran-anti-israel-legislation/.

Times of Israel (2020) 'Iran MPs Ban Work with Israel, Including Using Its Software, as Acts against God' *The Times of Israel*, 18 May 2020, available at https://www.timesofisrael.com/iran-to-hold-limited-quds-day-events-against-israel-amid-pandemic/.

Vahdat, A, Gambrell, J (2020) 'Iran Leader Says Israel a "Cancerous Tumor" to be Destroyed' Yahoo News, 22 May 2020, available at https://au.news.yahoo.com/iran-leader-says-israel-cancerous-085723535.html.

VOA News (2021) 'Sudan's Cabinet Votes to Remove Anti-Israel Law' *VOA News*, 6 April 2020, available at https://www.voanews.com/a/africa_sudans-cabinet-votes-remove-anti-israel-law/6204231.html.

Weber, M ([1922] 1978). *Economy and Society: An Outline of Interpretive Sociology* (Berkeley, CA, University of California Press).

25

Revolutions and Legal Cultures. Perspectives and Reflections

HANNE PETERSEN

I. INTRODUCTION

IN APRIL 2010, a minor volcano under the Icelandic glacier Eyiafjallajökull erupted and disrupted air travel in northern Europe and the northern hemisphere for several weeks. During this period, one of Iceland's many well-known authors, Einar Már Gudmundsson,[1] wrote an essay in a Danish newspaper called *Revolutionary Volcanoes*. Here he linked the outbreak to the impact of the biggest ever volcanic eruption of Iceland's history from 1783–1784 (Gudmundsson 2010), where roughly a quarter of the Icelandic nation died – most from indirect effects, including changes in climate and illnesses in livestock in the following years caused by the ash and poisonous gases from the eruption. The 1783 eruption is estimated to have erupted the largest quantity of lava from a single eruption in historic times.[2] Gudmundsson wrote that this eruption not only caused crop failures in Iceland, but also affected Europe, including French agriculture, leading to famine and the starvation of many farmers. He claimed that connected and deteriorated living conditions were perhaps an (indirect) cause of the French Revolution. He also considered and compared the economic consequences of the volcanic eruptions of 1783 to the economic consequences Iceland suffered after the financial crisis in the fall of 2008. It is well known that the French Revolution changed the political, economic and legal system not only of France but also gradually of the whole continent – introducing, among other things, a change of values, governance and the important codifications of law, which are still characteristic of continental European legal culture. So far, the economic, political and legal consequences of the 2008 financial crises have not led to major legal disruptions.

---

[1] Einar Már Gudmundsson (b 1954) is the most well-known and highly regarded Icelandic fiction writer. Besides fiction he has also written about the financial crisis in Iceland, both in his Whitebook, *Hvidbogen – Krisen på Island* (2009), and in essays in Bankstræde nr. 0 [Bank Strait] (2017), thus transcending the boundary of fiction and combining it with non-fiction.

[2] Wikipedia: Volcanism of Iceland (accessed October 2022).

The heritage of the financial crisis and the Covid-19 pandemic, combined with consequences of several intermittent crises, may cause a tempering of a neoliberal political and legal culture subjugated to market relations, values, norms and attitudes, which have so far dominated the world since 1979. That was the year when Margaret Thatcher introduced neoliberal politics into the UK, but also the year of the Iranian Islamic Revolution. Revolutions and crises have an impact on legal cultures as well as on relations between law and society, which is sociology of law and what Reza Banakar spent much of his life working with. In this chapter, I will take a brief and superficial look at relations between revolutions, legal cultures and law and on the way that societies relate to past turbulent changes.

II. ON REVOLUTIONS – CAUSES AND CONSEQUENCES

Jack Goldstone, an American professor of sociology, who hardly deals with law or legal culture, writes in *Revolutions. A Very Short Introduction* (2014) that revolution can best be defined in terms of:

> *both* observed mass mobilization and institutional change, *and* a driving ideology carrying a vision of social justice. *Revolution* is the forcible overthrow of a government through mass mobilization (whether military or civilian or both) in the name of social justice, to create new political institutions. (Goldstone 2014: 4)

He later writes that revolutions are like earthquakes, and that geologists can identify major fault zones, where earthquakes are most likely to arise (ibid: 15). However, knowing the general mechanisms does not lead to predictions of them. 'Similarly, social scientists can identify societies that seem to have major faults and growing tensions – these may be evident from signs of social conflict or heightened difficulties of institutions or groups carrying out accustomed tasks or meeting their goals' (ibid: 16). But, again, that does not lead to exact predictions about when and where revolutions and dramatic changes may occur. Nonetheless, scholars of revolutions generally agree upon five elements that they consider necessary and sufficient for an unstable social equilibrium to arise, which may lead to a revolution (ibid: 16). These are, briefly summarised:

(1) economic and fiscal strains (leading to increased taxes or heavy borrowing, often seen as unjust);
(2) growing alienation and opposition among elites (who are always competing for position);
(3) some form of increasingly widespread popular anger at injustice (amongst eg peasants, workers, students, mothers);
(4) an ideology that presents a persuasive shared narrative of resistance (religious movements, nationalist liberation) creating a shared identity and righteousness;
(5) favourable international relations, as revolutionary success often depends on foreign support (ibid: 16–18).

When these five conditions coincide, the normal social mechanisms that restore order in crises are not likely to work. However, as they seldom coincide, revolutions are also rather rare. In addition, *structural* and *transient causes* have to be in place. The first are long-term and large-scale trends that undermine existing social institutions and relationships, and the second are contingent events or actions by particular individuals or groups. Goldstone also lists *five structural causes*, which are: (1) demographic change (eg a 'youth bulge'); (2) a shift in the pattern of international relations (eg after wars or crises); (3) uneven or dependent economic development; (4) new patterns of exclusion or discrimination against particular groups; (5) the evolution of personalist regimes evolving into personalist dictatorships (ibid: 20–23). *Transient causes* are sudden events that push a society out of stability (ibid: 24).

III. THE FRENCH REVOLUTION – NEW INSTITUTIONS AND NEW LEGAL CULTURE

In 1919 the Norwegian professor of law, Francis Hagerup (1853–1921), who was also a politician and diplomat, published a book called *Ret og Kultur i det nittende Århundrede* [*Law and Culture in the Nineteenth Century*]. Here he underlined the importance of enlightenment and the French Revolution for legal culture – especially regarding the principles of freedom and equality of individuals as well as the demand for protection of individuals (Hagerup 1919: 1). As a reaction to the American and French revolutionary movements, the first third of the nineteenth century saw a strong conservatism, which influenced both the perception of law and legislation. Legal ideas and institutions, which have the same origin, have often been marked in ways that give them very different characteristics (ibid: 2).

British historian William Doyle comments on Thomas Carlyle's influential history of the French Revolution from 1837 (translated into many languages) which Carlyle to some extent defended. Doyle in that context writes that the French Revolution was 'an explosion of popular violence, understandable if scarcely defensible resentment' (Doyle 2019: 5). It was a *series* of developments, a *process* bewildering to most contemporaries, which stretched over a number of years. It was a sustained period of uncertainty, disorder, and conflict, reverberating far beyond the borders of France. It began between 1787 and 1789 (ibid: 19), and it was triggered by several lost wars, financial overstretch of Louis XVI and international rivalry among empires as well as competition for dominance over resources from the colonies. The government of the *ancien régime* was very heterogeneous, exemplified in the structure of privilege and exemption, which gave each and every institution, group or area a status not like any other. Clergy and nobility owned most and paid least. 'The burden of taxation ... fell disproportionately on those least able to pay' (ibid: 26). This historic heritage is described in detail in Thomas Piketty's recent book on *Capital and Ideology*, where his first chapter deals with this 'three-part society' and its 'trifunctional inequality' (Piketty 2020: 59 ff).

Even if reforms were overdue, nobody was able to bring them about:

> The judiciary, for example, was perceived to be overstaffed, underemployed and its procedures slow, expensive and unreliable ... magistrates were recruited by heredity or purchase rather than tests of competence. The labyrinthine complexities of the law, where attempts at codification had petered out in the 1670s were sustained by innumerable local and

provincial customs and privileges, many of them repeatedly confirmed in return for cash payments over the centuries. (Doyle 2019: 29)

The king had sold public offices for centuries as a source of income and borrowing (ibid: 23). The end of monarchy as well as bankruptcy was near in the ensuing vacuum of power, and the French Revolution:

was the process by which this vacuum was filled ... But hardly anybody foresaw the events, or the moment, which brought its collapse. Historians are instinctively reluctant to invoke chance or accidents, in bringing about great events, but in this case they played a crucial part ... Even the weather was hugely influential in what happened next. (ibid: 37)

Civil war – and terror – became an important part of the process. The guillotine was introduced in April 1792 'and designed as a humane means of execution by rational men who failed to foresee the effect of the rivers of blood it released when used on large numbers of victims' (ibid: 56). Over time, the memory of this terror was submerged or put out of sight – perhaps by later atrocities. Hagerup does not mention it in his book from 1919 – at a time where even more war and terror during World War I was fresh in everyone's memory.

The French Revolution influenced upheavals for the centuries to come, from the Bolshevik Revolution to Germany, China and countless other countries (ibid: 9). The Code Napoleon remained the basis of civil law in parts of Germany for all of the nineteenth century, in Poland until 1846 and in Belgium and Luxemburg until today. It influenced the Universal Declaration of Human Rights in 1948, where the preamble and 14 out of its 30 articles were taken from the Declaration of 1789 (ibid: 17). It continues to be disputed and contested. According to Doyle, however, the most influential and lasting innovation was the introduction of the decimal metric system of weights and measures zealously promoted under Napoleon (ibid: 12). To this author it seems a rather technical focus – which also underlines the difficulties in measuring value changes.

IV. NON-EUROPEAN INFLUENCES AND CONTRIBUTIONS BY AN ELITE INDIVIDUAL

We normally consider revolutions to be the results of social, economic and political forces and developments. However, in this context of commemoration of the work of an individual scholar, I also want to draw attention to a few important scholars whose thoughts and ideas have influenced their own and later times. Revolutions and the related social (and legal) change they produce are influenced by intellectual ideas promoted by individuals.

A year before the French Revolution, which led to a social and legal eruption with a European but also global impact, the German philosopher Arthur Schopenhauer (1788–1860) was born as a son of a wealthy merchant in the city of Danzig. After Danzig had come under Prussian rule in 1793, the family moved to the free city of Hamburg (still a city-state today). Arthur was expected and persuaded to take over his father's business by an offer of a tour of Europe, where he learnt a number of languages through prolonged stays, amongst others in England. However, as his father died early, Arthur never took over the business. His status and considerable inheritance allowed him to survive as an independent philosopher after having left the University in Berlin in 1820 due to competition with Hegel. He fled from the cholera epidemic in Berlin in 1831 and moved to Frankfurt, where he survived and lived an isolated life, but kept himself informed beyond the fragmented German political world, through foreign language literature. He was influenced by and knowledgeable about Indology and Buddhism, and was a regular reader of *Asiatic Researches*, established by a colonial society in Bengal (Ñanajivako 1970).[3] Schopenhauer was (and is) one of the most widely read German and European philosophers. He may perhaps be seen as a representative of an alienated elite, who contributes to paving the way for social and intellectual change. He has considerably influenced a number of later philosophers, musicians and artists including Richard Wagner, Friedrich Nietzsche, Leo Tolstoy, Sigmund Freud, Carl Gustav Jung, Thomas Mann and Ludwig Wittgenstein in both the nineteenth and twentieth centuries, and he has been called the philosopher of pessimism. His work is amongst others an example of – and a reaction to – the widespread importance of religious (Christian) values and norms, still dominant in many parts of the Western world in relation to law and legal culture also after the French Revolution. We still speak about 'world religions', and we are presently witnessing a changing global order, where the Eastern values and normative cultures, which interested Schopenhauer, are growing in influence.

Religion and philosophy were the most important fields of knowledge contributing to the understanding of societies in a changing world in the eighteenth and nineteenth centuries. The gradual process of secularisation took place particularly in Western societies, at a time when sociology had not yet emerged as a discipline. When religion and philosophy lost their status and power of explanation, economy, law and sociology to some extent took over – particularly in the West.

V. THE RUSSIAN REVOLUTION

Goldstone describes a 'stable equilibrium' as one where the response to a moderate disturbance, revolt or strike is 'for rulers and elites and even most popular groups to act to restore the existing social order' (Goldstone 2014: 14). Thus, relations between law, legal culture and society have often been relations of (mutual) support and legitimisation of frequently hierarchical and patriarchal institutions and orders. Institutions, forms and cultures of government, politics and law have, however, sometimes changed, when the equilibrium has been disrupted by revolutions or radical reforms as in the case of the Russian empire. The mutual but also delicate support between religious authorities, monarchs or emperors and ruling classes gradually changed into more or less secularised institutions (of eg education and science).

---

[3] Bhikkhu Ñanajivako was himself born as Cedomil Veljacic in Yugoslavia, and resided as a Buddhist monk in Sri Lanka from 1966.

Democratised forms of (party based) government emerged – also interrupted by periods of dictatorship:

> On February 1917 thousands of female textile-workers and housewives took to the streets of Petrograd, the Russian capital to protest about the bread shortage and to mark International Women's Day. The following day, more than 200,000 workers were on strike and demonstrators marched from the outlying districts into the city centre, hurling rocks and lumps of ice at police as they went. (Smith 2002: 5)

Demonstrations continued and a revolution had broken out, but not until 27 February did any of the revolutionary parties manage to give leadership to it. On 2 March 1917, Emperor Nicholas abdicated and the 300-year-old Romanov dynasty ended. Demography had changed considerably in the half century before the revolution. The population had grown from 74 to 164 million between 1860 and 1914. Russia had become increasingly urbanised and by 1913, it had become the fifth largest industrial country in the world. Nonetheless, it was still a backward poverty-stricken country menaced by deep social tensions. Average peasants lived lives of poverty, deprivation and oppression, while infant mortality was the highest in Europe. In the cities, overcrowding, high rents, and appalling squalor were the norm, and St Petersburg was considered the unhealthiest capital in Europe, where 14,000 people died in a cholera epidemic in 1908 (Smith 2002: 6–9). World War I marked a watershed in Europe's history, destroying several empires while also discrediting liberal democracy, which prepared the way for the totalitarian politics of 1920 and 1930s (ibid: 12). Soviets were the new institutions and the 'principal organ of political expression for the workers and soldiers' (ibid: 17). They sprang up rapidly and in big numbers, and saw themselves as organs of the 'revolutionary democracy'. The economy suffered serious deterioration, production of fuel and raw materials fell, the transport system was in increasing chaos, leading to a shortage of bread in cities. Prices rose fourfold and the real value of wages plummeted (ibid: 29). Even if the October Revolution generated a sense that in a new world justice and equality would triumph over arbitrariness and exploitation, the culture of democracy and law was both thin and fragile (ibid: 40, 45). At the end of the civil war between the Red and the White factions – which also deepened national identities – the Red Army had become the largest institution of the state, enjoying absolute priority in the allocation of resources (ibid: 54, 60). With a near fatal attack on Lenin at the end of August 1918, terror became elevated to official policy – at a time when 600,000 British and French troops had already been sacrificed at the Somme River in World War I 'in order to advance seven miles' (ibid: 63 ff). By 1920–1921, a system of what came to be called 'War Communism' was introduced. The 'command-administrative system and militarised ideology that it engendered proved to be the lasting elements of the Soviet system' (ibid: 85). By 1920, the basic features of the Communist system were in place, 'rule by a single party, extreme centralisation of power, intolerance of dissent, the curtailment of independent organisations, and readiness to use force to solve political and economic tasks' (ibid: 97). Smith writes that the culture of the party was profoundly changed by civil war:

> The atmosphere of pervasive violence and destruction, the unremitting popular hostility, sharpened dictatorial and brutal reflexes. The Bolshevik ethos had always been one of ruthlessness, authoritarianism and 'class hatred', but in the context of civil war these qualities transmogrified into cruelty, fanaticism, and absolute intolerance of those, who

thought differently. The invasion of foreign powers, the failure of revolution to spread across Europe, bred a mentality of encirclement, of Russia as an armed fortress, as well as an obsession with enemies. (ibid: 98)

Economic policy and plans were the major instruments for implementation of this policy. In the socialist states in the twentieth century, law was of limited importance both as an expression of (liberal) values and as a tool for social change but it did not disappear fully. The period of New Economic Policy (NEP) had abandoned terror as an instrument of political rule. In 1922 a Criminal Code was enacted, that 'drew to a surprising degree on elements of tsarist jurisprudence ... Moreover the Bolsheviks, in continuing to see law principally as a means of defending the state, unconsciously served as perpetuators of Russian tradition' (ibid: 118). Smith finishes his introduction by underlining the role of 'geography, geopolitics, economic and political structures, the specific conjunctures thrown up by revolution, civil war, and a shattered economy, and not least, events that no one foresaw' as critical features in shaping the institutions and practices of the Soviet state (ibid: 159).

VI. 1968 CULTURAL REVOLUTION IN CHINA AND 1979 ISLAMIC REVOLUTION IN IRAN

American emeritus professor Richard Curt Kraus wrote the very short introduction to the Oxford University Press 2012 publication, *The Cultural Revolution*. He notes in the preface that the revolution was violent 'yet it was also a source of inspiration and social experiment' (Kraus 2012: xiii). Kraus stresses the connection between the Cultural Revolution and the present globalised world, where the status of China has changed considerably. He marks that each of the revolutionary waves that swept over twentieth-century China was 'passionately concerned with transforming culture' (ibid: 5). Further, he points out three broad explanations for the Cultural Revolution, which he also describes as a revolution within a revolution: (1) conflict within the political elite; (2) tensions within Chinese society; and (3) China's international position (ibid: 20). He also links revolution and tradition, writing that it 'is easy to see in Cultural Revolutionary ritual and behavior the impact of hierarchical Chinese tradition' (ibid: 22). However, the Cultural Revolution also coincided with a global movement of radical politics, he points out. In the US, it was black power, feminism, hippies and opposition to the Vietnam War. In Europe it was the Paris riots and the Prague spring which marked broad cultural and political shifts (ibid: 84). In the present where:

the West wrestles with China's rise in the international community, the Cultural Revolution remains a useful and perhaps irresistible propaganda point. An imagined Western moral superiority is clarified by a typical and mistaken Cultural Revolution narrative: the economy was a shambles, education destroyed, but Deng Xiaoping rescued China by copying *our* free market. Kicking Mao's corpse strengthens the position of globalism, proves that socialism does not work and reveals China as unstable and dangerous. (ibid: 117)

Of course, these extremely brief reflections on decades of social unrest and tension over time and in the world cannot give due credit to nuances. However, the very short introductions provide food for thought on the present era and the somewhat changing ideological lenses through which we are investigating the world. There is no short OUP introduction to the Iranian Islamic revolution, but Goldstone deals with this revolution on four pages based to a large degree on Charles Kurzman's interesting book *The Unthinkable Revolution in Iran* (Goldstone 2014; Kurzman 2004).

Kurzman (like Kraus) presents a quite positive approach to the revolution he describes, contrary to the later (increasingly anti-Muslim) perspectives and interpretations, which may have been particularly dominant in media strongly influenced by contemporary and later political developments. The Iranian absolutist monarchy enjoyed widespread political, military and economic support from the Americans, who until the regime fell considered a revolution 'unthinkable'. According to Kurzman, what made the Islamic Revolution possible in Iran after all, was the emergence and existence of a *'viable movement'*, which could produce an alternative to the corrupt and authoritarian rule of the Shah. This movement consisted primarily of young students at the religious seminaries particularly in Qom, a city considered holy and known as the largest centre for Shi'a scholarship in the world. These students were strongly influenced by Khomeini, who had been in exile in Iraq for several years, and who became the leader of the religious government after the Revolution on 11 February 1979. As already mentioned, Thomas Piketty in his book on *Capital and Ideology* describes the dominant 'trifunctional' society in most of Europe until (after) the French Revolution, where monarch, clergy and the general population constituted the powerful agents. This can perhaps be said to constitute also Iranian society before the revolution. In Iran, religious agents and movements were sufficiently powerful to produce 'an ideology that presents a persuasive shared narrative of resistance', which supported a revolt against an immoral ruler, thus creating a shared identity (Goldstone 2014: 18). Iran, which had been part of the Persian Empire, had – like many parts of the former Ottoman Empire, notably Turkey under Atatürk (after 1923) – carried out what might be called 'forced modernisation', which often includes secularisation, education (of both gender) and westernisation of dress codes and calendar.

According to Goldstone, an area where:

> revolutionary outcomes have consistently disappointed their followers is women's rights ... Alongside ethnic and religious minorities women have consistently been let down by revolutionary promises for equality. They have made progress only where they have undertaken their own mass campaigns for the right to vote and women's rights. (ibid: 40)

The strongest example of this is probably the French Revolution itself, where it took more than 150 years before the revolutionary values would also include women, who were only granted voting rights at the end of World War II.

The Iranian elections from 2021 indicate that the outcomes of the Islamic revolution have disappointed both the large group of young people in the country, as well as women. However, there is probably no 'viable alternative' at present, either inside the country or in an international context, that might bring about change.

In 2020 Shirin Ebadi, Iranian political activist, lawyer and former judge wrote an article on just this topic, 'Iran's revolution has failed its women'. She wrote that Ayatollah Khomeini had insisted on equality among all Iranians in his many speeches and declarations, but had also declared a month after he took power that women who worked in the public sector should wear a veil. 'Women in Iran are not against the veil, they are against the fact that it is compulsory'. Ebadi claims that women want a secular and democratic government and are at the forefront of protests against the government, and that the feminist movement in Iran has not been opposed by men (Ebadi 2020). In spite of this optimistic inside view, the Iranian revolution has nonetheless – as is well known – produced a diaspora of refugees, who have suffered under the repression of violent regimes. Shahrnush Parsipur (2013) and Shirin Neshat are some of the female representatives, and Reza Banakar was another.

VII. HAROLD BERMAN – LAW AND REVOLUTION – AND THE END OF AN ERA

Besides the French Revolution, the Russian Revolution has probably led to the most important upheaval and to social and legal change in the twentieth century, not only in the West but in the world at large. The collapse of the Russian monarchy may have had equal global impact in ending an era, as claimed by Harold J Berman (1918–2007) born the year after the Russian Revolution and just before the end of World War I. His most important and historical work is *Law and Revolution: The Formation of the Western Legal Tradition*, published in 1983, two years before Mikhail Gorbachev was elected General Secretary of the Communist Party of the Soviet Union from 1985 until 1991 and president from 1988–1991 leading the period of *Glasnost* (openness) and *Perestroika* (restructuring). Berman claims in the preface that we are at the end of an era and that this:

> is not something that can be proved scientifically. One senses it or one does not. One knows by intuition that the old images … have lost their meaning … Because the age is ending, we are now able to discern its beginnings. In the middle of an era, when the end is not in sight, the beginning is also hidden from view. (Berman 1983: v)

Berman became a very influential American legal scholar, professor of law at Harvard and an expert in comparative, international and Soviet/Russian law as well as legal history, philosophy of law and the intersection of law and religion. His knowledge about the Soviet Union and its political culture and system probably gave him this intuition of the ending of an age. This end meant not just the end of state communism in the Soviet Union and the countries of former Eastern Europe. He mentions also a sense of the 'decline of unity and common purpose in Western civilization as a whole … Perhaps the most hopeful prospect is that of economic, scientific and cultural interdependence on both a regional and worldwide basis' (ibid: vi). He underlines that we need to overcome the reduction of law to a set of technical devices for getting things done, 'law has to be believed in or it will not work; it involves not only reason and will but also emotion, intuition and faith. It involves a total social commitment' (ibid: vii), and he continues that in periods of crisis we need a larger vision. Twelve years later, in 1995, he wrote a short article called 'World Law', where he indicated that all humanity has now entered a new era. He claimed that the right name for this era of global interdependence was 'emerging world society' and the right name for the law governing it was a term able to encompass the many regulatory and normative activities, taking place beside and beyond nations, which would be 'world law'. World law goes beyond the law of world economy and world trade, which has played a dominant role for centuries. It includes both customary law and international and transnational law. It especially also includes the 'voluntary not-for-profit non-governmental world organizations with members from many different countries' (Berman 1994). The term has not really taken hold (yet), perhaps because the discussion on globalisation and everything 'global' started shortly after from the mid-1990s after the collapse of the Soviet Union.

VIII. 1989: THE 'NEOLIBERAL CULTURAL REVOLUTION' AND THE 'DILEMMA OF LAW'

Sociology of law has had a more critical view of both law and society than most (Western modern) jurisprudence, which has been more prone to become decontextualised and ahistorical in the twentieth century. However, sociology of law – which Reza Banakar called a 'stepchild' of jurisprudence – has also tried to gain recognition from this 'father figure' of modern (Western) law. The second half of the twentieth century witnessed both the Cold War, and the feminist and environmental movements, with a continued emphasis on the values of equality, liberty and fraternity/solidarity. The collapse of state socialism and the victory of market-oriented neoliberalism heralded an era of values emphasising (individual) choice, consumption, competition and security. This 'cultural neoliberal revolution' has also had a strong impact on Western (and global) legal culture, leading to a shift of norms, attitudes and values. At the time of writing, it seems as if the neoliberal culture – and its influence on the relation between law and society – may be on the decline, particularly after the financial crisis in 2008 and strengthened after the climate crisis and linked to the pandemic in the period from 2019 to the present.

In 2010 Dominique Moïsi, a French political scientist, whose father was an Auschwitz-survivor published *The Geopolitics of Emotion – How Cultures of Fear, Humiliation, and Hope are Reshaping the World* (Moïsi 2010). He described the culture of the United States as dominated by fear, while Middle Eastern culture was shaped by humiliation. He also claimed that a culture of hope was to be found in Asia, not least in China, at a time when China had opened up towards the West after joining the WTO and had just held the Olympics, which started on 08.08.2008. The way he included the role of emotions is (still) quite unusual for political science – as well as for law. It is perhaps a harbinger of change in our perception of the forces that influence the world we have always been part of.

Laurence Smith, a professor of geography and earth and space sciences at UCLA (1996–2019), who left the university (as emeritus professor) and became Professor of Earth, Environmental and Planetary Sciences at Brown University, addressed a general audience in his book *The New North – The World in 2050* (Smith 2012). It analysed four key 'megatrends': population growth and migration; natural resource demand; climate change; and globalisation. The book projects a world that by mid-century will have shifted its political and economic axes radically to the 'north', which for Smith is the geographical north. 'I loosely define this "New North" as all land and oceans lying 45 N latitude or higher currently held by the United States, Canada,

Iceland, Greenland (Denmark) Norway, Sweden, Finland and Russia' (ibid: 6–7). This differs from the views that see a one-way geopolitical shift towards mainly 'the East'.

Since the beginning of 2020, the world has experienced the global impact of Covid-19, which started in China at the end of 2019. Wuhan is a transportation hub and, like other Chinese cities, it has grown tremendously over recent decades. The Covid-19 phenomenon – and crisis – may become one of the global developments that will demonstrate (again) how different parts of an 'emerging world society' deal with major existential challenges, and what strategies, norms and practices are used or developed in different localities, societies and regions as well as legal cultures.

According to Frank M Snowden, professor emeritus of history and the history of medicine at Yale, epidemics have altered societies they have spread through, affecting personal relationships, the work of artists and intellectuals, and the man-made and natural environments. In an interview in *The New Yorker* from 3 March 2020, he explained that 'Epidemic diseases are not random events that afflict societies capriciously and without warning … On the contrary, every society produces its own specific vulnerabilities. To study them is to understand that society's structure, its standard of living, and its political priorities'. Snowden considers that 'Epidemics are a category of disease that seem to hold up the mirror to human beings as to who we really are'. Epidemic diseases have touched all areas of human life profoundly and they have had tremendous effects on social and political stability (Chotiner 2020). Snowden's book *Epidemics and Society. From the Black Death to the Present* started as a course in medical history at Yale in the immediate aftermath of a series of public health emergencies – SARS, avian flu and Ebola at the beginning of the twenty-first century. He considers that '(H)ow the global community deals with these issues may well be an important factor in determining the survival of our society, and perhaps even of our species' (Snowden 2019: 3). In his 2020 preface, Snowden writes:

> Epidemics afflict societies through the specific vulnerabilities people have created by their relationships with the environment, other species and each other … A world with nearly eight billion people, the majority of whom live in densely crowded cities and all linked by rapid air travel, creates innumerable opportunities for pulmonary viruses. At the same time, demographic increase and frenetic urbanization lead to the invasion and destruction of animal habitat, altering the relationships of humans to the animal world. (Snowden 2020: preface)

Revolutions, climate change and pandemics are amongst the powers forcing or causing people to leave places they have been linked to by family ties, birth and upbringing.

Reza Banakar's Swedish PhD dissertation from 1994 probably reflects several of his own experiences as a migrant in Sweden and Europe. It is called *Rättens Dilemma. Om konflikthantering i ett mångkulturellt samhälle* [*The Dilemma of Law. On Conflict Handling in a Multicultural Society*]. He notes in the introduction that law is not the best instrument that may protect vulnerable social or ethno-cultural groups against different forms of injustices. 'These rights must be created through informal spontaneous socio-cultural processes – which might only come into being outside the legal system – in order that they achieve a cultural anchoring in the population' (Banakar 1994: 19). Under the present crisis, the dilemma of law is again apparent, this time also in the relation between human and non-human environments.

REFERENCES

Banakar, R (1994) *Rättens Dilemma. Om konflikthantering i ett mångkulturellt samhälle* (Bokbox Förlag).

Berman, H (1983) *Law and Revolution. The Formation of the Western Legal Tradition* (Cambridge, MA, Harvard University Press).

—— (1994) 'World Law' 18 *Fordham International Law Journal* 1617, available at https://ir.lawnet.fordham.edu/ilj/vol18/iss5/4.

Chotiner, I (2020) 'How Pandemics Change History', An interview with Frank M Snowden, *The New Yorker*, 3 March.

Doyle, W (2019) *The French Revolution. A Very Short Introduction*, 2nd edn (Oxford, Oxford University Press).

Ebadi, S (2020) 'Iran's Revolution has Failed its Women' *thenationalnews.com* (last accessed 2 October 2022).

Goldstone, JA (2014) *Revolutions. A Very Short Introduction* (Oxford, Oxford University Press).

Gudmundsson, EM (2010) 'Revolutionære vulkaner' [Revolutionary Volcanoes]. *Politiken*, 18 April.

Hagerup, F (1919) *Ret og Kultur i det nittende Århundrede* (Copenhagen, Gyldendalske Boghandel, Nordisk Forlag).

Kraus, RC (2012) *The Cultural Revolution* (Oxford, Oxford University Press).

Kurzman, C (2004) *The Unthinkable Revolution in Iran* (Harvard, Harvard University Press).

Moïsi, D (2010) *The Geopolitics of Emotion – How Cultures of Fear, Humiliation, and Hope Are Reshaping the World* (New York, Anchor Books).

Neshat, S (2009) 'Women without Men, 2009' (feature film based on Shahrnush Parsipur's novel *Women Without Men*).

Ñanajivako, B (1970; reprint 1988) 'Schopenhauer and Buddhism' *The Wheel Publication* 144/145/146.

Parsipur, S (2013) *Kissing the Sword. A Prison Memoir* (transl Sara Khalili) (New York, The Feminist Press at the City University of New York).

Piketty, T (2020) *Kapital og Ideologi* (Copenhagen, DJØF forlag of Informations Forlag).

Smith, L (2012) *The New North – The World in 2050* (London, Profile Books).

Smith, SA (2002) *The Russian Revolution. A Very Short Introduction* (Oxford, Oxford University Press).

Snowden, FM (2019) *Epidemics and Society. From the Black Death to the Present* (New Haven, Yale University Press).

—— (2020) *Epidemics and Society. From the Black Death to the Present* (New Haven, Yale University Press) (Kindle edition).

Part V

Sociology of Law as Science

26

Reza Banakar and the Quest for a Sociology of Law

OLE HAMMERSLEV AND MIKAEL RASK MADSEN

I. INTRODUCTION

REZA BANAKAR WAS an extraordinary person in so many ways. To young scholars, he was always very generous with both his ideas and time, and he spent endless time helping them (and us) to develop research projects and publications. We both benefited immensely from his generosity when we first entered academia. Although already an established authority in the field, he became not just a mentor but also a dear friend and travel companion from China to Canada. We also both sympathised with his broader projects of internationalising Nordic sociology of law and developing sociology of law as a distinct discipline situated equally between law and sociology. Reza was determined to disrupt the relative closure of Nordic sociology of law, which at the time was largely organised around intra-Nordic exchanges and conferences. He wanted it to adapt and speak to the latest developments in international sociology of law. While critical of the state of the art, his project was above all a testament to his great respect for the many insights generated by Nordic sociologists of law over the decades. His fear was that without a sufficiently international outlook, Nordic sociology of law would lose intellectual momentum and risked being marginalised in both law and sociology. His push for change was largely successful, as we have demonstrated in surveying the situation of the sociology of law in Scandinavia (Hammerslev and Madsen 2014).

His second and perhaps even bigger project concerned sociology of law more generally. Somewhat provocatively naming sociology of law a 'stepchild' of its parent-disciplines of law and society (Banakar 1998b), his writings sparked a Nordic debate about the state and character of the sociology of law (see for example Dalberg-Larsen 2000; Hellum 2000; Hydén 1999; Mathiesen 1998; Petersen 2000; Sand 2000). Reza, however, did not stop with his diagnosis of the identity crisis of sociology of law but took it upon himself to develop the intellectual tools necessary to solve the crisis. The result was a series of texts on sociological theory and methodology, which are now fundamental reading for scholars and students of sociology and law (Banakar 2000; 2003; 2013; Banakar and Travers 2005; 2002).

As well as instigating two crucial debates on sociology of law in Scandinavia and beyond, Reza also made many other contributions. He was an unfaltering defender of sociology of law and always fought for better research conditions for the discipline. He did that at the universities where he found employment over the years as well as through the discipline's various professional bodies, such as the International Institute for the Sociology of Law in Oñati, the Research Committee on the Sociology of Law and the Socio-Legal Studies Association. He was in many ways the dearest friend of the discipline, just as he was a dear friend to many of his colleagues, including ourselves.

It is impossible to do justice to his immense contribution in a short chapter. We have therefore opted to focus on his theoretical and methodological contributions to sociology of law. We also know that these subjects were very close to Reza's heart and ambitions. We first outline some of the central tenets of his theoretical engagement with sociology of law before turning to his methodological contributions and how they are reflected in his empirical work, notably his fieldwork in Iran.

II. TAKING SOCIOLOGY OF LAW SERIOUSLY

Having submitted his PhD in Lund in 1994, an empirical work on the Swedish ombudsman institution (Banakar 1998a; 1994), Reza quickly turned towards theoretical and methodological inquiries into the state of sociology of law, notably in the Nordic countries. At the time, Nordic sociology of law was to a certain extent marked by regional and linguistic closure (for an early description of Scandinavian sociology of law see, eg, Eckhoff 1968 and Hydén 1986). The well-organised and well-oiled set-up of Nordic conferences and journals in the field further made scholars focus on objects of inquiries particularly relevant to the Nordic countries. Research into the welfare state played a considerable role but that was at the expense of other relevant socio-legal issues of a globalising world. Regardless of the relative success of *Nordic* sociology of law, Reza could see that the discipline was somewhat marginalised at both law faculties and sociological departments across the region. The problem, according to Reza, was that sociology of law was the unfortunate stepchild of two much more powerful parents, law and sociology. Sociology of law was effectively under pressure from both law and sociology, neither of which – for different reasons – was likely to come to its rescue regardless of the parental relationship. He wrote:

> Sociologists – if they read socio-legal work – complain because it does not live up to their theoretical and methodological sophistication and epistemological purity. Those few academic lawyers who might read sociological analysis of law raise their eyebrows in amazement (if not in disapproval and disdain) and wonder what it has to do with the law they know. (Banakar 1998b: 3)

Reza's diagnosis was very clear. Sociology of law was '… placed somewhat precariously at the intersection of the disciplines of law and sociology, each of which in turn fosters its own distinct mode of conceptualizing, describing, analysing and experiencing social life' (Banakar 2003: 1). Reza further argued that the discipline of sociology of law was dangerously close to being pulled apart by the adversarial forces arising from these disciplines, generally causing socio-legal studies to fail to grasp the whole sociological complexity of the law and its institutions (Banakar 2003). All of this resulted in a fragmented field of inquiry, which lacked basic paradigms, common concepts and theories as well as methods. Accordingly, the fundamentals for making socio-legal studies a distinct and valuable scientific discipline were in jeopardy (ibid).

Drawing on Bourdieusian sociology, Reza was also very conscious that research is always positioned in a research field shaped by its own distinctive power hierarchies and funding opportunities. Reza reflected on the significance of these material constraints, arguing that until sociology of law managed to build its own strong theories and methodologies, it would be difficult for it to gain a more powerful and respectable position in the broader academic field.

This reflection is found across Reza's theoretical and methodological work, where he took up the perhaps most central distinction of socio-legal studies, namely the dichotomy between law's inside and outside or, put differently, law's internal operations and doctrine and its engagement with society (Weber 1978; Cotterrell 1998; Nelken 1993; Habermas 1996; Friedman 1986). This dichotomy reflects a disciplinary tension which in turn has made socio-legal scholars produce a new set of dichotomies, such as 'law on the books' versus 'law in action', or 'formal law' versus 'informal law', all of which are essentially designed to reflect the different research agendas of the two 'parental' disciplines. If it was not capable of including both perspectives, Reza feared that sociology of law would end as blinded or even empty. In this regard he drew on Habermas, who had argued:

> The philosophical discourse of justice misses the institutional dimension, toward which the sociological discourse on law is directed from the outset. Without the view of law as an empirical action system, philosophical concepts remain empty. However, insofar as the sociology of law insists on an objectivating view from the outside, remaining insensitive to the symbolic dimension whose meaning is only internally accessible, sociological perception falls into the opposite danger of remaining blind. (Habermas 1996: 66)

Rather than accepting the state of affairs, Reza argued that sociology of law should merge the two sides of the dichotomy while being open to their liquid and blurred boundaries, noting:

> ... the question is whether sociology is able to climb out of its own skin and get inside the law to understand and explain the law's 'truth', namely, the motives and meanings of legal phenomena from within. (Banakar 2000: 274)

Reza further developed his position by focusing on how the legal field managed to generate and legitimise its relative autonomy by constructing law as a 'pure science' – to use the Kelsen's (1960) notion – and thus detach law from its social context. Law's detachment from the social and its success in establishing itself as a closed discursive formation created particular methodological difficulties for sociology of law if it should traverse the boundaries between outsiders' and insiders' perspectives:

> These methodological obstacles, which are not specific to the sociology of law, and which also exist in other sub-branches of sociology, concern the tension between the 'experience-near' concepts and perspectives of insiders (such as lawyers, doctors, clients, and so on) on their field of activity, and the 'experience-distant' theoretical concepts of the outsiders

(in this case the sociologist studying law, medicine, and so on) on the insiders' perceptions, beliefs, intentions, and actions. (Banakar 2000: 274)

Reza did not claim to provide *the* solution as to how to overcome this inherent categorisation and problem of the sociology of law. Instead, he offered a well-argued reflection on how to incorporate the essential insights of the various dichotomies in a more constructive and interpretive – indeed reflexive – socio-legal research methodology and agenda. From the outset, the distinction between research theory and methods was blurred in Reza's work (see eg Banakar 2001b). His goal was fundamentally to bring reflexivity into socio-legal research as a means for a self-reflection, which should in turn help legal sociologists produce more original research with regard to law, sociology and ultimately sociology of law.

Reza took no shortcuts in his attempt to formulate his solution. In his important book *Merging Law and Sociology: Beyond the Dichotomies in Socio-Legal Research* (Banakar 2003), he divides the analysis into three parts on respectively 'The Theoretical State of the Sociology of Law', 'Revisiting the Classics,' and a 'Sociological Theory of Legislation'. The first part is by far the longest section of the book, at more than 160 pages. In this section, following an analysis of the scientific status of the field of sociology of law, notably its theoretical fragmentation and discontinuity, he called for the need to implement what he called a reflexive matrix: an analytical framework that considered both mainstream sociological features of law and the perceptions and logics of legal insiders, such as lawyers and judges.

The path suggested by Reza is in many ways straightforward. While the respective and irreconcilable research agendas of law and sociology, and the equally incompatible habitus of legal scientists and sociologists, have made socio-legal research something of a scientific no-man's land, Reza sought to advance socio-legal research which bridged legal insights and sociological insights: law as normative, formal, informal, internal, external, etc. Importantly, Reza was not arguing for relaunching the 'law in context' approach, a tradition which to him was an example of sociology of law when it was neither fish nor fowl, but rather emphasising his reflexive matrix as a framework for genuine socio-legal research capable of bridging the two disciplines. According to Reza, sociology of law, particularly when it took a strong sociological starting point, needed to develop a greater sensibility towards law and its many actors as the means for acquiring the fundamental insights that will broaden both the horizons of the discipline and its audience. These insights have not been lost on scholars, and new forms of legal realism build on similar premises, including our own work at the crossroads of sociology of law and legal realism (see for example Holtermann and Madsen 2015; 2016).

Having recognised the dichotomy between the inside and outside of the law, and the related difficulty of making sociology of law relevant to both law and sociology, Reza directed his research towards understanding law and other normative systems based on sound epistemological foundations (Banakar 2014; 2003). In *Merging Law and Sociology*, he outlined the basics of what he termed a 'sociological theory of legislation'. This is also where he seemed to have realised that to develop the agenda further, there was a need for extensive empirical studies. In *Merging Law and Sociology*, he illustrated his theory with an analysis of Swedish anti-discrimination legislation which generally confirmed his central theoretical points. His case studies clearly showed how law is always a process influenced not only by the fact that it is the most direct outcome of modern democratic decision-making but also that it is furter produced, reproduced and altered by agents and institutions, not all of which pay much attention to the label of their activities. Hence, law is both formal and informal, normative and objective, and produced by legal insiders as well as outsiders. Therefore, it necessarily has to be understood in the context of this multitude of stakeholders. These empirical findings gave him further appetite for empirical studies and the related methodological questions that empirical sociology of law raises.

III. THE TURN TO METHODOLOGY

Reza's methodological work was largely a collective enterprise undertaken with Max Travers. It was with Travers that Reza published some of the first textbooks on sociolegal theory and methodology, although the textbook label might be misleading considering the intellectual ambitions of these works. The authors acknowledged the existence of numerous textbooks on social scientific methods, yet they argued that most of these books failed to explain how these many methods could be applied when studying law. Nowhere were there instructions to be found for interviewing judges or analysing legal documents (Banakar and Travers 2005: x). In other words, they wanted to focus on the full range of different theories and methodologies that were relevant to socio-legal scholars and students when conducting research. The output of this endeavour was their path-breaking books on theory (Banakar and Travers 2002) and methodology (Banakar and Travers 2005). Two decades after their publication, they are still the go-to books in the field for both students and established scholars.

In addition to the collective work with Travers, Reza also analysed the classics of the sociology of law work with a view to unearthing their methodologies. Reza revisited, for instance, Gurvitch (Banakar 2001a), Petrażycki, Timasheff, Podgórecki and Ehrlich (Banakar 2013; 2003) to devise relevant methodological approaches for contemporary sociology of law. Through these studies, Reza found ways in which cultural understandings of law, when seen in the context of the agents' positions in society, could help further develop his analytical matrix.

Reza's engagement with the classics of sociology of law was anything but backward-looking. Besides locating methodological tools, he sought to apply these theories directly in studies of contemporary globalisation. In one of his texts on the classics, Reza (2013) uses the example of the Chinese 'Guanxi', ie a personal relation enmeshed in values of connectedness, harmony and long-term mutual benefit rather than individualism, profit maximization and competition. According to Reza, the institution of Guanxi produces a system of norms based on long-term contacts and contracts which might best be described as a contemporary example of living law. At the same time, Guanxi produces nepotism, closed networks in Chinese firms, which influence the choice of partners, etc. This system, according to Reza, is not in alignment with the approaches of Western companies and investors and their attempt at creating more transparent rule based systems on the global market. Guanxi can be seen as compensating for local legal systems' inadequacy as a form of living law.

Reza undoubtedly had a rare and deep knowledge of the classics and his scholarship in this regard could easily be the subject of a separate chapter. However, rather than resting on his theoretical and methodological laurels, Reza turned increasingly towards new empirical studies. Reflecting his Iranian origins and the long time he had spent in the United Kingdom, Reza went on to conduct empirical studies in Iran regarding cultural practices of law and on the legitimacy of the European Union and Brexit. In the next section we change focus and outline how Reza tried to use his theoretical and methodological insights in conducting empirical studies.

IV. THE EMPIRICAL TURN – NEW EMPIRICAL INQUIRIES

Reza's Iranian work illustrates well the arguments outlined already in his stepchild article and further developed in subsequent publications. Inspired by Bourdieusian research tools (Bourdieu and Wacquant 1992), Reza's cultural approach to law enabled him to explain how different positions in the Iranian legal field reproduced and applied different forms of law. In the book *Driving Cultures in Iran* (Banakar 2016), Reza starts out by considering how, despite its strict traffic laws, which include 'severe fines for dangerous and reckless driving' (ibid: 7), Iran has extremely high rates of road traffic accidents, indeed one of the highest rates in the world. Drawing on interviews with Iranians from different social backgrounds, Reza argues that their driving behaviour originates not from the law but from Iranian culture, which is shaped by rules informed by both pre-modern and extra-legal normative orders. The empirical situation of Iranian driving culture in terms of a medley of multiple legal cultures, formed by religion, and legal and political polycentricity and class (ibid), illustrates a key dimension of law, namely that it is 'living' – to use Ehrlich's (2001) notion – and thus in tension with both law in books and law in action. As Reza consistently argues, law in Iran is therefore much more than black letter law; on the contrary, it is materially grounded in, whilst also shaping, Iranian outlook and practices. This legal cultural approach bridges the inside-outside dichotomy and challenges perspectives that focus solely on black letter law and accept legal systems' self-presentation as socially detached.

In Reza's co-authored chapter on the Iranian legal profession (Banakar and Ziaee 2020) he further illustrates this living law perspective. Here he and his co-author present a study of law in practice as viewed by citizens and different kinds of lawyers, and analysed against their positions in specific social spaces. More specifically, the chapter empirically examines how, since the 1979 Revolution, the clerical regime has been increasingly limiting the legal profession's autonomy by preventing members of the Iranian Bar Association (IBA) from freely electing their Board of Directors and by establishing a new and competing body of lawyers – so-called legal advisers of the judiciary – to contest the IBA's professional monopoly. As a result, the profession tripled between 2005 and 2015. For these advisers, entry into the legal profession was via religious studies, an easier route than the traditional legal one, but also implying their subjection to political and theocratic, rather than professional, control. Thus, these polar positions in the Iranian legal field exemplify the co-existence of two different legal cultures, which reflect in turn the dichotomy built into Iranian society following the revolution. Whereas legal advisers seek to deliver substantive justice through the application and reconstruction of Islamic jurisprudence, regular attorneys continue to attempt to practise law consistent with 'the ideals of due process, certainty and uniformity in legal decision-making' (Banakar and Ziaee 2020: 581). However, the contemporary character of Iranian society and politics also means that regular lawyers encounter difficulties in obtaining clients, and that winning cases most often requires various forms of corrupt practices. Reza's expansive approach to law, with its exploration of the various legal cultures and practices performed by lawyers with different backgrounds placed differently in the legal field, provides a unique and highly complex account of the Iranian legal field.

Another interesting aspect of Reza's Iranian studies is their pragmatic approach to methodology. The approach was based on Reza's own methodological guidelines for comparison (Banakar 2003; Banakar and Travers 2005; see Hammerslev and Sommerlad 2021). First, a pragmatic (and cautious) approach was necessary when conducting this form of research in an authoritarian regime like Iran. Not only could research be dangerous, it was also impossible to know what kind of data it was possible to gather at the start of a project. The chapter on the legal profession developed radically during the research period as Reza realised it had in fact become possible to conduct qualitative interviews in Iran. Second, because he did not start with a pre-definition of law and lawyers, he was able to include forms of normative orders other than those stipulated by black letter law and therefore also different kinds of professionals who recognised and complied with different forms of normative orders. This complex picture of legal professionals was then situated in a larger context, in which the profession was examined in relation to the Iranian field of state power. The result is a distinct analysis of the plurality of the Iranian legal profession.

From the very beginning of his academic career, Reza was clearly inspired by Jürgen Habermas' focus on how the system continuously colonised the life worlds and thus displaced the democratic power of the people to elites and large organisations (Habermas 1984). This has followed him one way or another through most of his studies. The Habermasian inspiration is particularly explicit in his last studies which focused on Brexit and the legitimacy of the law (Banakar 2019). Using Santos' (1987) cartographic tools of inter-legality and scale, Reza argues that the political system in the United Kingdom (as well as Brussels) was detached from ordinary citizens' life worlds, causing friction and misunderstandings. According to Reza, EU law has disintegrative effects caused by the power disparity which hierarchically forms the relationship between the EU, its Member States and citizens. When the EU's inter-legality flows top down, its authority is based on the EU itself but meditated through the Member States' legal systems, a long way from the life worlds of the citizens. However, when it flows bottom up, the law is created and potentialised by Member States mediated to the EU. In both ways, the EU's inter-legality lacks legitimacy of its own; ie the legitimacy of the law is not based in citizens' life worlds (Banakar 2019). In his Iranian studies, the Habermasian inspiration is more discreet but it nevertheless offers a tool for better understanding his complex analysis. Put simply, law needs to make sense and give meaning for both professionals and ordinary citizens. The results are complex social assemblages which can only be fully comprehended using sociological reflexivity.

V. CONCLUSION

While the Iranian studies are empirical masterpieces in their own right, they are also clear illustrations of what Reza sought to achieve with his ambitious project of relaunching sociology of law as a distinct and worthy discipline. In some ways, Reza did come full circle with the Iranian studies. Not only did they allow him to come back to his country of origin and connect with a distant past, but they also offered him the perfect terrain for conducting the kind of 'inside-out/outside-in' reflexive sociology of law which he advocates throughout his entire oeuvre. Here he was both an insider and an outsider, capable of analysing the different components of the objects studied. This sets the bar high for other sociologists of law and underlines the level of ambition necessary if sociology of law is to merge law and sociology and thus establish itself as a scientific discipline not marginalised between the mother disciplines.

Since Reza's thought-provoking 'stepchild' article, Nordic sociology of law has undoubtedly opened up and moved towards international agendas and audiences. Following his recommendations, students coming into the field are now much more concerned with theory and methodology than had often been the case previously. The field is still somewhat fragmented, but sociology of law clearly relates to international and Nordic sociology, whilst carefully not losing sight of law. The relative success of contemporary sociology of law may be illustrated by the regularity with which socio-legal research applications receive grants from both national and European research foundations and the fact that Nordic socio-legal scholars are taking part in leading large-scale international research projects. A great part of this achievement can be ascribed to Reza's insistence on the importance of global outlook and firm theoretical and methodological foundations.

Let us conclude on a very personal note. As noted, throughout our research careers – from being young students coming into the field of sociology of law to today – Reza has always been there as a solid rock guiding us scientifically and professionally. As a friend, he was always there for us with his great humour and caring personality. His nickname among insiders was 'den tandløse tiger', although he always had bite. Thank you for everything! You are deeply missed.

REFERENCES

Banakar, R (1994) *Rättens Dilemma: Om konflikthantering i ett mångkulturellt samhälle* (Lund, Bokbox Publishing).

—— (1998a) *Doorkeepers of the Law: A Socio-Legal Study of Ethnic Discrimination in Sweden* (Aldershot, Dartmouth/Ashgate).

—— (1998b) 'The Identity Crisis of a "Stepchild": Reflections on the Paradigmatic Deficiencies of Sociology of Law' 21 *Retfærd.Nordic Legal Journal* 3.

—— (2000) 'Reflections on the Methodological Issues of the Sociology of Law' 27 *Journal of Law and Society* 273.

—— (2001a) 'Integrating Reciprocal Perspectives: On Gurvitch's Theory of Immediate Jural Experience' 16 *Canadian Journal of Law and Society* 67.

—— (2001b) 'A Passage to "India": Toward a Transfomative Interdisciplinary Discourse on Law and Society' 24 *Retfærd.Nordic Legal Journal* 3.

—— (2003) *Merging Law and Sociology: Beyond the Dichotomies in Socio-Legal Research,* (Berlin, Galda + Wilch Verlag).

—— (2013) 'Klassisk retssociologi – og dets relevans for nutidig forskning' in O Hammerslev and MR Madsen (eds), *Retssociologi* (Copenhagen, Hans Reitzels Forlag).

—— (2014) *Normativity in Legal Sociology: Methodological Reflections on Law and Regulation in Late Modernity* (London, Springer).

—— (2015) *Driving Culture in Iran: Law and Society on the Roads of the Islamic Republic* (London, IB Tauris).

—— (2019) 'Brexit: A Note on the EU's Interlegality' in BL Kristiansen, K Mitkidis, L Munkholm, L Neumann and C Pelaudeix (eds), *Transnationalisation and Legal Actors: Legitimacy in Question* (London, Routledge).

Banakar, R and Travers, M (eds) (2002) *An Introduction to Law and Social Theory* (Oxford, Hart Publishing).

—— (2005) *Theory and Method in Socio-Legal Research* (Oxford, Hart Publishing).

Banakar, R and Ziaee, K (2020) 'Iran: A Clash of Two Cultures?' in RL Abel, O Hammerslev, H Sommerlad and U Schultz (eds), *Lawyers in 21st Century Society, vol 1: National Reports* (Oxford, Hart Publishing).

Bourdieu, P and Wacquant, L (1992) *An Invitation to Reflexive Sociology* (Chicago, University of Chicago Press).

Cotterrell, R (1998) 'Why Must Legal Ideas Be Interpreted Sociologically?' 25 *Journal of Law and Society* 171.

Dalberg-Larsen, J (2000) 'Sociology of Law from a Legal Point of View' 23 *Retfærd.Nordic Legal Journal* 71.

Eckhoff, T (1968) 'Sociology of Law in Scandinavia' in R Treves and JFG Van Loon (eds), *Norms and Actions: National Reports on Sociology of Law* (The Hague, Martinus Nijhoff).

Ehrlich, E (2001) *Fundamental Principles of the Sociology of Law* (New Brunswick, Transaction Publishers).

Friedman, LM (1986) 'The Law and Society Movement' 38 *Stanford Law Review* 763.

Habermas, J (1984) *Theory of Communicative Action: Reason and the Rationalization of Society* (London, Heinemann).

—— (1996) *Between Facts and Norms* (Cambridge, Polity Press).

Hammerslev, O and Madsen, MR (2014) 'The Return of Sociology in Danish Socio-Legal Studies: A Survey of Recent Trends' 10 *International Journal of Law in Context* 397.

Hammerslev, O and Sommerlad, H (2021) 'Comparison as a Socio-Legal Tool: A Celebration of Reza Banakar and His Work on Methodology' 168 *Retfærd. Nordic Journal of Law and Justice* 39.

Hellum, A (2000) 'How to Improve the Doctrinal Analysis of Legal Pluralism' *Retfærd. Nordic Journal of Law and Justice* 40.

Holtermann, JVH and Madsen, MR (2015) 'European New Legal Realism and International Law: How to Make International Law Intelligible' 28 *Leiden Journal of International Law* 211.

—— (2016) 'Toleration, Synthesis or Replacement?: The "Empirical Turn" and its Consequences for the Science of International Law' 29 *Leiden Journal of International Law* 1001.

Hydén, H (1986) 'Sociology of Law in Scandinavia' 13 *Journal of Law and Society* 131.

—— (1999) 'Even a Stepchild Eventually Grows Up: On the Identity of Sociology of Law' 22 *Retfærd.Nordic Legal Journal* 71.

Kelsen, H (1960) *Reine Rechtslehre: Mit einem Anhang: Das Problem der Gerichtigkeit* (Wien, Franz Deuticke).

Mathiesen, T (1998) 'Is it All That Bad To Be a Stepchild? Comments on the State of Sociology of Law' 21 *Retfærd.Nordic Legal Journal* 57.

Nelken, D (1993) 'The Truth about Law's Truth' *European Yearbook of the Sociology of Law* (Milan, Giuffre).

Petersen, H (2000) 'Forging New Identities in the Global Family? Challenges for Prescriptive and Descriptive Normative Knowledge' *Retfærd. Nordic Journal of Law and Justice* 46.

Sand, I-J (2000) 'A Future or a Demise for the Theory of the Sociology of Law' 90 *Retfærd. Nordic Journal of Law and Justice* 55.

Santos, BDS (1987) 'Law: A Map of Misreading. Towards a Postmodern Conception of Law' 14 *Journal of Law and Society* 279.

Weber, M (1978) *Economy and Society* (Berkeley, CA, University of California Press).

27

Governing through Covid Indicators

DAVID NELKEN

I. INTRODUCTION

W̶E ARE CURRENTLY living through a difficult period during which enormous efforts have been expended in trying to overcome the worldwide threats posed by the mutating Covid 19 virus. Sociologists of law and other behavioural scientists are not in the front line in the same way as those in the health, caring and service delivery professions. But they too are called upon to make a contribution in helping policymakers choose how to frame their interventions and assess their outcomes.[1] This includes trying to understand the way people have reacted to messages about the spread of Covid and how this has affected its diffusion. Hence this chapter will discuss the role played in this process by what I shall be calling Covid indicators (see further Nelken and Siems 2021).

I have gained much from my late friend's Reza Banakar's insights into questions of theory and method in our field (see, eg, Banakar 2003; 2015; Banakar and Travers 2005; 2013). Not knowing what he would have said about the events we are now going through makes me feel his loss even more. But I am pretty certain that he would agree with the idea that sociology of law should try to offer something here. So I will begin by picking out three of the ways this would be suggested by his work.

First, Reza never shied away from the big questions, as in his writing about the 2007–2008 financial global crisis (Banakar 2013) or the Brexit decision in 2016 (Banakar 2019). His 2013 paper used the financial crisis, for example, as a backdrop

---

[1] Their role is evidenced also by the inclusion of representatives of the behavioural sciences in the relevant scientific advisory bodies, albeit in a minority with probably less clout than say health professionals, epidemiologists and statisticians. Of course, this does not mean that all such representatives speak with one voice. The UK Scientific Advisory Group for Emergencies (SAGE) committee includes, for example, Susan Michie a brilliant leading psychologist of public health (and 'card-carrying communist', as some newspapers never tired of repeating), who was noted for a cautious approach to easing of restrictions, alongside Robert Dingwall, an influential health sociologist (and sociologist of law), more often quoted in the same newspapers as calling for the relaxation of restrictions sooner rather than later.

against which to formulate concerns regarding the limits of legal regulation in late modernity and explore the formation and operations of the late modern state, asking if power is separated from politics and has moved to the level of global organisations. He went on to ask what kind of law was emerging de facto in response to the fluidity of late modernity, and how legal imagination envisaged the future of law. One of the striking things about the response to Covid, perhaps consistent with a hiatus in some aspects of globalisation, was the weakness of transnational bodies such as the World Health Organisation or the European Union and the way nation-states chose or were left to do the heavy lifting of responding to the pandemic.

In the second place, researching the responses to Covid offers the chance to observe interrelations between law, medicine, social control, expertise, and politics in ways that would have piqued Reza's interest. For example, some time ago, he authored a wide-ranging paper that was concerned with the different significance of social control for law as compared to medicine (Banakar 2000). Following up a debate about how sociologists can get at law's 'truths', he explains why he thought that there was more resistance to sociological approaches on the part of lawyers than from the medical profession. He argued that sociology offered more direct competition to law, in claiming to offer alternative interpretations of legal questions. By contrast, it played a complementary role in medicine. In addition, both law and sociology were manifestly about social control whereas this was only a latent function of medicine. In this paper, as elsewhere, he also discussed questions of institutionalisation and legitimacy, all matters which are relevant to working out when communications about Covid are authoritative. More could be said about the linkages between law and social control, both from an external and an internal perspective.[2] Equally important, the challenge here is less to work out how to decide whether sociology can know the truths about indicators and more to appreciate how it plays a role linking up with law and medicine so as to persuade us that they have got things right.

Last but not least, Reza Banakar's familiarity with places as different as the UK, Sweden and Iran (Banakar 2016), means that he certainly could have had an interest in comparing the way different places dealt with the pandemic. He would also have agreed, I think, that compliance levels can be used to illustrate differences in legal culture (Nelken 2016a), and, as we shall see, the results were often not as might have been predicted. What he would have found new, perhaps, was the extent to which comparison of such levels itself served as a means of social control, a way of justifying and spreading new rules and restrictions.

Hopefully, this discussion of Covid indicators will show how Reza's analyses of law, medicine and social control can be taken further. In what follows I shall first describe the various roles of Covid indicators and their normative significance. I then

---

[2] As we shall see in this study of social indicators, other things than law may be doing the job of social control without using this terminology. It is possible that Reza exaggerated the significance of the fact of legal actors using the language of social control more than those in the health professions.

discuss the success of Covid indicators in proving and producing compliance. I end by examining the ways comparison may itself play a role in social control.

II. THE LAW OF THE INDICATOR

When we speak about social indicators, we need to distinguish (at least) three kinds. We can speak of explanatory indicators, meaning by this the indices, proxies, or variables that quantitative social scientists (in particular) develop when seeking to study variance. Alternatively, we could be discussing policy indicators, ie the targets or benchmarks used in setting and assessing the results of social interventions so as to see if they have achieved their intended outcomes. Finally, we could be concerned with what are known as global social indicators, measures or standards formulated as part of large-scale ranking exercises that stipulate and compare the performance of units. Our main concern here is with the last of these indicators. But global social indicators sometimes build on or incorporate the other two kinds of indicators[3] (see, eg, Karstedt 2011), and, in actual practice, there can be some blurring or even confusion between the scientific, pragmatic, and programmatic purposes of social indicators (see Nelken 2015a; 2016b; 2019).

A global social indicator has been defined by leading commentators as:

> a named collection of rank-ordered data that purports to represent the past or projected performance of different units. The data are generated through a process that simplifies raw data about a complex social phenomenon. The data, in this simplified and processed form, are control used to compare units of analysis (such as countries or institutions or corporations), synchronically or over time, and to evaluate their performance by reference to one or more standards. (Davis et al 2012: 6)

Sally Merry, who also sadly passed away recently, was one of the pioneers in studying these instruments. She explained that global social indicators have 'knowledge effects', meaning that they themselves often bring into being the categories – such as failed states – whose performance they claim to be measuring (Merry 2011). The knowledge they retail is also often flawed. Indicators count only what can be counted and often provide only a partial and misleading picture that risks mistaking the map for the territory. For example, the 'raw' information on which comparisons are based is typically collected and compiled by workers near the bottom of organisational hierarchies, and the pressures and priorities of those on the ground may often be different from or incompatible with accurate record-keeping (see, eg, Park 2015).

Indicators also have what Merry called 'governance effects'. What is presented as a technical exercise in fact involves political decision-making with significant

---

[3] In seeking to rank performance they may rely on social science explanations, including, for example, those that link legal regimes and economic success. Conversely, social scientists sometimes take indicators developed for comparative evaluations of performance and use them as stand-in variables for empirical studies geared to providing explanation of variation. See, for example, Karstedt 2011.

distributional consequences. In addition, typically, it is countries from the Global North that get to define what counts as the global standard, as in the way 'development' is measured in terms of specific local accomplishments rather than as a reflection of the structural relationship between the local and the global.

The wide adoption of such social indicators has been linked to the rise of the so-called 'audit society'. As Shore and Wright tell us:

> virtually every aspect of contemporary professional life and organisational behaviour is now subject to elaborate systems of audit and inspection: everything from the provision of public services, education, policing, and security, to health care, safety, energy conservation, information systems, and the performance of individuals. Even intangible phenomena such as levels of 'trust', 'perceptions of corruption', 'quality of life years', and 'gross national happiness' are now routinely quantified, measured, and ranked in competitive national and international league tables that purport to offer at-a-glance comparisons. (Shore and Wright 2015: 22)

Global social indicators therefore do much more than just provide information. They form part of practices designed to measure or produce compliance and (thereby) stimulate change.[4] As Figure 1 suggests, such indicators can be placed along a continuum of normative regulation from the most to the least counterfactual.

Figure 1 A Continuum of Normative Regulation

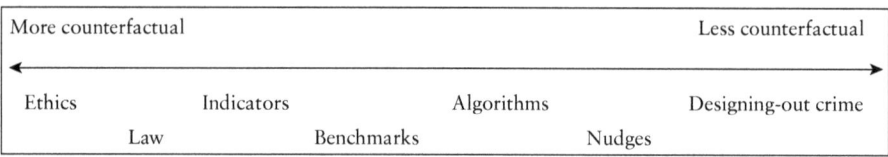

At the more counterfactual end of the continuum we can locate those standards (as with religious, moral and ethical statements) that appeal to people to behave in certain ways without this necessarily being accompanied by formal efforts to enforce them. At the other, more instrumental end, we find efforts to engineer changes in social behaviour without those subject to this being always made aware that they are being manipulated (for example, when the shape of seats in train stations are designed so as to prevent people sleeping on them, or the architecture of public spaces is constructed to make people hurry through them). Other kinds of normative material such as soft law, global social indicators, codes of conduct professional, technical standards, and hyper-nudges, can then be placed at intermediate places along the continuum. Generally speaking, if norms are understood to impose 'counter-factually stabilized

---

[4] It would be interesting to relate the roles played by Covid indicators to what Sullivan (2020) in the sphere of international law calls the 'Law of the List'. That too, according to him, opens up issues concerning accountability, authority claims, normative conflicts, and governance practices. For other related discussions of governance through social problems, whether domestic or transnational crime, see Simon 2007; Findlay 2008; 2021.

behavioural expectations' (Luhmann 2014: 33), then indicators can be considered as, on the one hand, less counterfactual than law, and on the other, more counterfactual than those ways of shaping behaviour that leave less room for choosing whether or not to comply.

Indicators interrelate and interact with all these other forms of normativity in a variety of local, national, and transnational spaces. Gaining a better understanding the role of social indicators in transnational governance requires us to explore how their similarities and differences allow them to interact with other sources of regulation.

According to Merry et al 'Indicators and law both embody standards, and for this reason both can operate as an expression of values and political commitments' and note that 'the motivations for producing law and indicators may not be that different' (Merry et al 2015: 19). As compared to domestic and international law for instance, they have their own normative force and can be used in schemes of social control involving incentives and sanctions, such as, for example, when the United States seeks to outlaw human trafficking, or when the European Union uses indicators to assess when candidate countries are ready to join the union. They can be employed to reveal when legal intervention is needed, or to extend law's reach. But there are also differences:

> as compared to law, the production process for indicators is subjected to less limitation and regulation from that of a formal legal standard. Participation in the law making process, committees or treaties, and even regarding 'soft law' such as domestic policies, usually requires slow and complex negotiation and adaptation, involving a large number of participants, and can be more influenced by, or targeted to political agendas, than the process of making an indicator. (Davis et al 2015: 20)

Nearer the other end of the continuum, when indicators are linked to schemes of social intervention, they offer 'an alternative way of assessing social facts against norms. In contrast to law (and more like benchmarking), they do not deal in the binary terms of legal/illegal of legal reasoning but in terms of degree, ie they determine where a given conduct is located in a performance scale (Restrepo-Amariles 2015). They may also be associated with efforts to use nudges so as to change behaviour.[5] When they are employed as part of 'algorithmic regulation',[6] indicators intervene in

---

[5] A nudge alters the environment so that when a given decision is made, the resulting choice will be the most positive or desired outcome for those who have set it up. Roger Cotterrell (in some comments he kindly sent me) asks, 'does law always operate in a binary manner? Eg law often adopts "reasonableness" standards that involve much discretion in application. Police discretions in application of law may only become binary when a court has to rule on their exercise in a particular case. Doesn't law often work by "nudging" conduct, attitudes etc?' He is surely right that law in practice often exercises all sorts of behavioural pressures, including nudges. But, for many legal theorists, most obviously Lon Fuller, 'legality' should require a high level of predictability in how it will be interpreted and applied. Whereas, as we move along the continuum, outcome is privileged over process.

[6] An algorithm is defined as 'a process or set of rules to be followed in calculations or other problem-solving operations, especially by a computer. See https://www.oxfordlearnersdictionaries.com/definition/english/algorithm.

entire populations of users over widely dispersed geographic areas, are dynamic and seek to shape conduct and produce given outcomes (Yeung 2017).

There is no well accepted typology of kinds of global social indicators (though see Siems and Nelken 2017); and many such indicators share only a 'family resemblance', with only some elements in common. There are important differences, for example, in using indicators for providing financial ratings of credit worthiness (which can even be self-fulfilling), and evaluating the performance of countries in respecting the rule of law or protecting human rights. In the case of the latter indicators, some commentators argue that we should concentrate less on their role in promoting immediate compliance and more on the way they can stimulate debate about the values at stake (see Rosga and Satterthwaite 2009). But where, as here, we are dealing with matters of life and death, calls for more debate as a value in itself are likely to sound unconvincing, and, in general, if indicators are to be reliable guides for decision-making, some limits to contestation need to be set (Nelken 2015b).

If indicators measure the success of others' performance, how is their own performance to be measured? Which of the many roles and audiences for a given indicator (as they change over time) should matter more for this purpose? Much depends on the definition of success we adopt. In terms of their extrinsic success we can certainly point to cases where the process of monitoring and ranking impacts the behaviour of states (Kelley and Simmons 2020). And management consultants insist that we can only change what we can measure. By contrast, it has been argued that it is not possible simultaneously both to measure and change a phenomenon (Goodhart 1975), especially where those being assessed are rewarded for given outcomes. Case studies of global indicators show us that it can be rather easy to game their metrics (see, eg, Zaloznaya and Hagan 2012, and, more generally, Muller 2018). Alternatively we may be interested in intrinsic definitions of success, such as whether a given indicator has been adopted and given credibility at the expense of other competing ones concerning the same issue. Or success can be taken to mean wide acceptance and 'normalisation' of the underlying theory, the idea, of what is being measured. We will say something about both these kinds of measures of success.

III. THE ROLE OF COVID INDICATORS IN ASSESSING AND PRODUCING COMPLIANCE

A case study of Covid indicators offers an opportunity for observing global social indicators at work. I will first describe some of the forms taken by such indicators, then ask what may have been special about them and how this may have affected their success.

Data about what was happening during the Covid pandemic was generated by national, international, and transnational organisations, and illustrated in maps, graphs, tables, and figures. Sometimes they were presented as 'snapshots', illustrating at any given date diachronic developments over time or synchronic differences between countries. Alternatively, they were displayed on dashboards[7] (some of which allowed for interaction with the user), that focused on day-by-day bulletins, or even minute-by-minute changes, and offered the possibility of interrogating the data with respect to given localities and times. Information provided included reported rates of testing, of infection (with and without symptoms), numbers of deaths, numbers in home isolation and hospitalised, those on ventilators, recovered, excess deaths as compared to previous years, etc (see, eg, Figure 2).

Figure 2 Media Communication about the spread of Covid in the UK

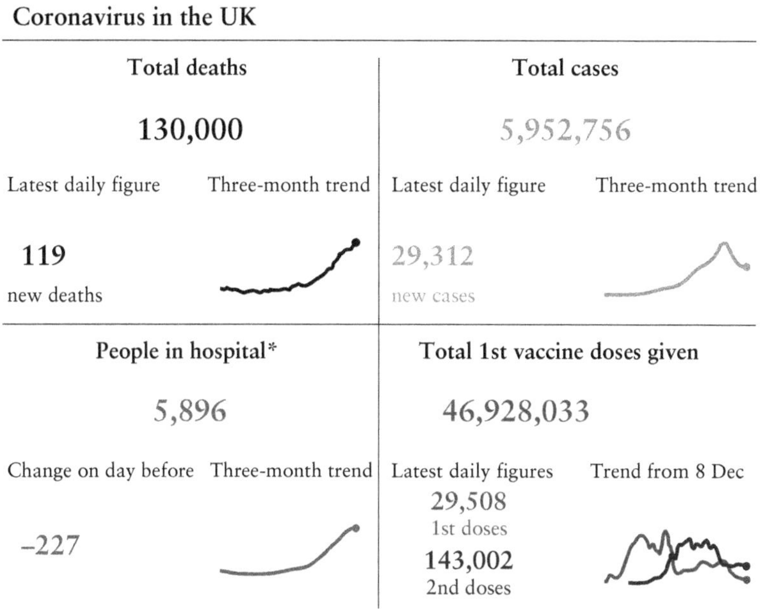

Coronavirus in the UK

Total deaths		Total cases	
130,000		5,952,756	
Latest daily figure	Three-month trend	Latest daily figure	Three-month trend
119 new deaths		29,312 new cases	
People in hospital*		Total 1st vaccine doses given	
5,896		46,928,033	
Change on day before	Three-month trend	Latest daily figures 29,508 1st doses	Trend from 8 Dec
−227		143,002 2nd doses	

*Publication dates differ by nation, most recent data for all nations to 3 Aug.
Source: Gov.uk dashboard.

Secondary re-purposing of Covid data focused on the progress of the epidemic[8] and/or, more explicitly, on evaluating the success of local policies for dealing with it (Petherick et al 2020; Infantino 2021). Examples of the first are the World Health Organisation (WHO)'s 'Covid-2019 situation reports', the European Centre for Disease Prevention and Control (ECDC)'s 'Covid-19 situation update worldwide',[9]

---

[7] See https://coronavirus.jhu.edu/map.html. See also Dong et al 2020.

[8] Johns Hopkins University has been amongst the leading collators of health data. See, eg, https://systems.jhu.edu/research/public-health/2019-ncov-map-faqs/ and https://coronavirus.jhu.edu/news. Other credible sources include https://ourworldindata.org/coronavirus; and https://ourworldindata.org/coronavirus-source-data; https://ourworldindata.org/Covid-media-coverage. See also https://www.healthdata.org/about/history; https://covid19.healthdata.org/united-states-of-america; https://www.healthdata.org/Covid/faqs; https://www.healthdata.org/Covid/media. *cf* https://www.bsg.ox.ac.uk/research/research-projects/coronavirus-government-response-tracker.

[9] See also the US CDC Global Covid-19 website, at https://www.cdc.gov/coronavirus/2019-ncov/global-Covid-19/index.html.

the Johns Hopkins University (JHU)'s 'Covid-19 Dashboard', Worldometer (WoM)'s and Our-World-in-Data (OWiD)'s statistics on the 'Coronavirus Pandemic', and the Institute for Health Metrics and Evaluation (IHME)'s 'Covid-19 Projections'. Examples of the second kind are the Oxford University's 'Covid-19 Government Response Tracker' (Ox-CGRT), the Deep Knowledge Group (DKG)'s 'Covid-19 Rankings and Analytics', the Centre for Civil and Political Rights (CCPR)'s 'State of Emergency Data', and Simon Porcher's 'Rigidity of Governments' Responses to Covid-19' dataset and index.[10]

In terms of the three different types of indicators that we have distinguished, Covid data may play a role in exercises seeking to explain different rates of infections and death; they may serve to document best practices and justify different policy choices, or they may be used to judge and rank performance by different countries. Covid indicators were used by governments, administrators, and citizens for such aims as predicting, deciding, justifying, coordinating, informing and shaming. Circulating such information was often deliberately intended to get people to take more care to avoid spreading the disease, increasing the take-up of vaccination and, as an indirect means to the same ends, shaming governments into taking more appropriate action or stimulating compliance by the public with rules intended to limit the spread of the disease. As with other global social indicators, ranking what was happening in different countries pointed to which places were safer for investors, for workers, and for travellers, etc. Less obviously, they may also have formed part of rituals to create solidarity and reassurance – attempts to undermine (false) confidence, to extend control, or to distract from other political issues and failings.

Thinking back to Figure 1, Covid indicators too can be placed along a continuum of counterfactuality, and both intersect and interact with other forms of normative regulation. At one end of the continuum, Covid indicators were pressed into service by governments to justify rules requiring compliance by citizens (in association with both nudging and enforcement) and helped justify legal crackdowns on those who failed to conform to health obligations. Indicators were also used to direct and to justify (police) enforcement of rules designed to limit the spread of Covid. At the other end, Covid indicators helped prepare the way for the obligatory use of artificial intelligence devices to measure one's own and other people's rates of infection in ways that leave little room for resistance.

Undoubtedly, Covid indicators played an ongoing role in the process of signalling danger and justifying – or attempting to justify – national and locally imposed curbs on supposedly risky behaviour.[11] But we need to be cautious in assessing how far Covid indicators were successful in ensuring compliance. Who should define

---

[10] https://www.nature.com/articles/s41597-020-00757-y.

[11] Of course the media also used qualitative evidence – including 'horror stories' about the dangers of the epidemic – and each followed their own agendas to increase circulation and meet the perceived expectations of their readers, by calling for more or for less restrictions and emphasising either the success or the failure of goverment campaigns.

success? Should we take into account the views of those who were doubtful about the fight against Covid, especially those who found problematic the immediate and longer-term potential political consequences some of the means adopted to ensure conformity? How far are the side and collateral effects of lockdowns and other restrictions relevant to our assessment? What about the effects on inequality as between these countries more and less able to afford to implement necessary measures?

As important, how far can the success of an indicator be distinguished from what happens with the larger project for which it is being mobilised? Could we say that Covid indicators provided a valuable service even when the project of controlling the disease was going badly – or *especially* in such cases? But how far should we go in evaluating indicators in terms of their intrinsic success? If we compare Covid indicators with some of the better known ones, such as those measuring business friendliness by the World Bank, or the OECD's Programme for International Student Assessment (PISA), measures of educational levels, or the ranking of corruption by Transparency International, it is arguable that they have been less successful in institutionalising themselves. Indeed, rather than legitimising the policy choices of more successful governments, some Covid indicators (such as the Deep Knowledge Group (DKG)'s 'Covid-19 Rankings and Analytics) themselves sought out endorsements from those countries whose relative success they had blandished – before falling silent (from May 2020) whilst the fortunes of different governments in their fight against Covid kept on changing.[12]

It is not that other better institutionalised global social indicators succeed more because they get things 'right'. Nor are they incontestable or uncontested. Far from it. But the repeated criticisms of the perceptions of corruption index put out by Transparency International, for example, itself presupposes that this indicator is widely cited and that a certain international hierarchy of ranking is widely shared – and therefore difficult to change without such contestation. Here, however, the changing Covid indicators meant that places kept altering their relative position as standard bearers of best practices. Countries such as Italy, which fared badly in the so-called first wave of the disease (Volpi and Serravalle 2020), were amongst the most successful in handling the threatened second wave; others, such as Israel, that were stars in the first wave, were trapped in escalating efforts at lockdown to deal with the second wave.[13] The UK and the United States did disastrously in stopping the spread of Covid, but were amongst those preeminent in rolling out vaccines. The sense of all being contingent and in flux was felt all the more keenly by the way that Covid numbers were produced daily (rather than annually) via dashboards. But even a previous, more leisured, effort to define which countries would be likely to

---

[12] https://www.dkv.global/.

[13] 'Prime Minister Benjamin Netanyahu's cabinet decided on Thursday to tighten Israel's coronavirus lockdown after he voiced alarm that a surge in infections was pushing the nation to "the edge of the abyss," the YNet news site said. Israel went back into lockdown on September 18. But over the past week, the number of daily new cases has reached nearly 7,000, severely straining the resources of some hospitals': https://www.globaltimes.cn/content/1201955.shtml.

do best in responding to a pandemic also turned out to have got things very wrong (see Figure 3).

Figure 3　The Indicator That Got it Wrong

The Countries Best Prepared To Deal With A Pandemic
Index scores by level of preparation to respond to an epidemic/pandemic*

United States 83.5
United Kingdom 77.9
Netherlands 75.6
Australia 75.5
Canada 75.3
Thailand 73.2
Sweden 72.1
Denmark 70.4
South Korea 70.2
Finland 68.7

*2019. 100 = greater level of preparation. Index benchmarks health security on factors critical to fighting disease outbreaks.
Source: 2019 Global Health Security Index.

This degree of uncertainty undermined one of the major functions of these kind of indicators, that of guiding decision-making. In addition, the often unpredictable and unpredicted messages about the spread of Covid encouraged doubt about whether experts and politicians really knew the answers anyway. In fact, there was considerable uncertainty, confusion, and contradiction about the exact ways to implement crucial prophylactic measures, such as social distancing, handwashing, and the wearing of masks. For example, it was said at first that people might become more complacent when wearing masks.[14] They might end up re-using them, which would be unhygienic, use masks sold on the black market, or wear homemade masks, which could be of inferior quality and essentially useless. Even where the experts seemed in agreement, people found it difficult to treat the latest decrees and accompanying set of rules as absolute – when only shortly before different advice was being given and they were informed that diametrically opposite rules were in force in other places.[15] In addition, some places did badly despite following recommended policies, as seen in the failure of stringent policies in France, or the level of excess death rates in Peru despite their long lockdown.[16] This was also a period when scientific expertise on matters of policy (as with climate change) was being openly ridiculed by some. Even for those more disposed to trust the experts, lack of clarity on whether politicians were following 'the science' (or just using what suited them) weakened their credibility. As important perhaps, the

---

[14] https://www.asiaone.com/lifestyle/doctor-says-wearing-face-mask-can-increase-your-risk-coronavirus-infection-heres-why.
[15] Changing advice over the need to wear masks was only the most obvious of these switches.
[16] See https://www.bbc.com/news/world-latin-america-53150808.

transnational level of policymaking tended to be subordinated here to the national level.[17] International authorities, such as the WHO, following a period of caution in handling earlier epidemics, tried to get traction for their warnings and recommendations. But they often went unheard. This was not helped by their own initial hesitation in declaring a pandemic and their equivocation over the benefits of wearing masks.[18] Their authority was also directly challenged by the President of the United States, who alleged that it had shown too much indulgence towards China, and threatened to withdraw funding.[19] Thus, the lead in policymaking to deal with Covid was usually taken by nation-states, sometimes – as in countries such as the United States and Brazil – led by politicians who were amongst the first to cast doubt on scientific expertise.

IV. COMPARISON AND CONTROL

It will be obvious by now that the uses and effects of Covid indicators were different in different places. Many of the communications about Covid pointed to such country-level differences (see Figures 4A and B). But the lessons to be learned were not always spelled out.

Figures 4A and 4B Comparing the Spread of Covid in Different Countries

Figure 4A

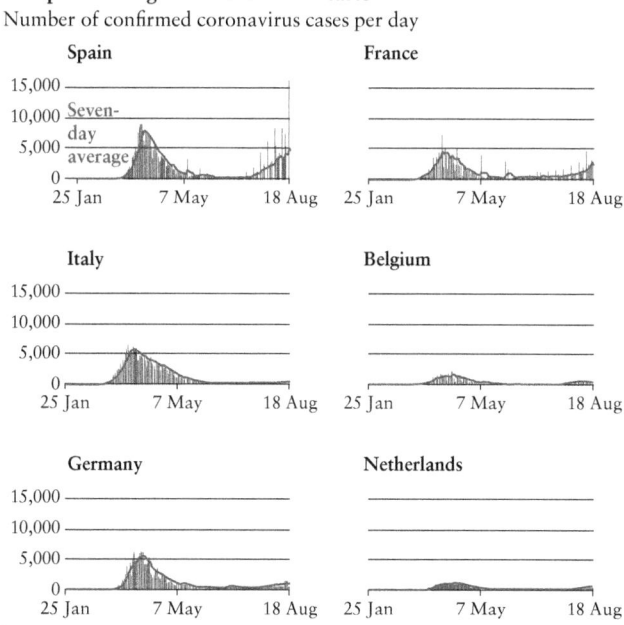

Source: ECDC, data to 18 August.

[17] On the continuing need for national endorsement of transnational standards even in successful efforts at governance, see the discussion of normative 'settlement' in Halliday and Shaffer (2014).

[18] The WHO was somewhat more authoritative later on, for example in its directives regarding the six requirements that needed to be satisfied before exiting from lockdown.

[19] See https://www.bbc.com/news/world-us-canada-53327906.

Figure 4B

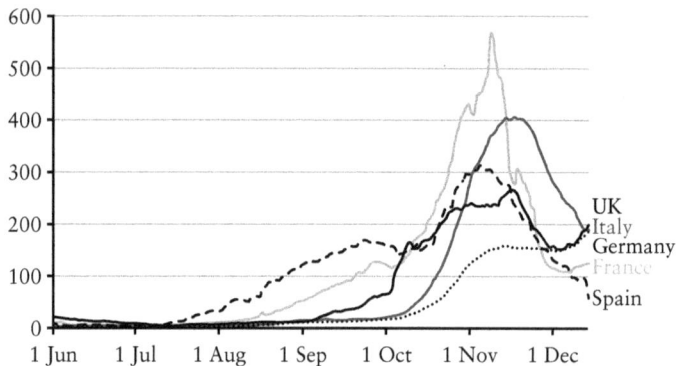

Cases in selected European countries
Total cases per 100,000 people by week up to 14 December

Note: Countries do not always release figures every day, which may explain some of the sharp changes in the trendlines.

Source: ECDC, data to 14 Dec.

Three issues concerning the role of such Covid indicators in comparison are worth further exploration. What were the factors, the similarities and differences, that were linked to different outcomes in the spread of Covid? What differences in policies were said to lead to better outcomes? And, crucially, what happened to comparative methodology when pressed to serve the goal of spreading best practices?

Early differences in the spread of Covid, and the reasons why some places suffered more than others, were attributed to a number of factors that were independent of policy choices (though potentially relevant to them). These included the presence of major international airports, as in the Netherlands and the UK, unhealthy populations, as in the United States, built-up resistance to antibiotics, in the case of Italy, the distractions of Brexit, again in the UK, or tensions between the Federal state and regional governments, for Spain. Outside of Europe the range of relevant factors increased. In Peru it was a challenge to enforce social distancing where so many live in overcrowded homes, the lack of refrigerators meant that people have to shop regularly and risk coming into contact with market vendors who may have the illness. The society relied on its informal economy and people had to use crowded public transport. It was difficult to deliver aid to those who needed it when only 38 per cent of the population had bank accounts.[20] In India, many people had a justified suspicion of top-down health interventions, as well as strong commitment to collective religious practices which can expose them to danger.

When it came to assessing the outcome of different policy choices, commentators tried to work backwards from differing outcomes. But it was sometimes difficult to identify what there was in common in policymaking between apparently more successful countries such as Australia and New Zealand, Norway, Germany, Taiwan,

---

[20] See https://www.bmj.com/content/373/bmj.n1442.

Singapore, South Korea – as well as central European countries such as Hungary, as compared to less successful ones, such as the United States, Brazil, Russia, the UK, Belgium, France, Spain, Peru, Mexico, Iran and India. It was noted that some of the more successful countries, such as Taiwan, Singapore and South Korea, had experienced SARS and MERS epidemics; South Korea, for example, had specifically learned from its mistakes last time round and had systems ready in place to deal with any new epidemic.[21] As regards the less successful countries, commentators pointed to failures of leadership in the way the crisis was handled, under-preparation and slowness in reacting,[22] and getting things wrong, including confusing Covid with influenza, using ventilators too soon, exposing old people in care homes to the disease, putting political logic before health, and not listening sufficiently to (the right) experts.

As for the causes of the epidemic spreading, we learnt of the heightened risks for care homes, for certain categories of victims, such as health workers, the old, Black and minority ethnic people, the poor, and those compelled to work and shop in dangerous conditions. We were told of the importance of reducing the period from the first appearance of symptoms to the isolation of the individual.[23] There was also a growing consensus that best practice included making tests extensive and affordable, tracing and isolating, imposing social distancing early, and keeping the public well informed and engaged. Closing borders, as was done quickly in Australasia, could also keep out those travellers who might bring with them infection.

More controversially, some argued that countries with more autocratic regimes, starting with China itself, were better able to respond quickly and decisively. It was suggested that we needed to understand 'why countries with more democratic political institutions experienced deaths on a larger per capita scale and sooner than less democratic countries'. It was said that more democratic regimes faced a dilemma if they were 'to respond quickly and more efficiently to future outbreaks of pandemics, or similar urgent crises'. Successful strategies had to:

> include expedited decision-making processes that place unpalatable restrictions on individual liberties … failure to deal effectively with pandemics poses a risk to the public's trust in democratic governance and could contribute to the democratic roll-back that is happening in some regions of the world. Giving up some liberties in the short-run within democratic institutions may be necessary to ensure liberties into the future with democratic institutions. (Cepaluni et al 2020)

On the other hand, they do concede:

> As the pandemic started in East Asia, the location of some of the best-managed autocracies, it may be that our sample disproportionately includes the autocratic governments with high state capacity. Therefore, it is an area for future research to see if our results hold when autocracies with lower state capacity are eventually included in the sample. (ibid: 25)

It should also be noted that it was in some of the countries with 'illiberal populist' leaders where the virus got most out of hand (Leonhardt and Leatherby 2020).

---

[21] This explanation is also offered for Italy's relative success in (so far) avoiding a second wave: https://www.theguardian.com/world/2020/sep/24/totally-awakened-how-tragedy-has-left-italians-alert-to-deadly-virus.

[22] See https://www.thetimes.co.uk/edition/news/government-underestimated-speed-of-surge-in-coronavirus-cases-0xzfkcvfh.

[23] See https://www.bbc.com/news/world-asia-51970379.

Reza might have looked for explanations of levels of compliance with Covid rules in terms of public law-abidingness. In his book about Iran, Banakar makes sense of driving (mis)behaviour by suggesting that people there act on the assumption that other people are likely to be breaking the law (Banakar 2016). By contrast, it seems that those who governed Sweden made the assumption that people would keep to safety rules even when not obliged by law to do so. Yet, in the case of Covid restrictions, countries such as the Netherlands or Germany, usually seen as basically law-abiding places, saw a remarkable level of resistance. In the Netherlands, people destroyed testing centres in Eindhoven and Amsterdam and a curfew had to be introduced. In Germany, resisting Covid rules help to spread the disease.[24] In Italy there was fierce criticism of Covid measures by some public intellectuals such as Georgio Agamben, who insisted that restrictions imposed in the name of health priorities should be seen mainly in the light of their function in tightening state control over the population (Agamben 2020). But, despite a fair number of news reports of resistance by members of the public, it seemed that there was better compliance with rules designed to stop the spread of the disease there than in the UK.[25] In fact, evidence is now emerging that those in charge in the UK took their decisions on the basis that they could not count on compliance by the public (Kahl and Wright 2021).

But it is one thing to seek explanation or choose best practices by highlighting similarities and differences (being careful only to combine 'like with like'). It is something else to try to commensurate, that is to seek to spread common standards and evaluate places in terms of their conformity to them. In the latter case, being able to make sense of current differences in local contexts in the possibility of reaching these standards is not the real point of the exercise. A key question for those studying global social indicators is thus how far those making and using such indicators are interested in combining both comparison and commensuration, and what happens when they try to do so (Espeland and Stevens 1998; 2008; Merry 2016). Put another way, what do comparisons of success do to the criteria of what makes a successful comparison?[26]

Some of the many publicly disseminated communications about Covid did make some attempt to compare 'like with like', controlling for those factors, such as the age of the relevant population, and whether different generations lived together, that might explain (away) differences in the rates of the disease. But this was by no means a consistent feature of such communications. Nor did they come near to including the very many possible contextual factors that distinguished one place from another (or even the same place over time). Rightly or wrongly, what was seen as mattering were levels of danger, not its causes.

---

[24] See https://www.aa.com.tr/en/europe/germany-adopts-national-virus-law-amid-protests/2216245; Lange and Monscheuer 2022.

[25] See 'Covid-19, la seconda ondata mette in crisi l'Europa. 'L'Italia resiste ancora, seguiamo le regole'. Gli scienziati: la situazione nel nostro Paese non sarà come in Spagna e Francia. 'Qui distanziamento e mascherine rispettati': https://www.quotidiano.net/cronaca/seconda-ondata-Covid-mette-in-crisi-l-europa-l-italia-resiste-seguiamo-le-regole-1.5530753.

[26] See, for my previous discussions of this issue, Nelken 2021a; 2021b.

Figures 5A and 5B Controlling for contextual differences in Covid Rates

Figure 5A Controlling for Intergenerational Ties and Case Fatality Rates[27]

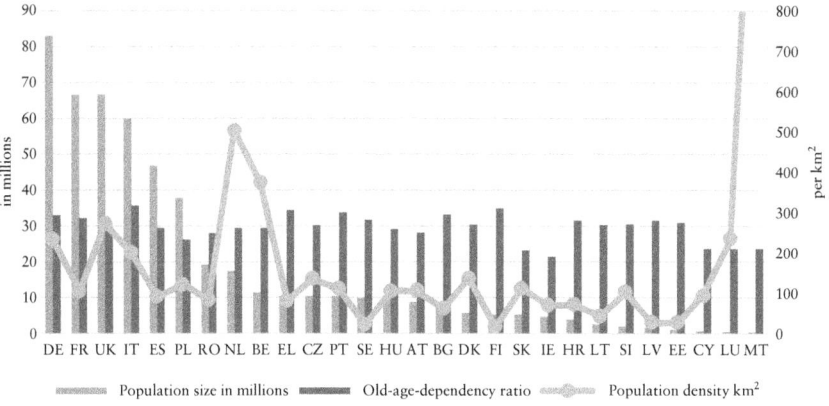

Figure 5B Death and Infection Rates for Covid, Controlling for Old Age, Dependency Ratio and Population Density[28]

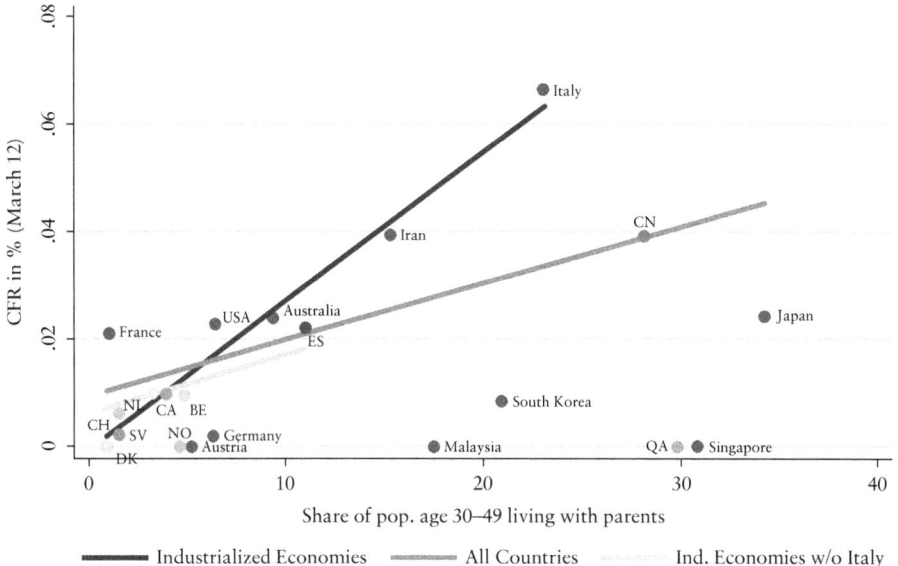

[27] See https://voxeu.org/article/intergenerational-ties-and-case-fatality-rates; https://www.google.com/search?q=BBC+total+cases+per+100,000+people+by+week+up+to+18+August&client=firefox-b-d&source=lnms&tbm=isch&sa=X&ved=2ahUKEwjQi8iWg4LsAhUKkMMKHWYnC544ChD8BSgCegQICxAE&biw=1086&bih=702#imgrc=k-PtsRZWZYkMjM.

[28] See https://blogs.lse.ac.uk/europpblog/2020/05/19/comparing-european-reactions-to-covid-19-why-policy-decisions-must-be-informed-by-reliable-and-contextualised-evidence/.

Just as problematic, when it came to the value of such comparisons, Covid indicators (like other global social indicators) disregarded the possibility that countries might have been trying to achieve different goals from those for which they were being evaluated. Rankings of countries' responses to Covid would be very different, for example, if the metric used had been progress towards the goal of achieving herd immunity,[29] or the costs imposed on the economy or on restrictions on political freedoms. Reducing communications about Covid to graphic presentations of the spread of the disease avoided the question of whether there could be a plausible trade-off between employment and health, especially as serious damage to the economy or reduction in public resources undoubtedly also has wider effects on health.[30]

Given his location in Lund, Reza would have found that the Swedish case offered a particularly interesting illustration of the difficulty of providing useful indicators where the goals of those assessed differ from those doing the assessing. Sweden (differently from most other countries in Europe) chose to follow a less strict approach, in particular seeking to avoid imposing a lockdown. Whilst some commentators saw this choice as one aimed at achieving herd immunity, or even as giving priority to the economy, the experts advising in Sweden argued that public health needed be viewed in the broadest sense. For them the kind of strict mandatory lockdowns imposed elsewhere were unsustainable over the long term and could have serious secondary impacts, including increased unemployment and mental health problems.[31] Their distinctive policy was held to steadily even at the expense of a greater number of infections and deaths as compared to their Scandinavian neighbours.[32] But, as numbers went up, there was considerable internal debate and heart-searching amidst recognition that, in economic terms, it was badly affected almost as much as its Scandinavian neighbours.

A disregard for the finer requirements of 'fair' comparison could perhaps be forgiven if the priority was basic data about absolute Covid levels. But even this could not be taken for granted. Beyond differences in goals there were also (sometimes for related reasons) differences in how Covid deaths and infections were defined cross-nationally. Even if this presupposed some a priori standardisation of the definitions and practices used for defining Covid in each country this (to date) has not been achieved. For example, Belgium was notorious for using an expansive definition of dying with the virus as dying from the virus; in the United Kingdom

---

[29] This approach was discredited because of the number of deaths that would have resulted, and the too great burden it would have placed on health systems. But the goal remained in the background, to be used as a yardstick regarding when a population is considered no longer at risk and for deciding how to distribute vaccines once they are developed.

[30] Some leaders openly gave priority to the economy. 'Mr Bolsonaro has repeatedly said that 70 per cent of Brazil's population of 211m would eventually be infected with coronavirus and "there's no running away from that,"' at https://www.ft.com/content/065c783e-2402-4c0d-ad40-1b5e38ae96d4. On the other hand, damage to the economy does also have direct and indirect implications for life and death (and vice versa): https://www.express.co.uk/news/uk/1341671/breast-cancer-screening-delayed-coronavirus-pandemic-NHS.

[31] See https://www.ft.com/content/5cc92d45-fbdb-43b7-9c66-26501693a371.

[32] Importantly, the number of infections and deaths was no greater than in those European countries that did opt for lockdown.

the definition of death figures included only people who died within 28 days of testing positive for the coronavirus, and other ways of measuring suggested that the number of deaths was higher. Both the WHO and the leading medical journal, *The Lancet*, pleaded for the introduction of similar criteria for all countries. In addition, once it became clear how often Covid can be present even without symptoms, the number of those infected came to be seen simply as a function of how much testing was being carried out – something that varied enormously between and within countries.[33] The alternative criterion, one that increasingly came to be recommended, was to measure 'excess' deaths in any one year as compared to the average of other years. But, arguably, what counts as (unacceptable) 'excess' in one place, facing one set of circumstances and challenges, may not be at all the same as in another.

The message that emerges from this and other uses of indicators is the need to be aware of the different purposes that may lie behind comparison. Can we square the circle of establishing standards that transcend contexts whilst also respecting the local differences that the universalising standard cannot and does not wish to reflect?[34] What happens in practice, insiders tell us, is that what counts as context is a work in progress – and is an exercise in persuasion. The issue is certainly 'problematised'; but it is also 'solved' for all practical purposes. Reporting on their experience in helping design UN indicators for application in the field, Desai and Shomerus describe what they call 'the relationing spectre of contextualized data and the generalizing exorcism of a call to action' (Desai and Shomerus 2018: 104). They explain that the academic role – or at least an academic stance – will seek to stress the importance of 'being true to context', whereas the advocate – or advocate role – is more about transforming it. For them, 'invoking "context" therefore functioned as a way of claiming certain types of (meso) work while disclaiming others by turning the local into an unsolvable problem' (ibid: 105). Balancing contextual knowledge with abstract and universal claims is not something easily achievable in the abstract, but most concessions to difference can be postponed to the moment of application (ibid: 109).

REFERENCES

Agamben, G (2020) *A che punto siamo? L'epidemia come politica* (Quodlibet).
Banakar, R (2000) 'Reflections on the Methodological Issues of the Sociology of Law' 27 *Journal of Law and Society* 273.
—— (2003) *Merging Law and Sociology: Beyond the Dichotomies of Socio-Legal Research* (Berlin, Galda and Wilch Publishing).

[33] The WHO calculated that one in ten of the world's population may have been infected as of October 2020, whilst 70 per cent of recorded cases came from only ten countries: https://www.bbc.com/news/world-54422023.
[34] For Barberet (forthcoming) 'there are a variety of very established and creative ways that intergovernmental organizations engage in comparative analysis that manage to both allow comparison as well as appreciate context'.

—— (2013) 'Law and Regulation in Late Modernity' in R Banakar and M Travers (eds), *Law and Social Theory*, 2nd edn (Oxford, Hart Publishing).

—— (2015) *Normativity in Legal Sociology: Methodological Reflections on Law and Regulation in Late Modernity* (London, Springer).

—— (2016) *Driving Culture in Iran: Law and Society on the Roads of the Islamic Republic* (London, IB Tauris).

—— (2019) 'Brexit: A Note on the EU's Interlegality' in BL Kristiansen, K Mitkidis, L Munkholm, L Neumann and C Pelaudeix (eds), *Transnationalisation and Legal Actors: Legitimacy in Question* (London, Routledge).

Banakar, R and Travers, M (eds) (2005) *Theory and Method in Socio-Legal Research* (Oxford, Hart Publishing).

—— (2013) *Law and Social Theory* (Oxford, Hart Publishing).

Barberet, R (forthcoming) 'Globalization, Gender, Sexual Identity and Crime' in D Nelken and C Hamilton (eds), *Handbook of Comparative Criminal Justice* (Cheltenham, Edward Elgar).

Cepaluni, G, Dorsch, MT and Branyiczki, R (2020) 'Political Regimes and Deaths in the Early Stages of the Covid-19 Pandemic', Working paper, Central European University, available at https://preprints.apsanet.org/engage/api-gateway/apsa/assets/orp/resource/item/5ea7229e5d762d001217da9a/original/political-regimes-and-deaths-in-the-early-stages-of-the-Covid-19-pandemic.pdf.

Davis, K, Fisher, A, Kingsbury, B and Merry, SE (eds) (2012) *Governance by Indicators: Global Power Through Classification and Rankings* (Oxford, Oxford University Press).

—— (2015) 'Introduction: the Local-Global Life of Indicators: Law, Power and Resistance' in SE Merry, KE Davis and B Kingsbury (eds), *The Quiet Power of Indicators* (Cambridge, Cambridge University Press) 1.

Desai, D and Shomerus, M (2018) 'There Was A Third Man …': Tales from a Global Policy Consultation on Indicators for the Sustainable Development Goals' 49 *Development and Change* 89.

Dong, E et al (2020) 'An Interactive Web-Based Dashboard to Track Covid-19 in Real Time' *Lancet Infect DIS* (19 February), at https://doi.org/10.1016/S1473–3099(20)30120-1.

Espeland, W and Stevens, M (1998) 'Commensuration as a Social Process' 24 *Annual Review of Sociology* 313.

—— (2008) 'A Sociology of Quantification' 49 *European Journal of Sociology* 401.

Findlay, M (2008) *Governing through Globalised Crime* (Willan).

—— (2021) *Globalisation, Populism, Pandemics and the Law: The Anarchy and the Ecstasy* (Cheltenham, Edward Elgar).

Goodhart, CAE (1975) 'Monetary Relationships: A View from Threadneedle Street' in *Papers in Monetary Economics*, vol 1 (Reserve Bank of Australia).

Halliday, TC and Shaffer, G (eds) (2014) *Transnational Legal Orders* (Cambridge, Cambridge University Press).

Infantino, M (2021) 'Hazards and Fallacies of Social Measurements: Global Indicators in the Pandemic' 17 *International Journal of Law in Context* 168.

Kahl, C and Wright, T (2021) *Aftershocks: Pandemic Politics and the End of the Old International Order* (Macmillan).

Karstedt, S (2011) 'Exit: The State, Globalisation, State Failure and Crime' in D Nelken (ed), *Comparative Criminal Justice and Globalisation* (Ashgate) 107.

Kelley, JG and Simmons, BA (2020) *The Power of Performance Indicators* (Cambridge, Cambridge University Press).

Lange, M and Monscheuer, O (2022) 'Discussion Paper: Spreading the Disease. Protest in times of Pandemics' (ZEWHU).

Leonhardt, D and Leatherby, L (2020) 'Where the Virus Is Growing Most: Countries with "Illiberal Populist" Leaders Brazil, Russia, Britain and the U.S. Have Something in Common' *NY Times* 2 June 2020.

Luhmann, N (2014) *A Sociological Theory of Law*, 2nd edn (Routledge).

Merry, SE (2011) 'Measuring the World: Indicators, Human Rights, and Global Governance' 52 *Current Anthropology* 583.

—— (2016) *The Seductions of Quantification* (Chicago, Chicago University Press).

Merry, SE; Davis, KE and Kingsbury, B (eds) (2015) *The Quiet Power of Indicators* (Cambridge, Cambridge University Press).

Muller, JZ (2018) *The Tyranny of Metrics* (Princeton, NJ, Princeton University Press).

Nelken, D (2015a) 'The Changing Roles of Social Indicators: From Explanation to Governance' in V Mitsilegas, P Alldridge and L Cheliotis (eds), *Globalisation, Criminal Law and Criminal Justice. Theoretical, Comparative and Transnational Perspectives* (Oxford, Hart Publishing) 25.

—— (2015b) 'Conclusion: Contesting Global Indicators' in SE Merry, KE Davis and B Kingsbury (eds), *The Quiet Power of Indicators* (Cambridge, Cambridge University Press) 317.

—— (2016a) 'Comparative Legal Research and Legal Culture: Facts, Approaches and Values' 12 *Annual Review of Law and Social Science* 45.

—— (2016b) 'From Pains-taking to Pains-giving Comparisons' 12 *International Journal of Law in Context* 390.

—— (2019) 'Whose Best Practices? The Significance of Context in and for Transnational Criminal Justice Indicators' 46 *Journal of Law and Society* S1 S31.

—— (2021a) 'Between Comparison and Commensuration: A Case Study of Covid 19 Rankings' in D Nelken and M Siems (eds), 'Numbers in an Emergency: The Many Roles of Indicators in the Covid 19 Crisis' 17 *Special Issue: International Journal of Law in Context.*

—— (2021b) 'Global Social Indicators, Comparison, and Commensuration: A Case-Study of Covid Rankings' in *The Global Community Yearbook of International Law and Jurisprudence 2020* (Oxford, Oxford University Press).

Nelken, D and Siems, M (eds) (2021) 'Numbers in an Emergency: The Many Roles of Indicators in the Covid 19 Crisis' 17 *Special Issue: International Journal of Law in Context.*

Park, SJ (2015) '"Nobody Is Going to Die": An Ethnography of Hope, Indicators and Improvisations in HIV Treatment in Uganda' in R Rottenburg and SE Merry (eds), *The World of Indicators: The Making of Government Knowledge through Quantification* (Cambridge, Cambridge University Press) 188.

Petherick, A et al (2020) 'Variation in Government Responses to Covid-19' Blavatnik School Working Paper, 29 April 2020, available at https://www.bsg.ox.ac.uk/sites/default/files/2020-05/BSG-WP-2020-032-v5.0_0.pdf,4–5.

Restrepo-Amariles, D (2015) 'Legal Indicators, Global Law and Legal Pluralism: An Introduction' 47 *The Journal of Legal Pluralism and Unofficial Law* 9.

Rosga, AJ and Satterthwaite, ML (2009) 'The Trust in Indicators: Measuring Human Rights' 27 *Berkeley Journal of International Law* 253.

Shore, C and Wright, S (2015) 'Governing by Numbers: Audit Culture, Rankings and the New World Order' 23 *Social Anthropology* 22.

Siems, M and Nelken, D (2017) 'Global Social Indicators and the Concept of Legitimacy' 13 *International Journal of Law in Context* 436.

Simon, J (2007) *Governing through Crime* (Cambridge, Cambridge University Press).

Sullivan, G (2020) *The Law of the List* (Cambridge, Cambridge University Press).

Volpi, R and Serravalle, E (2020) *Coronovirus: No, non è andate tutto bene* (Leone Verde).

Yeung, K (2017) 'Algorithmic Regulation: A Critical Interrogation', King's College Research Paper No 2017-27, https://ssrn.com/abstract=2972505.

Zaloznaya, M and Hagan, J (2012) 'Fighting Human Trafficking or Instituting Authoritarian Control? The Political Cooptation of Human Rights Protection in Belarus' in K Davis, A Fisher, B Kingsbury and SE Merry (eds) *Governance by Indicators: Global Power Through Classification and Rankings* (Oxford, Oxford University Press) 344.

28

Safe but not Secure? Risk Management, Communication and Preparedness for a Pandemic in Aviation

JOHN WOODLOCK

I. INTRODUCTION

S OCIOLOGISTS HAVE LONG described contemporary society as a 'risk society' which must perpetually deal with the risks it has manufactured for itself. By extension, if risk society theory holds good, even to some degree, then scholars argue that the idea of a 'risk regulatory state' should not be construed as a surprising development (Black 2010; see also Beck 1992). Notwithstanding, the globalisation processes of late modernity[1] have witnessed a gradual change to the nation-state in a way that has 'recast the relationship between law, state and society' (Banakar 2015: 2). A defining feature of twenty-first century globalisation and the transnational forces that shape late modern law are forms of legal regulation that increasingly focus on the management of risk and instrumentally seek to control and rationally regulate specific societal domains (ibid: 189–90). Aviation is one such sector which 'operates in a labyrinth of norms' and where the risk-critical nature of this industry sector requires that risk management techniques are primarily developed to deal with safety and security as regulated phenomena. As such, the design and implementation of risk management plans regarding safety and security in aviation now rely on effective regulation and its implementation where 'law plays a predominant role' (Leloudas and Haeck 2003: 150).

More broadly speaking, at the core of risk-based regulation is 'the prioritising of regulatory actions in accordance with assessments of the risks' that may hinder a regulator achieving its objectives (Baldwin et al 2012: 281). Scholars suggest that these 'risk-based regulatory frameworks are not neutral, technical instruments' but, rather, involve complex decision-making and evaluation processes to determine which risks

---

[1] The notion of late modernity employed here follows from Banakar's three-fold understanding regarding the transformation of the state under the conditions of globalisation (see Banakar 2015: 16).

are to be prioritised and how they are to be defined. This also involves decision making about which risks are not to be prioritised (ibid: 282–83). Consequently, two main challenges are understood to face risk-based regulators: (i) accurately identifying the risks to the achieving of objectives, so that these may be evaluated and controlled by the regulator; and (ii) exploring 'the extent to which managerial attitudes will affect the level of risk presented' by a company or organisation. Scholarship has duly noted that the 'quality and character' of organisational management and the risk controls they employ will affect the probability, response and consequences of a harmful event and its occurrence (ibid: 283–85).

This chapter addresses these two challenges to critically discuss cross-sectorial risk management strategies surrounding global public health and aviation in relation to the spread of infectious diseases and the context of the global Covid-19 pandemic. Two questions regarding regulated risk management and 'preparedness' concerning crisis situations within global aviation guide the essay. First, why is the Covid-19 pandemic commonly portrayed as an 'unprecedented' event for global aviation? Second, do public health organisations and aviation regulatory bodies share a common perception of risk for the effective cross-sectorial risk management of exogenous events such as the pandemic crisis? To answer these questions, the chapter discusses the notion of 'the availability heuristic' in relation to institutional thinking and communication (cognition) about risk. The availability heuristic infers that social actors' experiences and vivid recollections of recent events significantly affect social thinking that these types of occurrences are more likely to happen again (Sunstein 2002: 33). Availability, as discussed here, inclusively considers effective risk communication in relation to major events for establishing reliable sectorial and cross-sectorial response capabilities to allow key social actors such as industrial entities, regulators, and legislators to adequately deal with sudden crisis events and related hazards (Berger-Sabatel and Journé 2018: 31; Slovic et al 2000: 104). As Cass Sunstein has importantly highlighted, public officials, lawmakers and organisations are often 'highly reactive to public alarm' and therefore 'prone to the availability heuristic' in a way that can limit risk assessment and leave less readily available risks problematically 'out of sight' (Sunstein 2002: 34; see Slovic et al 2000: 105–109).

II. RISK MANAGEMENT IN AVIATION – REGULATING SAFETY AND SECURITY

Civil aviation has a multi-level regulatory character, where the ICAO[2] promotes international aviation standards and recommended practices (SARPs), agencies such as EASA[3] govern aviation regionally (European Union), and the civil

---

[2] International Civil Aviation Organisation (ICAO) is a United Nations (UN) body established in 1947. ICAO standards do not supersede national legislation and it is not regarded as a global aviation regulator per se (ICAO 2021f; see Huang 2009).

[3] European Union Aviation Safety Agency was established in 2002 'to promote the highest standards of safety and environmental protection' in European civil aviation (EASA 2021).

aviation authorities of sovereign states implement international standards and enforce regional regulations at a national level (ICAO 2021f; Dempsey and Chen 2013: 516; Harrison 2009: 27; Huang 2009; see Regulation (EU) 2018/1139[4]). Although global aviation safety and security policies are ultimately the responsibility of ICAO, which lays down the basic international standards that Contracting States to the Chicago Convention[5] must adhere to, national states remain highly influential in that they retain sovereignty over their own airspace. This means that states can exercise much freedom 'to flesh out the details' for meeting their own safety and security regulatory expectations when implementing ICAO's universal standards (Harrison 2009: 4; Huang 2009: 8; see Ratajczyk 2015).

As two long-standing pillars of the aviation industry, safety and security as questions of risk and risk management are regulated as distinct phenomena in this sector. Safety is associated with the safe operation of aircraft and involves personnel licensing and airworthiness. Security primarily concerns protecting international civil aviation 'against acts of unlawful interference' (Huang 2009: 7; see Eurocontrol 2021). A fundamental difference between these two terms is that international standards for aviation safety are generically designed around protecting against unintentional harm and *internal* threats. Security regulations and standards are more specifically designed to prevent against intentionally harmful acts and threats from the *external* environment (Cusick et al 2017: 426; see Wright 2021).[6] Common to both phenomena, however, is that failures of risk management, whether safety and/or security related, often lead to serious financial consequences for an airline. In times of major crisis these failures have the potential to devastate the aviation industry globally. Given that law and regulation play a primary role in contemporary aviation risk management strategies, failures of risk management are often consonant with failures of law and regulatory governance.

Key events such as the 9/11 attacks in New York in 2001 prompted an international increased awareness of the need to (re)assess the risks the aviation industry faced. Consequently, the security landscape of global aviation has changed over time, including significant regulatory changes (Leloudas and Haeck 2003: 150; see ICAO 2021a). With few major airlines experiencing serious accidents since the early 1990s, perceived danger concerning aviation safety among airline passengers is low, with safety increasingly becoming more a question of public expectation than a worrying concern. In contrast, security-related events maintain long-term public

---

[4] Regulation (EU) 2018/1139 of the European Parliament and of the Council of 4 July 2018 on common rules in the field of civil aviation and establishing a European Union Aviation Safety Agency, and amending Regulations (EC) No 2111/2005, (EC) No 1008/2008, (EU) No 996/2010, (EU) No 376/2014 and Directives 2014/30/EU and 2014/53/EU of the European Parliament and of the Council, and repealing Regulations (EC) No 552/2004 and (EC) No 216/2008 of the European Parliament and of the Council and Council Regulation (EEC) No 3922/91, https://eur-lex.europa.eu/legal-content/EN/TXT/PDF/?uri= CELEX:32018R1139&from=EN.

[5] The Convention on International Civil Aviation in 1944 (see Havel and Sanchez 2014).

[6] SARPs for international aviation security are designated as Annex 17 to the Chicago Convention. The SARPs for aviation safety entail several Annexes to the Convention with Annex 19 covering Safety Management.

alarm and are highly publicised in mainstream and social media. It is not surprising then that people exhibit greater awareness of dangers perceived as security risks. As a direct consequence of the 9/11 attacks, members of the global flying public have, for over two decades, directly experienced austere aviation security measures embedded in multi-level politico-legal security policies that specifically address global anti-terrorism, border management, passenger screening, and use of passenger data (Havel and Sanchez 2014: 214; Fitzgerald 2012; Harrison 2009; Wilkinson and Jenkins 1999; see ICAO 2021b).

In a broader sense this suggests that risk communication surrounding key events in aviation differs depending on how risk is defined and generically perceived – whether as an internal question of airline safety and/or as an external threat to aviation industry security. Air travel, it would seem, is publicly perceived as a safe activity but not always experienced as a secure phenomenon. Given the devastating effect of the Covid-19 pandemic on global aviation (see Amankwah-Amoah 2020: 2; Gössling 2020; Forsyth et al 2020; GARS 2020; European Parliament 2021: 36; IATA 2020b; OECD 2020; EASA 2020), it merits asking how risk and risk management in relation to security, public health, and preparedness are perceived and communicated between the aviation sector and public health authorities.

III. INTERNATIONAL AND REGIONAL CROSS-SECTORIAL RISK MANAGEMENT – CAPSCA AND RAGIDA

To understand how risk is perceived and communicated requires understanding how risk is defined and by whom. Ulrich Beck's risk society theory contrasts modes of risk definition in industrial and risk societies (Mythen 2004: 53). For Beck, this is a question of 'relations of definition' that involves 'an arsenal of institutions' including state and regional governments, scientific organisations, the civil service, and the legal system. As Mythen points out, the multiple functions of these institutions and relations of definition are 'absolutely crucial in informing and moulding public understandings of risk' (ibid: 21–22; see Beck 2009: 24–46). The role of social institutions must therefore be considered to understand how risk is or is not deemed calculable and made meaningful (Mythen 2004: 53). In the current context, this entails exploring risk communication and risk reduction preparedness in relation to the transmission of infectious diseases and the global airline sector. This is because the rules and capacities that structure how risk is identified and assessed as social environmental problems, and as risks, are established and legally regulated in and through social institutions (ibid: 21). As Reza Banakar importantly reminds us, although risk is not a legal concept it can and does influence legal decision-making (Banakar 2015: 190).

In security scholarship, risk research has long faced a struggle to determine whether the spread of infectious diseases 'represents an existential threat to both national and international security'. However, the Covid-19 pandemic and its immense effect on human and bio security has exposed an acute need to 'reexamine the relationship between ID and global security' (Albert et al 2021). In fact, scholars have long argued that the globalisation of health security is a double-edged sword that, on the one hand, presents new threats and challenges but, on the other, also provides new opportunities to better deal with health threats (Hough 2008: 187). For example, the proliferating securitisation of global health law incurs a potential for abusive and arbitrary state power, such as using invasive cell phone technology to trace infected persons. Yet, if understood as not only a health crisis but also a human crisis, dealing with the pandemic crisis requires a primary focus on 'the capability of national and global institutions to address this essential threat to human health and life' (Halabi 2020: 1608–11). In this sense, the Covid-19 pandemic has exposed vulnerabilities and weaknesses in how states and international organisations interact when dealing with public health crises. Recognition of these shortcomings presents an opportunity to (re)assess how risks are perceived and communicated across geopolitical and sectorial boundaries (Alvarez 2020; see ICAO 2020c). As Leitmeyer highlights:

> … the perception of a risk plays a crucial role in its assessment and the decision for contact tracing. Assessments are influenced not only by the societal environment in which events occur and decisions are being made, but also by politics and the economic situation in a country. (Leitmeyer 2011: 4)

According to ICAO, the expansive growth of international aviation passenger numbers over the past two decades increases the risk for the spread of infectious diseases. Therefore, protecting global health has become a major priority for airlines, airports, passengers and personnel, but also for governments regarding their 'health, safety and security oversight responsibilities under the Chicago Convention and the International Health Regulations (IHR)' (ICAO 2021e). In that the rapid spread of infectious diseases across continents and between countries has been attributed to air travel (Naboush and Alnimer 2020; Macilree and Duval 2020), the global commercial air carrier fleet was almost completely grounded in a matter of weeks in the early Spring of 2020 following the WHO declaration that Covid-19 was a pandemic (European Parliament 2021; Gössling 2020). This action was primarily a public health and security strategy (human and bio) of containment by nation state governments who mandated travel restrictions and implemented quarantine measures to prevent the spread of the Covid-19 virus within and across national borders (see Gössling 2020; see IATA 2020a; IATA 2020b; ICAO 2021c).

ICAO crucially recognises that different states have different levels of preparedness for dealing with a crisis like a pandemic and the waves that follow. Accordingly, the 'ICAO Handbook for CAAs on the Management of Aviation Safety Risks related to Covid-19' (Doc 10144) outlines how tackling the global pandemic to uphold aviation safety must rely on 'the 3Cs' – cooperation, collaboration and communication (ICAO 2020c). Beyond these sector specific safety-focused guidelines, international organisations and transnational agencies have also worked cross-sectorially in the area of global health and human security in the context of aviation. These collaborations have interactively led to the drafting of rules and guidelines regarding the transmission of infectious diseases via aircraft. They especially address working with variations in national regulations and different levels and styles of enforcement between countries to establish standardised processes, not least regarding contact tracing concerns (ICAO 2021e).

At the international level, the ICAO has, since 2006, also managed the CAPSCA[7] programme which is a 'voluntary cross-sectorial, multi-organizational collaboration programme' that is also supported by the WHO. CAPSCA works to improve preparedness, planning and response by bringing international, regional, national and local organisations together for dealing with public health events which affect the global aviation sector (ICAO 2021e). Amongst others, two key objectives outlined by CAPSCA are: (i) to assist states or territories with the implementation of ICAO Standards and Regulations (SARPs) and WHO International Health Regulations (IHR); and (ii) to build capacity by providing assistance to states or territories to establish national aviation pandemic preparedness plans and to develop core capabilities (ICAO 2021e).

Regionally, the European Centre for Disease Prevention and Control (ECDC), an agency of the European Union, has issued a technical report (on MERS-CoV) in January 2020 – 'Risk assessment guidelines for infectious diseases transmitted on aircraft (RAGIDA)'. This shows how, prior to the Covid-19 outbreak, infectious diseases have long been a concern on the risk assessment agenda of the EU regarding the European aviation sector (ECDC 2020). The RAGIDA project was initiated in 2007 to assist EU Member States' national public health authorities in 'assessing the risks associated with the transmission of infectious agents on-board aircrafts and to help in the decisions on the most appropriate, operationally feasible public health measures for containment' (ECDC 2020: 1). Importantly for the Covid-19 focus of this chapter, the report notes that during the process of developing the MERS guidance, a new outbreak of a novel coronavirus had been identified in Wuhan in China. Pending further assessment, the ECDC report recommended that the MERS guidance be used when dealing with this new infectious agent, Covid-19, 'until further evidence warrants a new review' (ibid: 2).

Although explicitly stating that implementing and enforcing containment measures through law was necessary, official assessment reports and reviewed research discussing contact tracing before and during the current pandemic identify the risk of transmission aboard aircraft as low (Rosca et al 2021; ECDC 2020). Yet the international (CAPSCA) and regional (RAGIDA) collaborations highlighted here share a common perception that compliance with guidelines is paramount for effective risk management of infectious diseases. A joint statement from the WHO and ICAO addressing Covid-19 exemplifies this focus on compliance regarding cross-sectorial collaboration between aviation and public health authorities;

> ICAO and WHO remind all stakeholders of the importance of following existing regulations and guidance, particularly the relevant standards contained within the various Annexes to the Convention on International Civil Aviation and the International Health Regulations (2005). Cross-sector collaboration at the national level is also important, and in this regard, States are reminded to coordinate between aviation and health authorities and to establish National Facilitation Committees that comprise all relevant groups, in line with ICAO guidelines. (ICAO 2020b)

---

[7] Collaborative Arrangement for the Prevention and Management of Public Health Events in Civil Aviation.

Yet compliance understood in this sense seems to assume that cross-sectorial risk assessment and guidelines for infectious diseases are readily accessible and effectively communicated to aviation sector stakeholders such as airline carriers and their managerial teams. As a question of availability and security, this also neglects how judgmental biases may problematically underpin assumed sectorial compliance with cross-sectorial drafted rules applied in national contexts.

IV. THE AVAILABILITY HEURISTIC – THE WRITING ON THE WALL FOR EFFECTIVE RISK-BASED REGULATION?

In discussing risk regulation and the notion of judgmental biases, Sunstein suggests that social actors often lack adequate information on risk, commonly display insufficient knowledge about the nature and extent of risks, and demonstrate poor understanding about the different consequences of risk reduction. Consequently, public demands for risk regulation are commonly steered by public alarm and frequently based on 'misunderstandings of facts' (Sunstein 2002: 33). To explain why people's judgements about risk and risk regulation are flawed, Sunstein discusses cognition and how using the 'availability heuristic' affects thinking about risk. In short, the availability heuristic implies that if people have experience of and can vividly recall recent incidents, they tend to think that there is a greater likelihood that these events will (re) occur (ibid: 33; see Tversky and Kahneman 1973). Accordingly, the continued focus on the threat of terrorism to aviation in the wake of the 9/11 events, including the much publicised failures in security and intelligence sharing, may well have amplified such risks in a way that has prolonged public alarm about and through aviation security measures (see Harrison 2009: 125). As Kasperson et al argue on the social amplification of risk, 'if the risks are already feared by the public' an increased amplification is most likely (Kasperson et al 2000: 242). However, it is not just ordinary citizens who are 'prone to use the availability heuristic'; public officials, lawmakers and organisations in democratic societies are often 'highly reactive to public alarm'. In particular, imagining worse-case scenarios can generate alarm where fear of consequences may serve to blot out more accurate assessments of risk (Sunstein 2002: 34). Availability in this sense can problematically 'lull people into complacency', where risks that are not readily accessible 'seem invisible' when 'what is out of sight is effectively out of mind' (ibid: 34; see Slovic et al 2000:105–109).

Despite the assessment of risk for infectious diseases and availability of formal information and guidance developed through the international and transnational collaborations discussed previously (CAPSCA and RAGIDA), it is surprising to find that it is commonly floated by mainstream media and sector specific actors that the effects of the pandemic were an 'unprecedented' shock. Related claims that international commercial aviation did not expect the magnitude of the economic devastation and market-crippling effects caused by the fallout from Covid-19 are similarly surprising (Gelles and Chokshi 2020; GARS 2020; IATA 2020a; ICAO 2020a). In fact, scholars have been quick to point out that the previous epidemic and pandemic outbreaks of SARS, swine flu, and MERS (and others) provided multiple opportunities for airline organisations to develop contingent preparedness plans for the financial and operational effects of public health scares on the airline sector, including for a worse-case scenario. Rather than showing strategic and effective management of risk, the Covid-19 outbreak has instead exposed that poorly informed airline managerial strategies, especially top management teams, were found wanting and dysfunctional in their preparedness despite these epidemic 'dry runs'. Scholarship accredits this widespread poor preparedness to poor scanning of the external environment by aviation companies to develop effective preparedness plans and management contingency strategies to deal with the shock of exogenous external events like pandemics on commercial airlines. An increasingly aggressive corporate culture and highly competitive air travel market may also have blinkered airline managers to the need for preparatory risk reduction plans that recognise the seriousness of the threats posed by ID outbreaks. Indeed, scholars have long raised concerns regarding 'future' epidemics if a more easily transmissible disease than, for example, SARS emerges. It has been argued that 'more uniform and planned responses' are vital for limiting loss of life and 'the economic devastation wrought by an outbreak' (Brown and Kline 2020: 1; Bowen and Laroe 2006: 143; Tisdall and Zhang 2020; see Burkle 2015; *cf* Linden 2021).

Explained in terms of the availability heuristic, the notion that the effects of the pandemic on aviation were unprecedented are highly questionable and suggest that although international governing bodies and regional agencies were actively engaged in cross-sectorial collaboration and working together to develop risk assessment and guidelines, the potential and magnitude of such risks appear to have remained out of sight for airline companies. In other words, the risk of an ID pandemic as an existential threat to the stability and survival of the aviation industry itself seemed smaller than it was (see Sunstein 2002: 289).

But can this really be the case? Is it feasible to claim, in a heavily regulated sector where safety and security are regulatory pillars, that the threat to the stability of the aviation sector from public health scares first became available as a serious risk concern for the airline companies because of rising public alarm, imposed travel restrictions, and falling passenger numbers with the onset of the Covid-19 pandemic? Was the worst-case scenario for a pandemic visible to the governing bodies of aviation and public health authorities but remained out of sight for airline firms? Or were airline companies themselves poor in scanning their external environment, given that the risk of pandemics have long been a visible concern for governing bodies of the aviation sector, such as ICAO? This chapter argues that these questions are ultimately questions of how risk is identified, how and by whom risk is defined, and how those defined risks are communicated through official rules and guidelines to get the long-term attention of affected industry actors. In other words, law and regulatory oversight should play a crucial role in processes of risk communication and vice versa. Indeed, as Reza Banakar has argued:

> … legal rules may be regarded as standards for action, or as one among many resources used to negotiate the boundaries of law. The interpretative and contextual nature of legal rules indicates that law consists not only of rules alone, but also communicative processes through which the interpretation and application of rules are realised in various social and

legal contexts. Sociologically, these communicative processes, rather than legal rules, are the units of analysis. (Banakar 2015: 27)

V. RELATIONS OF DEFINITION OF RISK – A PROBLEM OF RISK COMMUNICATION?

In discussing risk and culture almost four decades ago, Douglas and Wildavsky argued that an 'operational rule of industrial firms that enables them to act is precisely to avoid attempting to know too much about future consequences' (Douglas and Wildavsky 1982: 93). Given the fallout of poor preparedness in aviation, it is fair to argue that within the broader risk management environment dealing with the Covid-19 crisis, avoiding knowledge of future consequences may well be regarded as a poor strategy of survival for air carrier firms in the slow-to-recover aviation sector. That said, what we may be witnessing is industry damage control to protect the immediate and long-term future of commercial flight, where risk communication strategies to limit collateral damage to aviation and organisational brands are crucial (see Eurocontrol 2021). If the global flying public, already alarmed by the public health threat, perceives that air carriers were complacent in managing risks posed by infectious diseases to commercial flight despite institutional awareness and cross-sectorial assessment, then it lies in the interests of airline firms to control their part of that narrative to reduce the collateral damage to their brand and their product. It must be reiterated that following the 9/11 attacks, the failure to communicate risks between security and intelligence agencies in the United States was considered a contributing factor to the events. Understood as a failure of risk management to predict such an event, the public alarm that followed undermined public trust in the aviation sector, and contributed to serious negative long-term economic effects for the global airline industry (see Harrison 2009: 125–36).

Yet communicating about a crisis is difficult, but even more so if one is in 'defensive mode', such as in the immediate wake of an accident, or being exposed as ill-prepared for a pandemic. On the one hand, media are often more interested in sensational news than informational speeches. On the other hand, airline firms themselves are not always comfortable about speaking publicly on safety and/or security issues which inevitably invites talk about accidents or safety/security shortcomings, phenomena that are never good for corporate reputation or public image. Therefore, organisations employ a pro-active form of safety communication to improve an organisation's image in the public arena (see Guérard 2018: 136–37). This is because reputation is one of the most valuable assets of an air carrier and 'is worthy of particular attention' (Leloudas and Haeck 2003: 155). But importantly, as Fitzgerald has noted, in the wake of a serious event, an airline which informs the public that it had consistently complied with the available rules and guidance, may be considered 'still guilty in the court of public opinion' (Fitzgerald 2012: 42). But does this entail that risk management communicated as compliance with guidelines and preparedness for the effective containment of a global pandemic has transmuted into impression management of corporate reputations to contain economic losses and adverse consequences of a global pandemic?

It seems relevant to refer back to Beck's theory of risk society to make sense of the calculable risks and apparent unprecedented shock of the Covid-19 pandemic on aviation. According to Beck, risk society can be described as:

> a phase of development of modern society in which the social, political, ecological and individual risks created by the momentum of innovation increasingly elude the control and protective institutions of industrial society. (Beck 1999: 72)

However, Mythen (citing Beck) further argues that the nature of risk is dynamic and has changed over time where risk as natural hazards are characteristic of premodern societies and manufactured risks the products of modern societies (Mythen 2004: 23). If we can assume that the Covid-19 virus is a natural hazard (dispelling laboratory-engineered theories), the rapid transmission and failure to contain the spread of the virus can be explained as a manufactured risk associated with human action but also, perhaps, institutional inaction. This understanding considers the unbridled proliferation and normalisation of 'frequent flyer' air travel in the neo-liberalised aviation sector of the twenty-first century (see Gössling 2020; Fitzgerald 2012). More specifically, we can situate and explain the pandemic as a decision-contingent manufactured risk generated by the profit-steered practices determining the actions and in-actions of 'people, firms, state agencies and politicians' in the risk society of a late modern world (Beck 1992: 98).

In contexts of high uncertainty, such as an unfolding public health crisis, 'information is gold' where accurate situational assessment is a necessary critical first step to make sense of the crisis and to build a reservoir of reliable knowledge to establish evidence-based response strategies (Bastide 2018: 106). Effective risk communication therefore plays a crucial role in establishing reliable sectorial response capabilities for dealing with unexpected events which lead to crisis (Berger-Sabatel and Journé 2018: 31). On the flip-side of that discussion, inadequate risk communication can seriously affect the effectiveness of a crisis response. The results of risk assessments must be communicated to the different social actors who are responsible for dealing with the hazards. Amongst others, these include industrialists, regulators, and legislators (Slovic et al 2000: 104). As Slovic et al have observed about risk and judgment:

> If these people do not see, understand or believe these risk statistics, then distrust, conflict and ineffective management can result. (Slovic et al 2000: 104)

Problematically, however, official risk communication is often confined to a limited audience and reduced to the transfer of formal information between those who prepare crisis response plans and those who should implement them, whether at a sectorial, national, or an organisational level. This means that significant parts of the external environment are often excluded in this transfer because 'effective commitment from the responders in the preparedness process' is not always required (Berger-Sabatel and Journé 2018: 33). The evolution of aviation has witnessed an increasing reliance on freely communicating information throughout the sector where economic, technical, safety, and security information is openly shared among industry stakeholders in the interest of industry prosperity (Harrison 2009: 5; see IATA 2020a). As Guérard argues, reliable safety communication can support safety management in the aviation industry, where learning from and sharing safety-related information is highly beneficial among organisations. However, in times of crisis, such as on the occurrence of a serious accident, 'the communication landscape changes dramatically'. On the one hand, aviation professional experts with knowledge of events provide valid information to reliable mainstream media to inform the public. But in the current information technology world, other information-providers have entered the communication scene and relay information of a different nature with different motivations for doing so. Importantly, key industry actors such as the air accident investigative authorities in some countries have recognised how poor or inadequate communication on their part negatively impacts their credibility and also public trust in commercial aviation. As such, these entities have adapted to this situation and initiated changes to their communication practices following major events, providing information to the public in a more effective and regular manner. These practices can include the use of social media platforms and holding daily press conferences (Guérard 2018:136). In sum, good risk communication inextricably entails good impression management during a crisis to allow authorities and organisations to protect their credibility lest poor risk management strategies be exposed as causal or contributing factors to the crisis.

VI. CONCLUDING DISCUSSION

Aviation-focused legal scholars have defined risk in aviation as the uncertainty arising from an aviation activity or as 'the exposure to losses' an aviation organisation faces from its activities (Leloudas and Haeck 2003: 152). However, Reza Banakar tells us that:

> Certainty and uncertainty are two sides of the same coin insofar as the experience of one presupposes at least the awareness of the other as a pending possibility. Certainty suggests knowledge and security, while uncertainty correlates with unforeseen threats, anxiety, risk and insecurity. (Banakar 2015: 12)[8]

Key to these insights is that certainty is associated with security and knowledge, but uncertainty with insecurity and risk. By discussing increasing uncertainty in relation to the social and cultural consequences of globalisation and the transnational forces reshaping political and legal landscapes, Banakar argued that two specific developments have speeded up this 'swing towards uncertainty'. At the micro-level, enhanced reflexivity of social actors has had implications for law and regulation where social actors reflect more about structures and the constraints imposed upon them by traditional institutions. At the macro level, uncertainty increases because decision-making and normativity has shifted from the local to the transnational levels of society. Citing Beck, Banakar further argued that social relations, networks and communications

---

[8] See Joormann 2019, who applies Banakar's insights on certainty and uncertainty to the context of legal decision making and asylum cases within the Swedish migration courts.

that were once territorially distinct to nation-states are now undermined by 'a new kind of capitalism, a new kind of economy, a new kind of global order and a new kind of personal life' (ibid: 14). This shift has given way to forms of social regulation where risk management is prioritised and dealing with social issues is a lesser concern (ibid: 251). In a cautionary tone, Banakar highlights that with globalisation come global problems such as environmental pollution, global warming, terrorism, and pandemics. These phenomena, he suggests, are in part a result of transnational forces which are difficult to gauge for precisely calculating risk or to develop effective policy and regulation, at least at a national level (ibid: 14–15).

Given the focus of this chapter, Banakar's insights, on the effects of globalisation and limits of transnational regulation to accurately evaluate risk, describe and in some sense predict the global problems facing international aviation in late modernity: environmental destruction, aggressive anti-terrorism regulations, and globe-spanning pandemics. It must be reiterated that the RAGIDA programme was initiated by the ECDC to assist EU Member States' national public health authorities in assessing the risks associated with the transmission of infectious diseases onboard aircraft. The project also sought to help national authorities in their decision-making processes for establishing 'the most appropriate, operationally feasible public health measures for containment' (ECDC 2020: 1). In other words, calculating risk and developing effective policy in this context are, as Banakar suggested, problematic at national level, especially when transnational forces are involved. A closer look at why the RAGIDA project was initiated shows that from its inception, it sought to provide a transnational solution to overcome the limitations of international and national law to manage the risk of ID transmission via aircraft. RAGIDA identified that even though world health regulations (WHR) are legally binding on 194 states, limited guidance exists for the public health management of infectious diseases onboard aircrafts and in airports. Moreover, it highlights that existing WHO guidelines (for tuberculosis, for example) may not reflect the epidemiological situation in different EU Member States, with national guidelines for some diseases often found to be inconsistent (ECDC 2020).

Against the backdrop of Banakar's association of certainty with security and knowledge, and uncertainty with insecurity and risk, it seems plausible to argue that security (and safety) regulation as a risk management strategy concerning aviation must be knowledge-based but also presuppose uncertainty, that is, awareness of the potential for unforeseen threats, insecurity and risk. Relatedly, it is fair to argue that the presupposition of insecurity and the risks identified in RAGIDA are not only related to the transmission of infectious diseases onboard aircraft, but also locate the limitations of ID containment in relation to the limitations between state-based laws and rules for dealing with a public health crisis. In other words, as discussed by Banakar, the limitations of risk management, in late modernity, are closely associated with the limitations of law. This is also clear regarding international standards, as highlighted in the ICAO handbook (Doc 10144) which recognises how different states have different levels of preparedness, and identifies that states are limited actors for ensuring implementation of rules and guidelines for the successful risk management of a pandemic crisis (ICAO 2020c).

For Banakar, therefore, the motivation behind processes of managing risk is not only to control uncertainty but also a matter of fulfilling law's quest for ensuring legal certainty. As he put it:

> Efforts to harmonise various categories of legal rules … across national boundaries are also motivated by the belief that by increasing similarities between legal systems we enhance certitude, thus improving law's efficiency. (Banakar 2015: 13)

Given that cross-sectorial collaborative projects such as CAPSCA and RAGIDA have been running for almost 15 years, and that other ID epidemic health scares have occurred around the globe during this time,[9] it seems far-fetched to report that the current Covid-19 pandemic was an 'unprecedented' event. Such claims not only suggest that the visibility and availability of sector specific and cross-sectorial guidelines may not be as readily accessible to airline firms as is required but should generate institutional and public concern as to why this is the case.

But this leads to the question whether poor risk communication is a consequence or an antecedent of poor availability. By considering the availability heuristic and how prolonged public alarm and 9/11-related security measures have shaped the risk-based regulatory environment for aviation security, it now seems timely that new questions on preparedness for crisis events in aviation should confront old problems that maintain prolongated fear surrounding the threat of terrorism. As a regulated risk management strategy with the primary focus on unlawful interference as the main threat to security, uncertainty is maintained around the likely occurrence of similar events so as to control the future, much as Banakar (2015: 194) has argued in relation to anti-terrorist law in the UK. However, the external threat currently stifling the airline industry is not the result of an unlawful act against aviation but rather, a natural hazard worsened by the structural, economic and politically manufactured risks surrounding the neoliberal market-focused global aviation sector. Among these manufactured risks is the failure of the aviation sector to adequately communicate the risks of a pandemic and prepare for the insecurity these events bring to the airline industry itself. That said, airline operators are already at a disadvantage to effectively manage risks for the worst-case scenario of a pandemic when that scenario has, for over two decades, been specifically defined in and through law as the threat of terrorism to the stability of international aviation. Perhaps the Covid-19 pandemic and its prolonged effects on the aviation industry have now brought public health concerns to the fore alongside the pillars of safety and security, to be now considered 'a third pillar of aviation' (see Eurocontrol 2021; see also ICAO 2021d).

REFERENCES

Albert, C, Baez, A and Rutland, J (2021) 'Human Security as Biosecurity: Reconceptualizing National Security Threats in the Time of Covid-19' 40(1) *Politics & the Life Sciences* 83.

[9] For example, pandemic influenza A(H1N1) in 2009, MERS- CoV in 2012 (see Leitmeyer 2011; ECDC 2020).

Alvarez, JE (2020) 'The WHO in the Age of the Coronavirus' 114(4) *American Journal of International Law* 578.

Amankwah-Amoah, J (2020) 'Stepping Up and Stepping Out of Covid-19: New Challenges for Environmental Sustainability Policies in the Global Airline Industry' *Journal of Cleaner Production* 271.

Baldwin, R, Cave, M and Lodge, M (eds) (2012) *Understanding Regulation: Theory, Strategy, and Practice*, 2nd edn (Oxford, Oxford University Press).

Banakar, R (2015) *Normativity in Legal Sociology: Methodological Reflections on Law and Regulation in Late Modernity* (Heidelberg, Springer).

Bastide, L (2018) 'Crisis Communication during the Ebola Outbreak in West Africa: The Paradoxes of Decontextualized Contextulaization' in M Bourrier and C Bieder (eds), *Risk Communication for the Future Towards Smart Risk Governance and Safety Management* (Cham, Springer).

Beck, U (1992) *Risk Society: towards a New Modernity* (London, Sage).

—— (1999) *World Risk Society* (Cambridge, Polity).

—— (2009) *World at Risk* (Cambridge, Polity).

Berger-Sabatel, A and Journé, B (2018) 'Organizing Risk Communication for Effective Preparedness: Using Plans as a Catalyst for Risk Communication' in M Bourrier and C Bieder (eds), *Risk Communication for the Future Towards Smart Risk Governance and Safety Management* (Cham, Springer).

Black, J (2010) 'The Role of Risk in Regulatory Processes' in R Baldwin, M Cave and M Lodge (eds), *The Oxford Handbook of Regulation* (Oxford, Oxford University Press).

Bowen, JT Jr and Laroe, C (2006) 'Airline Networks and the International Diffusion of Severe Acute Respiratory Syndrome (SARS)' 172(2) *The Geographical Journal* 130.

Brown, RS and Kline, WA (2020) 'Exogenous Shocks and Managerial Preparedness: A Study of US Airlines' Environmental Scanning before the Onset of the Covid-19 Pandemic' 89(1) *Journal of Air Transport Management.*

Burkle, FM Jr (2015) 'Global Health Security Demands a Strong International Health Regulations Treaty and Leadership From a Highly Resourced World Health Organization' 9(5) *Disaster Medicine and Public Health Preparedness* 568.

Cusick, SK, Cortes, AI and Rodrigues, CC (2017) *Commercial Aviation Safety*, 6th edn (McGraw Hill Education).

Dempsey, PS and Chen, K-W (2013) 'Aviation Safety and Security Requires Global Uniformity' 38 *Annals of Air and Space Law* 515.

Douglas, M and Wildavsky, AB (1982) *Risk and Culture: An Essay on the Selection of Technological and Environmental Dangers* (Berkeley, CA, University of California Press).

EASA (2020) https://www.easa.europa.eu/newsroom-and-events/press-releases/aviation-must-keep-strong-focus-safety-pandemic-and-eye-greener (accessed 3 October 2022).

—— (2021) https://www.easa.europa.eu/the-agency/faqs/agency#category-about-easa (accessed 3 October 2022).

ECDC (2020) https://www.ecdc.europa.eu/sites/default/files/documents/infectious-diseases-transmitted-on-aircrafts-ragida-risk-assessment-guidelines.pdf (accessed 3 October 2022).

Eurocontrol (2021) https://www.eurocontrol.int/article/life-beyond-covid-19-how-will-aviation-need-change (accessed 3 October 2022).

European Parliament (2021) https://www.europarl.europa.eu/RegData/etudes/STUD/2021/662903/IPOL_STU(2021)662903_EN.pdf (accessed 3 October 2022).

European Union (2020) *EUR-Lex, Access to European Law.* http://eur-lex.europa.eu/homepage.html?locale=en (accessed 3 October 2022).

Fitzgerald, PP (2012) 'Questioning the Regulation of Aviation Safety' 37 *Annals of Air and Space Law* 1.

Forsyth, P, Guiomard, C and Niemeier, H-M (2020) 'Covid-19, the Collapse in Passenger Demand and Airport Charges' 89 *Journal of Air Transport Management* 89.

GARS (2020) https://unitingaviation.com/news/economic-development/the-coronavirus-outbreak-the-unprecedented-shock-to-aviation/ (accessed 3 October 2022).

Gelles, D and Chokshi, N (2020) '"Almost without Precedent": Airlines Hit Hard by Coronavirus' *New York Times*, 5 March, available at https://www.nytimes.com/2020/03/05/business/coronavirus-airline-industry.html (accessed 3 October 2022).

Guérard, M (2018) 'How Safety Communication can Support Safety Management: The Case of Commercial Aviation' in M Bourrier and C Bieder (eds), *Risk Communication for the Future Towards Smart Risk Governance and Safety Management* (Cham, Springer).

Gössling, S (2020) 'Risks, Resilience, and Pathways to Sustainable Aviation: A Covid-19 Perspective' 89 *Journal of Air Transport Management*.

Halabi, SF (2020) 'The Origins and Future of Global Health Law: Regulation, Security, and Pluralism' 108(6) *Georgetown Law Journal* 1607.

Harrison, J (2009) *International Aviation and Terrorism: Evolving Threats, Evolving Security* (London, Routledge).

Havel, BF and Sanchez, GS (2014) *The Principles and Practice of International Aviation Law* (New York, Cambridge University Press).

Hough, P (2008) *Understanding Global Security*, 2nd edn (London, Routledge).

Huang, J (2009) *Aviation Safety through the Rule of Law, ICAO's mechanisms and Practices* (Netherlands, Kluwer).

IATA (2020a) https://www.iata.org/en/iata-repository/publications/economic-reports/covid-19-has-been-an-unprecedented-shock/ (accessed 3 October 2022).

—— (2020b) https://www.iata.org/en/iata-repository/publications/economic-reports/air-passenger-monthly-analysis---apr-20202/ (accessed 3 October 2022).

ICAO (2020a) https://unitingaviation.com/news/economic-development/the-coronavirus-outbreak-the-unprecedented-shock-to-aviation/ (accessed 3 October 2022).

—— (2020b) https://www.icao.int/Security/Covid-19/PublishingImages/Pages/Statements/Joint%20ICAO-WHO%20Statement%20on%20Covid-19.pdf (accessed 3 October 2022).

—— (2020c) https://www.icao.int/safety/SafetyManagement/Doc10144/Doc%2010144.pdf (accessed 3 October 2022).

—— (2021a) https://www.icao.int/Meetings/AVSEC2021/Pages/Commemoration-911-attacks.aspx (accessed 3 October 2022).

—— (2021b) https://www.icao.int/Security/Pages/default.aspx (accessed 3 October 2022).

—— (2021c) https://www.icao.int/sustainability/Documents/Covid-19/ICAO%20Covid%202021%2007%2021%20Economic%20Impact%20TH%20Toru.pdf (accessed 3 October 2022).

—— (2021d) https://www.icao.int/Security/Security-Culture/Pages/YOSC-2021.aspx (accessed 3 October 2022).

—— (2021e) https://www.icao.int/safety/CAPSCA/Pages/About-CAPSCA.aspx (accessed 3 October 2022).

—— (2021f) https://www.icao.int/about-icao/Pages/default.aspx (accessed 3 October 2022).

Joormann, M (2019) *Legitimized Refugees: A Critical Investigation of Legitimacy Claims within the Precedents of Swedish Asylum Law* (Doctoral Thesis, Lund University).

Kasperson, RE, Renn O, Slovic, P, Brown, HS, Emel, J, Gobel, R, Kasperson, JX and Ratick, S (2000) 'The Social Amplification of Risk; A Conceptual Framework' in P Slovic, *The Perception of Risk* (London, Earthscan).

Leitmeyer, K (2011) 'European Risk Assessment Guidance for Infectious Diseases Transmitted on Aircraft – the RAGIDA Project' *Euro surveillance: bulletin Europeen sur les maladies transmissibles = European communicable disease bulletin* 16(16).

Leloudas, G and Haeck, L (2003) 'Legal Aspects of Aviation Risk Management' 28 *Annals of Air and Space Law* 149.

Linden, E (2021) 'Pandemics and Environmental Shocks: What Aviation Managers Should Learn from Covid-19 for Long-term Planning' 90 *Journal of Air Transport Management*.

Macilree, J and Duval, DT (2020) 'Aeropolitics in a Post-Covid-19 World' 88 *Journal of Air Transport Management*.

Mythen, G (2004) *Ulrich Beck: A Critical Introduction to the Risk Society* (London, Pluto).

Naboush, E and Alnimer, R (2020) 'Air Carrier's Liability for the Safety of Passengers during Covid-19 Pandemic' 89 *Journal of Air Transport Management*.

OECD (2020) https://www.oecd.org/coronavirus/policy-responses/covid-19-and-the-aviation-industry-impact-and-policy-responses-26d521c1/ (accessed 3 October 2022).

Ratajczyk, M (2015) *Regional Aviation Safety Organisations. Enhancing Air Transport Safety through Regional Cooperation* (Alphen aan den Rijn, Kluwer).

Rosca, EC, Heneghan, C, Spencer, EA, Brassey, J, Plüddemann, A, Onakpoya, IJ, Evans, D, Conly, JM and Jefferson, T (2021) 'Transmission of SARS-CoV-2 Associated with Aircraft Travel: a Systematic Review' 28(7) *Journal of Travel Medicine*.

Slovic, P, Fischoff, B and Lichtenstein, S (2000) 'Cognitive Processes and Societal Risk Taking' in P Slovic, *The Perception of Risk* (London, Earthscan).

Sunstein, CR (2002) *Risk and Reason: Safety, Law, and the Environment* (Cambridge, Cambridge University Press).

Tisdall, L and Zhang, Y (2020) 'Preparing for "Covid-27": Lessons in Management Focus – An Australian General Aviation Perspective' 89 *Journal of Air Transport Management*.

Tversky, A and Kahneman, D (1973) 'Availability. A Heuristic for Judging Frequency and Probability' 185 *Science* 1124.

Wilkinson, P and Jenkins, BM (eds) (1999) *Aviation Terrorism and Security* (London, Frank Cass).

Wright, SJ (2021) *Aviation Safety and Security. Utilizing Technology to Prevent Aircraft Fatality* (Boca Raton, CRC Press).

29

The Interlegal Evocation
of Peace in Colombia

NICOLÁS SERRANO C

I. INTRODUCTION

SOCIOLEGAL SCHOLARS IN Colombia have often addressed what seems to be a local phenomenon worthy of research: the existence of a large production of laws and the population's affection for legal provisions in a context of recurrent legal inefficacy and widespread violence (Rodriguez Garavito 2009). The capacity of the law to connect symbols in society has been suggested as an explanation (García Villegas 2014). From this perspective, the law stands primarily on its power to evoke and inspire rather than on its formal observance in Colombia.

On the one hand, this thesis is sustained by the inertia of the colonial tradition, according to which Spanish law was the source for the legitimacy of the king's authority but not the foundation for compliance with his commandments. On the other hand, it is explained by the aspirational character of the 1991 Constitution: the chart projects a non-existent but desired reality that fosters collective affection for the law (García Villegas 2012).

Following these arguments, the relationship to the law in Colombia has also been described in terms of 'the enjoyment that progressive legal decisions produce ... in excess of their real possibilities of application' (Lemaitre 2007: 18). As the political and cultural meanings invoked by the law are the predominant source for legal enthusiasm, social actors experience legal change as a political victory, a step in the process of cultural and social change, and not necessarily as deceiving (Lemaitre 2009).

When analysing the role of the law in the production of social and cultural meaning, most Colombian sociolegal scholars have focused on either the national legal level or on social movements. Building on Banakar's bottom-up/top-down law contextualisation method (Banakar 2015) and his analysis of the EU's interlegality (Banakar 2019), I will explore the role of the municipal level in reproducing the symbolic function of the law in Colombia.

As Vivian (2021) suggested, Banakar's understanding of the law is fluid, multiform, and multidimensional: the law appears unified only as sections that constitute its regulatory monopoly through forms of knowledge and communication (Banakar 2003).

The perceived momentary stability of the law emerges by the intersection between its external and internal realities within a given context. In other words, social life is an integral part of the law's manifestations, and thus the relation between law and social forces is not of mirroring but of interaction.

Banakar was sensitive to the different levels in which social life manifests in late modernity. While the micro level involves increased reflexivity of agency against social and institutional structures, the macro level encompasses the decentralisation of normativity sources and the search for risk and uncertainty management (Banakar 2015). The law travels through legal, social, and institutional settings by its interpretative and contextual character.

Banakar suggests contextualising the law by integrating its macro applications and micro usages to describe 'how the law interacts with and simultaneously manifests itself at the macro, micro and intermediary meso levels of society over time' (ibid: 7). This approach proposes to look at the interaction between law as a body of rules and society at the macro level, the interpretation and enforcement at the meso level, and law's uses, experiences, and expectancies at the micro level. The direction of the movement – from above or from below – is shaped by different power relations involved in the journeys of the law. The analytical focus does not lie on rules or social forces but on the communicative interactions between them, connecting the internal and external standpoints of law and the top-down and bottom-up processes (ibid: 160).

Banakar (2019) relied on Santos' notion of interlegality (1987) to analyse the different top-down and bottom-up legal interactions involved in Brexit. From such a viewpoint, the outcome of the 2016 referendum was the expression of an internal UK crisis of law, identity, politics, and democracy as much as a sign of the failure of the EU integration project (Banakar 2019: 62). The hierarchical structure supporting the EU's interlegality was the source of the crisis.

According to Santos, sociolegal life is constituted by the simultaneous and network-like operation of different legal spaces. Because of their interactions and intersections, the actors' legal experiences are inevitably made out of transitions and trespassings through and within them. Santos' interlegality aims to trace the uneven dynamic process that entails understanding the relationships within and between legal spaces and their correlative social experience.

For Santos – as for Banakar – legal orders search for a regulatory monopoly, a process that can be unveiled through a cartographic analogy. Law – like cartography – does not mirror but inevitably distorts reality to handle complexity. Scale (the detail by which legal objects are defined), projections (the definition of a centre and periphery expressed in terms of accepted interpretative frames), and symbolisation (the communicative style) are the cartographic properties by which legal spaces achieve their exclusivity. As a result, different legal spaces create dissimilar legal objects upon the same social object.

Taking this a step further, Banakar addressed the power dimension of the interactions between legal spaces generating the EU interlegality. He analysed how the sequences of actions of interlegality are shaped differently by the EU's power architecture. Top-down interlegality (from small to large scale) is instrumental, strategic, universal, and charged with the force of law and politics. Bottom-up interlegality (from large to small scale) is tactical, edifying, particular, transitory, and driven by social and cultural forces (Banakar 2019: 66). The attempts to reduce the difference between legal spaces by fostering a collective identity (from the top) and through a democratisation process (from the bottom) failed. The European search for legal harmonisation clashed with local concerns regarding the protection of the job market and the defence of culture. As a result, the integrative properties at the macro level operated as disintegrative at the micro level (ibid: 70).

Inspired by this framework, I will explore how different manifestations of the law evoke peace as non-violence in Colombia. I will address the municipal level of Bogotá (the country's capital city) as an actor participating in a broader interlegal archi-tecture. From this standpoint, municipal regulations and practices emerge from the interactions between the legal system, municipal governments, and communities as a recalibrated map searching for social intelligibility (Drummond 2011). I will describe how Bogota's interpretative and communicative governmental practices articulated constitutional aspirations with social experiences reassuring the interlegal evocation of peace.

I will develop the arguments by following the journey of the constitutional right to life. First, I will address the role of the Constitution as a symbolic antidote to violence in Colombia. Second, I will describe how in 2001, the government of Bogotá interpreted the right to life within municipal concerns of public order as 'Life is Sacred', a motto inscribed amidst one of the municipal symbolic practices in the city's central cemetery. Finally, I will explore how such a funerary space – in a bottom-up movement – was reinterpreted through the artwork '*Anonymous Auras*' in 2007 as a place of memory, allowing social movements to reclaim the space and relate to legal frames aimed at symbolically repairing the victims of the conflict.

II. THE RIGHT TO LIFE

The enactment of a new Constitution in 1991 has become a landmark for the social, legal, political, and economic life of Colombia. The 1991 Chart replaced the 1886 Constitution that emphasised the centralist, Hispanic and catholic character of the Colombian nation (Camacho 1997). Despite numerous constitutional changes during the twentieth century, by the end of the 1980s, the enforceability of rights in Colombia still depended on the will of the executive power. The 1886 Constitution was commonly understood as an obstacle to contemporary democracy to the point that 'its existence was dependent on the systematic suspension of its validity' (Melo 2017: 270). Indeed, Colombia was governed under a state of exception for 32 years, between 1949 and 1991 (García Villegas 2017).

The initiative to change the old Constitution emerged from the student social movement. The liberal government of the time – pursuing the country's insertion into global economic dynamics – swiftly supported the enterprise. The constitu-tional change in Colombia was an institutional answer to the historical crisis of the state (Negretto 2013), expressed in the incapacity to solve fundamental inequalities – land distribution and the provision of social services – upon which rested economic and social disparities. The new Constitution attempted to respond to what has been traditionally considered sources of violence in Colombia: the supremacy of the executive power and the correlative exclusion of social and political groups with progressive social change agendas.

The Colombian nation-state was born out of a political field dominated by bipartisanship. The centralist and federalist views that arose immediately after independence from the Spanish Empire developed into two traditional and opposing Colombian political parties (conservatives and liberals). Their power struggle gave rise to several civil wars during the nineteenth century, fostered the promotion of armed guerrillas in rural areas at the beginning of the twentieth century, and led the country to one of its most violent periods between 1945 and 1958, known as *La Violencia* (The Violence period).

A milestone of this phase was the 1948 assassination in Bogotá of Jorge Eliécer Gaitán, a liberal leader who was likely to become president. In response, a popular uprising burnt and looted infrastructure, businesses, and homes for several days. After public order was re-established, between 2,000 and 3,000 people were counted dead or missing. These events (known as the *Bogotazo*) persist in the Colombian collective memory as the assassination of an anti-elitist leader loved by the people. The uprising itself survives as a reminiscence of chaos.

In 1956, liberals and conservatives reached a political agreement by which they would alternate presidential power every four years until 1974. Amidst these convulsed decades, different guerrilla groups emerged, inspired by the conviction that legal and peaceful channels for political and social change had been exhausted.[1]

The political and social process that gave life to the new Constitution brought the impetus for social change into the realm of law once again. The popular election of a National Constituent Assembly allowed a wide range of actors to obtain political participation. Despite the strength of traditional parties, the representatives of students, women's organisations, indigenous communities, and academia, among other social forces, found a place in the assembly. The participation of the recently demobilised M-19 guerrilla group – now organised as a political party – was significant, as they occupied approximately a quarter of the assembly seats. The Constitution was labelled as an act of peace through which violence was to be dissipated by dealing with political conflicts within institutional democratic channels (Gutiérrez-Sanín 2011).

The 1991 Constitution ended up being a complex assemblage of two transnational global projects at the time (Rodríguez Garavito 2011): on the one hand, the neoliberal project, whose understanding of the rule of law focused on providing security to the market (predictability and guarantees to property rights); on the other, the neo-constitutionalist paradigm, inspired by the human rights movement and embodied in a generous bill of rights and well-defined judicial review mechanisms. As a result, since 1991, Colombia has been formally a constitutional, social, democratic, environmental state under the rule of law (*Estado constitucional, social, democrático y ambiental de derecho*), establishing the supremacy of the Constitution, now including civil, political, economic, social, and cultural rights.

---

[1] The most influential guerrilla groups of Colombia have been the FARC-EP, the ELN, the EPL, the *Quintín Lame* and the M-19.

The 1991 constitutional framework has enabled moderate possibilities for social change due to the new direct mechanisms established to protect citizens' rights and the renewed vigour of the High Court (Uprimny and García 2004; Santos and Rodríguez Garavito 2007). However, the promise of peace has not yet been fully realised. Although the new Constitution was the basis for new peace processes between the government, guerrilla groups, and paramilitary forces, domestic conflict did not cease. Warfare became increasingly a struggle for territorial control between the state forces, guerrillas, paramilitary, drug lords, and other armed groups looking to exploit legal and illegal economies. Hand in hand, abuses from the state forces increased, while the effects of the neoliberal economic policies created social unrest in numerous social groups that did not see substantive changes in terms of equity.

In Colombia, 'violence is equated to lawlessness and the remedy for violence is assimilated to the expansion of the social rule of law, the State form that embodies the rule of law in the Colombian Constitution' (Lemaitre and Restrepo-Saldarriaga 2019: 2). The relation between law, peace, and violence emerged from the power of law to give meaning to the social world. For Colombia, this is one in which law 'symbolically reconstructs the value of human life and dignity, denied daily by the experience of violence' (Rodriguez Garavito 2009: 20). The enthusiasm for legal reform lies in 'the idea of human dignity that the law demands, which owes much to natural law, from which it inherits that everything human is sacred and equivalent to other human beings' (Lemaitre 2007: 390).

Within this understanding, the right to life is fundamental in the constitutional frame. Its total reach lies in several articles of the Constitution and the ample jurisprudence developed by the Constitutional Court. It goes from granting territorial autonomy to indigenous communities – there is no dignified life outside the expression of their territorially embedded worldviews – to the provision of social services and the regulation of abortion. However, the right to life is often associated with a single article of the Constitution: 'The right to life is inviolable. There shall be no death penalty' (Constitution, Article 11). A conflict-oriented interpretation is yet prominent in the legal narrative, as described by the Colombian Commission of Jurists:

> The right to life is one of the fundamental axes of the new Constitution. The 1991 Chart has in its origins a peace agreement between the State and several demobilised guerrilla groups and includes a coexistence agreement between the members of Colombian society. Hence, one of its objectives, if not the most important, is to contribute to the fight against violence. (Barreto Soler and Sarmiento Anzola 1997: 20)

The right to life is fundamental to Article 22 of the Constitution, by which in Colombia 'peace is a right and duty of which compliance is mandatory'. Such interpretation bound the law (in its constitutional expression) to peace (as an absence of internal conflict) as the primary source of order in opposition to violence (non-legal use of force). Moreover, the conflict-oriented understanding of this constitutional principle encompasses the promise of protecting life by the hand of 'a power capable of building and maintaining a peaceful coexistence scenario, in which killing each other is not the way to respond to situations of conflict or social tension. It gives rise to the State's duty to establish or keep the peace' (García 2005: 211). This duty found a particular local expression in the municipal government of Bogotá in 2001.

III. LIFE IS SACRED

The assurance of order is a central feature of urban legality, being the regulation of public health and the use of space, two of its fundamental axes (Azuela 2021). Bogotá's development plans exemplify urban planning thinking: they are technical and financial documents approved by the city council upon a text proposed by the municipal administration that ought to mirror citizens' concerns.

The basic structure of development plans is the staging of a desired future, following the identification of critical problems addressed by suggested solutions expressed in strategies, programs, projects, objectives, goals, indicators, and the financial resources to operationalise them. This structure establishes the criteria for pertinence, efficiency, and effectiveness and provides the ground for social, political and fiscal accountability. Once approved, development plans become byelaws, the official route of action for city governments. Development plans are frames via which local governments claim legality – through their links to a higher legal disposition – and legitimacy – based on their political approval. The municipal level is constitutionally bound by the principles of concurrence, coordination, and subsidiarity but has relative autonomy to interpret the legal frames to find ways to answer the demands of citizens.

The backbone of the 2001–2004 development plan for Bogotá was a 'civic culture' strategy, whose goals were to increase voluntary compliance with norms, to foster citizens' ability to enter into and comply with agreements and mutual help, to help citizens act according to their conscience and in harmony with the law, and to promote communication and solidarity (Bogotá 2001).

'Sacred Life' was the name of one of the leading civic culture programmes. Its objectives were to discourage the use of weapons, reduce the number of violent deaths in the city, promote healthy lifestyles, and generate confidence, security, and tranquility so people can enjoy their rights and fulfil their duties (ibid: 9). It was an explicit reference to the constitutional principle of protecting life, which was a principle of the development plan itself (Vélez Arango 2016).

Civic Culture was an approach developed by the municipal government of Bogotá in 1997. It aimed to promote peaceful coexistence between the city's inhabitants by fostering a minimal set of shared urban social rules (Londoño 2003). From this perspective, the divorce between legal, cultural, and moral norms was the source of most of the city's problems. Applying an 'intensified communication' informed by Habermas' and Bernstein communicative theories, Civic Culture sought a continuum between moral, cultural, and legal argumentation as a tool to bind them (Mockus 2001). The strategy set the law as a background for such harmonisation: the law should incorporate collective minimum agreements, articulate cultural differences, and provide relative stability to abstract moral principles. Civic Culture has systematically relied on protecting life as one of its communicative axes for local governance. Such a communication effort mainly relied on what the municipal government labelled a pedagogical approach. Its ruling principles were the dialogical communication in search of mutual understanding and free agreement, the formation of the will through processes of expression and interpretation using artistic practices, and out-of-school pedagogical practices that included an ethical and political dimension in terms of coexistence (Saenz 2017).

The municipal government set the goals for the 'Sacred Life' programme in terms of urban security: reduction of violent deaths, homicides, personal injuries, and thefts. Similarly, it aimed at encouraging voluntary disarmament and increasing the perception of security. The reduction of violent deaths and injuries responded to the local understanding of the Colombian conflict and the epidemiological interpretation of violence common in urban policy since the 1990s (Silva et al 2009). The end of the twentieth century in Colombia was marked by the peace negotiation process between the government and the FARC guerrilla group. The peace process ultimately failed in 2002 amidst increased military actions between paramilitary militias, guerrillas and the state forces. Bogotá was also a field of warfare, and its impact was understood as a matter of urban order.

In January 2002, the FARC-EP guerrilla group attacked the city's water supply, an act considered by the city government to be a violation of the International Humanitarian Law and a transgression of the minimum rules of war (Sáenz 2003: 37). It was the starting point of an institutional campaign for civil resistance that sought to promote the peaceful rejection of violent acts. Its focus was to protect public goods (eg energy and water supply infrastructures, schools, hospitals, and the food chain distribution) and to promote – with the participation of the inhabitants of the city – collective acts against any form of violence (assassinations, bombings, kidnappings, and death threats to citizens or public officers, among others). The campaign promoted the avoidance of violence in private or public life, acting non-violently in the face of violence, responding to acts of destruction with construction, and externalising the rejection of violence and life-threatening acts as key messages (Saenz 2007: 175).

As part of the civil resistance activities, and in line with the performative character of Civic Culture, the municipal government organised monthly public meetings at the columbaria[2] at the Central Cemetery. The columbaria, built between 1947 and 1956, stands on what was known as 'the cemetery of the poor', in contrast with the mausoleums of the Central Cemetery where Colombian personalities lie. Under the columbaria, the unidentified bodies from the '*Bogotazo*' were buried in 1948. In 2000, burials at the columbaries were suspended, and the remains were removed in the following years. The site was meant to be turned into a recreational area. Before 2002, no living memory was attached to the site.

The purpose of the gatherings at the cemetery was to ritualise and ratify the value of life against the normalisation of violence in the city. The meetings at the cemetery were held for two years, during which artists, social movements, victims of violence, and other social and political actors gathered in what became one of the local government's signature actions. As part of the activities, the city's Mayor presented the decreasing rates for homicides amidst artistic and performative acts having the columbaria as a scenario (youngsters, for example, were seated in the empty graves as a symbol of life). Also, as part of the civil resistance meetings, the administration temporarily closed them with a banner displaying the message 'Political Constitution

---

[2] Columbarium are funerary monuments or buildings with niches or cavities in the walls to place the cinerary urns or bodies.

of Colombia, Article 11: The right to life is inviolable. There shall be no death penalty'. The normative claim 'Life is Sacred' (*La Vida es Sagrada*) was written in the finial of the columbaria. A peculiar official graffiti (Hermer and Hunt 1996): an open rule reduction evoking authority and legitimacy from the Constitution, indicating that the law and the derived municipal regulations are justifiable cultural codes of conduct. Life's victory over death was associated with the triumph of the constitutional order upon which the municipal order stood.

The civil resistance strategy was criticised by social peace-seeking organisations, as they considered it an illegitimate irruption of the state power in what should have been the field of civil society. In the National Peace Congress of 2002, there was an explicit rejection of the campaign based on the consideration that the civil resistance processes in Colombia should be led by social actors, not by the state in any of its manifestations (Vélez Arango 2016). The local government understood itself as a promoter of much broader collective actions (Saenz 2007) and, as such, an ally to the citizenry in the fight against the violence that 'hurt them both', problematically equating the local administration with civil society and forgetting the active role of the state in the conflict.

Nevertheless, Civic Culture and the civil resistance activities were not controversial for most of the public opinion. The media swiftly echoed the performative practices. Besides, Civic Culture communicative efforts conveyed an intelligible sense of order to most of the city's inhabitants, simultaneously articulating the national legal system – expressed paradigmatically in the Constitution – with municipal governmental practices and the daily urban experiences.[3] 'Life is Sacred' soon became a well-known trope in Colombia, still used and reproduced today as a symbol of the constitutional spirit. Today, the Life is Sacred rubric still remains on top of the columbaria.

IV. ANONYMOUS AURAS

In 2003, Doris Salcedo – a well-known Colombian artist – approached the municipal government of Bogotá with a special request: to revoke the renovation project seeking to build a soccer field and a skating rink on the columbaria land. The municipal administration consented and declared the columbaries as a cultural heritage asset of the city based on their historical and memorial character (Bogotá 2003). Only uses that were consistent with their architectonic, symbolic, and cultural character were to be allowed. In 2003, Ms Salcedo convened the seminar *Art, Memory and City*, where Colombian and international artists discussed the site's future. They recommended that the city commission an artist to carry out a project inspired by site-specific artistic principles and the counter-monument movement (Cerón 2010). The future artwork should overcome the modern practice of making people remember by perpetually giving objects the function of linking places to memory, usually via a written description and the alienation of the object from its surroundings. On the contrary, counter-monumentalism aimed at incorporating the state's role

---

[3] Notable exceptions were the street vendors, whose use of urban space was a constant source of conflict with the city administration.

into the national memorial landscape (Young 1992). The suggestion was to blend temporary artistic works with the architectural and symbolic surroundings of the cemetery without imposing narratives or replacing the act of reminiscence, but rather activating and questioning the memory (Cerón 2010).

The municipality agreed on the artistic intervention, but the project got a green light only until 2007. The artist commissioned was Beatriz González, a well-known Colombian artist who developed the oeuvre '*Anonymous Auras*' (*Auras Anónimas*). She covered almost 9,000 empty open graves of the columbaria with variations of the same structural image in which two black silhouettes carry a corpse. The aim was – symbolically – to not let the auras wander while reproducing the repetition of the acts of violence of the conflict: 'I want to capture the auras of the thousands of deaths that may be floating here and offer a space for those who want to be able to mourn them' (González 2019a). The 'Life is Sacred' heading was kept on top of the structures, as in the words of Ms González, it was one of the layers of the site.

The artwork did not claim a victory over death through law but attempted to reconcile life and death by the hand of a symbolic burial. The oeuvre ended up not being temporary. As the artist once declared in an interview, 'I am sure that this work does not expire because it has a useful memory' (González 2019b; Bustos 2019). The call to mourning activated the memory for the thousands of unidentified deaths of 1948 and, by extension, for all the contemporary unknown victims of the socio-political conflict.

In 2012, *Anonymous Auras* became spatially part of the Centre for Memory, Peace, and Reconciliation of Bogotá (CMPR). Initially proposed by social organisations, the CMPR was created by the city's Coexistence and Public Security policy in 2011 and was grounded on the national Act for the Victims of the Conflict (Law 1448 of 2011) aimed at providing attention, assistance, and comprehensive reparation to the victims of the Colombian conflict. This Act comprises measures for symbolic reparation understood as actions aimed at ensuring the preservation of historical memory, non-repetition of victimising events, public acceptance of the facts, the request for public forgiveness, and restoration of the dignity of the victims (Article 41). The Centre for Memory is an institutional space whose primary objective is to gather social organisations to foster peace through promoting memory processes.

The CMPR is a local expression of a national attempt to repair and pay homage to the victims of the conflict by acknowledging the state as an active armed force in the conflict and recognising its omissions as a guarantor of citizens' rights. It is located in a new building amidst the funeral complex, just to the right-hand side of Ms González's work, in lands owned by the city. Since then, *Anonymous Auras* has been spatially considered part of the Centre for Memory as an open exhibit.

In 2019, the National Heritage Council declared the columbaria as an area of affectation of the Central Cemetery, making them by extension an asset of cultural interest of national character. Thus, the efforts to invoke peace and reconciliation narratives found an institutional and spatial expression. The artistic attempt to trigger memory transited to an institutionalised search for the historical memory of the Colombian conflict.

Various disparate groups have used *Anonymous Auras* as a space for memory. It has been the gathering place for demonstrations in favour of peace processes, for remembering state crimes, and a setting for further artistic interpretations of the conflict. Its capacity to activate the memory still survives. In 2020, while the city government was urging the inhabitants to stay at home and 'take care of life' amidst the Covid pandemic, the Indigenous Guard (*Guardia Indígena*), an autonomous force of the indigenous peoples of Colombia, recorded a video of their anthem with the columbaria as a setting. 'Forward, comrades, ready to resist. Defending our rights, even if we have to die', says the chorus.[4] The video was released while thousands of members of indigenous communities reached Bogotá to join a nationwide strike against the national central government.

V. CONCLUDING REMARKS

The journey of the right to life through different legal spaces outlines the organic role of the municipality amidst an interlegal network. The municipal government participated as a privileged interpreter between the legal system and the daily city legal experience. The intensive communication of the municipal authorities preserved the interlegal network intelligibility, enabling a comprehensible legal flow through the legal system – expressed paradigmatically in the Constitution – and the social expectancies of the city inhabitants –marked by the longing for peace and safety.

The municipal interpretation of the constitutional duty of protecting life as Sacred Life created a space to fill the constitutional principle with the objects created by the distortions of the municipal level: fight delinquency, control road safety, discourage non-aggressive interpersonal relations, reject political violence, promote civil resistance, abide norms. The performative and symbolic communication of the city authorities exalted the law as a source of peace and a rejection of different expressions of violence, meeting widespread social expectations about the law captured under the notions of peaceful coexistence and urban public order. The municipal goal of harmonising law, culture, and morals involved portraying a coherent broader interlegal architecture.

The interpretation of the constitutional duty to protect life as municipal-driven civil resistance practices was challenged by social movements that, in a bottom-up trajectory, did not lose sight of the state as an active participant in the Colombian conflict. For them, the municipal power, despite its in-between position, was a state's local expression: the suggested interlegal consistency was an illusion.

Social forces transited their way up the interlegal network by the concurrence of artistic practices and the municipal interest on the columbaria back in 2003. While consistent with the communicative style of governance of the time, the artistic intervention in the funerary space also endorsed a new set of meanings coming out of social movements and beyond specific municipal administrations. In such a route, social forces ultimately met the legal spaces created to acknowledge the state's role amidst the Colombian conflict. Over time, the development of the interlegal network

---

[4] Himno de la Guardia Indígena – Guardia Fuerza- Parranderos del Cauca ft. Andrea Echeverry, Ali Aka Mind, Chane Meza et al, 21 October 2020, music video: www.youtube.com/watch?v=OA96avuk1aQ.

made the columbaria a layered memory space that emerged from the consecutive interactions of social forces, municipal authorities, and national legal concerns. Still today, past and present experiences of violence grow, associated with a memory architecture standing on the belief that law conjures peace.

REFERENCES

Azuela, A (2021) Cities and Urbanisation. *Routledge Handbook of Law and Society* (Routledge).
Banakar, R (2003) *Merging Law and Sociology: beyond the Dichotomies of Sociolegal Research* (Berlin, Galda and Wilch Publishing).
—— (2015) *Normativity in Legal Sociology* (Springer).
—— (2019) 'Brexit: A Note on the EU's Interlegality' in B Lemann Kristiansen et al (eds), *Transnationalisation and Legal Actors: Legitimacy in Question* (London, Taylor & Francis).
Barreto Soler, M and Sarmiento Anzola, L (1997) *Constitución Política de Colombia comentada por la Comisión Colombiana de Juristas, Título II de los derechos, las garantías y los deberes* (Bogotá).
Bogotá, AMD (2001) Plan de Desarrollo Económico, Social y de Obras Públicas para Bogotá DC 2001–2004 'BOGOTÁ para VIVIR todos del mismo lado'.
—— (2003) Decreto 396 de 2003. Por el cual se declaran algunos bienes de interés cultural y se dictan otras disposiciones (Bogotá).
Bustos, OEB (2019) 'Gracias, Beatriz González, por recuperar los columbarios del Cementerio Central', available at www.las2orillas.co/gracias-beatriz-gonzalez-por-recuperar-los-columbarios-del-cementerio-central.
Camacho, RP (1997) 'La Constitución de 1991 y la perspectiva del multiculturalismo en Colombia' 7 *Alteridades* 107.
Cerón, J (2010) 'Auras anónimas: Beatriz González en el Cementerio Central de Bogotá' 9 *Art Nexus: el nexo entre América Latina y el resto del mundo* 66.
Drummond, S (2011) *Mapping Marriage Law in Spanish Gitano Communities* (UBC Press).
García, GMG (2005) 'El derecho a la vida en la constitución colombiana: principios constitucionales y derechos fundamentales' *Nuevo Foro Penal* 188.
García Villegas, M (2012) 'Constitucionalismo aspiracional: derecho, democracia y cambio social en América Latina' 25 *Análisis Político* 89.
—— (2014) *La eficacia simbólica del derecho. Sociología política del campo jurídico en América Latina* (Bogotá, Random House).
—— (2017) *El orden de la libertad* (Bogotá, Fondo de Cultura Económica).
González, B (2019a) 'Columbarios-protegidos-por-Consejo-Nacional-de-Patrimonio', *Periódico Arteria*, 11 October 2019, availabe at https://www.periodicoarteria.com/noticia/Columbarios-protegidos-por-Consejo-Nacional-de-Patrimonio.
González, B (2019b) 'Gracias, Beatriz González, por recuperar los columbarios del Cementerio Central', interview by Oscar Emilio Bustos, *Las Dos Orillas Periódico*, 20 November 2019, availabe at https://www.las2orillas.co/gracias-beatriz-gonzalez-por-recuperar-los-columbarios-del-cementerio-central/.
Gutiérrez-Sanín, F (2011) 'La Constitución de 1991 como pacto de paz: discutiendo las anomalías' 13 *Estudios socio-jurídicos* 419.
Hermer, J and Hunt, A (1996) 'Official Graffiti of the Everyday' *Law and Society Review* 455.
Lemaitre, J (2007) *Fetichismo legal: Derecho, violencia y movimientos sociales en Colombia* (Bogotá, Universidad de Los Andes Sela).

—— (2009) *El derecho como conjuro: fetichismo legal, violencia y movimientos sociales* (Bogotá, Siglo del Hombre, Uniandes).

Lemaitre, J and Restrepo-Saldarriaga, E (2019) 'Law and Violence in the Colombian Post-Conflict: State-Making in the Wake of the Peace Agreement' 67 *Revista de Estudios Sociales* 2.

Londoño, R (2003) 'Líneas de investigación e intervención en los programas de cultura ciudadana de Bogotá (1995–1997, 2001–2004)' *Pensar Iberoamérica: Revista de cultura* 8.

Melo, JO (2017) *Historia mínima de Colombia* (El Colegio de Mexico AC).

Mockus, A (2001) *Cultura ciudadana, programa contra la violencia en Santa Fe de Bogotá, Colombia, 1995–1997. Estudio técnico* (Banco Interamericano de Desarrollo).

Negretto, GL (2013) *Making constitutions: presidents, parties, and institutional choice in Latin America* (Cambridge, Cambridge University Press).

Rodriguez Garavito, C (2009) 'Prólogo: Violencia, legalismo y fetichismo: el desciframiento de la paradoja colombiana' in J Lemaitre, *El derecho como conjuro: fetichismo legal, violencia y movimientos sociales* (Bogotá, Siglo del Hombre, Uniandes).

—— (2011) 'Toward a Sociology of the Global Rule of Law Field' in Y Dezalay and B Garth (eds), *Lawyers and the Rule of Law in an Era of Globalization* (Routledge).

Sáenz, J (2003) 'La cultura ciudadana: una pedagogía para la democracia, la civilidad, la seguridad, la comunicación y el disfrute' *Bogotá para vivir 2001–2003*.

—— (2007) *Desconfianza, civilidad y estética: las prácticas formativas estatales por fuera de la escuela en Bogotá, 1994–2003* (Bogotá, Universidad Pedagógica Nacional).

—— (2017) 'Antanas Mockus as a Pedagogue: Communicative Action, Civility and Freedom' in C Tognato (ed), *Cultural Agents Reloaded: The Legacy of Antanas Mockus* (Harvard, Harvard University Press).

Santos, BDS (1987) 'Law: A Map of Misreading. Toward a Postmodern Conception of Law' 14(3) *Journal of Law and Society* 279.

Santos, BDS and Rodríguez Garavito, CA (2007) *El derecho y la globalización desde abajo: hacia una legalidad cosmopolita* (Anthropos).

Silva, AE, Pérez, F, Ruiz, F and Martín, T (2009) *Bogotá, de la construcción al deterioro 1995–2007* (Bogotá, Universidad del Rosario).

Uprimny, R and García, M (2004) 'Corte Constitucional y emancipación social y violencia en Colombia' in BDS Santos and M García, *Emancipación social y violencia en Colombia* (Bogotá, Norma) 463.

Vélez Arango, C (2016) *Nuevas formas de resistencia civil: la propuesta de Antanas Mockus en Bogotá* (Maestría en Ciencia Política).

Vivian, MM (2021) 'Law, Justice and Reza Banakar's Legal Sociology' 11 *Oñati Socio-Legal Series* 1.

Young, JE (1992) 'The Counter-monument: Memory against Itself in Germany Today' 18 *Critical Inquiry* 267.

Part VI

Applied Sociology of Law

30

Trade Union Solidarity and the Issue of Minimum Wage Regulation in the EU

ANN-CHRISTINE HARTZÉN

I. INTRODUCTION

T HIS CONTRIBUTION AIMS to critically assess the understanding of solidarity within the position of the Swedish trade unions in relation to the issue of a minimum wage regulation at the EU level. The idea is to highlight challenges for Social Europe in the form of difficulties for the European trade union movement to identify a common ground and a strong strategy for the improvement of working conditions. The focus on solidarity is thus centred on international trade union solidarity, or as I will coin it in this contribution, 'EU transnational trade union solidarity'.

The topic as such is currently at the centre of attention for any socio-legal scholar with interests in Social Europe due to the legislative debate about a Directive concerning the regulation of minimum wages at EU level[1] (European Commission 2020; discussed by Hartzén and Hettne 2021). This initiative has, from the outset, met sharp resistance from Swedish social partners, whereas the overall attitude from EU level social partners – especially trade union organisations – has been positive. Sweden is one of the countries with the highest levels of minimum wages (Hartzén 2021; Hällberg and Kjellström 2020; Nelson and Fritzell 2019) and the Swedish trade union opposition towards improvements of working conditions for workers worse off can thus be questioned as lacking solidarity from a broader EU perspective. At the least it can be considered a potential obstacle for the European trade union movement in establishing a much-needed strategy directed towards the improvement of working conditions for the worst off workers in the EU (Hartzén 2017). As a Swedish labour law scholar, the Swedish model and the role of Swedish social partners in the European project is naturally of specific interest to me.

---

[1] The Directive on adequate minimum wages in the European Union was approved by the Council on 4 October 2022. This text is based on results from a study conducted in the earlier phase of the legislative initiative and as such the final approval of the Directive does not affect the results.

This chapter therefore aims to critically assess the understanding of solidarity within the position of Swedish trade unions in relation to the issue of minimum wage regulation at EU level. To do so the chapter draws on findings from an empirical study of the contents of communication from Swedish trade union organisations. In order to provide an understanding of how I conceive of solidarity, specifically in the form of EU transnational trade union solidarity, within the ambit of this contribution, this concept will be discussed in the next section. After that, I will provide a discussion on how I have constructed a critical study of the presence of EU transnational trade union solidarity in the communication of Swedish trade unions concerning the proposed EU directive on regulation of minimum wages. This will then be followed by an analysis of the empirical findings and the final section will provide my conclusions.

II. THE CONCEPT OF SOLIDARITY

Grasping the meaning and definition of the concept of solidarity can be a challenge because 'Solidarity is an elusive and multidimensional concept which indicates different things to different people in different times and places' (Banakar 2018: 81). The challenge is not lessened in an international and/or transnational setting such as the EU, and this is expressed in a rich academic debate concerning the concept of solidarity in the EU (eg Banakar 2018; de Witte 2012; Garben 2022; Karageorgiou 2018; Krunke et al 2020; Martinico 2016; Sangiovanni 2013). This is not to say that it is impossible to distinguish certain core characteristics inherent in the concept of solidarity, nor that the conception of such characteristics within the context of EU transnational trade union solidarity cannot be defined or explained. Instead, identifying the main characteristics of solidarity and explaining how those characteristics can be conceived in relation to EU transnational trade union structures will form the basis for the further analysis in this text.

Solidarity as a concept needs to be understood in the specific context within which an analysis of its existence and function is conducted. Since the focus here is on EU transnational trade union solidarity, it is therefore important to seek to comprehend how solidarity can be understood in a transnational setting such as the EU. Sangiovanni (2013) has explained well how the EU as a project of integration involves cooperation between the Member States in order to achieve aims that the Member States otherwise would have been unable to achieve, but that cooperation also comes with specific risks in terms of the capacity for each Member State to yield benefits. Therefore, Member States need to assess what costs they are willing to accept in order to offset specific risks associated with integration in a form of insurance-based rational assessment of opportunity costs (ibid). Instead of seeking to answer the question of how all benefits and burdens generated by the EU cooperation should be distributed, Member States need to assess the risks and costs associated with trade-offs between different goals and opportunities in a form of a reciprocity-based cooperation where reciprocity and common goals yielding benefits for all (albeit those benefits may be unevenly distributed) form the core of Member State solidarity (ibid).

A similar reasoning can be applied to EU trade union cooperation, since such cooperation can provide ground for achieving aims that in an integrated EU labour market it would not be possible for national trade union movements to achieve on their own (Hartzén 2017). In this sense, EU transnational trade union solidarity could thus be understood in terms of a cooperation based on the willingness of national trade unions to collaborate transnationally in the EU, by investing certain costs in order to offset risks associated with the further integration of the EU labour market. As such, national trade unions will thus need to accept certain trade-offs in order to assure reciprocity in their striving towards common goals that may provide benefits to all workers in the long-term perspective even though such benefits might not be evenly distributed, especially in the short-term perspective. Measures that would assure an increase in wages for those workers in the EU earning the least, could in this sense be considered such a common objective, likely to yield benefits for all workers in the EU. For those earning the least, the benefits would be fairly evident as well as immediate, and for those earning higher wages there could be long-term benefits in the form of a decreased risk of social dumping through low-wage competition, by for example posted workers.

Further elaborated, the idea of solidarity in the EU transnational setting can be understood based on the idea that the EU provides a type of common societal scheme from which it is expected that all Member States will benefit in the long run. This form of cooperation, however, requires a certain level of civil solidarity which will be difficult to attain and uphold if social inequalities between certain groups of citizens become permanent and structural features (Garben 2022). In other words, the participation in a common project of this kind cannot be conditioned on guaranteed net benefits and the value produced within such a common system also needs to be redistributed from winners to losers of the system in a manner that shows solidarity. This in turn generates a need for a reinforcing solidarity structure based on deliberate participation of all, without expectations of guaranteed short-term gains and that those subject to structural disadvantages are compensated in the long-term perspective without having their self-worth and agency undermined (ibid).

In relation to EU transnational trade union solidarity, this can be understood in terms of seeking to achieve the goal of improving the conditions for the workers who are worst off and that national trade unions representing workers who are better off do so without expecting short-term guaranteed benefits for their own members, but that the long-term value of bottom-line improvements will also provide benefits for the initially better off trade unions and their members. In principle, this is how the global International Transport Workers' Federation's Flag of Convenience Campaign has been constructed, from which the short-term benefits have yielded clear improvements of the working conditions for the seafarers worst off, whereas the better off seafarers, for example from Sweden, have seen longer-term benefits in the form of decreased downward pressure on wages and lessened risks of losing jobs to seafarers from low-wage countries (Hartzén 2017).

Understanding solidarity in this manner also highlights the importance of full participation from all in both stages of the reciprocity-based solidarity act. Half-hearted participation whereby some members would not commit fully to the first act of solidarity, but rather choose only to participate when they anticipate immediate net benefits would most likely spur on crises of solidarity instead of contributing to solving them (Garben 2022). In other words, when solidarity is framed in an instrumental manner serving the short-term needs currently preferred by some participants in the common project, then it will risk bolstering negative solidarity (Butler and Snaith 2020), providing ground for rising protectionism, xenophobia and scepticism against the common project (Banakar 2018).

This means that EU transnational trade union solidarity needs to be understood in terms of an idea of reciprocity-based cooperation, where efforts are made in order to promote the overall good of workers and sacrifices from national trade unions need to be made in order to achieve that common good. Such sacrifices are justified on the basis that the overall good will also benefit those making the initial sacrifice in the long-term perspective in spite of being perceived as having a negative impact for that same national union in the short-term perspective. Refusing to participate in the common project due to self-perceived negative consequences for a specific national trade union movement will undermine the fostering of further developed EU transnational trade union solidarity (*cf* Garben 2022; Banakar 2018). In such a case, the possibility for developing a strong EU-level trade union strategy focusing on improving the conditions for the worst off workers within the EU, would be hindered, limiting the possibilities for identifying a strategy more likely to provide benefits to all in the long term (Hartzén 2017). The understanding of EU transnational trade union solidarity as consisting of the deliberate participation of all with the requirement to accept certain costs without immediate guaranteed benefits in order to achieve a common good that will provide benefits to all workers in the EU in the long term will thus form the basis for the further analysis.

III. UNDERSTANDING TRADE UNION SOLIDARITY BY STUDYING COMMUNICATION

As has been explained above, trade union solidarity as defined for the purpose of this paper, needs to be understood as a reinforcing solidarity structure involving striving towards improving conditions for the worst off workers. In my view, it is a concept framed in terms of the promotion of a normative value. The idea of normative values reflects, in my opinion, ideals of how society ought to be or to function (Hartzén 2017; 2019). The idea that transnational trade union solidarity ought to be framed towards the aim of improving conditions for the worst off workers thus results in trade union solidarity being conceived of as a normative value. Such values can be understood as part of the programs applied by autopoietic systems in the recursive production of communication of the system (Luhmann 2013). In this sense the system produces communication, which through the system's programme is aimed at the promotion of specific societal values (Luhmann 1995), or in my words normative values. As I have argued elsewhere (Hartzén 2017; 2019), it is possible to discern and study such values by carefully examining language used in communication produced within a system. Those arguments have been developed in relation to studies holding ambitions of identifying what a regulatory system is, what results it produces, and why. That requires a two-step analysis of empirical material containing communication produced by the system under study. Such a two-step analysis is enabled by making use of Luhmann's distinction between observation and interpretation

(King and Thornhill 2003) when studying empirical material. In the first step, the empirical material is analysed on the basis of an observation of what can be found in the empirical material in terms of positivistic values that enable the researcher to identify what the binary code of the system categorises as part of the system. In the second step, the analysis focuses on interpretation of the content of the empirical material in order to identify the normative values that frame the programming of the communication and thus provide ground for understanding the meaning of that communication. Such an analysis requires a careful examination of both the wording and the structure of the communication in terms of what normative values are expressed, in what order and to what extent different normative values are recurrent or even absent (Hartzén 2019).

However, the aim here is to critically assess the understanding of solidarity within the position of Swedish trade unions in relation to the issue of the minimum wage directive. Therefore, the empirical study I have conducted for this paper holds a more narrowly defined ambition. The ambition is not to explain what a regulatory system is, nor why it is what it is. Instead, the focus is on communication produced by specific organisations, ie Swedish trade unions. Nevertheless, the method of studying system communications by this two-step analytical approach will be useful for this study. The reason is that it is possible to identify organisations which contribute to the production of communication within an autopoietic system (Drepper 2005). In this sense, organisations can be understood as the location for specific communication within the system and thus make the communicative structures of the system observable (Nassehi 2005).

Within the European Social Dialogue a vast number of organisations contribute to the production of communication; amongst these organisations we can identify trade union organisations at both EU and national level. Since the EU level organisations are complex, not least in the sense that their members are also representatives of other organisations, they face specific challenges in the production of communication. I have identified such challenges in terms of difficulties in enacting clear membership premises that also result in difficulties in forming strong and clear goal-oriented decision premises (Hartzén 2017). Swedish trade unions can, in my view, be understood as organisations that are structurally coupled with the EU level trade union movement since they have representatives as members in the EU level trade unions. I therefore find the communications from Swedish trade unions interesting to study, because the structural coupling and complex membership structures are likely to also trigger effects for the communications of the EU-level trade unions. Critically assessing the position of Swedish trade unions with regard to EU transnational trade union solidarity in relation to the issue of minimum wage regulations at EU level can therefore be used as an example for to shed light on some of the challenges for the EU-level trade union movement in formulating a clear and strong strategy to strive towards the improvement of conditions for the worst off workers in the EU.

The empirical material used for analysis in this contribution therefore consists of publicly expressed opinions from Swedish trade union organisations and/or their representatives concerning the issue of regulation of minimum wages in the EU. Similar forms of texts where representatives of employers' organisations are also listed amongst the signatories have been left out, in order to ensure that the opinions expressed are purely representative of trade unions. Even though the issue as such has formed a clear consensus between both parties of the labour market in Sweden, the involvement of a representative from an employers' organisation in the formulation of a text could imply a slight shift in the balancing of interests expressed. In order to minimise the risks that such a shifted balance could bear for the analysis, those documents have been left out. The selection of publicly expressed opinions has been done on the basis that it is written by representatives having a clear mandate to express the view of the trade union organisation as such or in other forms published through a formal channel of communication from a trade union or federation of trade unions, such as a formal webpage. Therefore, the material taken up consist of texts either written by the president of a trade union organisation, consisting of a formally recognised interview with such a person or being signed by presidents of several trade union organisations. These texts have been published either as debate articles in daily press, as statements on trade union webpages or as opinion statements from trade union organisations to the Swedish government and to the Commission. Most of these opinions were published before the publication of the proposed directive and as such they do not contain comments relating to the contents of the directive and regulations prescribed therein; instead, the opinions are directed to the broader question of regulating minimum wage at EU level as such. The discussion will therefore also consider the statements in these opinions from this broader perspective in relation to EU transnational trade union solidarity.

The focus of my analysis of this material is on the issue of EU transnational trade union solidarity. This concept, which I have explained above, needs to be understood as requiring from the involved actors, such as Swedish trade unions, the acceptance of initial costs without requiring guaranteed net benefits. The overall aim of such solidarity is to achieve the improvement of working conditions for the worst off workers, since this is also an aim that will provide benefits to all in the long-term view. In this sense, I understand EU transnational trade union solidarity as a normative value that can be identified in communication through the examination of what interests are expressed (improving conditions for the worst off workers or something else) as well as what costs the actors involved are willing to accept and what benefits they expect. The presence of the normative value of EU transnational trade union solidarity is, as such, possible to identify through its elements of *interests* aligning with the concept of solidarity and the acceptance of *costs* without requiring immediate *benefits*. These elements of trade union solidarity have thus been of importance in the analysis of the empirical material where the expressed interests are used to identify to what extent solidarity as a value is present in the communications studied, ie the first step of observation. In the next step, I have interpreted how the value of solidarity is given meaning by seeking to identify how it is applied in terms of accepted costs and required benefits. The focus of this analysis has therefore been on identifying expressions that focus on the interests of Swedish social partners and Swedish workers from both a short-term and long-term perspective; expressions concerning the needs of workers in other countries, especially workers subject to poorer conditions and/or weaker social dialogue institutions, as well as expressions directed at some form of common aim for EU transnational trade union cooperation. The extent to which these communications express willingness to participate in the common project in order to yield long-term benefits for all in spite of cost for the Swedish trade union movement in the short term has been thoroughly examined. In this analysis I have sought to identify what the communications studied express as the main focus and most important interest to protect, what costs are considered acceptable and what potential benefits are expected, by taking into account the structure of the communication and repetitions of values expressed in the communications. In the next section I discuss the results of this study and relate the position of Swedish trade unions to the context and aim of the proposal.

IV. SWEDISH TRADE UNIONS, SOLIDARITY AND EU MINIMUM WAGE

The overall aim of the proposed directive on the regulation of minimum wages in the EU is to ensure that all workers in the EU are entitled to a wage that allows for a decent standard of living (European Commission 2020). This falls in line with an overarching aim for EU transnational trade union cooperation of improving the conditions for workers across the EU, especially those who are the worst off, since those workers are more likely to not earn a decent wage (Hartzén 2017). The acknowledgement of such a form of common aim is partly found in three of the five studied texts (PTK 2020; Arrius et al 2020; Risgaard et al 2020), whereas the other two (Arrius 2020a; 2020b) contain no reference to such transnational aims, but instead focus fully on the protection of national interests of safeguarding the Swedish (or Nordic) model of collective bargaining. Martin Linder, the chair of the congregation of private white-collar workers in Sweden (in Swedish: *Privattjänstemannakartellen*, hereinafter PTK), clearly states that there is a problem with low wages in the European labour market and acknowledges an aim of coming to terms with that problem (PTK 2020). Arrius et al (2020) also acknowledges that there are problems with the EU labour market and that conditions need to be improved, but the focus here is rather on problems relating to low collective agreement coverage rates and insufficient models for wage-setting. Such issues can indirectly be linked, however, to an overall aim of improving conditions for workers subject to poor working and employment conditions. Similarly, Risgaard et al (2020) point to the need to support capacity-building for social partners and promote collective bargaining across the EU as well as the issue of poor wages in some Member States, indirectly acknowledging that there is an overarching aim of improving working conditions, especially for workers at the bottom-end of the labour market.

Nevertheless, in spite of at least indirectly acknowledging an EU transnational common aim, the main focus in the communications centre around the need to protect the Swedish (or Nordic) model for wage-setting exactly as it is and assure that this model is not subject to any risks of intervention. Willingness to accept any forms of costs for minimising risks associated with a common EU-level aim of improving conditions for the worst off workers is strikingly absent from most of these communications. Arrius et al (2020) recognise the necessity of accepting a certain level of uncertainty in the common EU project, but emphasises that EU regulation concerning minimum wages would create an unbearable degree of uncertainty for the Swedish model. Risgaard et al (2020) highlight some suggestions for supporting developments of collective bargaining structures, but rather in a manner that would imply costs for other parties instead of requiring Swedish (or in this specific case Nordic) trade unions to accept costs. The other communications are, as stated, centred on the need to protect the Swedish model as it is, clearly expressing unwillingness to accept any form of interventions or risk-bearing for the Swedish model in relation to this issue (Arrius 2020a; 2020b; PTK 2020). Arrius (2020a; 2020b) highlights the need to preserve a wage-setting model which has yielded benefits for the Swedish economy for more than 20 years and to ensure that this model is protected from any risks of intervention associated with the common EU project in relation to the issue of minimum wages. In a similar vein, these national protective interests are also clearly expressed by Linder (PTK 2020).

The interest of protecting the Swedish model and the concerns of the Swedish trade unions shines through all of the studied communications, which also clearly express the proposed EU intervention as a threat to these interests (Arrius 2020a; 2020b; Arrius et al 2020; PTK 2020; or from the Nordic perspective Risgaard et al 2020). The proposal is highlighted as a threat that could negatively affect Swedish growth (Arrius 2020a), would risk undermining the Swedish model (PTK 2020), and generate a risk of judicial review of the Swedish model for collective bargaining as a whole by the Court of Justice of the European Union (Arrius et al 2020). Expectations of guaranteed net benefits from the EU common project in the form of guaranteed protection of the Swedish model without adjacent risks for the same model are instead portrayed in various forms by highlighting that there are no water-tight exceptions for this model in the current proposal (Arrius et al 2020; Arrius 2020b; Risgaard et al 2020).

In this sense, these communications clearly express a negative form of solidarity (Butler and Snaith 2020), distinct from the form of EU transnational trade union solidarity as explained above. Such negative solidarity is not new within EU, nor has it solved previous crises. As well explained by Banakar (2018), the deficits in relation to the social dimensions of solidarity at EU level have created

> a political vacuum at the national and local levels, which is exploited by populist and nationalist groups whose aim is to bolster a negative form of solidarity. As Brexit has shown, besides spreading tribal mentality and xenophobia, these populist groups work proactively against the very idea of a European Union (ibid: 82).

The position taken by Swedish trade unions, as found in the studied communications concerning the issue of EU minimum wage regulation, is therefore worrying for several reasons. First, the vague and indirect acknowledgement of a common EU transnational trade union aim of improving conditions for the worst off workers in the EU points to challenges for taking a very first step towards EU transnational trade union solidarity. Second, the unwillingness to accept any form of costs or risks associated with a common EU transnational trade union aim in relation to this issue make the Swedish trade unions incapable of participating in the first act of such a form of solidarity. This, in combination with the clearly expressed national protectionist interests, bears the risk of bolstering negative solidarity instead of fostering EU transnational trade union solidarity. As such, the potential to further and promote improvements in conditions for the worst off workers through the development of EU transnational trade union solidarity diminishes. Even though these conclusions can only be applied in relation to the specific issue of a proposal for regulation of minimum wages in the EU and therefore cannot be generalised to the overall strategy of Swedish trade unions, there is a need for reflection concerning future choices of strategy and possibilities for achieving the long-term gains of a common EU trade union cooperation.

V. CONCLUDING REMARKS

As I have explained in this text, EU transnational trade union solidarity needs to be understood in terms of a reinforcing solidarity structure. Such a structure requires all national trade union movements to deliberately participate in the push towards a common aim of improving conditions for the worst off workers in the EU, accepting that this cooperation comes with certain costs and without immediate guaranteed benefits, but the attainment of the common aim will yield long-term benefits for all. Since the basis for analysis is limited to one specific issue, there is no basis for drawing general conclusions on the presence of such a form of solidarity within the position of Swedish trade unions in relation to the EU project as a whole. The conclusions drawn, therefore, relate only to the isolated and specific issue of a proposed EU Directive on the regulation of minimum wages. Any claims reaching beyond that scope would require further analysis outside the realm of this chapter. I hope that such an analysis would render a different understanding of the situation, because in relation to EU minimum wage regulation the picture is of concern. The position of Swedish trade unions in relation to this specific issue is very far from a position that could foster EU transnational trade union solidarity. A common aim of EU transnational trade union cooperation is only vaguely and indirectly acknowledged; any costs for achieving such a potential aim are rejected and – in terms of potential benefits – short-term guaranteed benefits seem to be expected whereas long-term common benefits seem neglected. The position of Swedish trade unions on this issue is more closely associated with a form of negative solidarity focusing on national protectionism, which risks the bolstering of nationalistic movements, increasing scepticism against the common project, and as such contributes to – rather than solving –solidarity crises for EU transnational trade union cooperation.

REFERENCES

Arrius, G (2020a) 'Stå emot EU:s minimilöner, regeringen', debate article published Arbetet 20 October 2020, available at https://www.saco.se/press/aktuellt-fran-saco/debatt/sta-emot-eus-minimiloner-regeringen/ (last accessed 4 October 2022).

—— (2020b) 'EU-direktivet om minimilöner kan pressa Svenska löner nedåt', press release from SACO available at https://www.saco.se/press/aktuellt-fran-saco/pressmeddelanden/eu-direktivet-om-minimiloner-kan-pressa-svenska-loner-nedat/ (last accessed 4 October 2022).

Arrius, G, Gideonsson, S and Svanström, T (2020) 'Sverige måste stoppa EU:s minimilöner', debate article published in *Svenska Dagbladet*, 20 November 2020, available at https://www.saco.se/press/aktuellt-fran-saco/debatt/sverige-maste-stoppa-eus-minimiloner/ (last accessed 4 October 2022).

Banakar, R (2018) 'Law, Love and Responsibility: A Note on Solidarity in EU Law' in R Banakar, K Dahlstrand and L Ryberg Welander (eds), *Festskrift till Håkan Hydén* (Lund, Juristförlaget i Lund).

Butler, G and Snaith, H (2020) 'Negative Solidarity: The European Union and the Financial Crisis' in H Krunker, H Petersen and I Manners (eds), *Transnational Solidarity: Concept, Challenges and Opportunities* (Cambridge, Cambridge University Press).

de Witte, F (2012) 'Transnational Solidarity and the Mediation of Conflicts of Justice in Europe' 18(5) *European Law Journal* 694.

Drepper, T (2005) 'Organization and Society – On the Desideratum of a Society Theory of Organizations in the Work of Niklas Luhmann' in D Seidl and KH Becker (eds), *Niklas Luhmann an Organization Studies Advances in Organization Studies* (Koege, Liber & Copenhagen Business School Press).

European Commission (2020) 'Proposal for a Directive of the European Parliament and of the Council on adequate minimum wages in the European Union' COM(2020) 682 final.

Garben, S (2022) 'Dignity- and Reciprocity-based Solidarity as the Normative Framework of the EU's Constitutional Settlement' in A-C Hartzén, A Iossa and E Karageorgiou (eds), *Law, Solidarity and the Limits of Social Europe: Constitutional Tensions for EU Integration* (Cheltenham, Edward Elgar).

Hällberg, P and Kjellström, C (2020) *Collective Agreements and Minimum Wages* (Stockholm, Swedish National Mediation Office).

Hartzén, A-C (2017) *The European Social Dialogue in Perspective: Its Future Potential as an Autopoietic System and Lessons from the Global Maritime System of Industrial Relations* (Doctoral dissertation, Lund University).

—— (2019) 'Aligning Normativity with Luhmann for a Critical Study of Industrial Relations' 19(2-3) *Retfaerd* 9.

—— (2021) *Working, Yet Poor: National Report Sweden* (Lund, Lund University).

Hartzén, A-C and Hettne, J (2021) 'Förslaget om minimilön i EU – en europeisk angelägenhet eller en svensk olägenhet?' 1 *Viewpoint Europe* (Centre for European Studies, Lund University).

Karageourgiou, E (2018) *Rethinking Solidarity in European Asylum Law: A Critical Reading of the Key Concepts in Contemporary Refugee Policy* (Doctoral dissertation, Lund University).

King, M and Thornhill, C (2003) *Niklas Luhmann's Theory of Politics and Law* (New York, Palgrave Macmillan).

Krunke, H, Peterson H and Manners, I (eds) (2020) *Transnational Solidarity: Concept, Challenges and Opportunities* (Cambridge, Cambridge University Press).

Luhmann, N (1995) *Social Systems* (transl J Bednarz, with D Baecker) (Stanford, Stanford University Press).

—— (2013) *Theory of Society*, vol 1 (transl R Barrett) (Stanford, Stanford University Press).

Martinico, G (2016) 'What Does Solidarity Mean in Multi-National Contexts: The Case of the European Union' 7(1) *Romanian Journal of Comparative Law* 7.

Nassehi, A (2005) 'Organizations as Decision Machines: Niklas Luhmann's Theory of Organized Social Systems' 53(1) *Sociological Review* 178.

Nelson, K and Fritzell, J (2019) *ESPN Thematic Report on In-work poverty in Sweden*. (Brussels, European Commission, Directorate-General for Employment, Social Affairs and Inclusion).

PTK (2020) 'Djupt oroande att EU-kommissionen presenterar förslag till direktiv om minimilöner', interview with Martin Linder, chair of PTK, published at https://www. ptk.se/press/djupt-oroande-att-eu-kommissionen-presenterar-forslag-till-direktiv-om-minimiloner/ (last accessed 4 October 2022).

Risgaard, L, Gabrielsen, H-C and Svanström, T (2020) 'EU legislation on minimum wages is not the solution', blog post for Social Europe, published 5 October 2020 at https://socialeurope.eu/ eu-legislation-on-minimum-wages-is-not-the-solution (last accessed 4 October 2022).

Sangiovanni, A (2013) 'Solidarity in the European Union' 33(2) *Oxford Journal of Legal Studies* 213.

31

Constitutional Imaginaries: A Socio-legal Perspective of Political and Societal Constitutions

JIŘÍ PŘIBÁŇ

I. INTRODUCTION

'WE IMAGINE THE happy state' states Plato in his *Republic* (Plato 2000: 111) and, to further illustrate this constitution of the ideal city, he employs a 'noble lie' as a founding myth of this imaginary polity. According to Plato, 'We want one single, grand lie which will be believed by everybody – including the rulers, ideally' (ibid: 107–10).

The lie is actually a fiction behind the imagined community, which makes it constituted by two different myths. The first is an autochthonous myth of the same descent of the entire population of the earth. The second is a myth of divine dispensation of different metals in the citizens' souls which constitutes the imagined polity's differentiated class structure. People are made to believe both myths and thus reconcile the principles of commutative and distributive justice by the symbolic constitution of the polity's unity.

This coeval constitution of the care for the city and for each other shows the legitimation function of imaginaries communicating the common good despite economic, political and other societal differences. This function was later elaborated by Polybius when he wrote in his *Histories*:

> it is the very thing which among other peoples is an object of reproach, I mean superstition, which maintains the cohesion of the Roman state. These matters are clothed in such pomp and introduced to such an extent into their public and private life that nothing could exceed it, a fact which will surprise many. My own view at least is that they have adopted this course for the sake of the common people. It is a course which perhaps would not have been necessary had it been possible to form a state composed of wise men, but as every multitude is fickle, full of lawless desires, unreasoned passion, and violent anger, the multitude must be held in by invisible terrors and suchlike pageantry. (Polybius in MacIntyre 2002: 104)

According to this view, symbols of power structures generate acceptance and unity in the absence of reason and rational consensus. They are more effective means of political and societal stability with stronger capacity to guarantee the common consensus than the rational discourse which is a privilege of wise and educated elites and therefore cannot be extended to the whole society.

In the modern language of social and political sciences, Polybius's description of 'superstition' would be grasped by the concept of *ideology* as collectively shared views of different social groups which stabilise the existing political system by obfuscating and covering its internal conflicts and contradictions. Karl Mannheim described ideology as the collective unconscious motives blurring the real state of society and thus stabilising its order. It is part of a typically modern conflict caused by the democratisation of the state and the plurality of political parties which need to justify and systemically explain and validate their struggle and position within the political and social order.

Value plurality is a consequence of democratisation of modern society (Mouffe 2000: 120–21). Ideology then replaces theology in its goal of constituting the total and only image of modern society. However, this goal is paradoxical exactly because modern society is defined by the pluralism of its value structure (Mannheim 1997: ch 2). Modern morally pluralistic and politically democratic societies subsequently consist of the plurality and conflict of ideologies mirroring structural conflicts between those who rule and those ruled by them.

Unlike philosophy, with its belief in objective validity and social indeterminacy of knowledge, sociology – according to Mannheim – analyses unconscious social motives connecting the existence of a particular social group with its cultural values, goals and ideological arguments (ibid: 30). Modern democratic and pluralistic politics then reveals how different groups and parties represent different ideas and use them to legitimise their political goals and programmes.

To the credit of Mannheim's sociology of knowledge, the concept of ideology ceased to be the subject of speculations of idealistic and critical philosophy and became an intrinsic part of sociological inquiries into the construction of social reality and meaning and the circularity of legitimation and delegitimation processes in different social systems including the systems of positive law and politics. In the last two decades, these problems have been particularly elaborated by different philosophies and theories of social imaginaries.

In this chapter, I adopt these theories to explore imaginaries constituted by the systems of positive law and politics. I draw on the conceptualisation of modernity as the state of societal, political and value plurality. The contrast between the polyvalence and functional differentiation of modern society and the transcendental validity claims generated by specific social systems and enforced through their imaginaries continues to be one of the central themes of both social and legal theory. I, therefore, analyse social imaginaries as background power communicating the common good in functionally differentiated society at national as much as global societal levels.

II. PHILOSOPHY AND SOCIOLOGY OF IMAGINARIES

Imaginary symbolic forms of communication are spontaneous expressions of the human nature as the 'animal symbolicum' (Cassirer 1944: 26). For instance, Ernst

Cassirer adopted the notion of symbolic forms which, unlike the Kantian notion of universal and transcendental forms, are constituted historically and established in the social context of language, myth, religion and art. According to him, these symbolic forms are rooted in 'metaphorical thinking' and have their historical 'laws of evolution' while unified by 'a final community of function' of the human mind and its spiritual creativity (Cassirer 1946a: 84; Přibáň 2007).

Cassirer's philosophical analysis of symbolic forms and communication draws on humanity as unity of the manifold and considers symbolic expression the common denominator of human culture present in myth and art as much as language, logic and science. The function of symbolic forms is the constitution of an objective social and cultural reality (Cassirer 1946b: 45). Despite its philosophical attraction as the potential nature of humanity, this final community of symbolic forms, however, has to be analysed by anthropological and sociological methods to such extent that, according to Cassirer, the very notion of symbolic forms is nothing more than Emile Durkheim's 'primitive forms of classification' (Cassirer in Bourdieu 2014: 165).

Philosophers and sociologists thus both agree that symbolic forms of communication constitute social reality. Indeed, it is possible to ask whether symbolically communicated imaginaries are reservoirs of the ultimate meaning of social and human existence. Speculations on homogeneity and heterogeneity, transcendence and immanence or objective and subjective validity are likely to continue informing general philosophical and specific jurisprudential and ethical arguments and their sociological criticisms. Nevertheless, the very existence of these forms of social communication means that the specific constitution, function and operations of imaginaries in legal, political and other social systems have to be examined from social theoretical and sociological perspectives.

What Durkheim described as society comes very close to what the anthropologists understand by culture. Durkheim's sociology of 'collective representations' is often described as a predecessor of more recent philosophical and sociological studies of social imaginaries and the imaginary constitution of society (Gilleard 2018: 320). These representations make social institutions and practices collectively both meaningful and functional and, as such, constitute social facts and reality.

Imaginaries, therefore, are not to be taken as expressions of a universal rule of humanity and its collective soul or mass psyche. Their function is not ontological in the sense that they would confirm the collective existence of humankind. The question of 'Who are we as a meaningful community?' cannot be answered by one 'real' voice of the collective mind and always remains to be constituted and articulated through functionally differentiated social systems and their imaginaries. This is why even the identity politics of modern imagined communities, for instance, cannot be freely manipulated and controlled by the technologies of political power and its existential narratives of populist imaginaries.

Imaginaries also do not belong to either the substructure of material power, or the superstructure of hegemonic ideology or symbolic order. They need to be distinguished from cultural myths and economic or political dogmas and cannot be treated as mere residues of mythological and ideological imaginations operating in otherwise functionally differentiated systems and falsely constituting idealisations of social unity and totality.

Imaginaries constitute 'the symbolic dimension of the social world, the dimension through which human beings create their ways of living together and their ways of representing their collective life' (Thompson 1984: 6). In this respect, Durkheim's analysis of society as an autonomous societal process of collective self-understanding and self-representation actually can be used and reformulated as a 'second order' communication of imaginary collective unity in contemporary complex and functionally differentiated society (Durkheim 1898: 300).

Rather than one ultimate and binding system of imaginaries guaranteeing social solidarity and collective trust, modern social imaginaries constitute polysemy which is diffuse and generated by different rationalities. In this chapter, therefore, I draw on theoretical arguments and conceptualisations of imaginaries elaborated by Benedict Anderson's sociology of imagined communities and Charles Taylor's philosophy of modern social imaginaries. I also employ Niklas Luhmann's autopoietic social systems theory and its elaboration by Gunther Teubner in the context of theory of societal constitutions to analyse the paradox of the imaginary unity of society constituted by differentiated social systems. I argue that polysemy and polyvalence of constitutional imaginaries is driven by functional differentiation and the internal paradoxes of social systems.

III. SOCIETAL POWER OF IMAGINARIES AND THE PARADOX OF VALUE LEGITIMATION

Social imaginaries are societal forces, *potentia*, which reconstitute functionally differentiated society as one legitimate polity. They evolve immanently through different social systems, but they are treated as transcendentally valid and constitute social subjects as members of *communitas* – the community of values. They operationalise the transvaluation of values and represent the societal constitution of transcendental validity.

The function of social imaginaries is the constitutionalisation of systemic *facts* of power as legitimising *values* of polity. They transform the plurality of social immanence and differentiated societal forces into the community of transcendental values and ideals.

Using the terminology of structuralism, the constitution of social imaginaries can be described as arbitrary and conventional because they are social and historical constructs relative to the semantics and structures of specific systems such as positive law and politics. At the same time, they generate principles and values transcending these specific structures and constituting general expectations of living in one legitimate polity. The imaginary constitution of society, therefore, is the paradoxical constitution of one social self by specific social systems which involves the possibility of communitas as a collective form of the ethically meaningful life constituted by shared values and legal rules (Cotterrell 1995: 325).

Nevertheless, the contrast between the purity of authentic values of community and their corruption by the state of politics and society, so much favoured by Rousseau and subsequent generations of revolutionaries and moralists, does not apply to the constitutional imaginaries because they are constituted by society itself.

They are internal symbolic constructs of self-constituted positive law and politics which make it possible to constitutionally imagine and describe functionally differentiated modern society and its power hierarchies, fragmentations and asymmetries as one polity and distinguish between legitimacies and illegitimacies in it (Browne 2019: 399).

The paradoxical imaginary self-constitution of functionally differentiated society as a symbolically unified whole thus reveals a second paradox related to the semantics of social imaginaries which consists of the fact that generally shared and valid social values are just momentary outcomes of different societal operations and legitimation strategies. Values thus can constitute only immanent waiting lists despite the fact that they are argumentatively formulated as transcendental foundations by politicians, judges, activists, citizens and even legal or social theorists.

This internal paradox of the community of values claiming transcendental validity but depending on their immanent enforcement and legitimation needs to be analysed within the context of positive law and politics. Using the methodology of social systems theory and its radical constructivist perspective eliminates a typical mistake of perceiving imaginaries as the meaningful opposites of systemic rationality which reveal the authentic human existence in the otherwise alienating modern society. Instead, imaginaries can be analysed as expanding the potential of the functional rationality of different social systems and contributing to their legitimation beyond efficiency and performativity by making them part of the symbolic constitution of society.

Instead of constituting the canon of legitimising social imaginaries, a theory of constitutional imaginaries has to adopt both the sociological analysis of systemic paradoxes and the genealogical perspective analysing polyvalence, polysemy, mutual conflicts and societal contingency of specific imaginaries. Imaginaries are a play of societal forces and it is our job to identify and analyse them and their permanent transvaluations of societal values and immanent subversions of rights and principles considered transcendentally justified and verified (MacIntyre 1990: 38–43). In other words, it is our job to identify and understand these self-referential and self-subversive forces of social imaginaries and the interdependence of legitimacies and illegitimacies in positive law, politics and other social systems.

Following this social theoretical perspective and adopting it in the context of positive law and politics, constitutional imaginaries can be defined as systemic constructs describing functionally differentiated modern society as one polity and distinguishing between legal and political legitimacies and illegitimacies in it. The systems of positive law and politics construct their imaginary of constitution as the legitimate form of government.

Constitutional imaginaries are semantic reflections of structural tensions in modern constitutions, such as the distinctions between hierarchical political mastery and civic horizontal autonomy, normative authority and factual self-creation, reason and will or transcendental validity claims and their immanent enforcement. They are responses to the most general question of the possibility of a legitimate political order and collective self-rule materialising in the rule of law.

It, therefore, does not make much sense to stage another replay of constitutional theory's conceptualisations, contradictions and paradoxes of democracy, self-determination and self-authorisation of popular and constitutional sovereignty. Instead, theoretical frameworks and their normative ambitions can be analysed against the background of social imaginaries showing that theories are part of the semantics and dramas evolving in modern constitutional politics. A sociology of constitutional imaginaries can show what their meaning and exercise look like and how they evolve and transform in the systems of positive law and politics.

IV. THE SOCIAL IMAGINARY OF POLITICAL CONSTITUTION: BEYOND THE UNITY OF *TOPOS-ETHNOS-NOMOS*

Imaginaries are both constituting and constituted by society (Blumenberg 1985: 37). Political constitutionalism reveals the duality of social imaginaries as both produced by social systems and stabilising them from the outside. Constitutions are imagined as a constructed artifact typical of historical and social contingencies, yet they are also treated as a natural fact validated by the very existence of its polity. The social construction of legal constitution is thus paradoxically imagined as a natural core of society (Giudice 2020).

Political constitution evolving through structural coupling between the systems of positive law and politics is a strong imaginary of legitimate government itself because of the generally shared belief that legality is the most efficient tool of limiting government and its political power as much as granting citizens their freedom and rights. The very idea of popular self-government and laws expressing the people's collective will and shared values draws on the imaginary of society as unity defined by legal rights and guaranteed by political force.

The constitution of society as one polity defined by the unity of *topos-ethnos-nomos*, that is the unity of territory, people and their laws, informed the rise of modern nations and nationalisms as much as constitutional democratic statehood and its liberal and republican regimes. Society imagines its collective self through the imaginary of legal constitution as expression of unity, commonality and meaningful existence. This imaginary of unity still persists in the current globalised society.

However, the imaginary of polity as one nation living on a given territory under the constitutional rule of law includes the problem of legitimation of legality itself which cannot be answered by exclusive reference to the systemic operations and efficiency of law and politics. Constitutions, therefore, internalise other imaginaries and knowledge regimes as background power of their societal operations to stabilise their legitimation by social and moral plurality, administrative steering, economic prosperity and social justice.

This co-dependence of the imaginary force of constitutions and their legitimation by non-legal social imaginaries is associated with but not limited by the modern constitutional state. Some imaginaries easily evolve beyond and independently of the classic constitutional imaginary of polity as the unity of topos-ethnos-nomos. Market spontaneity and performativity of economic constitutionalism is easy to imagine in the context of European and global constitutionalism. The same can be said about social steering of constitutionalism by administrative governance and reason. On the other hand, the politically mobilised democratic community, so easily imagined and politically used and abused within the structures of modern nation-states, is harder to constitute at supranational and transnational levels.

The post-1945 history and general process of European integration and its legal and political forms thus offer a unique opportunity to study constitutional imaginaries beyond structural and semantic limitations of the modern nation-state and its imaginary unity of topos-ethnos-nomos. Like the modern nation-states, the history of transnational European integration has been informed by two general political goals, namely economic prosperity and social stability. These goals are formulated through imaginaries which are also typical of the nation-states, that is market as free exchange of mutual advantages and benefits, rights equally shared by their subjects and power democratically accountable and operating and conditioned by the public sphere.

However, these typically modern liberal imaginaries cannot be simply translated from the nation-state to the transnational supra-state constitutional structures of the EU which are expected to be socially and morally pluralistic, efficiently and rationally governed, economically prosperous and sufficiently democratised to challenge populist and illiberal responses to the European integration. The imaginaries of constitutional pluralism, administrative calculemus, economically prosperous imperium and the politically mobilised transnational democratic community, therefore, have evolved and operate as societal background power constituting and legitimising European polity.

These imaginaries are constituted by different social systems of administration, economy and politics and further transform and transvaluate the imaginary of political constitution beyond the classic unity of topos-ethnos-nomos. A study of constitutional imaginaries subsequently has to comprehend this transformation and transvaluation of the concept of constitution as much as validations of political constitutions by other social imaginaries and knowledge regimes. A social theory of constitutional imaginaries, therefore, moves from the question of *what* is the social self as constitutional polity to the question of *how* this imaginary of self as societal unity is constituted by different systems and their semantics.

V. IMAGINARIES AND SOCIETAL CONSTITUTIONALISM: A THEORETICAL PERSPECTIVE

As briefly demonstrated, the concept of imaginary is an intrinsic part of social philosophy and theory. Apart from Cassirer and Durkheim's legacies, it is particularly Charles Taylor who engaged in explorations of modern social imaginaries (Taylor 2004).

Normative theoretical and political claims and philosophical speculations are associated with the concept of imagination of *the world as it ought to be* while the sociological concept of imaginary describes *the world as it is* and signifies the specific semantics behind legitimation of existing practices, institutions and societal norms (Loughlin 2015; Přibáň 2018). Unlike the theorised and politically instrumentalised concept of imagination, social imaginaries, however, are neither practical, nor theoretical political constructs. They precede ideological practices and theoretical knowledge of the sociological or any other scientific imagination.

According to Taylor, they are 'common understanding that makes possible common practices and a widely shared sense of legitimacy' (Taylor 2004: 23). They, therefore, provide for meaning to whatever presents itself in society and thus constitute the imaginary order out of the semantic chaos.

A social theoretical inquiry into the imaginary constitution of political power and legal authority subsequently cannot be limited by either jurisprudential matters of legal principles and reasoning, or political matters of power institutions and constellations. It has to dig much deeper into the constitution of modern functionally differentiated society and its pluralistic value structures, unified only through the semantics of higher abstraction of imaginaries. It has to address the following questions: What enables the very process of legitimation of political power by legal rules? What background power operates in political constitutions and their legitimacy? What societal forces constitute the distinction between legitimacies and illegitimacies in law and politics?

I respond to these questions by arguing that constitutional imaginaries function as this societal force (*potentia*) behind political power (*potestas*) and legal authorisation (*auctoritas*). This approach uses different theoretical and methodological sources, especially the combination of Taylor's theory of social imaginaries and Luhmann's autopoietic social systems theory which inspired recent theories of societal constitutionalism, especially the theory of globally operating and fragmented societal constitutions elaborated by Gunther Teubner.

Luhmann's theory of autopoietic social systems showed that social subsystems are constituted by their self-referential constitution of internal meaning. Meaning became part of function. All subsystems of society, such as economy, politics, law, science, religion, and art, are normatively closed, self-referential and self-created – *autopoietic*. In this theoretical framework, society is constituted through autopoiesis of specific functionally differentiated systems. Law and politics perform only specific operations in this general self-constitution of society.

Luhmann famously criticised external and ultimate source of legal validity and reformulated the problem of legitimacy and the principle of justice as an intrinsic value (*Eigenvalue*) of the legal system manifested in its procedures, operations, internal coherence and, most importantly, efficiency as the internal criterion of legitimacy. According to him, justice is 'a contingency formula' and 'the concept of substantive justice ... transforms a tautology into a sequence of arguments and makes something that is seen as highly artificial and contingent from the outside appear quite natural and necessary from the inside' (Luhmann 2004: 445).

The systemic semantics of validity by decisions means that the content of these decisions is indeterminate, but acceptable and validated through generalised 'dispositions of procedures' (Luhmann 1981: 122–50). Political values and principles of representative democracy and human rights are thus turned into internal operations of the constitutional system and, as long as constitutions are considered legally valid and their principles uncontested, no recourse to the idea of substantive political justice and legitimacy is needed and political values are treated as internal sources of the legal system.

According to this view, legitimacy by substantive values and justice is merely an externality of the system of positive law which has no effect on its functionality and potential deficits. Legitimacy is generated through legal procedures and legal validity is secured through decisions made according to these procedures (Luhmann 1983: 28). Political principles and operations such as democratic will-formation, majority rule, constitutional separation of power, individual freedom, security and protection against the abuse of power and violence, are internalised by the system of positive law as procedures imposing constraints on arbitrary political decisions by virtue of their systemic operations and not by their principal nature and normative supremacy in a social and political order.

However, persistent and repetitive jurisprudential, political and public debates regarding constitutional principles, supra-legal values and their legal transvaluations also show that the systems of positive law and politics are expected to be meaningful beyond their function even if this meaning is impossible to achieve by rational consensus or intersubjectively shared experiences. This general expectation of meaning constituted by societal values and its change in the process of transvaluation of values is part of the imaginary self-constitution of society as one constitutional polity.

In this respect, Teubner's theory of societal constitutions represents an original reinterpretation of Luhmann's systems theory by expanding the concept of constitution into non-political systems, regimes and sectors of society. According to Teubner, polity and constitution are not merely political and legal concepts. They signify societal processes of systemic, sectorial, regime and organisational self-constitution. Instead of state-centred political constitutionalism, societal constitutionalism thus draws on a fragmented multiplicity of constitutions evolving in modern society beyond politics (Teubner 2012).

Another important hallmark of Teubner's societal constitutionalism is the epistemological shift from state hierarchies and authority-driven vertical forms of communication to horizontal relations between law and society. This shift has been inspired by Georges Gurvitch's perspective of the sociology of law as science studying the horizontal relations of law (Gurvitch 1947) to other social processes of norm making, the legal formalisation of informal and diffuse social norms, and the multitude of social normativities within the code of law (Teubner 1992).

Against Luhmann's concept of constitutions as organisations of structural coupling between politics and law using the primary coding of power and secondary coding of legality, Teubner argues that it is non-political societal constitutions which externally limit power operating in the systems of politics and law.

According to this view, it is necessary to look for the normative force in society and contrast it to other rules, principles and norms with their different regimes of validity and enforcement. Unlike Luhmann's procedural notion of legitimation, Teubner critically revisits the problem of legitimation but links the question of constitutional subjects to the self-constitution of the system's *episteme* as the source of the system's constitutional authority. This self-constitution includes the intrinsic political tension between the semantics and imaginaries of democracy and technocracy, respectively the public and expert reason.

If constitutional modernity means the differentiation of the economic, political and legal rationalities, part of which was the process of inventing the people as the imaginary subject of sovereign power (Morgan 1998), constitutional postmodernity of societal constitutionalism, according to Teubner, involves abandoning this ultimate subject of politics and constituting non-human and non-political subjects imaginable as fragmentation and the plurality of knowledge regimes and networks within the system of global law (Teubner 2012: 71).

VI. CONCLUDING REMARKS: TOO MUCH POTENTIA, TOO LITTLE AUCTORITAS IN GLOBAL SOCIETAL CONSTITUTIONALISM

Teubner admits that democratic legitimacy and its deficits are 'the Achilles' heel' of transnational regimes and societal constitutionalism (Teubner 2018: 7). Addressing the 'universal core of democracy' (ibid: 11), he even argues that the conditions of global transnationalisation of law require a re-thinking and re-contextualisation of democracy including its relational aspect and self-identification of the authors of rules and decisions and those affected by them even if these new 'constituencies' and 'demoi' of transnational regimes are fluctuating and involve the affected outsiders as much as the corporate members in possession of expert knowledge which are 'the sources of regime authority' (Teubner 2018: 21).

Teubner's comment on democratic legitimacy as the Achilles' heel of transnational constitutionalism indicates a more general problem of global society that is the surplus of power and the shortage of authority. The absence of a global constitutional polity and its fragmentation into different subjects of the varied societal constitutions cannot obscure the fact that these constitutions are power organisations impossible to be exclusively legitimised by their social efficacy and steering capacity.

Using Unger's concept of 'institutional imagination' (ibid: 13), Teubner invites his reader to engage in the construction of new imaginaries of legal legitimation and authorisation suitable for transnational European and global law operating independently of the differences between international and transnational, public and private, or substantive and procedural law. However, Teubner's approach also shows that the theory of societal constitutions cannot ignore constitutional imaginaries of modern national and international politics and law and their potential to address legitimation deficits in globalised societal constitutionalism.

The power of expert knowledge is the source of authority in societal constitutions due to its ability to produce social norms and establish the conditions and criteria of efficient governance. The tension between democracy and technocracy in societal constitutions may be managed by internal constitutions of demoi with the potentia of dissent and its execution through the procedures of self-contestation.

The theory of societal constitutions, therefore, has to analyse not only power without legitimacy but also powerful imaginaries constituting the possibility of legitimation and the 'jurisprudence' of different knowledge regimes – economic, administrative, clinical, educational, scientific, digital etc (Foucault 2003: 36). Understanding this jurisprudence of different disciplines of knowledge assumes identifying and analysing their constitutional imaginaries evolving in different social systems and constituting new subjects of both political and societal constitutions.

The theory of societal constitutions and their jurisprudence of both legal and non-legal knowledge regimes must involve a genealogy of constitutional imaginaries and their legitimation potential. It has to take the opposite direction to the recent sociological theories of legal pluralism and reflexive law promising to replace state law and formal institutions with civil society and informal networks. Power would not become more legitimate if it is constituted in the transnational private and public spheres of global society instead of coercive apparatuses of the nation-state and international organisations. The sheer number of books published on 'global trans-formations' of law, ethics, politics and society in the last several decades actually warns any researcher against hasty promises of new legitimation formulas evolving in this context.

Societal constitutionalism should not disconnect from the idea of sovereignty and territorial control only to reconnect with some reflexive ideas of the collective self-rule of the multitude and the plurality of political subjects constituted at global level. It is not subjects and their actions that constitute the subsystems of societal constitutions and legitimise their power because the subject is constituted by the system itself. Systems do not recognise subjects but produce them. New imaginaries of globally reflexive constitutional identities of the multitudinous self cannot fulfil the promise of substituting the reified essentialist images of nationhood and statehood and legitimise transnational polities by the contested collective identity because these contestations, rather than on the political will and subjects' actions, depend on the systemic rationality of transnational regimes.

The reflexive and differentiated images of demoi pushing back the expansive power of expert knowledge and conditioning it by the varied procedures of democratic legitimation are not enough for the legitimation of transnational societal constitutions. It, rather, is important to analyse how these constitutions manage to turn the affected populations into legitimate demoi and how they translate their specific expert knowledge to the generally shared rules and normative regimes.

REFERENCES

Blumenberg, H (1985) *Work on Myth* (Cambridge, MA, MIT Press).

Bourdieu, P (2014) *On the State: Lectures at the College de France, 1989–1992* (Cambridge, Polity).

Browne, C (2019) 'The Modern Political Imaginary and the Problem of Hierarchy' 33(5) *Social Epistemology* 398.

Cassirer, E (1944) *An Essay on Man: An Introduction to a Philosophy of Human Culture* (New Haven, CT, Yale University Press).

—— (1946a) *Language and Myth* (New York, Harper).

—— (1946b) *The Myth of the State* (New Haven, CT, Yale University Press).

Cotterrell, R (1995) *Law's Community: Legal Theory in Sociological Perspective* (Oxford, Clarendon Press).

Durkheim, E (1898) 'Représentations individuelles et représentations collectives' 6(3) *Revue de Métaphysique et de Morale* 273.

Foucault, F (2003) *'Society Must Be Defended': Lectures at the College de France, 1975–76* (New York, Picador).

Gilleard, C (2018) 'From Collective Representations to Social Imaginaries: How Society Represents Itself to Itself' 5(3) *European Journal of Cultural and Political Sociology* 320.

Giudice, M (2020) *The Social Construction of Law: Potential and Limits* (Cheltenham, Edward Elgar).

Gurvitch, G (1947) *The Sociology of Law* (London, K Paul, Trench, Trubner & Co).

Loughlin, M (2015) 'The Constitutional Imagination' 78(1) *Modern Law Review* 1.

Luhmann N (1981) *Ausdifferenzierung des Rechts: Beiträge zur Rechtssoziologie und Rechtstheorie* (Frankfurt, Suhrkamp).

—— (1983 [1969]) *Legitimation durch Verfahren* (Frankfurt, Surhkamp).

—— (2004) *Law As a Social System* (Oxford, Oxford University Press).

MacIntyre, A (1990) *Three Rival Versions of Moral Enquiry* (London, Duckworth).

—— (2002 [1967]) *A Short History of Ethics* (London, Routledge).

Mannheim, K (1997 [1936]) *Ideology and Utopia* (London, Routledge).

Morgan, ES (1998) *Inventing the People: The Rise of Popular Sovereignty in England and America* (New York, Norton).

Mouffe, C (2000) 'For an Agonistic Model of Democracy' in N O'Sullivan (ed), *Political Theory in Transition* (London, Routledge) 113.

Plato (2000) *The Republic* (ed GRF Ferrari, transl T Griffith; Cambridge, Cambridge University Press).

Přibáň, J (2007) *Legal Symbolism: On Law, Time and European Identity* (Aldershot, Ashgate).

—— (2018) 'Constitutional Imaginaries and Legitimation: On Potentia, Potestas, and Auctoritas in Societal Constitutionalism' (2018) 45(S1) *Journal of Law and Society* 30.

Taylor, C (2004) *Modern Social Imaginaries* (Durham, Duke University Press).

Teubner, G (1992) 'The Two Faces of Janus: Rethinking Legal Pluralism' 13 *Cardozo Law Review* 1443.

—— (2012) *Constitutional Fragments: Societal Constitutionalism and Globalization* (Oxford, Oxford University Press).

—— (2018) 'Quod Omnes Tangit: Transnational Constitutions without Democracy?' 45(S1) *Journal of Law and Society* 5.

Thompson, JB (1984) *Studies in the Theory of Ideology* (Berkeley CA, University of California Press).

32

Public Sentiments on Justice, Legal Consciousness, and the Study of Marginalised Groups

PETER SCHARF SMITH

I. INTRODUCTION

THERE IS A rich international literature on legal consciousness – the many ways in which people understand and use the law. This literature has until recently arguably had a somewhat limited impact in the Nordic countries. Instead, Nordic scholars have studied public sentiments on justice in great detail. However, an unfortunate disconnect between these Nordic studies and the international research on legal consciousness remains. A couple of years ago, I discussed this matter with Reza, who urged me to pursue the idea of bridging the gap between these two schools of research. Hence, it seems very fitting to address this topic in this particular volume where we honour Reza's impressive socio-legal legacy.

Therefore, in this chapter, I will try to combine research on legal consciousness with Nordic studies on public sentiments of justice and I will do this in a discussion of the families and children of prisoners and their marginalised position in the legal system. I will describe this Nordic research as a form of what Ewick and Silbey (1998) called 'legal consciousness as attitude' and as belonging to what has recently been termed the mobilisation school within legal consciousness studies (Chua and Engel 2019). I will go on to explain how the very instrumental and empirically strong Nordic research on public sentiments of justice can help us better understand the possible ways in which the views, values, and attitudes of marginalised groups can achieve representation in our criminal justice systems. With regard to the latter I will use prisoners' families and children as a case study; an example of a group in society that risks experiencing significant inequality and social injustice (Bülow and Lindblom 2020; Condry and Smith 2018) as well as 'legal alienation' (Hertogh 2018). Finally, I argue that adopting a human rights approach is a sound way of addressing this problem in a way that brings the legal consciousness of these families and children to bear on the criminal justice system.

In other words, this chapter aims to synthesise literature on legal consciousness and public sentiments on justice in order to discuss possibilities for creating a more socially just application of the law.

II. PUBLIC SENTIMENTS, SOCIAL JUSTICE AND PRISONERS' CHILDREN

One of my favourite classroom exercises is when I ask my students, often sociology of law and law students, to act as policy makers and decide if and in what way public opinion should inform criminal justice policies and punishment practices. Such a discussion articulates numerous fundamental questions about the role of law and legal institutions in our societies, and I am happy to note that the necessity of adopting a socio-legal perspective becomes immediately apparent even for the most positivistic law students. What is the role of penal law, punishment, and prisons? What do we want to achieve with these institutions? What is justice and who should decide that? And how do we implement policies of punishment? By asking such questions we have begun delving into, for example, retributive and utilitarian perspectives on criminal justice, issues concerning the role of judges and possibly lay-judges when passing sentences, as well as basic questions concerning law making and the autonomy of law in democracies. Who should influence the production and execution of laws and legal standards?

One of the many issues that interest me personally in that regard is the degree to which marginalised groups risk experiencing further marginalisation in the criminal justice system and often do not receive proper representation of their views, situation, and problems (Smith 2018). An example from one of my own areas of research involves the way in which prisoners' families and children easily find their perspective excluded because they become associated with the offender and are not primarily seen as individual law-abiding citizens and rights-holders. The children of prisoners – those who have a meaningful relationship with their imprisoned parent – are a perfect example in that regard. They are innocent and yet punished in the sense that they experience profound loss when a parent is sentenced and often face severe challenges and hardship in maintaining contact during the incarceration (Smith 2014). According to Bülow and Lindblom, these children endure two types of 'objectionable inequalities' when viewed from a social justice perspective, by being 'deprived of resources that are important for ensuring fair equality of opportunity in adulthood, but also because they are likely to suffer inequalities in terms of childhood welfare' (Bülow and Lindblom 2020: 1).

Yet lawmakers are often completely ignorant about the perspective, the legal consciousness, and the rights of these children (Minson 2021). For example, when the then Danish Minister of Justice, Lene Espersen, published a bill in 2005, which, based on the Danes' alleged public sense of justice, ordered three months' home leave suspension for prisoners who appeared late for their commitment to prison, she stated: 'I think it has a pedagogical effect if you cannot visit your family for three months or participate in your child's birthday' (Smith 2014: 222). The Minister of Justice in other words focused exclusively on the prisoner and completely failed to even consider how the children would feel about such legislation. Breaking the contact between children and parents was in this particular context framed as something that was positive for the state and allegedly reflected the public sense of justice. As a result, the children of prisoners (who had a meaningful relationship with their incarcerated parent) were marginalised and their sentiments on justice completely ignored.

Below I will first discuss relevant definitions of *legal consciousness* and *public sentiments on justice*, whereafter I will apply these concepts, along with the term *legal alienation* (Hertogh 2018), in a discussion of prisoners' families and children and their situation vis-à-vis the legal system. Following that, I will suggest a way in which the Nordic research on sentiments on justice can be used as a tool that justifies and enables us to include the perspective of the families of prisoners and ultimately helps us create a more socially just application of the law.

III. LEGAL CONSCIOUSNESS AND SENTIMENTS ON JUSTICE – DEFINITIONS AND SCHOOLS OF RESEARCH

A significant socio-legal literature has accumulated over the years which in various ways deals with how people understand, engage with, and relate to law and legal norms. Some will date this literature back to Eugen Ehrlich and his concept of 'living law' which ventured beyond the written code of law and was meant to capture the 'rules of conduct' which 'a plurality of human beings' considered binding (Ehrlich 1936: 39). Today, this literature is sometimes portrayed as being grouped into studies about either legal culture or legal consciousness (Friedman 2016: 208 ff), where Friedman defines the former as 'people's ideas, expectations, and attitudes about law and the legal system' (ibid: 208). Others talk mainly about a literature on legal consciousness (Hertogh 2018; Chua and Engel 2019) which can be defined as 'the ways in which people experience, understand, and act in relation to law' (Chua and Engel 2019: 336). According to Chua and Engel, legal consciousness thus defined 'comprises both cognition and behaviour, both the ideologies and the practices of people as they navigate their way through situations in which law could play a role' (ibid: 336).

In my opinion, and for the purpose of this chapter, it makes sense to talk about two schools of research, where one comprises research on legal culture and legal consciousness, while the other studies public sentiments on justice, often in the form of sentiments on punishment. I find that these two schools are often separated and, as already stated, part of the point of this chapter is to bring these two fields of research together.

Studies on legal consciousness have been driven especially by American research (Ewick and Silbey 1998; Chua and Engel 2019) and, as explained above, have been directed mainly at ordinary people's relationship with the law. Methodologically speaking, this school has been mostly qualitative and in a number of important cases ethnographic in its approach (Hertogh 2018: 76). In their overview of studies on legal consciousness Chua and Engel divide the literature into three schools: the identity school (focusing on the subjectivity of the individual, their sense of who they are etc); the hegemony school (which sees law as a pervasive and powerful instrument of state control); and the mobilisation school (which is preoccupied with laws potential for transforming society) (Chua and Engel 2019: 337 ff).

Research on public opinion and public sentiments on justice has been both qualitative and quantitative, and aimed especially at sentiments on punishment (Roberts et al 2003; Ryberg and Roberts 2014; Balvig et al 2015). This school of research has been prominent in the Nordic countries where public sentiments on justice have been studied in great detail over the years and large amounts of empirical data have been created through the use of both qualitative and quantitative methods (Balvig 2006; Olaussen 2014; Balvig et al 2015). These Nordic studies have been aimed at measuring people's attitudes and sentiments towards punishment and have studied public opinion with regard to what the level of punishment should be in connection with different types of offences (Balvig 2006; Olaussen 2014; Balvig et al 2015). Some of these studies have included public opinion on different forms of punishment and thereby the execution of punishment itself (Balvig 2015; Frøset et al 2016). The philosophical aspects of public sentiments on justice have also been studied (Ryberg 2006) and it has been attempted to apply this research on the situation of marginalised groups (Smith 2018). The term '*retsfølelse*' (in Danish) or '*rettsfølelse*' (in Norwegian) has often been used in Scandinavia about these sentiments on justice and Ryssdal defines this term as 'an attempt to anchor sentiments on punishment deeply in the Norwegian spirit of the people' which points towards 'a sentiment, a value-based perception or a consciousness of what the *just* solution is' (Ryssdal 2007: 2).

One could arguably label this Nordic research on public sentiments of justice as a form of what Ewick and Silbey (1998) called 'legal consciousness as attitude' and as belonging to the mobilisation school within legal consciousness studies (Chua and Engel 2019). However, the extensive use of quantitative methods (along with qualitative methods) distinguishes the Nordic research from most of the studies on legal consciousness (Hertogh 2018: 77) and arguably so does the pre-occupation with people's visions of what a just application of the law *should* be. The latter, however, make this research very practically useful if one wants to somehow include public sentiments in policy making and law making.

A key feature of much of the Nordic research on public sentiments on justice, which is to a large degree based on Balvig's original Danish study (Balvig 2006), is the analytical distinction between three different forms of sentiments: the general; the informed; and the concrete sense of justice (Balvig et al 2015). The general sense of justice, also sometimes known as the uninformed sense of justice, consists of people's immediate attitude towards general questions such as 'Do you think punishments in this country are too lenient, about right or too harsh?' (Balvig et al 2015: 346). The informed and the concrete senses of justice, on the other hand, are based on increasing levels of knowledge – in the case of the Nordic studies, knowledge about specific criminal acts, their consequences and their context. Together, the three forms of sentiment on justice constitute what Ryberg describe as people's 'normative opinions on punishment' (Ryberg 2006: 19). It is a key finding in the Nordic studies that people's will and wish to punish is significantly reduced when their knowledge and level of information goes up. In other words, while the general sense of justice proscribes high levels of punishment, the informed sense of justice produces much lower levels of punishment, and the concrete sense of justice even lower (Balvig 2006; Balvig et al 2015).

In the following I shall turn to the case of prisoners' families and invoke concepts from the school of legal consciousness research in order to understand the situation and perspective of these families and especially their children. Following that I will employ the Nordic school of research on public sentiments on justice and the concepts of informed and concrete sense of justice in an attempt to sketch out some basic elements in a more socially just application of law in this area.

IV. UNDERSTANDING PRISONERS' FAMILIES – THEIR LEGAL CONSCIOUSNESS AND THEIR SENTIMENTS ON JUSTICE

Prisoners' families and their children of course constitute a huge and varied group of people which likely have very different views on justice and punishment. For some families and children, it will be positive to have a violent and disruptive partner/parent removed from the home and, in that sense, imprisonment can have not only negative but also positive effects. Nevertheless, all those families and children who have a meaningful contact with the imprisoned parent are at risk of encountering a legal system, a prison system, a police force, and more generally representatives of the state which, and who, they find have little focus on their views, needs, and problems. This has been described as an 'upside down' experience of the penal system and the criminal justice system (Smith 2014: 79): a situation where prisoners' families and children risk experiencing state authorities as enemies rather than allies in a 'process towards social end even administrative exclusion' (ibid: 81).

Examples are abundant from many different jurisdictions. A Dutch study, for example, describes how witnessing a violent arrest can leave traces and 'sensations the child will never forget' (Nijnatten 1998), and Danish research demonstrates how such arrests can result in more or less traumatic experiences for all involved parties, including the police (Smith 2014). An English study demonstrates how families of long-term prisoners find themselves caught up in a 'web of shame', suffering from stigmatisation from being associated with serious offenders (Condry 2007: 66) and an influential American study describes how prisoners' relatives experience 'secondary prisonization', meaning that the negative effects of imprisonment are transferred to the relatives in various ways (Comfort 2008). For example, as demonstrated in a study of a mother-child visitation programme in an American prison, children of incarcerated parents experienced 'changes in their schedules and routines' and visits provoked 'anxiety, confusion, concern and attention' over 'the jail's effort to discipline their bodies and regulate their emotions' (Aiello and McCorkel 2018: 16). Very concrete examples include a Danish boy, who remembers a prison officer who said 'visiting time is over' as a 'stupid pig', and a girl who witnessed her father's arrest and henceforth became afraid of the police (Smith 2014: 80). According to French psychologist Alain Bouregba, a child's sense of community can be destroyed in such situations and replaced by withdrawal and isolation, and eventually antipathy towards society (ibid: 81).

Again, all this of course depends very much on the family situation and especially the relationship between the child and the incarcerated parent. In some cases, imprisonment can be beneficial for the involved children (Smith 2014: ch 13). But, as illustrated above, many families and children suffer in such situations and experience significant problems accordingly. And, as demonstrated, this can seriously affect the way that these families and children experience society and state representatives such as police officers and prison officers. Several studies also report how encountering the legal system and all the laws governing remand, imprisonment, prison visits etc can be a stressful and overwhelming experience. For example, many families know little about their rights regarding visitation and sometimes they are not even notified about the detention (Condry and Smith 2019). A British study found that 'the initial process of arrest and remand' was associated with disruption of the family income, disorientation, loss, and uncertainty (Codd 2008: 52). As explained by Condry 'It is important to look at the whole criminal justice process (…) relatives are often very involved with each stage of the investigation and some cases can take years to process from discovery to sentencing' (Condry 2007: 4). Unfortunately, this in no way means that the legal system and its institutions are well designed to take the perspective and rights of these families into account. On the contrary, the criminal justice system is typically designed to balance the state's use of power against the rights of prisoners, while third parties such as prisoners' relatives have been left out of the equation (Smith 2018; Lanskey et al 2018).

Taken together, one could say that the legal consciousness and the sentiments on justice of these families and children has generally been overlooked or simply ignored in the continuous development of the criminal justice system. Using Ewick and Silbey's terminology, we can speculate that many families of prisoners are at risk of experiencing a sliding scale in terms of their legal consciousness, where they might start out displaying a 'before the law' attitude towards the law which could easily change to a 'with the law' and finally an 'against the law' legal consciousness given the problems and situations they face and the way they are met by the state (Ewick and Silbey 1998: 47 ff).

Employing Hertogh's innovative approach, it seems reasonable to argue that many prisoners' families risk experiencing 'legal alienation' (Hertogh 2018). Hertogh defines legal alienation 'as a cognitive state of psychological disconnection from official state law and the justice system' and goes on to explain that when 'people are listening to the discourse of the law, they are no longer able to identify their voice at all' (ibid: 14).[1] This seems to be a very precise description of the above-quoted boy's experience of having a visit with his imprisoned father stopped as well as the girl's recollection of her father being arrested. These citizens could clearly not identify with the law they encountered in those particular situations.

Hertogh introduce four normative profiles to describe people's attitudes towards law: 'legalists', 'loyalists', 'cynics' and 'outsiders' (ibid: 57 ff). Two of these are especially relevant in the present context, namely the 'cynics' and the 'outsiders'. The former display what Hertogh calls 'informed alienation', while the latter exhibit 'uninformed alienation' (ibid: 58). Both positions are likely for those who find themselves harmed by the imprisonment of a relative in extensive ways and who will have a hard time finding the law and the practical workings of the criminal justice system and its institutions fair and just.

---

[1] Hertogh distinguishes between four dimensions of legal alienation, 'legal meaninglessness', 'legal powerlessness', 'legal cynicism' and 'legal value isolation', which all seem relevant in a further description of the legal consciousness of prisoners' families (Hertogh 2018: 49 ff).

Hertogh furthermore criticises classic legal consciousness research for not treating law as a dependent variable – ie law is treated as state law, a fixed entity that people keep coming back, despite not achieving the results they want (ibid: 68 ff). Instead Hertogh urges us to make law part of the enquiry and not only ask how people relate to the law but also ask what people 'experience as law' (ibid: 69). Interestingly, the Scandinavian research on sentiments on justice also ventures beyond understanding how people think about the law by posing a different but extremely useful question, namely how people think the law *should* operate. I will return to this dimension below, which arguably let us come even closer to sentiments about what justice is and what it looks like in practice.

The critical perspective of legal consciousness research in general, and the application of the term legal alienation in particular, can help us understand the situation of prisoners' families and children vis-à-vis the legal system. The Nordic studies on public sentiments on justice and the distinction between the three different levels of sentiments can arguably help us understand what to do about it. At least, it can form a starting point from which we can plot a way out of the legal alienation of marginalised groups such as the children of prisoners. In the following I will try to demonstrate how.

V. FROM THE UNINFORMED TO THE INFORMED SENSE OF JUSTICE – THE NORDIC STUDIES

The Nordic research on public sentiments on justice began in earnest with Balvig's large scale study of Danish attitudes towards punishment (Balvig 2006). The background was a wave of penal populism, with politicians constantly arguing that stiffer sentences should be introduced to satisfy the public sentiments on justice – a phenomenon which has only become more prolific since and has characterised the legal policy debate in many countries for decades (Roberts et al 2003; Ryberg and Roberts 2014; Frøset et al 2016). The Danish study from 2006 has since been repeated in the Nordic countries of Norway, Sweden, Finland, and Iceland, as well as several times in Denmark (Balvig et al 2015) and in Greenland (Balvig 2015).

All this Nordic research clearly demonstrates that the general sense of justice calls for tougher punishment, but that this attitude rests on misunderstandings and a lack of knowledge about the criminal justice system, sentences and punishment (Balvig 2006; Balvig et al 2015; Olaussen 2014). Measuring the informed and the concrete sense of justice produces very different results and it becomes clear that the will and wish to punish diminishes as the level of knowledge increases (Balvig et al 2015). The Nordic studies uniformly show how in six different cases of criminal behaviour people tended to punish milder than the courts would when they knew the facts and circumstances surrounding the case – that is, when their informed and concrete sense of justice was probed (ibid). The problem is that these informed attitudes are generally not uncovered or included in the daily media/political debate on crime and punishment. On the contrary, the politicians are speaking directly to the uninformed sense of justice when they campaign for more and tougher punishment. And indeed, international research demonstrates that studies of the general sense of justice will always produce a wish for more punishment, regardless of whether or not sentences have been stiffened in the preceding years (Balvig 2006: 11). In that sense, the general perception of justice can be described as a sort of bottomless reservoir of attitudes and emotions proscribing more and more revenge and punishment based on wrongful assumptions about the crime, punishment and the criminal justice system (Smith 2007). Interestingly, this seems to be the very way in which law makers in Denmark have envisaged the use of public sentiments on justice in connection with prison law in the sense that every time such sentiments are invoked as a legal consideration in the law they are done so in way that presupposes their punitive nature (Engbo 2005). But as we have seen, people's informed and concrete sentiments on justice generally support milder forms, and lower levels, of punishment.

VI. GIVING MARGINALISED GROUPS AND THEIR SENTIMENTS ON JUSTICE REPRESENTATION

It is beyond the scope of this chapter to fully discuss in what way (or if) public sentiments on justice should be reflected in the punishment system. Indeed, there no general agreement among scholars exactly as to how – or indeed whether or not – public sentiments on justice are relevant and should feed into actual policies on, and practices of, punishment. Ryberg and Roberts distinguish between three different models in that regard: (a) a 'direct importation model', according to which 'community values should be directly imported into sentencing practice'; (b) an 'exclusionary model', according to which 'community values are explicitly excluded from the evolution of any penal policies'; and (c) a 'qualified public input' model, which represents 'an intermediate position' between the other two (Ryberg and Roberts 2014: 5). Several authors follow the last model and many argue that some level of public input is required in a democracy (Hough and Roberts 2012; Olaussen 2014), which is also a starting point here in the present chapter.

It seems clear to me that, if we want to acknowledge and incorporate the emotions and experiences of prisoners' families in a model of 'qualified input' of public sentiments on justice, we should, in other words, disregard the uninformed and turn to the informed and the concrete public sentiments on justice.[2] The Nordic research demonstrates the relative mildness and leniency displayed by the public when their informed and concrete sentiments on justice are measured and these attitudes would be much more inclusive and more understandable for many families of prisoners (and would also help us avoid adopting overly punitive policies that risk disrupting utilitarian purposes of punishment in general). This would logically help minimise the risk of these families experiencing legal alienation. In that sense, it would arguably strengthen social cohesion in society if informed and concrete sentiments on justice were to influence criminal justice policy towards marginalised groups in society in general.

---

[2] Olaussen argues similarly and highlights how the more punitive general sentiments of justice are voiced by people 'who don't know the actual level of punishment, and underestimate it' (Olaussen 2014: 98).

Unfortunately, it is not an easy task to limit and control the influence of general sentiments on justice. Seen from an academic point of view it is furthermore problematic that researchers interested in what has been termed *principled sentencing* seems to have focused almost exclusively on the effects of punishment on the offender, whereas the broader effects on society and on, for example, prisoners' families have been ignored (Smith 2018).

Regardless, if we accept the 'qualified public input' model outlined earlier, and then proceed using the informed and concrete sense of justice, then this arguably makes for a very sensible way of imbedding the sentiments of prisoners' families in our criminal justice practices. By including these informed and concrete sentiments on justice, we arguably create a system of punishment that increasingly takes the involved parties and the social context of the crime into account and as a result produces a more lenient and balanced criminal justice system that will cause less harm. Below I will argue that a human rights perspective makes for a sound way of operationalising such an approach. First, however, we have to deal with a potential problem, namely victims of crime and their sentiments on justice.

VII. VICTIMS OF CRIME AND THE FAMILIES OF PRISONERS

Naturally, if we begin to give increasing voice to the sentiments of certain groups in society we might risk affecting the sentiments of other groups. Again, it is beyond the scope of this chapter to fully engage in a thorough discussion of the possible consequences in this regard but it seems obvious that we need to consider victims of crime in the present context. Indeed, the lobbying of victim interest groups has in some jurisdictions contributed to increasingly punitive policies (Hoyle 2012: 406). Nevertheless, other victim interest groups have refrained from commenting on sentencing (ibid: 405) and supporting victims' rights does not necessarily lead to harsher punishment but can, among many other things, be a matter of securing victim participation in the criminal justice process and during the trial (Laugerud and Langballe 2017). As explained by Hoyle, this is not a zero-sum question, as the use of restorative justice demonstrates (Hoyle 2012: 414 ff). The introduction of restorative justice and victim-offender mediation has shown that it is possible to help victims while at the same time introducing alternatives to imprisonment. Although the evidence is not uniform, there is generally high victim satisfaction with restorative justice programs (ibid: 418) even though these often entail meeting out a milder sanction for the offender. In the words of Hoyle, restorative justice can therefore 'serve as a 'cooling device' to our current 'hot criminological climate' (ibid: 419) and in that sense help create policies that will aid victims of crime as well as the families of prisoners. Additionally, and crucially, the relatives of the incarcerated are typically victims themselves and in that sense in some ways share fate with the direct victims of the criminal act. This is particularly evident in the case of the involved children, who in most cases are clearly innocent casualties of an act of crime (even though it was not directed at them personally) and the way that the criminal justice system has chosen to deal with that.

VIII. MARGINALISED GROUPS, SENTIMENTS
ON JUSTICE AND HUMAN RIGHTS

There are of course many possible ways of adjusting the criminal justice system in order to include the views, values, and sentiments of certain groups in society more than presently. What I will do in the following is point to one possible avenue in this regard which has been more or less universally designed to include and secure the rights of minorities, marginalised groups, and more generally those at risk of oppression in society.[3] I am thinking about international and regional human rights systems, which not only aim to secure the rights of families and children in general but which in recent years have also witnessed significant development with regard the families of prisoners in particular (Smith 2016). Human rights soft law and human rights standards have in recent years increasingly taken the perspective of this group, and especially the involved children, into account (Smith 2018). During the last 15 years or so human rights standards have been influenced significantly by research on the families of prisoners and especially on the children of prisoners. As a result, the UN and the European Council (along with many others) have developed very concrete recommendations and standards describing how the rights and needs of the children of prisoners should be respected throughout every stage of the criminal justice system (Donson and Parkes 2021; Smith and Villman 2021). Such standards include everything from taking the situation and needs of children into account during the arrest of the parent to, for example, identifying and considering the best interest of the child in connection with sentencing. Broadly speaking, respecting such standards will likely go a long way towards making sure that the views and sentiments of the children and families of prisoners are taken much more into account. Indeed, this development in human rights standards has been accompanied by reforms in some jurisdictions which to a certain extent have begun to implement the rights of these children and thereby, arguably, have increased the chance of making them feel more included and less alienated. Concrete examples include reform projects in Denmark, Sweden and Norway, which have created much more child-friendly visiting conditions in prisons (Smith 2015).

Taken together, and based upon the above theoretical reflections concerning legal consciousness and legal alienation, the empirical research on public sentiments on justice, as well as the case of prisoners' families and children, I think that there is good reason to hypothesise that adopting a 'qualified public input' model in criminal justice reforms, and invoking informed and concrete sentiments on justice when doing so, can form the basis for a more inclusive and a more socially just application of the law towards marginalised groups in society. And, in the case of the children of prisoners, an increasing implementation of human rights standards in the area is very likely a sound way of operationalising such an approach, since these standards are designed to take the best interests of the child into account throughout every stage of the criminal justice process.

---

[3] For a discussion of the more or less universal nature of human rights in light of post-colonial theory (among other things), see Mende 2021.

REFERENCES

Aiello, BL and McCorkel, JA (2018) '"It Will Crush You Like a Bug": Maternal Incarceration, Secondary Prisonization, and Children's Visitation' 20(3) *Punishment & Society* 351.

Balvig, F (2006) *Danskernes syn på straf* (Copenhagen, Advokatrådet).

—— (2015) 'Retsfølelse og retsfornuft – i Grønland' 102(1) *Nordisk Tidsskrift for Kriminalvidenskab* 1.

Balvig, F, Gunnlaugsson, H, Jerre, K, Tham, H and Kinnunen, A (2015) 'The Public Sense of Justice in Scandinavia: A Study of Attitudes towards Punishments' 12(3) *European Journal of Criminology* 342.

Bülow, W and Lindblom, L (2020) 'The Social Injustice of Parental Imprisonment' 7(2) *Moral Philosophy and Politics*.

Chua, LJ and Engel, DM (2019) 'Legal Consciousness Reconsidered' 15 *Annual Review of Law and Social Science* 335.

Codd, H (2008) *In the Shadow of Prison: Families, Imprisonment and Criminal Justice* (Cullompton, Willan).

Comfort, M (2008) *Doing Time Together: Love and Family in the Shadow of the Prison* (Chicago, University of Chicago Press).

Condry, R (2007) *Families Shamed: The Consequences of Crime for Relatives of Serious Offenders* (Cullompton, Willan).

Condry, R and Smith, PS (2018) *Prisons, Punishment and the Family. Towards a New Sociology of Punishment?* (Oxford, Oxford University Press).

—— (2019) 'A Holistic Approach to Prisoners' Families – from Arrest to Release' in M Hutton and D Moran (eds), *The Palgrave Handbook of Prison and the Family* (Palgrave).

Donson, F and Parkes, A (eds) (2021) *Parental Imprisonment and Children's Rights* (Routledge).

Ehrlich, E (1936) *Fundamental Principles of the Sociology of Law* (Harvard University Press).

Engbo, HJ (2005) *Straffuldbyrdelsesret* (Jurist- og Økonomforbundets forlag).

Ewick, P and Silbey, SS (1998) *The Common Place of Law: Stories from Everyday Life* (Chicago, University of Chicago Press).

Friedman, LM (2016) *Impact. How Law Affects Behavior* (Harvard, Harvard University Press).

Frøset, AM, Gröning, L and Wandall, RH (2016) *Rettsfølelse i strafferettssystemet: Perspektiver fra teori og praksis* (Gyldendal Juridisk).

Hertogh, M (2018) *Nobody's Law. Legal Consciousness and Legal Alienation in Everyday Life* (Palgrave).

Hough, M and Roberts, J (2012) 'Public Opinion, Crime, and Criminal Justice' in R Morgan et al (eds), *The Oxford Handbook of Criminology*, 5th edn (Oxford, Oxford University Press) 279.

Hoyle, C (2012) 'Victims, the Criminal Process, and Restorative Justice' in R Morgan et al (eds), *The Oxford Handbook of Criminology*, 5th edn (Oxford, Oxford University Press) 398.

Lanskey, C et al (2018) 'Prisoners' Families and the Referred Pains of Imprisonment' in R Condry and PS Smith (eds), *Prisons, Punishment and the Family: Towards a New Sociology Of Punishment* (Oxford, Oxford University Press).

Laugerud, S and Langballe, Å (2017) 'Turning the Witness Stand into a Speaker's Platform: Victim Participation in the Norwegian Legal System as Exemplified by the Trial against Anders Behring Breivik' 51(2) *Law & Society Review* 227.

Mende, J (2021) 'Are Human Rights Western – and Why Does It Matter? A Perspective from International Political Theory' 17(1) *Journal of International Political Theory* 38.

Minson, S (2021) *Maternal Sentencing and the Rights of the Child* (Palgrave).

Nijnatten, C (1998) *Detention and Development: Perspectives of Children of Prisoners* (Forum Verlag Godesberg).

Olaussen, LP (2014) 'Concordance between Actual Level of Punishment and Punishments Suggested by Lay People – but with Less Use of Imprisonment' 2(1) *Bergen Journal of Criminal Law & Criminal Justice* 69.

Roberts, J, Stalans, L, Indermaur, D and Hough, M (2003) *Penal Populism and Public Opinion* (Oxford: Oxford University Press).

Ryberg, J (2006) *Retsfølelsen. En bog om straf og etik* (Copenhagen, Roskilde).

Ryberg, J and Roberts, J (eds) (2014) *Popular Punishment. On the Normatice Significance of Public Opinion* (New York, Oxford University Press).

Ryssdal, A (2007) 'Den allmenne rettsfølelse' 11 *Veiviser eller villeder i strafferetten, Advokatbladet* 1.

Smith, PS (2007) 'Straf, retsfølelse og reality TV' 1 *Social Politik*.

—— (2014) *When the Innocent Are Punished: The Children of Imprisoned Parents* (Basingstoke, Palgrave).

—— (2015) 'Reform and Research – Re-connecting Prison and Society in the 21st Century' 4(1) *International Journal for Crime, Justice and Social Democracy* 33.

—— (2016) 'Prisons and Human Rights – Past, Present and Future Challenges' in L Weber, E Fishwick and M Marmo (eds), *The Routledge International Handbook of Criminology and Human Rights* (Routledge) 525.

—— (2018) 'Prisoners' Families, Public Opinion, and the State: Punishment and Society from a Family and Human Rights Perspective' in R Condry and PS Smith (eds), *Prisons, Punishment and the Family. Towards a New Sociology of Punishment?* (Oxford, Oxford University Press).

Smith, PS and Villman, E (2021) 'Prisons, Families and Human Rights: from Prisoners' Rights to Rights of Prisoners' Children' in F Donson and A Parkes (eds), *Parental Imprisonment and Children's Rights* (Routledge).

33

Challenging Legal Orthodoxy: New Orientations in Space and Time in Discourses Over Land Tenure

ANNE GRIFFITHS

I. INTRODUCTION

I FEEL HONOURED to be making a contribution to an anthology commemorating the scholarship of Reza Banakar. Over his career, Reza was passionate about engaging with law and legal processes from a variety of social-scientific standpoints with different methodological orientations. This is evident from his two editions of [*An Introduction to*] *Law and Social Theory* (2002; 2013) that he co-edited with Max Travers, along with their volume on *Theory and Method in Socio-Legal Research* (2005) to which I, and many others, had the privilege to contribute. Working as a lawyer at Edinburgh Law School I very much appreciated his open-mindedness towards legal studies in general and his willingness to engage with a wide variety of perspectives. His approach was instrumental in encouraging me to develop my ideas about legal pluralism that involved an interdisciplinary perspective, drawing on anthropological approaches centred on the acquisition of empirical data through ethnography in the global South.

My chapter for this anthology is founded on my recent book *Transformations on the Ground: Space and the Power of Land in Botswana*, published by Indiana University Press in 2019. It is based on research carried out on and off in Botswana, southern Africa over 30 years and draws on a variety of sources. These include archival records, examination of formal laws in court, and land board records. It covers fieldwork on unwritten oral customary law and participant observation of disputes and interviews with government personnel, members of non-governmental organisations and local citizens. It also draws on extended oral life histories on everyday life of families from Molepolole village that cover five generations. Thus it draws on a diverse range of methods in its acquisition of data.

The book formed part of an inter- and trans-disciplinary international project on Framing the Global at Indiana University's Centre for the Study of Global Change.

This was funded by Indiana University Press and the Mellon Foundation (USA). I think Reza would have approved of this project given its breadth of vision and cross disciplinary nature. As part of our fellowship, the 15 fellows were asked to pick a topic through which to address the global. Topics included, 'displacement', 'materiality', 'affect' and 'genealogies' I opted for the study of land and its legal regulation, and I hope to do justice to Reza's pioneering spirit by challenging legal orthodoxy in this area by moving beyond a linear model of space and time on which it is based.

II. LAND AS A LENS FOR EXPLORING NOTIONS OF SPACE AND TIME?

Land is a global resource that has come under pressure driven by the demands of world population growth and dispossessed populations brought about by war, famine and economic migration. It has also been promoted by the need to generate food security and energy. These imperatives, along with longer term goals of securing environmental sustainability and responses to climate change, constitute formidable challenges to control over and use of land worldwide. Thus, the pressure on access to and control over land, and the uses to which is it put not only transcends nation-states. It forms a core component of macro-perspectives that centre on national, international and transnational engagement with trade and commerce in the global market place. At the same time it also forms a critical component at the micro-level of individual, family and household provision for shelter, livelihoods and processes of capital accumulation.

Thus land embodies a space that not only embraces a grounded, physical and territorial place, but also represents a more intangible universe, where space is viewed as a product that embodies social relationships with intersecting dimensions. These make it clear, as Lefèbvre (1991) has observed, that space cannot be divorced from ideology or politics because it cannot be viewed as 'a natural medium that stands outside of the way it is conceived' (Crang and Thrift 2000: 3).

Adopting this perspective on space allows for diverse interpretations of how relations to land are constituted and makes visible the ways in which they may vary, complement, overlap, or even come into conflict with one another and with the broader competing global perspectives in operation at any moment in time. Time and space are intertwined to differing effect: on the one hand, adopting a linear approach to time with the goal of annihilating certain types of space (Harvey 1990); and on the other, by making time subservient to space in the recognition of social states of being. Thus the temporal dimensions of space are important for 'space without time is as impossible as time without space' (Crang and Thrift 2000: 3) so that temporality forms an integral part of space (Khan 2009). This relationship exists because human behaviour, including the realm of law, 'is located in and constructed in space' (Low and Lawrence-Zúñiga 2003: 1) that is linked through time to human experience. As such, it involves a plurality of spheres that, as Fabian (1983) demonstrates, give rise to a number of different interpretations of time at different moments in history.

III. CONTEXTUALISING LAW: HOW LAND IS DEALT WITH IN BOTSWANA

Debates on land in Botswana are shaped by the country's encounter with colonialism. Formerly known as the Bechuanaland Protectorate, it was under British indirect rule from 1885 to 1966 when it acquired independence. It inherited a framework within which the use, control over and allocation of land was regulated according to how it was classified. As a result three types of land tenure exist.

The first involves tribal land held in customary land tenure under the Tribal Land Act (Cap 32.02) enacted in 1968 and re-enacted in 2018. This recognised the communal forms of tenure that are the basis of Africans relationship to land. The second type is state land, previously crown land administered by the Bechuanaland Protectorate. Most of this type of land is found in the urban areas. The third type of land is freehold land, created for settlers during the colonial era. This type of tenure recognised individual ownership in land with a right to free and undisturbed possession, largely in relation to agricultural land.

The different types of land tenure have different legal rules governing them. They are the product of different spatial and temporal logics that reveal how social and property relations are maintained at any given historical moment, providing scope for differing and contested claims to land today. Among these systems a major distinction is drawn between tribal land, that is communal land (which is 70 per cent of the land in Botswana), and state or freehold land.

The former, that is tribal land, while enshrined in statute, derives from understandings about oral, unwritten customary law as compared to the written statutory laws that apply to state and freehold land. All three systems have their roots in the colonial past. As Chanock (1985: 5) has noted, law was 'the cutting edge of colonialism' and it continues to play a major role today in the way that land is dealt with. It combines aspects of unwritten customary law that apply to 'tribal' land as well as statutory law (involving registration of title) derived from European and Cape colonial law. Indeed, Morolong and Ng'ong'ola observe (2007: 143) that 'the unique features of contemporary tribal or customary land tenure in Botswana can be retraced to the manner in which the country's plural land tenure system was constructed during the first few decades of colonial rule'.

This land tenure system was one that promoted a particular colonial vision of social order and property rights that has come to reflect traditional legal orthodoxy when it comes to property rights worldwide. It reflected an ideological quest for power through the inscription of law on territory. For as the Benda-Beckmanns and Wiber (2006: 2) observe, property regimes 'cannot be captured in one-dimensional political, economic or legal models'.

Nonetheless, the colonial model of law sought to make them so by creating separate legal regimes that distinguished between them, and that were applicable to, the colonisers and the colonised. This approach, which embodied separate and parallel systems of law (Hooker 1975), was one in which one land regime applied to the colonisers while another applied to the colonised assigned to 'tribal areas'[1] by their colonial

---

[1] The term 'tribe' continues to feature as a formal legal term under the formal legal and administrative structure in Botswana today.

overlords. As a result colonialism 'created and maintained boundaries through dualistic or pluralistic legal structures, boundaries in physical space defined and managed by laws and regulations' (Home 2012: 9).[2] This resulted in complex relations to land through spaces embodying territorial, political, economic, and social relations. These underpin contemporary dilemmas that transformations over time have brought about with regard to pursuing policies on land and legal reform.

IV. CONTEMPORARY AND INTERNATIONAL APPROACHES TO LAND TENURE

How land is dealt with is not just of importance to Botswana. It also features at the heart of international and transnational approaches to sustainable development and the eradication of poverty. A 2008 report by the Commission on the Legal Empowerment of the Poor and the United Nations (UN) Development Program identified property (which includes land) as one of four pillars of legal empowerment (Commission on Legal Empowerment of the Poor 2008). This was along with access to justice and the rule of law, labour, and business rights. The report marked a recognition of the need to adopt a more holistic approach to development and poverty, including attention to human rights as more broadly construed to include social and economic rights (such as rights to food, housing, water, and health), along with concepts of good governance, accountability, and transparency.

All these aspects form part of the 2030 UN Agenda for Sustainable Development that was agreed to by 193 world leaders in 2015 (UN 2015a; 2015b). In doing so, they sought to create an international, overarching framework within which transnational organisations such as the UN and World Bank can promote global development. The range of its remit, in space both territorial and normative, represents what Walker (2014: 60) observes is an 'unprecedented ... planetary legal regime'. Its global focus is aimed, in particular, at meeting the needs of 'developing countries-including African countries' (UN 2015b: 25).

Although the agreed-on agenda seeks to balance economic and humanistic needs, the functional vehicle within which these needs are being met is based on a strategy that focuses on a particular paradigm of governance based on the legal protection of a Western conception of property rights. This strategy provides for a systematic identification of land, often through a cadastral survey, that confers ownership on an individual through registration of title in a public institution such as the Registry of Deeds. In adopting *this* approach to property rights, it is argued that greater certainty in land rights will be created, which will empower the poor to unlock their capital in land through obtaining access to credit that can be used to generate greater economic productivity and wealth.

The assumption on which this argument is based derives from a view that the main cause of poverty for the poor is their lack of access to formal property rights

---

[2] This demarcation of legal systems into separate spheres was one advanced by the coloniser. However these systems did not stand in isolation to one another but did interact. For a discussion on this see Griffiths (1997).

resulting in their inability to use their land productively to engage with market forces. This view has been, and continues to be, adopted by the World Bank, a view heavily influenced by the work of Hernando de Soto (2000), who has championed the adoption of formal property law in the developing world in order to facilitate economic development for the poor.[3] Economic development, he maintains, would be achieved through the legalisation of assets (currently considered dead capital because it is held on an informal basis) that would enable the poor to benefit from the functions of formal capital to maximise their assets.

The concept of universal legal protection also informs the report of the Commission for the Legal Empowerment of the Poor (2008), which posits that universal legal protection is necessary in order to promote access to justice and effective property rights that are currently lacking because poor people do not have access to a well-functioning justice system that ensures their property and businesses are legally recognised. This Western approach to property rights forms part of a broader, neoliberal approach to a global agenda geared toward the opening up of borders and markets through the free flow of capital, supported by access to financial services, including credit.

This approach has been subject to much criticism because it makes particular assumptions about causal connections between formal property, economic development, and poverty. It has also been subject to criticism because it 'pays little attention to locally owned definitions of human being and well-being' that are crucial factors in creating globally sustainable and equitable human progress (CIGI 2012: 3). This is because of its narrow focus on a particular form of land tenure, which is presented as part of an inevitable historical process based on an evolutionary and linear theory of rights. This follows on from Sir Henry Maine's observations on the evolution of society as being one based on a move from status to contract (1861: ch V).

As a result, the underlying basis on which the governance framework is based is never questioned, but rather where there are failures in the achievement of sustainable development goals they are simply 'attributed to the people, systems, and governments of the Global South, or sub-Saharan Africa' (CIGI 2012: 3). This attitude is inferred in observations such as the following: 'Sub-Saharan Africa is not on track to achieve any of the Millennium Development Goals (that preceded Sustainable Development Goals) and extreme poverty persists on every continent' (Commission on Legal Empowerment of the Poor 2008: 1). This assumption is founded on a Western construct, grounded in aggregation and averages, that fails to address the needs of the very poorest. Indeed, as Home (2012: 11) has noted, neoliberal aid and policies that include land titling 'as a precondition of World Bank structural adjustment from the 1980s' hardly address 'the basic inequalities in ownership and access to land'.[4] The failure to take adequate notice of existing inequalities subsisting in the South often leads to misguided assertions, such as that Mozambique

---

[3] For critiques of de Soto's position see Benda-Beckmann (2003); Manji (2006); Nyamu-Musembi (2007) and Peters (2007).

[4] Manji (2001) addresses this point, noting that what is really at stake here is not so much property rights but issues of democratisation and governance.

'is way "off track" despite strong improvements' (CIGI 2012: 3). Such statements gloss over the need for an analysis of structural interests, access, and equity in addressing questions of sustainable development (Amanor and Moyo 2008) rather than focusing on the more narrow and limited technical management of land and resources. As a result, despite the global agenda to empower the poor through land ownership what has resulted in Botswana is 'a persistent narrowing in the definition of those with primary rights to land' (Peters 2004: 292). Such a development is not an isolated occurrence. For Thompson (1993) has documented how the wider range of rights associated with the 'commons' in Britain were gradually narrowed and whittled away in favour of property owners. Resort to legal regulation in courts played an important part in this process that resulted in 'the right of use ... [becoming] not a use but a property [right]' (Thompson 1993: 135). For Peters (1994: 190) this represents a process in which:

> holders of (usually) small areas of customary land in Africa are represented as 'backward', or 'conservative' and obstacles to the 'modernisation' of agriculture'. It was accompanied by the use of law 'to force registration and titling to land', thus 'converting socially managed land into a fungible property, freeing it for the market. (Peters 2014: 190)

What is clear is that the agenda for change, promoting land reform around the world, deals more with policies and techniques of implementation rather than addressing underlying substantive concerns referred to by Amanor and Moyo about redistributing land more equitably.

V. BOTSWANA'S RESPONSE TO GLOBAL APPROACHES TO LAND TENURE

Botswana did not opt to introduce radical changes to land reform when it became independent in 1966. Instead it elected to pursue a strategy of 'adaptation' (Bruce 1998), which sought to merge 'some aspects of traditional tenure arrangements with the modern, that is characterized by private ownership and the creation of the land market' (Ijagbemi 2006: 318). This strategy, manifested in the creation of the Tribal Land Act, continues to guide Botswana's governmental approach to land reform today, as evidenced by Botswana's (National) Land Policy approved by Parliament in 2015 and in its reformulated Tribal Land Act of 2018.

VI. THE ROLE OF SPACE AND TIME IN CONSTRUCTING LAND TENURE RELATIONS

In these processes, in which social relations to land are constituted, it is important to acknowledge the role that space and time play in their construction. For it is clear, as Blomley (1994: 24) observes, that all 'social and political life occurs in time and space'. As Massey (2013) notes, a site in space 'isn't so much about physical locality as much as relations between human beings'. Thus space is not a pre-determined, fixed entity, but is flexible and multi-faceted. Thus, where space represents that dimension of the world in which we live, it is one, according to Massey (ibid), within which 'distinct trajectories co-exist'. However, while space represents 'the domain of things being, existing at the same time' (ibid) it is clear that space and time 'are intimately connected' (ibid) to the extent that Crang and Thrift (2000: 3) observe that space 'cannot be divorced from time'. For spaces within which social relations to land are created exist in time which has two dimensions. The first relates to its existence at a particular moment in time, involving a synchronic aspect. The second takes account of how social relations to land endure through time, and involves a diachronic aspect. Both these aspects of space are at work in social relations to land.

VII. DIMENSIONS OF TIME AND SPACE AS THEY PLAY OUT IN BOTSWANA

The past can be seen to be at work in Botswana's approach to land reform. This is one in which its current land provisions clearly derive from an adaptive strategy that stems from historical developments going back to the colonial era. It includes the retention of plural legal systems that continue to operate in Botswana today. Thus, attempts to extensively reform customary law in relation to land have been rejected on the basis that 'widespread departures ... are neither feasible nor necessary', as it was sufficient to engage in alterations based on 'the existing policy and legal framework' (Government of Botswana 2003: para 1.05 p 2).

In engaging with the past in the present, and with a view to the future, for the benefit of future generations, it is important to acknowledge the different temporalities that are at work. These may involve time in relation to a longer-term perspective, geared towards a more distant future, along with a more instrumental set of shorter-term strategies on land management. They may also involve approaches based on a 'linear' notion of time, as well as on a notion of 'social time'. The former, that is a linear notion of time, adopts an evolutionary trajectory associated with constantly moving forward, emphasising 'historical forms in its continual juxtaposition of equivalent intervals' (Greenhouse 1989: 1637). It represents an approach to time that is evident in the way in which Botswana deals with the spaces for action in allocating land, repossessing undeveloped land, or hearing disputes under land boards that administer tribal land. What is important about this approach to temporality is that it acts in an exclusionary manner. This comes about because temporality is formulated in terms of a trajectory that is built on a narrative of 'ongoing intervals in time that give rise to a single principle of selection' (ibid: 1631). Such a principle and approach negates any other construction of time or space.

This depiction of time and space may be contrasted with the concept of 'social time' that allows for the recognition of 'multiple forms of time that are simultaneously available in a single context' (ibid: 1633). So, just as space may represent what Massey (2013) calls 'a sphere within which distinct trajectories co-exist; as the sphere of co-existing heterogeneity', so time may also embody a multiplicity of forms that may be used to organise different dimensions of space in ways that give rise to contestations over people's entitlements to it. It allows for a more multi-dimensional perception of time, that in the case of customary land tenure allows for a movement back and forth from communal land tenure to individual or household land tenure according to cycles of agricultural development during the year.

It is important to comprehend which temporality is being invoked, for a linear perspective is one that establishes itself as the only authentic, authoritative and legitimate model for constructing relations between space and time. As such, the power that it exercises may be used to silence other accounts or narratives in a way that is not readily apparent. To provide an example, international discourses concerning 'developed' and 'undeveloped' countries provide an illustration of this power to silence what is at work. For, as Massey (2013) has observed, classifying a country as 'developed' or 'undeveloped' on the global stage gives rise to a situation where an 'undeveloped' country is no longer viewed as being on a par with a 'developed' country. This is so, even although an undeveloped country exists at the same time in space as a developed country. This comes about because its temporal location is as 'a country which is following our path to becoming a developed country like us' (ibid). Massey argues that what this form of categorisation does, through a linear trajectory of time, is to deny 'the simultaneity, the multiplicity of space' that would 'acknowledge the co-existence of such countries of state'. For it effectively turns all these differences between countries into a single historical trajectory that follows an evolutionary course. As such, it represents an aspect of the global and globalisation that is premised on moral superiority or hegemonic discourse (Fassin 2012). This discourse, according to Fassin, relies as much on exclusion as inclusion. It is able to achieve this exclusionary power by 'turning space into time, turning geography into history' (Massey 2013). As a result, such a model operates to deny 'the possibility of something different' and of opening up 'politics to the possibility of alternatives' (ibid).

It is important to recognise that the approach adopted under this model of time and space is based on *a* particular set of assumptions, derived from a particular ideological approach to development. Nonetheless this approach is treated as the foundational base for policy-making and regulation in international, transnational, national and local domains. Challenging its claims to authority and legitimacy can, however, provide space for constructing other accounts of social relations that may allow for alternative visions. In doing so, by confronting claims to an historical authenticity that is based on the 'natural order' of things, *a* particular reconstruction of the past may be displaced. As a result, the dominant narrative of what Lund has called 'the inevitability of history' becomes 'unsettled' (Lund 2013: 30).

VIII. CONCLUDING OBSERVATIONS

My research in Botswana treats land as a site of action involving social relations embedded in space and time. It highlights the need to view concepts, such as the 'global', the 'local' and 'globalisation' in relational terms and not as delimited entities. The domains featuring in my study vary in scale from international agencies, such as the UN and the World Bank, to national institutions, such as the Ministry of Land and Housing, to district administration in the form of Kweneng Land Board and Bakwena Tribal Administration, through to more circumscribed units involving families and households located in Molepolole village. They highlight varying standpoints on land. However, although these arenas vary in range and scope, they nonetheless have connective threads operating through the numerous forms of access, control and management of land. These embody a nexus of relations that take shape between families, communities, the state and the globe. In adopting a dialectical perspective my study dissolves opposites and entertains internal contradictions. In other words, rather than juxtaposing these concepts as bounded entities that stand in opposition to one another, as for example, constructs in an ideological discourse, or as representing a purely bounded, territorial jurisdiction that does not extend beyond the nation-state, my study explores the ways in which these concepts interact and intersect in multiple dimensions.

The importance of this approach is that it counteracts what Ferguson (1992) has termed the mythology of globalisation in so far as it purports to represent a large-scale phenomenon that promotes culturally homogenising forces over all others. It also provides a corrective to the depiction of globalisation as time-space compression, characterised by an all embracing 'speed up in time' with a singular trajectory (Harvey 1990: 240), for it highlights the ways in which 'social groups are very differentially placed in relation to this reorganization' (Massey 1994: 121) that are 'highly complicated and extremely varied' (ibid: 150) and that reveal their uneven and differentiated effects with respect to the distribution of resources such as land.

My research on land, in keeping with other empirical studies, demonstrates the extent to which law is articulated within a wider social, political and economical structure that engages with local, national, international and transnational domains. It raises questions about the relationship between law and power that vary according to the various models that apply to law's recognition. These reflect diverse interpretations according to the differing methodological and epistemological approaches that underpin them. It is important to acknowledge where power is located, how it is constituted and what forms it takes. For as Fassin (2012: 106) has observed 'globalization is more than anything else a contemporary expression of power: the power to act on people and things as well as on ideologies and subjectivities'.

Reza had a keen interest in exploring how different methods could be used to research law and legal phenomenon and with what results, transcending the boundaries of established disciplines such as law, sociology, political science and social anthropology. He helped establish a context within which sociology of law could flourish 'due to its strong capacity for interdisciplinary engagement and links to other scientific concepts, methodologies and research fields ' (Přibáň 2021: 2). I hope my discussion of space and time in relation to the legal regulation of land can make a contribution to the ongoing development of this field.

REFERENCES

Amanor, KS and Moyo, S (2008) *Land and Sustainable Development in Africa* (London, Zed Books).
Banakar, R and Travers, M (eds) (2002) *An Introduction to Law and Social Theory* (Oxford, Hart Publishing).
—— (2005) *Theory and Method in Socio-Legal Research* (Oxford, Hart Publishing).
—— (2013) *Law and Social Theory*, 2nd edn (Oxford, Hart Publishing).

Benda-Beckmann, F von (2003) 'Mysteries of Capital or Mystification of Legal Property?' 41 *European Journal of Anthropology* 187.

Benda-Beckmann, F von, Benda-Beckmann, K von and Wiber, M (eds) (2006) *Changing Properties of Property* (New York, Berghahn Books).

Blomley, NK (1994) *Law, Space and the Geographies of Power* (New York, Guilford).

Botswana, Government of (2003) *Review of Botswana National Land Policy: Final Report*, vol 1 (31 January), National Resources Services (pty) in association with LANDflow Solutions (Pty) (Ministry of Lands and Housing, Department of Land, Gaborone, Government Printer).

—— (2015) Botswana Land Policy. Government Paper No 4, Approved by the National Assembly (16 July) (Ministry of Lands and Housing, Gaborone, Government Printer).

Bruce, J (1998), 'Learning from the Comparative Experience with Agrarian Reform' in M Barry (ed), *Proceedings of the International Conference on Land Tenure in the Developing World* (Cape Town, University of Cape Town Press).

Chanock, M (1985) *Law, Custom and Social Order: The Colonial Experience in Malawi and Zambia* (Cambridge, Cambridge University Press).

CIGI (2012) Centre for International Governance Innovation (CIGI) and Korea Development Institute 'Post-2015 Development Agenda: Goals, Targets, Indicators', Special Report by B Carin, N Bates-Earner, MH Lee, W Lim and M Kapila, available at www.cigionline.org/publications/post-2015-development-agenda-goals-targets-and-indicators.

Commission on Legal Empowerment of the Poor (2008) *Making the Law Work for Everyone*, vol 1, available at https://www.un.org/ruleoflaw/blog/document/making-the-law-work-for-everyone-vol-1-report-of-the-commission-on-legal-empowerment-of-the-poor/.

Crang, M and Thrift, N (eds) (2000) *Thinking Space* (London, Routledge).

De Soto, H (2000) *The Mystery of Capital: Why Capitalism Triumphs in the West and Fails Everywhere Else* (New York, Basic Books).

Fabian, J (1983) *Time and the Other: How Anthropology Makes its Object* (New York, Columbia University Press).

Fassin, D (2012) 'That Obscure Object of Global Health' in MC Inhorn and EA Wentzell (eds), *Medical Anthropology at the Intersections: Histories, Activisms and Futures* (North Carolina, Duke University Press) 95.

Ferguson, M (1992) 'The Mythology about Globalization' 7 *European Journal of Communication* 69.

Greenhouse, C (1989) 'Just in Time: Temporality and the Cultural Legitimation of Law' 98 *Yale Law Journal* 1631.

Griffiths, A (1997) *In the Shadow of Marriage: Gender and Justice in an African Community* (Chicago, University of Chicago Press).

—— (2019) *Transformations on the Ground: Space and the Power of Land in Botswana* (Bloomington, Indiana University Press).

Harvey, D (1990) 'Between Space and Time: Reflections on the Geographical Imagination' 80 *Annals of the Association of American Geographers* 418.

Home, R (2012) 'The Colonial Legacy in Land Rights in Southern Africa' in B Chiagra (ed), *African Development Community Land Issues: Towards a New Sustainable Land Relations Policy* (Oxford, Routledge) 8.

Hooker, MB (1975) *Legal Pluralism: An Introduction to Colonial and New-Colonial Laws* (Oxford, Clarendon Press).

Ijagbemi, B (2006) 'Land Tenure Reforms and Social Transformation in Botswana: Implications for Urbanization' (dissertation, University of Arizona), available at https://repository.arizona.edu/bitstream/handle/10150/196133/azu_etd_1972_sip1_m.pdf?sequence=1.

Khan, LA (2009) 'Temporality of Law' 40 *McGeorge Law Review* 55.

Lefèbvre, H (1991) *The Production of Space* (Oxford, Blackwell), first published in French (1974) *La Production de l'espace* (Paris, Anthropos).

Low, SM and Lawrence-Zúñiga D (eds) (2003) *The Anthropology of Space and Place: Locating Culture* (Oxford, Blackwell Publishing).

Lund, C (2013) 'The Past and Space: On Arguments in African Land Control' 83 *Africa* 14.

Maine, HS (1861) *Ancient Law, Its Connections with the Early History of Society, and Its Relations to Modern Ideas* (London, John Murray).

Manji, A (2001) 'Land Reform in the Shadow of the State: The Implementation of New Land Laws in Sub-Saharan Africa' 22 *Third World Quarterly* 327.

—— (2006) *The Politics of Land Reform in Africa: From Communal Tenure to Free Markets* (London, Zed Books).

Massey, D (1994) 'A Global Sense of Place' in D Massey, *Space, Place and Gender* (Minneapolis, University of Minnesota Press) 146.

—— (2013) 'Doreen Massey on Space', a dialogue between Doreen Massey and Nigel Warburton, *Social Science Bites*, 1 February 2013, available at www.socialsciencespace.com/2013/02/podcastdoreen.massey-on-space/.

Morolong, ST and Ng'ong'ola, C (2007) 'Revisiting the Notion of Tribal Land' in CM Fombad (ed), *Essays on the Law of Botswana* (South Africa, Juta Law)142.

Nyamu-Musembi, CN (2007) 'De Soto and Land Relations in Rural Africa: Breathing Life into Dead Theories about Property Rights' (2007) 28 *Third World Quarterly* 1457.

Peters, PE (1994) *Dividing the Commons: Politics, Policy and Culture in Botswana* (Charlottesville, University Press of Virginia).

—— (2004) 'Inequality and Social Conflict over Land in Africa' 4 *Journal of Agrarian Change* 269.

—— (2007) 'Challenges in Land Tenure and Land Reform in Africa: An Anthropological Perspective' CIS Working Paper Series (Cambridge, Harvard University Press) available at www.hks.harvard.edu/sites/default/files/centers/cid/files/publications/faculty-working-papers/141.pdf.

—— (2014) 'Analysing Land Law Reform' 46 *Development and Change* 167.

Přibáň, J (ed) (2021) *Research Handbook on the Sociology of Law* (Cheltenham, Edward Elgar Publishing).

Thompson, EP (1993) *Customs in Common* (New York, New Press).

UN (2015a) 2030 UN Agenda for Sustainable Development, available at www.un.org/sustainable development/development-agenda/.

—— (2015b) Sustainable Development Goals, available at https://www.un.org/sustainable development/sustainable-development-goals/.

Walker, N (2014) *Intimations of Global Law* (Cambridge, Cambridge University Press).

34

Sexual Violence, Standard(s) of Proof, and Arbitrariness in Judicial Decision-Making

HILDUR FJÓLA ANTONSDÓTTIR

I. INTRODUCTION

I N HIS BOOK, *Normativity in Legal Sociology: Methodological Reflections on Law and Regulation in Late Modernity* (2015), Reza Banakar argues for the integration of top-down and bottom-up approaches into one single methodological framework to capture the complexity of socio-legal transformations and reconstructions. Banakar's (2015) meta-methodological framework includes three levels of analysis: (1) How does the law, as a body of rules, interact with society at the macro level? (2) How are legal rules interpreted at the intermediary level of legal institutions? (3) How is law identified, employed, and experienced by ordinary citizens at the level of social action? The purpose of this chapter is to conduct a meta-methodological exercise to explore the value of Banakar's approach. The focus of analysis is the legal phenomenon of different standards of proof in evidentiary law, which I will explore in the context of sexual violence.

Studies have shown that for people who have been subjected to sexual violence it is of paramount importance to have these experiences acknowledged and recognised (McGlynn and Westmarland 2019; Daly 2017). Criminal law is the justice paradigm within which allegations of sexual violence are traditionally evaluated (Henry et al 2015). However, in the European countries (and beyond), most cases of sexual violence do not result in conviction (Lovett and Kelly 2009; Krahé 2016), this also applies to Iceland (Antonsdóttir and Gunnlaugsdóttir 2013) as well as other Nordic countries (Brå 2019). Attrition rates in sexual offence cases remain high, particularly in cases of rape, which the law attributes to insufficient evidence or lack of evidence against the backdrop of a high standard of proof ('beyond reasonable doubt') (Antonsdóttir and Gunnlaugsdóttir 2013; Brå 2019). In addition, international research spanning decades has shown that rape myths can influence judicial decision making to the detriment of victims' credibility (Ehrlich 2001; Temkin and Krahé 2008; Walklate 2008; Edwards et al 2011; Dinos et al 2015; Ívarsdóttir 2019).

In that sense, the criminal justice system perpetually misrecognises most cases of sexual violence, which can be understood as a form of symbolic violence (Bourdieu 1987) given the power of law to impose its norms on society.

Although criminal law can be said to dominate the 'imaginative space of justice' (Henry et al 2015: 6) in cases of sexual violence, the criminal justice system is not the only legal procedure through which legal recognition becomes possible. Legal recognition can also be obtained in, for example, civil tort cases, where the standard of proof is considered lower than in criminal cases. However, in Iceland, as well as in the other Nordic countries, standalone civil lawsuits in cases of serious sexual violence, such as rape, are seemingly very rare (Antonsdóttir 2014).

Some policy discussions have taken place in Iceland on this topic, including a cross-party parliamentary resolution tasking the Minister of Justice to prepare a bill on the statutory right to legal aid for victims of violence in close relationships and sexual violence. This measure would allow them to pursue a civil case outside the criminal court if their claims have not been addressed in the criminal case (parliamentary document no 153, 2018–2019). In addition, the Ministry of Justice has had a commissioned policy paper under review on ways to strengthen the legal rights and status of victims of sexual violence, which also includes a recommendation on affording victim-survivors the right to legal aid to pursue civil claims and for the state to partially guarantee the amounts awarded (Antonsdóttir 2019).

To better understand the socio-legal forces at play that shape the way in which sexual violence is viewed according to different standards of proof, I use Banakar's (2015) meta-methodological approach to explore how standards of proof are conceptualised, practised, and experienced in the context of sexual violence in the Icelandic and, to some extent, the greater Nordic context. More specifically, using Banakar's (ibid) three-level analysis, I ask: How are conceptualisations of rules about different standards of proof constructed at the macro level? How are standards of proof applied by the courts on the intermediary level of legal institutions? How are standards of proof experienced by people who have been subjected to sexual violence? The analysis is conducted within a Bourdieusian framework, coupled with Banakar's socio-legal thinking.

II. LEGAL CONSTRUCTIONS OF THE STANDARD(S) OF PROOF

The legal definition of standard of proof is the level of certainty and the degree of evidence necessary to establish proof in a criminal or civil proceeding. However, the way in which the standards of proof are conceptualised differs between legal systems and jurisdictions. Constructions of the standards of proof within legal theory are the domain of legal scholars and there exist numerous theories about the way in which standards of proof should be conceptualsed, understood, and applied.

In the common law countries, there are different standard of proof which are conceptualised based on probabilities. In US law, for example, there are three different standards of proof: in criminal law, the case must be proven 'beyond a reasonable doubt', while in civil law plaintiffs have to prove their case on the basis of 'preponderance of the evidence'. In a limited number of civil law matters, which are deemed to be of particular gravity for the defendant, the intermediate required standard of proof is 'clear and convincing evidence' (Clermont and Sherwin 2002).

In principle, continental law does not distinguish between civil law and criminal law when it comes to the standard of proof. In many civil law countries, judges are supposed to use the same (high) standard proof in both criminal and civil matters or 'intime conviction', which prescribes that judges and jurors must be personally convinced whether a factual claim is true or not, according to their conscience (Engel 2009). However, studies from civil law countries on how the standard of proof is applied in practice indicate that judges apply a lower standard of proof in civil matters (Schweizer 2016; Arnalds and Jónsson 2014).

The term Nordic law emphasises the considerable similarities between the law, legal systems, and legal cultures of the Nordic countries (Husa et al 2008). All the Nordic jurisdictions apply the principle of free evaluation of evidence and there are generally no rules on the admissibility of evidence (Brienen and Hoegen 2000). While Nordic evidentiary theory had a common platform, it has developed in different ways under the free evidentiary system and different schools of thoughts dominate in different countries. Three models have been identified in this regard: the Swedish model is akin to the German one; the Norwegian model is similar to the US approach; and the Danish model contains no main rule, and the standard of proof varies based on legal areas, rules, and cases. In the field of evidentiary law, Nordic legal scholarship is characterised by normative language, descriptive statistics and/or mathematical formulas (Strandberg 2012).

So-called Nordic frequency theories (in Norwegian, *nordiske frekvensteorier*) have been influential in Norwegian and Swedish evidentiary law in relation to the theorisation of the standards of proof, but not in Denmark. These theories are understood to be anchored in statistics, maths, the natural sciences or descriptive social sciences. They use axioms from probability theory and many advocates of these methods use frequencies to quantify probability. These are, however, fictitious frequencies and have no basis in social reality. In Nordic legal scholarship it is emphasised that the judge can seldom quantify these probabilities and therefore cannot practise the axioms as arithmetic problems. The idea is, however, that this is in principle the right way to think about the evidentiary problem and that these are the recommended guidelines for evidentiary assessment (ibid).

Icelandic evidentiary law is influenced by Danish evidentiary law but, in comparison to the other Nordic countries, is theoretically underdeveloped. Generally, the prescribed standard of proof is high, or beyond reasonable doubt, and the burden of proof rests with the plaintiff filing the claim. However, Supreme Court case law indicates that the standard of proof is not so strict in practice (Arnalds and Jónsson 2014). For example, in Supreme Court verdict no 49/2005, a woman filed a civil tort claim for non-pecuniary damages against three men for having 'violated her sexual freedom by having sex with her against her will'. The woman won the case against the three defendants, even though before filing the civil claim the woman had reported the case to the police and the State Prosecutor decided not to issue charges.

This shows that there can be a degree of tension, or a gap, between the way in which legal scholars conceptualise standards of proof and the way in which judges apply these standards. As Banakar notes, legal philosophy 'is awash with attempts to justify law as a rational system of rules' (2015: 10). Western legal scholarship is shaped by the modernist project of rationalising and systematising social organisation which has served to transform law into a formal system of legal norms which is understood to generate decisions based on legal authority as opposed to arbitrary decisions based on moral or political motivations. Importantly, this affords autonomy to the legal order, which also functions to disembed the law from its socio-historical context, and which allows the law to disregard extra-legal considerations. Indeed, the hallmark of legal positivism, the dominant ideology within Western legal scholarship, is to continually attempt to separate facts and values, law from morality and legal certainty from justice (Banakar 2015).

Drawing on Bourdieu's (1987) socio-legal thinking, this tension, or gap, between scholarly attempts to rationalise and justify the standards of proof and the judicial application of these rules, can be explained by the division of labour within the juridical field. The juridical field is characterised by competition for the monopoly of the right to determine the law. In this context, legal scholars and judges are in permanent interpretative conflict over the legitimate exercise of juridical power. While legal scholars pull the law in the direction of pure theory, ordinary judges are charged with its adaptation to reality. However, the relationship between legal scholars and judges is also characterised by functional complementarity. Judges take refuge behind the appearance of simply applying the law, while the juridical canon functions as a reserve authority providing guarantee for juridical acts. However, as judges carry out acts of jurisprudence, they, thereby, contribute to juridical construction. And while legal rules might diminish the variability of judicial decision making, a degree of arbitrariness remains in legal decisions (ibid).

III. INSTITUTIONAL APPLICATION OF THE STANDARD(S) OF PROOF

In the late 2000s, a public debate ensued between a law professor at the University of Iceland and a Supreme Court Judge about the evidentiary assessment in cases of sexual violence. The main bone of contention was how judges should assess direct versus indirect evidence in cases of sexual violence in criminal cases. While direct evidence is considered to support the truth of an assertion, for example the guilt or innocence in criminal law, indirect evidence supports the creation of an inference that the matter asserted is true, such as the condition of a victim after the alleged crime (Tómasson 2007). The then Supreme Court Judge held that judges were giving increased weight to indirect evidence in rape cases and warned that external pressure from the general public to convict in such cases leads to convictions without establishing legal proof (Gunnlaugsson 2008; 2010). The law professor, on the other hand, argued that even if indirect evidence generally has less evidentiary value than direct evidence, the use of indirect evidence has been used in Icelandic criminal law for centuries (Tómasson 2007).

A study from 2014, based on 26 interviews with legal practitioners within the criminal justice system in Iceland, found that, according to participants, victim testimonies and indirect evidence had been given increased weight over the years. Participants described how these changes stemmed from better police investigations, increased knowledge about the nature and consequences of sexual violence and, not least, a generational change within the legal institutions that make up the criminal justice system, and a change in attitudes towards these crimes. However, defence lawyers interviewed in the study thought that due to public pressure, the standard of proof in cases of sexual violence was no longer as high as in other types of criminal offences (Antonsdóttir 2014).

In the same study, participants were asked if the character of the judge and their life experience was important in the way in which judges assess cases of sexual violence. Participants generally agreed that that was the case. One judge said:

> The legal standard in criminal cases is simply to assess if it is beyond reasonable doubt that the crime has been committed and all judges follow that standard, but then it is of course possible that judges' personal opinions have some effect in the way in which they make that assessment. (ibid: 60)

Judges were also asked if they received any training to ensure that their evidentiary assessment is independent from social class, age, gender and the appearance and behaviour of the victim and the accused. The general response was, in short, no. One judge said:

> Well, we of course simply rely on our legal education and our knowledge and experience. No one is of course born a perfect judge; it takes years of experience. [...] Judges have to be knowledgeable about human nature, but people are of course created differently, or, yes, not equally sensitive in making that assessment. (ibid: 62)

Notably, legal practitioners, including judges, freely admit that judicial decision-making is not only a question of law but also very much a human affair that is shaped by the character and world view of individual judges and subject to the influence of social forces, external to the law. Bourdieu points out that 'the more or less extensive freedom of interpretation granted to them in the application of rules, judges introduce the changes and innovations which are indispensable for the survival of the system' (1987: 824). Otherwise, the system would 'risk closing itself into rigid rationalism if it were left to the theorists alone' (ibid: 824). However, the pendulum can swing both ways.

The Icelandic Appeals Court was established with law no 50/2016 and started its operations on 1 January 2018. Before its establishment, the Icelandic Supreme Court had both functioned as an appeals court and a supreme court. In May 2021, news broke in the media that the Icelandic Appeals Court had lowered the sentences or turned convictions into acquittals in 42 per cent of all sexual offence cases over the last three years. This percentage is much higher than in drug cases and cases of physical violence, in which sentences were lowered or convictions overturned in 25 per cent of cases. This pattern is also evident when looking at the number of cases where an acquittal in the District Courts was turned into a conviction or sentences increased in the Appeals Court, ie in every third of drug cases and in every sixth of physical violence cases, but in every eighth of sexual violence cases (Guðmundsson 2021).

In an interview with the media, a member of parliament, who is also a former prosecutor, was quoted saying:

> What is also important to consider here is that these are cases that the prosecution authorities have assessed as being likely to result in a conviction, issued charges, these are cases that have resulted in a conviction in the district courts. This is an indication that there is

not full consistency in the way in which the prosecution authorities, the district courts and the Appeals Court view these cases. (Sigurðardóttir 2021)

In another interview, a victim lawyer is quoted as saying:

> Amongst us colleagues who work in this field, it is our feeling that the Appeals Court has set a higher standard of proof in cases of sexual violence than what the Supreme Court had directed, for example as it relates to indirect evidence. Such as psychological evaluations and testimonies of witnesses. (ibid)

These examples clearly show that the judicial application of the standards of proof is a human affair, influenced by institutional culture, embedded in socio-historical contexts, and can oscillate between legal formalism and substantive justifications. It further shows how legal decisions are characterised by a level of arbitrariness which also functions to reveal what Bourdieu (1987) calls the symbolic violence of the law.

IV. NOT GUILTY OF A CRIME BUT LEGALLY RESPONSIBLE FOR THE CONSEQUENCES

In the Nordic countries, as in many other civil law countries, victims in criminal cases have the right to file a civil tort claim in conjunction with the criminal case (Brienen and Hoegen 2000). In most Nordic countries, however, judges do not evaluate such civil claims if the accused is acquitted. That has to do with the so-called same-direction principle (in Danish *ensretningsprincippet*), which means that the outcome of the tort claim should be in line with the outcome of the criminal case. In Norway, however, judges are not required to follow the same-direction principle, and can consider these compensation claims even if the accused is acquitted, based on a civil standard of proof, ie clear and convincing evidence (in Norwegian *klart sannsynlighetsovervekt*). It is, therefore, not uncommon that if the accused is acquitted of the crime, he is still found liable for damages for the wrong and harm of his actions (NOU 2000; 2016).

This practice by the Norwegian courts of assessing compensation claims independently after an acquittal in the criminal case has been challenged several times before the European Court of Human Rights (ECtHR), particularly on the basis of Article 6(2), which states: 'Everyone charged with a criminal offence shall be presumed innocent until proven guilty according to law'.[1] All three cases concerned sexual offences where the accused had been acquitted of the crime but found liable to pay damages. The applicants' arguments include that having been found liable for damages means that the acquittal in a criminal case can be questioned. While the decisions vary in favour of the applicant or Norway, in short, the ECtHR finds that to evaluate the civil claim on the basis of a lower burden of proof does not, in and of itself, violate Article 6(2) as long as the practice is not contrary to domestic legislation, and the boundaries between the compensation claim and the criminal case

---

[1] See *Y v Norway* 2003 (56568/00); *Ringvold v Norway* 2003 (34964/97); *Orr v Norway* 2008 (31283/04).

are not blurred in the legal assessment and the subsequent wording of the verdict.[2] This Norwegian legal practice offers a stark example of how it is possible to reach two different legal outcomes based on different standards of proof in cases of sexual violence – even in the same case.

There has been considerable debate among legal scholars in Norway and Denmark about this Norwegian legal practice. Some find it preferable on the basis of efficiency arguments, ie if the civil claim can be assessed in conjunction with the criminal case, victims do not need to pursue a standalone civil suit after the completion of the criminal case, and this provides victims with better access to tort law, given that financial risk can prevent them from pursuing a civil case (Garde 1998; Strandbakken 1998; Strandbakken and Garde 1999; NOU 2000; Betænkning 2010). Others think that the same-direction principle should apply to ensure that an acquittal in a criminal case cannot be questioned (Smith 1999; 2004a; 2004b; 2007). This Norwegian practice has also been questioned due to its unforeseen legal effects on the treatment of the case, ie it is possible that judges find it easier to acquit the accused if it is also possible to find him liable to some degree or that judges can be reluctant to award victims compensation after having acquitted the accused (NOU 2016).

Interestingly, the primary concerns in this debate have to do with extra-legal factors. Even if Norwegian law allows for different standards of proof, based on legal rationality, there is discernible legal anxiety about the way in which this legal practice can impact judicial psychology and affect the perception of the law among the public. This concern over the psychological effects on judges, reveals judges as human beings ruled by emotional or psychological instincts as opposed to legal rationality which risks exposing the degree of arbitrariness inherent in judicial-making and is, therefore, understood to pose a threat to the legitimacy of the legal system.

V. EXPERIENCES OF THE STANDARDS OF PROOF

Survivors of sexual violence can find different standards of proof to be perplexing. In 2007, the Icelandic Parliament passed law no 26/2007 on the appointment of a committee charged with investigating historic violence and abuse against children in state-run treatment facilities and boarding houses in Iceland. The committee (henceforth the Committee) was led by a professor at the law department of the University of Iceland and was also comprised of scholars in the field of psychology and social work. The Committee conducted an extensive investigation of nine facilities and boarding houses which included review of documents and interviews with former employees and residents, and subsequently published three reports on their findings (Spanó et al 2009; 2010; 2011). In the reports it is stated that the Committee used the 'balance of probabilities' standard, or 'more probable than not' standard, to assess, in its totality, the truth of the accounts they gathered based on the interviews.

When the findings were published the law professor who chaired the Committee was interviewed in the media, where he said that – according to the findings of the

---

[2] *Y v Norway* 11 February 2003 (56568/00).

investigation –the Committee found that it was 'more likely than not' that violence and abuse, including sexual violence, had been committed against children in many of these facilities at certain time periods. Subsequently, two women, who were former residents of these facilities and had been subjected to sexual violence, were interviewed in the media and criticised the report for not having included a more extensive discussion on the sexual abuse perpetrated against children at one of the facilities, and, importantly, they criticised the language used by the committee, ie that it was considered 'more likely than not' that the children had been subjected to sexual violence (Afdráttarlaus um sannleiksgildið 2013). Here, the sense is that they did not feel that the language 'more likely than not' adequately reflected that the accounts of the former residents had been fully believed and, therefore, that there was doubt that the sexual abuse had actually taken place. The chair of the Committee came before the media and was at pains to explain to the public that the Committee had not been charged with deciding on people's guilt or innocence as is the case in criminal trials.

A study based on interviews with survivors of sexual violence in Iceland about their views on a favourable judgment in a civil tort lawsuit, indicates that legal recognition of the wrong and harm they had suffered can be of great importance (Antonsdóttir 2020a). It did, however, come as a surprise to many that criminal and civil law used different standards of proof. One participant, a 35-year-old woman, was, however, aware of this difference and said:

> I find it a bit strange that there is some kind of double justice, and now I put justice in quotation marks. I find it very strange that there are different standards of proof. It somehow upsets my sense of justice that you can look at the same man and either see him as guilty or as innocent based on different standards of proof. But I have found myself jumping for joy when someone has been found guilty in a private case who was acquitted in a criminal case, like in the O.J. Simpson case. … At the same time as I felt a sense of justice it also underscored how wrong the verdict in the criminal case had been.[3]

Here, the interviewee expresses discomfort with what she calls 'double justice', or a double standard of justice, indicating that the rationalisation of different standards of proof serves to reveal how the law creates a separation between law and justice, which, in itself, upsets her sense of justice. As Bourdieu (1987) notes, the process of continual rationalisation that characterises the law contributes to establishing a social division between ordinary people and legal professionals. This process functions to constantly increase the separation between judgment based on law and everyday understandings of fairness (ibid). And as Banakar (2015) points out, even while ordinary people might share the same concept of the law as legal professionals, that does not mean that they experience the relationship between law and morality in the same way. This highlights the importance for socio-legal theory to 'transcend the internal/external dichotomy which mainstream jurisprudence employs to place the contradictory outcomes of legal operations outside the juridical gaze' (ibid: 74).

---

[3] Unpublished interview conducted as a part of my PhD thesis (Antonsdóttir 2020b).

VI. SUMMARY AND CONCLUDING REMARKS

Here, I have shown how constructions of standards of proof are a product of the division of labour within the juridical field and the interpretive conflict between legal scholars and judicial decision makers over the right to determine the law. While legal scholars attempt to rationalise and define standards of proof in terms of pure theory, using normative language, descriptive statistics and/or mathematical formulas, ordinary judges contribute to their juridical construction by way of carrying out acts of jurisprudence, continuously adapting them to the reality of individual cases. This tension is perhaps particularly discernible in many civil law countries, where there is a degree of inconsistency, or a gap, between the formal standard of proof, as outlined by legal scholars, and the standard of proof applied in case law.

Based on interviews with judges and other legal practitioners in Iceland, the application of the standards of proof is not only a question of the legal rules but is also understood to be a human enterprise affected by extra-legal forces which can change over time. As shown by the example of the newly established Appeals Court in Iceland, the degree of arbitrariness in legal decisions is detectible not only on the level of individual judges but also on an institutional level, which, arguably, reveals the symbolic violence of the law. In the case of Norway, where accused persons can be found not guilty yet liable in the same case based on different standards of proof, there is discernible anxiety among legal scholars that although legal rationality allows for the use of different standards of proof, its application risks exposing the social embeddedness of the law, which is understood to pose a threat to its legitimacy.

Due to its quality of indeterminacy, the rational language of probability used to conceptualise civil standards of proof can be experienced by survivors of sexual violence as hurtful and offensive, even though the legal decision is in their favour. In that sense, the legal rationalisation of different standards of proof highlights law's self-described separation between law and justice, which contributes to the social division between ordinary people and legal professionals, and can be experienced as a moral conundrum by survivors.

While the discussion in this chapter has been limited in scope, I hope to have been able to exhibit how using Banakar's (2015) meta-methodological approach, coupled with a Bourdieusian socio-legal analysis, has revealed how the construction, application, and experiences of different standards of proof are subject to the ongoing interaction between the legal and social fields. This shows the legal phenomenon of standards of proof to be embedded in socio-historical contexts, which transcends the self-described internal/external dichotomy of the law.

REFERENCES

Afdráttarlaus um sannleiksgildið (2013) *Mbl.is*, 9 January, available at https://www.mbl.is/frettir/innlent/2013/01/09/afdrattarlaus_um_sannleiksgildid/.

Antonsdóttir, HF (2014) 'Viðhorf fagaðila til meðferðar nauðgunarmála innan réttarvörslukerfisins og tillögur að úrbótum' (Report) (Reykjavík, EDDA – Center of Excellence at the University of Iceland).

—— (2019) 'Réttlát málsmeðferð með tilliti til þolenda kynferðisbrota. Greinargerð um leiðir til að styrkja réttarstöðu brotaþola' (Report), prepared for the Office of the Prime Minister of Iceland, available at https://www.stjornarradid.is/lisalib/getfile.aspx?itemid=c9ee2c0c-927f-11e9-9442-005056bc530c.

—— (2020a) 'Compensation as a Means to Justice? Sexual Violence Survivors' Views on the Tort Law Option in Iceland' 28 *Feminist Legal Studies* 277.

—— (2020b) 'Decentring Criminal Law: Understandings of Justice by Victim-Survivors of Sexual Violence and their Implications for Different Justice Strategies' (PhD dissertation, Lund University).

Antonsdóttir, HF and Gunnlaugsdóttir, ÞS (2013) 'Tilkynntar nauðganir til lögreglu á árunum 2008 og 2009: Um afbrotið nauðgun, sakborning, brotaþola og málsmeðferð' (Report) (Reykjavík, EDDA – Center of Excellence at the University of Iceland).

Arnalds, SR and Jónsson, R (2014) 'Sönnun orsakatengsla í líkamstjónamálum' in *Afmælisrit: Viðar Már Matthíasson Sextugur, 16. ágúst 2014* (Reykjavík, Bókaútgáfan Codex).

Banakar, R (2015) *Normativity in Legal Sociology. Methodological Reflections on Law and Regulation in Late Modernity* (Springer).

Betænkning (2010) Reform af den civile retspleje VI. Behandling af forurettedes civile krav under straffesager (Adhæsionprocessen) no 1522 (Justitsministeriet).

Bourdieu, P (1987) 'The Force of Law: Toward a Sociology of the Juridical Field' 38 *Hastings Law Journal* 805.

Brå (2019) 'Våldtäkt från anmälan till dom. En studie av rättsväsendets arbete med våldtäktsärenden' Rapport 2019:9 (Stockholm, The Swedish National Council for Crime Prevention).

Brienen, MEI and Hoegen, EHH (2000) *Victims of Crime in 22 European Criminal Justice Systems: The Implementation of Recommendation (85) 11 of the Council of Europe on the Position of the Victim in the Framework of Criminal Law and Procedure* (Netherlands, Wolf Legal Publishers).

Clermont, KM and Sherwin, E (2002) 'A Comparative View of Standards of Proof' *Cornell Law Faculty Publications* Paper 222.

Daly, K (2017) 'Sexual Violence and Victims' Justice Interests' in E Zinsstag and M Keenan (eds), *Restorative Responses to Sexual Violence: Legal, Social and Therapeutic Dimensions* (London, Routledge).

Dinos, S, Burrowes, N, Hammond, K and Cunliffe, C (2015) 'A Systematic Review of Juries' Assessment of Rape Victims: Do Rape Myths Impact on Juror Decision Making?' 43(1) *International Journal of Law, Crime and Justice* 36.

Edwards, KM, Turchik, JA, Dardis, CM, Reynolds, N and Gidycz, CA (2011) 'Rape Myths: History, Individual and Institutional-Legal Presence, and Implications for Change' 65 *Sex Roles* 761.

Ehrlich, S (2001) *Representing Rape: Language and Sexual Consent* (London, Routledge).

Engel, C (2009) 'Preponderance of the Evidence versus Intime Conviction: Behavior Perspective on Conflict between American and Continental European Law 33(3) *Vermont Law Review* 435.

Garde, P (1998) 'Adhæsionsprocessens brister' *Ugeskrift for Retsvæsen* (UfR) 31.

Guðmundsson, BÞ (2021) 'Milda dóma frekar í kynferðisbrotum en öðrum málum' *Ruv.is*, 8 May, available at https://www.ruv.is/frett/2021/05/08/milda-doma-frekar-i-kynferdisbrotum-en-odrum-malum.

Gunnlaugsson, JS (2008) 'Mál af þessu tagi' 2 *Tímarit Lögréttu*.

—— (2010) 'Guðlegt vald?' 2 *Tímarit lögfræðinga*.

Henry, N, Flynn, A and Powell, A (2015) 'The Promise and Paradox of Justice: Rape Justice beyond the Criminal Law' in A Powell, N Henry and A Flynn (eds), *Rape Justice beyond the Criminal Law* (Palgrave Macmillan).

Husa, J, Nuotio, K and Pihlajamäki, H (2008) 'Nordic Law – Between Tradition and Dynamism' Tilburg Institute of Comparative and Transnational Law, Working Paper no 2008/10.

Ívarsdóttir, EH (2019) 'Um sönnun í nauðgunarmálum. Saklaus uns sekt er sönnuð?' (Master's thesis, Faculty of Law, University of Iceland).

Krahé, B (2016) 'Societal Responses to Sexual Violence Against Women: Rape Myths and the "Real Rape" Stereotype' in H Kury, R Sławomir and E Shea (eds), *Women and Children as Victims and Offenders: Background, Prevention, Reintegration* (Switzerland, Springer International).

Lovett, J and Kelly, L (2009) 'Different Systems, Similar Outcomes? Tracking Attrition in Reported Rape Cases across Europe (Final report)' (London, Child and Woman Abuse Studies Unit, London Metropolitan University).

McGlynn, C and Westmarland, N (2019) 'Kaleidoscopic Justice: Sexual Violence and Victim-Survivors' Perceptions of Justice' 28(2) *Social & Legal Studies* 179.

NOU (2000) 'Erstatning til ofrene hvor tiltalte frifinnes for straff' NOU 2000:33 (Oslo, Justis- og politidepartementet).

—— (2016) 'Ny straffeprosesslov. NOU 2016:24' (Oslo, Justis- og beredskapsdepartementet).

Schweizer, M (2016) 'The Civil Standard of Proof – What is it, Actually?' 20(3) *The International Journal of Evidence & Proof* 217.

Sigurðardóttir, K (2021) 'Landsréttur strangari í kynferðisbrotum en Hæstiréttur' *Ruv.is*, 9 May, available at https://www.ruv.is/frett/2021/05/09/landsrettur-strangari-i-kynferdisbrotum-en-haestirettur.

Smith, E (1999) 'Frifundet i straffesagen – dømt til offererstatning. En Kafkask retstilstand' *Ugeskrift for retsvæsen* 200.

—— (2004a) 'Frikändt for brott, men ändå skyldig' 89 *Svensk Juristtidning* 773.

—— (2004b) 'Mere om erstatning til offeret efter frifindelse af tiltalte' 1 *Juristen* 22.

—— (2007) 'The Presumption of Innocence' 51 *Scandinavian Studies in Law* 489.

Spanó, RS, Sigurðsson, JF, Bjarnadóttir, R, Júlíusdóttir, S and Sigurjónsdóttir, ÞB (2009) 'Skýrsla nefndar samkvæmt lögum nr. 26/2007. Áfangaskýrsla nr. 1 Könnun á starfsemi Heyrnleysingjaskólans 1947–1992, vistheimilisins Kumbaravogs 1965–1984 og skólaheimilisins Bjargs 1965–1967' (Reykjavík, Forsætisráðuneytið).

—— (2010) 'Skýrsla nefndar samkvæmt lögum nr. 26/2007, áfangaskýrsla nr. 2: könnun á starfsemi vistheimilisins Silungapolls 1950–1969, vistheimilisins Reykjahlíðar 1956–1972 og heimavistarskólans að Jaðri 1946–1973' (Reykjavík, Forsætisráðuneytið).

—— (2011) 'Skýrsla nefndar samkvæmt lögum. 26/2007. Áfangaskýrsla nr. 3 Könnun á starfsemi Upptökuheimilis ríkisins 1945–1971, Unglingaheimilis ríkisins 1971–1994 og meðferðarheimilisins í Smáratúni og á Torfastöðum 1979–1994 (Reykjavík, Forsætisráðuneytið).

Strandbakken, A (1998) 'Frifunnet for straff – idømt erstatningsansvar – Om beviskravet i straffesaker og sivile saker' *Lov og rett* 540.

Strandbakken, A and Garde, P (1999) 'Erstatningsdommen, den frifundne og uskyldsformodningsreglen' *Ugeskrift for Retsvæsen* 237.

Strandberg, M (2012) *Beviskrav I sivile saker* (Bergen, Fagbokforlaget).

Temkin, J and Krahé, B (2008) *Sexual Assault and the Justice Gap: A Question of Attitude* (Oxford, Hart Publishing).

Tómasson, E (2007) 'Sitt er hvað, sönnunarbyrði og sönnunarmat: umfjöllun um dóm Hæstaréttar 20. október 2005 í máli nr. 148/2005' 60(3) *Úlfljótur, tímarit laganema*.

Walklate, S (2008) 'What is to be Done about Violence against Women? Gender, Violence, Cosmopolitanism and the Law' 48 *British Journal of Criminology* 39.

Index

'adaptation strategy' (Botswana), 446
agency and social forces, 222–3
'algorithmic regulation' and global social
    indicators, 359–60
American Bar Association, Jurimetrics
    Committees set up, 230–1
'anomie', 87, 185
anonymity of cars and car-driving, 301–2
'Anonymous Auras' (artwork), 398–400
anti-Israel law (Iran, 2020), 321–3
  abolition of state of Israel and, 323–4
  contact and communication with Israel and, 323
  internal and external factors of, 323
  passing of and penalties under, 322–3
anti-semitism (Iran), 324, 325–6
'appreciation' (fieldwork strategy), 253
arrest and remand procedure, effect on families,
    433–4
artificial intelligence (AI) and legal informatics, 233
Association of American Law Schools, Jurimetrics
    Committee set up by (1960), 231
'audit society' (Shore and Wright), 358
authorisation, Teubner on, 426
authoritarian governments, attitudes to, 303–4
automobile industry (Iran), 297–8, 299
  car ownership, 299
automobiles' role in internationalism, 301
automotive society, sociological literature on, 299–300
autopoiesis, 74–5
  non-living systems, application to, 74–5
'availability heuristic', 376
  risk and, 381
aviation:
  certainty and risk in, 385
  collateral damage to, risk communication
    strategies limit, 383
  companies, poor-preparedness for public health
    scares, 381–2
  public health authorities and, collaboration
    between, 380–1
  risk, in, 15, 385
  safety and security and, 375, 376–8

Banakar, Reza:
  case studies, 27–9
  publications of, 24–5, 28
  see also specific subjects

'Before the Law' (Kafka parable), 204–5, 206
Berman, Harold J (legal scholar), 339–40
'best interests of the child principle, the' (Egypt), 153
black letter law, 38–9
  Banakar on, 38–9
  conflict and consensus and interpretative
    sociology tradition, 38–9
  definition of, 38–9
Botswana:
  land discourses, 18–19
  land tenure in, 443–4
Bourdieu, Pierre, on fields, 50
'Brexit: A Note on the EU's interlegality'
    (Banaker, 2019), 29
bribery offences, TeliaSonera's prosecution over,
    118–19
Bulgaria, KoL instruction given in, 170

Cairo Appeal Court, judgment in favour of
    Elhinnawy, 152–3
'Can Legal Sociology Account for the Normativity
    of Law' (Banakar, 2013), 27
'Can Sociology and Jurisprudence Learn from
    Each Other' (Banakar, 2006), 27
CAPSCA programme, 380, 387
cars and car-driving, anonymity of, 301–2
case handling process, citizens' experience of, 244
caseworkers:
  citizens' rights and obligation,
    interpretation of, 245
  law, view of, 244–5
  practices and formal law and, 243
causality in society, 64
Center for Egyptian Women Legal Assistance
    (CEWLA), 150, 152, 154
Central Fine Collection Agency (CJIB)
    (Netherlands), 312, 314, 315
Centre for Memory, Peace and Reconciliation of
    Bogotá (CMPR), 399
certainty and risk in aviation, 385
chief clerks' duties, 254
'child is affiliated to the conjugal bed,
    the' (Egypt), 153
children:
  prisoners' see prisoners' children and families
  violence and abuse cases against (2007 Iceland
    committee report), 459–60

Chinese Cultural Revolution (1968), 337–8
citizens:
  compliance rules for Covid 19 indicators for,
    362–3
  rights and obligations of, case workers'
    obligation to explain, 245
  role and concept of, 99–100
citizenship:
  imperialism and, 101–2
  laws, examples of, 101, 104
  military recruitment and, 99–100
  military service (Austria) and, 104
  national and German unification, 104
  Prussian and military expansion, 103
civil resistance (Colombia), 397–8
  columbaria meetings, 397–8
  strategy, criticism of, 398
Coca-Cola Corporation, CSR policy, 137
collective representation (Durkheim), 419
columbaries:
  civil resistance meetings at, 397–8
  cultural heritage asset, become, 398–9
Columbia:
  civic culture and resistance, 396–8
  guerrilla groups, in, 341, 396
  law, relationship to, 391
  nation-state political background, 394
  violence in, 395
Columbian Constitution 1991, 393–4
  global projects and social change opportunities
    in, 394, 395
Columbian nation-state political background, 394
'Commonplace of Law: Stories from Everyday
    Life, The' (Ewick and Silbey, 1998), 206
common societal scheme (EU) and solidarity, 407
communication:
  EU transnational trade union solidarity and,
    408–11
  Swedish trade unions and, 409–11
  symbolic forms of, 419
compensation claims (Norway), assessment of
    after acquittal in criminal cases, 458–9
concepts and correspondences, 223
conceptualisation of law, state's, 54–5 (fig)
conflict:
  solving (Hungary), reluctance to use
    rights-conscious way, 175
  tradition and black letter law, 38–9
conflicts, ethical and political dimensions of, 284
constitutional imaginaries, 417–18, 420–1, 421–2
  transnational European integration and, 423
constitutional law:
  imperialism and, 96
  military emphasis of, 104–5
  pluralism and, 98

constitutional legitimacy principles, 98–9
constitutions:
  imaginaries as, background of, 422
  social imaginaries and, 422–3
contemporary societies and integrative
    function of law, 321
co-option, policy-science, and legal practice, 56
cooperation, collaboration and communication
    (safety-focused guidelines), 379
corporate lawyers:
  'pathetic dots', as, 129–30
  social discourse's effect on, 131
corporate legal structure, CSR and, 136
corporate regulations:
  cross-border, 133
  juridical capital and, 119
corporate social responsibility (CSR), 128, 131
  Coca-Cola Corporation and, 137
  corporate legal structure and, 136
  legitimacy of and soft law, 133–4
  operational change, effect on, 135, 136
  transnational corporate governance and,
    135–7
corporations, powers of, 112
correspondences and concepts, 223
Cotterrell, Roger, on legal literature, 286, 287
court clerks (Turkey):
  criminal legal aid fieldwork,
    participation in, 254–6
  duties of, 254–5
  judges and, relationship between, 255
court files (Turkey), accessing, 255–6
Covid 19:
  'best practice' data, 363–4 (fig)
  deaths, standardisation of definition of, 370–1
  media communication of spread of, 361 (fig)
  pandemic data, methods of generation of,
    360–1
  Rankings and Analytics, 362, 363
  restrictions, examples of resistance to, 368
  situation reports on, 361–2
  Sweden, in, 370
Covid 19 indicators, 362, 370
  citizens' compliance, rules for, 362–3
  contextual differences, controlling for, 369 (figs)
  decision-making, guiding, 364–5
  evaluation of success of, 363
Covid 19, spread of:
  autocratic countries' response to, 36
  comparison of and factors in, 365–6
  police enforcement of rules to limit, 362
  policy choices, results and consequences of,
    366–7
  risk factors and people at risk, 367
  reasons for, 366

criminal:
   behaviour, attitudes to punishment for
      (Nordic studies), 435–6
   justice practice and prisoners' families'
      sentiments, 437
   law firms (Turkey), access to, 256–7
criminal legal aid fieldwork (Turkey), 249
   court clerks' participation, 254–6
   judges' participation in, 251–2, 253–4
   methodology, 250–1
crises, public safety communication about, 383–4
critical realism, 63
cultural:
   dependence, 284
   differences, preservation of and legal systems,
      321
   lag and social integration, 70
   'neoliberal revolution', effect of, 340
   values, social norms' contribution to, 70
culture:
   concept of discussed, 285
   definition of, 202, 320
   law and, 320
   modernisation of (Iran), 325
customary marriages, 6, 7, 145, 148–9, 151, 153
'cynics' (people's attitude to law), 434

danger in modern life, 301
decentralisation in Indonesia, consequences of, 90
decision-making:
   Covid 19 indicators guide, 364–5
   lawyers' and sociology, 62
   studies on, 39
Deep Knowledge Group (DKG), 362, 363
democracy:
   cultural, 90
   emergence of, sociological reconstruction of,
      216
democratic legitimacy, Teubner on, 436
'dependence on strangers', 301
desire for justice, paradox of (Banakar), 204–5
deterrence:
   Iranian traffic rules and 310
   Netherlands traffic rules and, 313
developed and undeveloped countries and space
      and time, 448
development plans:
   Bogotá (2002–4), 396
   structure and aims of, 396
*Dilemma of Law: Conflict Management in Multi-
      cultural Society, The* (Banakar, 1994),
      202–3, 341
'direct importation model' (public sentiments on
      justice), 436
'disconnected from society at large', 301

Discovery of Grounded Theory, The (Glaser and
      Strauss), 195
DNA testing:
   conception after rape and, 153–4
   evidence of, 7, 145, 148, 149, 151–2, 154–6
Doorkeepers of the Law (Banaker, 1998), 28
'double movement' of law, 83–4, 87–8
   examples of, 87–8
'Double-Thinking and Contradictory
      Arrangements in Iranian Law and
      Society' (Banakar 2018), 28–9
driving culture:
   discipline of driving, 302
   driving violations accepted, 304
   social norms and, 305
   veiled and unveiled, is part of, 303
Driving Culture in Iran (Banakar, 2016), 28,
      299–300, 307, 350
Dutch drivers, analysis of survey results, 315

ecological system, 77
   normativity of, 77
economic considerations:
   hard cases, in, 136–7
   social responsibility and, 136–7
economic system, normativity of, 76
Egyptian family law, overview of, 6–7
Elhinnawy v Fishawy (2006), 145, 146, 148–9,
      152–3
employment case handling process, 240–1, 242–3
   data collection, 243
epidemics, consequences of for society, 341
epistemic relativism, 63
ethics and normativity, 72–3
ethno-cultural conflicts, Banakar's interest in, 28
European Centre for Disease Prevention and
      Control (ECDC), 380, 386
European Union (EU):
   law, solidarity in (Banakar), 29
   trade union cooperation and solidarity, 406–7
European Union Aviation Safety Agency (EASA),
      376, 378
European Union transnational trade union
      solidarity, 406–7, 408
   communication and, 408–11
evidence, direct or indirect, in sexual violence
      criminal cases, 456–7
'exclusionary model' (public sentiments on
      justice), 436
external and internal culture, Engel on, 284

families:
   arrest and remand procedure, effect on,
      433–4
   prisoners' *see* prisoners' children and families

'family resemblance' (Wittgenstein), 86, 199,
    201, 360
Febbrajo, Alberto, on legal culture, 286
feminist scholarship and sociology of law, 215–16
field (*champ*):
    Bourdieu on, 50
    definition of, 112
fields of action, 50, 51 (fig), 52
    triangle of, 51–2
fiqh, development of, 147
formal law:
    caseworkers' practices and, 243
    law in society, starting point for, 242
forum shopping, 114, 119, 122
French Revolution, 333–4
    causes and influence of, 333–4
    women failed by, 338
frequency theories (Nordic), 455
'frequent flyer' air travel and risk, 384
functional differentiation and individuality, 222

gender images and roles (Germany),
    modernisation of (data analysis), 166
General Data Protection Regulation (GDPR),
    233–4
German Democratic Republic's opinions on
    families and family law (1966), 164
German unification (1864–71) and national
    citizenship, 104
Germany:
    KoL instruction given in, 170
    migration background of population, 167
    public's needs and interests, opinions on (1973),
        164
global:
    financial crisis, Banakar on, 355–6
    resource, land as, 442
    security and ID, relationship between, 378–9
global social indicators:
    'algorithmic regulation' and, 359–60
    comparisons of success and, 368
    continuum of normative regulation and,
        358–9 (fig)
    definition of, 357
    governance and knowledge effects, 357–8
    law and, 359
    measurement of, 360
    social intervention and, 359
globalisation:
    late modernity and, 375
    mythology of, 449
'governance effects' (global social indicators),
    357–8
grounded theory, 195
Guanxi and sociology of law, 349

guerrilla groups (Colulmbia), 394
    FARC-EP group, 397

Habermas, Jürgen, Banakar on, 351
hard cases, economic considerations of,
    136–7
hard law, 103
    socially-orientated changes via, 137
    solutions legalise social discourse, 131
harmony, definition of, 88
'Having One's Cake and Eating It'
    (Banakar, 2011), 26–7
Heimat (Banakar), 211–12
Hertogh, Marc:
    law profiles and legal alienation in, 207
    legal consciousness research, on, 435
history and sociology, 265
human rights:
    international and regional systems,
        438
    standards, 438
    TeliaSonera and, 116–17 (case law)
Hungary:
    Civil Liberties Union (TASZ), 178–9
    legal knowledge assessed in (1965), 164
    rights consciousness *see* rights consciousness
        (Hungary)

Icelandic Appeals Court, sexual offences cases,
    sentences lowered for, 457–8
Icelandic evidentiary system, 455
'Identity Crisis of a "Stepchild", The', (Banakar,
    1998), 24, 59–60
    assumptions of, 60
    criticism of, 60–1
ideology, concept of and sociological inquiries,
    418
imaginaries, 419–20
    constitutional *see* constitutional imaginaries
    constitutions, as backgrounds of, 422
    modern social, 420
    social *see* social imaginaries
'immediate jural experience' (Gurvitch), 26
immigrant communities and Western and Islamic
    legal cultures, tensions between, 28
imperialism:
    citizenship and, 101–2
    constitutional law and, 96
    legal pluralism and, 94–5
    warfare and, 100
indicators, types of, 357
individuality:
    functional differentiation and, 222
    practice of science and, 220–1
individuals and science, 218

infectious diseases (ID):
  global security and, relationship between,
    378–9
  spread of and international aviation passenger
    numbers, 379
institutional legitimacy (Iranian traffic rules), 311
  Netherlands traffic laws and, 314
institutional practices (Iran) and rule of law,
    279–80
interlegality (Santos), 392
  top-down and bottom-up legal interactions
    and, 392
international:
  aviation passenger numbers and spread of
    infectious diseases, 379
  crimes, Swedish legislation applied to, 121
  law, Lundin Oil's violation of (Sudan,
    1997–2003), 120–2
International Civil Aviation Organisation (ICAO),
    376–8
  SARPS, 376, 380
internationalism, automobiles' role in, 301
Introduction to Law and Social Theory (Banakar
    and Travers, 2002), 35, 189–90, 191–2
  theory and practice debate in, 192–3
'Iran: A Clash of Two Cultures?' (Banakar and
    Keyvan, 2020), 29
'Iran: A Clash of Two Legal Cultures?' (Banakar
    and Ziaee), 294
Iranian:
  driving culture, 350
  legal profession, 294, 350–1
  social structure, 280
  society and legal culture, Banakar's study of,
    28–9
Iranian drivers:
  deterrence effect on, 312
  personal norms followed, 312
Iranian traffic rules:
  deterrence and, 310
  motorists' socio-economic and demographic
    characteristics, 312
  non-compliance with, 310–12
  peer opinion, 310–11
  personal legitimacy and morality in, 311
  procedural justice, 311
Islam, post-9/11 changes, 325
Islamic Revolution in Iran (1979), 338
  women failed by, 338–9
Israel:
  abolition of State of Israel and anti-Israel law,
    323–4
  contact and communication with and anti-Israel
    law, 323
IT systems and legal informatics, 234

judges:
  court clerks (Turkey) and, relationship between,
    255
  criminal legal aid fieldwork (Turkey),
    participation in, 251–2, 253–4
  independence of (Iran), 295
judiciary (Iran), legal culture of, 294
juridical capital and corporate regulation, 119
jurimetrics, 229–31
  committees on set up, 230–1
  Journal, 230–1
  Loevinger on, 230
  Swedish development and publications of, 231
justice, public sentiments on (Nordic research),
    436

Kafka, language and law, on, 202–3, 205
'Kafkaesque', concept of, 203
  late modernity and, 203
knowledge:
  production of and science, 218–19
  transitive and intransitive directions of, 65
Knowledge and Opinion about Law (KoL), 7–8
  Bulgaria, in, 170
  conference sessions on, 162
  German research (1970), 164–5
  Germany, instruction given in, 170
  legal rules, acceptance of, and, 163
  migrant communities, in, 167–8
  1960s-1980s research, 163–4
  research on, 161–2
  young people, teaching to, 168–9
'knowledge effects' (global social indicators), 357

*Lack of Rights Consciousness in the Legal
    Cultures of Central Europe and The
    Balkans. Myth or Reality?*, 162, 173
  attorneys, negative views of, 184
  conflicts with institutions, reluctance to act
    (finding), 177–81
  court trial experience, beneficial effect of, 184
  discussion transcripts, 177
  focus groups of, 175–7
  law and rights as last hope, 179–80
  legal alienation and negative impact of law,
    181–2
  legal experience, positive impact of, 181–6
  main findings, 174–5
  money's importance in conflict-solving, 180–1
  online format's disadvantages and advantages,
    177
  reference to law or rights, reluctant, 178–9
land:
  global resource, as, 442
  ownership, empowering the poor through, 446

property rights and, 444–5
reform (Botswana) and time and space, 447–8
sustainable development and, 444
time and space and, 442
tribal (Botswana), 443
land tenure:
Botswana, in, 443–4
time and space's role in, 446–7
language:
concept of, 201
Kafka on, 203
philosophy of, 201
late modernity:
globalisation and, 375
Kafkaesque and, 203
law and, 27, 28–9, 41–2, 87, 216, 356
legal culture and, 200
rights discourse in, 28
social structure and, 216
law:
autonomy of, and legal culture, 284
Banakar's view of, 202, 391–2
caseworkers' view of, 244–5
contextualisation of, 26–7
definition of, 85, 320
dis-embedding and displacement of, 86–7
global social indicators and, 359
humanistic study of, 201
in-depth interviews on, 278
integrative function of and contemporary
        society, 321
Kafka on, 202–3, 205
late modernity, under, 27, 216
law in society, understanding of, 205–6
legal culture and, 288
limitations of, and limitations of risk
        management (Banakar), 386
negative impact of and *Lack of Rights
        Consciousness*, 182
people's attitudes to profiles, 434
personal experience of (Hungary), 175
profiles of (Hertogh), 207
social control for (Banakar), 456–7
social practices generate, 281
sociological elements of, 64–5
sociology of law and, 53–4, 55 (fig), 66
state conception and conceptualisation of, 54, 96
Swedish, Banakar on, 202
law and culture, literature on, 320
law and enforcement, interviews on, 279
law and legality, Kafka as a 'modern' and 'late
        modern' writer on, 204–5
law and literature:
Movement, Banakar's contribution to, 199–200
similarities with sociology of law, 201–2

law and morality, legal positivists on, 42
law and regulatory oversight and risk
        communication, 382–3
law and social order, interviews on, 278
Law and Social Theory (Banakar and Travers,
        2013), 35, 41–2
law and society, 49
Association (US), 229
Iran, in, 295
studies (US), 52–3
tension between (Banakar), 61–2
law enforcement and jurisdiction, interviews on,
        278
law, perceptions of inform practices, 244–5
'Law, Love and Responsibility' (Banakar, 2018), 29
'Law, Rights and Justice in Late Modern Society'
        (Banakar 2010), 27
law shopping, 114, 122
law-society dichotomy, Banakar on, 61–3
sociological study of law and, 66
Stepchild Controversy, in, 61
'Law, Sociology and Method' (Banakar and
        Travers 2005), 26
'Law Through Sociology's Looking Glass'
        (Banakar 2009), 25
lawyers, 269
decision-making and sociology, 62
legal culture of (Iran), 294
legal:
argumentation (Robert Alexy), 27
certainty, ensuring of by law, (Banakar), 387
codification (France), 103
constitution, social construction of, 422
cynicism (legal alienation), 207
empowerment, women's need of, (Germany),
        166–7
experts, significance of, 121
legitimacy (Iranian traffic rules), 311
legitimation, Teubner on, 426
meaninglessness (legal alienation), 207
methodology, SoL, for, 9
obligation, 95
orders and normative orders, distinguishing
        between, 85
philosophy and normativity, 74
political reforms (Iran), and, conditions and
        opportunities for, 326–7
positivism, literature on, 27
positivists on law and morality, 42
powerlessness (legal alienation), 207
regulation, external, company's operational
        change through, 136
sociology neglects normativity of justice, 40
solutions and legal informatics and sociology
        of law, 235

theory, 127–8
value isolation (legal alienation), 207
legal alienation:
  Hertogh on, 207
  Lack of Rights Consciousness and, 181–2
  legal hearings and texts, 182–4
'Legal awareness of Polish society: diagnosis,
    types, ways of shaping' (Skapska, 2018),
    162
legal consciousness, 162, 244
  attitude, as, 432
  definition, 163
  Ewick and Silbey on, 206
  negative, 166
  prisoners' families and children, of, 434
  research, Hertogh on, 435
  social legal research, in, 162
  studies on, 431
legal culture, 11–12, 282–3
  anthropologists' views on, 264
  approach to and presentation of, 265
  authors' views on, 263–4
  autonomy of law and, 284
  Cotterrell on, 286, 287
  definition of, 264–5, 282–3, 431
  external and internal, 279, 282
  Febbrajo on, 286
  interviews on, 279
  Islamic, 326
  late modernity and, 200
  law and, 288
  non-Western-centred perspective, 266
  post-Soviet era, in, 266–7
  problems of, 285
  sociologists' views on, 264
  sociology of law and, 287–8, 290
legal education:
  aims of, 8
  women's need of, (Germany), 166–7
legal formalism:
  military order and, 94–8
  Russia, in, 267–8
legal informatics, 232
  AI and, 233
  field of research, becomes, 232
  IT systems and, 234
  legal solutions and, 235
  scientific application of, 233
legal knowledge:
  Hungary, in, 164
  Iran, in, 281–2
legal mobilisation, 145, 150–2
  bringing cases to court, 174–5
  individual claimants and social interest groups,
      agency of, 155–6

legal experience and, 181
Muslim personal status, in, 146
scholarship, 146
legal norms, 71
  formal system of, 456
legal pluralism, 106–7
  analysis of, 96–7
  Banakar on, 37–8
  definition of, 113
  imperialism and, 94–5
  multinational comparisons' use of, 114
  normative pluralism and, distinction between,
      86
  transnational, 111, 113
legal professions:
  authoritarian states, in, 295–6
  common language of, 296–7
legal rules:
  acceptance of and KoL, 163
  parallel (TeliaSonera), 118–19
legal spaces, 392–3
  fields of, 39
legal systems:
  normativity of, 77–8
  presentation of cultural differences and, 321
legality:
  Ewick and Silbey on, 206
  law and (Kafka), 204–5
legitimacy, Luhmann on, 424–5
legitimation, Teubner and Luhmann on, 425
'Life of the Law in the Islamic Republic of Iran,
      The' (Banakar and Keyvan, 2018), 29
'Light, The' (Furugärde), 209–11, 212
literature, 200–1
  law and, similarities with sociology of law,
      201–2
  law representations in, Banakar on, 26
'living law' (Ehrlich), 26, 431
  sociology of, 56
Loevinger, Lee, on jurimetrics, 230
'Love, Law and Responsibility' (Banakar, 2018), 29
Luhmann, Niklas, on normativity, 74–5
Lundin Energy (Swedish company), 115
Lundin Oil, international law, violations of
      (Sudan, 1997–2003), 120–2

*Merging Law and Sociology: Beyond the
    Dichotomies in Socio-Legal Research*
    (Banakar 2003), 24–5, 26, 28, 348–9
Merry, Sally, 357, 359
methodologies and methodology:
  Banakar's studies' approach to, 351
  combining top-down and bottom-up
      approaches, 245–6
migrant communities, KoL in, 167–8

migrant groups (Germany)
  integration classes and initiatives, 167–8
  law and state institutions, distrust of, 167
military:
  codification, 97–8
  desertion, 102
  expansion and Prussian citizenship, 103
  order and legal formalisation, 97–8
  recruitment and citizenship, 99–100
minimum wages (EU)
  regulation of, texts on, 411–12
  Swedish trade unions, regulation on, 412–13
mobilisation:
  judicial, 151–2
  legal (Egypt), 150–2
modern law (Iran) and politics, 324–5
modern state constitutions, 95–6
modernity, social life manifested in, 392
Moïsi, Dominique, (French political scientist), 340
moral rules and norms, 70–1
*Multicultural Jurisdictions – Cultural Differences
    and Women's Rights* (Shachar), 90
multiculturalism, 89
  Banakar's interest in, 28
  liberal, 89
multinational corporations, legal pluralism,
    use of by, 114
Muslim family law, codification of, 147

nation building (Italy), 104
nationalism defined, 301
naturalism defined, 63
Netherlands traffic laws:
  deterrence and, 3
  institutional legitimacy (Iranian traffic laws)
      and, 311
  legal legitimacy, 314–15
  peer opinion in, 313–14
  personal legitimacy and morality in 314
  procedural justice and, 314
  reasons for non-compliance with, 312–15
New Economic Policy (NEP) (Russia), 337
New North – The World in 2050, The (Smith),
    340–1
*Nobody's Law: Legal Consciousness and Legal
    Alienation in Everyday Life* (Hertogh,
    2018), 206–7
non-living systems, autopoiesis applied to, 74–5
Nordic:
  frequency theories, 455
  labour market, 16–17
  sociology of law (Banakar), 345, 346–7
normative orders:
  legal orders and, distinguishing between, 85
  literature on, 86

non-state, 85
  plural, justice under, 90–1
normative pluralism, 84–5
  legal pluralism and, distinguishing between, 86
normative regulation, continuum of, 358–9 (fig)
normativity, 39–41
  definitions of, 72, 74
  ecological system, of, 77
  economic system, of, 76
  ethics and, 72–3
  force in society, as, 65–6
  Islamic, pluralism of, 146
  legal philosophy and, 74
  legal sociology neglects, 40
  legal systems, of, 77–8
  Luhmann on, 74–5
  political administrative systems, in, 76
  psychology and, 73–4
  reason and, 73
  social systems and, 75
  sociology and, 288–9
  technical systems, of, 77
Normativity in Legal Sociology (Banakar, 2015),
    39–40
normativity's prediction, 78–80
  political and administrative system, in, 79
  social and technical systems, in, 79
norms, 41, 70, 73
  bureaucratic, 71
  descriptive, 278, 280, 303
  economic, 71, 79–80
  ethnic, Global South, in, 89
  injunctive, 278, 280, 303
  internalisation of, 70
  legal *see* legal norms
  methodological, 217
  moral rules and, 70–1
  personal, Iranian drivers follow, 312
  scientific research and, 217–18
  social *see* social norms
  technical, 71–2, 79
  types of, 69–72
  values and, relationship between, 320
Norwegian Center for Computers and Law
    (NRCCL) (1970), 232

operational change:
  CSR's effect on, 135
  external legal regulation, through, 136
Outline of Social Psychology, An (Sherif),
    70–1
'outsiders' (people's attitudes to law), 434

parental authority, Polish opinions on (1963), 164
'Passage to "India", A' (Banakar, 2001), 24

paternal filiation (Egypt):
  reforms, 148
  twin sons, for, 153 (case law)
paternity:
  claims, use of technology in, 153–4 (case law)
  establishment of, 150–1
paternity (Egypt):
  gestation period, 148
  Hanafi doctrine establishes, 148
pathetic dots, 129–30
  corporate lawyers as, 126–30
Peasants into Frenchmen (Weber, 1976), 301
peer opinion:
  Iranian traffic rules, in, 310–11
  Netherlands traffic laws, in, 313–14
personal legitimacy:
  Iranian traffic rules, in, 311
  Netherlands traffic laws, in, 314
personal morality:
  Iranian traffic rules, in, 311
  Netherlands traffic laws, in, 314
personal status bill (Egypt), 155–6
personalism, 300–1
  Iran, in, 300
pluralism:
  constitutional law and, 98
  Islamic normativity, of, 146
pluralistic legal theory, 95–6
'Poetic Injustice' (Banakar, 2008), 28
Poland:
  constitutional development of (1772-), 105–6
  parental authority, opinions on (1963), 164
policy audience, 50
political:
  constitutions, evolution of, 422
  power, legitimation of, 424
political/administrative systems, 75–6
  normativity in, 76, 79
politics (Iran) and modern law, 324–5
'Politics of Legal Cultures, The' (Banakar, 2008), 28
poor, the, empowering through land ownership, 446
'Power, Culture and Method in Comparative Law' (Banakar, 2009), 26–7
prisoners' children and families:
  criminal justice practices and, sentiments of, 437
  justice and punishment, views on, 433
  legal consciousness of, 434
  marginalisation of, 430–1
  sentiments and, 18, 437
procedural justice:
  Iranian traffic rules, in, 311
  Netherlands traffic laws, in, 314

process of law (Iran), 280–1
professionalised law developed in Russia, 270
property rights:
  land and, 444–5
  Western approach to, 444–5
psychology and normativity, 73–4
public health:
  authorities and aviation, collaboration between, 380–1
  scares, aviation companies' poor preparedness for, 381–2
public sentiment and opinion on justice, 432
  'legal consciousness as attitude', as, 432
  Nordic research on, 432
punishment:
  Danish attitudes towards (Balvig), 435
  public support for leniency, 436

'qualified public input' model (public sentiments on justice), 436
quantitative representative surveys (Germany), 165

RAGIDA project, 380, 386, 387
rape, conception of daughter after, 153–4
reason and normativity, 73
'Rechtsreport' (Roland Legal Cost (Protection) Insurance) (annual report), 165, 166
reckless driving (Banakar), structure of, 278–81
'Reflections on the Methodological Issues of the Sociology of Law' (Banakar, 2000), 24
reflexive mechanisms, 289–90
research, theory-led and empirical, 332–3
restorative justice, 437
revolutions, definitions and elements of, 332–3
right to life (Columbia), 395
rights consciousness (Hungary), 173
  conflict solving and, 175
Rights in Context (Banakar, 2010), 28
risk:
  'availability heuristic' and, 381
  aviation, in, and certainty and uncertainty, 385
  'frequent flyer' air travel and, 384
  social institutions' understanding of and preparation for, 378
  society theory (Beck), 378, 384
risk-based regulators, challenges to, 376
risk communication:
  effective, inadequate, and official, 384
  law and regulatory oversight and, 382–3
  mainstream and social media, via, 384
  strategies limited by collateral damage to aviation, 383

risk management:
aviation, in, 15, 375
international and regional cross-sectorial, 378–81
limitations of and limitations of law (Banakar), 386
social regulation and, 386
rule of law and institutional practice (Iran), 279–80
Russian:
civil cases, 271
commercial cases, 272
courtroom practice, 271
courts' use of written evidence, 272–3
criminal cases, 272
legal system, historical development of, 269–70
legal tradition, 268–9
monarchy, impact of collapse of, 339
Revolution (1917), 335–7

'Sacred Life' programme (Columbia), 396
urban security under, 397
safety communication, 385
same-direction principle, 458
Sarbanes-Oxley Act 2002, 137, 138
Schopenhauer, Arthur (1788–1860), 334–5
influence over later philosophers, 335
science:
addressees of, 219
co-construction of society and, 219
individuals and, 218
practice of and individuality, 220–1
production of knowledge and, 218–19
sociology of law and, 217, 221
scientific activity is part of society, 220
sexual offence cases:
Icelandic Appeals Court lowers sentences, 457–8
lack of convictions in, 453–4
sexual violence cases:
double standard of justice in, 460
indirect evidence in (Iceland, 2014 study), 456–7
sexual violence in criminal cases, direct or indirect evidence in, 456–7
Sharia, development of, 147
Smith, Laurence, 340–1
social:
forces and agency, 222–3
institutions and risk, 378
integration, 'cultural lag' as threat to, 70
intervention and global social indicators, 359
life manifested in modernity, 392
media, risk communication via, 358
practices generate law, 281
regulation and risk management, 386
responsibility and economic considerations, 136–7

structure and late modernity, 216
systems and normativity, 75, 79
social discourse:
corporate lawyers, effect on, 131
hard law solutions legalise, 131
loss of control in society and, 279–80
social imaginaries, 420, 423–4
constitutions and, 422–3
duality of, 422
self-referential and self-subversive forces of, 421
semantics of, 421
social norms:
cultural values, contribution of to, 70
driving culture and, 305
'social time' (time and space), 447
societal constitutionalism (Teubner), 425, 426–7
society:
causality in, 64
co-construction of and science, 219
epidemics' consequences for, 341
law and, 52–3, 61–2, 229, 295
loss of control in and social disorder, 279–80
Luhmann on, 424
Mannheim on, 418
normativity and, 65–6
scientific activity is part of, 220
unity of *topos-ethnos-nomos* and, 422
socio-legal:
enterprise, 47, 48
legal inquiry, 48, 62
studies and theories (Banakar), 347–8
socio-legal research, 49–50
Banakar on, 348–9
origins of, 56–7
socio-legal theory, 26
criticism of (Banakar), 26
methodology and, Banakar on, 349–50
sociological jurisprudence:
Banakar on, 36–7
definition of, 36
jurists and thinkers on, 36–7
sociological knowledge (Iran), 281–2
sociology, 40, 265
lawyers' decision-making and, 62
normativity and, 288–9
paradigms in, 62
sociology of law (SoL):
analysis of, 16
history of, 49
literature on, 4–5
mission of, 51
origins of and approaches to, 228
pre-conditions, 56
theoretical aspects of, 228

'Sociology of Law: From Industrialisation to
Globalisation, The' (Banakar, 2011), 25
soft law, 6, 128, 132–3
consequences of, 131
definition of, 130
'law', as, 132
legitimacy of and CSR, 133–4
soft regulation, attitudes to, 132
solidarity, 406–8
common societal scheme and, 407
EU law and (Banakar), 29
EU trade unions and, 406–7, 408
negative form of, 412
standard of proof:
definition, 454
Icelandic example of, 455–6
probabilities, based on, examples of, 454–5
state:
bureaucracy, in-depth interviews on, 278
control, sociology of law, of, 52
law, top-down and bottom-up perspectives, 282
legal pluralism, aspects of, 146
'stepchild':
concept of, 47–8
development of (Banakar), 239–40
project (Banakar), 345
Stepchild Controversy, 59–60
law-society dichotomy in, 61
Sunni jurisprudence schools, 147
'supplication' (fieldwork strategy), 252–3
sustainable development:
goals, 445–6
land and, 444
Sweden, jurimetrics development and publications,
231
Swedish Law and Informatics Research Institute
(IRI) (1968), 232
Swedish trade unions:
communication and, 409–11
EU minimum wage regulation, attitude to, 412–13
symbolic forms, 418–19

technical systems and normativity, 77, 79
TeliaSonera (Swedish company), 115
bribery offences, prosecution over, 118–19
human rights violation allegations, 116–17
Theory and Method in Socio-Legal Research
(Banakar and Travers 2005), 189–90, 191–2
'theory and practice' debate in, 192–3
time and space:
developed and undeveloped countries and, 448
land and, 442
land reform (Botswana) and, 447–8
land tenure, role in, 446–7
multiple forms of time, 447

tolerance, 88–9
top-down and bottom-up approaches (Banakar):
analysis of, 453
study of law and, 239–46, 292–3, 453
top-down and bottom-up legal interactions:
formal law structure interactions and, 242–3
interlegality and, 392
topos-ethnos-nomos and society, 422
traffic laws (Iran and Netherlands):
congruence between state law and living law,
316–17
instrumental and normative values, 316
legal compliance through legal legitimacy, 316
traffic research, 308–10
Australia, in, 309
compliance models, 308–9
Ghana, in, 309
legitimacy of, 309–10
Scotland, in, 309
*Transformations on the Ground: Space and the
Power of Land in Botswana*,
(Griffiths), 441–2
transnational:
corporate regulation, 134
European integration and constitutional
imaginaries, 423
rules and regulations, 134
transnational corporate governance:
changes to, 135–8
CSR and, 135–7
operational and structural change, 135
transnational corporations, 134
public pressure on, 117
regulation of, 113–14
Trial, The (Kafka), 204–5
law discussed in, 207–8

uncertainty and risk in aviation, 385
Understanding Law and Society (Travers 2010), 36

value plurality in modern society, 418
values and norms, relationship between, 320
'variable geometry' triangle, 51
veiled and the unveiled, 302–4
driving culture as, 303
public and private sphere distinguished, 303
public sphere is veiled, 302–3
victim-offender mediation, 437
victimology, 208
victims:
crime, of, 437
sexual offences, of, right to legal aid to pursue
civil claim, 454
violence, abuse cases (Iceland) against children
(2007 committee report), and, 459–60

War Communism (Russia), 336–7
warfare and imperialism, 100
Western civilization, Berman on, 339
'Who Needs the Classics?' (Banakar, 2012), 26
'Whose Experience is the Measure of Justice?' (Banakar 2007), 27
women:
  French Revolution fails, 338
  Islamic Revolution in Iran fails, 338–9

lawyers (Germany), KoL research on, 165
legal education and empowerment, need of (Germany), 166–7
Working Group on Documentation in sociology of law (International Sociological Association), 229
bibliographical appendix on jurimetrics published (1968), 231
'World Law' (Berman article), 339–40
written evidence, Russian courts' use of, 272

Ingram Content Group UK Ltd.
Milton Keynes UK
UKHW051806200323
418598UK00029B/31